Imitation in Animals and Artifacts

Complex Adaptive Systems (selected titles)

John H. Holland, Christopher G. Langton, and Stewart W. Wilson, advisors

Imitation in Animals and Artifacts

edited by Kerstin Dautenhahn and Chrystopher L. Nehaniv

A Bradford Book
The MIT Press
Cambridge, Massachusetts
London, England

This book was set in Melior and Helvetica Condensed on 3B2 by Asco Typesetters, Hong Kong. Printed and bound in the United States of America.

Library of Congress Cataloging-in-Publication Data

Imitation in animals and artifacts / edited by Kerstin Dautenhahn and Chrystopher L. Nehaniv.
    p. cm. — (Complex adaptive systems)
  "A Bradford book."
  Papers presented at a meeting held in Edinburgh, Scotland, Apr. 7–9, 1999.
  Includes bibliographical references and index.
  ISBN 0-262-04203-7 (alk. paper)
  1. Imitation—Congresses. 2. Learning in animals—Congresses. 3. Machine learning—Congresses. I. Nehaniv, Chrystopher L., 1963– II. Dautenhahn, Kerstein. III. Series.
BF357 .I47 2002
591.5′14—dc21   2001054644

Contents

Preface

Imitation has traditionally been regarded as easy, and often scornfully dismissed as trivial, "cheating," or unworthy in comparison to higher cognitive abilities. Yet this is an illusion. What does it even mean for two behaviors to be the "same?" Explaining the imitative abilities of humans and other animals has proved to be a complex subject. The mechanisms are not well understood and the connection to sociality, communication, and learning is deep, as recent research from various disciplines has started to reveal. Building robots and software agents that can imitate other artificial or human agents in an appropriate way is an endeavor that involves the deepest problems of connecting perception, experience, context, and action. These are some of the main issues treated in this book.

This book grew out of the "Imitation in Animals and Artifacts" Symposium, which we organized in Edinburgh, Scotland (7–9 April 1999), under the auspices of the Society for the Study of Artificial Intelligence and Simulation of Behaviour (AISB). Owing to generous support by the Engineering and Physical Sciences Research Council (EPSRC), we were able to invite a number of established researchers in the field of imitation. This first interdisciplinary symposium attracted a very high level of interest from researchers from a broad spectrum of scientific disciplines ranging from animal behavior to artificial intelligence; from computer science, software engineering, and robotics to experimental and comparative psychology, neuroscience, primatology, and linguistics. This diversity is also reflected in the contents of the present volume. Issues of imitation, behavior matching, and observational learning arise in all of these fields, although little or no communication of results on the closely related ideas has been established between most of these disciplines. Together with more than forty participants from the United Kingdom and other countries, this mixture gave rise to an exciting and thought-provoking first attempt at integrating research on imitation from two distinct communities, namely, those researchers working in the sciences of the natural (i.e., studying imitation in humans and other animals), and those working in the sciences of the artificial (i.e., studying imitation via the construction of artifacts, in software or hardware).

The symposium comprised invited and keynote lectures by Josep Call, Cecilia M. Heyes, Louis M. Herman, Henry Lieberman, Martin Loomes, Elisabetta Visalberghi, and Andrew Whiten, along with twenty-three other oral and several poster presentations.[1] In this way, the symposium was different from previous international meetings on imitation that had generally focused on either the animal or the artifact perspective on imitation. The symposium demonstrated the breadth of different theories, methodologies, and experimental approaches used in research on imitation. It became clear that despite the large differences in practical work on imitation with animals as opposed to artifacts, many common research issues can be identified that can benefit from an interdisciplinary perspective. This point became perhaps most obvious in presentations that addressed robotic imitation: here, it is necessary to be very precise about what exactly is meant by cognitive, behavioral, or perceptual concepts and theories, and how these can be effectively specified, modeled, and tested. Thus, constructing and programming robots that imitate requires one to implement concepts and theories on the level of information processing (mechanisms that mediate perception and motor control in robot control programs) while the agent (robot) is situated via action and perception in a particular environment.

The great enthusiasm and excited exchange of ideas between researchers from these widely scattered areas revealed the desirability of a book that students, researchers, and others intrigued by imitation could turn to for a perspective on the work on imitation across the various disciplines. There are excellent books and reviews of imitation within particular disciplines, but only with much more specialized scope.[2] This, and the lack of any book that examines imitation from a broad interdisciplinary scope, inspired us to undertake editing this volume. Keynote lecturers and some other presenters from the symposium were invited to contribute chapters written especially for this book with an interdisciplinary audience in mind, as were other researchers representative of many fields in which the study of imitation arises but who were not able to attend. The chapters were peer reviewed by at least two referees and subsequently improved. A short overview of the chapters is given in the Introduction (chapter 1), which also presents a unifying, interdisciplinary, agent-based perspective on imitation and discusses a selection of key research issues in the field. In the following, we outline the basic motivation for initiating interdisciplinary work on imitation.

Imitation is often considered an important mechanism whereby knowledge can be transferred between agents (biological, computational, or robotic autonomous systems). Over the last decade, the topic of imitation has emerged in various areas close to artificial intelligence including cognitive and social sciences, developmental psychology, animal behavior, robotics, programming by demonstration, machine learning, and user-interface design. The importance of imitation has grown increasingly apparent to psychologists, ethologists, philosophers, linguists, cognitive scientists, computer scientists, mathematicians, biologists, anthropologists, and roboticists. Yet the workers confronted with the need to understand imitation are often unaware of relevant research in other disciplines. Until now, the study of imitation has lacked a rigorous foundation, with no major interdisciplinary framework available on the subject for workers in computer science, robotics, or the biological sciences. This volume is aimed toward remedying this. In this volume, we bring together work by established researchers on imitation from these different areas, writing with an interdisciplinary audience in mind, to produce a reference suitable as an introduction to the state-of-the-art work on imitation across disciplines.

Recently, imitation has begun to be studied in domains dealing with such nonnatural agents as robots, and as a tool for easing the programming of complex tasks or endowing groups of robotic agents with the ability to share skills without the intervention of a programmer. Imitation can play an important role in the more general context of interaction and collaboration between agents and humans—for example, between software agents and human users. Intelligent software agents need to get to know their users in order to assist them and do productive work on behalf of humans. Imitation is therefore a means of establishing a "social relationship" and learning about the actions of the user, in order to include them into an agent's own behavioral repertoire.

Imitation is, on the one hand, suggested as an efficient mechanism of social learning both for artifacts and a number of animal species, including humans. Moreover, experiments in developmental psychology suggest that infants use imitation to get to know others as persons, perhaps by applying a "like-me" test: "persons are objects which I can imitate and which imitate me." On the other hand, imitation methods, as in programming by demonstration set-ups in robotics and machine learning, have primarily focused on technological dimensions, while disregarding the more social and developmental functions. Additionally, the split between imitation research in natural sciences and the sciences of the artificial has been difficult to bridge, as we have lacked a common framework supporting an interdisciplinary approach. From a constructive viewpoint, studying imitation for an embodied system inhabiting a nontrivial environment leads one to address all major artificial intelligence (AI) problems from a new perspective: perception-action coupling, body-schemata, learning of sequences of action, recognition and matching of movements, contextualization, reactive and cognitive aspects of behavior, the development of sociality, or the notion of "self," just to mention a few issues. As we elaborate in chapter 1, research on imitation can benefit from an agent-based perspective that treats imitation as more than an isolated mechanism, mapping between perception and action (possibly via elaborate neural architectures for learning and associations). Instead, we argue that the full complexity and potential of imitation only unfold when viewing imitation in the context of the behavior of an autonomous agent that is situated and embodied[3] in a particular environment that includes other agents as well as other sources of dynamic change.

Imitation involves at least two agents sharing a context of which they have some corresponding perceptions, and may allow one agent to learn from the other. The exchange of skills, knowledge, and experience between natural agents cannot be achieved by brain-to-brain communication in the same way computers can communicate via the internet. It is mediated via bodies, the environment, the verbal or nonverbal expression or body language of the "sender," which in return has to be interpreted and integrated in the "recipient's" own understanding and behavioral repertoire. Moreover, as imitation games between babies and parents show, the metaphor of "sender" and "receiver" is a deceptive oversimplification, since the game emerges from the engagement of both agents in the interaction (compare the notions of situated activity and interactive emergence).

Thus, learning by imitation and learning to imitate are not just topics specific to machine learning, but can be seen as benchmark challenges for successful real-world artifacts in robotics and artificial intelligence. At the same time for psychologists and biologists, the building of artifacts that imitate could provide invaluable insights into understanding and validating mechanisms and theories that result from observation and experimental testing with animals. With respect to primate (social) intelligence, Nicholas K. Humphrey proposed as early as 1976:

However, the trouble is that too much of the evidence is of an anecdotal kind; we simply do not have agreed definitions or agreed ways of measuring either of the relevant parameters. What, I think, is urgently needed is a laboratory test of "social intelligence." The essential feature of such a test would be that it places the subject in a transactional situation where he can achieve a desired goal only by adapting his strategy to conditions which are continually changing as a consequence partly, but not wholly of his own behavior. The "social partner" in the test need not be animate (though my guess is that the subject would regard it in an "animistic" way); possibly it could be a kind of "social robot," a mechanical device which is programmed on-line from a computer to behave in a pseudo-social way. (Humphrey 1976)[4]

Several chapters in this book outline different state-of-the-art approaches in robotics for building robots that imitate, with a particular focus on humanoid robots. Thus, maybe Humphrey's dream will come true in the near future, namely, that a socially skilled robot is available that can be used as a research platform for studying imitation and social intelligence in interactions with other robots, humans, and nonhuman primates. Such robotic social partners might even be useful in studies with parrots or dolphins (see the chapters by Pepperberg, Lieberman, and Herman) whose enculturation allows them to accept humans (and possibly humanoid robots) as social interaction partners. However, despite a variety of technical problems, it remains to be seen if similarity on the level of basic morphological and behavioral characteristics suffice, or whether other sensor modalities need to be addressed (e.g., smell, touch) in building such social interaction partners.

The following list, adapted from the call for papers for the 1999 AISB Symposium "Imitation in Animals and Artifacts," indicates the breadth of research topics relevant to interdisciplinary work on imitation:

- Trying to Imitate—solving the correspondence problem between differently embodied systems
- Learning by Imitation—harnessing imitation as a means to bootstrap acquisition of knowledge and appropriate behaviors
- Imitation in Animals (examples of imitation, theories, comparisons to mechanisms of social learning)
- Imitation in Developmental Psychology
- Imitation Games and Language Games
- Imitation in Play and Creativity
- Memetics and Cultural Transmission
- Evolution of Symbolic Communication
- Social Intelligence (the role of cognitive capacities, emotions, internal states, and behavioral competencies, understanding of self and others)
- Mimicry and Deception
- Robot Imitation (experiments, architectures, role of memory and prediction, learning sequences of actions)
- Algebra and Dynamics of Imitation
- Formalization and Mechanisms of Imitation and Behavior Matching: (1) metrics on imitative behaviors as observed externally or monitored internally, (2) specification of the agent's internal/ cognitive processes resulting in matching the observed behavior
- Applications in Interactive Systems (computer-assisted instruction, user-interface design, cognitive technology, customization, mimetic agent technology, social intelligence, semiotic and linguistic systems, automated software generation)
- Neuroscience and Machine Approaches to Motion Perception and Imitative Actions
- Imitation and Intent (relations to cognitive robotics, theory of other minds, empathy, first-/second-person metaphors, affective computing, deliberation versus reactivity, situated planning, and teamwork).

This list is not meant to be exhaustive, but it demonstrates the scientific challenges that are posed by research on imitation, and the need for interdisciplinary work and collaboration in order to advance knowledge in these areas. The basic take-home message after reading this book might be: "Do as I do" is more difficult than it seems! Humans and other animals (e.g., dolphins) seem to imitate with great ease, but as soon as one attempts to build artifacts that imitate and learn how to imitate, one discovers a whole universe of challenging research problems.

We gratefully acknowledge the help and support of the following organizations: the Society for the Study of Artificial Intelligence and Simulation of Behaviour (AISB), the University of Hertfordshire, the Engineering and Physical Sciences Research Council (EPSRC) for Grant Number GR/M59129. For their enthusiasm, kindness, and help we thank Martin Loomes, Geraint Wiggins, the AISB symposium participants and scientific committee members, all the authors, referees, and reviewers of the chapters in this book, and Bob Prior and the staff at The MIT Press.

Notes

1. A list of presentations and speakers at the symposium is on the web at ⟨http://homepages.feis.ac.uk/~nehaniv/AISB-program.html⟩. The papers on which the contributed talks were based have been published separately in *Proceedings of the AISB '99 Symposium on Imitation in Animals and Artifacts (7–9 April 1999, Edinburgh, Scotland)*, K. Dautenhahn and C. L. Nehaniv (eds.), by the Society for the Study of Artificial Intelligence and Simulation of Behaviour, 1999 (ISBN: 1-902956-05-2). A related special issue of the international journal *Cybernetics and Systems* (published by Taylor and Francis) on "Imitation in Natural and Artificial Systems," guest edited by C. L. Nehaniv and K. Dautenhahn, reports on the some of the latest work on imitation and appears as the first issue of that journal for 2001 (see appendix).

2. Some excellent but much more specialized sources on imitation include C. M. Heyes and B. G. Galef Jr. (eds.), *Social Learning in Animals: The Roots of Culture* (Academic Press, San Diego, 1996); J. Nadel and G. Butterworth (eds.), *Imitation in Infancy* (Cambridge University Press, Cambridge, UK, 1999); T. R. Zentall and B. G. Galef Jr. (eds.), *Social Learning: Psychological and Biological Perspectives* (Lawrence Erlbaum Associates, Hillsdale, NJ, 1988); T. R. Zentall, Imitation in animals: Evidence, function, and mechanisms, *Cybernetics and Systems* 32(1–2): 53–96, 2001; and A. Cypher (ed.), *Watch What I Do: Programming by Demonstration* (MIT Press, Cambridge, MA, 1993).

3. Our notions of the terms *situated* and *embodied* are based on definitions used in the field of behavior-based artificial intelligence, compare R. C. Arkin: *Behavior-Based Robotics*, MIT Press, Cambridge, MA, 1998 and R. Pfeifer and C. Scheier: *Understanding Intelligence*, MIT Press, Cambridge, MA, 1999. Here, situatedness refers to an agent being surrounded by the real world, where a continuous stream of sensory inputs is the only source of information about the environment while the agent interacts with the environment. The situated agent acts on reality itself rather than abstract representations of reality. Embodiment is used with respect to an agent having a spatial reality—that is, possessing a physical body and dynamically interacting with the world. Another more-precise and operational definition of embodiment that is not restricted to the physical body stresses the structural coupling of an agent with its environment; see discussions in T. Quick, K. Dautenhahn, C. L. Nehaniv, and G. Roberts, "On bots and bacteria: Ontology-independent embodiment," *Advances in Artificial Life*, Lecture Notes in Artificial Intelligence, vol. 1674, Springer Verlag, Berlin, pp. 339–343, 1999. An extended version is available on-line at ⟨http://www.cs.ucl.ac.uk/staff/T.Quickpapers/quick_casys99.ps⟩.

4. Nicholas K. Humphrey, The social function of intellect, in P. P. G. Bateson and R. A. Hinde (eds.), *Growing Points in Ethology* (Cambridge University Press, Cambridge, UK, 1976), pp. 303–317.

© 1994 FarWorks, Inc. All Rights Reserved/Dist. by Creators Syndicate

So let's go over it again: You're about a mile up, you
see something dying below you, you circle until it's
dead, and down you go. Lenny, you stick close
to your brothers and do what they do."

1 *The Agent-Based Perspective on Imitation*

Kerstin Dautenhahn and Chrystopher L. Nehaniv

1.1 Introduction

This chapter presents the agent-based perspective on imitation. In this perspective, imitation is best considered as the behavior of an *autonomous agent* in relation to its environment, including other autonomous agents. We argue that such a perspective helps unfold the full potential of research on imitation and helps in identifying challenging and important research issues. We first explain the agent-based perspective and then discuss it in the context of particular research issues in studies with animals and artifacts, with reference to chapters presented in this book. At the end of the chapter, we briefly introduce the individual contributions to this book and provide a roadmap that helps the reader in navigating through the exciting and highly interwoven themes that are presented in this book.

In order to focus discussions, we explain the agent-based perspective with particular consideration of the *correspondence problem*, an important issue in research on imitation that is discussed in more detail in chapter 2. For the purpose of this chapter, the correspondence problem can be characterized as follows: given an imitator (a biological or artificial system) trying to imitate a model (the biological or artificial system to be imitated), how can the imitator identify, generate, and evaluate appropriate mappings (perceptual, behavioral, cognitive) between its own behavior and the behavior of the model? In order to illustrate this problem, figure 1.1 shows different tetrapod bodies. Arrows indicate where one would intuitively, and based on knowledge of the tetrapod body plan, identify structural correspondences. Movements of these agents and their interactions with the environment are, however, different. For example, what is the corresponding movement of a human to a dolphin flapping its tail? Even two members of the same species have different embodiments, due to individual differences, developmental differences (ontogeny), environment, experience, and other factors.

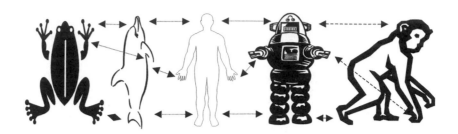

Figure 1.1 Structural homologies among tetrapod animals/artifacts.

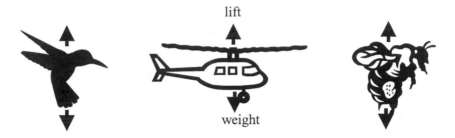

Figure 1.2 Achieving hovering behavior with dissimilar bodies.

However, even systems with very dissimilar bodies and body plans such as a hummingbird, a helicopter, and a humble bee can achieve the same behavior, "hovering," exploiting the same laws of physics (figure 1.2). Thus, even among agents with very dissimilar bodies, it makes sense to talk about imitation being realized, if appropriate correspondences exist.

1.2 The Agent-Based Perspective: Imitation in Context

In this chapter (see also chapter 2) we discuss correspondences between systems (animals or artifacts) with different or similar bodies. Often, research on imitation with artifacts views imitation as an efficient *mechanism* that can be exploited to implement socially mediated learning and adaptation. What we would like to argue in this chapter is that in order to better understand the whole scope and potential of imitation in animals and artifacts, as well as its phylogeny and ontogeny in biological systems, an agent-based perspective is beneficial and necessary. This means imitation is best considered as the behavior of an *autonomous agent* in relation to its environment. In other words, viewing imitation solely as a *mechanism* that can be isolated from the system, its embodiment, and its environment and then generalized as a general-purpose mechanism (e.g., for social learning) significantly narrows the field of study, and is likely to unnecessarily confine the application of research on imitation to the area of machine learning. As we will show below when discussing this viewpoint in the context of particular research questions, an agent-based perspective prevents us from a too narrow interpretation of what imitation is and what the important parameters are that need to be considered in research on imitation. What can be gained from this perspective? To give two examples: historically, in robotics research, research on imitation is often devoted to the development of a robot control architecture that identifies salient features in the movements of an (often visually observed) model, and maps them appropriately to motor outputs of the imitator (compare one of the first examples of robotic imitation in Kuniyoshi, Inoue, and Inaba 1990, 1994). Model and imitator are usually not *interacting* with each other, nor are they sharing and perceiving a common *context.* Also, the *social dimension* of imitation (and corresponding issues of when and why should an agent imitate) is usually ignored. Robotics research is easily biased toward separating the *mechanism* of, for example, learning by imitation from the phylogenetic and ontogenetic history of imitation, and the particular embodied and situated context in which imitation occurs in nature. Thus, robotics research has often been limited to the question *how* to imitate, focusing on the "here and now," that is, focusing on a particular robotic system and its imitation "task," prespecified by the experimenter. Not surprisingly, this has led to very diverse approaches to robot controllers for imitative learning, and the difficulty to generalize to different contexts and different robotic platforms. An exception and example where an architecture developed for *learning by imitation* has been applied to different robot platforms and contexts is described by Billard (chapter 11 of this volume). However, it remains to be seen how such an approach could be realized for *learning/trying to imitate*—an at present unsolved and open research problem. So far, the exploration of the design space of architectures and models for imitation is usually neither systematic nor theory-driven.

Novelty and other issues regarding the general nature of imitation as discussed in animal imitation research usually do not play a significant role in robotics imitation research. However, as we discuss below, an agent-based perspective has a broader view and includes five central questions ("Big Five") in designing experiments on research on imitation—namely, *who*, *when*, *what*, and *how to imitate*, in addition to the question of *what makes a successful imitation*. A systematic investigation of these research questions could therefore shed light on the full potential of imitation from an agent-based perspective. That might lead to robots that can recognize good teachers, select what to imitate on their own, and imitate when appropriate; for example, imitate in order to acquire new skills or imitate as a means of communication with other agents. Such agents might be able to apply and control imitation as part of their larger behavior repertoire, part of their strategy to survive in a social world, rather than being machines that are designed solely as imitating machines.

The possible contribution of the agent-based perspective to research on animal imitation is quite different: it might help in concretizing models and theories on animal imitation by drawing attention to the *how* question: How are particular elements of a model or theory based in mechanisms at a level of description such that agent-based physical or computational models can be built that might validate these models or theories? Biologists try to understand a biological system by analyzing and describing it, but they traditionally do not attempt to synthesize a machine that might look and behave like the animal. But a robotic experiment that is based on the implementation of a particular model of animal imitation could validate the model, in the sense that it can show that the model really works, at least for a particular agent and environment set up. Conversely, it could reveal gaps, inconsistencies, levels of detail not fleshed out in theory, as well as overlooked issues and assumptions. Experiments with artifacts can confirm whether a particular model is *sufficient* to generate imitative behavior. Of course, such experiments cannot replace studies with animals that need to show whether the model holds true for animal systems. But studies with robotic and computational agents might identify new research questions and inspire studies with animals. For example, the correspondence problem, which has been identified as an important problem in imitation with artifacts (see chapter 2), has not been discussed extensively in research on animal imitation. A potential explanation might be that animals that do imitate "naturally" tend to imitate conspecifics—that is, members of the same species having bodies very similar to their own. Size differences might still be obvious (e.g., if an infant chimpanzee imitates her mother), but generally we do not ask questions like "why is the infant responding to arm movements with arm movements?" Building a robot that responds to a particular observed movement with a particular response lets us appreciate the full complexity of the correspondence problem, which is seemingly solved with ease by animals that imitate (compare chapter 3 on dolphin imitation).

In order to justify the agent-based perspective on imitation, we now first explain and define the concept of *autonomous agent* and show the implications of applying this concept to the study of imitation. We then give examples from the study of imitation in animals and artifacts that support this agent-based perspective.

Biological and Constructed Agents

Recently, the concept of agents and autonomous agents has attracted significant attention in areas as diverse as artificial intelligence, economics, artificial life, and social sciences (for overviews and reviews on agent-based modeling and agent research, see for example, Wooldridge and Jennings 1995; Bradshaw 1997; Jennings, Sycara, and Wooldridge 1998; Dautenhahn 1998a, 2000b). The concept of agent goes back to Carl Hewitt's computational *actor* model published in 1977, which suggested to model problem-solving as the activity of a society of primitive objects, the actors, that cannot be decomposed further (cf. Minsky 1085). In the actor programming methodology, actors are executed concurrently and interact purely locally by sending messages to each other. Control is therefore decentralized in a society of self-contained actors that locally know about each other.

Particularly in the 1990s, the terms *agent* and *autonomous agent* became widely used in both the robotics as well as the artificial intelligence community. Based on an interest in animals and robotic agents, Luc Steels (1995) characterized an autonomous agent as (1) a system, consisting of a set of elements interacting with each other and the environment; (2) performing a particular function for another agent or system; and (3) as capable of maintaining itself—that is, a self-sustaining system. In the area of software systems, a variety of properties of agents have been identified and discussed by Wooldridge and Jennings (1995):

- *Autonomy:* agents operate without direct intervention of humans or others and have some kind of control over their actions and internal state.
- *Social ability:* agents interact with other agents and possibly humans via some kind of agent-communication language.
- *Reactivity:* agents perceive their environment (the physical world, a user via graphical user interface, a collection of other agents, the Internet, combinations of these), and respond in a timely fashion to changes that occur in it.
- *Proactiveness:* agents do not simply act in response to their environment, they are able to exhibit goal-directed behavior by taking the initiative.

Other, more specific attributes of agency, like mobility, rationality, and others are often added to the above list in stronger notions of agency. A widely known definition of *autonomous agent* was proposed by Franklin and Graesser (1997):

An autonomous agent *is a system situated within and a part of the environment that senses that environment and acts on it, over time, in pursuit of its own agenda and so as to affect what it senses in the future.*

This definition is very attractive since it applies easily to both animals and artifacts. Franklin and Graesser (1997) propose a natural kinds taxonomy of agents. Figure 1.3 shows a modification of this taxonomy adapted to the specific subject of this chapter.

Biological agents are historical agents, situated in time and space, their morphologies and behavior reflect the "history" of

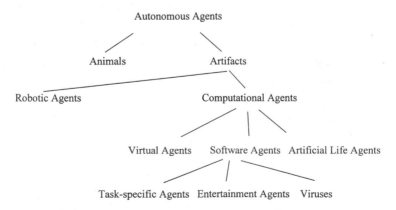

Figure 1.3 A taxonomy of autonomous agents, modified from Franklin and Graesser, (1997).

phylogeny and ontogeny, which also makes every biological agent unique. This applies to a single-cell organism such as *E. coli* or *Paramecium* as well as to multicellular organisms. Experiences during the lifetime of an organism are shaping its body, behavior, and mind. This is particularly developed in organisms that can actively remember the past and reconstruct their history. In Dautenhahn (1996), the term *autobiographic agent* is defined as follows: "Autobiographic agents are agents which are embodied and situated in a particular environment (including other agents), and which dynamically reconstruct their individual *history* (autobiography) during their lifetimes."[1] An autonomous agent perspective on imitation means that an agent is more than a Xerox machine that is producing photocopies, more than a puppet-on-a-string robot tele-controlled by a skilled operator (such a perspective is therefore narrower than the definition of imitation as discussed by Mitchell in chapter 17 of this volume). An *autonomous, autobiographic agent* is able to represent, access, and to some extent control its behavior and relationship to the (social) environment, based on experiences in the past and predictions about the future. Based on its phylogeny and ontogeny, an animal agent anticipates what is likely to happen next, and prepares itself to act appropriately in response (Smith 1996). This does not mean that the remembering, anticipation, and prediction need to be "conscious" in any sense. Indeed, these notions apply as much to bacteria and bugs as they do to mammals, including humans.

Now, what does this short review of the concept of autonomous agents contribute to imitation and the correspondence problem? To begin with, it provides a common viewpoint applicable to both animals and artificially constructed agents and thus bridges biology and the sciences of the artificial. If animals, robots, and software agents are all instances of *agents*, then general principles and problems of autonomous autobiographic agents inhabiting a shared context arise repeatedly in the designs of their imitative and social learning abilities. Such designs may be those of nature, whose secrets biologists and psychologists attempt to unravel, or they may be artificial ones, which roboticists and other system builders seek to engineer.

It is an interesting observation that in fields as diverse as software engineering, cognitive science, and robotics, where researchers try to understand natural intelligence and attempt to describe, model, simulate, and build systems that show (aspects of) natural intelligence, the concept of *autonomous agents* has proved to be valuable, despite the fact that, particularly in the early years, the concept was often used very vaguely and diversely. It is obviously advantageous to think about distinct, self-contained, autonomous entities as the basic objects of study. We might even speculate about the evolutionary origin of this tendency to conceptualize the world in terms of interacting agents: According to the *Social Intelligence Hypothesis*, the evolution of primate intelligence is linked with an increase of the complexity of primate social life (see articles in Byrne and Whiten 1988; Whiten and Byrne 1997). The argument suggests that during the evolution of human intelligence, a transfer took place from social to nonsocial intelligence so that hominid primates could transfer their expertise from the social to the nonsocial domain (see review in Gigerenzer 1997). An interesting aspect of this kind of transfer is given by Mithen (1996), who explains the evolution of anthropomorphic thinking with an accessibility between the domains of social intelligence and natural history intelligence so that "people could be thought of as animals, and animals could be thought of as people" (p. 224).

Furthermore, the accessibility between the domains of social and technical intelligence led to the possibility of thinking about people as objects to be manipulated, similar to the way physical objects can be manipulated. If this overlap between the technical and social domain is mutual, then this could explain why we tend to think of artifacts in terms of social entities. Reeves and Nass (1996) have convincingly shown that humans tend to treat computers (and media in general) as people, and the same is suggested for robots (Bumby and Dautenhahn 1999). Treating robotic and software agents as people opens up a rich source of knowledge of the social world, knowledge about relations, communication, cooperation, and so forth. Recognizing the power of harnessing such correspondences between natural agents for predicting each other's behavior suggests that they might be profitably applied in developing certain artificial ones. As a design paradigm to help ground meaning in interactive constructive biology and computational systems, Nehaniv (1999a,b) has advocated the application of such "egomorphic principles"—that is, useful metaphors and mappings in design that exploit correspondences of an agent's *first-person* embodiment with that of other agents, in effect making them into *second persons*. Similarly, using an agent-based perspective in the study of imitation can give us access to a rich source of knowledge

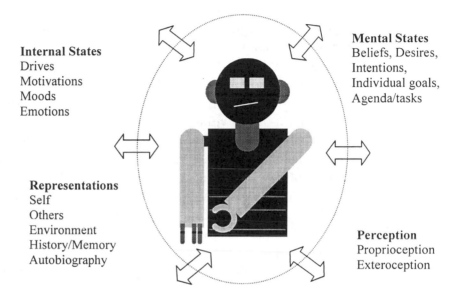

Behavior Repertoire
Instincts
Individually learned behavior
Explicitly taught behavior
Socially acquired behavior

Mental States
Beliefs, Desires,
Intentions,
Individual goals,
Agenda/tasks

Internal States
Drives
Motivations
Moods
Emotions

Representations
Self
Others
Environment
History/Memory
Autobiography

Perception
Proprioception
Exteroception

Figure 1.4 A hypothetical *autonomous, autobiographic agent:* situated in time and space, historically grounded, and structurally coupled with its environment (embodied).

that we have on biological agents. An agent is situated in time and space, agents are not identical, they have a unique perspective and life history reflected in their behavior and their bodies. Also, a biological agent occupies a particular *ecological niche* representing its particular biotic and abiotic relationships with the environment; it is, as such, experiencing, responding to, creating, and being part of its *Umwelt*, its own individual surrounding world (Uexküll 1909); compare also Fritz and Kotrschal's ethological approach to avian imitation (chapter 5 of this volume).

Figure 1.4 shows a hypothetical agent and aspects of its embodiment that can be modeled in order to make it an autonomous, autobiographic agent (the list is not exhaustive, and depending on the particular design philosophy adopted by the designer, those issues might be addressed in a variety of ways and with different emphasis).

Let us now discuss a few consequences of this agent-based perspective on imitation, with a particular focus on the correspondence problem.

Agents Are Part of a (Social) Environment: The Case of Enculturated Agents

Autonomous *social agents* are embedded in a social and cultural environment. As pointed out, for example, by Herman (chapter 3 of this volume) and by Call and Carpenter (chapter 9 of this volume), the issue of *enculturation* plays an important part in discussions on the interpretation of experiments that are designed to show whether certain animals can imitate or not (Tomasello et al. 1993; Whiten and Custance 1996; Hayes and Hayes 1952). Apes who are raised by humans and grow up in a typically human social and cultural environment are more likely to demonstrate imitative abilities than apes who are mother reared. Herman (chapter 3 of this volume) discusses that enculturation might play a role in his studies with captive dolphins who have intensive daily contact with humans. Distinctive differences between imitative abilities of mother-reared versus enculturated apes are also noted. Tomasello, Savage-Rumbaugh, and Kruger (1993) systematically studied the skills of apes to reproduce modeled actions. Subjects included mother-reared chimpanzees and bonobos, enculturated chimpanzees and bonobos, and 2-year-old human children. Results show that the mother-reared nonhuman apes hardly show any imitative learning of novel actions (both with respect to ends and means of the actions). In contrast, the enculturated apes and the human children showed much more frequent imitative learning, without any significant differences in frequency between species.

Call and Carpenter (chapter 9 of this volume) argue for an enhanced ability of enculturated apes to pay attention to actions, rather than to results, as compared to mother-reared apes. For some animals, being immersed in human culture may influence the ontogeny of imitative abilities—social animals such as apes show the ability to respond to exposure to human culture. How these influences work is still an open question. According to Call and Carpenter, enculturation might influence the development of attention mechanisms so that animals focus on different sources of information in the environment (in particular, in the behavior of the animal to be imitated). A similar hypothesis is discussed by Tomasello (1999), who suggests that in humanlike cultural environments, apes receive a kind of *socialization of attention*. Being surrounded by humans who show them things, point toward objects, encourage (and even reinforce) imitation, and teach them special skills—all of which involve a referential triangle of human, ape, and a third entity—seems to encourage a development of cognitive achievements in apes similar to those of human children, although differences between cognitive skills in enculturated apes and human children remain apparent. However, enculturation seems to affect cognitive skills and imitation in apes. In the context of the correspondence problem, the enculturation effect might change the animal's attention to different aspects of the corresponding behavior and the relationship of demonstrator, imitator, and possibly other objects. If the enculturation effects on attention proposed by Call and Tomasello can be confirmed (at least for human-raised apes), trying to account for these effects will pose an interesting challenge for theories and models of imitation.

Other types of influences may play a role. Growing up in a human family means that a lot of time is spent on social interactions. In particular, young animals receive an enormous amount of attention. Imitative and rhythmic interaction games (comprising, e.g., vocalizations and body movements) between infants and caretakers—such as imitation and turn taking—play an important part in the development of social cognition and communication in the young human animal (Bullowa 1979; Užgiris et al. 1989; Meltzoff 1996; Meltzoff and Moore 1999; Nadel et al. 1999; Trevarthen 1977; Trevarthen, Kokkinaki, and Fiamenghi 1999; Heimann and Ullstadius 1999; Butterworth 1999; Užgiris 1999). Imitation plays an important part in play and social learning in humans, including adults and children. An animal that grows up in close contact with humans may experience an enormous amount of attention, engagement, and positive feedback with respect to imitative and coordinated behavior between humans and the nonhuman animal. This might have several influences on the cognitive development of the animal. To name a few: The fact that an imitative action—even an accidental one—may receive positive feedback and attention could increase the animal's motivation and tendency to imitate. Without this encouragement to imitate during social development an animal might not consider imitation to be a desirable goal. Also, in a human-populated environment an animal is likely to frequently observe imitated actions—humans imitating each other or the animal. This might influence the way sequences of actions are observed, structured, and organized—the reader may compare discussions on action- versus program-level imitation, string parsing, or sequence versus hierarchy copying (Byrne and Russon 1998; Byrne 1999; Whiten, chapter 8 of this volume). Also,

the structure of observed behavior needs to be mapped on corresponding structures of behavior that can be generated by the
observer. Thus, enculturation might influence processes involved
in the correspondence problem. In particular, the *motivation* to
observe an action and its *salience* for the animal may be strongly
affected by the details of enculturation. Often, humans serve as
models for tests on imitation in nonhuman apes. However, from a
nonhuman ape's point of view, the behavior of humans, who also
come in various other roles (for example, as keepers, experimenters, observers, etc.) and who are not necessarily considered
part of the family, might not necessarily be mapped to their own
behavior. Similarly, Whiten (chapter 8 of this volume), when
describing experiments where humans serve as models for chimpanzee imitation, discusses the need to do comparable studies
with chimpanzee models.

Enculturated bottlenosed dolphins are a good example of animals who seem to readily "solve the correspondence problem"
and identify mappings between their own actions and those of
conspecifics or of humans (Herman, chapter 3 of this volume),
although differences between the body shapes and behaviors of
dolphins and humans are larger than differences between humans
and nonhuman apes. Perhaps enculturated animals understand
better what they are "supposed" to do in an imitation task, given
that they had been exposed to numerous examples of social interactions and imitation with and among humans. This does not
exclude the possibility that imitative behavior might also be prevalent in natural populations of the highly social dolphin, as evidenced, for example, by signature whistle matching recently
documented for wild dolphins (Janik 2000). Animals with strong
individual-specific social relationships generally employ communication systems including signature signals for recognition (Tyack
2000). The imitation of signaling and other behaviors thus appears
to be strongly connected with such sociality, and with the evolution of symbolic communication.

Social relationships between model and imitator might also influence the readiness of an animal to imitate. In children's play or
interactions between infants and human caretakers, imitation usually occurs spontaneously. In research into animal imitation, the
animals often go through an intensive training period in order to
make an experimental approach possible. In contrast, social learning in the wild happens spontaneously, influenced by social net-

works and relationships among group members, as in the socially transmitted behavior in Japanese macaques described by Huffman (1996). As in the case of dolphins, captive animals with intensive human contact often socially bond with their trainers. They might be highly motivated since they want to please the human, in addition to wanting positive feedback (such as food rewards).

An interesting example of the importance of social roles and relationships for teaching African Grey parrots the correct labels of objects and other skills is described by Pepperberg (chapter 4 of this volume). A *model/rival technique* is used in order to teach the bird: This technique involves two humans and the bird. One human serves as a model for the bird's correct responses, shows aversive consequences for errors, and is also competing with the bird for the trainer's attention. The trainer and model/rival then switch roles. This method has proved to be most effective, and shows that the specific (social) structure of this training procedure is, in comparison to other training techniques, most likely to result in successful vocal learning.

To summarize, the autonomous agent perspective that acknowledges individualized social and historical grounding (phylogenetic and autobiographic) suggests that research on imitation should consider the social and cultural influences, including relationships, social networks, and the individual kinds of interactions an animal is involved in during its ontogeny. Controlling these parameters is problematic, if not impossible, for experimental approaches to animal imitation. However, experiments with advanced artifacts that can engage in social interactions with humans and that will be able to build up relationships with them (Breazeal and Scassellati, chapter 14 of this volume) might give valuable insights into this area.

Understanding Others' Minds (and Perceptions)

Heyes and colleagues (Heyes and Dawson 1990; Heyes, Dawson, and Nokes 1992) reported evidence of observational learning or imitation using a bidirectional control procedure where a trained rat (demonstrator) pushes a joystick in either of two directions. Later, an observer rat is placed in the chamber with the joystick. Observer rats seemed to show the tendency to push the joystick in the same direction (in space as well as relative to the body) as the demonstrators. However, later studies showed that odor cues on the joystick are sufficient if not necessary to account for the results (Mitchell et al. 1999). For olfactory-dominant species like rats or dogs, experiments that test for imitation via visual observation are therefore likely to be affected. This example shows the difficulty in interpreting an imitation experiment with animals: one often cannot know (and/or control) what goes on in an animal's mind, what it is currently perceiving, and which sensory inputs provide salient features that influence the animal's behavior. For humans and other primates, vision is generally an important sensory modality, but even within the sensory modality different inputs can have different salience. Generally, one needs to consider the possibility that different types of sensory input might have different salience for different kinds of species. To give an example: the salience of species-typical features (which might be substantially different from humans) plays an important role in discussions on self-recognition/self-awareness in primates. Gallup (1970) developed an experimental procedure that is intended to formally test for self-awareness—the *mirror test*. The first step of this procedure is to expose the animal to a mirror. Then, a dye mark is applied to the animal's eyebrow or ear (or other visually inaccessible parts of the body/head) while the animal is anesthetized (or some other way it could be made sure that the animal is unaware of the changes to his body). Then, the animal is again exposed to a mirror and the responses are recorded. Humans more than about 2 years old and great apes show self-recognition, typically inspecting their "modified" body part in the mirror, trying to remove the mark, and so on. Many subsequent studies show that humans older than 2 years, chimpanzees, gorillas, and orangutans, but not most monkey species showed self-directed behavior when tested by Gallup's procedure (compare Parker, Mitchell, and Boccia 1994). Mirror-guided body inspection is often taken as a sign of self-recognition/ self-awareness—that is, to realize that the reflected image represents "one's self," and not a different animal, with important implications for questions on animals' understanding of the social world (theory of mind, mindreading, e.g., Premack and Woodruff 1978; Baron-Cohen 1995; Heyes 1998). The results have therefore often been interpreted in terms of fundamental cognitive differences of apes and other primates (e.g., Povinelli and Preuss 1995). Experiments with the mirror test and its implications have been critically analyzed (e.g., Mitchell 1993; Heyes 1994), and also challenged experimentally. Yet Hauser and colleagues published experimental evidence in 1995 of self-recognition in cotton-top tamarins (*Saguinus oedipus*), using a variation of Gallup's mirror-test: instead of placing a dye mark on the eyebrow, the white hair on the tamarins' head was color dyed. Among many species of tamarins, only the cotton-top tamarin has a distinctive and species-typical tuft of white hair on the top of its head. Discussions on methodological problems of both the original mirror test, as well as results of Hauser and colleagues can be followed up, for example, in Anderson and Gallup (1997) and Hauser and Kralik (1997). New experimental paradigms will shed more light on the question of individual, developmental, and species differences of self-awareness and performance in the mirror test (see discussion in Tomasello and Call 1997, 331 ff.). The importance of this discussion for imitation lies in the question of why animals might fail the mirror test. They might fail because of an absence of the concept of "self," but they might fail, for example, because of the lack of salience of the dye-mark. For all monkey species, staring is typically an aggressive threat. Thus, monkeys tend to only stare briefly at the mirror, which, according to Hauser and colleagues (1995), does not suffice to recruit the attention necessary to discover correspondences between the animal's own body and the mirror image. The mirror test might therefore be an appropriate test for self-recognition in humans, for whom mirrors are an important cultural artifact and who spend a significant amount of time in front of a mirror. However, for other animals less visually oriented or who pay different attention to specific features of another animal's body, this test might be inappropriate. Similarly, testing whether an animal can imitate or not requires an insight into how animals perceive the world. An agent-based perspective on imitation and the correspondence problem demands an analysis of different ways in which animals understand and perceive the world. Artifacts might provide interesting tools in order to investigate the "other minds" problem. Building an artifact with possibly very different ways and modalities of perceiving the world (e.g., a robot with infrared or ultrasonic sensors, a software agent getting input from the environment via streams of data following a fixed protocol), requires different types of correspondences between the model and the imitator's perceptions. Such types of experiments could go far beyond the traditional robotics approach to imitation that involves two robots of the same kind imitating each other.

Novelty: Can There Be Imitation without Learning?

Often, imitation is discussed as a form of social or observational *learning*. Early on, imitation had been defined as "learning to do an act from seeing it done" (Thorndike 1898). Indeed, the investigation of imitation in robotics and software-agent research is deeply motivated by the promise of having an effective and efficient means of teaching the robot or agent new skills and competencies. A new paradigm of robot programming could be achieved using such "programming by showing." Likewise, many definitions of imitation require the imitated action or behavior either to be novel in contrast to "instinctive tendencies" (Thorpe 1956; Visalberghi and Fragaszy, chapter 18 of this volume), or, in broader definitions of imitation, to be novel in contrast to "designed" and familiar actions that are already in the behavioral repertoire of an animal or artifact (Mitchell 1987). Recognizing that no imitation can be exact, Whiten and Ham (1992) define imitation as a process in which an individual "learns some aspect(s) of the intrinsic form of an act" from another.

Nevertheless, there are several fundamental problems with demanding novelty and learning of imitated behavior. In degenerate cases, it may be that only the sequencing or combination of actions already in the repertoire is novel in an observed behavior (compare the discussion of "horizontal processes" in the associative sequence learning theory of Heyes and Ray 2000 and Heyes, chapter 19 of this volume). Such a combinatorially novel sequence might be copied immediately, or even as it is being performed by a demonstrator. It might not be retained at all, so there may be no grounds to claim that anything has been learned; or it might be performed after a long delay and possibly in similar or more general contexts. So even in blind copying, there can at least be the novelty of sequencing. A novel behavior can consist of a new combination of familiar actions. In saying that an animal is "copying a novel act," novelty is always relative; there are degrees of novelty, and in particular, any behavior is always related to acts already in the repertoire (Whiten 1999, personal communication). For example, experiments on tool use often involve manipulations and actions that in themselves are not novel (e.g., Nagell, Olguin, and Tomasello 1993, studying social learning with chimpanzees and human children involving rakelike tools to access food; the same task studied with orangutans by Call and Tomasello 1994; or Whiten, chapter 8 of this volume, studying chimpanzees and children manipulating an artificial fruit to access food). Such tasks involve basic actions like picking up, pushing, pulling, and turning objects, which are familiar to the animal, but only a specific subset of all possible combinations of actions in a sequence of actions leads to success—for example, in terms of food access. Also, what kind of action is "novel" for a particular animal is impossible to judge without knowing its complete *history* from birth, a requirement that is unrealistic to fulfill for field studies, and immensely difficult even in the case of animals reared under close observation by humans. Moreover, even exactly the same behavior can have a different meaning when applied to a different context. In these cases, there can be novelty in the sequencing or organization of familiar behavioral components, or novelty in the application of familiar behavioral patterns in a new context or for a new purpose. If a human infant learns by observation that an umbrella protects from rain, using exactly the same tool for protection from intense sunlight cannot be judged "novel" from the point of view of tools and actions involved, but fulfills the novelty criterion with respect to environmental features. But what if the child later uses the umbrella to hide from her parents, or to fight off an aggressive dog? Such examples indicate that an infant observing an adult using an umbrella for protection against rain can potentially use many different sources of information in the observed action in constructing an imitative action: information on actions (exact movements and sequences of movements for opening the umbrella and positioning it correctly above one's head), state changes or results (standing under the umbrella away from the rain), and goals (not getting wet); see also the discussion by Call and Carpenter in chapter 9 of this volume. Additionally, the observing child can learn about more generic affordances of the umbrella, as a means to actively control and protect oneself from the impact of the environment (raindrops, sunbeams, eye gaze). There seems to be no clear way for an observer to draw a line in the sand demarcating imitation. There is a continuum when a behavior is applied in contexts increasingly removed from the context in which the behavior was observed. This continuum extends from, on the one hand, *imitation* (or even *"blind-copying"*) and, on the other hand, *generalization* (or even *insight*) in the application of old or observed behaviors in new contexts, including, possibly, the application of known actions or tools in new settings in ways that have never been observed. Since imitated actions are constructed by an agent, they depend on the agent's embodiment and the way the agent interacts with the environment. In addition to learning very specific behaviors, an agent might learn about general means to control its interactions with the environments—that is, by using tools as extensions of its embodiment. Thus, although a behavior itself might not be novel, a novel usage in a different context can be an important generalization step for an agent with potentially great adaptive value. Like any behavior produced by an agent, an imitated behavior does not exist in a vacuum, it is constructed by a particular agent, dependent on its specific embodiment, and mediated by the environment.

But even if the imitating agent's behavior does not change and if it does not learn anything, imitation—in the sense of producing similar behavior—may have great adaptive value. Navigating in an unknown landscape is greatly simplified if roads exist, that is, if one can follow the paths other people took, either by following particular cars or following the roads, which as cultural artifacts represent collective experiences. Likewise, one can follow directions literally—that is, without trying to understand the directions, without creating a mental map. A great advantage of such a following strategy (either literally following another agent in space, or following instructions) is the simplicity in processing the information. Observation of actions may be supplanted by communication, with explicit instructions, possibly yielding something akin to imitation (see Goodenough, chapter 22 of this volume). If the instructions are robust and come from a reliable source, then such a strategy might work well. However, it can break down if the environment and/or the relationship of the agent toward its environment changes. For example, the instructions say "take the exit at junction 11" (but junction 11 is closed), or the robot's batteries are going down so that "turn left 90 degrees" results in turning left 78 degrees, or the robot learned to grasp a cup and is confronted with a wine glass. Thus, in addition to identifying results and goals, the capacity for generalization is important for being able to apply an imitated behavior in a new context. Without such generalization, the matching action will be limited to a particular context—identical or very similar to the context where the behavior was originally observed. In extreme cases, with no learning or novelty present, the matching behavior could only occur in an extremely limited context while the behavior to be matched is simultaneously being observed. *Imitation* here does not require memorizing, learning, or generalizing behavior, it only requires:

1. identifying the appropriate model behavior
2. mapping the model behavior to a corresponding behavior of the imitating agent
3. selecting and executing this corresponding behavior

In robotics experiments, the *following strategy*, which implements such a procedure in the context of movements in a two-dimensional space, has proved quite successful for certain kinds of learning by imitation, whereby imitation and correspondences of behavior were "engineered" (not learned) according to the above-mentioned procedure (Dautenhahn 1994; Hayes and Demiris 1994; Demiris and Hayes 1996; Dautenhahn 1995; Gaussier et al. 1998; Billard and Dautenhahn 1997, 1998, 1999; Billard, chapter 11 of this volume). Once two agents share a common context and enough corresponding perceptions of the environment (see Nehaniv and Dautenhahn 2001), a follower agent could learn by imitation from a teacher agent, for example, how to travel a maze or how to label its experiences with "words" from a common vocabulary. Thus, for an autonomous agent, imitation can be adaptive—that is, beneficial to the survival of the individual agent, without involving any explicit learning of the imitated behavior. In such cases, the results of the imitated behavior might be beneficial (i.e., when the imitating agent follows another agent to a specific area of interest, for example, a charging station), or the imitative behavior can serve as a powerful "social bonding" mechanism that creates a shared context that supports social learning (see discussions in Billard and Dautenhahn 1998, 1999). Based on recent discussions on "mirror" neurons and the neurobiological origin of imitation in primate evolution, one might speculate that *mirror neurons* are nature's solution—at least in some primates—to solving the correspondence problem, namely, in creating a common shared context and shared *understanding* of actions and affordances (see below) between two agents (see discussion by Arbib, chapter 10 of this volume).

Imitation, Development, Communication, and Culture

In human primates, imitation plays an important role for the individual's social acquisition of a variety of skills, ranging from vocal imitation in language games to imitation of body movements (e.g., when instructed how to tie shoelaces). However, imitation has important implications at the level of human culture also: social learning is an important requirement for the development of culture in animals (Bonner 1980; Whiten et al. 1999; Reader and Laland 1999) and in particular, human culture (Dawkins 1976). Imitated behaviors or "memes"—are said to be *replicators* in human culture (although the meme is still a rather unsatisfactorily delimited unit of replication)—and are spreading through various forms of imitation, very broadly construed; varieties are formed and selected in a Darwinian dynamic by the biological and cultural environment, which they may, in turn, shape (Dawkins 1976; Blackmore 1999, 2001; Goodenough, chapter 22 of this volume).

Also, as already indicated by Byrne and Russon (1998), at least in human culture imitation is an important *medium of communication*. Imitation is an important mechanism of social learning in human culture, but also a powerful means of signaling interest in another person, used for purposes of communication. According to Nadel and colleagues (1999), *immediate imitation* is an important *format of communication* and milestone in the development of intentional communication, linking the imitator and the imitatee in synchronized activity that creates intersubjective experience, sharing topics and activities, important for the development from primary to pragmatic communication (see also Billard, chapter 11 of this volume). Infants are born ready to communicate by being able to reciprocate in rhythmic engagements with the motives of sympathetic partners (Trevarthen, Kokkinaki, and Fiamenghi 1999). It is important to note that the development of human social cognition and communication is so deeply dependent on the imitative, social encounters of the developing infant that these encounters are likely to shape human culture. This presents an exciting area for further studies on the origins and mechanisms of human culture (compare Užgiris 1999; Butterworth 1999).

Imitating another person, particularly on the level of characteristic vocal or body-movement behaviors, is often used by actors to impersonate historical or contemporary characters. Conspicuous imitation of someone's behavior can be an indication of disapproving mockery. Even unconscious temporal synchronization and rhythmic coordination of movements between people plays an important role in communication and interaction in human culture and proxemics (for the study of humans' perception and use of space, compare Hall 1968, 1983). Temporal synchronization of behavioral dynamics has also been implemented in studies with robot-human interaction (Dautenhahn 1999). Children are encouraged to emulate role models who exhibit desirable behavior and character. In fashion and sports, imitation can also be a kind of flattery: copying a particular style invented by a colleague means paying a compliment in human culture. Even in science the invention of new techniques, methods, and theories by a single individual will only survive in the scientific culture if they are imitated and adopted by others. As cultural replicators, scientific theories are modified and refined through generations of Hegelian dialectic, Popperian falsification, and paradigm shifts of scientific discourse (Kuhn 1962).

Just Puppets on Strings?

For generations humans have been entertaining with circus animals that were trained to "imitate" human behavior (bears riding bicycles, chimpanzees dressed up like humans and smoking a cigar, etc.). In satire, cartoons with nonhuman animals that undoubtedly represent politicians and other human contemporary figures are a widely used artistic vehicle. Surprisingly, as Mitchell discusses in chapter 17 of this volume, although children's imitation skills are generally highly regarded and a rich source of entertainment and amazement ("Look, he uses the spoon like his father!"), imitation in nonhuman animals is often dismissed as "just imitating," particularly when the cognitive abilities of nonhuman animals are at stake. Similar to the circus bear riding a bicycle, or the animal actor showing greater-than-life intelligence on television, in public opinion we are possibly biased to believe that a "trick" is used when we are shown nonhuman animals imitating. Notably, robots (especially humanoid robots that have a similar body shape and movement repertoire to humans) that show imitative abilities often attract huge public (media) attention, as described in Atkeson and colleagues (2000). It is relatively easy to give the impression of, for example, a humanoid robot imitating a human, from an observer point of view: theoretically, instead of having the robot imitating a human, a human who is skilled enough can (with imperceptible delay) imitate the robot, or, knowing the robot's behavior in advance, could "demonstrate" actions that the robot is then sure to "imitate," even if the robot has no perception of the human at all. Playback of a captured data stream of human joint articulations on a robotic hand or humanoid body is an instance of matching behavior, but is even weaker than "blind copying" since the hand or body never perceives the actions it later matches, like a marionette on strings. Similarly, a compact-disc player does not imitate nor even blindly copy vocal performance. Thus, the observation that a biological and an artificial agent are nearly simultaneously performing the same movements does not necessarily reveal anything about imitation. However, programming a robot to perform interesting movements (particularly humanlike, smooth movements as they can be observed in dancing) is substantially more difficult than training a dog to dance, let alone the question of imitation (compare Atkeson et al. 2000). In the case of the dog, we are already dealing with an animal that is capable of showing a variety of different behaviors. Also, it is a very social and socially susceptive animal that is bonded with a human trainer and tries to please him. Thus, a dog is already a socially intelligent autonomous agent and in training it we can build on these skills. Building truly autonomous robots that can be taught a variety of skills in a variety of situations has become more realistic than 10 years ago, but it is still a challenging and exciting research endeavor (see contributions by Demiris and Hayes, Billard, Breazeal and Scassellati, and Matarić in this volume). Two major problems in agent imitation that become apparent in robot imitation are:

1. The problem of *perception*, comprising information on states in the environment as well as states of the agent itself with respect to the environment—that is, proprioception and kinesthesis. These are highly developed in humans and other animals, playing a central part in motor control and regulating animal-environment interactions, but are often extremely underdeveloped and impoverished in robots.

2. The "Big Five" central issues for designing experiments on imitation with autonomous agents[2]: *whom* to imitate (Who is a good teacher? Can a learner become a teacher?[3]), *when* to imitate (play context, teaching, exploration, etc.), *what* to imitate (states, actions, goals, as discussed in chapter 2, or results, actions, goals in Call and Carpenter's terminology, chapter 9 of this volume), *how to map* observed to imitated behavior (*the correspondence problem*[4]),

and *how to evaluate* the success of the attempt at imitation (degrees of success; see chapter 2 and Nehaniv and Dautenhahn 1998b, 2001).

From an autonomous agent perspective on imitation, we might distinguish two cases of when imitation can be observed in an agent: the imitative behavior might result from specific imitation mechanisms that are part of the agent's cognitive and behavioral architecture, or they might result from the interaction of the agent with its environment, so that the "imitated behavior" (as perceived and described by a human observer) is an emergent behavior that is based on simpler mechanisms (compare discussion by Noble and Todd in chapter 16 of this volume). Generally, humans show a tendency for anthropomorphism or *behavior reading* (Mitchell and Hamm 1997). However, many (particularly social) behaviors that appear well organized and structured result from principles of self-organization and local agent-agent plus agent-environment inter-actions. The organization of social insect societies gives a good example of impressive global patterns (e.g., termite mounds) that emerge from distributed interactions (see discussions in Theraulaz and Bonabeau 1999; Bonabeau, Dorigo, and Theraulaz 1999; Dautenhahn 2000a). Such studies (and supporting evidence from simulations with computer programs and mobile robots) show convincingly that complex behavior need not result from the cognitive or behavioral complexity of the animal, or the complexity of the control program of a robot.

Interactive Emergence: Niches and Design Spaces

In the domain of social interactions, self-organization of social behavior is not limited to social insect societies. Often, even in a small group of agents or in dyadic interactions, being endowed with a set of mechanisms that allow local interaction with the environment produces behavior that appears to be based on complex mechanisms of social control.[5] Hendriks-Jansen (1996) discusses the notion of *interactive emergence* with respect to behavior-based robots (e.g., see Brooks 1991) and mother-infant interactions. Imitation games between infants and their caretakers and peers are an example of the emergence of imitation: although from an observer point of view it appears as if the players follow an external rhythm, the rhythm and turn-taking behavior is created by the "players" in a particular social context. For the study of imitation, this has important implications and points toward the importance of research into the emergence of imitation: how can imitative behavior emerge from nonimitative behavior, what are the basic behavioral (perceptual? cognitive?) components and conditions that are *necessary and sufficient* to produce imitation in a particular social context? Also, how do transitions from nonimitative to imitative behavior occur and how can this approach be exploited to control social interactions, for example, in robot-human interaction? Research into the interactive emergence of imitation is sparse (compare Breazeal and Scassellati, chapter 14 of this volume), but might help us explore the design space of robotic solutions to the Big Five challenges. Also, this design space needs to be linked with sets of requirements determined by the concrete properties of the agent and its embodiment with respect to the environment. Aaron Sloman has called these sets of requirements *niche spaces* (1995). Different types of robotic control architectures might map to (different sets of) requirements for different types of robots or other agents. To date, most robotic research is a priori constraining the design space (e.g., by fixing whom, when, and what to imitate) and focusing on a particular architecture providing a fixed solution to the question of how to imitate. Likewise, the evaluation of the success of imitation is then often based on techniques specific to the concrete experimental setup. This approach has been necessary primarily for practical reasons—that is, due to the difficulty of working experimentally with physical robots. Such proof-of-concept implementations have demonstrated what is possible, but they make it difficult to make comparisons and evaluations across different experimental setups. However, for the long-term vision of interdisciplinary research on imitation, an autonomous agent viewpoint might help in developing a *science of imitation* by systematically exploring design spaces, niche spaces, and mappings between the two.

For biological systems, design and niche spaces of different species are interrelated by an evolutionary history. It is speculation to suggest that, for example, all primates, all mammals, or all vertebrates might share the same neurobiological mechanisms underlying imitation. It is, however, unlikely that choices are arbitrary, and discussions have begun on whether the neurobiology of human imitative skills is based on mirror neurons first discovered in monkeys (see discussions in Arbib, chapter 10 of this volume;

Gallese et al. 1996; Rizzolatti et al. 1998). In addition to informing models and architectures on imitation for robotic agents (e.g., Demiris 1999; Demiris and Hayes, chapter 13 of this volume; Billard 2001), such findings can provide data on the internal structure of the design space. Such knowledge can even make the link to other cognitive human skills like language (see Arbib, chapter 10 of this volume; Rizzolati and Arbib 1998) and even social understanding and empathy (Gallese and Goldman 1998). Thus, research on imitation addresses different fascinating facets of animal social minds, in the case of human primates ranging from "do as I do" as a means of teaching/instruction/play, to "you are like me" and imitation games that build scaffolding for the development of social cognition and social bonding, to potential (at present still speculative) implications for "I could be you" (Dautenhahn 1997)—that is, empathic understanding as the strongly bonding mechanism between human beings and possibly other nonhuman animals (compare O'Connell 1995; Gallese and Goldman 1998). For artificial agents such as robots, empathic skills could be the first step toward becoming truly socially intelligent agents (Dautenhahn 1997; Dautenhahn 2000c).

1.3 Overview of Chapters

The twenty-two chapters in this book address different aspects of research on imitation. We deliberately avoided grouping the chapters into the two categories "animals" and "artifacts," since this would have been counterproductive to an integrated, interdisciplinary viewpoint. Instead, we have adopted an agent-based perspective as outlined above and arranged the chapters along common themes that would have been obscured by a "traditional" split into the natural, the artificial, and the theoretical sections. The book thus follows a thread of related issues and topics that meanders through the key aspects of the field of imitation. A pictographic overview and "roadmap" is shown in figure 1.5.

In the following, we trace this thread to briefly introduce the remaining chapters.

In chapter 2, Chrystopher L. Nehaniv and Kerstin Dautenhahn discuss "The Correspondence Problem," already mentioned briefly in this chapter. The authors provide a framework that allows a unified treatment of the problem of imitation for possibly dissimilar bodies (correspondence problem) with respect to animals and

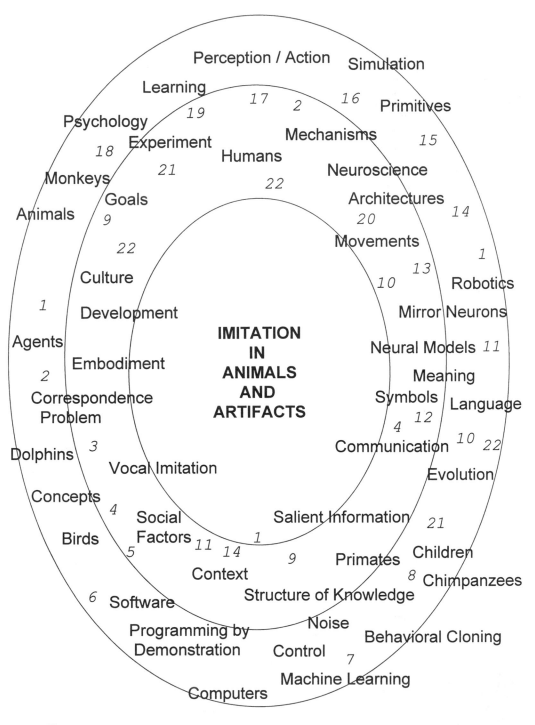

Figure 1.5 Roadmap showing the structure of this volume. Numerals indicate chapter numbers, and serve to situate chapters with respect to relevant nearby issues and topics. See table of contents for chapter titles and authors. Note that some chapter numbers occur more than once in the roadmap.

artifacts by clarifying what it means for the behaviors of different agents to match, and the measures of such matching.

In chapter 3, "Vocal, Social, and Self-Imitation by Bottlenosed Dolphins," Louis M. Herman reviews experimental evidence for imitation of self and others by enculturated bottlenosed dolphins. He gives a comprehensive overview of the study of imitation in dolphins during intra- and interspecies interaction. The studies investigate a variety of different modalities of imitation, comprising auditory and visual imitation, behavioral synchrony, imitation controlled by gestures, imitation of televised models and human body postures, imitation of self, and so on. Particularly intriguing are data where dolphins seem to instantaneously and simultaneously imitate each other. Other cases of dolphin imitation illustrate that they employ appropriate correspondences in mapping movements and body parts when imitating human trainers.

Another highly social species of animals is studied by Irene M. Pepperberg in chapter 4, "Allospecific Referential Speech Acquisition in Grey Parrots (*Psittacus erithacus*): Evidence for Multiple Levels of Avian Vocal Imitation." Her results indicate an elaborate interspecies correspondence here in the vocal and auditory domain, as well as evidence of an interspecific correspondence in conceptual abilities and the referential and predicative use of speech by the parrots. As with Herman's discussion of dolphin imitation, enculturated Grey parrots learn from human trainers and generalize their knowledge to interactions with others when provided a particular social context, as exemplified by Pepperberg's highly successful model/rival technique with role reversal adapted from Todt (1975).

Johannes Fritz and Kurt Kotrschal discuss "On Avian Imitation: Cognitive and Ethological Perspectives" in chapter 5. In contrast to Herman's and Pepperberg's chapters, which show interspecies imitation (human-dolphin, dolphin-dolphin [but human mediated], human-parrot), this chapter focuses on social learning among birds. Research on social learning in a variety of different bird species is addressed. Experiments on social learning and imitation in different bird species are reviewed in the light of possible social cognitive mechanisms. An ethological perspective on the study of social learning in common ravens (*Corvus corax*) is discussed, focusing on food scrounging. The authors argue for taking into account the social, ecological, and life-history contexts of social learning that are often neglected in laboratory studies. Discussions of experiments with common ravens and other bird species lead to the development of a model of the relationship between scrounging and learning. Social conditions (social relationship between "producer" and "scrounger") and ecological conditions are important factors in this model. This work is put in the broader context of a synthesis of cognitive and ethological approaches.

In Henry Lieberman's chapter "Art Imitates Life: Programming by Example as an Imitation Game" (chapter 6), the social context of imitation is quite different from the previous chapters. Here, social learning is studied as a means of machine learning in which an artifact (software) learns tasks from a human. This programming-by-example (PBE) approach can result in more natural human-computer interfaces where humans can demonstrate to the computer what to do, rather than going down to the level of arcane programming languages. It is interesting to note that Lieberman is also currently studying the PBE paradigm with Irene Pepperberg's Grey parrots. Future experiments in this domain may show whether one day, nonhuman animals could program computers by example.

A machine-learning perspective is also given in chapter 7, "Learning to Fly," by Claude Sammut, Scott Hurst, Dana Kedzier, and Donald Michie—a classic paper reprinted here that shows the application of behavioral cloning techniques to the problem of learning to fly a simulated aircraft by observing the control actions of human pilots. The authors show how subsymbolic skill-level knowledge can be extracted from the behavior of humans—knowledge that is normally not or cannot be articulated explicitly. For example, humans usually cannot explain how it is that they ride a bicycle, walk, or catch a ball. The authors illustrate how techniques of behavioral cloning build up decision trees, giving rules capturing such knowledge from the behavior of human pilots, whereby different trees control behaviors appropriate in different subgoal contexts along an overall flight plan. The decision trees, given current state and sensory readings, determine control actions on the aircraft's various actuators. This allows an autopilot, which is a "behavioral clone" of the human pilot, to successfully take off, circle back, and land the aircraft.

The structure of knowledge that is necessary in order to transfer skills from one system to another is also an important component of Andrew Whiten's chapter, "Imitation of Sequential and Hierarchical Structure in Action: Experimental Studies with Children and Chimpanzees" (chapter 8). Imitation of sequential and hierarchical structure in object manipulation is studied with the "artificial-fruit" paradigm, involving an artifact that can be manipulated only in particular ways and (if operated successfully) then provides a reward. Results suggest that hierarchy copying and sequence copying are two separate and important aspects of what constitutes the copying of a behavioral "program." Whiten argues for further extensive comparative studies with different animal species, which might shed more light on these two types of imitation and their natural occurrence.

Josep Call and Malinda Carpenter's "Three Sources of Information in Social Learning" (chapter 9) clarifies the relationship between emulation and other types of social learning. The chapter then discusses differences of what kind of information an imitator might focus on while observing a demonstrator, and how this could result in different types of social learning. Call and Carpenter outline a new, multidimensional framework for investigating social learning that is based on analyzing different types of information (goals, actions, results) that imitating agents are able to extract from observing the model agents. Shifting between and exploiting various sources of information is discussed with respect to humans, apes, and individuals with autism. Advantages of this framework for animals and artifacts are discussed. Similar to Whiten's chapter, the proposed framework points to the need for extensive comparative studies across different species, in order to clarify the nature of different types of social learning as they can be observed in biological systems.

Michael Arbib's chapter "The Mirror System, Imitation, and the Evolution of Language" (chapter 10) bridges the gap between imitation as it can be observed today, and the neurobiological evolutionary "history" of imitation in humans. Based on recent experiments with monkeys, Arbib outlines a hypothetical history of human imitation, ranging from "I know what you do" to "I understand what you say." This argument includes an interesting link between body movements, body language, gestural communication, sign language, and "human" language. The latter is often described as "unique" to humans and in this way isolating humans from the rest of the animal kingdom. Arbib's ideas might therefore have important implications for studies on teaching nonhuman animals sign language, accounting for the language-readiness of human infants, and reconstructing an evolutionary history of human language.

Aude Billard's chapter gives a concrete example of how implementations of minimal systems with languagelike features could employ imitation as a social-bonding mechanism that allows an imitator robot to learn a vocabulary from a demonstrator robot. In "Imitation: A Means to Enhance Learning of a Synthetic Proto-Language in Autonomous Robots" (chapter 11), the learning architecture (a recurrent neural network) is tested in different experimental setups, including robot-robot as well as robot-human interaction. Robots equipped with such a learning architecture can be taught a vocabulary of "words" (symbolic body movements or labels) if a skilled teacher is available that provides consistent behavior. Particularly important in these experiments is the fact that the "meaning" of "words" is experienced by the learner robot based on its own proprioceptive and extero-perceptions.

In chapter 12, "Rethinking the Language Bottleneck: Why Don't Animals Learn to Communicate?" Michael Oliphant discusses experiments that demonstrate that learning word-meaning pairs is neither computationally expensive nor even difficult, and can be realized with relatively simple neural networks. Unlike in simulations, "meaning" in nature does not exist independently of agents (Nehaniv 1999a,b). Oliphant argues that the fact that learned symbolic systems of communication (verbal or movement based) seem not to be widespread in the animal kingdom might therefore be due to the problem of detecting the "meaning" of symbols in learning such a system. This nicely links back to the issue of mirror neurons and Michael Arbib's chapter relating between primate imitation and language. The mirror-neuron system and areas of the human brain associated with language might thus support language readiness in humans by providing access to the meaning of others' movements and gestures in terms of what the corresponding movements and their affordances could mean for oneself.

The mirror system and data from developmental psychology on imitation in infants have also inspired the development of robot control architectures, as described by John Demiris and Gillian Hayes in chapter 13, "Imitation as a Dual-Route Process Featuring Predictive and Learning Components: A Biologically Plausible Computational Model." This model of primate imitation mechanisms is experimentally tested with simulated robots, where an observing robot is imitating particular movements—namely, sign language "words" that are part of the international standard semaphore code (ISSC). The model combines a passive route to imitation (perceive–recognize–reproduce) with an active route that internally generates movements wherein the imitator puts itself in the place of the demonstrator. Then, it selects one that predicts the demonstrator's behavior best. Experimental results with this computational model yield interesting predictions that might inspire future experiments on primate imitation mechanisms and, in particular, the mirror-neuron system. This chapter presents the first experimentally tested robot control architecture for imitation that is inspired by the mirror-neuron system.

While the chapter by Demiris and Hayes focuses on the plausibility of the robot's control architecture for imitation, in chapter 14, "Challenges in Building Robots that Imitate People," Cynthia Breazeal and Brian Scassellati focus on designing and programming a humanoid robot so that it produces imitative and other socially plausible behaviors in interaction with humans. The chapter discusses main problems and challenges of this approach. Of particular interest is that social interaction (for example, imitative turn-taking games) can emerge from the dynamics and regulation of meaningful social interaction, in the same way as the structure and rhythms of imitation games played by an infant and her caretaker, which are not imposed by an external or internal clock or supervisor.

This focus on face-to-face interaction dynamics contrasts with Maja J. Matarić's discussion of "Sensory-Motor Primitives as a Basis for Imitation: Linking Perception to Action and Biology to Robotics" (chapter 15). She proposes a model of imitation based on sensory-motor primitives, supported by evidence on movement perception in humans and the neurobiological basis of motor control. Different robotics test beds and experimental methods are discussed, involving a variety of different artifacts—for example, a simulated humanoid and different types of mobile robots. Results of these experiments are interpreted with respect to the proposed model of imitation. This chapter illustrates a particular design perspective based on sensory-motor primitives. These primitives could also serve as atomic units in building up a partial solution to the correspondence problem (compare chapter 2). Ultimately, one can expect that a synthesis is required between work on correspondences, a focus on the control architecture (as it is done, for example, in Demiris and Hayes's work, chapter 13), and the consideration of the social context, as we see it in Billard's and Breazeal and Scassellati's work (chapters 11 and 14).

In research that is constructing robots that imitate, usually the term "imitation" is not clearly distinguished from other forms of social learning or copying, since any kind of social learning or copying at all, for example, with a humanoid robot, is difficult to accomplish. From a conceptual point of view, this is, however, an important issue and is discussed in more detail by Jason Noble and Peter Todd in chapter 16, "Imitation or Something Simpler? Modeling Simple Mechanisms for Social Information Processing." Here, the authors address the perennial question "what is imitation?" in the more general context of social-learning mechanisms, from a bottom-up point of view that is concerned with building minimal systems that achieve particular behavior. They describe how some simple mechanisms applied in a collection of robotic agents could give rise to various well-known phenomena that look, at first sight, very much like imitation (e.g., contagion and stimulus enhancement). An important aspect is hereby the role of the observer.

"Imitation as a Perceptual Process" (chapter 17), by Robert W. Mitchell, complements this approach by starting off with a definition of imitation that can be applied across biological and artificial systems. Applying this definition, he identifies different types of design processes that lead to different types of imitation. Mitchell then discusses the important role of perceptual matching in animal imitation—in particular, kinesthetic-visual matching. He argues that perceptual matching is a significant factor in imitation, and that one particular form of perceptual matching, namely, kinesthetic-visual matching, is essential for bodily and facial imitation and self-recognition, and probably also is important for pretense and for recognizing that one is being imitated by another. The argument is discussed with respect to different species of animals (humans at different stages in their ontogeny, children with autism, apes, monkeys and other mammal species, birds). Implications for the design of machines that imitate are outlined.

Elisabetta Visalberghi and Dorothy Fragaszy's "'Do Monkeys Ape?'—Ten Years After" (chapter 18) gives an excellent example of problems and issues involved in animal imitation research, based on their long-term research with capuchin monkeys. The authors here use a definition of imitation that demands novelty of the acquired behavior. The results suggest that social partners do affect many aspects of behavior in capuchins, but that they do not imitate or learn unlikely behaviors from one another. Since capuchin monkeys are social learners, but do not show imitation, the same might be true for many, if not all monkey species. Data on social learning in capuchin monkeys support the domain-general view of their social learning abilities, namely, what they learn socially seems consistent with what they learn in individual contexts. The authors discuss this conclusion in the general context of research on animal imitation and recent findings on the mirror-neuron system. Controversies on mechanisms and the nature of social learning and imitation in different species of animals are certain to be ongoing in the field of animal behavior research; compare the recent suggestion of true imitation in marmosets (*Callithrix jacchus*) by Voelkl and Huber (2000).

"Transformational and Associative Theories of Imitation" (chapter 19), by Cecilia Heyes, reviews a range of existing theories of the proximate psychological mechanisms of imitation distinguishing *transformational theories* (which suggest that most of the information required for behavioral matching relies on internal cognitive processes for its generation) from *associative theories* (which claim that this information is principally derived from experience). She outlines a new, *Associative Sequence Learning Theory (ASL)*, which makes testable predictions. ASL suggests that imitation is mediated by associative processes establishing correspondences in *horizontal* (temporal sequencing) and *vertical* (sensory-motor) dimensions. She argues that this approach provides a more satisfactory and predictive framework than existing theories, particularly, for handling the important problem of *perceptual opacity* of some imitated behaviors that yield very dissimilar sensory inputs when observed than when executed—for example, facial expressions as opposed to the movement of distal appendages or vocalizations.

"Dimensions of Imitative Perception-Action Mediation" (chapter 20), by Stefan Vogt, addresses the question of how action is informed by perception (perception-action mediation), an important issue for cognitive-psychological research on imitation. Experiments with human subjects are reviewed in order to illustrate the important research issues. In light of such experiments and other evidence from the behavioral and neuroscience literature, Vogt proposes a distinction between *parameter imitation* (via a dorsal stream), which focuses on only specific aspects of a model's behavior and *action imitation* (via a ventral stream) for complete actions (or sequences of actions). He argues that neither type of imitation is guided by a detailed representation derived from the model. The former type allows for fast incorporation of highly particular aspects of the model's behavior into the observer's, while in the latter type the observer's own motor action repertoire is accessed on a high level of coding.

In "Goal Representations in Imitative Actions" (chapter 21), Harold Bekkering and Wolfgang Prinz discuss possible cognitive mechanisms that underlie imitative performance in human infants and children. They focus on the "when," "how," and "what" of imitation, surveying and presenting evidence from imitation in children for a *goal-directed theory of imitation*. This theory argues that the action recognition process is guided by an interpretation of observed motor patterns as goal-directed behaviors, and that these goals can later activate a motor program to attain corresponding effects (possibly organized in a sequence or hierarchy). This is related to what, in the artifact community, has been called *functional imitation* (Demiris and Hayes 1997) or *effect-level imitation* (Nehaniv and Dautenhahn 1998b, 2001). The authors briefly overview other approaches, such as the active intermodal mapping theory (AIM) of Meltzoff and Moore (e.g., Meltzoff 1996; Meltzoff and Moore 1999) and statistical parsing theories (e.g., of Byrne and Russon 1998; Byrne 1999), arguing that these do not account for certain data on imitation in children, but that the goal-directed theory does. Their analysis suggests that data on imitation in children cannot be explained without the assumption that it relies on observable goals and inferences about the actor's intentions in an observed act.

The final contribution in this volume, "Information Replication in Culture: Three Modes for the Transmission of Culture Elements through Observed Action" (chapter 22), by Oliver R. Goodenough, addresses imitation from the point of view of cultural transmission. Goodenough argues that cultural transmission occurs through the imitation of *actions*, rather than of ideas, giving rise to a significant transmission bottleneck in that the action must actually be observed and lead to another (replicated) action. He classifies cultural transmission into three general modes of action: uncoded (nonlinguistic behavior), partially coded (stories), and fully coded (formulas). He also discusses how external storage (e.g., in writing) and how compression via language help avoid this transmission bottleneck. For example, multiple streams of replication go through stories—relating to the actions that the story encourages and relating to the replication of the story itself. Such a role for storytelling in cultural transmission need not be limited to human agents, but also has an interpretation for constructed agents via the notion of transmission of partially coded episodic experiences of auto-biographic agents (Dautenhahn 1996; Nehaniv 1997; Nehaniv and Dautenhahn 1998a; Nehaniv, Dautenhahn, and Loomes 1999; Dautenhahn, to appear). Goodenough's three modes could provide a useful conceptual framework for such analogues of human story-telling in autonomous agents by shedding light on connections to imitation. By focusing on human cultural transmission, this final chapter of the book completes the circle back to the issues discussed here and in the other chapters—namely, the social context of imitation.

Notes

1. The notion of autobiographic agent is strongly inspired by research in psychology on human autobiographical memory, e.g., in Nelson 1993; Conway 1996.
2. See also Breazeal and Scassellati, chapter 14 of this volume, Noble and Todd, chapter 16 of this volume, and Bekkering and Prinz, chapter 21 of this volume.
3. This particular scenario is studied in Billard and Dautenhahn 1999. Here, in a group of nine (simulated) robotic agents, learner agents can become teachers once they are "confident" enough of a vocabulary they have learned by imitation; see also Billard, chapter 11 of this volume.
4. The correspondence problem is particularly obvious in the case of dissimilar bodies—for example, when a robot imitates a human. Correspondences apply to positions, postures, and movements of the bodies of both model and imitator, and to actions (which need *not* be movements) and the state changes these induce, as well as to *correspondences of perception*, which are necessary so that model and imitator can share perceptions of a *shared context*; see discussions in Nehaniv and Dautenhahn 2001; Billard, chapter 11 of this volume.
5. In Dautenhahn 1998a, 1998b we explain the issue in more detail and its implications. The phrase "the social world is its own best model," inspired by Brooks 1991, captures the principle of interactive emergence of social behavior.

References

Anderson, J. R., and G. G. Gallup Jr. Self-recognition in *Saguinus*? A critical essay. *Animal Behaviour* 54: 1563–1567, 1997.

Atkeson, C. G., J. G. Hale, F. Pollick, M. Riley, S. Kotosaka, S. Schaal, T. Shibata, G. Tevatia, A. Ude, S. Vijayakumar, E. Kawato, and M. Kawato. Using humanoid robots to study human behavior. *IEEE Intelligent Systems* 15(4): 46–56, 2000.

Baron-Cohen, S. *Mindblindness: An Essay on Autism and Theory of Mind*. Cambridge, Mass.: MIT Press, 1995.

Billard, A. Learing motor skills by imitation: A biologically inspired robotic model. *Cybernetics and Systems*, special issue on "Imitation in Natural and Artificial Systems," 32(1–2): 155–193, 2001.

Billard A., and K. Dautenhahn. Grounding communication in situated, social robots. In *Proceedings TIMR UK 97 Towards Intelligent Mobile Robots.* Technical Report Series of the Department of Computer Science, Manchester University, 1997.

Billard, A., and K. Dautenhahn. Grounding communication in autonomous robots: An experimental study. *Robotics and Autonomous Systems,* 24(1–2): 71–81, 1998.

Billard, A., and K. Dautenhahn. Experiments in social robotics: Grounding and use of communication in autonomous agents. *Adaptive Behavior,* special issue on "Simulation Models of Social Agents" 7(3–4): 415–438, 1999.

Blackmore, S. *The Meme Machine.* Oxford U.K.: Oxford University Press, 1999.

Blackmore, S. Evolution and memes: The human brain as a selective imitation device. *Cybernetics and Systems,* special issue on "Imitation in Natural and Artificial Systems" 32(1–2): 225–255, 2001.

Bonabeau, E., M. Dorigo, and G. Theraulaz. *Swarm Intelligence: From Natural to Artificial Systems.* New York: Oxford University Press, 1999.

Bonnerj, J. T. *The Evolution of Culture in Animals.* Princeton: Princeton University Press, 1980.

Bradshaw, J. M. (ed.). *Software Agents.* Cambridge, Mass.: MIT Press, 1997.

Brooks, R. A. Intelligence without reason. In *Proceedings of the 1991 International Joint Conference on Artificial Intelligence,* pp. 569–696, Cambridge, U.K.: Cambridge University Press, 1991.

Bullowa, M. (ed.). *Before Speech.* Cambridge, UK: Cambridge University Press, 1979.

Bumby, K., and K. Dautenhahn. Investigating children's attitudes towards robots: A case study. In *Proceedings of the Third International Cognitive Technology Conference* (CT '99), pp. 391–410. San Francisco: August 1999. Available: ⟨http://www.cogtech.org/CT99⟩.

Butterworth, G. Neonatal imitation: Existence, mechanisms, and motives. In J. Nadel and G. Butterworth (eds.), *Imitation in Infancy,* pp. 63–88. Cambridge, U.K.: Cambridge University Press, 1999.

Byrne, R. W. Imitation without intentionality. Using string parsing to copy the organization of behaviour. *Animal Cognition* 2: 63–72, 1999.

Byrne, R. W., and A. E. Russon. Learning by imitation: A hierarchical approach. *Behavioral and Brain Sciences* 21: 667–709, 1998.

Byrne, R. W., and A. Whiten. *Machiavellian Intelligence.* Oxford: Clarendon Press, 1988.

Call, J., and M. Tomasello. The social learning of tool use by orangutans (*Pongo pygmaeus*). *Human Evolution* 9: 297–313, 1994.

Conway, M. A. Autobiographical knowledge and autobiographical memories. In D. C. Rubin (ed.), *Remembering Our Past: Studies in Autobiographical Memory,* pp. 67–93. Cambridge, U.K.: Cambridge University Press, 1996.

Dautenhahn, K. Trying to imitate—A step towards releasing robots from social isolation. In P. Gaussier and J.-D. Nicoud (eds.), *Proceedings From Perception to Actions Conference (Lausanne, Switzerland).* Los Alamitos, Calif.: IEEE Computer Society Press, pp. 290–301, 1994.

Dautenhahn, K. Getting to know each other—Artificial social intelligence for autonomous robots. *Robotics and Autonomous Systems* 16: 333–356, 1995.

Dautenhahn, K. Embodiment in animals and artifacts. In *Embodied Cognition and Action,* AAAI Fall Symposium Technical Report FS-92-02. Menlo Park, Calif.: American Association for Artificial Intelligence Press, pp. 27–32, 1996.

Dautenhahn, K. I could be you—The phenomenological dimension of social understanding. *Cybernetics and Systems* 25(8): 417–453, 1997.

Dautenhahn, K. The art of designing socially intelligent agents: Science, fiction, and the human in the loop. *Applied Artificial Intelligence,* special issue on "Socially Intelligent Agents" 12(7–8): 573–617, 1998a.

Dautenhahn, K. Grounding agent sociality: The social world is its own best model. In R. Trappl (ed.), *Cybernetics and Systems '98: Proceedings of the 14th European Meeting on Cybernetics and Systems Research,* vol. 2, pp. 779–784. Austrian Society for Cybernetic Studies: Vienna, Austria, 1998b.

Dautenhahn, K. Embodiment and interaction in socially intelligent life-like agents. In C. L. Nehaniv, ed. *Computation for Metaphors, Analogy, and Agents*, Lecture Notes in Artificial Intelligence, vol. 1562, pp. 102–142. Berlin: Springer Verlag, 1999.

Dautenhahn, K. Reverse engineering of societies—A biological perspective. *Proceedings AISB Symposium Starting from Society—The Application of Social Analogies to Computational Systems*, pp. 21–31. Society for the Study of Artificial Intelligence and the Simulation of Behaviour, 2000a.

Dautenhahn, K. (ed.). *Human Cognition and Social Agent Technology*. Amsterdam: John Benjamins Publishing, 2000b.

Dautenhahn, K. Socially intelligent agents and the primate social brain: Towards a science of social minds. In *Proceedings AAAI Fall Symposium Socially Intelligent Agents—The Human in the Loop*. Menlo Park, Calif.: American Association for Artificial Intelligence Press, 2000c.

Dautenhahn, K. Stories of lemurs and robots—The social origin of story-telling. In P. Sengers and M. Mateas (eds.), *Narrative Intelligence*. John Benjamins Publishing (to appear).

Dawkins, R. *The Selfish Gene*. Oxford: Oxford University Press, 1976.

Demiris, J. *Movement Imitation Mechanisms in Robots and Humans*. Ph.D. thesis, University of Edinburgh, Scotland, U.K., 1999.

Demiris, J., and G. Hayes. Imitative learning mechanisms in robots and humans. In *Proceedings of the Fifth European Workshop on Learning Robots*. Bari, Italy, July 1996.

Demiris, J., and G. Hayes. Do robots ape? In K. Dautenhahn (ed.), *Socially Intelligent Agents: Papers from the 1997 AAAI Fall Symposium* (November, MIT, Cambridge, Massachusetts), pp. 28–30. Menlo Park, Calif.: American Association for Artificial Intelligence Press, 1997.

Franklin, S., and A. Graesser. Is it an agent, or just a program? A taxonomy for autonomous agent. In *Proceedings of the Third International Workshop on Agent Theories, Architectures, and Languages*, published as *Intelligent Agents III*. Springer-Verlag, pp. 21–35, 1997.

Gallese, V., L. Fadiga, L. Fogassi, and G. Rizzolatti. Action recognition in the premotor cortex. *Brain* 119: 593–609, 1996.

Gallese, V., and A. Goldman. Mirror neurons and the simulation theory of mind-reading. *Trends in Cognitive Sciences* 2(12): 493–501, December 1998.

Gallup, G. G. Jr. Chimpanzees: Self-recognition. *Science* 54: 1563–1567, 1970.

Gaussier, P., S. Moga, J. P. Banquet, and M. Quoy. From perception-action loops to imitation processes: A bottom-up approach to learning by imitation. *Applied Artificial Intelligence*, special issue on "Socially Intelligent Agents" 12(7–8): 701–729, 1998.

Gigerenzer, G. The modularity of social intelligence. In A. Whiten and R. W. Byrne (eds.), *Machiavellian Intelligence II: Extensions and Evaluations*. Cambridge, UK: Cambridge University Press, pp. 264–288, 1997.

Hall, E. T. Proxemics. *Current Anthropology* 9(2–3): 83–95, 1968.

Hall, E. T. *The Dance of Life: The Other Dimension of Time*. New York: Anchor Books, Doubleday, 1983.

Hauser, M. D., J. Kralik, C. Botto, M. Garrett, and J. Oser. Self-recognition in primates: Phylogeny and the salience of species-typical traits. In *Proceedings of the National Academy of Sciences* 92: 10811–10814, 1995.

Hauser, M. D., and J. Kralik. Life beyond the mirror: A reply to Anderson and Gallup. *Animal Behaviour* 54: 1568–1571, 1997.

Hayes, G., and J. Demiris. A robot controller using learning by imitation. In A. Borkowski and J. L. Crowley (eds.), *SIRS-94, Proceedings of the 2nd International Symposium on Intelligent Robotic Systems*, LIFIA-IMAG, pp. 198–204. Grenoble, France: July 1994.

Hayes, K. J., and C. Hayes. Imitation in a home-raised chimpanzee. *Journal of Comparative Psychology* 45: 450–459, 1952.

Heimann, M., and Eva Ullstadius. Neonatal imitation and imitation among children with autism and Down's syndrome. In J. Nadel and G. Butterworth (eds.), *Imitation in Infancy*, pp. 235–253, Cambridge, UK: Cambridge University Press, 1999.

Hendriks-Jansen, H. *Catching Ourselves in the Act: Situated Activity, Interactive Emergence, Evolution, and Human Thought.* Cambridge, Mass.: MIT Press, 1996.

Hewitt, C. Viewing control structures as patterns of passing messages. *Artificial Intelligence* 8: 323–364, 1977.

Heyes, C. M. Reflections on self-recognition in primates. *Animal Behaviour* 47: 909–919, 1994.

Heyes, C. M. Theory of mind in nonhuman primates. *Behavioral and Brain Sciences* 21: 101–148, 1998.

Heyes, C. M., and G. R. Dawson. Demonstration of observational learning using a bidirectional control. *Quarterly Journal of Experimental Psychology* 42B: 59–71, 1990.

Heyes, C. M., G. R. Dawson, and T. Nokes. Imitation in rats: Initial responding and transfer evidence. *Quarterly Journal of Experimental Psychology* 45B: 81–92, 1992.

Heyes, C. M., and E. D. Ray. What is the significance of imitation in animals? *Advances in the Study of Behaviour* 29: 215–245, 2000.

Huffman, M. A. Acquisition of innovative cultural behaviors in nonhuman primates: A case study of stone handling, a socially transmitted behaviour in Japanese macaques. In C. M. Heyes and B. G. Galef Jr. (eds.), *Social Learning in Animals: The Roots of Culture*, pp. 267–289. New York: Academic Press, 1996.

Janik, V. M. Whistle matching in wild bottlenose dolphins (*Tursiops truncatus*). *Science* 289: 1355–1357, 2000.

Jennings, N. R., K. Sycara, and M. Wooldridge. A roadmap of agent research and development. *International Journal of Autonomous Agents and Multi-Agent Systems* 1(1): 7–38, 1998.

Kuhn, T. S. *The Structure of Scientific Revolutions.* Chicago: University of Chicago Press, 1962.

Kuniyoshi, Y., H. Inoue, and M. Inaba. Design and implementation of a system that generates assembly programs from visual recognition of human action sequences. In *Proceedings IEEE International Workshop on Intelligent Robots and Systems IROS '90*, pp. 567–574, 1990.

Kuniyoshi, Y., H. Inoue, and M. Inaba. Learning by watching: Extracting reusable task knowledge from visual observation of human performance. *IEEE Transactions on Robotics and Automation* 10(6): 799–822, 1994.

Meltzoff, A. N. The human infant as imitative generalist: A twenty-year progress report on infant imitation with implications for comparative psychology. In C. M. Heyes and B. G. Galef Jr. (eds.), *Social Learning in Animals: The Roots of Culture*, pp. 347–370. New York: Academic Press, 1996.

Meltzoff, A. N., and M. K. Moore. Persons and representation: Why infant imitation is important for theories of human development. In J. Nadel and G. Butterworth (eds.), *Imitation in Infancy*, pp. 9–35. Cambridge, UK: Cambridge University Press, 1999.

Minsky, M. *The Society of Mind.* New York: Simon and Schuster, 1985.

Mitchell, C. J., C. M. Heyes, G. R. Dawson, and M. R. Gardner. Limitations of a bidirectional control procedure for the investigation of imitation in rats: Odour cues on the manipulandum. *Quarterly Journal of Experimental Psychology* 52B: 193–202, 1999.

Mitchell, R. W. A comparative-developmental approach to understanding imitation. In P. P. G. Bateson (ed.), *Perspectives in Ethology 7*, pp. 183–215. Now York: Plenum Press, 1987.

Mitchell R. W. Mental models of self-recognition: Two theories. *New Ideas in Psychology* 11: 295–325, 1993.

Mitchell, R. W., and M. Hamm. The interpretation of animal psychology: Anthropomorphism or behavior reading? *Behaviour* 134: 173–204, 1997.

Mithen, S. *The Prehistory of the Mind.* Thames and Hudson, 1996.

Nadel, J., C. Guerini, A. Peze, and C. Rivet. The evolving nature of imitation as a format of communication. In J. Nadel and G. Butterworth (eds.), *Imitation in Infancy*, pp. 209–234, Cambridge, UK: Cambridge University Press, 1999.

Nagell, K., K. Olguin, and M. Tomasello. Processes of social learning in the tool use of chimpanzees (*Pan troglodytes*) and human children (*Homo sapiens*). *Journal of Comparative Psychology* 107: 174–186, 1993.

Nehaniv, C. L. What's your story?—irreversibility, algebra, autobiographic agents. In K. Dautenhahn (ed.), *Socially Intelligent Agents: Papers from the 1997 AAAI Fall Symposium* (November, MIT, Cambridge, Mass.), pp. 150–153. Menlo Park, Calif.: American Association for Artificial Intelligence Press, 1997.

Nehaniv, C. L. Introduction, and The second person—Meaning and metaphors. In C. L. Nehaniv (ed.), *Computation for Metaphors, Analogy, and Agents*, Lecture Notes in Artificial Intelligence, vol. 1562, pp. 1–10, 380–388, Berlin: Springer Verlag, 1999a.

Nehaniv, C. L. Meaning for observers and agents. *IEEE International Symposium on Intelligent Control/Intelligent Systems and Semiotics (ISIC/ISAS '99)*, pp. 435–440. Cambridge, Mass.: Institute of Electronic and Electrical Engineers Press, 1999b.

Nehaniv, C., and K. Dautenhahn. Embodiment and memories—Algebras of time and history for autobiographic agents. In R. Trappl (ed.), *Cybernetics and Systems '98: Proceedings of the Fourteenth European Meeting on Cybernetics and Systems Research*, vol. 2, pp. 651–656. Vienna: Austrian Society for Cybernetic Studies, 1998a.

Nehaniv, C., and K. Dautenhahn. Mapping between dissimilar bodies: Affordances and the algebraic foundations of imitation. In J. Demiris and A. Birk (eds.), *Proceedings European Workshop on Learning Robots 1998 (EWLR-7)*. Edinburgh, Scotland, 1998b.

Nehaniv, C. L., and K. Dautenhahn. Like me?—Measures of correspondence and imitation. *Cybernetics and Systems*, special issue on "Imitation in Natural and Artificial Systems" 32(1–2): 11–51, 2001.

Nehaniv, C. L., K. Dautenhahn, and M. J. Loomes. Constructive biology and approaches to temporal grounding in post-reactive robotics. In G. T. McKee and P. Schenker (eds.), *Sensor Fusion and Decentralized Control in Robotics Systems II*, Proceedings of SPIE, vol. 3839, pp. 156–167, Bellingham Was.: SPIE—the International Society for Optical Engineering, 1999.

Nelson, K. The psychological and social origins of autobiographical memory. *Psychological Science* 4(1): 7–14, 1993.

O'Connell, S. M. Empathy in chimpanzees: Evidence for theory of mind? *Primates* 36(3): 397–410, 1995.

Parker, S. T., R. W. Mitchell, and M. L. Boccia (eds.), *Self-awareness in Animals and Humans*. New York: Cambridge University Press, 1994.

Povinelli, D. J., and T. M. Preuss. Theory of mind: Evolutionary history of a cognitive specialization. *Trends in Neurosciences* 18(9): 418–424, 1995.

Premack, D., and G. Woodruff. Does the chimpanzee have a theory of mind? *Behavioral and Brain Sciences* 4: 515–526, 1978.

Reader, S. M., and K. N. Laland. Do animals have memes? *Journal of Memetics—Evolutionary Models of Information Transmission* 3, 1999. Available: ⟨http://www.cpm.mmu.ac.uk/jom-emit/⟩.

Reeves, B., and C. Nass. *The Media Equation: How People Treat Computers, Television, and New Media Like Real People and Places*. New York: Cambridge University Press, 1996.

Rizzolatti, G., and M. A. Arbib. Language within our grasp. *Trends in Neurosciences* 21(5): 188–194, 1998.

Rizzolatti, G., L. Fadiga, V. Gallese, and L. Fogassi. Premotor cortex and the recognition of motor actions. *Cognition and Brain Research* 3: 131–141, 1998.

Sloman, A. Exploring design space and niche space. In *Proceedings Fifth Scandinavian Conference on Artificial Intelligence (SCAI 95)*. Trondheim, Amsterdam: IOS Press, 1995.

Smith, W. J. Communication and expectations: A social process and the cognitive operations it depends on and influences. In M. Bekoff and D. Jamieson (eds.), *Readings in Animal Cognition*, pp. 244–255. Cambridge, Mass.: MIT Press, 1996.

Steels, L. When are robots intelligent autonomous agents? *Robotics and Autonomous Systems* 15: 3–9, 1995.

Theraulaz, G., and E. Bonabeau. A brief history of stigmergy. *Artificial Life* 5(2): 97–116, 1999.

Thorndike, E. L. Animal intelligence: an experimental study of the associative process in animals. *Psychological Review Monographs* 2(8): 551–553, 1898.

Thorpe, W. H. *Learning and Instinct in Animals.* London: Methuen, 1956.

Todt, D. Social learning of vocal patterns and modes of their applications in Grey parrots. *Zeitschrift für Tierpsychologie* 39: 178–188, 1975.

Tomasello, M. Do apes ape? In C. M. Heyes and B. G. Galef, Jr. (eds.), *Social Learning in Animals: The Roots of Culture*, pp. 319–346. New York: Academic Press, 1996.

Tomasello, M. *The Cultural Origins of Human Cognition.* Cambridge, Mass.: Harvard University Press, 1999.

Tomasello, M., and J. Call. *Primate Cognition.* New York: Oxford University Press, 1997.

Tomasello, M., E. S. Savage-Rumbaugh, and A. C. Kruger. Imitative learning of actions on objects by children, chimpanzees, and enculturated chimpanzees. *Child Development* 64: 1688–1705, 1993.

Trevarthen, C. Descriptive analyses of infant communicative behaviour. In H. R. Schaffer (ed.), *Studies in Mother-Infant Interaction.* New York: Academic Press, 1977.

Trevarthen, C., T. Kokkinaki, and G. A. Fiamenghi Jr. What infants' imitations communicate: With mothers, with fathers, and with peers. In J. Nadel and G. Butterworth (eds.), *Imitation in Infancy*, pp. 128–185, Cambridge, U.K.: Cambridge University Press, 1999.

Tyack, P. L. Dolphins whistle a signature tune. *Science* 289: 1310–1311, 2000.

Uexküll, J. von. *Umwelt und Innenwelt der Tiere.* Berlin: J. Springer, 1909.

Užgiris, I. C. Imitation as activity: Its developmental aspects. In J. Nadel and G. Butterworth (eds.), *Imitation in Infancy*, pp. 186–206. Cambridge, U.K.: Cambridge University Press, 1999.

Užgiris, I. C., J. Benson, J. Kruper, and M. Vasek. Establishing action-environment correspondences: Contextual influences on imitative interactions between mothers and infants. In J. Lockman and N. Hazen (eds.), *Action in Social Context.* New York: Plenum, pp. 103–127, 1989.

Voelkl, B., and L. Huber. True imitation in marmosets. *Animal Behaviour* 60(2): 195–202, 2000.

Whiten, A. Remarks on novelty in keynote lecture Cognitive issues in imitation: Studies with child and chimpanzee, at AISB Symposium on "Imitation in Animals and Artifacts," personal communication, Edinburgh, Scotland, 7 April 1999.

Whiten, A., and R. W. Byrne. *Machiavellian Intelligence II: Extensions and Evaluations.* Cambridge, UK: Cambridge University Press, 1997.

Whiten, A., and D. Custance. Studies of imitation in chimpanzees and children. In C. M. Heyes and B. G. Galef Jr. (eds.), *Social Learning in Animals: The Roots of Culture*, pp. 291–318. New York: Academic Press, 1996.

Whiten, A., J. Goodall, W. C. MacGrew, T. Nishida, V. Reynolds, Y. Sugiyama, C. E. G. Tutin, R. W. Wrangham, and C. Boesch. Cultures in chimpanzees. *Nature* 399: 682–685, 1999.

Whiten, A., and R. Ham. On the nature and evolution of imitation in the animal kingdom: Reappraisal of a century of research. In P. J. B. Slater, J. S. Rosenblatt, C. Beer, and M. Milinski (eds.), *Advances in the Study of Behavior, 21*, pp. 239–283. New York: Academic Press, 1992.

Wooldridge, M., and N. R. Jennings. Intelligent agents: Theory and practice. *The Knowledge Engineering Review* 10(2): 115–152, 1995.

2 The Correspondence Problem

Chrystopher L. Nehaniv and Kerstin Dautenhahn

2.1 Matching and Imitation

The identification of any form of social learning, imitation, copying, or mimicry presupposes a notion of *correspondence* between two autonomous agents. Judging whether a behavior has been transmitted socially requires the observer to identify a *mapping* between the demonstrator and the imitator. If the demonstrator and imitator have similar bodies—for example, are animals of the same species, of similar age, and of the same gender—then to a human observer an obvious correspondence is to map the corresponding body parts: left arm of demonstrator maps to left arm of imitator, right eye of demonstrator maps to right eye of imitator, tail of demonstrator maps to tail of imitator. There is also an obvious correspondence of actions: raising the left arm by the model corresponds to raising the left arm by the imitator, production of vocal signals by the model corresponds to the production of acoustically similar ones by the imitator, picking up a fruit by the demonstrator corresponds to picking up a fruit of the same type by the imitator. Furthermore, there is a correspondence in sensory experience: audible sounds, a touch, visible objects and colors, and so on, evidently seem to be detected and experienced in similar ways.

What to take as the correspondence seems relatively clear in this case. As humans, we are good at imitating and at recognizing such correspondences. It is also clear that most other animals, robots, and software programs may in fact generally fail to recognize any such correspondences. To judge a produced behavior to be a copy of an observed one, we require at least that it respects some such correspondence. The faithfulness or precision of the behavioral match can obviously vary, and no absolute cutoff or threshold exists defining success as opposed to failure of behavioral matching. But one can study the degree of success using various metrics and measures of correspondence (Nehaniv and Dautenhahn 2001; also see below).

Moreover, it turns out that the "obvious" correspondences between similar bodies mentioned above are not the only ones possible. Consider a human imitating another one that is facing her: if the demonstrator raises her left arm, should the imitator raise her own left arm? Or should she raise her right, to make a "mirror image" of the demonstrator's actions? If the demonstrator picks up a brush, should an imitator pick up the same brush? Or just another brush of the same type? If the demonstrator opens a container to get at chocolate inside, should the imitator open a similar container in the same way—for example, by unwrapping but not tearing the surrounding paper, or is it enough just to open the container somehow? The different possible answers to these questions presuppose different correspondences.

If a child watches a teacher solving subtraction problems in arithmetic, and then solves for the first time similar but not identical problems on its own, social learning has occurred. But what type of correspondence is at work here? In China and Japan, the ideographic character for "to imitate" also means "to learn" or "to study." By going through the motions of an algorithm for solving sample problems, students everywhere are able to learn how to solve similar ones—of course without necessarily gaining understanding of why the procedures they have learned work.

In this chapter, for lack of a better term, we shall use the word "imitator" to refer to any autonomous agent performing a candidate behavioral match. The use of this word here does not entail any particular mechanism of matching or any particular type of social learning. In what follows, we shall describe how different matching phenomena arise depending on the criteria employed in generating the behavior of the imitator. For example, goal emulation, stimulus enhancement, mimicry, and so on, will all be cast as solutions to correspondence problems with different particular selection criteria.

Dissimilar Bodies

A correspondence need not be a one-to-one mapping, but could also be a one-to-many, many-to-one, or many-to-many relation. If the number of *degrees of freedom* (DOFs) in, for example, the joints of two agents' arms are different, then there can be no simple one-to-one correspondence between their actions. A robot might imitate a human nodding or waving successfully even without requiring that it has the same number and type of joints in its head and neck or arms and hands as the human whose behavior it emulates.

In fact, exact copying, even with similar embodiment, is almost never possible: one never has exactly the same agents with exactly the same kinds of bodies in exactly the same setting when the behavior of one agent is said to match that of another, as they must differ at least in their situatedness in time and/or space, not to mention numerous other details (Whiten and Ham 1992; Nehaniv and Dautenhahn 2001).

A useful correspondence could also be a *partial* mapping. That is, it need not be defined on all possible states and actions of the model: it may describe corresponding states and actions in the imitator for only some of these. For example, a robot might be able to successfully imitate me waving my arms using a particular correspondence between the angles it observes between my shoulder and arm and at my elbow, but this does not mean that the correspondence gives any information on how to relate my legs to its legs. Indeed, it might not even have legs!

To achieve a behavioral match, of whatever sort, a correspondence must explicitly or implicity be present. In trying to imitate or learning socially by observing, an autonomous agent must somehow solve the *correspondence problem*.

Informal Statement of the Correspondence Problem

Given an observed behavior of the model, which, from a given starting state, leads the model through a sequence (or hierarchy) of subgoals (in states, action, and/or effects, while possibly responding to sensory stimuli and external events), find and execute a sequence of actions using one's own (possibly dissimilar) embodiment, which, from a corresponding starting state, leads through corresponding subgoals (in corresponding states, actions, and/or effects, while possibly responding to corresponding events).

Thus, such a correspondence can require relating aspects of actions of the model to actions that one can carry out, or states of the model in its environment to states of one's own body and environment, or both. It may also require relating sensory and external events of the demonstrator to those experienced by the imitator. A simple correspondence recognized between hummingbirds

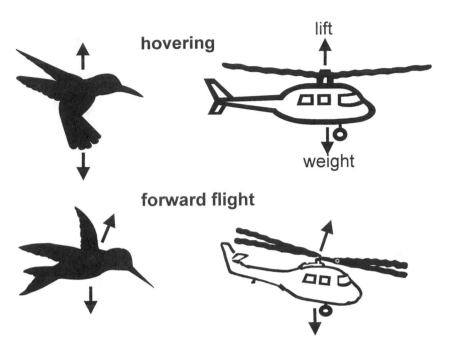

Figure 2.1 A simple correspondence between helicopters and hummingbirds. For states, rotor angle relates to wing angle. For actions, changing rotor angle relates to change in wing angle. For hovering behavior, the angles are horizontal, and lift balances weight exactly. As the angle increases from horizontal, the component of thrust in any horizontal direction generates horizontal motion. All other aspects of state, action, and environment are ignored for purposes of matching hovering, backward, and forward motion. (Compare Alexander, 1992.)

and helicopters is given in figure 2.1 (Nehaniv and Dautenhahn 2001).

When creatures with less similar embodiments, such as dolphins, parrots, orangutans, chimpanzees, and bonobos, exhibit vocal or motor or goal-oriented behaviors matching those of human demonstrators, the correspondences between the bodies of the animals and the humans become more abstract than those between similarly embodied model and imitator. Nevertheless, these animals, at least when enculturated with humans, do display behaviors matching those of the human models (Herman, chapter 3 of this volume; Pepperberg, chapter 4 of this volume; Russon and Galdikas 1993, 1995; Tomasello, Savage-Rumbaugh, and Kruger 1993). This means that either they or at least the human experimenters observing their behavior employ correspondences between the bodies, sensory and effector systems of these animals and the bodies, and sensory and effector systems of their human models. Such correspondence may indeed be attributed to be present by the experimenters. Although we may not conclude that the animals in question are necessarily aware of the correspondence, these animals are at least able to act in a manner strongly suggesting that they have solved a partial correspondence problem between their own bodies and that of a human demonstrator.

Referring to Louis Herman's results on dolphin imitation of humans (chapter 3 of this volume), the dolphins were tested for imitation of human demonstrators using an unstated correspondence and showed that they are largely able to imitate the humans according to it: human forearms waving with bent elbow relate to wiggling pectoral fins; a human propelling her body partially out of water corresponds to a leap out of the water by the dolphin; human and dolphin underwater somersaults correspond; human head and dolphin head correspond; but human legs correspond to the dolphin's tail when raising them out of the water or slapping them on its surface. One could speculate that possibly the dolphin understands how its body plan relates to that of a human. Referring to Irene Pepperberg's data on Grey parrots (chapter 4), Alex and other parrots show acoustical production of humanlike speech sounds using very different vocal apparatus. Both they and we have employed a correspondence between the sounds although these do not have identical acoustical formants and spectra. Moreover, these parrots use their speech to refer to and describe properties of objects in a manner related to how we as humans use similar sounds.

Furthermore, by the use of more "exotic" correspondences, it is possible to set up unusual temporal synchronizations of perceived behavior and action. For example, Dautenhahn (1999) describes experimental couplings between hand movements of a human and the behavior of a "dancing" mobile robot moving on the ground.

2.2 Successful Correspondence?

When does a candidate behavior actually match an observed behavior? In stating the correspondence problem, we required that a sequence or hierarchy of corresponding subgoals be attained. This notion of *subgoal* in the statement of the correspondence problem should not be taken to necessarily imply any intentionality on the part of the demonstrator or imitator. For biological and autonomous agents, it is useful to accept a notion of "on behalf of"

(Kaufmann 2000). Biological agents engage in behavior that is generally somehow beneficial to them. *E. coli* follow a gradient likely to lead them to food, and growing plants may turn toward sunlight. These behaviors are on behalf of the agent, helping it attain its goals. Having goals does not imply any intentional mental state. It is in this sense that *goal* is used here. A subgoal here is thus either a state of affairs that would promote the "on behalf of" the autonomous agent or which is observer-attributed as such. Goals do not arise independently of autonomous agents. (See also the agent-based discussions of *meaningful information* as information that is *useful* for an autonomous agent in achieving its goals [Nehaniv 1999; Nehaniv, Dautenhahn, and Loomes 1999].)

Whether or not behavior is judged as matching seems to be very much a subjective issue. Different observers of a candidate matching behavior may attribute a vast range of differing mechanisms and goals to the imitator and/or the demonstrator. The imitator itself might use yet another mechanism and unknown criteria in responding to stimuli and perceptions of its own surrounding world (*Umwelt*) in order to generate the behavior. This does not mean that it is hopeless to endeavor to formalize what is meant by such terms as *imitation*, *mimicry*, and so on, but it does point to the central role of the observer (who might coincide with the demonstrator, the learner, or be a third party) in deciding whether or not an exhibited behavior matches that of a model. (See also the discussion of the role of the observer in chapter 1.)

Clearly, different observers may have different answers to the question of whether or not a corresponding behavior has occurred: suppose, for example, that a certain fictional species of bird learns to produce an ultrasonic signal by repeated exposure to the sound of a dog whistle. A naive human observer would hear no sound when observing this bird produce this call and could not say to what extent the call was similar or not to the sound the whistle produces. But an observer equipped with listening equipment to transpose the sounds to the human-audible range would be able to give some evaluation of how well the bird's call matched that of the whistle.

2.3 Correspondences in Actions, States, and Goals

In imitation, emulation, mimicry, stimulus enhancement, and other behavioral areas of learning and matching, we take account of mapping (and more generally relations) in:

- *State* of the system (body), objects, and environment
- *Action* (and sequences of actions) that transform the state, including internally generated actions and external ones (sensory stimuli and other events)
- *Goals*—the configurations of state (and/or possibly action sequences) that meet an external or internal criterion

These aspects have also been identified by Call and Carpenter (chapter 9 of this volume) as three major sources of information in social learning, which researchers may use to categorize different types of matching behavior and social learning. (They also use the term "result" as an alternative to "state," but we do not in order to avoid the suggestion of a goal implicit in the word "result.")

Our formalization of correspondences takes all of the above into account. Degree of success of attempted matching behavior can be formalized by metrics on states and actions with respect to attainment of sequences of subgoals, as we explain in the next section. Different types of error measures—variously emphasizing state, actions, or goals, and granularity—in this formalization describe different types of observational behavior matching.

2.4 Formalization of Correspondences

In this section, we give a simple mathematical framework to describe the notion of correspondence between two autonomous agents in a rigorous way. We have tried to do this in a manner that will be useful for an interdisciplinary reader. No specialized mathematical training is required to benefit from this discussion, which provides a broadly applicable framework useful in understanding various solutions of the correspondence problem.

States and Events

For two autonomous agents, animals, robots, or software systems, identify the set of each one's possible states and actions. Denote the states (of the body and environment) of the first agent as X and the states of the second as Y. Denote the set of elementary actions of the first agent by Σ and those of the second agent by Δ. The set of all finite sequence of actions of the first agent is denoted Σ^* and the set of all finite sequences of action of the second is denoted Δ^*. Effects on the environment will be reflected in state. One may also

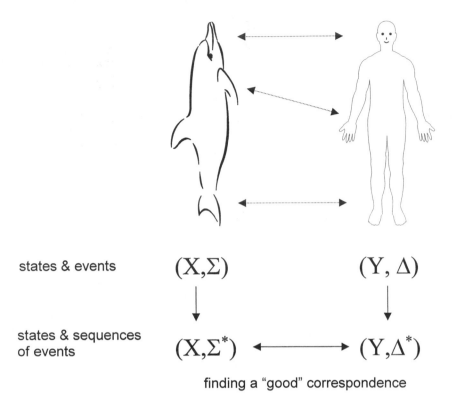

states & events $\qquad$ (X, Σ) $\qquad\qquad$ (Y, Δ)

states & sequences
of events $\qquad$ (X, Σ^*) $\longleftrightarrow$ (Y, Δ^*)

finding a "good" correspondence

Figure 2.2 Correspondence of states and of event sequences of imitator and model. States include states of the body and relevant aspects of the environment. Events include actions that the agent can perform (internally generated events) as well as sensory perceptions and other externally generated events. The set Σ^* consists of all finite sequences of events from the basic set of events Σ for the imitator, and similarly for the model. A correspondence between the imitator and model is represented as a partial relational mapping relating states of the imitator with states of the model, and relating sequences of action-events for the imitator with sequences of action-events for the model.

speak of particular properties of action/events or of sequences of action/events.

From the description of an agent by a set of states and set of action/events (X, Σ), we derive an extended description with the same states and all finite sequences of events (X, Σ^*).[1] Using sequences of events rather than such individual ones allows for the fact that a single action—for example, of the demonstrator—might correspond in the imitator to several actions, or vice versa. This situation is illustrated in figure 2.2.

The identification (collapsing) of sequences of actions that always have the same effects allows one to pass from the description of states and elementary action/events (X, Σ) to an algebraic invariant of the agent called its *transformation semigroup* (X, S). This will not be described further here, but we wish only to note that correspondences can be constructed at this level. For details, see Nehaniv and Dautenhahn (2001). Mathematical techniques for solving the problem of making a correspondence many-to-one (rather than many-to-many) are given by Nehaniv (1996).

Correspondences as Relational Mapping

Formally, a *correspondence* (or *relational mapping*) between the two autonomous agents is a relation of states $\Phi \subseteq X \times Y$ and a relation of sequences of actions $\Psi \subseteq \Sigma^* \times \Delta^*$, satisfying:

For all $x \in X$ and $y \in Y$, if $(x, y) \in \Phi$ and $(s, t) \in \Psi$ then $(x\,s, y\,t) \in \Phi$.

Let us consider what this means in plainer language. A state relation Φ consists of those pairs of states of the two agents that are said to correspond. Similarly, an action relation Ψ consists of those pairs of sequences of elementary actions that are said to correspond. In words, the above condition says: "If state x of the first system corresponds to state y of the second system, and action sequence s in the first is related to action sequence t in the second, then the corresponding resulting states must correspond." More briefly: "When starting with corresponding states, corresponding actions lead to corresponding states."

An attempted correspondence might be a one-to-one function, or many-to-many relation as discussed above. It need not be fully defined. Of course, there will, in general, exist many correspondences between two autonomous agents. Whether or not a particular candidate relation is a good solution to the correspondence problem depends on the evaluation of how appropriate the correspondence is from the viewpoint of some observer. This might be an external observer, a demonstrator, or an imitator.

Using the concepts and notation given above, a simple formalization of the correspondence problem is given by the following:

Formal Statement of the Correspondence Problem

Given an observed behavior of the model, parse this behavior into action sequences $t_1, \ldots, t_k$, starting in state y_0 with states $y_1, \ldots, y_k$, the states that successively result from carrying out the t_i in order.

Find a correspondence, Φ on states and Ψ on action sequences, relating one's own actions and states to those of the observed model, and from a corresponding state x_0, execute corresponding behaviors $s_1, \ldots, s_k$ such that the resulting behavior is as similar as possible, where the degree of dissimilarity is measured by summing an error measure $\mathbf{d}((y_i, t_i), (x_i, s_i))$ over i.

In fact, the "actions" in this formulation are actually "action/events," but we have tried to make the statement as concise as possible and so have included the events within the notion of action: experiencing an event such as a particular sensory perception is taken to be a particular kind of action/event.

Behavior matching according to a correspondence is schematically illustrated in figure 2.3. (Also in the figure, s_0 and t_0 are "null

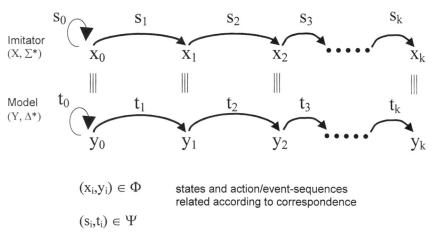

Given a correspondence

$$(X, \Sigma^*) \rightarrow (Y, \Delta^*)$$

attempted matched behavior is given by:

$(x_i, y_i) \in \Phi$ states and action/event-sequences related according to correspondence

$(s_i, t_i) \in \Psi$

Figure 2.3 Schematic view of behaviors matched according to a formal correspondence. Vertical links indicate corresponding states (according to the state component Φ of the relational mapping) and action/event sequences (according to the event component Ψ of the relational mapping)—links for Ψ not shown. In the model's behavior, successive sequences of events $t_1, \ldots, t_k$ take its state from y_0 successively through states $y_1, \ldots, y_k$, while for the imitator, successive corresponding sequences of events $s_1, \ldots, s_k$ take its state from x_0 successively through corresponding states $x_1, \ldots, x_k$. (Evaluation of the attempted behavioral match is done by a separate dissimilarity measure. See below.)

actions," included for mathematical convenience in computing dissimilarity as the error sum with index i going from 0 to k.) Note that a correspondence that works for generating one behavioral match may or may not work well for matching other observed behaviors. But a good, detailed correspondence, such as the dolphins' evident identification of actions of its body parts with those of human trainers mentioned above, provides reusable knowledge that applies across many situations to yield successful imitative behaviors.

We emphasize here that our formalization is a method of description helpful in modeling an imitator matching an observed behavior. We are certainly not claiming that animals are using such a framework to guide their own matching behavior, but only that the framework provides a useful description of behavioral matching that is independent of the particular mechanisms actually employed. A designer of an autonomous agent that is trying to imitate another agent could have this agent use this framework for selecting among possible correspondences. An observer—for example, a scientist studying behavioral matching in animals—can usefully employ this framework to describe the particular correspondence in any matching observed—in particular, whether aspects of state, actions, or goals are most descriptive (or predictive) of observed imitative behavior and which type of dissimilarity measure best describes (or predicts) the aspects that are matched. In addition, by casting results on matching behavior in this framework, different research on imitation and matching behavior can be compared.

Metrics and Measures of Success in Behavior Matching

Metrics and *error measures* (1) can capture the notion of the difference of performed actions from desired actions, (2) can measure the difference of attained states from desired states, or (3) can measure the difference of sequences of both. Such measures can take discrete or continuous values. This is the role of the dissimilarity measure **d** in the formal statement of the correspondence problem above.

Evaluation of a candidate for behavioral matching depends in the formalization very much on the error measure **d**. Different kinds of measures result in different types of matching and would lead to types of learning of behaviors that ethologists and psychologists would classify as different types of social learning or copying. For example, if the error measure **d** in the above formulation of the correspondence problem ignores the state component, then only actions are salient to the success of attempted matching behavior.

Granularity refers to the fineness of the imitation—for example, in the number of states, actions, or subgoals matched. If the measure **d** ignores the action component, then only the sequence of states attained is salient. The number k in the formal statement of the correspondence problem gives the granularity of the attempted behavioral match. If $k = 1$, then only the overall end result is salient for determining successful correspondence. The measure of dissimilarity can require that certain states or actions are attained or closely matched; thus, it can be used to evaluate whether a sequence of subgoals has been attained or not, and to what degree. Matching the "right" subgoals can be forced, for example, by making the measure take value zero when they are achieved but a high error value otherwise.

Types of Behavior Matching

Learning a correspondence means learning a piece of such a relational mapping. Metrics and measures on state, actions, and goals can guide this learning. The type of social learning (or any of the related phenomena involving matching) depends on the metrics used and which aspect or aspects of a behavior they measure. More details are in Nehaniv and Dautenhahn (2001). (For a review of mechanisms of social learning and simpler phenomena see Call and Carpenter, chapter 9 of this volume; Noble and Todd, chapter 16 of this volume; Zentall 2001.) Various areas of matching and learning can be classified according to different aspects of the relational mapping in a particular attempted correspondence:

- Construction of correspondence in actions and their sequencing using an action relation Ψ required by the metric characterizes *mimicry*, or *copying* (without goal or state matching).
- Construction of correspondences in actions Ψ and states Φ at high granularity matching attributed goals of demonstrator characterizes forms of *imitation* such as *action-level imitation* (Byrne and Russon 1998) or *string parsing* (Byrne 1999) (with metric reflecting subgoal salience).

- Construction of correspondence in states required by the metric restricting the state relation Φ characterizes *emulation* (Tomasello 1990; see discussion by Call and Carpenter, chapter 9 of this volume).
- Construction of correspondence using state relation Φ via metrics requiring matching of an attributed goal characterizes *goal emulation* (Whiten and Ham 1992) (with low granularity) or *stimulus enhancement* (Galef 1988) (with low granularity and only state matching).
- Construction of a correspondence in the action relation Φ with effect information in the states and metric reflecting subgoal salience characterizes learning *tool affordances* or *action affordances* (Tomasello and Call 1997).
- The above types of correspondence, in which matching is required for hierarchically structured tasks and subtasks involving behavioral loops and conditionals, characterize various forms of *program-level imitation, hierarchical procedure imitation, procedural matching,* or *programming by example* (Byrne and Russon 1998; Whiten, chapter 8 of this volume; Cypher 1993; Lieberman, chapter 6 of this volume; Furse 2001).
- Understanding and matching higher-level structures characterizes various other forms of observational learning and matching involving *theory of mind* or *mind-reading* (Premack and Woodruff 1978; Byrne and Whiten 1988; Povinelli and Preuss 1995; Whiten and Byrne 1997; Gallese and Goldman 1998), *empathy* (O'Connell 1995, Dautenhahn 1997, 2000), or a *body-plan correspondence* (this chapter).

The reader may like to compare a similar classification of behavioral matching and types of social learning given by Call and Carpenter (chapter 9 of this volume). As they have emphasized, in studying such behavior in animals, it is a good idea to try to identify which types of information the subject animal is using. Competing predictive models could be constructed using the above formalizations and different error measures reflecting various types of observational behavior matching. To help identify the mechanism being used by the animal, these competing models could then be evaluated by comparing their predictions with experimentally observed behavioral matching.

Conversely, in building artifacts and employing appropriate measures of dissimilarity on different aspects of state, actions, goals, and granularity of desired matching behavior, one can implement various forms of behavioral matching and social learning. For example, in agent-based computer simulations, Aris Alissandrakis and the authors have studied the results of applying different metrics and different granularities to generate different corresponding behaviors in the imitation of sequences of moves by differently embodied agents. These agents are embodied as chess pieces, whose movement constraints provide a well-known example of dissimilar "bodies" in a simple, discrete shared world—namely, a chess-board. A chess-world knight or bishop, for example, may imitate a zig-zag of three moves by a demonstrator queen, but each such agent is subject to the constraints on how it is allowed to move (its embodiment) and so can only roughly approximate the queen's precise behavior. Nevertheless, the knight and bishop or other pieces can successfully imitate the behavior to varying degrees with respect to particular granularities (e.g., end-result or trajectory matching) and various metrics. Varying the granularity and metrics for assessing attempts at imitation in this experimental setting illustrates the profound influence of these factors on the qualitative features of the resulting imitative behavior (Alissandrakis, Nehaniv, and Dautenhahn 2000). Similarly, differently embodied animals, robots, or other autonomous agents whose behavior matches those of others can be modeled as using correspondences between their own states and actions and those of a demonstrator, using various granularities and measures of dissimilarity.

2.5 Perception-Action Correspondences

Another particular application of the relational mapping formalism is to perception-action correspondence. A perceived state corresponds to one's own state under the state component (Φ) of a relational mapping, perceptual stimuli from an action correspond under an action component (Ψ) to one's own action. The new perceived state—that is, the perceived state following the perceived action—should correspond to one's own new state after one's action. This is similar to interagent correspondence but applies to the case that the first system is given by one's perceptions of one's own state and of one's own actions—for example, by sensory kinesthetic and proprioceptive feedback (or also via external

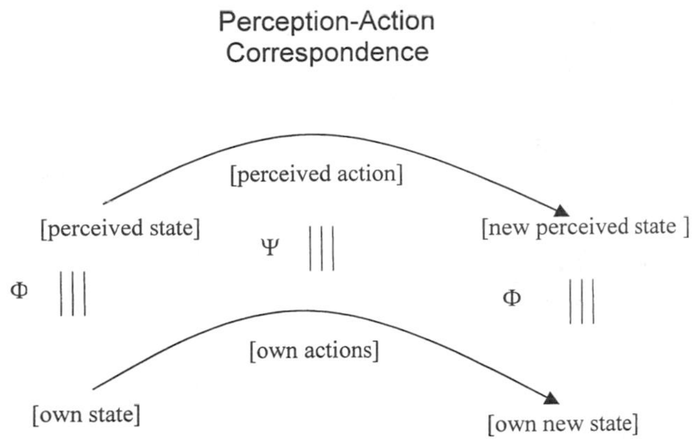

Perception-Action
Correspondence

[perceived action]

[perceived state]   [new perceived state]

Ψ $|||$

Φ $|||$ Φ $|||$

[own actions]

[own state]   [own new state]

Figure 2.4 A perception-action correspondence can be interpreted for the case of observing the self (through proprioceptive, kinesthetic, and other feedback—e.g., via mirrors). Φ denotes correspondence of states, while Ψ denotes correspondence of action-events. Learning a correspondence is learning a piece of a relational mapping. Metrics on state, actions, goals can guide this learning. Type of learning depends on metrics used and which aspect(s) they measure. Learning to control one's own body implies learning a correspondence between feedback about one's states and actions and what one's states and actions actually are (physically). Possibly some of this correspondence may be innate, although different theories disagree on the extent to which this is so in various species.

feedback—for example, via mirrors or from others responding by imitating one's behavior)—while the second system is given by one's own states and actions. Solving the correspondence problem in this case means learning to control one's own body in the sense of relating one's sensors and effectors to the perceptual feedback they produce. Such a correspondence is schematized in figure 2.4.

Associative Sequence Learning Theory

For example, in the Associative Sequence Learning Theory (ASL) of C. M. Heyes and E. D. Ray (2000) (see also Heyes, chapter 19 of this volume), associations between sensory data and motor representations of behavior ("vertical" links) can be viewed as parts of a correspondence in the formal sense described above. Learning these sensory-motor associations corresponds to building up a solution to the correspondence problem between perceived stimuli (generated by either one's own action or another's action) and one's own motor actions. Complementing this, representation of patterns of behavior is encoded during the learning of temporal sequencing of actions or of higher-level behavioral programs that make use of perception-action correspondence. Currently, ASL does not address the effect of actions on objects or the environment, but we believe that it can be fruitfully extended to incorporate these effects.

The Mirror System

An example of a candidate natural mechanism at the neurological level for solving the correspondence problem is the mirror system present in the brains of at least some primate species, in which certain neurons fire both when performing a particular motor action, such as grasping a piece of food, and when seeing another performing such an act. Some of these neurons appear to encode the particular affordances of movements in relation to objects in the animal's environment (Gallese et al. 1996; Gallese and Goldman 1998; Hari et al. 1998; Rizzolatti et al. 1998; Rizzolatti and Arbib 1998; Arbib, chapter 10 of this volume). As such, the mirror system could mediate a relational mapping between the action of an agent on its environment and those of others it observes. This has also inspired the use of a similar mechanism in robots (Demiris 1999; Demiris and Hayes, chapter 13 of this volume).

Mechanisms, Representations, and the Structure of Socially Learned Information

The structure of imitated behavior can often reveal something of the way in which observed behavior is represented in the imitator. This realization is apparent in the animal imitation literature in such distinctions as action- versus program-level imitation (Byrne and Russon 1998), sequential versus hierarchical structuring of observationally acquired behavior (Whiten, chapter 8 of this volume), and statistical string parsing without intentionality (Byrne 1999).

The methods for extracting socially observed information are by no means unique and the spectrum of representations for organizing observationally acquired information into procedural representations is broad. Some representational formats, techniques, and paradigms used in sciences of the artificial include finite-state automata (e.g., Hopcroft and Ullman 1979); epsilon machines (Crutchfield 1994); generalized Hebbian temporal learning (Billard, chapter 11 of this volume); behavioral cloning and rule extraction (Sammut et al. 1992, chapter 7 of this volume); programming by example (Cypher 1993; Lieberman, chapter 6 of this volume); case-based reasoning (e.g., Kolodner 1993); and stories (Nehaniv 1997; Goodenough, chapter 22 of this volume).

2.6 Discussion

Whatever form of behavioral matching one considers, regardless of the mechanisms behind it, at its heart must lie a notion of correspondence between autonomous agents. Together with such correspondences between the possible states and sequences of action/ events of the respective agents, measures of dissimilarity in matching behavior are enough to classify these phenomena into different classes used by ethologists and psychologists. Various forms of imitation and related phenomena such as emulation, mimicry, blind copying, and social learning correspond to different aspects of constructing a relational mapping between possibly dissimilar bodies (or autonomous agents)—in particular, to whether actions, states, goals, or some combination of these are required to correspond in the course of the behavior. If an animal learns to match the behavior of another, the type of correspondence problem being solved may be indicated by the aspects in which the matching actually occurs. This can be used to distinguish one form of matching from another (for example, mimicry from goal emulation, etc.). Metrics encoding goals relate to intentionality, tool affordances, reinforcement, and the judgment of whether situations are equivalent or not. The structuring of behavior in sequences of actions, hierarchies, or behavioral programs is relevant for studying how solutions of the corrrespondence problem are utilized by an animal. The representation of procedural knowledge as a program, string of actions, hierarchically organized collection of subgoals, and so on, can be used in artificial systems to make use of attempted correspondences and perception-action relations in applications such as programming by example, behavioral cloning, and robot and agent social learning.

All these aspects—action and state correspondences, metrics encoding goals, and the structuring of behavior—need to be considered in studying observational learning and imitation. One should ask: what type of novelty occurs in each of these aspects? (See also the discussion of novelty in chapter 1.) In which of these aspects is there a consistent correspondence? In regard to animals, psychologists and ethologists are interested in uncovering the structure of observational learning, while, in the realm of artifacts, engineering such structure and tinkering with its various aspects affords the possibility to introduce biologically inspired social learning mechanisms into artificial systems.

Solutions to the correspondence problem are a result of successful attempts at imitating (*trying to imitate* [Dautenhahn 1994]) or at mimicry or learning socially. In contrast, in building artifacts, or sometimes even in education (rote or pattern learning), it can be useful to harness *learning by imitation*: here, the correspondence problem is solved at the outset, imitation has been engineered in, but by imitating a teacher, a learner agent comes to experience situations where learning of other skills takes place. (See Hayes and Demiris 1994; Demiris and Hayes 1996; Billard and Dautenhahn 1997, 1998, 1999; Billard, chapter 11 of this volume for examples of such learning that is facilitated by imitation. See Nehaniv and Dautenhahn 2001 for further discussion of the distinction between trying to imitate and learning by imitation.)

We have endeavored to provide a framework with solid mathematical foundations in which one can address matching phenomena in both natural and artificial systems. The algebraic framework presented here for the correspondence problem was initiated by Nehaniv and Dautenhahn (1998). We hope this will be useful in revealing hidden assumptions and observer-dependent aspects of criteria for judging whether or not social learning, imitation, or matching has taken place. Moreover, the notions of relational mapping and metrics provide one with a toolkit for studying what type of correspondence is being constructed, whether one is observing it in controlled experiments with humans and animals, or in other settings involving the matching of behaviors. For workers building artificial systems that can learn by observing, this framework provides a language and mathematical tools for analyzing the aspects of any artificial system that should learn by observing another agent—whether human, animal, robotic, or of another type. By studying which components of a relational mapping need to be engineered—what aspects of a correspondence are to be built in and what aspects are to be learned—a designer may approach the various aspects of a social learning artifact in a systematic manner. Introducing this common framework for correspondence to the study of imitation in animals and artifacts also gives us a way to compare, evaluate, and relate research on imitation and behavior matching in widely disparate studies ranging from animal studies involving various different species to research studies on robots and software agents that seek to engineer and harness such social learning phenomena into artifacts.

Note

1. Mathematically, this can be described as deriving, in a canonical manner, a *free transformation semigroup action* from an automaton.

References

Alexander, R. M. *Exploring Biomechanics: Animals in Motion*, chapter 5. New York: Scientific American Library, 1992.

Alissandrakis, A., C. L. Nehaniv, and K. Dautenhahn. Learning how to do things with imitation. In *Proceedings AAAI Fall Symposium on Learning How to Do Things*. Menlo Park, Calif.: American Association for Artificial Intelligence Press, 2000. Available: ⟨http://homepages.feis.herts.ac.uk/~nehaniv/chessworld.ps⟩.

Billard, A., and K. Dautenhahn. Grounding communication in situated, social robots. In *Proceedings TIMR UK 97 Towards Intelligent Mobile Robots*. Technical Report Series of the Department of Computer Science, Manchester University, 1997.

Billard, A., and K. Dautenhahn. Grounding communication in autonomous robots: An experimental study. *Robotics and Autonomous Systems* 24(1–2): 71–81, 1998.

Billard, A., and K. Dautenhahn. Experiments in social robotics: Grounding and use of communication in autonomous agents. *Adaptive Behavior*, special issue on "Simulation Models of Social Agents" 7(3–4): 415–438, 1999.

Byrne, R. W. Imitation without intentionality. Using string parsing to copy the organization of behaviour. *Animal Cognition* 2: 63–72, 1999.

Byrne, R. W., and A. E. Russon. Learning by imitation: A hierarchical approach. *Behavioral and Brain Sciences* 21: 667–709, 1998.

Byrne, R. W., and A. Whiten (eds.). *Machiavellian Intelligence*. Oxford: Clarendon Press, 1988.

Crutchfield, J. Observing complexity and the complexity of observation. In H. Atmanspacher (ed.), *Inside versus Outside*. Springer Verlag, pp. 234–272, 1994.

Cypher, A. (ed.). *Watch What I Do: Programming by Demonstration*. Cambridge, Mass.: MIT Press, 1993.

Dautenhahn, K. Trying to Imitate—A step towards releasing robots from social isolation. In P. Gaussier and J.-D. Nicoud (eds.), *Proceedings From Perception to Actions Conference (Lausanne, Switzerland)*, pp. 290–301. Los Alamitos, Calif.: IEEE Computer Society Press, 1994.

Dautenhahn, K. I could be you—The phenomenological dimension of social understanding. *Cybernetics and Systems* 25(8): 417–453, 1997.

Dautenhahn, K. Embodiment and interaction in socially intelligent life-like agents. In C. L. Nehaniv (ed.), *Computation for Metaphors, Analogy, and Agents*, Lecture Notes in Artificial Intelligence, vol. 1562, pp. 102–142. Berlin: Springer Verlag, 1999.

Dautenhahn, K. Socially intelligent agents and the primate social brain: Towards a science of social minds. In *Proceedings AAAI Fall Symposium Socially Intelligent Agents—The Human in the Loop*. Menlo Park, Calif.: American Association for Artificial Intelligence Press, 2000.

Demiris, J. *Movement Imitation Mechanisms in Robots and Humans*. Ph.D. thesis, University of Edinburgh, Scotland, 1999.

Demiris, J., and G. Hayes. Imitative learning mechanisms in robots and humans. In *Proceedings of the 5th European Workshop on Learning Robots*, Bari, Italy. July 1996.

Furse, E. A model of imitation learning of algorithms from worked examples. *Cybernetics and Systems*, special issue on "Imitation in Natural and Artificial Systems" 32(1–2): 121–154, 2001.

Galef, B. G. Jr. Imitation in animals: History, definition, and interpretation of data from the psychological laboratory. In T. R. Zentall and B. G. Galef Jr. (eds.), *Social Learning: Psychological and Biological Perspectives*, pp. 3–28. Hillsdale, N.J.: Erlbaum, 1988.

Gallese, V., L. Fadiga, L. Fogassi, and G. Rizzolatti. Action recognition in the premotor cortex. *Brain* 119: 593–609, 1996.

Gallese, V., and A. Goldman. Mirror neurons and the simulation theory of mind-reading. *Trends in Cognitive Sciences* 2(12): 493–501, December 1998.

Hari, R., N. Forss, S. Avikainan, S. Salenius, and G. Rizzolatti. Activation of human primary cortex during action observations: A neuromagnetic study. *Proceedings of the National Academy of Sciences* 95: 15061–15065, 1998.

Hayes, G., and J. Demiris. A robot controller using learning by imitation. In A. Borkowski and J. L. Crowley (eds.), *SIRS-94, Proceedings of the 2nd International Symposium on Intelligent Robotic Systems*, LIFIA-IMAG, Grenoble, France, pp. 198–204. July 1994.

Heyes, C. M., and E. D. Ray. What is the significance of imitation in animals? *Advances in the Study of Behavior* 29: 215–245, 2000.

Hopcroft, J. E., and J. D. Ullman. *Introduction to Automata Theory, Languages, and Computation*. Reading, Mass.: Addison-Wesley, 1979.

Kauffman, S. Remarks on goals and purpose in biological agents during a lecture delivered to the Working Group on Evolvability. Santa Fe Institute, New Mexico, pers. communication, April 2000.

Kolodner, J. *Case-Based Reasoning*. San Francisco: Morgan Kaufmann Publishers, 1993.

Nehaniv, C. L., From relation to emulation: The covering lemma for transformation semigroups. *Journal of Pure and Applied Algebra* 107: 75–87, 1996.

Nehaniv, C. L. What's your story?—Irreversibility, algebra, autobiographic agents. In K. Dautenhahn (ed.), *Socially Intelligent Agents: Papers from the 1997 AAAI Fall Symposium* (November 1997, MIT, Cambridge, Mass.), pp. 150–153. Menlo Park, Calif.: American Association for Artificial Intelligence Press, 1997.

Nehaniv, C. L. Meaning for observers and agents. In *IEEE International Symposium on Intelligent Control/Intelligent Systems and Semiotics (ISIC/ISAS '99)*, pp. 435–440. Cambridge, Mass.: Institute of Electronic and Electrical Engineers Press, 1999.

Nehaniv, C. L., and K. Dautenhahn. Mapping between dissimilar bodies: Affordances and the algebraic foundations of imitation. In J. Demiris and A. Birk (eds.), *Proceedings European Workshop on Learning Robots 1998 (EWLR-7)*, Edinburgh, Scotland. 1998.

Nehaniv, C. L., and K. Dautenhahn. Like me?—Measures of correspondence and imitation. *Cybernetics and Systems*, special issue on "Imitation in Natural and Artificial Systems" 32(1–2): 11–51, 2001.

Nehaniv, C. L., K. Dautenhahn, and M. J. Loomes. Constructive biology and approaches to temporal grounding in post-reactive robotics. In G. T. McKee and P. Schenker (eds.), *Sensor Fusion and Decentralized Control in Robotics Systems II*, Proceedings of SPIE vol. 3839, pp. 156–167. Bellingham, Wash.: SPIE—The International Society for Optical Engineering, 1999.

O'Connell, S. M. Empathy in chimpanzees: Evidence for theory of mind? *Primates* 36(3): 397–410, 1995.

Povinelli, D. J., and T. M. Preuss. Theory of mind: Evolutionary history of a cognitive specialization. *Trends in Neurosciences* 18(9): 418–424, 1995.

Premack, D., and G. Woodruff. Does the chimpanzee have a theory of mind? *Behavioral and Brain Sciences* 4: 515–526, 1978.

Rizzolatti, G., and M. A. Arbib. Language within our grasp. *Trends in Neurosciences* 21(5): 188–194, 1998.

Rizzolatti, G., L. Fadiga, V. Gallese, and L. Fogassi. Premotor cortex and the recognition of motor actions. *Cognition and Brain Research* 3: 131–141, 1998.

Russon, A., and B. M. F. Galdikas. Imitation in ex-captive orangutans. *Journal of Comparative Psychology* 107: 147–161, 1993.

Russon, A., and B. M. F. Galdikas. Contraints on great apes' imitation: Model and action selectivity in rehabilitant orangutan (*Pongo pygmaeus*) imitation. *Journal of Comparative Psychology* 109: 5–17, 1995.

Sammut, C., S. Hurst, D. Kedzier, and D. Michie. Learning to fly, *Proc. 9th International Machine Learning Conference (ML '92)*. San Francisco: Morgan Kaufmann, 1992.

Tomasello, M. Cultural transmission and tool use and communicatory signaling of chimpanzees? In S. Parker and K. Gibson (eds.), *"Language" and Intelligence in Monkeys and Apes: Comparative Developmental Perspectives*. Cambridge, UK: Cambridge Unviersity Press, 1990.

Tomasello, M., and J. Call. *Primate Cognition*. New York: Oxford University Press, 1997.

Tomasello, M., E. S. Savage-Rumbaugh, and A. C. Kruger. Imitative learning of actions on objects by children, chimpanzees, and enculturated chimpanzees. *Child Development* 64: 1688–1705, 1993.

Whiten, A., and R. W. Byrne. *Machiavellian Intelligence II: Extensions and Evaluations*. Cambridge, UK: Cambridge University Press, 1997.

Whiten, A., and R. Ham. On the nature and evolution of imitation in the animal kingdom: Reappraisal of a century of research. In P. J. B. Slater, J. S. Rosenblatt, C. Beer, and M. Milinski (eds.), *Advances in the Study of Behavior, 21*, pp. 239–283. San Diego, CA: Academic Press, 1992.

Zentall, T. R. Imitation in animals: Evidence, function, and mechanisms. *Cybernetics and Systems*, special issue on "Imitation in Natural and Artificial Systems" 32(1–2): 53–96, 2001.

3 Vocal, Social, and Self-Imitation by Bottlenosed Dolphins

Louis M. Herman

3.1 Imitation by Animals

Despite a long history of behavioral research on imitation (e.g., see reviews in Galef 1988, 1998; Whiten and Ham 1992), the definition of imitative behavior and which animals may exhibit imitation remain areas of discussion and debate (cf. Heyes 1993; Byrne and Russon 1998; Byrne and Tomasello 1995; Moore 1996; Tomasello 1996; Tomasello and Call 1997; Whiten and Custance 1996; Zentall 1996). In its most basic sense, imitation is a type of social behavior in which one animal copies the form of the behavior of another (Whiten and Ham 1992). Apparent copying may be seen in such elementary social events as flocking, schooling, or phonoresponses (e.g., wolves howling). However, these acts do not necessarily imply any learned or cognitive component that, for example, would allow for generalization of the imitative act to other types of observed behaviors, including behaviors new to the observer's experience (cf. Thorpe 1963).

Much recent work has focused on developing tasks that might clearly reveal an animal's ability to learn through imitation, and that can distinguish apparent imitative success from other explanations for the behavior, such as stimulus enhancement, local enhancement, contagion, or emulation (see, e.g., Tomasello 1996; Whiten and Ham 1992; Zentall 1996). One of these tasks is the two-action test. For example, some observer animals watch a demonstrator move a rod to the left for food reinforcement and others watch a movement to the right (e.g., Heyes and Dawson 1990). Imitation is inferred if the observer animals subsequently move the rod significantly more often in the same direction as the demonstrator. However, this test hardly taps the range or flexibility of imitative behavior possible in the species studied (also see Moore 1996, for a similar critique), and is not itself immune from artifacts that may control responding (e.g., odor cues for rats—Gardner 1997). Complex versions of the two-action test, comprising sequences of actions, are more successful in demonstrating the flexibility of imitative response that can be achieved. In a study reported by Whiten (chapter 8 of this volume), each of four chimpanzee subjects observed a human opening an "artificial fruit" through a sequence of four steps. Each step was actually a two-action test. The sequences were different for each chimpanzee, yet after four or five demonstrations each successfully copied their particular sequence. Views of researchers differ as to the developmental levels or experiences required for the realization of imitative behavior by chimpanzees. Tomasello, Savage-Rumbaugh, and Kruger (1993) reported imitation of novel actions on objects by "enculturated" chimpanzees (raised by humans in a humanlike culture), but not by mother-reared chimpanzees, suggesting that enculturation was a necessary precursor for the emergence of imitative ability (also see Tomasello 1996). Whiten and Custance (1996) argued, however, that their chimpanzees, which successfully imitated some of the actions of a human opening an artificial fruit, did not fit the enculturated standards of Tomasello (1996).

The range and flexibility of imitative behavior attainable can also be assessed by examination of the ability of animals to copy motor acts or postures of a model. Custance, Whiten, and Bard (1995) replicated the mimicry work with chimpanzees of Hayes and Hayes (1952). Custance and colleagues (1995) demonstrated that their subjects were able to imitate a variety of postures and motor behaviors of the experimenter on the command *do this* (the chimps successfully imitated 18 to 19 of 48 motor acts, as judged by independent observers). Call and Tomasello (1995) reported similar findings for their orangutan subject, Chantek. It is not clear, however, whether the *do this* command was semantically processed as an instruction to imitate (there was no contrasting term in either the chimpanzee or orangutan studies indicating *don't do this* or *do something different*), or whether imitation was simply elicited by the experimental context. In the latter case, *do this* would function only as a releasing stimulus.

These various data with chimpanzees give support to the imitative capacity of this species. However, which other animals are able to learn through imitation is still largely unresolved. Visalberghi and Fragaszy (1990), after reviewing studies of imitative learning in various species of monkeys, concluded, "optimistically, imitation plays a limited role in the acquisition of novel behaviors in monkeys" (p. 266). Visalberghi (chapter 18 of this volume) reported that her statement remains unchanged despite almost ten years of further study of monkeys. Heyes (1993) claimed that only two published studies, one with budgerigars and the other with rats, have provided convincing evidence of nonvocal imitation in animals. In each case, the two-action test was used. Rats were significantly more likely to move a lever in the direction demonstrated by another rat (Heyes and Dawson 1990); on their first two trials, budgerigars were more likely to remove a bottle cap in the way demonstrated, by using their beak or their feet (Galef, Manzig, and Field 1986). Heyes's conclusions were strongly contested by Byrne and Tomasello (1995) who stated, "by everyone's definition imitation ... should involve the animals learning a new response" (p. 417). These authors then argued that the budgerigars were not learning a new response, and that the behavior of rats, tested in a two-action task, could also be explained by a variety of factors other than imitation (see, e.g., Gardner 1997).

The precision or exactness with which the model's behaviors are copied also intrudes on the definition of imitation and on the assessment of apparent imitative acts. Whiten and Ham (1992) argued that exact copying is unlikely, and that imitation is more often partial than complete. This exemption seems preferable to an all-or-none definition of imitation and would allow more species to be credited with at least some degree of imitative ability (e.g., Caldwell, Whiten, and Morris 1999). Nehaniv and Dautenhahn (chapter 2 of this volume) discuss the different possible correspondences between the actions of model and imitator, and Nehaniv and Dautenhahn (2000) provide an analysis of various ways of measuring the degree of success of the imitator.

The following sections review a variety of studies of imitation by dolphins that address some of the issues discussed above. These include the range and flexibility of imitative acts that can be performed by dolphins, whether novel acts can be imitated, and whether dolphins can acquire a generalized concept of "imitate." Other issues considered are cross-species imitation, vocal as well as motor imitation, and self-imitation. Thus, no one test is put forth as prima facie evidence for imitation by dolphins. Instead, the various topic areas listed provide for a series of convergent approaches to the study of imitative processes that eventually yield an appreciation for the rich imitative capacities of dolphins.

3.2 General Principles: Definition and Premises in the Study of Imitation by Dolphins

Three premises have guided our laboratory's approach to the study of imitation by dolphins:

1. Evidence for imitative ability is strongest if imitation can be demonstrated in a variety of ways and in a variety of contexts.
2. Although the genesis of imitative ability may derive from social factors, its expression may also appear in nonsocial contexts.
3. If imitation is understood conceptually by the subject, it should generalize to many situations, and be controllable by abstract symbols.

Like any concept, imitation has many dimensions. Its expression, breadth, and limitations are therefore best understood by examining for imitative capability in a variety of contexts, procedures, and even modalities. In broad terms, imitation may be defined as the process of accessing a mental representation of an experienced event to reproduce that event through one's own behavior. This definition allows imitation to apply to events experienced though any sense—auditory, visual, or proprioceptive/kinesthetic. The strongest evidence for any putative imitative capacity would then be the demonstration of a variety of imitative acts in a variety of contexts and through a variety of modalities, capacities that are readily observed in humans. The human ability for both vocal and motor mimicry, for example, represents different types of imitation achieved through different modalities. Imitation of self (repeating one's own behavior if requested to do so), as well as imitation of others (social imitation), adds further dimensions to the human's robust imitative repertoire. Additionally, it is abundantly clear that humans can develop a generalized concept of "imitate" that includes semantic knowledge of the abstraction "imitate," and that the term applies not only to the observer's own imitative acts but also to the recognition of the imitative acts of others.

To what extent can this suite of imitative abilities characterizing human performance, including the understanding of imitation as a concept, be found in dolphins? Herman, Pack, and Morrel-Samuels (1993) provided summaries of a variety of studies showing capabilities of bottlenosed dolphins for vocal imitation of computer-generated arbitrary sounds and for motor imitation of dolphin or human models. Further discussion and details of these studies are provided here, as well as summaries of recent studies reporting the ability of dolphins to reproduce their own motor behaviors in response to an abstract gestural command. These various capabilities represent, respectively, vocal, social, and self-imitation and each can be elicited and controlled by abstract symbols. The elicitation of an imitative act by an abstract symbol and the dolphin's ability to generalize the imitative act to a variety of different experienced events illustrate the understanding of imitation conceptually.

3.3 The Dolphin Subjects

The imitative abilities of four bottlenosed dolphins (*Tursiops truncatus*) housed at the Kewalo Basin Marine Mammal Laboratory in Honolulu were studied. Three of the dolphins are females (Akeakamai, Phoenix, and Elele) and the fourth is a male (Hiapo). All were wild born and arrived at our laboratory at about the age of two. The imitation studies were carried out over a number of years, with at times considerable intervals between studies with a given dolphin. During some of the studies, the dolphin subject was relatively young (e.g., about 5–6 years of age in the vocal mimicry study of Akeakamai ["Ake," for short] by Richards, Wolz, and Herman 1984; about 2–3 years of age in the motor imitation studies of Hiapo and Elele by Xitco 1988; and 11–12 years of age in the motor mimicry study of Ake and Phoenix, also by Xitco 1988). The self-imitation studies with Hiapo and Elele (Mercado et al. 1998; Mercado et al. 1999) were carried out when the pair was about 12 years of age.[1] In addition to the studies of imitation, these four dolphins also participated in studies investigating other capacities, including sensory abilities, cognition, and communication (e.g., Herman 1986; Herman, Pack, and Hoffmann-Kuhnt 1998; Herman, Pack, and Morrel-Samuels 1993; Herman, Pack, and Wood 1994; Herman, Richards, and Wolz 1984). Because of these diverse experiences and training, all four dolphins are highly test-sophisticated and are familiar with a variety of human manual gestures or sequences of gestures that can direct their behavior.

The bottlenosed dolphin is a cosmopolitan, social species, found in temperate to tropical waters throughout the world. The social world of these animals is highly complex, and is often referred to as a fission-fusion society in which individuals may have many different associates ranging from transient affiliations to long-term enduring relationships (Wells 1991). Coordination of behaviors occurs frequently in activities as diverse as foraging, predator defense, allo-parental care, and reproduction. Our laboratory procedures acknowledge and respond to the highly social nature of these

Figure 3.1 The dolphin Phoenix with a familiar staff member (A. A. Pack) in close social interaction.

animals. Each day, there is approximately 8–10 hours of dolphin-human contact, ranging from formal test sessions, to husbandry work, to play interactions. These activities are structured to be positive rewarding experiences for both dolphin and human participants. The result is a close bidirectional social and emotional bond between dolphins and humans (e.g., figure 3.1). The dolphins remain very interested in us and in our activities, participate eagerly in our studies, and typically show sustained attention throughout. The extensive daily contact with humans might merit the dolphins being labeled currently as "enculturated."

3.4   Vocal Imitation: Imitation of Arbitrary Computer-Generated Sounds; Imitation of Signature Whistles

In principle, there would seem to be few physical or physiological constraints that of themselves would preclude mammals or birds from demonstrating some form of motor imitation, if the cognitive underpinnings for imitative ability were present. On the other hand, there appear to be many such constraints on vocal imitation in mammals. In primates, for example, a lack of vocal imitation ability may reflect vocal tract limitations or insufficient neurological control of voice production, rather than a cognitive limitation (Lieberman 1968). No comparable vocal constraint exists for dolphins.

Bottlenosed dolphins are highly vocal animals and use sounds for echolocation, communication, and emotional expression (Herman and Tavolga 1980). Short, broadband clicks are used for echolocation. Narrow-band, frequency-varying sounds—termed whistles—are thought to be primarily for communication, and "pulse-bursts," which resemble the graded signals of most other mammals (Caldwell and Caldwell 1967), occur in emotional contexts ranging from aggression to pleasure. In an early paper, Caldwell and Caldwell (1965) reported that each dolphin appeared to produce its own unique whistle sound, which they termed its "signature." The signature was defined as the most commonly occurring whistle, at times constituting as much as 90% of the whistles produced. There is some variation in the signature, such as the number of repetitions, the amplitude, and whether or not the complete signature contour is produced (Caldwell, Caldwell, and Tyack 1990). Whistles other than the signature are also produced (e.g., McCowan and Reiss 1995). In captive situations, spontaneous vocal mimicry of artificial sounds introduced into the dolphin's habitat has been observed (Caldwell and Caldwell 1972; Herman 1980, Richards 1986; Reiss and McCowan 1993). Of most interest, imitation by one dolphin of another's signature whistle has also been observed (Richards 1986; Tyack 1986). Our earliest formal study of imitation investigated a dolphin's ability to vocally mimic a variety of electronically generated sounds broadcast into its habitat through an underwater speaker (Richards, Wolz, and Herman 1984). A sequence of three sounds elicited vocal mimicry by the dolphin Ake: (a) a 9-kHz frequency-modulated tone called Ake to the listening station at an underwater speaker; (b) a short 4-kHz pure-tone sound, glossed as "mimic," alerted Ake to "get ready" for the model sound that followed; and finally (c) the "model" sound to be imitated was broadcast. In response to the model sound, Ake vocalized into an adjacent hydrophone. Imitations were judged in real time in a remote studio by an experienced observer listening to the sounds from the hydrophone and, at the same time, watching a frequency-versus-time visual representation of the sound on an oscilloscope. Audio tape recordings allowed for subsequent detailed analyses. Figure 3.2 shows spectrograms of nine different model sounds and the dolphin's imitation of these sounds. In each case, the arrow points to the beginning of the dolphin's imitation.

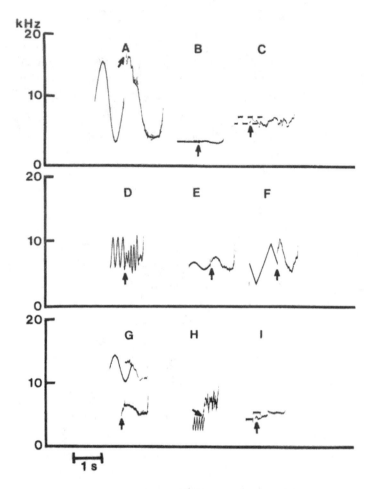

Figure 3.2 Vocal imitation of nine computer-generated model sounds by dolphin Akeakamai. The model sound is shown on the left of each panel and the dolphin's imitation on the right. The arrow points to where the dolphin's imitation begins. See text for additional details. (After Richards, Wolz and Herman, 1984)

It is apparent that many different waveforms were mimicked, including slow frequency modulation (model A), an unmodulated 6-kHz tone (B), a dual-frequency pulsed tone (C), and a triangle wave (F). Ake's mimics were usually recognizably similar to the model sound, although with successive exposure to a model sound, her accuracy at mimicry improved. Some models, however, were imitated accurately on the first attempt (for example, model I in figure 3.2), illustrating the development of a generalized concept of vocal mimicry. Models G and H show imitations one octave removed, down or up, from the model's frequency range. Octave generalization (recognizing a tune, or frequency contour, as the same across octaves) is elementary for humans, is apparently outside the abilities of birds (Hulse 1989), but is well within the capabilities of dolphins (Ralston and Herman 1995). Reliability of mimicry by the dolphin was excellent. Figure 3.3 shows the consistency attained in mimicking multiple times each of four different model sounds. The four model sounds were presented in eight blocks of four trials. Within blocks, the four sounds occurred in a counterbalanced order as determined by a Latin square design. Clearly, these results reveal an impressive vocal imitative ability. None of the model sounds was taken from natural vocalizations of bottlenosed dolphins, and some were not of a type found in the real world of the dolphin (e.g., models C, F, and I).

3.5 Behavioral Imitation of Others (Social Imitation)

Behavioral Synchrony

In the wild, synchronous behaviors, such as surfacing and leaping together, characterize many of the actions of closely affiliated pairs of dolphins and may serve, in part, to affirm that relationship. Some synchronous behaviors may involve mutual or reciprocal imitation, as in a "follow-the-leader" game with perhaps some exchange of leadership. At our laboratory, we have built on the dolphin's naturally occurring synchronous behaviors to demonstrate that dolphins can develop a concept of "togetherness." We taught the dolphins a gestural symbol, which we call *tandem*, that directs two (or more) dolphins to perform any particular requested behavior together. For example, if each of two trainers on opposite sides of the dolphins' tank gives his or her dolphin the *tandem* sign followed by the specific gestural sign for *back dive*, the dolphin pair will join underwater and then leap out of the water together backwards in a closely spaced and timed maneuver. If a dolphin is not given the *tandem* sign, it will not attempt to join with another dolphin. Even complex sequences of behaviors can be executed in tandem. For example, in response to three sequential gestures, glossed as *tandem + kiss + jump*, the two instructed dolphins execute a forward leap together while touching each other's rostrum (beak). These kinds of directed synchronous behaviors clearly require close attention to each other's body movements

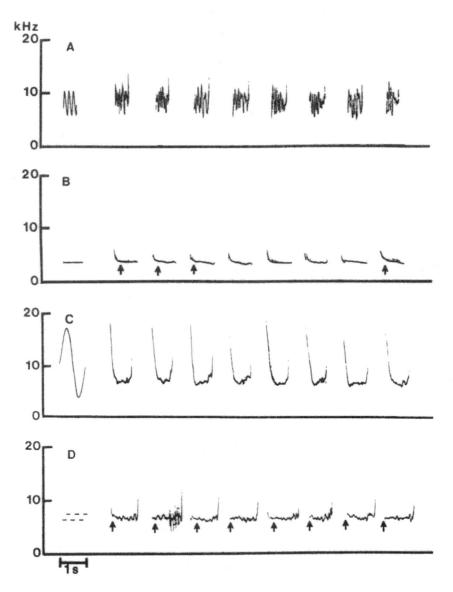

Figure 3.3 Reliability of eight imitations of each of four different model sounds by dolphin Akeakamai. The model sound is shown on the left of each panel, with the eight successive imitations, each obtained at a different time, on the right. For clarity of presentation, the model sound occurring before each imitation was removed from the figure. (After Richards, Wolz and Herman, 1984)

and body positioning, an obvious general requirement for social mimicry.

Additionally, in response to a sequence of two gestures glossed as *tandem + create*, the dolphins will self-select a behavior and perform it together. Braslau-Schneck (1994) documented 79 different behaviors performed together by the dolphins Elele and Hiapo in response to *tandem + create* instructions. Twenty-three of these behaviors were novel, in that they were not under control of established gestures. Mimicry of one dolphin's behavior by the other offers the most likely explanation for their joint performance. Videotape analyses of successful responses revealed that in most cases the dolphins appeared to be in virtual synchrony. However, on 30 of 44 occasions when a difference in timing could be detected, Elele performed the behavior slightly ahead of Hiapo; on the remaining occasions, Hiapo performed slightly ahead. Typically, behaviors did not occur immediately after a *tandem + create* instruction was given, but only after several seconds of swimming together underwater, apparently "organizing" their response. It is unclear, however, whether any intentional communication is occurring before the pair executes a behavior. At times, vocalizations can be heard, but it has been difficult to associate these reliably with specific behaviors. With improved acoustic monitoring capabilities, now being planned, it may be possible to answer the question of intentionality more decisively.

Imitation Controlled by an Abstract Gesture

A variety of informal reports from oceanariums have described apparent spontaneous imitative behaviors occurring among the resident dolphin species (reviewed in Herman 1980). These reports have included copying of the postural or motor behaviors of non-cetacean species such as seals, imitations of the actions of human divers, and imitation of the complex trained motor sequences of other dolphin tank mates. To study social imitation formally and to investigate whether a dolphin can develop a concept of imitate, we developed a gesture we termed "mimic" that elicited imitation of a model's motor behaviors by an observer dolphin (Xitco 1988). We used a limited number of behaviors to train imitative responses in the presence of the gesture, and then tested for generalization using other behaviors, some familiar and some novel. The model for the behaviors was either another dolphin or a human.

Dolphin-Dolphin Imitation

In the formal social imitation procedure (Xitco 1988), one dolphin acted as the demonstrator (model) and the other as the imitator. The dolphins Ake and Phoenix easily acted in either role. The two dolphins were stationed side by side, each facing a different trainer. A wooden partition extending outward from the tank wall prevented each dolphin from seeing the other's trainer, but because the board did not extend to the water surface, the dolphins could see each other. The trainer for the demonstrator dolphin gave a gesture or sequence of gestures asking for some particular behavior. The trainer for the observer dolphin then gave either the gestural *mimic* sign, asking that the dolphin copy the model's behavior or, alternatively, gave a gestural sign asking for some particular behavior different from that of the model. Imitating versus performing the alternative behavior was a highly reliable discrimination yielding virtually no error for either dolphin. This success demonstrated that the *mimic* sign was semantically processed, in that that the observer only imitated in the presence of the sign. Behaviors copied successfully included simple motor behaviors as well as actions on objects. In the latter case, the object itself did not elicit the behavior, as might be suggested by a stimulus enhancement explanation, because a variety of behaviors were demonstrated to each object and the observer copied the particular action performed. This might include, for example, leaping over the object, touching it with the tail, or touching it with the pectoral fin.

Phoenix and Ake were trained to respond to the *mimic* gesture through the following steps:

1. No partition in place. The two trainers stand side by side and simultaneously give *tandem + specific behavior* gestural instructions. Dolphins perform behaviors together.
2. No partition in place. Trainer 2 (imitator) slightly delays her *tandem* sign instruction relative to trainer 1 (demonstrator). Dolphin 2 follows dolphin 1 and executes same behavior.
3. Partition introduced. Trainer 1 gives a sign for a specific behavior. Almost simultaneously, trainer 2 gives *mimic* sign followed by the same specific behavior gesture.
4. On probe trials, specific behavior sign is deleted after *mimic* sign.
5. Training sessions continue until a criterion of 85 percent correct responses over two sessions is reached on trials using the *mimic* sign alone.

Table 3.1 Dolphin-dolphin behavioral mimicry: behaviors used to train mimicry for dolphins Phoenix and Akeakamai

BEHAVIOR DEMONSTRATED
Inverted swim*
Wiggle pectoral fins while in upright stance
Leap over object
Touch object with pectoral fin
Pirouette with head out of water
Somersault underwater
Corkscrew swim underwater
Spit water at object
Leap out of water, reenter head first
Leap out of water while somersaulting

* Behavior dropped from training set after session 14.

Ten different familiar behaviors were used to train the concept (table 3.1), after which each dolphin was tested on 15 additional transfer behaviors. Each training session consisted of two to four blocks of 12 trials each, with the two dolphins alternating roles as model or mimic for each block. At each block, there were ten mimic trials and two nonmimic trials (model performs a behavior, but imitator is given a sign for a different specific behavior). Inverted swimming was dropped from the training set for both dolphins after session 14, because neither dolphin was exhibiting successful imitations. For the remaining behaviors, Phoenix reached the performance criterion on her seventeenth session, and Ake on her twenty-sixth session.

After training was complete with a given dolphin, transfer testing began. Each dolphin was tested with 15 transfer behaviors (table 3.2). For each dolphin, 12 behaviors were from the preexisting repertoire of the dolphin and were under control of specific gestural signs. An additional three were novel to the observer dolphin, having been specifically taught only to the demonstrator. Of the 12 familiar behaviors in the transfer set, nine were the same for both dolphins (shared behaviors), but three were different (not shared). Shared behaviors were given to each dolphin in different

Table 3.2 Dolphin-dolphin behavioral mimicry: behaviors used to test transfer of the *mimic* concept for dolphins Phoenix and Akeakamai

BEHAVIOR DEMONSTRATED	PHOENIX IMITATES	AKE IMITATES
Touch object with tail	*D* (1) [3]	*D* (2) [2]
Back dive	*D* (−)	*D* (−)
Turn belly up at station	*D* (2) [2]	*D* (−)
Back swim waving pectoral fins	*D* (−)	—
Blow bubbles underwater	—	*D* (−)
Retrieve object	*D* (3) [3]	*D* (3) [3]
Spiraling leap	*D* (6) [1]	*D* (5) [3]
Shake head side to side	*D* (−)	*D* (−)
Twirl Frisbee on rostrum	*D* (2) [3]	—
Swim backwards, tail first	—	*D* (−)
Swim through a hoop	*D* (1) [3]	*D* (1) [3]
Slap tail on water	*D* (1) [3]	*D* (2) [1]
Nod head up and down	*D* (−)	*D* (−)
Backwards tail walk	*D* (−)	—
Throw ball	—	*D* (1) [2]
Press paddle with rostrum (novel)	*D* (2) [3]	—
Pull rope and ring bell (novel)	*D* (2) [3]	—
Slide out on platform (novel)	*D* (−)	—
Place ring on stick (novel)	—	*D* (3) [3]
Push buoy down with belly (novel)	—	*D* (−)
Carry towel on dorsal fin (novel)	—	*D* (−)

Note: D means behavior was demonstrated for indicated dolphin. Numbers in parentheses are the number of demonstrations required for the first successful imitation. A minus sign (−) indicates that the behavior was not imitated within the maximum of ten demonstrations. Numbers in brackets indicate the total number of successful imitations achieved (maximum = 3). All behaviors except those designated novel were familiar behaviors under gestural control for each dolphin.

Table 3.3 Results of dolphin-dolphin behavioral mimicry of familiar and novel behaviors for Phoenix and Akeakamai

MIMICKING DOLPHIN	NO. BEHAVIORS GIVEN		NO. IMITATED FIRST TRIAL		NO. IMITATED SUCCESSFULLY	
	Familiar	Novel	Familiar	Novel	Familiar	Novel
Phoenix	12	3	3	0	7	2
Akeakamai	12	3	2	0	6	1

blocks. Thus, the same dolphin never both demonstrated and imitated a given behavior within the same testing session. The 15 behaviors for each dolphin (table 3.2) were grouped and tested in three successive sets of four behaviors and one final set of three, the latter consisting entirely of the novel behaviors. Each testing session within a set consisted of 12 trials: three were behaviors from the transfer set, and nine were behaviors from the training set. Seven behaviors from the training set were used for mimic trials and two for nonmimic trials. An observer described the mimic dolphin's behavior in real time using the laboratory's standard nomenclature for behaviors. Videotape records provided for subsequent verification, as necessary. Successful mimics were defined as fully developed imitations occurring within the first ten demonstrations of that behavior (there was only one demonstration per testing session). Unsuccessful mimics were those behaviors not copied within ten demonstrations. If a behavior was copied successfully, it continued to be presented in subsequent sessions until the criterion of ten demonstrations had been achieved, or until three successful imitations had occurred. This procedure allowed for a measure of repeatability of the imitation.

Table 3.2 also gives the number of demonstrations required for the first successful mimic response and the number of successful imitations attained (maximum = 3). Table 3.3 provides an overall summary of each dolphin's performance over the 12 familiar and three novel behaviors given during the transfer tests. First-trial mimicry occurred on three of 12 familiar behaviors for Phoenix and on two for Ake. With repeated exposure to demonstrations of a behavior, more behaviors were imitated successfully. If a behavior was imitated successfully once, it tended to be imitated successfully again one or two more times. For Phoenix, in addition to the three familiar behaviors successfully imitated after the first demonstration, two others were successfully imitated after the second demonstration, one after the third, and a final one after the sixth demonstration. For Ake, in addition to her two successes after the first demonstration, two other familiar behaviors were imitated successfully after the second demonstration, one after the third, and one after the fifth. Two novel behaviors were successfully imitated by Phoenix (pressing a paddle and ringing a bell). In both cases, the first successful imitation occurred after the second demonstration. Ake successfully imitated one novel behavior (placing a ring on a stick) after the third demonstration. For Phoenix, eight of the nine behaviors she successfully imitated were imitated more than once, and for Ake six of the seven behaviors she successfully imitated were imitated more than once. The fact that most of the behaviors were not successfully imitated after the first demonstration, but the majority were successfully imitated eventually, suggests that successive exposures served to better define the model's behavior for the observer, yielding a richer representation of the behavior on which to base the imitative act. Overall, these data suggest that the difficulty for the dolphin was not so much in learning to imitate the other dolphin, or in performing the modeled behavior, but in attending to and representing the characteristics of the demonstrated behavior.

A possible weakness of the study was that the observer labeling the imitator's behaviors could usually also see the demonstrator's behaviors, inasmuch as the two behaviors occurred closely together in time. A delay procedure was subsequently instituted by Xitco (1988) that not only controlled for this potential observer bias, but also examined the extent to which mental representations of observed behaviors could be maintained over time. Six behaviors from the training set (table 3.1: wiggle pectoral fin, leap over object, touch object with pectoral fin, pirouette, somersault, and spit water at object) and one from the transfer set (table 3.2: swim through hoop) were used to test for delayed mimicry abilities of Phoenix and Ake. The observer dolphin was first habituated to waiting until the demonstrator had completed her behavior and had returned to her trainer before receiving a gestural instruction from her own trainer (termed "baseline" delay condition). The individual labeling the observer's responses was cued to visually attend to the dolphins only after the demonstrator had returned to her trainer, and was therefore unaware of what behavior had been demonstrated.

After completion of habituation training, imitation ability was tested after delays ranging up to 80 sec after completion of the demonstrator's behavior. The same set of seven behaviors used for habituation was again employed. Ake's imitative abilities were tested using three sets of delay values (8, 20, and 50 sec; 10, 25, and 80 sec; and 10, 25, and 60 sec, with the sets tested in the order listed). Additionally, each set contained the baseline delay condition used in the training procedure. Baseline performance in all cases yielded 95% correct imitations or better. On set 1, performance declined relatively slowly to approximately 91% and 86% correct imitations after 8- and 20-sec delays, respectively, and then declined more steeply to 69% correct after the 50-sec delay. Sets 2 and 3 showed an improved ability to imitate behaviors at long delays: approximately 95% correct imitations after a 25-sec delay, 74% after the 60-sec delay, and 59% after the 80-sec delay, all significantly above chance performance (estimated as $1/7$, $p < .001$ by the summed binomial test).

Phoenix was tested using a modified delay procedure in which six different delays, some short and some long, were tested during each session. Over sessions, delay lengths were gradually incremented. Under this procedure, Phoenix's imitations overall were less often correct than were Akeakamai's imitations ($p < .001$ by χ^2 test). Nonetheless, at delays ranging between 3 and 20 sec, 88% of her imitations were judged as correct, and at delays between 50 and 80 sec, 57% were judged as correct ($p < .001$ by summed binomial test).

The ability of the dolphins to copy a behavior successfully after delays implies a reliance on mental representations of the demonstrated behavior (Zentall and Galef 1988). An alternative explanation, however, is that the dolphins adopted a stereotyped posture during the delay interval, or rehearsed the behavior motorically (e.g., by slightly wiggling the pectoral fins during the delay interval if that had been the behavior modeled). In additional work, Herman, Morrel-Samuels, and Brown (1989) guarded against the use of such behavioral mediators by requiring the dolphin to perform one of several distractor behaviors, such as swimming on her back, during the delay interval. The ability to mimic the demonstrated behavior accurately, even after performing a distractor behavior, provided compelling evidence that the dolphins were using mental representations of behaviors to achieve imitations, rather than relying on motoric or kinesthetic cues to remember displayed behaviors.

Dolphin-Dolphin Imitation Replicated

Bauer and Johnson (1994) reported a replication of the Xitco (1988) imitation study with Phoenix and Ake. Two male bottlenosed dolphins (Toby and Bob) were tested using procedures closely following those described by Xitco. Each dolphin served as model for the other, with the roles as model and imitator reversed once within a session. The authors used a set of nine familiar behaviors to teach the *mimic* gestural command and to establish reliable behavioral imitation. Extensive training ("hundreds of trials for Toby and more than 1000 trials for Bob") was required before each reached a criterion of 75% correct imitations or better on each training behavior. During training, three of the ten behaviors were deleted for Bob and one for Toby, for lack of progress. After training was complete, transfer testing began, using ten additional behaviors familiar to the dolphins. Each transfer behavior was demonstrated for a maximum of ten times if no successful imitations occurred or for a maximum of nine additional trials after the first successful imitation. Toby successfully imitated four of the transfer behaviors (ball toss, back dive, somersault, and pirouette). Three of the four were imitated more than once. Additionally, a fifth behavior (retrieving a ring from the tank bottom) was modeled only once but was imitated successfully. Bob succeeded only in imitating the back dive, but imitated it successfully four times. As a final test of transfer, two novel behaviors were demonstrated for Toby, and a different two for Bob, but none of these were imitated within the ten-trial limit. The authors noted that the performance of Toby and Bob was less proficient than that displayed by Phoenix and Ake, but that their results nevertheless gave further support for a motor imitative ability of dolphins. The authors pointed to the more extensive learning experience of Phoenix and Ake, including experience with tandem behaviors and the manipulation of objects, as likely contributions to their superior imitative performance.

Human-Dolphin Imitation

The procedures used with the dolphins Phoenix and Ake were actually outgrowths of a preceding, less formal study by Xitco (1988) with the young dolphins Hiapo and Elele. The pair (each approximately 2–3 years of age) was housed in a separate facility from Phoenix and Ake during the study. The human model was in the water next to the particular dolphin being tested. In part 1 of the study, the emphasis was on teaching these naive dolphins the meaning of specific gestural signs for eliciting specific behaviors, by presenting the gestural sign immediately before the model's demonstration of the associated behavior. Two or three behaviors were demonstrated at each session, and repeated demonstrations of these behaviors occurred over several sessions. Some shaping of behavior may have occurred through social reinforcement for approximations. Under these procedures, there was little evidence that the gestural signs for specific behaviors were learned. However, table 3.4 shows that of 13 different behaviors demonstrated for Hiapo, 11 were imitated successfully at least once during the course of the study. Seven of these were imitated successfully after the first demonstration. Elele successfully imitated nine of 14 behaviors at least once. Four were imitated after the first demonstration. Most of the imitations were carried out concurrently with the model's demonstration. Hence, the model's behavior and not the preceding specific gestural sign for that behavior seemed to be the stimulus eliciting the dolphins' behaviors.

In the second part of the study, the generic *mimic* gestural sign was introduced. The procedures were as in part 1, except that the specific gestural signs that had preceded a demonstration of a behavior were no longer given. Instead, the *mimic* sign was given after the model had completed the demonstration. However, the dolphin was permitted to respond during the model's demonstration, and most often did so; therefore, the dolphin was not necessarily under control of the *mimic* sign. Ten of the behaviors successfully imitated during part 1 (table 3.4) were used to teach the *mimic* sign, but again Xitco's (1988) report does not provide any measure of whether control of imitation by the *mimic* sign was achieved, inasmuch as the dolphins were free to begin their imitation behavior contemporaneously with the model's demonstration.

After "training," four new behaviors were demonstrated for each dolphin, as shown in table 3.5. Two of these were the same for

Table 3.4 Human-dolphin behavioral mimicry: initial behaviors used to test ability of dolphins Elele and Hiapo to imitate human in-water demonstrator (*mimic* gesture not used)

HUMAN DEMONSTRATION	DOLPHIN REQUIRED BEHAVIOR	ELELE IMITATES	HIAPO IMITATES
Wave forearms with bent elbow	Wiggle pectoral fins[a]	D (−)	D (1) [3]
Propel body partially out of water	Leap out of water[a]	D (1) [3]	D (1) [1]
Somersault underwater	Somersault underwater[a]	D (2) [3]	D (1) [3]
Swim through hoop	Swim through hoop[b]	D (−)	D (1) [3]
Push floating object to trainer, using head	Bring floating object to trainer[b]	—	D (1) [2]
Rest chin on tank wall	Rest rostrum on tank wall	D (−)	D (−)
Head down, legs in air	Head down, tail in air	D (4) [3]	D (8) [3]
Lift object above surface with head	Lift object above surface	D (9) [3]	D (1) [3]
Lie horizontal on tank bottom	Rest on tank bottom	D (1) [3]	D (1) [3]
Rotate body in horizontal position	Rotate body in horizontal position	D (−)	D (−)
Push object below surface using chest	Push object below surface of water	D (2) [3]	D (3) [2]
Propel kickboard with head	Propel kickboard with rostrum	D (1) [2]	D (4) [2]
Swim under object	Swim under object	D (1) [3]	D (2) [3]
Slap legs on water while floating face down	Slap tail on water	D (3) [3]	—

Note: D means behavior was demonstrated for indicated dolphin. Numbers in parentheses are the number of demonstrations required for the first successful imitation. A minus sign (−) indicates that the behavior was not imitated within the maximum of ten demonstrations. Numbers in brackets indicate the total number of successful imitations achieved (maximum = 3).
[a] Behavior used in imitation training of Phoenix and Ake (table 3.1)
[b] Behavior used in transfer testing of Phoenix and Ake (table 3.2)

both dolphins and two were different. The new behaviors were demonstrated twice each during each session, for up to five sessions. Table 3.5 shows that Hiapo successfully imitated two of the four behaviors, one after the first demonstration. Elele also imitated two behaviors, one after the third demonstration and one after the fourth. Hiapo, but not Elele, successfully repeated an imitation more than once.

Overall, Hiapo and Elele produced many successful imitations, most of them occurring contemporaneously with the model's demonstration. This first study was valuable in identifying useful pro-

Table 3.5 Human-dolphin behavioral mimicry: behaviors used to test ability of dolphins Elele and Hiapo to imitate human in-water demonstrator (*mimic* gesture is used)

HUMAN DEMONSTRATION	DOLPHIN REQUIRED BEHAVIOR	ELELE IMITATES	HIAPO IMITATES
Slap legs on water while floating face down	Slap tail on water[a]	—	D (−)
Rotate horizontally from face-down to face-up	Turn belly up at station[b]	D (4) [1]	D (2) [3]
Scull backwards feet first, face-down	Swim backwards, tail first[b]	D (−)	—
Bring bottom object to surface using hands and head	Retrieve object from tank bottom	—	D (1) [3]
Rest chin on paddle	Rest rostrum on paddle	D (−)	—
Put object in basket with hands	Put object in basket (uses rostrum)	D (3) [1]	D (−)

Note: D means behavior was demonstrated for indicated dolphin. Numbers in parentheses are the number of demonstrations required for the first successful imitation. A minus sign (−) indicates that the behavior was not imitated within the maximum of ten demonstrations. Numbers in brackets indicate the total number of successful imitations achieved (maximum = 3).
[a] Behavior used in imitation training of Phoenix and Ake (Table 3.1).
[b] Behavior used in transfer testing of Phoenix and Ake (Table 3.2).

cedures and in calling attention to needed controls that were incorporated within the subsequent studies with Phoenix and Ake, described earlier, and within further studies of human-dolphin imitation presented in the following sections.

Imitation of Dolphin or Human Model

Using the same apparatus and procedures developed for Phoenix and Ake by Xitco (1988), Herman, Morrel-Samuels, and Brown (1989) reported on results of a study comparing imitation of a dolphin model with imitation of a human model. The subjects were again Phoenix and Ake. Each served as a model for the other in dolphin-dolphin imitation, and each served as the imitator when a human was the model. The human model was in the dolphin's tank in place of the model dolphin. Table 3.6 lists the 12 behaviors demonstrated by the dolphin models and by the human model. Eight of the behaviors were the same. An additional four

Table 3.6 Behaviors used to compare behavioral mimicry of dolphin model and human model

BEHAVIOR DEMONSTRATED	DOLPHIN MODEL	HUMAN MODEL
Pirouette, head out of water[a]	D (2)	D (2)
Somersault underwater[a]	D (1)	D (2)
Spit water at object[a]	D (2)	D (1)
Slap tail (feet) on water[b]	D (2)	D (2)
Throw a ball in air*	D (0)	D (0)
Twirl Frisbee on rostrum (finger)[b]	D (2)	D (2)
Pull rope and ring bell[b]	D (2)	D (2)
Throw ball into suspended basket*	D (1)	D (0)
Leap out of water, reenter head first[a]	D (0)	—
Spiraling leap[b]	D (1)	—
Wiggle pectoral fins in upright stance[a]	D (2)	—
Blow bubbles underwater[b]	D (0)	—
Swim through a hoop[b]	—	D (2)
Place ball in floating basket*	—	D (1)
Place ring on stick[b]	—	D (0)
Swim over surfboard*	—	D (0)

Note: D means behavior was demonstrated by indicated model; numbers in parentheses indicate number of successful imitations (out of two possible).
[a] Behavior modeled during training (Xitco 1988)
[b] Behavior modeled during transfer testing (Xitco 1988)
* Behavior not modeled in prior study (Xitco 1988)

behaviors were only modeled by the dolphins and a different four only by the human. Of the eight behaviors modeled in common by dolphin and human, three were from the training set of Xitco (1988), three were from the transfer set, and two were used for the first time in this paradigm. Of the four modeled only by the dolphin, two were from the training set and two from the transfer set. Finally, the four modeled only by the human included two from the transfer set and two behaviors new to the paradigm.

Each of the 12 behaviors assigned to dolphin models was performed once by each dolphin model while the other dolphin observed and acted as imitator. Each of the 12 behaviors demonstrated by the human model was performed once for each dolphin in a counterbalanced order across dolphins. Table 3.6 also gives the number of demonstrations of each behavior mimicked successfully by the pair of dolphins, with the maximum score per behavior being two. With the dolphin as model, 15 (62.5%) of 24 demonstrations were imitated successfully, and with the human as model, 14 (58.3%) were imitated successfully. Table 3.6 shows that for the eight behaviors demonstrated in common by dolphin and human models there was little difference in performance attributable to the different models. The correlation between performances on the eight behaviors across models was high ($r = .73$, $df = 7$, $p < .05$) and the difference in mean performance across models was not significant (t [$df = 7$] $= .55$, $p = .60$). Thus, behaviors that proved easy and difficult were largely the same across models. Two behaviors unique to this paradigm were imitated successfully by one of the dolphins; throwing a ball into a suspended basket was imitated successfully after a dolphin demonstration, and placing a ball in a floating basket was imitated successfully after a human demonstration. The results thus suggest that a key aspect for the imitating dolphin was the functional behavior rather than the particular model performing the demonstration or the exact form of the model's demonstration, which might differ to various degrees across models. Possibly, preserving the functional aspects of the model's behavior might be interpreted as goal emulation, as distinct from true imitation (Tomasello 1990, 1996; Zentall 1996; but cf. Whiten and Custance 1996; Whiten and Ham 1992). However, it is clear that although the exact form of the behavior was not preserved, the imitator's action nevertheless preserved the major components of the form (e.g., the imitating dolphin did not attempt to swim through the hoop while inverted, although inverted swimming is very common). As stressed by Whiten (Whiten and Custance 1996; Whiten and Ham 1992), no imitation will preserve all the details of the demonstration (also see the correspondence problem discussed by Nehaniv and Dautenhahn, chapter 2 of this volume). The results of table 3.6 also indicate that ancillary cues, such as vocalizations, or postural responses of a dolphin demonstrator that might guide the imitator's response, were not necessary for performance, as these would be absent or different for the human model.

Dolphin Imitation of Human Body Posture

The dolphin can readily learn to understand semantic references to its own body parts (e.g., rostrum, mouth, melon, pectoral fin, side, dorsal fin, belly, genital, tail), and can use those parts in various ways on command to touch or toss objects, or simply to shake the part or display it (Herman et al. 1999). It can also relate its body image to the human body plan, by adopting postural or behavioral responses analogous to those of the human. Inasmuch as the body plans of the two species differ considerably, the dolphin must analogize certain of its body parts to those of the human. In particular, the human's raised leg corresponds to the dolphin's raised tail, and the human's extended or waving arms correspond to comparable postures or movements of the dolphin's pectoral fins. Figure 3.4 shows three sets of panels illustrating examples of the dolphin Elele imitating various postures and behaviors of a human. The top panel of set A shows Elele imitating the human model who is leaning over backwards. Note that the dolphin is partially erect and has its upper body and pectoral fins out of water, analogous to the human's posture. In the bottom panel, the human has raised her leg in the air; the dolphin, in turn, raises its tail in the air, which of necessity requires that its body lie flatter. In the top panel of set B, the human stands erect facing the dolphin and bends her head and upper body far back. The dolphin imitates that posture, standing on its tail and leaning its own head and body backwards. In the bottom panel, the human leans forward and bends her head and upper body downward. The dolphin lowers its own head, hunching forward at the water surface. Finally, in set C, the human first faces sideways with her arms bent and raised at chest level. The dolphin also assumes this sideways posture, its body erect and pectoral fins out of water. In the bottom panel, the human has leaped into the air from the position illustrated in the top panel. Note that the human's knees are now about level with the top of the tank wall. In turn, the dolphin quickly thrusts itself upward, raising its body well above the surface of the water. In each of the three sets, the two behaviors modeled by the human were closely spaced in time, with the behavior in the top panel preceding that in the bottom panel. There was no specific formal training for these imitations, or for others not illustrated. Each of the four dolphins at our laboratory has a similar imitative capability, and each will attempt to imitate any new posture or motor sequence demonstrated by the human.

Figure 3.4 Examples of motor imitation of a human by dolphin Elele. Each imitation is a dynamic process characterized by the human performing the action and the dolphin closely following that in real time. The two frames in each panel were photographed closely in time using a Canon 35-mm single lens reflex camera with a 70–200 mm lens. See text for additional descriptions.

Figure 3.5 The dolphin Akeakamai watches the television screen through an underwater window. An image of a trainer, located in a remote studio and televised live, appears on the screen. A television camera, located in the window well next to the television set, films the dolphin. The dolphin's image is transmitted to a TV screen in the remote studio, allowing the trainer to observe the dolphin. The dolphin and human are thus together in a closed-circuit television link.

Dolphin Imitation of Televised Models

Herman, Morrel-Samuels, and Pack (1990) demonstrated that dolphins can spontaneously interpret live television displays of humans gesturing to them. The dolphins viewed the television screen through an underwater window and responded to the televised trainer in the same manner and about as reliably as they did to a live trainer at tank side (figure 3.5). Further, if the human performs a behavior on screen, such as a pirouette, head nod, head shake, or leg lift, the dolphin will imitate that behavior reliably. Imitation of television scenes was first attempted using video clips of dolphins or humans performing some simple behaviors, such as somersaulting or throwing a ball into a basket (Herman et al. 1989). However, this did not result in immediate copying of the behaviors by the observing dolphin. Possibly, this was because of the small size of the images appearing on the screen. This was corrected by tighter focusing of the television camera on the model. A second, and probably more basic, problem may have been that the dolphins did not understand that imitation was expected. This was corrected by having the human model on screen give the *mimic* gesture (Xitco 1988) after demonstrating the behavior, or by having a trainer on screen give the *mimic* gesture after a dolphin model had completed a behavior. Once these new conditions and procedures were established and familiarization training completed, successful imitations of either human or dolphin models occurred (reviewed in Herman, Pack, and Morrel-Samuels 1993).

Television images are not exact replicates of real-world images, so that the essential components of the postures or behaviors demonstrated must be abstracted from the television scene. We recently demonstrated spontaneous and accurate imitation of even degraded television images, produced by presenting the trainer's image in mosaic form, or as a negative image (reversal of blacks and whites).[2] These degraded images nonetheless preserved the movement components of the trainer, which were copied faithfully by the dolphins.

3.4 Self-Imitation: Repeating Arbitrary Directed Behaviors and Self-Selected Behaviors under Control of an Abstract Gesture

The origins of imitative ability may lie in the social context and the advantages of learning by observation, or perhaps reflect the benefits of synchronizing one's activities with another to achieve some goal or as a demonstration of affiliation. However, the link between motor imitation of others and of oneself is that both access mental representations of behaviors. The stimuli leading to those representations may differ—one external and the other internal—but the question is not about the origin of the representation but whether the animal can create a mental representation of a behavior, whatever its source, and replicate that behavior.

Self-Imitation Studies with the Dolphins Elele and Hiapo

Self-imitation can be defined as copying one's own behaviors. We have examined the dolphin's ability to copy its own behaviors in several contexts. For this purpose, we trained the dolphins Elele and Hiapo in the concept we called "repeat," signified by a unique gesture (Mercado et al. 1998, 1999). For example, if the dolphin is requested through a specific gesture to leap over an object, and then, upon completion of the act, is given the gestural sign "repeat," it should leap over again ("repeat" trial). To demonstrate that the dolphin's repetitive acts are under control of the gestural symbol, it must also be shown that it will only repeat its behavior in the presence of the symbol. Thus, after leaping over an object, the dolphin can instead be directed through some other specific gesture, say, to swim on its back ("nonrepeat" trial). The intent of the gestural contrasts is to show that the *repeat* gesture is processed semantically, and that context alone does not determine for the dolphin whether it should repeat its behavior or not.

In the study by Mercado and colleagues (1998), there were 32 different behaviors altogether; eight of these involved an action to an object and 24 involved no object. The dolphin's ability to repeat or not repeat an action was tested within sets of eight different behaviors; four were taken from a "baseline" training set and four were "transfer" behaviors not used during training. The training set established proficiency in the formal procedure and consisted of five sessions of 24 trials for Elele and Hiapo, plus a sixth session of 18 trials for Hiapo. *Repeat* and *nonrepeat* trials were intermixed nonsystematically within training sessions. To strengthen the concept, if necessary, trials were given occasionally on which the *repeat* sign was immediately followed by the specific behavior sign. During training, Elele's proficiency at the task (87% correct responses) significantly exceeded Hiapo's proficiency (62% correct) ($\chi^2[1, n = 258] = 19.6$, $p < .001$). Transfer testing followed immediately after completion of training.

Table 3.7 summarizes the results of transfer testing. Results are expressed as the number of correct repetitions out of four opportu-

Table 3.7 Self imitation: Number of correct repetitions (of four possible) of 8 different transfer behaviors to objects and 24 different transfer behaviors not involving objects, for dolphins Elele and Hiapo

NO. CORRECT REPETITIONS (MAX. = 4)	ELELE		HIAPO	
	Object (n = 8)	*No object (n = 24)*	*Object (n = 8)*	*No object (n = 24)*
4*	6	17	1	9
3*	1	4	1	3
2	1	2	2	—
1	—	1	2	4
0	—	—	2	8

Note: All 32 behaviors were under control of specific gestures before initiation of this study.
* $p < .05$, summed binomial test, with probability of correct repetition equal to .125.

nities for each of the 32 different transfer behaviors. For example, table 3.7 shows that Elele successfully repeated six of eight transfer behaviors involving an action to an object each of the four times it was tested. One of the remaining two behaviors was repeated successfully three times and the other twice. Three or four correct repetitions significantly exceeded chance, taken as .125 (there were eight different behaviors in each set tested, four transfer behaviors and four baseline behaviors). During transfer testing, performance on baseline behaviors was virtually flawless for both dolphins and on *nonrepeat* trials was at 90% correct responses or better. Although both dolphins were clearly capable of repeating behaviors under control of the *repeat* gesture, Elele's performance on transfer behaviors (89.3% correct repetitions overall) significantly exceeded Hiapo's performance (56.9% correct) $(\chi^2[1, n = 240] = 33.01, p < .001)$.

All of the behaviors in table 3.7 had been under sign control before the beginning of the formal *repeat* study. As an additional test of the *repeat* concept, therefore, four behaviors not previously under gestural sign control were selected and placed under sign control. These were pirouetting with head and torso out of water, submerging below the surface, repeatedly throwing a ball in the air and catching it with the mouth, and pressing a paddle. These four were then tested in the *repeat* procedure, using the same procedures as previously. Table 3.8 shows that Elele correctly repeated the two object-oriented behaviors either three or four times, and the two behaviors not involving objects twice each. Hiapo repeated the two object-oriented behaviors either once or twice, and the two not involving objects either once or all four times. The important result is that some newly acquired behaviors, as well as many familiar behaviors, could be repeated successfully.

The Mercado and colleagues (1999) study tested the dolphin Elele's ability to repeat action sequences involving responses to specified objects. For example, a sequence of three gestures glossed as Frisbee + Pectoral + Touch directed Elele to touch the floating Frisbee with her pectoral fin. After completing the specified action to the specified object, Elele might be given the *repeat* sign, requiring her to reproduce that specific response. Unlike the Mercado and colleagues (1998) study in which only a single object was present in the dolphin's tank, three different objects were now present (a Frisbee, a basket, and a ball). Thus, not only the action taken (there were six different possible actions) but also the specific object acted on had to be represented in memory for reliable

Table 3.8 Self-imitation: The number of correct repetitions (of four possible) of two different novel transfer behaviors to objects and two different novel transfer behaviors not involving objects, for dolphins Elele and Hiapo

NO. CORRECT REPETITIONS (MAX. = 4)	ELELE		HIAPO	
	Object (n = 2)	No object (n = 2)	Object (n = 2)	No object (n = 2)
4*	1	—	—	1
3*	1	—	—	—
2	—	2	1	—
1	—	—	1	1
0	—	—	—	—

Note: None of the four behaviors were under control of specific gestures before initiation of this study.
* $p < .05$, summed binomial test, with probability of correct repetition equal to .125.

responding to occur. The probability of responding correctly by chance to a *repeat* instruction was therefore considered to be one in eighteen (three objects multiplied by six actions). Over the 72 *repeat* instructions she was given, Elele responded wholly correctly to 30 (41.7%) ($p < .0001$, by the summed binomial test). Selecting the correct object again (50.0% correct, $p = .0025$) was more difficult than reproducing the correct action (80.6% correct, $p < .0001$). Nonetheless, the results demonstrate that the repeating rule generalized to the new requirement to recall a specific object.

Formal Training and Further Testing of the *Repeat* Concept with the Dolphin Ake
Although the training of Elele and Hiapo in the *repeat* concept was done initially as an informal exercise by several different trainers, and the procedures were not well documented, the dolphin Ake was more recently taught the concept through a formal procedure analogous to that used to teach social imitation controlled by a gesture. The steps were:

1. Trainer gives a gestural sign for a specific behavior (e.g., "somersault").
2. Dolphin executes behavior, hears a short whistle blast, and returns to trainer's station.

3. Trainer gives *repeat* sign followed immediately by the same specific behavior gesture (cueing procedure).
4. Dolphin repeats behavior and is rewarded.
5. On subsequent probe trials, specific behavior sign is deleted after *repeat* sign.
6. *Nonrepeat* trials also occur to insure that *repeat* sign is semantically processed.
7. Training sessions continue until a criterion of 80% correct responses over two sessions is reached.

Four behaviors were used to teach Ake the *repeat* concept. Two were object related (jump over an object and touch the object with your tail) and two were not (somersault, and swim on your back while waving your pectoral fins). Under these procedures, Ake reached the stated criterion in five sessions comprising a total of 67 *repeat* trials interleaved among 51 *nonrepeat* trials. Cueing was used only during portions of the first three sessions for a total of 29 trials. During the following two sessions, Ake responded correctly to 26 (83.9%) of the 31 *repeat* trials and made only one error on the *nonrepeat* trials.

Transfer tests using 15 new behaviors were then given to examine for generalization of the *repeat* concept. The transfer behaviors were interleaved among trials requiring repetitions of the four training behaviors and also trials on which a transfer behavior was given but a different behavior was requested subsequently (*nonrepeat* trial). A transfer behavior was tested twice each session that it appeared. Table 3.9 summarizes performance on each transfer behavior over the 24 sessions used for testing, each session of 24 or 30 trials. Behaviors are classified by whether they required an action to an object or not. Table 3.9 indicates the transfer session number on which the behavior was first tested, the total number of trials testing that behavior through all sessions, the number of correct repetitions, and the number of attempts required for the first successful demonstration. Behaviors that were repeated reliably early were retained in the pool of behaviors, and the others were deleted from the pool. It is apparent that there was a difference in repeatability of the different behaviors. Four of the behaviors involving an action to an object, and four not involving an object, were repeated successfully on the first attempt. Two behaviors not involving objects were never repeated. Overall, the percentage of trials on which a behavior was repeated successfully was significantly greater for behaviors involving an object (84.5%) than

Table 3.9 Self-imitation: The number and percentage of correct *repeat* responses given by the dolphin Akeakamai to each of 15 transfer behaviors

BEHAVIOR TO BE REPEATED	SESSION FIRST GIVEN[a]	TOTAL TRIALS	NO. CORRECT[b]
Object-Oriented Behaviors			
Toss an object	1	45	35 (1)
Swim under an object	1	37	35 (1)
Place mouth about object	9	28	27 (1)
Touch object with pectoral fin ("pec")	13	20	19 (1)
Inverted swim, object held between pecs	17	12	4 (6)
Behaviors Not Involving Object			
Shake head left and right	1	41	40 (1)
Lean over backward	1	10	0 (0)
Pirouette, head and torso out of water	1	12	6 (5)
Swim with head hunched over	1	12	4 (9)
Blow bubbles underwater	9	28	28 (1)
Swim with head held high	9	12	0 (0)
Wave tail in air	13	20	20 (1)
Leap out of water, belly-up	13	12	7 (1)
Arch body on top of tank scupper	17	12	3 (9)
Swim underwater while spiraling	17	12	10 (2)

[a] Indicates session number (of 24) on which behavior was first tested.
[b] Numbers in parentheses indicate on which attempt the behavior was first successfully repeated (e.g., 1 = successful on first attempt).

for those not involving an object (69.0%) ($\chi^2[1, N = 313] = 10.23$, $p < .01$).

All behaviors that were repeated, were repeated multiple times thereafter. Only one error was made on *nonrepeat* trials, giving strong evidence that the *repeat* gesture was semantically processed. The results of this study thus revealed that under the procedures used, only relatively minimal training was necessary to establish behavioral control by the *repeat* gesture. Further, the results showing successful transfer of many of the behaviors, as well as immediate (first trial) transfer of some, establish that the *repeat* gesture was understood conceptually. Overall, the results are consistent with those reported earlier by Mercado and colleagues (1998) and demonstrate a robust capacity for self-imitation by dolphins.

Repeating Self-Selected Behaviors

In the repeat paradigm, did the dolphin remember the initial behavior or remember the gesture that directed the initial behavior? Mercado and colleagues (1998, 1999) presented several arguments why remembering the gesture was unlikely. For example, the dolphin was able to repeat the initial behavior several times in succession if multiple repeat commands were given each time the dolphin returned to station. Additionally, the dolphin Elele successfully repeated three of four self-selected behaviors, and Hiapo one of four. A self-selected behavior was elicited using the generic *creative* gestural sign (Braslau-Schneck 1994).

In further studies, we developed an alternative procedure that allowed the dolphin Phoenix to self-select and execute a behavior from among a subset of five different object-oriented behaviors, in response to a gesture we termed *any* (Taylor 1995; Taylor-Gaines and Herman 1993). The five were leaping over an object, swimming under it, touching it with the tail, touching it with the pectoral fin, and opening the mouth about it. After executing a behavior of her choice, a further rule was that if the *any* sign were given again, a behavior different from the one just executed should be performed. Thus, if Phoenix leaped over an object, and was then given the *any* sign, she should then perform any one of the remaining four behaviors. Under these procedures, Phoenix reliably selected new behaviors when given the *any* sign.

Phoenix had also been taught the *repeat* gesture. Cutting (1997) studied Phoenix's ability to repeat the behavior she had performed last or to choose a different behavior, depending on whether she observed the *repeat* sign or the *any* sign. A trial began with the dolphin given a gesture to perform a specific behavior, such as "over" (leap over an object). A sequence of three gestures followed, consisting of *repeat* and *any*, alone or in combination. After each gesture, the dolphin was required to execute the appropriate behavior. Reward occurred only for the completion of the entire sequence. The trial was terminated immediately without reinforcement if any element of the sequence was responded to inappropriately.

An example of a specific sequence given to Phoenix was *over-any-repeat-any*. In response, Phoenix first leaped over the object, then touched it with her tail, then repeated the tail-touch, and finally again leaped over the object. Her successful completion of the sequence was rewarded. A different sequence given her was *mouth, repeat, any, repeat*. Here, she correctly mouthed the object, repeated that behavior, leaped over the object, and finally leaped over again. Table 3.10 lists eight different sequences of these types given to Phoenix, grouped by whether the final element in the sequence ended in an *any* command or a *repeat* command. Note that the two sequences in each row are identical, except for the final element. The total number of completed sequences of each type ranged from 79 to 81 (the target of 80 completed sequences was not always attained, because of scheduling errors). Each of the five behaviors began a sequence approximately an equal number of times (15–17 times, with the target having been exactly 16). In addition to the 318 completed sequences ending in *any*, as tabulated in table 3.10, 39 were not completed, an error having being made on one of the elements preceding the final one. This resulted in immediate termination of that trial. There were fewer early terminations for sequences ending in *repeat*. In addition to the 320 completed sequences shown in table 3.10, 14 were terminated early because of an error on one of the first three elements.

Table 3.10 Self-imitation: The number and percentage of correct responses given by the dolphin Phoenix to each of the four-element behavioral sequences

SEQUENCES ENDING IN *ANY*		SEQUENCES ENDING IN *REPEAT*	
B-A-A-A	60/79 (75.9%)	B-A-A-R	77/79 (97.5%)
B-A-R-A	75/80 (93.8%)	B-A-R-R	77/81 (95.1%)
B-R-A-A	65/79 (82.3%)	B-R-A-R	73/80 (91.3%)
B-R-R-A	79/80 (98.8%)	B-R-R-R	79/80 (98.8%)
ALL	279/318 (87.7%)	ALL	306/320 (95.6%)

Note: Responses are shown as (number correct)/(number of trials).
B, a specific behavior of five possible behaviors; R, an instruction to *repeat* the previous behavior; A, an instruction to choose *any* behavior from the set of five, other than the one performed previously.

Table 3.10 shows that performance was 76% correct or better for all sequence types. For each type, performance on the last element significantly exceeded chance ($p < .001$ by summed binomial, assuming an equal probability of choosing an *any* behavior or a *repeat* behavior). Overall, Phoenix responded correctly to significantly more sequences ending in *repeat* (95.6%) than to those ending in *any* (87.7%) ($\chi^2[1, N = 638] = 13.03$, $p < .001$).

The most pertinent sequence type in table 3.10 for determining unequivocally Phoenix's ability to repeat a self-selected behavior may be *B-any-any-repeat*. For this sequence, Phoenix must first execute the specific behavior signaled gesturally by the trainer, then self-select and execute a different behavior, then self-select and execute a behavior different from her previous self-selected behavior, and finally repeat that last self-selected behavior. The two successive *any* requirements insure that no gestural remnant remains of the initial behavior signaled by the trainer. It might be argued, for example, that for the first *any* behavior, the dolphin was remembering the gesture that elicited her first behavior and used that (wholly or in part) to select a different behavior. Selection of her second *any* response, however, can no longer rely on memory for the initial gesture since the initial gesture would not indicate what behavior had been self-selected. Thus, the final *repeat* requirement must be entirely based on memory for the last self-selected behavior. Of the 79 completed sequences of this type, Phoenix was correct on 77 (97.5%). Clearly, she was able to repeat a self-selected behavior, indicating that it was the behavior that was represented in memory and acted on, and not a specific gesture. A similar argument, using the sequence *B-any-any-any*, can be made that her final *any* responses were based on an encoded behavior and not on an encoded gesture. Her performance with this sequence type—60 of 79 (75.9%) sequences responded to correctly—was significantly below that for the corresponding sequence ending in *repeat* ($\chi^2[1, N = 158] = 15.87$, $p < .001$), but still well above chance. The overall results established that Phoenix discriminated semantically between the two gestures, *any* and *repeat*, in that she was able to repeat (imitate) her prior behavior or not depending on which gesture was given. Her ability to do this required that she maintain a representation of the behavior last performed, update that regularly as each new behavior was executed, and use that representation to choose the next behavior, depending on which gestural sign was received subsequently.

3.6 Summary and Discussion

What can be concluded about dolphin imitative abilities from the studies reviewed? First, dolphins are capable vocal mimics. This ability appears spontaneously under natural circumstances, as well as in the laboratory, in the form of mimicry of whistle "signatures" of other dolphins (Caldwell and Caldwell 1972; Caldwell, Caldwell, and Tyack 1990; Richards 1986). Possibly, imitation of another's whistle is a means of calling that dolphin or referring to it. Vocal mimicry also appears spontaneously in the laboratory in nonsocial contexts, in the form of copying of artificial sounds introduced into the habitat (McCowan and Reiss 1995; Richards 1986). This vocal mimicry tendency can be brought under experimental control, and precise mimicry of computer-generated model sounds, including novel sounds, can be developed (Richards, Wolz, and Herman 1984). Vocal imitation is rare among nonhuman mammals, but occurs among several marine mammal species in addition to the bottlenosed dolphin, including humpback whales that converge on similar song renditions each winter season (Helweg et al. 1992), and a harbor seal maintained in an aquarium that spontaneously began to mimic several English words (Rawls, Fiorelli, and Gish 1985).

Second, dolphins can imitate the behaviors of other dolphins. This occurs under natural circumstances and is evident in the close synchrony observed among dolphins during swimming and leaping. In the laboratory, imitation of arbitrary motor behaviors or of actions on objects has been demonstrated (Herman et al. 1989; Xitco 1988). In these studies, some novel behaviors were copied after only two or three demonstrations.

Third, dolphins are also capable of imitating the behaviors of human models (Herman, Morrel-Samuels, and Brown 1989; Xitco 1988). To do so, the dolphin must relate its body image to the human body plan (E. Herman et al. 1999), including representing some human body parts by analogy with its own body parts.

Fourth, dolphins can spontaneously generalize and extend their imitative ability to action images of humans on television screens, including degraded images (L. Herman 1999; Herman, Pack, and Morrel-Sanders 1993).

Fifth, dolphins are capable of copying their own behavior (self-imitation) and can faithfully repeat their arbitrary motor actions, as well as their actions on objects (Cutting 1997; Mercado et al. 1998, 1999; Taylor 1995; Taylor-Gaines and Herman 1993).

Finally, these imitative acts can be controlled and elicited by learned arbitrary symbols, as demonstrated throughout the studies of vocal-, social-, and self-imitation.

Thus, the premises that guided these studies of dolphin imitation can now be restated as broad general conclusions:

· The imitative abilities of dolphins extend to a variety of behaviors and contexts.
· The imitative abilities of dolphins are evident in social situations, but they also extend to nonsocial situations.
· The imitative act appears to be understood conceptually by dolphins, and can be elicited by arbitrary abstract symbols.

The abstract gestural symbols eliciting social- and self-imitation were semantically processed in that they were successfully discriminated from other abstract symbols requiring behaviors other than imitation.

The variety of demonstrated behaviors that were copied by the dolphins provided compelling evidence that these copies were true imitations and not a product of alternative mechanisms (e.g., stimulus or local enhancement). As discussed by Custance, Whiten, and Bard (1995), the imitation of a variety of actions controls for other explanations based on stimulus enhancement or contagion. Actions on objects provide particularly strong evidence against such alternative explanations. Thus, different actions to the same object (e.g., leaping over or touching with the tail) were demonstrated and copied, and the same action (e.g., touching with the pectoral fin) was demonstrated at different times with different objects, and was copied faithfully. Clearly, the object itself does not evoke the behavior.

The different settings and contexts in which motor behaviors were copied provide additional evidence against alternative explanations for apparent imitative behaviors. Included here are imitations of dolphin or human models, imitation of human models in-water or out-of-water, and imitation of behaviors of normal or degraded televised images of humans. The different models, settings, and contexts used for demonstration of a given behavior underscore that although the behavior may be modeled somewhat differently in each case, the dolphin nevertheless extracts the essential components of the behavior, and acts on those. The ability for imitation of human postures and movements requires that the dolphin be able to relate its body image to the human's body plan, even though the body plans are so different (also see E. Herman et al. 1999, for evidence of the dolphin's conscious awareness of its own body parts). That the dolphin nonetheless imitates the human successfully, sometimes by analogy (e.g., it uses its tail as an analogy to the human's leg, and its pectoral fins as an analogy to the human's arms), is further evidence for the flexibility and robustness of its imitative behavior.

The successful imitation of behaviors demonstrated on television indicates that ancillary components of live behaviors, such as the vocalizations of demonstrators or the percussive sounds of a body striking the water after a jump, are not necessary cues for effective imitation. The spontaneity with which the imitation of televised images occurred illustrates a conceptual leap in that a behavior far removed from the normal context was nevertheless immediately recognized, represented, and copied.

What does it mean to have a generalized concept of "imitate?" It implies that the capacity is not reserved or restricted to functionally significant events, or to events tied to the organism's natural repertoire, ecology, or habitat, but is broadly understood as applicable to any arbitrary experienced event. The dolphin is obviously an imitative generalist, evidenced not only by the variety of motor acts imitated and the different contexts in which imitation occurred, but also in the different types of imitation achieved— vocal-, social-, and self-imitation. Self-imitation, as well as the vocal imitation of arbitrary sounds, illustrates that the imitative act is not restricted to a social context.

What aspects of the demonstrated motor behaviors are represented in memory? It may be partly the form of the behavior (imitations are not always exact or complete—as stressed, for example, by Whiten and Custance 1996; Whiten and Ham 1992), and partly the intent (function) of the behavior. In our studies, the functional component appears in actions on objects. For example, the imitator may observe the demonstrator leaping over an object. A successful imitation preserves the functional component of leaping over the object, but the approach to the object and exactly where the leap is executed relative to the object may differ from that of the demonstrator. As defined here, specifically in reference to the dolphin studies reviewed, behaviors involving an action on an object are classified as "functional" behaviors whereas those not involving an object are defined as "nonfunctional." Do demonstrations of functional behaviors yield more reliable imitative performance than do demonstrations of nonfunctional behaviors? Table 3.11 regroups the behaviors listed in table 3.2 by whether they involved an action on an object (functional behaviors) or not (nonfunctional behaviors). The table shows that Phoenix successfully imitated all six of the functional behaviors she observed, including a novel one, but only three of nine nonfunctional behaviors. Similarly, Ake successfully imitated five of the seven functional behaviors demonstrated for her, including a novel one, but only two of eight nonfunctional behaviors. Although these data suggest the superiority of functional behaviors, and imply that their representation in memory may be richer, the data on delayed mimicry presented by Xitco (1988) were inconclusive as to whether this apparent advantage for actions on objects was maintained over time. Put simply, there was no reliable trend for functional behaviors to be more successfully imitated over delays than were nonfunctional behaviors. On the other hand, the data on self-imitation by Ake (table 3.9) suggested that functional behaviors were repeated more reliably than nonfunctional behaviors. Hence, further studies are needed to examine how imitation may vary in success depending on the class of behavior demonstrated or repeated.

The dolphin appears to share its capacity for both vocal and motor mimicry with one other nonhuman species, the African Grey parrot (*Psittacus erithacus*) (Moore 1992, 1996). A major difference, however, lies in the real-time copying of observed sounds or behaviors by the dolphin, and the "private" and greatly delayed imitations of the parrot, typically occurring only after a long "incubation" period (Moore 1992, 1996). For example, the parrot fully copied Moore's habit of waving goodbye and saying "Ciao" as he left the room only after a year of frequent observation of the act, and only waved its wings in Moore's presence after 37 months of having observed the act repeatedly. Further, there is no evidence that the parrot learned a concept of "imitate" that might enable it to copy a sound or behavior when requested by an abstract symbol. Instead, imitations, either vocal or motor, seemed to emerge spontaneously, albeit delayed. In contrast, the timing and contexts of the motor imitative acts of the dolphin are more similar to those of the chimpanzees studied by Hayes and Hayes (1952) and Custance, Whiten, and Bard (1995). However, chimpanzees or other great apes evidencing motor imitation are not able to extend their imitative ability to vocal reproductions of sounds, possibly because of vocal tract limitations (Lieberman 1968).

Table 3.11 Comparison of imitation success of functional behaviors (action to an object) and nonfunctional behaviors (motor act not involving an object)

BEHAVIOR	PHOENIX IMITATES SUCCESSFULLY	AKE IMITATES SUCCESSFULLY
Functional Behaviors (n = 10)		
Touch object with tail	*Yes*	*Yes*
Retrieve object	*Yes*	*Yes*
Twirl Frisbee on rostrum	*Yes*	—
Swim through a hoop	*Yes*	*Yes*
Throw ball	—	*Yes*
Press paddle with rostrum (novel)	*Yes*	—
Pull rope and ring bell (novel)	*Yes*	—
Place ring on stick (novel)	—	*Yes*
Push buoy down with belly (novel)	—	No
Carry towel on dorsal fin (novel)	—	No
Nonfunctional Behaviors (n = 11)		
Back dive	No	No
Turn belly up at station	*Yes*	No
Back swim waving pectoral fins	No	—
Blow bubbles underwater	—	No
Spiraling leap	*Yes*	*Yes*
Shake head side to side	No	No
Swim backward, tail first	—	No
Slap tail on water	*Yes*	*Yes*
Nod head up and down	No	No
Backward tail walk	No	—
Slide out on platform (novel)	No	—

Note: *Yes* means behavior was successfully imitated at least once. "No" means behavior was not successfully imitated within the limit of 10 demonstrations given.
— indicates behavior not modeled for indicated dolphin.

Is vocal imitation different conceptually from motor imitation? Both require that an event be experienced, represented, and then executed as an imitation. Some have attempted to distinguish between the two because in vocal imitation the individual is attending to the imitation, listening to his or her own vocalizations, and matching that against the stored representation, as in pattern matching (e.g., Noble and Todd 1999). However, recent neurological work on humans and monkeys has suggested that, for each species, either executing a motor act or watching another execute that act produced similar activation in the premotor cortex, among the so-called mirror neurons (Arbib, chapter 10 of this volume; Gallese and Goldman 1998; Hari et al. 1998; Rizzolatti et al. 1998). Hence, "pattern matching," at least on a neural level, may also occur in motor imitation through comparison of the stimulated motor neurons activated by visual observation of another's behavior and those activated within the imitating organism by execution of the motor act or preparation for its execution. This viewpoint also brings into question the value of distinguishing between vocal and motor imitation by claiming that only intramodal matching occurs with the former but cross-modal matching occurs with the latter (see, e.g., Noble and Todd 1999).

The findings on mirror neurons also provide a link between the ability to imitate another's actions and the ability to imitate one's own behavior. It is likely that these same neurons play a key role in moderating each type of imitation. At another level, all three types of imitations demonstrated for the dolphin—vocal, social, and self—are linked cognitively through the dolphin's understanding in each case of the imitative act as a concept that extends to any observed event within that domain. That a capability for robust, flexible real-time imitation may be reserved to more "intelligent" species is in keeping with views of imitation as an important social mechanism for transferring knowledge and skills, and as a complex psychological process (e.g., Heyes 1996).

Self-imitation requires that the individual represent its own recent behaviors in memory. It has not escaped our attention that this implies a level of self-awareness—specifically, awareness of one's own recent behaviors. The ability to either repeat a behavior or to choose one different from that just performed, each dependent on a different abstract symbol (Cutting 1997; Taylor 1995; Taylor-Gaines and Herman 1993; Mercado et al. 1998, 1999), only seems possible if the dolphin remains aware of which behavior it last performed and updates that record with each new behavior executed. Self-awareness has many dimensions, and awareness of one's own behavior provides but one perspective. Another perspective we have studied is awareness of one's own body parts, recently demonstrated in a dolphin subject (E. Herman et al. 1999).

In conclusion, the suite of findings summarized reveals unequivocally a generalized and highly flexible capability for imitative acts by dolphins that extend over a broad range of behaviors and contexts. To carry out these various imitative acts, the dolphin must be able to represent in memory sounds heard, motor behaviors observed visually, abstracted representations of real-life motor behaviors (as in television displays), and the kinesthetic and proprioceptive feedback of one's own motor behaviors (as in self-imitation). The foundation for these diverse and extensive imitative abilities may lie in the dolphin's natural ability to carry out highly synchronized social behaviors, and in its ability to imitate the vocalizations of other dolphins. Each skill may provide advantages to the individual: behavioral synchrony provides for more efficient foraging, feeding, and defensive maneuvers, and may affirm relationships between individuals; and vocal mimicry serves to maintain contact between closely allied individuals. The highly complex society of bottlenosed dolphins, and the close and intricate associations formed between individuals within that society, may provide intense selection pressures for the development of social learning skills and the ability to learn through observation. Finally, the ability to develop a robust generalized concept of "imitate," well illustrated in the studies reviewed here, is consistent with other data showing that dolphins can generalize rules and learn abstract concepts (e.g., Herman, Pack, and Wood 1994).

Acknowledgments

Preparation of this report was aided by grants from the Center for Field Research and The Dolphin Institute. Adam A. Pack, Sean Smeland, and Rebecca Cowan made helpful comments on earlier versions of the chapter. My thanks go to the many postdoctoral and graduate students at the Kewalo Basin Marine Mammal Laboratory, whose research and research assistance provided for much of the data reported here on dolphin imitative abilities, including Stacy Braslau-Schneck, Amy Cutting, Douglas Richards, Kristen Taylor, Eduardo Mercado, James Wolz, and Mark Xitco. Finally, I thank Sean Smeland for his help in the preparation of the figures.

Notes

1. The bottlenosed dolphin life span extends into the 40s or even 50s, in the wild or in captivity. Sexual maturity for females occurs at about the age of 7–9 years, and for males at about the age of 10–12. Physical maturity occurs at about the age of 15.
2. Video records of the dolphin imitating normal and degraded television images were presented at the AISB'99 Symposium on Imitation in Animals and Artifacts, 7–9 April 1999, Edinburgh, Scotland (Herman 1999).

References

Bauer, G. B., and C. M. Johnson. Trained motor imitation by bottlenose dolphins (*Tursiops truncatus*). *Perceptual and Motor Skills* 79: 1307–1315, 1994.

Braslau-Schneck, S. Innovative behaviors and synchronization in bottlenosed dolphins. Unpublished master's thesis, University of Hawaii, Honolulu, 1994.

Byrne, R. W., and A. E. Russon. Learning by imitation: A hierarchical approach. *Behavioral and Brain Sciences* 21: 667–709, 1998.

Byrne, R. W., and M. Tomasello. Do rats ape? *Animal Behavior* 50: 1417–1420, 1995.

Caldwell, C. A., A. Whiten, and K. D. Morris. Observational learning in the marmoset (*Callithrix jacchus*). In K. Dautenhahn and C. L. Nehaniv (eds.), *Proceedings of the AISB '99 Symposium on Imitation in Animals and Artifacts (Edinburgh, Scotland, 7–9 April)*, pp. 27–31, Brighton, U.K.: Society for the Study of Artificial Intelligence and Simulation of Behaviour, 1999.

Caldwell, D. K., and M. C. Caldwell. Vocal mimicry in the whistle mode in the Atlantic bottlenose dolphin. *Cetology* 9: 1–8, 1972.

Caldwell, D. K., M. C. Caldwell, and P. L. Tyack. Review of the signature whistle hypothesis for the Atlantic bottlenosed dolphin. In S. Leatherwood and R. Reeves (eds.), *The Bottlenose Dolphin*, pp. 199–234. New York: Academic Press, 1990.

Caldwell, M. C., and D. K. Caldwell. Individualized whistle contours in bottlenosed dolphins, *Tursiops truncatus*. *Nature* 207: 434–435, 1965.

Caldwell, M. C., and D. K. Caldwell. Intraspecific transfer of information via the pulsed sound in captive odontocete cetaceans. In R.-G. Busnel (ed.), *Animal Sonar Systems, Biology and Bionics*, pp. 879–936. Jouy-en-Josas, Laboratoire de Physiologie Acoustique, France, 1967.

Call, J., and M. Tomasello. The use of social information in the problem-solving of orangutans and human children. *Journal of Comparative Psychology* 109: 301–320, 1995.

Custance, D. M., A. Whiten, and K. A. Bard. Can young chimpanzees (*Pan troglodytes*) imitate arbitrary actions? Hayes and Hayes (1952) revisited. *Behaviour* 132: 837–859, 1995.

Cutting, A. E. Memory for self-selected behaviors in a bottlenosed dolphin (*Tursiops truncatus*). Unpublished master's thesis, University of Hawaii, Honolulu, 1997.

Galef, B. G. Imitation in animals: History, definition, and interpretation of data from the psychological laboratory. In T. R. Zentall and B. G. Galef (eds.), *Social Learning: Psychological and Biological Perspectives*, pp. 3–28. Hillsdale, NJ: Lawrence Erlbaum, 1988.

Galef, B. G. Recent progress in studies of imitation and social learning in animals. In M. Saborin, F. Craik, and M. Robert (eds.), *Advances in Psychological Science: Volume 2, Biological and Cognitive Aspects*, pp. 275–300. Hove, UK: Psychology Press, 1998.

Galef, B. G., L. A. Manzig, and R. M. Field. Imitation learning in budgerigars: Dawson and Foss 1965 revisited. *Behavioural Processes* 13: 191–202, 1986.

Gallese, V., and A. Goldman. Mirror neurons and the simulation theory of mind reading. *Trends in Cognitive Science* 2: 493–501, 1998.

Gardner, M. Imitation: The methodological adequacy of directional control tests. Unpublished doctoral dissertation. University of London, 1997.

Hari, R., N. Forss, S. Avikainan, S. Salenius, and G. Rizzolatti. Activation of human primary cortex during action observations: A neuromagnetic study. *Proceedings of the National Academy of Sciences* 95: 15061–15065, 1998.

Hayes, K. J., and C. Hayes. Imitation in the home-raised chimpanzee. *Journal of Comparative and Physiological Psychology* 45: 450–459, 1952.

Helweg, D. A., A. S. Frankel, J. R. Mobley Jr., and L. M. Herman. Humpback whale song: Our current understanding. In J. R. Thomas, R. A. Kastelein, and A. Ya. Supin (eds.), *Marine Mammal Sensory Systems*, pp. 459–483. New York: Plenum, 1992.

Herman, E. Y. K., D. Matus, S. Abichandani, M. Invancic, A. A. Pack, and L. M. Herman. Body awareness and identification of body parts by a bottlenosed dolphin. Poster presentation at the thirteenth Biennial Conference on the Biology of Marine Mammals. 28 Nov.–3 Dec., Wailea, Maui, Hawaii, 1999.

Herman, L. M. Cognitive characteristics of dolphins. In L. M. Herman (ed.), *Cetacean Behavior: Mechanisms and Functions*, pp. 363–429. New York: Wiley Interscience, 1980.

Herman, L. M. Cognition and language competencies of bottlenosed dolphins. In R. J. Schusterman, J. Thomas, and F. G. Wood (eds.), *Dolphin Cognition and Behavior: A Comparative Approach*, pp. 221–251. Hillsdale, NJ: Lawrence Erlbaum Associates, 1986.

Herman, L. M. Imitation of self and others by dolphins. In K. Dautenhahn and C. L. Nehaniv (eds.), *Proceedings of the AISB '99 Symposium on Imitation in Animals and Artifacts (Edinburgh, Scotland, 7–9 April)* Abstract. Brighton, U.K.: Society for the Study of Artificial Intelligence and Simulation of Behaviour, 1999.

Herman, L. M., P. Morrel-Samuels, and L. Brown. Behavioral mimicry of live and televised models by bottlenosed dolphins. Paper presented at the thirtieth Annual Meeting of the Psychonomic Society, Atlanta, GA, 1989.

Herman, L. M., P. Morrel-Samuels, and A. A. Pack. Bottlenosed dolphin and human recognition of veridical and degraded video displays of an artificial gestural language. *Journal of Experimental Psychology: General* 119: 215–230, 1990.

Herman, L. M., A. A. Pack, and M. Hoffmann-Kuhnt. Seeing through sound: Dolphins perceive the spatial structure of objects through echolocation. *Journal of Comparative Psychology* 112: 292–305, 1998.

Herman, L. M., A. A. Pack, and P. Morrel-Samuels. Representational and conceptual skills of dolphins. In H. R. Roitblat, L. M. Herman, and P. Nachtigall (eds.), *Language and Communication: Comparative Perspectives*, pp. 273–298. Hillside, NJ: Lawrence Erlbaum, 1993.

Herman, L. M., A. A. Pack, and A. M. Wood. Bottlenosed dolphins can generalize rules and develop abstract concepts. *Marine Mammal Science* 10: 70–80, 1994.

Herman, L. M., D. G. Richards, and J. P. Wolz. Comprehension of sentences by bottlenosed dolphins. *Cognition* 16: 129–219, 1984.

Herman, L. M., and W. N. Tavolga. The communication systems of cetaceans. In L. M. Herman (ed.), *Cetacean Behavior: Mechanisms and Functions*, pp. 149–209. New York: Wiley Interscience, 1980.

Heyes, C. M. Imitation, culture, and cognition. *Animal Behavior* 46: 999–1010, 1993.

Heyes, C. M. Introduction: Identifying and defining imitation. In C. M. Heyes and B. G. Galef Jr. (eds.), *Social Learning in Animals: The Roots of Culture*, pp. 211–220. New York: Academic Press, 1996.

Heyes, C. M., and G. Dawson. A demonstration of observational learning using a bidirectional control. *Quarterly Journal of Experimental Psychology* 42: 59–71, 1990.

Hulse, S. H. Comparative psychology and pitch pattern perception in songbirds. In R. J. Dooling and S. H. Hulse (eds.), *The Comparative Psychology of Audition: Perceiving Complex Sounds*, pp. 331–352. Hillsdale, NJ: Lawrence Erlbaum, 1989.

Lieberman, P. Primate vocalizations and human linguistic ability. *Journal of the Acoustical Society of America* 44: 1574–1584, 1968.

McCowan, B., and D. Reiss. Whistle contour development in captive-born infant bottlenose dolphins (*Tursiops truncatus*): Role of learning. *Journal of Comparative Psychology* 109: 242–260, 1995.

Mercado, E. III, S. O. Murray, R. K. Uyeyama, A. A. Pack, and L. M. Herman. Memory for recent actions in the bottlenosed dolphin (*Tursiops truncatus*): Repetition of arbitrary behaviors using an abstract rule. *Animal Learning and Behavior* 26: 210–218, 1998.

Mercado, E. III, R. K. Uyeyama, A. A. Pack, and L. M. Herman. Memory for action events in the bottlenosed dolphin. *Animal Cognition* 2: 17–25, 1999.

Moore, B. R. Avian movement imitation and a new form of mimicry: Tracing the evolution of a complex form of learning. *Behaviour* 122(3–4): 231–263, 1992.

Moore, B. R. The evolution of imitative learning. In C. M. Heyes and B. G. Galef Jr. (eds.), *Social Learning in Animals: The Roots of Culture*, pp. 245–265. New York: Academic Press, 1996.

Nehaniv, C. L., and K. Dautenhahn. Of hummingbirds and helicopters: An algebraic framework for interdisciplinary studies of imitation and its applications. In J. Demiris and A. Birk (eds.), *Interdisciplinary Approaches to Robot Learning*, pp. 136–161. World Scientific Press, 2000.

Noble, J., and P. M. Todd. Is it really imitation? A review of simple mechanisms in social information gathering. In K. Dautenhahn and C. L. Nehaniv (eds.), *Proceedings of the AISB '99 Symposium on Imitation in Animals and Artifacts (Edinburgh, Scotland, 7–9 April)*, pp. 65–73. Brighton, U.K.: Society of the Study of Artificial Intelligence and Simulation of Behaviour, 1999.

Ralston, J. V., and L. M. Herman. Perception and generalization of frequency contours by a bottlenose dolphin (*Tursiops truncatus*). *Journal of Comparative Psychology* 109: 268–277, 1995.

Rawls, K., P. Fiorelli, and S. Gish. Vocalizations and vocal mimicry in captive Harbor seals, *Phoca vitulina*. *Canadian Journal of Zoology* 63: 1050–1056, 1985.

Reiss, D., and B. McCowan. Spontaneous vocal mimicry and production by bottlenosed dolphins (*Tursiops truncatus*): Evidence for vocal learning. *Journal of Comparative Psychology* 107: 301–312, 1993.

Richards, D. G. Dolphin vocal mimicry and object labeling. In R. J. Schusterman, J. A. Thomas, and F. G. Wood (eds.), *Dolphin Cognition and Behavior: A Comparative Approach*, pp. 273–288. Hillsdale, NJ: Lawrence Erlbaum Associates, 1986.

Richards, D. G., J. P. Wolz, and L. M. Herman. Vocal mimicry of computer generated sounds and vocal labeling of objects by a bottlenosed dolphin, *Tursiops truncatus*. *Journal of Comparative Psychology* 98: 10–28, 1984.

Rizzolatti, G., L. Fadiga, V. Gallese, and L. Fogassi. Premotor cortex and the recognition of motor actions. *Cognition and Brain Research* 3: 131–141, 1998.

Taylor, K. B. Self-selection and self-monitoring of behavior by bottlenosed dolphins (*Tursiops truncatus*). Unpublished master's thesis, University of Hawaii, Honolulu, 1995.

Taylor-Gaines, K., and L. M. Herman. Self-selection and self-monitoring of actions by bottlenosed dolphins. *Abstracts: Tenth Biennial Conference on the Biology of Marine Mammals*, Galveston, Texas, p. 11. November 1993.

Thorpe, W. H. *Learning and Instinct in Animals*. London: Methuen, 1963.

Tomasello, M. Cultural transmission in the tool use and communicatory signaling of chimpanzees? In S. Parker and K. Gibson (eds.), *Language and Intelligence in Monkeys and Apes: Comparative Developmental Perspectives*, pp. 274–311. Cambridge, UK: Cambridge University Press, 1990.

Tomasello, M. Do apes ape? In C. M. Heyes and B. G. Galef Jr. (eds.), *Social Learning in Animals: The Roots of Culture*, pp. 319–346. New York: Academic Press, 1996.

Tomasello, M., and J. Call. *Primate Cognition*. New York: Oxford University Press, 1997.

Tomasello, M., S. Savage-Rumbaugh, and A. C. Kruger. Imitative learning of actions on objects by children, chimpanzees, and enculturated chimpanzees. *Child Development* 64: 1688–1705, 1993.

Tyack, P. L. Whistle repertoires of two bottlenosed dolphins, *Tursiops truncatus*: Mimicry of signature whistles? *Behavioral Ecology and Sociobiology* 18: 251–257, 1986.

Visalberghi, E., and D. Fragaszy. Do monkeys ape? In S. Parker and K. Gibson (eds.), *"Language" and Intelligence in Monkeys and Apes: Comparative Developmental Perspectives*, pp. 247–273. Cambridge, UK: Cambridge University Press, 1990.

Wells, R. S. The role of long-term study in understanding the social structure of a bottlenosed dolphin community. In K. Pryor and K. S. Norris (eds.), *Dolphin Societies: Discoveries and Puzzles*, pp. 199–225. Los Angeles: University of California Press, 1991.

Whiten, A., and D. Custance. Studies of imitation in chimpanzees and children. In C. M. Heyes and B. G. Galef Jr. (eds.), *Social Learning in Animals: The Roots of Culture*, pp. 291–318. New York: Academic Press, 1996.

Whiten, A., and R. Ham. On the nature and evolution of imitation in the animal kingdom: Reappraisal of a century of research. *Advances in the Study of Behavior* 21: 239–283, 1992.

Xitco, M. J. Jr. Mimicry of modeled behaviors by bottlenose dolphins. Unpublished master's thesis, University of Hawaii, Honolulu, 1988.

Zentall, T. R. An analysis of imitative learning in animals. In C. M. Heyes and B. G. Galef Jr. (eds.), *Social Learning in Animals: The Roots of Culture*, pp. 221–243. New York: Academic Press, 1996.

Zentall, T. R., and B. G. Galef. *Social Learning: Psychological and Biological Perspectives*. Hillsdale, NJ: Lawrence Erlbaum, 1988.

Zentall, T. R., J. E. Sutton, and L. M. Sherburne. True imitative learning in pigeons. *American Psychological Society* 7(6): 343–346, 1996.

4   Allospecific Referential Speech Acquisition in Grey Parrots (Psittacus erithacus): Evidence for Multiple Levels of Avian Vocal Imitation

Irene M. Pepperberg

4.1   Introduction

Avian vocal learning is often ignored in studies of imitation—it is usually considered a special irrelevant case (e.g., Shettleworth 1998) because the imitated actions are observable auditorially rather than visually. I propose, however, that allospecific vocal learning (acquiring vocalizations of another species) is a most interesting case of imitation because it is one of the few acts in which the copied behavior is, in accord with Thorpe's (1963) definition, completely novel—that is, the copying of an otherwise improbable act. Moreover, for just that reason, allospecific vocal imitative acts are less likely confounded with acts of social facilitation, stimulus enhancement, or other forms of nonimitative socially mediated learning (Fritz and Kotrschal, chapter 5 of this volume). In this chapter, I examine the replication of referential human speech by Grey parrots; explain why I believe it is both referential and a true instance of imitation; show how various forms of input (e.g., my model/rival training procedure) affect such learning; and use my experimental results as supporting evidence for the suggestion that imitation likely occurs at more than one level of complexity (e.g., Byrne and Russon 1998).

4.2   Vocal Learning as an Imitative Act

True vocal imitation is uncommon. Even vocal *learning* occurs in few species other than humans (Lachlan and Slater 1999), and in those species in which it does occur, in only rare instances can it be labeled an imitative act. For most oscine songbirds, for example, an individual learns songs or calls of conspecifics but the behavior is not necessarily imitation. Although a model is necessary because development in the absence of a model is abnormal (e.g., Marler 1970), the modeled act is not improbable (Thorpe 1963)— that is, some predisposition generally exists toward learning such conspecific vocalization (Petrinovich 1985), and the resultant behavior is rarely identical in form to that of the model (see Kroodsma

1996). Only when a subject engages in goal-directed learning of allospecific utterances (e.g., dolphins, *Tursiops truncatus*, reproducing computer-generated whistles, McCowan and Reiss 1997; white-crowned sparrows, *Zonotrichia leucophyrs*, learning the song of a strawberry finch, *Amandava amandava*, Baptista and Petrinovich 1984), can the case be made for true vocal imitation.

Given that avian vocal learning can be a form of imitation, of interest are data on how different types of input affect such learning. For some species (see Baptista and Gaunt 1994), socially interactive input is necessary for vocal imitation, which I define as the acquisition of *exceptional* vocalizations (see Pepperberg 1985, 1986a,b): communication characterized by vocal learning unlikely to occur in the normal course of development, such as acquisition of allospecific forms. Few researchers, however, examine in detail the exact nature of the input necessary to engender such learning, or the implications of results that suggest that successful imitation depends on the form of input. I study these problems in what may seem an unusual species—the mimetic Grey parrot (*Psittacus erithacus*). I study both the precise reproduction of human speech and the referential use of such sounds by these birds. Because the vocalizations are often used as requests, such imitation, although auditory/vocal, is as goal directed as that in studies involving physical actions (e.g., Akins and Zentall 1996; Fritz et al. 1999).

4.3 Fidelity of Vocal Learning in Grey Parrots

To the human ear, Grey parrot speech sounds almost indistinguishable from that of its trainers. But some researchers (e.g., Greenewalt 1968; Lieberman 1991) argue that birds cannot inherently produce human speech sounds and that human listeners simply interpret a bird's distorted acoustic signal as speech. Is the similarity really a matter of human perception, or do physical characteristics of a bird's utterances match those of humans? If the latter, are the characteristics the same ones scientists use to describe human speech? If so, such data would strengthen the case for Grey parrot vocal learning as an imitative act. To search for and examine possible acoustic and articulatory parallels between human and psittacine vowels and consonants, a student and I analyzed spectrograms and videotapes of speech samples from a 15-year-old, human-raised, male Grey parrot, Alex (Patterson and Pepperberg 1994, 1998). After his first year (spent at his breeder and a pet store), he interacted with humans 8 hours a day, including daily training on various cognitive concepts and English labels.

Methods of Analysis

For vowels, we measured fundamental frequency, F_0 (source vibration at the avian syrinx; syringeal constriction at the base of the trachea functionally resembles that of human vocal folds in phonation; see Gaunt and Gaunt 1985; Scanlan 1988), and used sonagraphic analyses to learn if Alex used one sound source (F_0) as do humans to produce speech, or two interacting sources, the mechanism used by songbirds for their vocalizations. We measured his first and second formants, F_1 and F_2, which are considered critical for vowel perception in humans (Borden and Harris 1984). Formants represent resonant frequencies in humans of the mouth opening (F_1) and oral cavity (F_2) and could represent specific areas of the parrot's vocal tract as well. A formant is not a harmonic of the fundamental frequency, F_0. Harmonics may also be present, but show up as odd multiples of F_0. The third formant, F_3, indicates whether constrictions that produce speech occur toward the front or the back of the human vocal tract. Alex's F_3 was rarely observed or was so close to F_2 as to be nearly indistinguishable from it.

For stops (consonants in which the flow of air is blocked), we measured equivalents of voice-onset timing (VOT, time between lip opening [in humans] to release air and the start of vibration of the sound source),[1] number of bursts (bursts result from release of air pressure built up by lip closure), and stop loci (high energy peaks associated with the voiceless aspirated portion of human stops). We collected three formant-related measures: (1) F_x onset—frequencies of F_1, F_2, and F_3 during the first 10 ms of voicing following a stop; (2) F_x target—average frequencies of F_1, F_2, and F_3 during the steady-state portion of the vowel following a stop; (3) duration (DUR)—time from the beginning of voicing to the first point where formants assume a steady-state pattern. We calculated $SLOPE_x$—the difference between F_x onset and target divided by DUR.

We then used standard phonetic and statistical techniques to compare Alex's and my utterances. I was chosen because I was Alex's principal trainer and most observers claim that his utterances closely resemble mine. The analysis methods were complicated, and I do not give details here (see Patterson and Pepperberg 1994, 1998). What are of interest are the results, and I present a summary of our findings.

Results

F_0 ANALYSES

F_0 analyses suggest that Alex, like humans and unlike most song-birds (Greenewalt 1968; Miller 1977), uses a single set of articulators to produce speech (Patterson and Pepperberg 1994). As noted above, some researchers suggest that a bird uses each half of the syrinx independently to produce two different sinusoidal pure tones, and that interaction of the two tones produces "formant frequencies of the original human speech sound that the bird is mimicking.... We perceive these nonspeech signals as speech because they have energy at the formant frequencies" (Lieberman 1984:156). Alex's data do not support that interpretation.[2] Parrot and human F_0's do not match exactly, but Alex has one F_0 and his absolute values are in the general range of an adult human (124–276 Hz, Peterson and Barney 1952).

COMPARISONS OF PSITTACINE AND HUMAN F_1 AND F_2

Accurate perception of human speech generally requires processing F_1, F_2, and often F_3 (Lieberman 1984). For a given sex and age, F_1 and F_2 vary across vowels and thus may be used to differentiate vowels for a class of speaker. We compared human and avian F_1's and F_2's, and tested if Alex's formant values could predict his vowels. We found (table 4.1; figure 4.1) differences and similarities between Alex's data and that of humans. For both F_1 and F_2, his range of values is less than those of humans and lacks humans' low-frequency values. For most vowels, Alex's F_1 differs considerably from mine and varies considerably less than mine with respect to vowel identity; his are almost invariant. Alex's vowels, like mine, are somewhat distinguishable by F_2; our F_2's are similar. Analyses also imply that his formants are, as in humans, associated with resonance of specific parts of his vocal tract (Warren, Patterson, and Pepperberg 1996).

Other ways to categorize human vowels, according to tongue placement with respect to height and distance from the front and back of the oral cavity (Remez et al. 1987), are important for Alex.

Table 4.1 Means of F_1 and F_2 for humans and Alex in Hz[a]

		/i/	/I/	/e/[b]	/E/	/æ/	/a/	/ə/	/o/	/U/	/u/[c]
F_1	M	270	390		530	660	730	640		440	300
		272	410		550	656	749	596	456	439	324
	W	310	430		610	860	850	760		470	70
		338	486		745	922	981	793	532	528	400
	C	370	530		690	1010	1030	850		560	430
		313	563		875	1116	1125	862	660	573	400
	Alex	932	805	821	812	848	872	806	684	837	844/829
	IMP	310	407	636	586	585	753	698	567	527	391/340
F_2	M	2290	1990		1840	1720	1090	1190		1020	870
		2209	1859		1740	1748	1192	1289	1176	1234	1396
	W	2790	2480		2330	2050	1220	1400		1160	950
		2837	2284		2123	2089	1440	1599	1419	1437	1617
	C	3200	2730		2610	2320	1370	1590		1410	1170
		2705	2615		2436	2345	1590	1627	1645	1558	1806
	Alex	2775	2330	2343	2117	2187	1433	1480	1360[d]	1604	1373/1637
	IMP	2988	2458	2520	2365	2382	1378	1505	1476	1626	2479/2148

Source: After Patterson and Pepperberg 1994.
[a] Values on the first line for M (man), W (woman), and C (child) are taken from Peterson and Barney (1952), values on the second line are from Zahorian and Jagharghi (1993). IMP represents myself.
[b] We do not include /e/ for M, W, C because no published values are available.
[c] Alex and IMP have two values for /u/ because they produce this vowel in two separate parts.
[d] This entry comprises a single sample.

Interestingly, frontness/backness, not height, of Alex's tongue relative to his oro-pharyngeal cavity (the equivalent of our oral cavity) correlates with different vowels. This finding is consistent with his flat F_1, which in humans roughly corresponds to tongue height, and his variable F_2, which in humans corresponds to front/back tongue position. Alex's /i, I, E, æ/ cluster together as "front" vowels; /U, ə, a/ cluster as "back" vowels. Although /u/ is a back vowel for most Standard American English speakers, it is a dipthong (has two parts, $/u_1/$ and $/u_2/$) for me and Alex. For me, the two parts are front vowels; for Alex, the two parts appear to be front and back vowels, respectively. All his vowels, however, cluster midrange with respect to the high/low distinction.

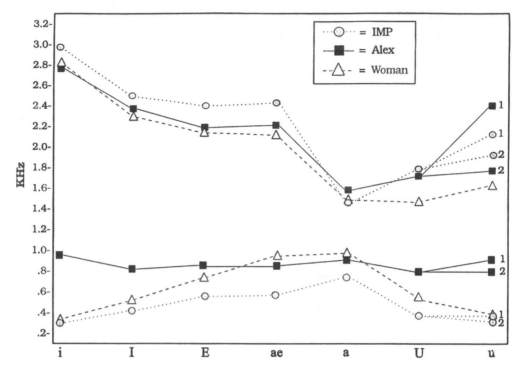

Figure 4.1 A comparative plot of F_1 (lower set of lines) and F_2 (upper set of lines) for Alex, me (IMP), and an "average" woman (from Peterson and Barney, 1952). (From Patterson and Pepperberg, 1994)

COMPARISONS OF PSITTACINE AND HUMAN STOP CONSONANTS (STOPS)

Acoustic analyses are more complex for stops than vowels but traditional measurements for human stops were generally applicable to Alex's. Similarities and differences exist for his and my stops (Patterson and Pepperberg 1998). Similarities involve statistically distinct acoustic characteristics and separation of stops into subsets based on voicing and place of constriction. Differences involve how stops separate into subsets and likely mechanisms used to produce speech. Alex's subsets are not identical to mine: His /b/ is an outlier, and his /p/ clusters nearer /d, g/ than /t, k/ (figure 4.2). Alex must produce /b, p/ without lips; he seems to compensate with mechanisms not available to humans.

EVIDENCE FOR PHYSICAL IMITATION

Our research suggests that Alex's fidelity of vowel and stop imitation is likely constrained only by the differences in human and avian vocal tracts, for example, lack of lips to produce bilabial /p/

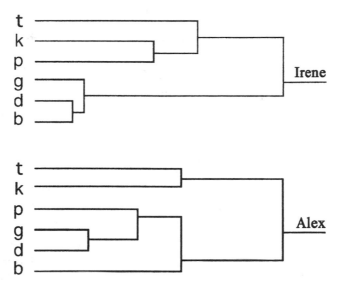

Figure 4.2 Cluster diagram of my (top) and Alex's (bottom) stops. Note the differences in placement of our /b/ and /p/. (From Patterson and Pepperberg, 1998)

and /b/. His vocalizations all resemble those of humans, and the characteristics used to describe human speech and the processes used to produce human speech (where possible) generally work equally well for him (Patterson and Pepperberg 1994, 1998). F_0 data, in particular, suggest that Alex, like humans, produces true resonances and not sinusoids at the appropriate formant frequencies. Such data support the interpretation of Alex's speech acts as a form of physical imitation.

4.4 Referential Use of Learned Vocalizations

Of importance, however, is not that Alex produces speech, but specifically *referential speech*. My point, discussed in detail below, is that his data indicate that imitation occurs at many levels of complexity. Purposeless duplication of an act, such as rote reproduction of human speech, lacks cognitive complexity and is a simple form of imitation, "mere" mimicry. But if the imitator performs the act because she or he understands its purpose—to reach a goal, be it an object or the ability to communicate, that is otherwise impossible to obtain—then the imitation is, in some sense, intentional and complex, an indicator of cognitive processing. Moreover, to use imitated speech referentially, Alex must discriminate among and appropriately categorize human sounds and understand that minor differences in speech are meaningful—that "want corn" and "want cork" have different results. Such ability also requires cognitive processing. Alex clearly exhibits these abilities. In studies lasting over two decades, Alex has learned to label more than 50 exemplars, seven colors, five shapes, quantity to 6, three categories (color, shape, material), and uses "no," "come here," "wanna go X" and "want Y" (X and Y are appropriate location or item labels). He combines labels to identify, request, comment upon or refuse approximately 100 items and alter his environment (Pepperberg 1990a). He processes queries to judge category, relative size, quantity, presence or absence of similarity/difference in attributes, and shows label comprehension (Pepperberg 1983, 1987a,b,c, 1988a,b, 1990b, 1992; Pepperberg and Brezinsky 1991). He semantically separates labeling and requesting (Pepperberg 1988a). Given an array of different numbers of intermingled red and blue balls and blocks, he can identify the number of blue balls (Pepperberg 1994a). Previous studies on mimetic birds, using standard conditioning techniques, failed to engender such learning (Pepperberg 1999); why did my work with Alex succeed?

4.5 Effects of Input on Vocal Learning in Grey Parrots

Background

My students and I compared various training systems for teaching Grey parrots referential labeling. We determined that one procedure, the model/rival (M/R) technique, was the most effective (see figure 4.3). To understand our results, I describe this system and contrast it with other forms that have been less successful, and discuss our findings. These studies were carried out with Alex and three juvenile Grey parrots, Kyaaro, Alo, and Griffin, whose living conditions were identical to those of Alex (e.g., Pepperberg 1994b). In each study, labels in various training conditions were counterbalanced with labels used in M/R training, and were always labels that could be imitated by Grey parrots.

Description of the Different Training Techniques

M/R TECHNIQUE
The model/rival (M/R) procedure was adapted from Todt (1975). Basic M/R training involves three-way interactions among two

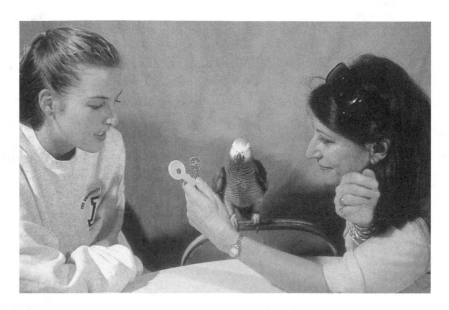

Figure 4.3 The model/rival protocol. (Photo courtesy of William Munoz)

humans and an avian student. M/R training primarily introduces labels and concepts, but also aids in shaping pronunciation. M/R training uses *social interaction* to demonstrate the targeted vocal behavior (Todt 1975). Sessions begin with a bird observing two humans handling an object in which the bird has shown interest. One human trains the second human (the model/rival), that is, presents and asks questions about the item ("What's here?" "What toy?"). The trainer rewards correct identifications with this item, thus demonstrating *referential* and *functional* use of labels, respectively, by providing a 1:1 correspondence between label and object, and by modeling label use as a means to obtain the object (details in Pepperberg 1981, 1990c, 1991). The second human not only is a model for the bird's responses and its rival for the trainer's attention, but also illustrates aversive consequences of errors: trainers respond to errors with scolding and temporarily hide the object. A model/rival is told to speak more clearly or try again when responses are garbled or incorrect, thereby allowing a bird to observe "corrective feedback" (see Goldstein 1984; Vanayan, Robertson, and Biederman 1985). The bird is included in interactions and rewarded for successive approximations to a correct response; thus, training is adjusted to its level. Model/rival and trainer reverse roles to show how the communicative process is used by either party to request information or effect environmental change. If birds do not see role reversal in training, they exhibit two behavior patterns inconsistent with interactive, referential communication: they do not transfer responses to anyone other than the human who posed questions during training, and do not learn both parts of the interaction (Todt 1975).

After using M/R input successfully, I designed studies to examine how various levels of reference, social interaction, and functionality might affect learning not only with respect to sound reproduction, but also with respect to comprehension and appropriate use (i.e., actions that require cognitive processing). To provide input that varied with respect to these factors, I contrasted sessions of M/R tutoring with sessions using different forms of human interaction, videotape, and audiotape input. Sessions could be designed so as to have varying components of input (table 4.2).

M/R VARIANTS

To eliminate as much reference and functionality as possible and still retain two trainers, I designed "M/R-variant 1" training (Pep-

Table 4.2 Training method, elements of input, and outcome

TECHNIQUE	REFERENCE	FUNCTIONALITY	INTERACTION	MODELING	ERROR[a]	REVERSAL	LEARNING
M/R	yes	yes	yes	yes	yes	yes	yes
M/R Variant-1	no	no	yes	yes	yes	yes	partial
Solo-1	yes	minimal	minimal	no	no	no	no
Basic Video	yes	partial	no	not live	yes	yes	no
V-Variant-1	yes	partial	minimal	not live	yes	yes	no
V-Variant-2	yes	potential	no	not live	yes	yes	no
V-Variant-3	yes	partial	yes	not live	yes	yes	no
V-L	yes	partial	yes	not live	yes	yes	no
Audio	no	no	no	not live	yes	yes	no
Operant[b]	no	minimal	minimal	no	no	no	no

Note: "Reference" means inclusion of physical objects to which the targeted label refers, "functionality" means that transfer of the object occurs after use of the targeted label, "interaction" refers to social interaction among trainers and subject, "modeling" indicates that one or two trainers demonstrate referential and functional use of a targeted label, "error" means that the effects of incorrect responses are demonstrated, and "reversal" indicates that two models interchange roles of querant and respondent.
[a] Denotes that corrective feedback was demonstrated after a model erred.
[b] Refers to standard operant conditioning training, like that used by Mowrer (1954). This entry is presented for comparison; I did not perform such experiments.

perberg 1994b). Two humans enacted the same roles as in basic M/R training, but now no longer modeled any connection between labels and specific objects or collections. As in the basic M/R procedure, roles were often reversed and Alex was included in the interactions. Correct responses garnered vocal praise and the opportunity to request anything desired (Pepperberg 1987a): although we usually reward Alex either with an item he has labeled *or* the opportunity to request a favored item ("I want X," Pepperberg 1987a), here we used only the latter reward; errors elicited scolding and time-outs. A sequence of eight number labels were trained without reference either to specific items or to Alex's previously acquired English number labels (Pepperberg 1994b, 1997); he saw only a string of pictured numerals. The labels were part of a study on ordinality, counting, and serial learning (Pepperberg and Silverstone, unpublished). The set, *il ee bam ba oo yuk chil gal*, was derived from Korean count labels, both to permit comparisons with children (Fuson 1988) and to be maximally different from English. *Bam* (/bæm/) and *ba* were substituted for the Korean *sam* and *sa* because of Alex's occasional difficulty in producing "ss." Training lacked functional meaning and all but minimal referentiality, but did maintain joint attention (known to be important for facilitating a child's label acquisition; e.g., Baldwin 1991) between bird, humans, and the pictured numbers.

To eliminate some functionality and as much social interaction as possible, and to examine the effect of joint attention on Grey parrot learning, I devised "solo-1" training (Pepperberg and McLaughlin 1996). The usual M/R procedure was amended such that the only aspects that remained were the use of a live trainer and a referential reward. A single trainer, rather than a pair, sat with her back to a bird, who was seated on a perch so as to be within reach of an object suspended by a pulley system. The trainer produced relevant phrases and sentences in which the object label was always stressed and in the final position (Pepperberg 1981)—for example, "You have a shiny *key*!" "You gonna get the *key*?" and so on, so as to replicate what is often heard during language learning in young children (see de Villiers and de Villiers 1978). Conceivably, parrots, like humans, most readily remember the ends of word strings (Lenneberg 1967; Silverstone 1989). The trainer never made eye contact with the bird nor did she ever present the object directly to the bird. This technique demonstrated reference and provided human input that could vary between sessions, but eliminated joint gazing and directional pointing. These sessions could

also provide limited interaction in the form of praise if the bird attempted the label. However, because interaction was otherwise absent, the bird did not observe more than a minimal level of functionality. Thus, for example, the bird would never see a demonstration of how the targeted vocalization could be used to obtain a particular item; the bird was merely simultaneously exposed to the item and several sentences about the label. Attaining more than this level of functionality was impossible for this particular protocol, given that pointing and joint gaze were prohibited.

VIDEO TRAINING

To provide training that closely followed the M/R procedure but eliminated social interaction and minimized functionality, I used a "basic video" procedure (Pepperberg 1994b). Here, I videotaped M/R sessions of the adult trained parrot, Alex, and showed a tape on each targeted label to the juvenile birds, Alo and Kyaaro. In the training videos, Alex occasionally erred or interrupted with requests for other items and changes of location (Pepperberg 1983, 1987a, 1994b), which allowed trainers to engage him in "corrective feedback." Thus, although Alex already knew the targeted labels (Pepperberg 1990a,b), tapes did not present the targeted material as a review but rather recreated training sessions. Too, as in live M/R presentations, trainers reversed roles and also occasionally erred. The tapes furthermore retained breaks for nonvocal exchanges (e.g., when trainers preened Alex) and trainers' departures by using, respectively, sconos of such nonvocal interactions or a blank screen. A zoom lens enabled us to include life-size images of Alex and the targeted objects in addition to the somewhat smaller images of the entire training scenario (the object, Alex, and two humans; Pepperberg, Naughton, and Banta 1998). For all video presentations, we spectrographically analyzed (Kay 5500 DSP Sona-Graph) the audio portion of the video to ensure that the sound was not degraded compared to that of Alex "live" (Pepperberg, Naughton, and Banta 1998). While watching these tapes, the juveniles sat on a perch in front of a television monitor in the absence of direct social interaction with trainers; no humans were present after a bird was situated on its perch. By watching a tape of a human or Alex produce a particular sound and either receive an item or be scolded, juveniles saw but did not experience directly the effect of a vocalization. Videos, therefore, demonstrated reference but lacked clear functional meaning. A previous study (Rutledge and Pepperberg 1988) showed that Alex could respond

to objects presented via a live video link; Grey parrots thus can at least recognize two-dimensional video representations.[3]

Given that children often learn from television (e.g., *Sesame Street*) best when they view programs with an *interactive* adult— for example, someone who questions them about the activities being viewed (Lemish and Rice 1986)—and because birds did not learn in basic video sessions, I decided to include live interaction with a human trainer in such sessions. For the children, the extent of interaction affected how much was learned (St. Peters, Huston, and Wright 1989). My students and I tested this possibility for Grey parrots with "video-variant 1" (Pepperberg, Naughton, and Banta 1998). We now included a "co-viewer": trainers who ensured that the birds attended to the monitor for the entire session. A trainer provided social approbation for viewing and pointed to the screen, making comments like "Look what Alex has!" Because we wished to separate out the effect of having a human present who interacted with the bird from the effect of having a human present who interacted with both the bird and the actions on the tape (Pepperberg, Gardiner, and Luttrell 1999), the co-viewer did not repeat new labels, ask questions, or relate the content to other training sessions. Any attempt a bird made at the label would be rewarded with vocal praise and not the object. Thus, the amount of social interaction was still somewhat limited, and the amount of functional meaning was the same as in the basic videotape session.

To ensure that lack of reward for an attempt at a targeted label was not what prevented learning from video, I devised the "video-variant 2" procedure (Pepperberg, Naughton, and Banta 1998). Although neither juvenile had used labels from basic video sessions in the vocal "practice" that we generally heard following M/R sessions (see Pepperberg, Brese, and Harris 1991), possibly they attempted to produce labels during video sessions and lack of reward had extinguished their behavior (Pepperberg 1994b). Thus, students and I repeated the basic videotape protocol, but included an "automatic" reward system (a pulley) so that a parrot could, in the absence of social interaction, receive the item if it attempted to produce the label. The pulley system was controlled by a student in another room who monitored the parrot's utterances through headphones. We taped sessions to test for (inter)observer reliability.

My students and I then tested two additional variations on the basic video design to see if such variations might engender learning from video input. First, to test the effect of additional interaction with co-viewers, we designed "video-variant 3." Second, to see if lack of learning from video was a consequence of habituating to (and thus ignoring) the single videotape that was used repeatedly, we devised "video-live" (VL) input: We taped Alex in typical M/R sessions and fed the live, taped input into Griffin's room. Although Alex's actions varied considerably over the course of each tape in the other video sessions, only one tape had been used for each label. In VL, in contrast, habituation was controlled because Alex's behavior differed across as well as during all sessions. Moreover, to counter habituation further, Griffin received VL sessions at 1- to 21-day intervals (on average, however, twice a week) so each presentation was an unexpected event (Pepperberg, Gardiner, and Luttrell 1999).

Video-variant 3 and VL sessions included highly interactive co-viewers. As in Pepperberg, Naughton, and Banta (1998), trainers not only ensured birds attended to the video, but also provided social approbation for viewing and pointed to the screen during and after interactions involving targeted objects, making comments like "See what Alex has!" Now, however, trainers repeated targeted labels, asked questions, handled objects, and rewarded label attempts with praise and the item. Sessions thus included modeling only via video, full reference, more social interaction, and more functionality for targeted items.

AUDIOTAPES

To test the effects of total absence of reference, context, and social interaction, I exposed the juveniles to audiotapes (Pepperberg 1994b). Audiotapes consisted of the audio portion of basic videotapes, and thus were still parallel to the M/R and video procedures. Juveniles received "basic audiotape" sessions in isolation (i.e., with no social interaction), and no objects or actions were associated with the sounds presented over the speaker. Note that this procedure replicated the conditions used in early studies of song learning in birds in social isolation (e.g., Marler 1970).

Results

I found that the birds did not learn *referential* labeling through any technique other than M/R training (table 4.2). For Grey parrots, at least, acquisition of referential English speech occurs when training involves two humans who: demonstrate referentiality and functionality of a label to be learned, socially interact with each other and the bird, exchange roles of questioner and respondent, portray the effects of labeling errors, provide corrective feedback, and adjust the level of training as the subject begins to learn. When training lacks some of these elements, birds fail to learn or acquire only limited associations rather than full referential use of targeted labels; that is, they cannot transfer label use from training to testing situations (Pepperberg, Naughton, and Banta 1998; Pepperberg, Gardiner, and Luttrell 1999; Todt 1975) or from the training exemplar to other instances of the relevant object or concept (Pepperberg, Naughton, and Banta 1998), or they reproduce but do not comprehend what they have learned (Pepperberg 1994b). Interestingly, conditions under which Grey parrots do acquire referential English labels are those (a) necessary for *exceptional* learning— learning that is unlikely during normal development but possible under certain conditions (Pepperberg 1985, 1988b, 1993, 1997)— and (b) required for language acquisition by children with specific impairments and who lack concomitant social skills (e.g., Rice 1991). Normal children, for example, but not impaired children or Grey parrots, learn from videotaped input in the absence of an interactive caretaker (review in Pepperberg, Gardiner, and Luttrell 1999). Normal children, but not Grey parrots, also learn labels during interactions with a single caretaker (Baldwin 1991; de Villiers and de Villiers 1978; Pepperberg et al., 2000).

4.6 Implications for Studies of Imitation

The results suggest three important ideas relevant to studies of imitation. These involve the difference between "mere mimicry" and the imitation of a goal-directed act; the fact that for a so-called mimetic bird, even "mere mimicry" is not easily acquired; and that the acquisition of an "improbable act" (Thorpe 1963) for purposeful behavior requires very specialized forms of input.

Mimicry versus Imitation

My experiments show that goal-directed imitation is different from "mere mimicry." The reason for this statement is that training that engenders the latter is usually incapable of engendering the former; the implication is that different learning—and possibly cognitive —processes are involved. Alex, exposed to M/R variant-1, learned to produce vocalizations—the string of vocal labels that were modeled—but the results of the experiment differed from those of M/R studies in two important ways. First, acquisition took 9 months, which was unusually long (Pepperberg 1981, 1994b; Pepperberg and Silverstone, unpublished). Second, and most striking, however, was that Alex was not immediately capable of using, nor could he subsequently learn to use, these labels in a referential manner—that is, with respect to either serial labeling or quantity. Even after we modeled 1:1 correspondences between eight objects and the string of labels, he was unable to use elements in the string to refer to smaller quantities, for example, to say "il ee bam ba" when presented with four items and asked to "Say number." Alex had thus learned to produce, but not comprehend the use of, these human vocalizations (Pepperberg 1994b). Given his previous success on both production and comprehension of human labels after M/R training (e.g., Pepperberg 1990b, 1992, 1994a), his failure was likely a consequence of the training protocol and not a lack of general cognitive capacity (Pepperberg 1994b). Interestingly, echolalia in autistic children is characterized by a similar lack of referential use of mimicked sounds (Fey 1986), and for such children, acquisition of normal communication appears to be a form of exceptional learning that is responsive to M/R training (Pepperberg and Sherman, 2000).

Input and Vocal Learning

My studies show that for a purportedly mimetic species, even simple mimicry does not occur under all conditions. Three Greys—Kyaaro, Alo, and Griffin—each failed to learn most labels in any video session, and the first two failed to learn from audiotapes (Griffin was not trained with audio). Tapes of solitary sound productions also revealed a total lack of "practice" (Pepperberg, Brese, and Harris 1991) of these labels, in contrast to frequent practice of labels trained in M/R sessions (Pepperberg 1994b; Pepperberg and McLaughlin 1996). Alo attempted to produce a label trained during video-variant 1 (nail), but failed to identify the object or even produce an approximation of the correct label on formal tests for labels trained in this and all other nonbasic M/R procedures. In contrast, on tests on labels taught via the basic M/R procedure, all birds appropriately identified several items (e.g., cork, paper, wood, wool). Thus, when input lacks certain aspects of reference, functionality, and/or social interaction, even a bird known for its mimetic abilities does not learn to produce allospecific utterances.

Elements of Input Needed for Referential Learning

We thus see that purposeful imitation requires considerable ability and specialized input: input that has reference, functionality, and social interaction. I will describe these elements in detail, so that their importance is clear. I will also emphasize how each element involves the need for cognitive processing. Without such elements, and thus without the need for cognitive processing, "more" mimicry results.

REFERENCE

Reference is, in part, what signals "are about" (Smith 1991). Reference, in principle, concerns the direct relationship between a signal and an object or action. Reference, however, is not always easily determined; for example, when we say "key," we generally mean a specific metal object (what Smith labels an "external" referent), but we may also mean an action, as to "key" in data. Similarly, a bird that emits an alarm call may refer to both the predator and the action it is about to take. Thus, not all information contained in a signal always involves a single referent. Determining the referent—and whether one "true" referent exists (and thus why arguments occur as to the actual referentiality of animal alarm calls)—often requires cognitive processing on the part of the receiver. If signal A is truly referential, the receiver cannot simply process the signal and remember and interpret it as being associated with situation X, but must decide, based on additional information, among the possibilities X, Y, and Z. The more explicit the referent of a signal, the more easily the signal appears to be learned.

FUNCTIONALITY

Functionality involves the pragmatics of signal use: when a signal is to be used and the effects of using information in the signal—for example, to achieve a goal, such as teaching our birds the difference between labeling and requesting (Pepperberg 1988a). Because use and effect of a signal may depend upon environmental context, functionality helps define reference—in the above example, it defines "key" as a noun or verb. Cognitive processes are again important for extracting the function of a signal from what may be many possibilities in a given situation. The more explicit a signal's functionality, however, the more readily the signal appears to be learned.

SOCIAL INTERACTION
Social interaction highlights which components of the environment should be noted, emphasizes common attributes—and thus possible underlying rules—of diverse actions, and allows input to be continuously adjusted to match the level of the receiver. Interaction may also provide a contextual explanation of the reasons for an action and demonstrate the consequences of an action (details in Pepperberg 1993, 1994b, 1997). Interactive input also appears to facilitate learning; and, again, cognitive processing is likely involved in sorting out the different facets of a given interaction.

ADDITIONAL ELEMENTS OF INPUT
Despite the importance of these major elements, further studies were needed to see if they were not just necessary, but sufficient for such learning to occur: the M/R technique also encompasses many minor elements of input (e.g., quality of input, role reversal of trainers; Pepperberg 1991), the effects of which were not initially examined. Subsequent work (Pepperberg et al., 2000) examined these issues, and reaffirmed that only the standard M/R technique, with all its elements of input, major and minor, is the most effective training for referential learning.

4.7 Conclusion

The "take home message" is that imitation is exceedingly complex, that different levels of imitation likely exist, and that the study of imitation has important implications for general learning theory. I am not the first to suggest that imitation encompasses a range of behavior patterns of varying complexity. Byrne and Russon (1998), for example, deconstruct the concept of imitation and propose a separation into "action level"—a specification of sequential acts—and "program level"—a description of subroutine structure and the hierarchical layout of a behavioral program. I additionally suggest that the level of imitation a given species—with a known range of cognitive capacity and learning ability—exhibits may depend upon the form of input to which it is exposed. The implication is that preexperimental generalizations with respect to species' imitation abilities will not necessarily be correct. Even a species known for its "mimetic" abilities, such as a parrot, will exhibit imitation only under certain conditions. Might other species, assumed incapable of any form of imitation, imitate if given appropriate input? My findings suggest that researchers must also search for correlates as well as homologies across species for those neuroanatomical areas recently found to be involved in simple mimetic acts (Iacoboni et al. 2000) and determine if different areas—in any species—are responsible for higher levels of imitation. Moreover, findings concerning the effect of input on learning and on the level of learning achieved may not be unique to imitation, but will likely hold true for other forms of behavior. Careful experimentation is thus necessary to determine the extent and range of any type of learning ability in any species, including humans (Pepperberg and Sherman, 2000).

Notes

1. In English, the lips separate *after* the vocal folds of the larynx begin to vibrate for "voiced" consonants /b, d, g/; for "voiceless" consonants, /p, t, k/, the vocal folds are vibrating when the lips part (Borden and Harris 1984). Thus VOT is extremely small for voiced consonants and somewhat longer for voiceless consonants in human speech. What Alex uses in place of lips is still under study (Patterson and Pepperberg 1998).

2. Although mynahs do not independently use two halves of their syrinx to produce formants from F_0's as Lieberman (1984) suggests, mynahs likely use a different strategy for formant production than Grey parrots. I do not compare mynah and parrot formant production; for details, see Klatt and Stefanski (1974). Recent studies (Banta Lavenex 1999) show that budgerigars do produce human vowels by amplitude modulation (as Lieberman suggests), but, because their syrinx cannot produce two independent sounds, they produce amplitude modulation via a somewhat different, as yet undetected, mechanism.

3. Recent studies (Ikebuchi and Okanoya 1999) suggest that standard cathode ray tubes in video monitors provide degraded visual input for a bird's visual system; we are presently studying the effects of using a liquid crystal display.

References

Akins, C. K., and T. R. Zentall. Imitative learning in male Japanese quail (*Conturnix japonica*) using the two-action method. *Journal of Comparative Psychology* 110: 316–320, 1996.

Baldwin, D. A. Infants' contributions to the achievement of joint reference. *Child Development* 62: 875–890, 1991.

Banta Lavenex, P. A. Vocal production mechanisms in the budgerigar (*Melopsittacus undulatus*): The presence and implications of amplitude modulation. *Journal of the Acoustical Society of America* 106: 491–505, 1999.

Baptista, L. F., and S. L. L. Gaunt. Advances in studies of avian sound communication. *Condor* 96: 817–830, 1994.

Baptista, L. F., and L. Petrinovich. Social interaction, sensitive phases, and the song template hypothesis in the white-crowned sparrow. *Animal Behaviour* 32: 172–181, 1984.

Borden, G. J., and K. S. Harris. *Speech Science Primer: Physiology, Acoustics, and Perception of Speech*. Baltimore: Williams and Wilkins, 1984.

Byrne, R. W., and A. E. Russon. Learning by imitation: A hierarchical approach. *Behavioral and Brain Sciences* 21: 667–721, 1998.

de Villiers, J. G., and P. A. de Villiers. *Language Acquisition*. Cambridge, Mass.: Harvard University Press, 1978.

Fey, M. E. *Language Intervention with Young Children*. San Diego: College-Hill Press, 1986.

Fritz, J., and K. Kotrschal. Social constraints and profitability of social learning. In K. Dautenhahn and C. Nehaniv, eds., *Proceedings of the AISB '99 Symposium on Imitation in Animals and Artifacts*, April, 1999. The Society for the Study of Artificial Intelligence and Simulation of Behaviour, Edinburgh, 1999.

Fritz, J., A. Bisenberger, and K. Kotrschal. Social mediated learning of an operant task in Greylag geese: Field observation and experimental evidence. *Advances in Ethology* 34: 51, 1999.

Fuson, K. C. *Children's Counting and Concepts of Number*. New York: Springer-Verlag, 1988.

Gaunt, A. S., and S. L. L. Gaunt. Electromyographic studies of the syrinx in parrots (Aves: Psittacidae). *Zoomorphology* 105: 1–11, 1985.

Goldstein, H. The effects of modeling and corrected practice on generative language and learning of preschool children. *Journal of Speech and Hearing Disorders* 49: 389–398, 1984.

Greenewalt, C. H. *Bird Song: Acoustics and Physiology*. Washington, DC: Smithsonian Institution Press, 1968.

Iacobonoi, M., R. P. Woods, M. Brass, H. Bekkering, J. C. Mazziotta, and G. Rizzolatti. Cortical mechanisms of human imitation. *Science* 286: 2526–2528, 2000.

Ikebuchi, M., and K. Okanoya. Male zebra finches and Bengalese finches emit directed songs to the video images of conspecific females projected onto a TFT display. *Zoological Science* 16: 63–70, 1999.

Klatt, D. H., and R. A. Stefanski. How does a mynah bird imitate human speech? *Journal of the Acoustical Society of America* 55: 822–832, 1974.

Kroodsma, D. E. Ecology of passerine song development. In D. E. Kroodsma and E. H. Miller, eds., *Ecology and Evolution of Acoustic Communication in Birds*, pp. 3–19. Ithaca, N.Y.: Cornell University Press, 1996.

Lachlan, R. F., and P. J. B. Slater. The maintenance of vocal learning by gene-culture interaction: The cultural trap hypothesis. *Proceedings of the Royal Society, London, B* 266: 701–706, 1999.

Lemish, D., and M. L. Rice. Television as a talking picture book: A prop for language acquisition. *Journal of Child Language* 13: 251–274, 1986.

Lenneberg, E. H. *Biological Foundations of Language*. New York: J. Wiley, 1967.

Lieberman, P. *The Biology and Evolution of Language*. Harvard University Press, Cambridge, MA, 1984.

Lieberman, P. *Uniquely Human: The Evolution of Speech, Thought, and Selfless Behavior*. Harvard University Press, Cambridge, MA, 1991.

Marler, P. A comparative approach to vocal learning: Song development in white-crowned sparrows. *Journal of Comparative and Physiological Psychology* 71: 1–25, 1970.

McCowan, B., and D. Reiss. Vocal learning in captive bottlenose dolphins: A comparison with human and nonhuman animals. In C. T. Snowdon and M. Hausberger, eds., *Social Influences on Vocal Development*, pp. 178–207. New York: Cambridge University Press, 1997.

Miller, D. B. Two-voiced phenomenon in birds: Further evidence. *Auk* 94: 567–572, 1977.

Patterson, D. K., and I. M. Pepperberg. A comparative study of human and parrot phonation: Acoustic and articulatory correlates of vowels. *Journal of the Acoustical Society of America* 96: 634–648, 1994.

Patterson, D. K., and I. M. Pepperberg. Acoustic and articulatory correlates of stop consonants in a parrot and a human subject. *Journal of the Acoustical Society of America* 106: 491–505, 1998.

Pepperberg, I. M. Functional vocalizations by an African Grey parrot (*Psittacus erithacus*). *Zeitschrift für Tierpsychologie* 55: 139–160, 1981.

Pepperberg, I. M. Cognition in the African Grey parrot: Preliminary evidence for auditory/vocal comprehension of the class concept. *Animal Learning and Behavior* 11: 179–185, 1983.

Pepperberg, I. M. Social modeling theory: A possible framework for understanding avian vocal learning. *Auk* 102: 854–864, 1985.

Pepperberg, I. M. Acquisition of anomalous communicatory systems: Implications for studies on interspecies communication. In R. Schusterman, J. Thomas, and F. Wood, eds., *Dolphin Behavior and Cognition: Comparative and Ecological Aspects*, pp. 289–302. Hillsdale, N.J.: Erlbaum, 1986a.

Pepperberg, I. M. Sensitive periods, social interaction, and song acquisition: The dialectics of dialects? *Behavioral and Brain Sciences* 9: 756–757, 1986b.

Pepperberg, I. M. Acquisition of the same/different concept by an African Grey parrot (*Psittacus erithacus*): Learning with respect to categories of color, shape, and material. *Animal Learning and Behavior* 15: 423–432, 1987a.

Pepperberg, I. M. Evidence for conceptual quantitative abilities in the African Grey parrot: Labeling of cardinal sets. *Ethology* 75: 37–61, 1987b.

Pepperberg, I. M. Interspecies communication: A tool for assessing conceptual abilities in the African Grey parrot (*Psittacus erithacus*). In G. Greenberg and E. Tobach, eds., *Cognition, Language, and Consciousness: Integrative Levels*, pp. 31–56. Hillsdale, N.J.: Erlbaum, 1987c.

Pepperberg, I. M. An interactive modeling technique for acquisition of communication skills: Separation of "labeling" and "requesting" in a psittacine subject. *Applied Psycholinguistics* 9: 59–76, 1988a.

Pepperberg, I. M. The importance of social interaction and observation in the acquisition of communicative competence: Possible parallels between avian and human learning. In T. R. Zentall and B. G. Galef Jr., eds., *Social Learning: Psychological and Biological Perspectives*, pp. 279–299. Hillsdale, N.J.: Erlbaum, 1988b.

Pepperberg, I. M. Cognition in an African Grey parrot (*Psittacus erithacus*): Further evidence for comprehension of categories and labels. *Journal of Comparative Psychology* 104: 41–52, 1990a.

Pepperberg, I. M. Some cognitive capacities of an African Grey parrot (*Psittacus erithacus*). In P. J. B. Slater, J. S. Rosenblatt, and C. Beer, eds., *Advances in the Study of Behavior*, vol. 19, pp. 357–409. New York: Academic Press, 1990b.

Pepperberg, I. M. Referential mapping: A technique for attaching functional significance to the innovative utterances of an African Grey parrot. *Applied Psycholinguistics* 11: 23–44, 1990c.

Pepperberg, I. M. A communicative approach to animal cognition: A study of conceptual abilities of an African Grey parrot. In C. A. Ristau, ed., *Cognitive Ethology: The Minds of Other Animals*, pp. 153–186. Hillsdale, N.J.: Erlbaum, 1991.

Pepperberg, I. M. Proficient performance of a conjunctive, recursive task by an African Grey parrot (*Psittacus erithacus*). *Journal of Comparative Psychology* 106: 295–305, 1992.

Pepperberg, I. M. A review of the effects of social interaction on vocal learning in African Grey parrots (*Psittacus erithacus*). *Netherlands Journal of Zoology* 43: 104–124, 1993.

Pepperberg, I. M. Evidence for numerical competence in an African Grey parrot (*Psittacus erithacus*). *Journal of Comparative Psychology* 108: 36–44, 1994a.

Pepperberg, I. M. Vocal learning in Grey Parrots (*Psittacus erithacus*): Effects of social interaction, reference, and context. *Auk* 111: 300–313, 1994b.

Pepperberg, I. M. Social influences on the acquisition of human-based codes in parrots and nonhuman primates. In C. T. Snowdon and M. Hausberger, eds., *Social Influences on Vocal Development*, pp. 157–177. New York: Cambridge University Press, 1997.

Pepperberg, I. M. *The Alex Studies: Cognitive and Communicative Studies on Grey Parrots*. Harvard University Press, Cambridge, MA, 1999.

Pepperberg, I. M., and M. V. Brezinsky. Acquisition of a relative class concept by an African Grey parrot (*Psittacus erithacus*): Discriminations based on relative size. *Journal of Comparative Psychology* 105: 286–294, 1991.

Pepperberg, I. M., and M. A. McLaughlin. Effect of avian-human joint attention on allospecific vocal learning by Grey parrots (*Psittacus erithacus*). *Journal of Comparative Psychology* 110: 286–297, 1996.

Pepperberg, I. M., and D. Sherman. Proposed use of two-part interactive modeling as a means to increase functional skills in children with a variety of disabilities. *Teaching and Learning in Medicine* 12: 213–220, 2000.

Pepperberg, I. M., and J. Silverstone. List learning by an African Grey parrot (*Psittacus erithacus*): Evidence for packaging and serial position effects. Unpublished manuscript.

Pepperberg, I. M., K. J. Brese, and B. J. Harris. Solitary sound play during acquisition of English vocalizations by an African Grey parrot (*Psittacus erithacus*): Possible parallels with children's monologue speech. *Applied Psycholinguistics* 12: 151–178, 1991.

Pepperberg, I. M., L. I. Gardiner, and L. J. Luttrell. Limited contextual vocal learning in the Grey parrot (*Psittacus erithacus*): the effect of interactive co-viewers on videotaped instruction. *Journal of Comparative Psychology* 113: 158–172, 1999.

Pepperberg, I. M., J. R. Naughton, and P. A. Banta. Allospecific vocal learning by Grey parrots (*Psittacus erithacus*): A failure of videotaped instruction under certain conditions. *Behavioural Processes* 42: 139–158, 1998.

Pepperberg, I. M., R. M. Sandefer, D. A. Noel, and C. P. Ellsworth. Vocal learning in the Grey parrot (*Psittacus erithacus*): Effect of species identity and number of trainers. *Journal of Comparative Psychology* 114: 371–380, 2000.

Peterson, G. E., and H. L. Barney. Control methods used in a study of the identification of vowels. *Journal of the Acoustical Society of America* 24: 175–184, 1952.

Petrinovich, L. Factors influencing song development in white-crowned sparrows (*Zonotrichia leucophrys*). *Journal of Comparative Psychology* 99: 15–29, 1985.

Remez, R., P. Rubin, L. Nygaard, and W. Howell. Perceptual normalization of vowels produced by sinusoidal voices. *Journal of Experimental Psychology: Human Perception and Performance* 13: 40–61, 1987.

Rice, M., Children with specific language impairment: Toward a model of teachability. In N. A. Krasnegor, D. M. Rumbaugh, R. L. Schiefelbusch, and M. Studdert-Kennedy, eds., *Biological and Behavioral Determinants of Language Development*, pp. 447–480. Hillsdale, N.J.: Erlbaum, 1991.

Rutledge, D. and I. M. Pepperberg. [Video studies of same/different.] Unpublished raw data, 1988.

Scanlan, J. Analysis of avian "speech": Patterns and production. Ph.D. diss., University College, London, 1988.

Shettleworth, S. J. *Cognition, Evolution, and Behaviour*. New York: Oxford University Press, 1998.

Silverstone, J. L. Numerical abilities in the African Grey parrot: Sequential numerical tags. Senior honors thesis, Northwestern University, 1989.

Smith, W. J. Animal communication and the study of cognition. In C. A. Ristau, ed., *Cognitive Ethology: The Minds of Other Animals*, pp. 209–230. Hillsdale, N.J.: Erlbaum, 1991.

St. Peters, M., A. C. Huston, and J. C. Wright. Television and families: Parental coviewing and young children's language development, social behavior, and television processing. Paper presented at the Society for Research in Child Development, Kansas City, KS, April 1989.

Thorpe, W. H. *Learning and Instinct in Animals*, 2d ed. Cambridge, Mass.: Harvard University Press, 1963.

Todt, D. Social learning of vocal patterns and modes of their applications in Grey parrots. *Zeitschrift für Tierpsychologie* 39: 178–188, 1975.

Vanayan, M., H. A. Robertson, and G. B. Biederman. Observational learning in pigeons: The effects of model proficiency on observer performance. *Journal of General Psychology* 112: 349–357, 1985.

Warren, D. K., D. K. Patterson, and I. M. Pepperberg. Mechanisms of American English vowel production in a Grey parrot (*Psittacus erithacus*). *Auk* 113: 41–58, 1996.

Zahorian, S. A., and A. J. Jagharghi. Spectral-shape features versus formants as acoustic correlates for vowels. *Journal of the Acoustical Society of America* 94: 1966–1982, 1993.

5   On Avian Imitation: Cognitive and Ethological Perspectives

Johannes Fritz and Kurt Kotrschal

5.1   Introduction

Cognition research in animals has thrived during the past few decades. Kamil (1998) refers to a "cognitive revolution" and advocates that this field of research needs to be combined with the Darwinian revolution. He used the term *cognitive ethology*, first defined by D. Griffin (1978), to characterize the field that synthesizes the Darwinian perspectives of contemporary ethology with the cognitive perspectives of psychology.

The field of social learning may be considered typical for this "cognitive revolution." It was developed primarily by psychologists who employed animals as models in laboratory experiments. The aim was primarily to investigate the continuity and generality of cognitive processes and mechanisms across species. However, biologists, especially ethologists, also study learning, but often with an evolutionary and functional focus. In general, research on social learning, which requires the social interaction and coordination of individuals (Coussi-Korbell and Fragaszy 1995), sometimes suffers from overly sterile, "nonsocial," laboratory situations and from a weak theoretical framework. The mechanism of imitation may serve as an example to point out the heuristic potential of "cognitive ethology."

As stressed by several sections of this book, another innovation in cognitive research that is well on its way involves modeling and the use of robots. Such approaches may help to integrate cognitive and ethological perspectives because modeling and simulation require simple and workable definitions of mechanisms and conditions (see Noble and Todd 1999).

In the following section (5.2), we give an overview of the research on imitation and related social cognitive mechanisms, restricting our examples to bird species. Research on this topic was mainly carried out under laboratory conditions. In section 5.3, we stress that an ethological approach is needed to tackle the functions of the learning mechanisms. Finally (5.4), we will reach some suggestions for a synthesis of the cognitive and ethological approaches.

5.2 Cognitive Approach

The majority of work on learning by observation was carried out on birds. They are primarily visually oriented and, therefore, research is less confounded by the potential influence of olfactory perception than in the case of mammals. Within the present framework we cannot include all empirical and theoretical studies performed over the last years, therefore we focus on studies that seem particularly pertinent to our present focus.

Nonimitative Socially Mediated Learning

Understanding imitation learning is facilitated by contrasting it with alternative, nonimitative social learning mechanisms. In the following, we present two examples of the transmission of feeding traditions in free-living birds where, at first glance, imitation seemed to be involved. However, for both examples, experimental laboratory studies indicated that nonimitative social mechanisms were sufficient to explain the formation of these traditions.

MILK BOTTLE OPENING BY BLUE TITS

In Great Britain, milk bottles are traditionally delivered at the doors of homes. Blue tits (*Parus caeruleus*) started to puncture bottle tops in order to gain access to the cream on top of the milk. This behavior became relatively common in a few isolated areas of Great Britain rather than appearing randomly all over the island. Therefore, Fisher and Hinde (1949) suggested that this innovation had been initiated independently in those areas by a few birds and was subsequently acquired by others as a result of interactions with milk-bottle-opening individuals. However, the authors emphasized that analyzing social influences on the spread of this skill required controlled experiments, which were later carried out by Sherry and Galef (1984, 1990). They exposed black-capped chickadees (*Parus atricapillus*) to a trained conspecific, who demonstrated the opening of milk bottle tops. In another group, the individuals' attention was drawn to a conspecific who just fed from opened bottles. Subsequently, birds in both groups were more likely to open bottles on their own than a third group, which had observed just an empty cage containing a closed milk bottle. Thus, birds observing a conspecific just drinking did as well as birds observing a conspecific opening the bottle before feeding. Sherry and Galef (1990) concluded that socially mediated processes other than imitation may have increased the frequency with which free-living British tits had learned to open milk bottles. The following example on behavioral transmission in a flock of geese points in the same direction.

BUTTERBURE BITING BY GREYLAG GEESE

In 1973, Konrad Lorenz established a free-living, semitame flock of Greylag geese (*Anser anser*) in the Upper Austrian Valley of the river Alm, which, over the years, fluctuated at around 130 individuals. In 1997, three geese were observed to bite through the stems of butterbure leaves (*Petasites hybridus*). During the following years, an increasing number of individuals began to bite and chew butterbure stems and at the end of the summer, 40 geese showed this behavior. In 1999, the number of stem biters increased to 95 individuals (Fritz, Bisenberger, and Kotrschal 1999). Within families, this behavior spread particularly fast. Ganders could be observed biting butterbure stems and that possibly attracted the attention of the goslings. As soon as a gosling had arrived, the gander stopped biting and left the stems to the exploring offspring. Therefore, as in the case of milk bottle opening, social influences were assumed to be involved in the spread of this tradition.

To examine the mechanisms involved, we performed an experiment with Greylag goslings (Fritz, Bisenberger, and Kotschal in press), which were hand-raised and, therefore, socially imprinted on humans. The task was to open the gliding lid of a box that contained pieces of apple (figure 5.1). To each of seven observer individuals, a human experimenter first tapped at a wooden handle on the lid and then pushed it open to disclose the reward. The seven naive control individuals were provisioned with the same reward, but out of the already open box. After these training trials, test trials followed. The closed box was presented for 30 seconds to each of the observer and the control individuals. In an alternation of training and test trials, all tutored observers learned to perform the task by manipulating the wooden handle whereas only one of the untutored control individuals succeeded. The observers also showed higher overall manipulation frequencies than the controls. In particular, they exhibited a higher frequency of wooden handle manipulations, which the tutor had tapped at and which allowed the opening of the lid (figure 5.2). Thus, our results indicate that the higher performance of the observers was due to their intense and handle-oriented exploratory behavior. This is evidence against

Figure 5.1 Opening of the experimental box by a Greylag goose. The lid could be pushed open at the wooden bar, offering the apple pieces beneath to the goose. The human tutor tapped at the bar to enhance the attention of the observer individuals.

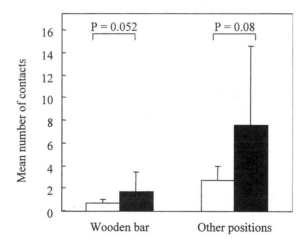

Figure 5.2 Mean + SD number of contacts with the wooden bar (compare figure 5.1) and other positions on the experimental box during the four trials of the first session in six unsuccessful controls (open rectangles) and the preopening trials of the first session in six successful observers (solid rectangles). To the observers, a human tutor demonstrated opening at the wooden bar, whereas the controls remained naive. Probability based on the Mann-Whitney U test.

imitation learning, where the observers would have been expected to solve the task by copying the motor pattern without so much exploration being necessary (Galef 1988; Bugnyar and Huber 1997).

NONIMITATIVE SOCIAL MECHANISMS

In both milk bottle opening and butterbure feeding, the birds seemed to learn a response reinforcer relationship (R-S learning) in a nonsocial way by trial and error,[1] which was accelerated in the observers. Therefore, Sherry and Galef (1990) suggested two possible nonimitative mechanisms as being involved in the transmission of the milk bottle opening behavior. First, the activity of competent birds may leave partially or entirely opened bottles to others, which then learn by themselves in the demonstrator's absence. This does not require the immediate interaction of the individuals. Second, the presence and activity of a conspecific on a bottle may simply enhance the attention of the naive bird toward this bottle.

In the Greylag geese, we could observe that the goslings' attention was attracted toward a particular butterbure stem when a gander bit there. The gander immediately stopped manipulating when a gosling arrived, which allowed the offspring to explore the partially or totally bitten stem. However, in our box-opening experiment, exploration opportunities did not differ between the observers and control individuals. The only additional source of information for the observers compared to that of the control individuals was the tutor's behavior. Therefore, we assumed that the socially enhanced attention toward the wooden bar (stimulus enhancement[2]) was responsible for the observers' performance.

STIMULUS ENHANCEMENT

Stimulus enhancement is defined as drawing an observer's attention to a particular object in the environment, where the individual then learns on its own (Zentall 1996; Giraldeau 1997). Heyes (1994) defined this as nonassociative one-stimulus learning (S-learning), referring to the theory of individual learning. Since paying attention to the actions of conspecifics in the contexts of feeding or predator avoidance is of high survival value, stimulus enhancement seems to be a general mechanism common to socially living animals. In several studies of socially mediated learning in birds it is discussed as the underlying mechanism (e.g., Krebs, Mac

Roberts, and Cullen 1972; Wechsler 1988) or, more often, as a possible alternative and more parsimonious explanation to imitation (see Fragaszy and Visalberghi 1996; Zentall 1996; Shettleworth 1998).

Stimulus enhancement seems to influence the observer in two ways. First, it focuses the observer's attention toward the specific stimulus and, second, it motivates the observer to act in a sustained way. For example, during the initial session of the study with Greylag geese (Fritz, Bisenberger, and Kotrschal in press), the observers tended to contact the position where the demonstrator had opened the lid more often as compared to the controls, whereas the manipulation frequencies at positions other than the bar were only slightly increased in the observers (figure 5.2). Therefore, due to observation of the tutor's behavior, observers focused their manipulation effort toward the relevant side and, additionally, manipulated more intensely and persistently.

Fryday and Greig-Smith (1994) reached similar conclusions in experiments with house sparrows (*Passer domesticus*), which were tested for their choice of red or yellow-colored food after observing a trained conspecific that fed on only one of the two colors. Compared to control birds, who were shown colored food without a model present, observers revealed a preference for the color chosen by the model and, additionally, they consumed more food.

This sparrow experiment does not reveal whether the demonstrator just drew the attention toward seeds of a specific color (S-learning; stimulus enhancement) or whether the bird learned by observation that seeds of a specific color were palatable (S-S learning; observational conditioning; Shettleworth 1998). In an additional experiment, Fryday and Greig-Smith (1994) could exclude observational conditioning. Again, the house sparrows had to choose one of two differently colored food patches, but now the model's food was quinine-treated. Therefore, if the observers learned by observation that the food chosen by the model was unpalatable (S-S learning), they should avoid it. This was not the case. On the contrary, the observers still preferred the food chosen by the model. This is consistent with results from rats (*Rattus norvegicus*; Galef, Wigmore, and Kennett 1993; Galef 1996; Tuci, Noble, and Todd 1999), where naive rats showed a substantial increase in preference for whatever food a demonstrator had eaten, regardless of whether the demonstrator was well or was suffering from gastrointestinal distress afterward.

The failure to learn to avoid food by observing others indicates that the observers do not associate the stimulus in question, whether it is a location in space, a kind of food, or a specific food smell, with the physical or even mental state of the demonstrator. Associative learning mainly seems to occur when the observer contacts and explores the stimulus on his own. This underlines the conclusion that in all the examples described above, stimulus enhancement (S-learning) was involved rather than imitation or observational conditioning.

Vocal Imitation

Many bird species learn elements of their song by listening to other individuals. Numerous studies have focused on the mechanism of vocal imitation (for reviews see Catchpole and Slater 1995; Shettleworth 1998) as well as on the function of learned songs (e.g., Marler et al. 1986; Kroodsma and Byers 1991; Nicol and Pope 1996). Even if details of avian vocal imitation vary markedly from one species to another (Slater 1989) it is regarded as having common features in determining long-lasting effects as a result of experiences during a sensitive period in which there is a preference for a species-specific quality of acoustic stimuli. In a way, this resembles sexual imprinting (Bolhuis 1991; Shettleworth 1998) and, therefore, is regarded as a specific kind of imitation. In contrast to motor imitation, however, the motor performance of the syrinx is not *visible* but the result is *audible*. Therefore, the learner can match its own vocal output to that heard from a model (equimodality).

Motor Imitation

Shettleworth (1998) assumes that the equimodality in song learning may be one of the reasons why this kind of imitation is common. Motor imitation, in contrast, implies that the observer must match the received visual inputs of an observed behavior with the proprioceptive feedback of its own motor action, what is called *visual-tactile cross-modal performance* (Meltzoff 1990; Heyes 1993). Therefore, motor imitation is considered to be the cognitively most demanding category of social learning (Galef 1988; Heyes 1993; Zentall 1996).

Even though the observation of skilled conspecifics often results in a matching behavior on the part of the observer, all studies failed to a varying degree to exclude the possibility of forms of social learning other than imitation. A general problem when working on social learning, and on motor imitation in particular, is the need for a diverse theoretical and methodological background in order to distinguish between the mechanisms. A wealth of definitions on imitation exist (Galef 1988; Zentall 1996), some of them including mental states such as "goal directedness," "perspective taking," or "mind reading" (see Whiten and Ham 1992; Zentall 1996; Heyes 1998), whereas other authors confine themselves to more operational definitions (Galef 1988; Heyes 1994). In contrast to psychologists, whose interest mainly rests at the cognitive mechanism, anthropologists and behavioral ecologists mainly focus on the functions of social-learning mechanisms for the acquisition and social transmission of behavior (Galef 1988; Shettleworth 1998). Consequently, the term *imitation* is often used in a rather general manner for processes leading to the forming of traditions.

Thus, so far there is still disagreement as to what "true" motor imitation is. As Shettleworth (1998) put it, imitation seems to be what is left over when all other conceivable routes for social learning have been ruled out (Zentall 1996). Therefore, the recent scarcity of conclusive studies for motor imitation abilities reflects methodological difficulties rather than a lack of imitation abilities in animals. Fortunately, recent studies have used more sophisticated experimental designs.

Research on Imitation Learning in Birds

MOVEMENT IMITATION

In a study on imitation learning in a Grey parrot (*Psittacus erithacus*) Moore (1992, 1996) used an ingenious method to eliminate the possibility of stimulus enhancement by focusing on the imitation of body movements rather than of goal-directed actions. The bird lived alone in a big laboratory room and was visited several times a day by an experimenter who performed various stereotyped movements, labeled by an identifying word or phrase. For example, the experimenter waved his hand while saying "ciao" or opened his mouth saying "look at my tongue." The parrot mimicked the movements together with the appropriate word or phrase, using its wings to simulate hand waving. By combining the movement with a label, imitation could be distinguished from behaviors resembling that of the human experimenter by chance.

Moore concluded that the parrot performed a great variety of movements, many of them novel and without explicit reinforcement, and, therefore, that the bird exhibited true movement imitation. However, the study was criticized for methodological features and for being too anecdotal (Shettleworth 1998). For example, the parrot was raised by humans and preexperiences with human movements could not be excluded. Even though this may not be an example of imitation, it is still an amazing instance of social learning by using existent physical actions in different contexts.

ACTION IMITATION

In contrast to the latter example, most studies on imitation employ goal-directed actions and since actions are related to specific stimuli, this approach requires controls for stimulus enhancement. The most widely acknowledged method to test for imitation skills was first developed by Dawson and Foss (1965) and has come to be known as the *two-action test* (Zentall 1996). In their experiment, budgerigars (*Melopsittacus undulatus*) watched demonstrators removing a lid from a food bowl either by stepping with their foot or by pecking with their bill. Thus, they moved the lid the same way but by either one of two topographically distinct behaviors. After observation, the observers preferred the method shown by the demonstrator. However, when Galef, Manzig, and Field (1986) replicated the experiment, they found only a transient effect of marginal significance.

In the following years, a number of experiments with variations of the two-action procedure followed (for a review, see Heyes and Galef 1996). One of the most revealing experiments was done with Japanese quail (*Coturnix japonica*) with a method similar to that used for the budgerigars (Akins and Zentall 1996). Again, the individuals had to uncover a food tray either by pecking with their bill or by stepping on it with their leg. Since the observers showed a clear preference for the version demonstrated by a trained conspecific model (figure 5.3), the authors concluded that this experiment provides strong evidence for motor imitation in these birds. In an additional experiment, Akins and Zentall (1998) confirmed their previous findings and found that the quails imitated a behavior only if they also observed that the demonstrator was rewarded.

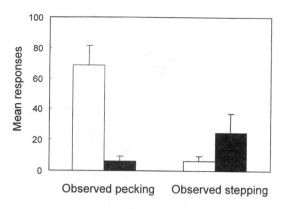

Figure 5.3 The mean + SEM frequency of pecks (open rectangles) and steps (solid rectangles) that were made by quails that observed pecking and by those that observed stepping for the first 5 min of the 30-min session. (Redrawn from Akins and Zentall 1996, with permission)

However, this evidence for imitative abilities was questioned since the motor patterns being copied were not novel or unusual behaviors, and, therefore, the observation of the models' behavior may have increased the probability of performing a contagious behavior (social facilitation; e.g., Campbell, Heyes, and Goldsmith 1999).

In the studies described above, the birds had to use two different parts of the body to perform the same task. In contrast, in a study by Lefebvre and colleagues (1997a) Carib grackles (*Quiscalus mexicanus*) had to remove a plug with their bill in two different directions, either by pecking it downward or by pulling it upward. One observer group could watch a trained conspecific using its open beak to pull the plug on a horizontal stick, whereas another group of observers watched a Zenaida dove pecking the plug downward with its closed beak. Consequently, individuals were more likely to perform the opening technique they observed. Even though the demonstrators were of a different species, the authors interpreted the result as evidence of imitative learning.

A similar experiment was done with European starlings (*Sturnus vulgaris*, Campbell, Heyes, and Goldsmith 1999). Observers watched a trained conspecific using its beak to remove one of two differently colored plugs from a hole. Both plugs could be removed by either pulling or pushing (two object/two action paradigm). There was a clear preference of the observer birds for the color as well as a for the opening technique demonstrated by the model. The preference for a color was interpreted as learning about a stimulus by observation, either by enhancement (S learning) or observational conditioning (S-S learning) whereas the preference for the technique was interpreted as motor imitation.

However, Campbell, Heyes, and Goldsmith (1999) discussed an alternative explanation to motor imitation for the behavioral matching in their own experiment as well as in the study with Carib grackles (Lefebvre et al. 1997a). The plug moved in different directions when the demonstrator pulled or pecked. Therefore, the observers may not have learned about the behavior of the demonstrators but about the different movements of the plug (emulation) or different positions of the removed plug (observational conditioning). An experimental way to investigate the possibilities would be to test observers in the absence of a demonstrator with an automatically moving plug. If *then* the observers show no bias in the direction of the plug, the evidence for motor imitation would be strengthened.

5.3 Ethological Approach

All these studies on imitation learning were carried out under laboratory conditions, involving the physical separation of the model and the observer in two compartments of the test apparatus (double-cage procedure). This may be suitable to test for general abilities and the presence of a specific learning mechanism. However, the ability and readiness to employ motor imitation or other learning mechanisms in a social context is not only a function of the species' evolutionary history and individual cognitive abilities, but seems to depend on the specific social and ecological conditions, notably on dyadic relationships and the profitability of the tactics employed (Coussi-Korbell and Fragaszy 1995; Fragaszy and Visalberghi 1996). Therefore, studies dealing with the social, ecological, and life history contexts of social learning are needed.

In the following section, we focus on food scrounging, which, for individuals in groups, is an alternative tactic to the execution of the food-producing task. Scrounging is defined as the ability to profit from food disclosed by a conspecific producer, who is experienced in performing the food-producing task (producer) (Giraldeau and Lefebvre 1987). Different studies indicate that the ability to scrounge inhibits individuals from learning the relevant task or, at the group level, prevents the transmission of the behavior (e.g., Barnard and Sibly 1981; Giraldeau and Lefebvre 1987; Beauchamp and Kacelnik 1991). However, theoretical models

(Coussi-Korbell and Fragaszy 1995; Fragaszy and Visalberghi 1996) and empirical studies (e.g., Prato Previde and Poli 1996; Terkel 1996; Fritz and Kotrschal 1999a) indicate that the opportunity to share a food source together with a producer may also support learning and further behavioral transmission. Based on a comparison of our study (Fritz and Kotrschal 1999a) with two other experiments (Nicol and Pope 1994; Giraldeau and Lefebvre 1987), we will in the following section develop a model of the relationship between scrounging and learning.

Social Learning in Common Ravens

In a study on semicaptive, hand-raised common ravens (*Corvus corax*; Fritz and Kotrschal 1999a) the double-cage procedure was avoided in order to investigate whether the presence of a conspecific can promote the acquisition of a motor task. Single observers were allowed to interact with a trained conspecific model at an experimental arena, which contained a superfluous number of testing devices (dyadic principle). To access three small pieces of meat out of a box, the birds had to open a lid in one of two ways, either by levering a lid open with the raven sitting on top of it, or by pulling the lid open while standing in front of the box (figure 5.4). When confronting experimentally naive individuals ($N = 6$) with the boxes, all of them opened the lids exclusively by levering. However, when a trained model demonstrated pulling, all observer birds ($N = 3$) initially showed both opening techniques, pulling (P) and levering (L; frequency within the first three actions of the observer birds: LPP, PLP, PLL). In two observer birds the pulling rates declined rapidly, and finally, they opened almost exclusively

Figure 5.4 A common raven opening one of the two lids of a box by pulling at the flap as demonstrated by the trained models. Alternatively, the lid could be opened by pushing at the inner rim of the lid while sitting on top of the box.

by levering, whereas the third observer retained pulling at a relatively high frequency over the entire duration of the experiment.

Usually, the two actions can be performed at the same part of the test apparatus to control for enhancement effects. In our experiment, however, the initial position of the test individual differed. Therefore, both motor imitation and stimulus enhancement were discussed as possible learning mechanisms involved.

Producing and Scrounging

Initially, the observer and the model were simultaneously present at the experimental arena. They remained within close spatial proximity to one another, offering the observer the opportunity to scrounge food disclosed by its conspecific. Even though the model tolerated the observer's scrounging attempts, all observers soon began to produce food on their own by either pulling or levering the lid open. Thus, the observers' fast acquisition of the appropriate skill shows that scrounging does not necessarily inhibit learning.

However, these data contrast with the outcome of a study by Nicol and Pope (1994) with domestic hens (*Gallus domesticus*), which had to learn a discrimination task by pecking the correct one of two differently colored keys in order to access food. First, a group of observer individuals were tested in a classical double-cage procedure, observing a trained conspecific model, which demonstrated pecking of the correct key behind a Perspex partition wall. Under such conditions, the observers did better than experimentally naive individuals in a control group. Thereafter, a group of observers was tested under the same conditions, but with the partition removed during the demonstration phase. These individuals did worse as compared to control individuals without a trained conspecific, indicating that being together has a negative influence on social learning.

Giraldeau and Lefebvre (1987) reached corresponding conclusions in their study with pigeons (*Columbia livia*). Their setup consisted of a row of 48 test tubes. Five randomly selected tubes contained two grams of millet seed each. To get access to the food, a pigeon had to peck on a wooden stick, causing the seeds to fall to the ground. In a group of 16 inexperienced pigeons only two became producers during 27 sessions of two hours each. All other individuals scrounged instead. However, when pairs of experienced and naive individuals were tested in a double-cage procedure, which prevents scrounging, the task to produce food was learned rapidly by each of the inexperienced observers. The authors concluded that the opportunity for scrounging appears to limit the cultural transmission of innovations.

A Model on the Relationship between Scrounging and Learning

We suggest that the relationship between scrounging and learning depends mainly on the social relationship between the producer and the scrounger (social conditions) and the quality and distribution of the food disclosed by a producer (ecological conditions; Fritz and Kotrschal 1999b).

The model is based on four assumptions: (1) Naive individuals have three opportunities to access the food. They can either scrounge, or learn by using social information (social learning; Heyes 1994), or learn on their own (asocial learning; Heyes 1994). (2) Scrounging reduces the costs of exploitation (Barnard and Sibly 1981) and, therefore, naive individuals in the presence of an experienced producer initially try to access the food by scrounging. (3) Whether an individual remains a scrounger or changes to another tactic depends upon the profitability and, therefore, on the ecological and social conditions. (4) Scrounging, as well as learning by observation, requires close proximity between the experienced and the inexperienced individual. Thus, for the naive individual, the ability to stay close to the experienced individual is a predictor for both the opportunity to scrounge and to learn by observation (Coussi-Korbell and Fragaszy 1995).

SOCIAL CONDITIONS

The studies with hens (Nicol and Pope 1994) and ravens (Fritz and Kotrschal 1999a) differ with respect to the social interactions of the observer and the model at the apparatus. In the study of Nicol and Pope (1994), three models seemed constrained to peck in the presence of observers because they occasionally turned and threatened the nearby conspecific. Two other hen models initially performed the task and were then displaced by the observers. Therefore, the decline in the performance of the hens without separation seemed to be due to aggressive dyadic interactions (figure 5.5). In contrast, the raven siblings, tested a few weeks after fledging, showed no aggressive interactions, and after opening the lid, the model accessed the reward together with the observer in all three model-

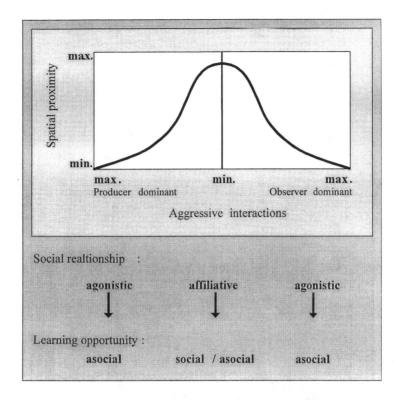

Figure 5.5   Model of the influence of the social relationship within a model-observer dyad. The model considers for a food resource, which has to be disclosed repeatedly. The spatial proximity between the two individuals (y-axis) is related to their social relationship, where the number of aggressive interactions serves as parameter (for x-axis). The more aggression occurs, the greater distance the individuals have to maintain between one another. The mean distance between the individuals is assumed to determine the opportunity to scrounge or to acquire information by observation (social learning). For both scrounging and learning, the conditions are optimal in an affiliative dyadic system where the individuals can stay in close proximity to one another. The probability that a scrounger should learn to perform the task on his own depends on his efficiency compared to that of the producer. If he gains the same amount of food as the producer he should remain a scrounger, if he gains less food it pays to become a producer. In an agonistic dyadic system, however, scrounging as well as social learning is restricted and individual learning remains as the proper tactic.

observer dyads. So, all of them first scrounged and then changed to perform the task using information gained by observation of the conspecific (social learning; figure 5.5).

ECOLOGICAL CONDITIONS

Comparing the studies with pigeons (Giraldeau and Lefebvre 1987) and ravens (Fritz and Kotrschal 1999a), no aggressive encounters occurred and naive birds had the opportunity to stay in close proximity to conspecifics. However, in contrast to the ravens, most pigeons remained scroungers. When comparing the experimental conditions, the quantity and distribution of the food and, therefore, the profitability of scrounging, differed markedly. For the pigeons, each apparatus contained numerous seeds (two grams). Pecking by the producer caused the food to fall to the ground and the producer as well as the scroungers had unrestricted access. Thus, the scroungers' tactic was at least as profitable as being a producer. In the experiment with the ravens, however, each compartment contained only three small pieces of meat. The producer obtained most of it before the observer arrived and, therefore, only 23–50% of the observers' scrounging trials were successful in gaining one of the three pieces of meat. Therefore, in the pigeons, the scroungers were successful scramble competitors, whereas in the ravens they were not.

We conclude that if the individuals stay in an *affiliative* social relationship, the scrounger's success in competing for the food seems to be crucial in determining whether scrounging prevents an individual from learning a task. If the scroungers' payoff is at least as high as that of the producers at the food source, scroungers should remain with their tactic. However, if the scroungers' payoff is lower than that of the producers' it pays to become a producer (figure 5.5).

5.4 Toward a Cognitive Ethology

Imitation, as any other cognitive mechanism, can only be regarded as a "natural" system and thus, as a topic of biological research, if it can be tackled and explained at the four levels of research introduced by Tinbergen (1963)[3]: all cognitive "mechanisms" should have (1) an evolutionary function (fitness consequence), (2) an underlying physiological mechanism, (3) an ontogenetic development, and (4) an evolutionary history. To explain a biological/

behavioral system, all four levels of Tinbergen need to be considered (Kamil 1998; Shettleworth 1998).

It becomes clear that blackbox approaches—considering the organism just as an input-output machine—suffer from severe heuristic limitations. Ontogeny and evolutionary history as well as physiological mechanisms may constrain behavior and, therefore, from the ethological point of view, a cognitive "mechanism" has to be investigated synthetically at all Tinbergian levels, called the field of cognitive ethology (Kamil 1998). In the following section we refer to the four levels to point out some lines of present synthetic research on social learning.

Physiological Mechanism

Research on imitation during the last decades employed more and more sophisticated definitions and adequate experimental setups. However, as pointed out in section 5.2, no conclusive evidence for imitation learning yet exists, neither in birds nor in other animals. The main reason for this discrepancy is the lack of a proper understanding of the physiological mechanism of motor imitation. In general, it was regarded as a "special" kind of social learning, that involves complex cognitive processes (see Galef 1988; Heyes 1999). However, recent developments cast doubt on this assumption. For example, Heyes (1999) proposes an "Associative Sequence Learning Theory" for imitation, suggesting that imitation is mediated by associative processes, which require no complex form of cognitive representation and cross-modal performance (see chapter 19 of this volume, written by C. Heyes).

An empirical step forward in the understanding of the cognitive mechanism is the finding of so called "mirror neurons" in the motor cortex of monkeys, which show the same firing pattern when the individual performs a single action or when it observes a human performing the same action (Rizzolatti et al. 1996). These neurons may be the unit allowing an observer to equate visual information with its own motor actions (visual tactile cross-modal performance; see section "Motor Imitation" and Heyes 1993). Despite these few open windows into the nervous system, the physiology behind the psychological phenomenon of social learning will remain hard to tackle. This is one of the reasons for the importance of models and simulations to generate hypotheses on the underlying mechanisms (Noble and Todd 1999).

Evolutionary Functions

In several studies with the two-action method, the observers first learned the more complex task, as demonstrated by the model. However, after an intervening trial-and-error phase, the observer usually changed to the more efficient opportunity to obtain the reward (e.g., Zentall, Sutton, and Sherburne 1996; Kaiser, Zentall, and Galef 1997; Bugnyar and Huber 1997; Fritz and Kotrschal 1999a). These findings are relevant for two reasons. First, imitation was often assumed to have an important function for the transmission of innovative behaviors (Galef 1988; Heyes 1993). However, the formation of a tradition requires not only an efficient way to acquire the behavior but also mechanisms to insulate it from modification (Heyes 1993; Fritz and Kotrschal 1999b; see section 5.3). Second, the assumption that imitation is the "Lamborghini" of social learning mechanisms (Giraldeau 1997) together with some remnant *scala-naturae* thinking may lead to the seemingly widespread idea that the ability for motor imitation may increase with increasing "intelligence" and exploratory abilities. From an evolutionary perspective, this is not necessarily the case. Motor imitation may be a quick way to learn a complex task, but it may not always be most adaptive, because it involves the risk of acquiring inefficient or even obsolete solutions. Artificial life simulations reach corresponding conclusions (Baldassarre and Parisi 1999). Thus, in terms of evolutionary function and adaptiveness, motor imitation may rather be a streetcar than a Lamborghini. It seems reasonable to examine under which conditions other mechanisms, like socially accelerated learning by trial and error, may be more functional than imitation in allowing an individual to generate optimal solutions and to learn more details about an object or a task than by motor imitation.

Ontogenetical Function

The ontogeny of imitation is an ill-researched field. At what time during life history are social mechanisms of learning employed and most beneficial for the individual, and what are the social/kinship relationships between potential tutors and observers? Some studies indicate that the parents' behavior in families accelerate learning on the side of the offspring. For example, Nicol and Pope (1994, 1996) found that the feeding display of the hen guides the young chicks to the food and that the hen responds with a high intensity of display if the chicks peck at the wrong items. In Greylag geese, we found that the gander leaves food he started to feed from to the arriving offspring. With increasing age, goslings become less attracted by the feeding behavior of the parents (Fritz, Bisenberger, and Kotrschal 2001). Corresponding with these findings, theoretical models are based on the assumption that the affiliative family group offers the best opportunities for close observation of experienced conspecifics, mainly of the parents (section 5.3; Coussi-Korbell and Fragaszy 1995; Fritz and Kotrschal 1999b). These findings also seem to indicate that the importance of, and readiness for, social learning changes during life history and with the social context. Further research is needed on this topic and it may be appropriate to consider age and social relationships when testing for social learning.

Evolutionary History

Early ethologists already maintained that different species have different learning capacities as a consequence of their evolutionary histories (innate schoolmaster concept; Lorenz 1943). This concept was rejected by behaviorists. However, today there is a broad acceptance that, even though the basic learning mechanisms are common to most animals, differences exist between species and even between individuals in their capabilities for learning. For example, Kotrschal, Van Staaden, and Huber (1998) showed that different fish species excel in different sensory domains and Lofebvre and colleagues (1997b, 1998) found a positive correlation between the relative forebrain size and the number of observed behavioral innovations in numerous bird species. Both findings indicate quantitative differences in learning abilities between species. Existing models on the evolutionary history of imitation learning are primarily speculative (e.g., Moore 1996). Thus, further models of and simulations on the evolution of imitation are necessary, related to new findings at all levels of research mentioned above.

Conclusion

A tentative conclusion on the present state of social learning in birds and other animals is easy to draw: speculations by far exceed what we know. This underlines the great importance of modeling and simulation in feedback with empirical research on social learning. Investigations along the lines of Tinbergen's four levels are needed to test the predictions gained from the models and, in turn, also to generate the necessary database for further modeling.

Acknowledgments

We are grateful to T. Bugnyar, J. Daisley, and J. Kendal for comments on the manuscript. Financial support came from the Austrian Academy of Science (grant for J. F.) and the FWF (project no. P 12472-BIO).

Notes

1. In contrast, referring to Heyes (1994), imitation is a special case of R-S learning, in which the individual does not learn due to trial-and-error but as a result of observing the model that performs the task.
2. Some authors distinguish between local enhancement and stimulus enhancement, where the former focuses the attention just to a single location and in the latter case the observer's attention is focused to stimuli of a specific quality. However, most experiments do not allow that distinction to be made (Galef 1988). Therefore, following Heyes (1994), we use the term *stimulus enhancement* only.
3. Tinbergen's paper (1963) was dedicated to Konrad Lorenz's sixtieth birthday. It systematizes the Lorenz-Tinbergen approach to behavioral research.

References

Akins, C. K., and T. R. Zentall. Imitative learning in male Japanese quail (*Coturnix japonica*) using the two-action method. *Journal of Comparative Psychology* 110: 316–320, 1996.

Akins, C. K., and T. R. Zentall. Imitation in Japanese quail: The role of reinforcement of demonstrator responding. *Psychonomic Bulletin and Review* 5: 694–697, 1998.

Baldassarre, G., and D. Parisi. Trial-and-error learning, noise, and selection in cultural evolution: A study through artificial life simulation. In K. Dautenhahn and C. Nehaniv, eds., *Proceedings of the AISB'99 Symposium on Imitation in Animals and Artifacts (7–9 April 1999)*. Brighton, U.K.: Society for the Study of Artificial Intelligence and Simulation of Behaviour, 1999.

Barnard, C. J., and R. M. Sibly. Producers and scroungers: A general model and its application to captive flocks of house sparrows. *Animal Behaviour* 29: 543–550, 1981.

Beauchamp, G., and A. Kacelnik. Effects of knowledge of partners on learning rates in zebra finches, *Taeniopygia guttata*. *Animal Behaviour* 41: 247–253, 1991.

Bolhuis, J. J. Mechanisms of avian imprinting: A review. *Biological Review* 66: 303–345, 1991.

Bugnyar, T., and L. Huber. Push or pull: An experimental study on imitation in marmosets. *Animal Behaviour* 54: 817–831, 1997.

Campbell, F. M., C. M. Heyes, and A. R. Goldsmith. Simultaneous testing for stimulus learning and response learning by observation in the European starling, *Sturnus vulgaris*, using a two object/two action test. *Animal Behaviour* 58: 151–158, 1999.

Catchpole, C. K., and P. J. B. Slater. *Bird Song: Biological Themes and Variations*. Cambridge, UK: Cambridge University Press, 1995.

Coussi-Korbell, S., and D. M. Fragaszy. On the relationship between social dynamics and social learning. *Animal Behaviour* 50: 1441–1453, 1995.

Custance, D. M., A. Whiten, and T. Fredman. Social learning of an artificial fruit task in capuchin monkeys (*Cebus apella*). *Journal of Comparative Psychology* 113: 13–23, 1999.

Dautenhahn, K., and C. Nehaniv, eds., *Proceedings of the AISB'99 Symposium on Imitation in Animals and Artifacts (7–9 April 1999)*. Brighton, U.K.: Society for the Study of Artificial Intelligence and Simulation of Behaviour, 1999.

Dawson, B. V., and B. M. Foss. Observational learning in budgerigars. *Animal Behaviour* 4: 222–232, 1965.

Fisher, M. S., and R. A. Hinde. The opening of milk bottles by birds. *British Birds* 42: 347–357, 1949.

Fragaszy, D. M., and E. Visalberghi. Social learning in monkeys: Primate "primacy" reconsidered. In C. M. Heyes and B. G. Galef Jr., eds., *Social Learning in Animals: The Roots of Culture*. San Diego: Academic Press, 1996.

Fritz, J., and K. Kotrschal. Social learning in common ravens, *Corvus corax*. *Animal Behaviour* 57: 785–793, 1999a.

Fritz, J., and K. Kotrschal. Social constraints and profitability of social learning. In K. Dautenhahn and C. Nehaniv, eds., *Proceedings of the AISB'99 Symposium on Imitation in Animals and Artifacts (7–9 April 1999)*, pp. 20–26. Brighton, U.K.: Society for the Study of Artificial Intelligence and Simulation of Behaviour, 1999b.

Fritz, J., A. Bisenberger, and K. Kotrschal. Social mediated learning of an operant task in Greylag geese: Field observation and experimental evidence. *Advances in Ethology* 34: 51, 1999.

Fritz, J., A. Bisenberger, and K. Kotrschal. Stimulus enhancement in Greylag geese, Social transmission of an operant task. *Animal Behaviour* 59: 1119–1125, 2000.

Fritz, J., A. Bisenberger, and K. Kotrschal. Coordination of food exploitation behaviour in families of Greylag geese. Submitted, 2001.

Fryday, S. L., and W. Greig-Smith. The effect of social learning on the food choice of the house sparrow (*Passer domesticus*). *Behaviour* 128: 281–300, 1994.

Galef, B. G. Jr. Imitation in animals: History, definition, and interpretation of data from the psychological laboratory. In T. Zentall and B. Galef, eds., *Social Learning: Psychological and Biological Perspectives*, 28. Hillsdale, N.J.: Erlbaum, 1988.

Galef, B. G., Jr. Social enhancement of food preferences in Norway rats: A brief review. In C. M. Heyes and B. G. Galef Jr., eds., *Social Learning in Animals. The Roots of Culture*. San Diego: Academic Press, 1996.

Galef, B. G. Jr., L. A. Manzig, and R. M. Field. Imitation learning in budgerigars: Dawson and Foss (1965) revisited. *Behavioural Process* 13: 191–202, 1986.

Galef, B. G. Jr., S. W. Wigmore, and D. J. Kennett. A failure to find socially mediated taste aversion learning in Norway rats (*Rattus norvegicus*). *Journal of Comparative Psychology* 97: 458–463, 1993.

Giraldeau, L. A. The ecology of information use. In J. R. Krebs and N. B. Davis, eds., *Behavioural Ecology*, 4th ed. Oxford, UK: Blackwell Science, 1997.

Giraldeau, L. A., and L. Lefebvre. Scrounging prevents transmission of food-finding behaviour in pigeons. *Animal Behaviour* 35: 387–394, 1987.

Griffin, D. R. Prospects for a cognitive ethology. *Behavioral and Brain Sciences* 1: 527–538, 1978.

Heyes, C. M. Imitation, culture, and cognition. *Animal Behaviour* 46: 999–1010, 1993.

Heyes, C. M. Social learning in animals: Categories and mechanisms. *Biological Review* 69: 207–231, 1994.

Heyes, C. M. Theory of mind in nonhuman primates. *Behavioral and Brain Science* 21: 101–148, 1998.

Heyes, C. M. Imitation, cognition, and culture: On the psychological mechanism and transmission function of imitation learning. *Advances in Ethology* 34: 9, 1999.

Heyes, C. M., and B. G. Galef Jr. *Social Learning in Animals. The Roots of Culture*. San Diego: Academic Press, 1996.

Kaiser, D. H., T. R. Zentall, and B. G. Galef Jr. Can imitation in pigeons be explained by local enhancement together with trial-and-error learning? *Psychological Science* 8: 459–460, 1997.

Kamil, A. C. On the proper definition of cognitive ethology. In R. P. Balda, I. M. Pepperberg, and A. C. Kamil, eds., *Animal Cognition in Nature*. London: Academic Press, 1998.

Kotrschal, K., M. J. Van Staaden, and R. Huber. Fish brains: Evolution and ecological relationships. *Journal of Fish Biology* 8: 1–36, 1998.

Krebs, J. F., M. H. Mac Roberts, and J. M. Cullen. Flocking and feeding in great tits (*Parus major*). *Ibis* 114: 507–530, 1972.

Kroodsma, D. E., and B. E. Byers. The functions of bird song. *American Zoologist* 31: 318–328, 1991.

Lefebvre, L., J. Templeton, K. Brown, and M. Koelle. Carib grackles imitate conspecific and Zenaida dove tutors. *Behaviour* 134: 1003–1017, 1997a.

Lefebvre, L., P. Whittle, E. Lascaris, and A. Finkenstein. Feeding innovations and forebrain size in birds. *Animal Behaviour* 53: 549–569, 1997b.

Lefebvre, L., A. Gaxiola, S. Dawson, S. Timmermans, L. Rosza, and P. Kabai. Feeding innovation and foraging size in australasian birds. *Behaviour* 135: 1077–1079, 1998.

Lorenz, K. Die angeborenen Formen möglicher Erfahrung. *Zeitschrift für Tierpsychologie* 5: 235–409, 1943.

Marler, P., A. Dufty, and R. Pickert. Vocal communication in the domestic chicken: I. Does a sender communicate information about the quality of a food referent to a receiver? *Animal Behaviour* 34: 188–193, 1986.

Meltzoff, A. N. Towards a developmental cognitive science: The implication of crossmodal matching and imitation for the development of representation and memory in infancy. *Annals of the New York Academy of Sciences* 608: 1–37, 1990.

Moore, B. R. Avian movement imitation and a new form of mimicry: Tracing the evolution of a complex form of learning. *Behaviour* 122: 231–263, 1992.

Moore, B. R. The evolution of imitative learning. In C. M. Heyes and B. G. Galef Jr., eds., *Social Learning in Animals: The Roots of Culture*. San Diego: Academic Press, 1996.

Nicol, C. J., and S. J. Pope. Social learning in small flocks of laying hens. *Animal Behaviour* 47: 1289–1296, 1994.

Nicol, C. J., and S. J. Pope. The maternal feeding display of domestic hens is sensitive to perceived chick error. *Animal Behaviour* 52: 767–774, 1996.

Noble, J., and P. M. Todd. It is really imitation? A review of simple mechanism in social information gathering. In K. Dautenhahn and C. Nehaniv, eds., *Proceedings of the AISB'99 Symposium on Imitation in Animals and Artifacts (7–9 April 1999)*. pp. 65–73. Brighton, U.K.: Society for the Study of Artificial Intelligence and Simulation of Behaviour, 1999.

Prato Previde, E., and M. D. Poli. Social learning in the Golden Hamster (*Mesocricetus auratus*). *Journal of Comparative Psychology* 110: 203–208, 1996.

Rizzolatti, G., L. Fadiga, V. Gallese, and L. Fogassi. Premotor cortex and the recognition of motor actions. *Cognitive Brain Research* 3: 131–141, 1996.

Sherry, D. F., and B. G. Galef Jr. Cultural transmission without imitation: Milk bottle opening by birds. *Animal Behaviour* 32: 937–938, 1984.

Sherry, D. F., and B. G. Jr. Social learning without imitation: More about milk bottle opening by birds. *Animal Behaviour* 40: 987–989, 1990.

Shettleworth, S. J. Varieties of learning and memory in animals. *Journal of Experimental Psychology: Animal Behaviour Processes* 19: 5–14, 1993.

Shettleworth, S. J. *Cognition, Evolution, and Behaviour*. Oxford University Press, New York, 1998.

Slater, P. J. Bird song learning. Causes and consequences. *Ethology, Ecology, and Evolution* 1: 19–46, 1989

Terkel, J. Cultural transmission of feeding behaviour in the Black rat (*Rattus rattus*). In C. M. Heyes and B. G. Galef Jr., eds., *Social Learning in Animals: The Roots of Culture*. San Diego: Academic Press, 1996.

Tinbergen, N. On aims and methods of ethology. *Zeitschrift für Tierpsychologie* 20: 410–433, 1963.

Tuci, E., J. Noble, and P. M. Todd. "I'll have what she's having:" A simulation analysis of the copying of food preferences in Norway rats. In K. Dautenhahn and C. Nehaniv, eds., *Proceedings of the AISB'99 Symposium on Imitation in Animals and Artifacts (7–9 April 1999)*, pp. 74–79. Brighton, U.K.: Society for the Study of Artificial Intelligence and Simulation of Behaviour, 1999.

Wechsler, B. The spread of food producing techniques in a captive flock of jackdaws. *Behaviour* 107: 267–277, 1988.

Whiten, A., and R. Ham. On the nature and evolution of imitation in the animal kingdom: Reappraisal of a century of research. In P. J. B. Slater, J. S. Rosenblatt, C. Beer, and M. Milinski, eds., *Advances in the Study of Behavior*. New York: Academic Press, 1992.

Zentall, T. R. An analysis of imitative learning in animals. In C. M. Heyes and B. G. Galef Jr., eds., *Social Learning in Animals: The Roots of Culture*. San Diego: Academic Press, 1996.

Zentall, T. R., J. E. Sutton, and L. M. Sherburne. True imitative learning in pigeons. *Psychological Science* 7: 343–346, 1996.

6   Art Imitates Life: Programming by Example as an Imitation Game

Henry Lieberman

6.1   Introduction

Having the computer imitate recorded human actions is the basis
for an experimental technology for programming, variously called
"Programming by Example" or "Programming by Demonstration."
This is an underappreciated technology that holds the promise of
revolutionizing programming and making it more accessible, especially to nonexpert programmers. Because imitation is a natural
learning strategy for people, it can help alleviate the barriers of abstraction and lack of short-term memory that makes programming
difficult for people. Much past work has focused on how to represent the recorded actions and how to generalize the resulting procedures so that they can be applicable to examples analogous to
those on which the system is taught. This chapter will survey past
work in the field and speculate on how the mechanics of imitative
behavior might inform future developments, especially the feedback loop of verifying that imitative behavior has the desired result
in new situations.

6.2   Monkey See, Monkey Do

Imitation can be a fundamental basis of learning, in both animals
and human beings. Early on, children learn by repeating what
adults do, and gradually learn more and more sophisticated ways
of incorporating aspects of the observed behavior of others into
their own behavior. We do not yet know to what extent we can
ascribe imitative behavior in animals to an instinct to copy others
or to some form of learning. It is clear, however, that observation
and imitation are central capabilities for many forms of learning.

Computers are funny things. They are not people, but since they
are designed and used by people, we can't help but incorporate
some aspects of our cognitive processing into their operation. We
can certainly make them imitate certain aspects of our own behavior, more or less closely. And just as we have trouble drawing
the line between simple instinctive copying and true learning in

humans and animals, we also have trouble drawing the line between simple repetition and true learning in computers. Clearly, as with animals, our interaction with computers can affect their behavior. Those changes in behavior can subsequently be observed in new situations that resemble the previous ones in which the imitation first occurred—whether or not we call it learning.

Programs are the instincts of computers. When we program computers, we are giving them behavior that then becomes automatic for the computer in the same way that instincts are automatic in animals. Certain animals, such as ourselves, may be endowed with an instinct to imitate observed behaviors, which forms the basis for learning. If we want machines to learn, can we endow them also with an instinct to imitate? Can a program that observes and imitates behavior of a human teacher enable a computer to learn? This is the question we will explore in this chapter.

6.3 Computer See, Computer Do

Programming by Example, also often referred to as Programming by Demonstration, is a technique that enables a user to teach new procedures to a computer. It consists of a learning program, or *agent*, attached to a conventional interactive graphical interface, such as a text editor, graphical editor, spreadsheet, or Web browser. The learning agent records the actions performed by the user in the user interface. The user demonstrates a concrete example of how to perform a procedure, using sample data objects that are meaningful to the user. The system then records the steps to form a program that can be used in situations that are analogous to, but not necessarily exactly the same as, those on which it was taught.

Programming by Example (PBE) can be seen as a way of trying to get the computer to imitate the user. By demonstrating a sequence of steps, the user is trying to get the computer to learn those steps so that the computer can in the future imitate what the user would have done, thereby saving the user time. Programming by Example also establishes a "show and tell" kind of interaction that is similar to the way people teach each other tasks, leading to a natural style of interaction. Because we all experience imitation as young children, computer novices can easily understand the idea of trying to get the computer to imitate them as a metaphor for the programming task.

Programming by Example was developed in response to a perceived difficulty in the skill of computer programming. Programming in a conventional programming language requires giving the computer an abstract description of steps it is to follow. This abstraction is difficult for people in all but the simplest of situations. It places high demands on the user's short-term memory. For most users who are not expert programmers, it is difficult to foresee the effect of a given programming language statement or expression, and to understand the consequences of a given program for the concrete cases of interest. With Programming by Example, the user can always see the direct consequences of an action, at least for the demonstrated examples, which makes it easier to decide what the next operation should be.

Many conventional applications already provide the ability to simply play back exactly a sequence of previously recorded user actions, also called a *macro*. Macros can be also seen as the simplest form of imitation. But macros tend to be brittle. If any minor aspect of the interface changes: positions of icons, slightly different data, different file names, and so on, the procedure may fail. In Programming by Example, the sequence of steps can be *generalized* by the agent. Some of the specific details of the sample data objects can be removed, or concrete actions generalized to a broader class of actions, so that the procedure then becomes useful in a wider variety of situations.

Generalization can take any of several forms—the agent can ask the user how to generalize the program and present lists of options; or the agent can use heuristics, perhaps dependent on the specific domain, to guess what the best generalizations are for each example and action.

The first true Programming by Example system was David Smith's Pygmalion (Smith 1993), in 1978. Pygmalion also introduced graphical programming, using icons to represent program elements and values, and using a graphic editor to manipulate the program. This was followed by a wide variety of systems in several domains, including desktop file systems, general Lisp programming, text editing, and several kinds of graphic editing. The state of the art in the early 1990s, including a general introduction to the topic, glossary, history, and other tutorial material is admirably covered in Cypher (1993b). The current state of the art as of this writing is presented in Lieberman (2000).

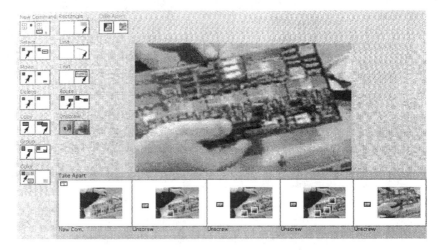

Figure 6.1   Mondrian is a graphical editor that learns new procedures through Programming by Example. Here, we teach the system how to take apart a circuit board.

As an example, Mondrian (Lieberman 1993) is typical of many Programming by Example systems. Mondrian is a graphical editor with an agent that records graphical procedures using Programming by Example (figure 6.1). The user demonstrates a procedure using the graphical editing operations on concrete graphical objects, indicating which ones are to be taken as examples.

The system then records a procedure that can be used later with new objects in place of the examples. Mondrian's learning procedure is similar to what is called in the literature *explanation-based generalization*, where a tree of dependencies among operations is constructed and the generalizations are propagated through this dependency tree (Lieberman 1993).

Mondrian also possesses the ability to learn declaratively as well as procedurally. The user could put graphical annotations on images or video frames to create a visual representation of objects that can be manipulated by the graphical editor. These graphical annotations name objects and establish a graphical part-whole hierarchy. The user could then operate on the graphical objects and the procedures would be recorded in terms of the relations described by the graphical annotations. In Lieberman and Maulsby (1996), the user can teach the agent how to take apart a motor by annotating a video of a human performing the same procedure in the real world. By asking the user to graphically annotate objects, there was no need to have computer vision procedures for recognizing objects in the scene. Graphical annotation represents a method for the user to communicate the meaning of demonstrated actions for the computer to imitate.

6.4   Imitation in Interface Agents

Imitation also plays a role as a metaphor in the movement toward *interface agents* in computer-human interaction (Bradshaw 1997). In contrast to traditional direct-manipulation icon-and-menu based software, the idea of an interface agent is to cast the computer in the role of a human assistant, such as a secretary or travel agent. This vision is related to that of PBE, but unlike PBE, where the user is explicitly trying to teach the machine a procedure, in many interface agent projects the user may not be explicitly trying to teach the machine, but simply performing tasks for other reasons. The agent then learns from more passive observation. The role of the user is then to provide feedback on the agent's actions, and perhaps also to provide advice that affects the agent's actions.

In some ways, this might be closer to the kind of imitation-based learning that may be occurring in some animals, in the sense that it usually occurs without explicit instruction or even feedback, from the teacher, as we did with Programming by Example. Communication in the other direction, from the agent to the user, is usually also limited, to avoid bothering the user with too many explicit requests for information.

Letizia (Lieberman 1997) is an example of this kind of agent. It is an agent that records selections of Web pages in a browser, and compiles a profile of the user's interests, without any explicit declaration of interest on the user's part. The agent then independently performs a breadth-first search surrounding the user's page, and filters the candidate pages through the user's profile. It produces a continuous display of recommendations of pages that the user may be interested in, representing the progress of the search in real time. Thus, Letizia's search seeks to imitate the user's browsing, producing a prospective evaluation of pages that saves the user time, which would otherwise be wasted in looking at irrelevant pages (figure 6.2).

However, Letizia specifically chooses *not* to imitate exactly the control structure of user browsing. Most Web browsers encourage a depth-first search of the Web space, since it's always easier to go "down" in a browser by following a link, than to go "sideways" and

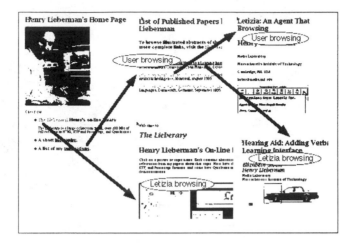

Figure 6.2 Letizia's breadth-first search doesn't precisely imitate, but rather *complements* the user's depth-first search.

visit sibling links to the page. The problem, which we observed in practice, is that users are tempted to go too deeply, following ultimately unfruitful "garden paths." So Letizia tries to adopt a complementary control structure, pursuing a breadth-first strategy to complement the user's presumed depth-first search, finding what would otherwise be ignored. This is an important lesson for learning—sometimes the goal is not to imitate the teacher exactly, but to understand what the teacher is doing in order to do something else complementary to it. This is clearly related to imitation, but there's no single word for it. I do not know whether or not this kind of imitative behavior is exhibited by animals or has been studied.

6.5 Can Programming by Example Imitate Imitation?

We can analyze the structure of many kinds of imitative behavior in the following steps:

- The learner observes the behavior of the teacher
- The learner interprets the teacher's behavior
- The learner tries to execute the interpretation of the behavior
- The learner receives feedback from the teacher or from the environment

Analysis of these stages—observation, interpretation, execution, and feedback—can also be applied to Programming by Example.

Observation amounts to the recording of the user actions in the interface. There is always the issue of at what granularity the actions are recorded. At the lowest level in an interactive graphical interface, the actions can be recorded as mouse movements, mouse clicks, and typed characters. At a higher level, the actions can be recorded as selection of menu operations, icons, ranges of text, spreadsheet cells, graphical objects, and so on. If the granularity is too small, recorded histories will get overwhelmed with data and place too much burden on the interpretive processes to follow. For example, we might record every mouse movement in an interface, but in most interfaces, not every mouse movement is significant, and recording all such movements produces prodigious amounts of data. If the granularity is too large, we might miss some significant events. For example, in the AppleScript language on the Macintosh, each application must declare what operations are recorded by the user interface recording facility, and many fail to declare enough operations to enable the computer to fully reproduce the user's actions. The granularity issue is discussed further in Lieberman (1990).

The issue of how to *generalize* a recorded program in Programming by Example is the step of interpreting the user's behavior. Generalization in Programming by Example typically means replacing constants in the program by variables to be filled in each time the program is subsequently executed, and also replacing descriptions of data and actions by more general descriptions that will have wider application in subsequent executions. When talking about data selected by the user, this is also sometimes referred to in Cypher (1993b) as the *data description problem*.

Among the systems described in Cypher (1993b), we can see a variety of approaches to the generalization problem. Some systems take the approach of asking the user to choose generalizations explicitly. Some ask the user to choose from a list of plausible generalizations computed heuristically in order to cut down the space of possible generalizations, which can grow very large when combinations of generalization characteristics are possible. Some choose generalizations automatically based on some domain knowledge, without user intervention. Some will accept user advice that alters how the generalization is chosen. None of these approaches is universally better, and Lieberman and Maulsby (1996) use a "spectrum of instructibility" to classify the dimensions of the unavoidable trade-off between convenience and control.

Key to the generalization problem is the related problem of *context*. Understanding which actions and objects are dependent upon the details of their context says whether or not they can be carried over to other contexts, and how. Traditional hardware and software design overlooks context because it conceptualizes systems as input-output functions. Systems take input explicitly given to them by a human, act upon that input alone and produce explicit output. But this view is too restrictive. Smart computers, intelligent agent software, and digital devices of the future will also have to operate on data that they observe or gather for themselves. They may have to sense their environment, decide which aspects of a situation are really important, and infer the user's intention from concrete actions. The system's actions may be dependent on time, place, or the history of interaction. In other words, dependent upon context. The impact and implications of the context problem are discussed further in Lieberman and Selker (2000).

The step of execution of the imitative behavior consists of the learner repeating the behavior of the teacher. Of course, there is hardly ever any such thing as exact repetition. What the learner does in imitation of the teacher will of course be dependent on the previous steps of what the learner has observed and interpreted in the teacher's behavior.

And if the teacher's behavior in question consists of multiple steps, then there may be interaction between the teacher and the learner at each step. The teacher may correct the student or give feedback, verbally or behaviorally, indicating approval or disapproval. The learner may observe directly his or her own success or failure by effects of the behavior on the environment. Thus, the phases of execution and obtaining feedback may be interleaved rather than occur one after the other.

In Programming by Example, there might be interaction between the user and the system during the execution and feedback phases. The user may be able to "step through" the recorded and generalized program to monitor execution and verify that it is having the intended effect. The user may be able to accept or reject various moves made by the system, or perhaps give it advice or critique that change its behavior, either during the demonstration or subsequently.

One system that perhaps went the farthest in providing feedback and monitoring of execution was Cypher's Eager (Cypher 1993a). Eager was a Programming by Example system for Hypercard that

recorded actions, and a prominent feature was its recognition of
looping behavior. When it noticed actions that tended to repeat a
sequence of earlier actions, it would provide *anticipatory feedback*. Every time the user took a step that led on a path that the
agent considered to be repetitive of past actions, the agent (represented by a green cat) would predict the next action, and unob-
trusively highlight it on the screen in green. The user was free to
confirm the prediction by choosing the action predicted, or to perform some other action, in which case the agent would abandon its
prediction. If the prediction was confirmed, the next action would
be predicted, until the entire loop was performed a second time.
At that time, the user would be given the option of repeating
the whole procedure, either a single time or until the data was
exhausted. Here, the cat was explicitly imitating the user's past
actions, and the user was cast in the role of "animal trainer" to
provide positive or negative feedback (figure 6.3).

It is in these last phases, execution monitoring and feedback,
that the connection between Programming by Example and imitative behavior in humans and animals needs to be developed in

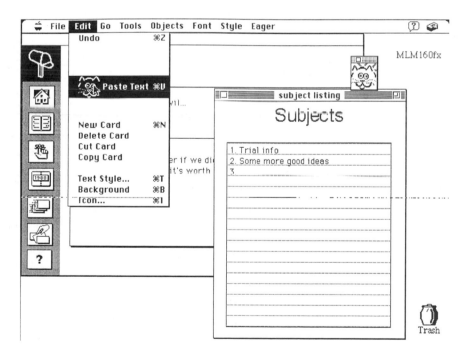

Figure 6.3 Eager's cat allows step-by-step confirmation by the user of the pattern of actions
recorded and generalized by the system.

greater depth. Programming by Example often has the problem of debugging and editing programs developed in this style, and enabling the user to visualize the process of recording, generalization, and execution. Imitation in humans and animals has produced highly developed strategies for dealing with these issues. Deeper understanding of these strategies might produce inspiration for providing better monitoring, editing, and debugging capabilities in our Programming by Example systems.

6.7 Can a Parrot Learn how to Program?

We are about to embark on an unusual test of the relationship between imitative behavior and programming. Cognitive studies on the higher primates have shown that they can be made to show simple communication and learning capabilities, although there still exists considerable controversy about the significance of these results.

Recently, however, surprising findings have surfaced about the communicative and cognitive abilities of African Grey parrots. The imitative vocalizations of parrots are, of course, well known, but Irene Pepperberg (1999) has shown that parrots are capable, at least under some circumstances and with careful long-term training, of using a languagelike code based on human speech for communication and problem solving. This, despite their relatively small brain size! See also chapter 4 of this volume.

In particular, such parrots are able to demonstrate some specific cognitive capabilities. They can remember and invoke sequences of events (up to a length limit imposed by short-term memory constraints, as is the case with humans). They can also understand, to some extent, categories of objects. They can, for example, be shown a yellow toy key, a yellow ball, and other yellow objects, and learn the category yellow such that they can respond "yellow" to a question "What color?" when shown a previously unseen yellow object. They can be taught other properties of an object, such as shape or material, so if you show them a blue key, they can say "key," knowing that the shape property does not refer to a specific object, and that shape, color, and material are independent properties of objects. This shows that they are somewhat capable of generalizing objects to categories.

It is our intuition that these two fundamental cognitive capabilities—sequencing and generalization—are at the root of the cognitive task of programming. Sequencing and generalization also happen to be the essential ingredients of a programming by example system. So we propose to try to teach a parrot how to program, using a Programming by Example system!

Media Lab student Ben Resner is building an experimental apparatus with which we can test these hypotheses. The apparatus consists of a set of stages of boxes containing a food reward, and a series of valves that allow the passage of food from one box to another, and eventually, accessible to the parrot. The box at each stage is controlled by a series of buttons, so that if the parrot presses a correct sequence of buttons, it can eventually obtain the food. The idea is that that the parrot could be taught to write a program to obtain the food, even if the sequence of buttons changes. The parrot will be taught to generalize over properties of the sequence (figure 6.4).

An early experiment by Radia Perlman (1976) at the Logo group of the MIT Artificial Intelligence Laboratory gives us some hope that this could be accomplished. The aim of the group was to teach

Figure 6.4 Parrot researcher Irene Pepperberg and parrot Wart play with an apparatus designed by Ben Resner for the parrot programming experiment.

Figure 6.5 Radia Perlman's 1974 Button Box (left) and Logo Turtle (right).

programming to young children, and Perlman set out to discover the minimum age at which children could be taught programming skills. She built a "Button Box" that consisted of a series of buttons that each launched a command to a small robot "turtle" (figure 6.5).

The programming operation consisted of a "Start Remembering" button that memorized a sequence of events that could subsequently be launched by a button that executed the stored procedure. Similar ideas were subsequently realized in the "Slot Machine," where computer-readable cards inserted into slots represented the programming operations, and "Instant Logo," a screen interface for programming macros consisting of Logo commands. The generalization operations of these systems were absent or quite limited, but the principle of programming was demonstrated. Children as young as four years old could learn to program the Button Box, well before they could learn to read. Thus, literacy skills were shown not to be essential to the fundamental task of creating procedures. They could well understand the idea of getting the computer to imitate the series of operations it was taught. Parrots can be shown to have performance on certain problem-solving tasks equivalent to three- or four-year-old children.

Teaching a parrot to program might sound a bit crazy, but we feel that the attempt should at least lead to some interesting results. To our knowledge, no one has ever tried to teach a non-human animal to exhibit any kind of programming activity. So, if it succeeds, we feel this will be a major result in the study of the cognitive capabilities of animals. And, in keeping with the theme of this book, it will provide evidence of the centrality of imitation in purposeful behavior by both animals and humans.

References

Bradshaw, J., ed. *Software Agents*. Cambridge, Mass.: MIT Press, 1997.

Cypher, A. Eager: Learning repetitive tasks by demonstration. In A. Cypher, ed., *Watch What I Do: Programming by Demonstration*. Cambridge, Mass.: MIT Press, 1993a.

Cypher, A., ed. *Watch What I Do: Programming by Demonstration*. Cambridge, Mass.: MIT Press, 1993b.

Lieberman, H. Tinker: A programming by demonstration system for beginning programmers. In A. Cypher, ed., *Watch What I Do: Programming by Demonstration*. Cambridge, Mass.: MIT Press, 1993.

Lieberman, H. Autonomous Interface Agents. *Proceedings of the ACM Conference on Computer and Human Interface CHI 97*, pp. 67–74. New York: ACM Press, 1997.

Lieberman, H. Integrating user interface agents with conventional applications. *ACM Conference on Intelligent User Interfaces*, San Francisco, January 1998. Revised version to appear in *Knowledge Systems Journal*.

Lieberman, H., ed. *Your Wish Is My Command*. San Francisco: Morgan Kaufmann, 2000.

Lieberman, H., and D. Maulsby. Instructible agents: Software that just keeps getting better. *IBM Systems Journal*, 35(3–4): 539–556, 1996. On-line at: ⟨http://www.research.ibm.com/journal/sj/mit/sectiond/lieberman.html⟩

Lieberman, H., and T. Selker. Out of context: Computer systems that adapt to, and learn from, context. *IBM Systems Journal*, 39(3–4): 617–632. 2000. On-line at: ⟨http://www.research.ibm/com/journal/sj/393/part1/lieberman.html⟩

Pepperberg, I. *The Alex Studies: Cognitive and Communicative Abilities of African Grey Parrots*. Cambridge, Mass.: Harvard University Press, 1999.

Perlman, R. Using computer technology to provide a creative learning environment for preschool children. AI Memo no. 360, Logo Memo 24, May 1976.

Smith, D. C. Pygmalion: An Executable Electronic Blackboard. In A. Cypher, ed. *Watch What I Do: Programming by Demonstration*, pp. 19–47. Cambridge, Massachusetts: MIT Press, 1993.

7 Learning to Fly

Claude Sammut, Scott Hurst, Dana Kedzier, and Donald Michie

7.1 The Problem

In this paper, we report on experiments that demonstrate machine learning of a reactive strategy to control a dynamic system by observing a controller that is already skilled in the task. We have modified a flight simulation program to log the actions taken by a human subject as he or she flies an aircraft. The log file is used to create the input to an induction program. The quality of the output from the induction program is tested by running the simulator in autopilot mode where the autopilot code is derived from the decision tree formed by induction.

A practical motivation for trying to solve this problem is that it is often difficult to construct controllers for complex systems using classical methods. Anderson and Miller (1991) describe a problem with present-day autolanders, namely that they are not designed to handle large gusts of wind when close to landing. Similar problems occur for helicopter pilots who must manoeuvre their aircraft in high winds while there is a load slung beneath the helicopter. Learning by trial-and-error could be used in simulation, but if we already have a skilled controller, namely, a human pilot, then it is more economical to learn by observing the pilot.

While control systems have been the subject of much research in machine learning in recent years, we know of few attempts to learn control rules by observing human behavior. Michie, Bain and Hayes-Michie (1990) used an induction program to learn rules for balancing a pole (in simulation) and earlier work by Donaldson (1960), Widrow and Smith (1964) and Chambers and Michie (1969) demonstrated the feasibility of learning by imitation, also for pole-balancing. To our knowledge, the autopilot described here is the most complex control system constructed by machine learning methods. The task we set ourselves was to teach the autopilot how to take off; fly to a set altitude and distance; turn around and land. We describe our experiments with a particular aircraft simulation and discuss the problems encountered and how they were solved. We also discuss some of the remaining difficulties.

7.2   The Flight Simulator

The source code to a flight simulator was made available to us by Silicon Graphics Incorporated. The central control mechanism of the simulator is a loop that interrogates the aircraft controls and updates the state of the simulation according to a set of equations of motion. Before repeating the loop, the instruments in the display are updated. The simulator gives the user a choice of aircraft to fly. We have restricted all of our experiments to the simulation of a Cessna, being easier for our subjects to learn to fly than the various fighters or larger aircraft available.

One feature of the flight simulator that has had a significant effect on our experiments is that it is non-deterministic. The simulator runs on a multi-tasking Unix system, not on a dedicated real-time system. Thus, it is not possible to give a guaranteed real-time response because the flight simulator can be interrupted by other processes for input-output (I/O) traffic. If nothing is done to compensate for these interruptions, a person operating the simulator would notice that the program's response to control actions would change. If no other processes were stealing CPU time it would respond quickly but it could become very sluggish when other processes were competing for the CPU.

To minimize the effects of variations in execution speed, the simulator regularly interrogates a real-time clock. This is used to calculate the number of main control loops being executed each second. If the simulation has slowed down since the last interrogation, the time interval used in solving the equations of motion is altered to allow the simulation to "catch up." The time interval is also changed in response to an increase in execution speed. To a human operator, who has a sense of time, this approximates uniform response. However, these adjustments do not ensure a perfectly uniform response. Therefore, to an autopilot that has no external sense of time, the effects of its control actions will be somewhat different from one run to the next and even during one flight.

We have chosen to treat this problem as a challenge. If we are able to devise rules that can control a noisy system, we will have done well and in fact, the rules that have been generated can handle considerable variation. Thus we can be optimistic that the methods we are developing can be extended to more complex systems that have real disturbances such as wind and genuinely noisy controls.

Another "feature" that we discovered about the Silicon Graphics flight simulator is that the rudder does not have a realistic effect on the aircraft. Fortunately this did not affect us since none of our pilots used the rudder. While a real pilot would frown upon this practice, it is possible to fly a real airplane without using the rudder (the rudder is used in turns to stop the plane from "sliding" with the result that the g-forces are not directed toward the floor as they should be).

7.3 Logging Flight Information

The display update has been modified so that when the pilot performs a control action by moving the control stick (the mouse) or changing the thrust or flaps settings, the state of the simulation is written to a log file. Initially, we obtained the services of 20 volunteers, believing that the more logs we had from a variety of subjects the more robust would be our rules. As we discuss later, we found that it was better to collect many logs from a small number of pilots. All the results presented below are derived from the logs of three subjects who each "flew" 30 times.

At the start of a flight, the aircraft is pointing North, down the runway. The subject is required to fly a well-defined flight plan that consists of the following manoeuvres:

1. Take off and fly to an altitude of 2,000 feet.
2. Level out and fly to a distance of 32,000 feet from the starting point.
3. Turn right to a compass heading of approximately 330°. The subjects were actually told to head toward a particular point in the scenery that corresponds to that heading.
4. At a North/South distance of 42,000 feet, turn left to head back toward the runway. The scenery contains grid marks on the ground. The starting point for the turn is when the last grid line was reached. This corresponds to about 42,000 feet. The turn is considered complete when the azimuth is between 140° and 180°.
5. Line up on the runway. The aircraft was considered to be lined up when the aircraft's azimuth is less than 5° off the heading of the runway and the twist is less than ±10° from horizontal.
6. Descend to the runway, keeping in line. The subjects were given the hint that they should have an "aiming point" near the beginning of the runway.
7. Land on the runway.

We will refer to the performance of a control action as an "event." During a flight, up to 1,000 events can be recorded. With three pilots and 30 flights each the complete data set consists of about 90,000 events. The data recorded in each event are:

on_ground	boolean: is the plane on the ground?
g_limit	boolean: have we exceeded the plane's g limit?
wing_stall	boolean: has the plane stalled?
twist	integer: 0 to 360° (in tenths of a degree, see below)
elevation	integer: 0 to 360° (in tenths of a degree, see below)
azimuth	integer: 0 to 360° (in tenths of a degree, see below)
roll_speed	integer: 0 to 360° (in tenths of a degree per second)
elevation_speed	integer: 0 to 360° (in tenths of a degree per second)
azimuth_speed	integer: 0 to 360° (in tenths of a degree per second)
airspeed	integer: (in knots)
climbspeed	integer: (feet per second)
E/W distance	real: E/W distance from centre of runway (in feet)
altitude	real: (in feet)
N/S distance	real: N/S distance from northern end of runway (in feet)
fuel	integer: (in pounds)
rollers	real: ±4.3
elevator	real: ±3.0
rudder	real: not used
thrust	integer: 0 to 100%
flaps	integer: 0°, 10° or 20°

The elevation of the aircraft is the angle of the nose relative to the horizon. The azimuth is the aircraft's compass heading and the twist is the angle of the wings relative to the horizon. The elevator angle is changed by pushing the mouse forward (positive) or back (negative). The rollers are changed by pushing the mouse left (positive) or right (negative). Thrust and flaps are incremented and decremented in fixed steps by keystrokes. The angular effects of the elevator and rollers are cumulative. For example, in straight and level flight, if the stick is pushed left, the aircraft will roll anti-clockwise. The aircraft will continue rolling until the stick is centered. The thrust and flaps settings are absolute.

A valid criticism of our data collection method is that we are not recording the same information that the subject is using and thus we make it difficult for the induction program to reproduce the pilot's behavior. For example, it was mentioned previously that subjects use an aiming point on the runway to adjust their trajectory while approaching the runway. No information directly related to an aiming point is recorded in the data. Our assumption is that enough other data are recorded to allow the induction program to do its job.

Response Times

When an event is recorded, the state of the simulation at the instant that an action is performed could be output. However, there is always a delay in response to a stimulus, so ideally we should output the state of the simulation when the stimulus occurred along with the action that was performed some time later in response to the stimulus. But how do we know what the stimulus was? Unfortunately there is no way of knowing. Human responses to sudden stimuli take approximately one second but this can vary considerably. For example, while flying, the pilot usually anticipates where the aircraft will be in the near future and prepares the response before the stimulus occurs.

Our approach has been as follows. Each time the simulator passes through its main control loop, the current state of the simulation is stored in a circular buffer. We estimate how many loops are executed each second. When a control action is performed, the action is output, along with the state of the simulation as it was some time before. How much earlier is determined by the size of the buffer. Of the three subjects used in these experiments, one operated the simulator with a delay of 40 loops (corresponding to a two or three second delay) and the other two subjects used a 20 loop delay (between one and one and a half seconds).

7.4 Data Analysis

Even with a well-specified flight plan such as the one we are using here, there is a large degree of a variation in the way different subjects fly. Because of this variation, the number of flights we have is not sufficient to allow an induction program to distinguish useful actions from noise using the raw data. However, it would not be very practical if it were necessary to fly hundreds of flights before anything useful could be obtained. So before applying the induction program to the data, we perform some analysis to assist it.

We have used C4.5 (Quinlan 1987) as the induction program in these experiments. Learning reactive strategies is a task for which C4.5 was never intended. However, we chose it for our initial investigation because we are familiar with it and it is reliable and well known. Having the source code also made it easier for us to generate the decision trees as if-statements in C. This was necessary so that the decision tree code could be inserted into the simulator.

Customized Autopilots

The learning task was simplified by restricting induction to one set of pilot data at a time. Thus, an autopilot has been constructed for each of the three subjects who generated training data. The reason for separating pilot data is that each pilot can fly the same flight plan in different ways. For example, straight and level flight can be maintained by adjusting the throttle. When an airplane's elevation is zero, it can still climb since higher speeds increase lift. Adjusting the throttle to maintain a steady altitude is the correct way of achieving straight and level flight. However, another way of maintaining constant altitude is to make regular adjustments to the elevators causing the airplane to pitch up or down. One of the subjects flew stage 2 by adjusting the throttle, the other two adjusted the elevators. We want the induction program to learn a consistent way of flying, so we are training it to emulate a particular pilot.

Flight Stages

The data from each flight were segmented into the seven stages described in section 7.3. In the flight plan described, the pilot must achieve several, successive goals, corresponding to the end of each stage. Each stage requires a different manoeuvre. Having already defined the sub-tasks and told the human subjects what they are, we gave the learning program the same advantage.

Decision Trees and Control Actions

In each stage we construct four separate decision trees, one for each of the elevator, rollers, thrust, and flaps. A program filters the flight logs generating four input files for the induction program. The attributes of a training example are the flight parameters described earlier. The dependent variable or class value is the attribute describing a control action. Thus, when generating a decision tree for flaps, the flaps column is treated as the class value and the other columns in the data file, including the settings of the elevator, rollers and thrust, are treated as ordinary attributes.

Determining Class Values

C4.5 expects class values to be discrete but the values for elevator, rollers, thrust and flaps are numeric. We will soon be experimenting with decision tree induction programs that have numeric output. However, for these experiments, a preprocessor breaks up the action settings into sub-ranges that can be given discrete labels. Sub-ranges are chosen by analysing the frequency of occurrence of action values. This analysis must be done for each pilot to correctly reflect differing flying styles. There are two disadvantages to this method. One is that if the sub-ranges are poorly chosen, the rules generated will use controls that are too fine or too coarse. Secondly, C4.5 has no concept of ordered class values, so classes cannot be combined during the construction of the decision tree.

Figure 7.1 shows the frequency of thrust values in stage 6 of the data for one pilot. Since thrust is controlled by a keystroke, it is increased and decreased by a fixed amount, 10% The values with very low frequencies are those that were passed through on the way to a desired setting. The graph reflects the facts that this pilot held the thrust at 100% until the approach to the runway began. The thrust was then brought down to 40% immediately and gradually decreased to 10% where it remained for most of the approach. Close to the runway, the thrust was cut to 0 and the plane glided down the rest of the way.

In this case, class values corresponding to 0, 10, 15, 20, 25, 30, 35, 40 and 100 were used. Anything above 40% was considered

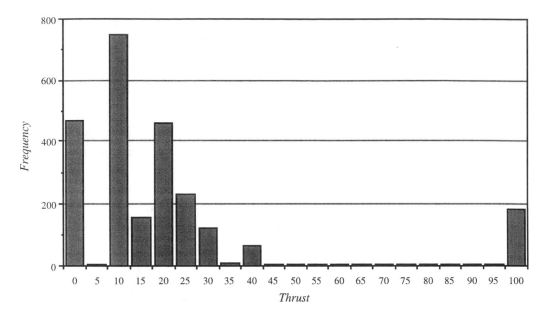

Figure 7.1 Frequency of thrust values in stage 6.

full-throttle. Anything below 10% was considered idle. Another reasonable clustering of values could be to group values from 15 to 35 together.

Absolute and Incremental Controls

An event is recorded when there is a change in one of the control settings. A change is determined by keeping the previous state of the simulation in a buffer. If any of the control settings are different in the current state, a change is recognized. For example, if the thrust is being reduced from 100% to 40%, all of the values in between are recorded. For thrust, these values are easily eliminated as noise during induction.

It is not so easy to eliminate spurious values from the elevator and rollers data. Both thrust and flaps can be set to a particular value and left. However, the effects of the elevator and rollers are cumulative. If we want to bank the aircraft to the left, the stick will be pushed left for a short time and then centered since keeping it left will cause the airplane to roll. Thus, the stick will be centered after most elevator or roller actions. This means that many low elevator and roller values will be recorded as the stick is pushed out and returned to the center position.

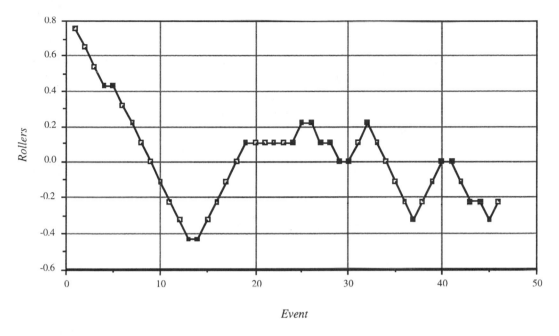

Figure 7.2 Change in rollers.

To ensure that records of low elevator and roller values do not swamp the other data, another filter program removes all but the steady points and extreme points in stick movement. Figure 7.2 shows a small sample of roller settings during a flight. Each point on the graph represents one event. Clearly many of the points are recorded as part of a single movement. The filter program looks for points of inflection in the graph and only passes those on to the induction program. In this graph, only the points marked in black will get through the filter.

7.5 Generating the Autopilot

After processing the data as described above, we can finally submit them to C4.5 to be summarized as rules that can be executed in a controller.

Pruning the Decision Tree

C4.5 has two parameters that can be varied by the user to adjust tree pruning. We have experimented with them to try to obtain the simplest workable rules. One parameter controls C4.5's confidence level. That is, the program will prune the decision tree so that it maintains a minimum classification accuracy with respect to test data. The second parameter controls the minimum number of instances required for a split. For example, if this parameter is set to 10, then no branch in the tree will be created unless at least 10 examples descend down that branch.

We proceed by generating decision trees using the default parameter settings, testing the rules in the simulator and then gradually adjusting the parameters to obtain simpler rules. This continues until the rule "breaks," i.e., it is no longer able to control the plane correctly.

Time and Causality

The rules constructed by C4.5 are purely reactive. They make decisions on the basis of the values in a single state of the simulation. The induction program has no concept of time or causality. In connection with this, some strange rules can turn up. For example, the rule below for thrust in the descent stage was derived from data that was not filtered as described above. There were 2,513 examples in the training set, the minimum split size was set to 5 (since the data from five flights were combined) and the confidence parameter was set to 0.1%.

airspeed > 127 : thrust_100
airspeed ≤ 127 :
| X_feet > 121.33 : thrust_30
| X_feet ≤ 121.33 :
| | elevation ≤ −43 :
| | | Z_feet > −11514.8 : thrust_0
| | | Z_feet ≤ −11514.8 :
| | | | climbspeed ≤ −13 : thrust_0
| | | | climbspeed > 13 :
| | | | Z_feet > −18475.8 : thrust_10
| | | | Z_feet ≤ −18475.8 :
| | | | | Y_feet ≤ 1535.21 : thrust_20
| | | | | Y_feet > 1535.21 : thrust_10
| | elevation > −43 :
| | | Y_feet ≤ 638.76 : thrust_25
| | | Y_feet > 638.76 :
| | | | Z_feet ≤ −26230.1 : thrust_15
| | | | Z_feet > −26230.1 : thrust_20

Only the first two lines of this rule are of interest at present. The first line states that when the airspeed is greater than 127 knots then the thrust should be 100%. When the airspeed is less than or equal to 127 knots the thrust is lower. The exact value being determined by the remainder of the decision tree. Thus C4.5 has correctly detected a correlation between speed and thrust. Unfortunately it uses the speed to determine the thrust when it should be the other way around.

By introducing the response time delays described in section 7.3 and the filtering in section 7.4 causality problems can be overcome to some extent, but rules like this sometimes still occur. At present the only way around this is to hope that savage pruning will improve the rule. For the case above C4.5 was re-run, this time with the minimum split size set to 500 resulting in the following rule:

$Z\_feet \leq -30642 : thrust\_100$
$Z\_feet > -30642 :$
$| \ elevation > -43 : thrust\_20$
$| \ elevation \leq -43 :$
$| \ | \ Z\_feet \leq -16382 : thrust\_10$
$| \ | \ Z\_feet > -16382 : thrust\_0$

This is quite sensible. Z_feet is the distance from the runway. As the airplane nears the runway, it descreases thrust progressively. The elevation rule says that if the nose is pointing down by more than 4.3° then increase the thrust to 20%. This will cause the nose to rise and then the thrust will be reduced to 0 or 10% depending on the distance from the runway. While we wish the aircraft to descend during this stage of the flight, it should not descend too steeply. This rule, working with the elevator rule controls the angle of descent.

We believe that learning could be improved by including some knowledge of causality in the system so that it is able to correctly identify dependencies among variables.

7.6 Linking the Autopilot with the Simulator

To test the induced rules, the original autopilot code in the simulator is replaced by the rules. A post-processor converts C4.5's decision trees into if-statements in C so that they can be incorporated into the flight simulator easily. Hand-crafted C code determines which stage the flight has reached and decides when to change stages. The appropriate rules for each stage are then selected in a switch statement. Each stage has four, independent if-statements, one for each action.

Delays

When the data from the human pilots were recorded, a delay to account for human response time was included. Since the rules were derived from this data, their effects should be delayed by the same amount as was used when the data were recorded. When a rule fires, instead of letting it affect a control setting directly, the rule's output value is stored in a circular buffer. There is one for each of the four controls. The value used for the control setting is one of the previous values in the buffer. A lag constant defines how far to go back into the buffer to get the control setting. The size of the buffer must be set to give a lag that approximates the lag when the data were recorded.

Averaging Control Settings

Earlier we had shown how we eliminate intermediate values in roller and elevator actions so that the induction program is not swamped with spurious data. The rules that result from this data can set values instantaneously as if the stick were moved with infinite speed from one position to another. Clearly this is unrealistic. When control values are taken from the delay buffer, they enter another circular buffer. The controls are set to the average of the values in the buffer. This ensures that controls change smoothly. The larger the buffer, the more gentle are the control changes. By experimentation, we have found that a buffer length of 5 approximates the speed with which the human pilots moved the controls.

7.7 Flying the Autopilot

We have succeeded in synthesizing control rules for a complete flight, including a safe landing. The rules fly the Cessna in a manner very similar to that of the pilot whose data were used to construct the rules. In some cases, the autopilot flies more smoothly than the human pilot. We demonstrate how these rules operate by describing the controllers built for the first four stages. The last three stages are too complex to include in this paper.

Stage 1

The critical rule at take-off is the elevator rule:

elevation > 4 : level_pitch
elevation ≤ 4 :
| airspeed ≤ 0 : level_pitch
| airspeed > 0 : pitch_up_5

This states that as thrust is applied and the elevation is level, pull back on the stick until the elevation increases to 4°. Because of the delay, the final elevation usually reaches 11° which is close to the values usually obtained by the pilot. *pitch_up_5* indicates a larger elevator action, whereas, *pitch_up_1* would indicate a gentle elevator action. The other significant control at this stage is flaps:

elevation ≤ 6 : full_flaps
elevation > 6 : no_flaps

Once the aircraft has reached an elevation angle of 6°, the flaps are raised.

Stage 2

In stage 2, the autopilot is required to attain level flight. Again this is done through the elevator rule:

climbspeed ≤ 13 : level_pitch
climbspeed > 13 : pitch_down_1

When the climb rate exceeds 13 feet/sec push the stick forward gently to bring climb rate down. While this rule makes sense, it does not completely stop the climb. The pilot timed the application of the control carefully so that by the time the stick was re-centered the climb rate was zero and remained so. This rule brings the climb rate down significantly but does not zero it. As a result, the aircraft climbs more than the pilot would have allowed it to.

Stage 3

Stage 3 requires a gentle right turn. The rollers rule is:

twist ≤ −23 : left_roll_3
twist > −23 :
| azimuth ≤ −25 : no_roll
| azimuth > −25 : right_roll_2

C4.5 was designed to handle categorical and numeric values, but it was not designed to handle values like angles and compass headings that are circular. To help it a little, values such as twist and azimuth (compass heading) which range from 0 to 360° were converted to ranges from −180° to +180°. Thus, the roll rule states that while the twist is less than 23° from horizontal and the aircraft is heading North, bank right. When the twist has reached 23° bank left to steady the aircraft. The azimuth rule ensures that the airplane will not bank right again if its heading is more than 25° off North.

Stage 4

The stage 4 rules are more complex than those for the previous stages. To make them understandable, they have been greatly simplified by over-pruning. They are presented to illustrate an important point, that is that rules can work in tandem although there is no explicit link between them. The following rules are for the rollers and elevator in a sharp turn left.

azimuth > 114 : right_roll_1
azimuth ≤ 114 :
| twist ≤ 8 : left_roll_4
| twist > 8 : no_roll
twist ≤ 2 : level_pitch
twist > 2 :
| twist ≤ 10 : pitch_up_1
| twist > 10 : pitch_up_2

A sharp turn requires coordination between roller and elevator actions. As the aircraft banks to a steep angle, the elevator is pulled back. The rollers rule states that while the compass heading has not yet reached 114°, bank left provided that the twist angle does not exceed 8°. The elevator rule states that as long as the aircraft has no twist, leave the elevator at level pitch. If the twist exceeds 2° then pull back on the stick. The stick must be pulled back more sharply for a greater twist. Since the rollers cause twist, the elevator rule is invoked to produce a coordinated turn.

The Complete Flight

The best way of measuring the performance of the rules is to compare a flight by a human pilot with a flight by the autopilot. Figures

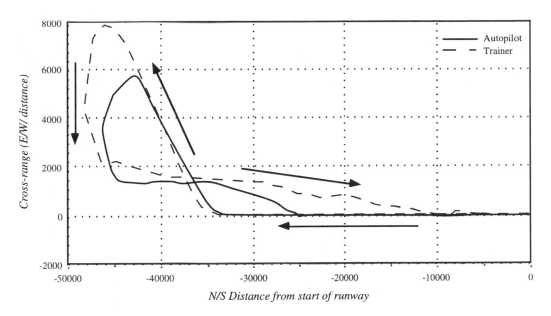

Figure 7.3 Cross-range Profile for Trainer and Autopilot.

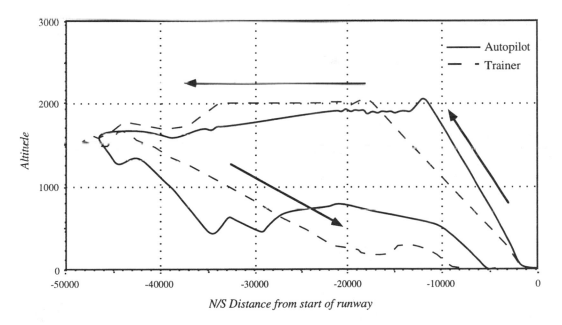

Figure 7.4 Altitude Profile for Trainer and Autopilot.

7.3 and 7.4 show profiles of a flight by one of the human pilots plotted with the profiles of a flight by the autopilot derived from that pilot's data. Figure 7.3 shows the ground track of the aircraft while figure 7.4 shows a horizontal view of the flight path. Note that the vertical and horizontal axes are shown at different scales.

7.8 Discussion

One of the interesting things we have learned in this study is that good pilots are bad! The autopilot whose profiles are shown in figures 7.3 and 7.4 was derived from a human pilot who had to make many course corrections during his flights. While such a flight is not a pretty sight, it provides useful data for the induction program. Pilots who are frugal in their use of the controls give few examples of what to do when things go wrong.

We have observed a "clean-up" effect noted in Michie, Bain and Hayes-Michie (1990). The flight log of any trainer will contain many spurious actions due to human inconsistency and corrections required as a result of inattention. It appears that effects of these examples are pruned away by C4.5, leaving a control rule which flies very smoothly. This effect was particularly noticeable in the approach stage of the flight when the trainer performed many roll manoeuvres to keep the aircraft lined-up on the runway. We have informally observed that the autopilot does a much better job of maintaining a steady glide path to the runway. Future experiments will attempt to quantify this difference in performance.

7.9 Conclusion

Almost all applications of inductive learning, so far, have been in classification tasks such as medical diagnosis. For example, medical records of patients' symptoms and accompanying diagnoses made by physicians are entered into an induction program which constructs rules that will automatically diagnose new patients on the basis of the previous data. The output is a classification. Just as diagnostic rules can be learned by observing a physician at work, we should be able to learn how to control a system by watching a human operator at work. In this case, the data provided to the induction program are logs of the actions taken by the operator in response to changes in the system. We have used a simple procedural model for inductively building sets of control rules. An induced rule-set constitutes a "strategy" for the given subtask—a kind of classifier that maps state records into action names, rather than mapping patient records into disease names. But in both the medical and control cases, there is a fundamental difference to be drawn between a purely symptomatic classification and one based on an understanding of the domain's causality. The latter requires declarative models able to support "what if" analysis, recognizing that actions (just like diseases) occur in response to, and result in, changes in the system being controlled. Symptomatic classification only deals with static data and does not cope explicitly with temporal and casual relations.

In our preliminary study we were able to demonstrate the feasibility of learning a specific control task. The next challenge is to build a generalized method that can learn basic skills that can be used in a variety of tasks. These skills become building blocks that can be assembled into a complete new controller to meet the demands of a specified task.

One of the limitations we have encountered with existing learning algorithms is that they can only use the primitive attributes supplied in the data. This results in control rules that cannot be understood by a human expert. Constructive induction (or predicate invention) may be necessary to build higher-level attributes that simplify the rules. A methodology for doing this, using the human expert as the source of the required backward-chained control hierarchy, is known as "structured induction" (Shapiro 1987). Our requirement now is for progress toward automating this kind of structuring (see Muggleton and Buntine 1988).

Machine learning of control systems may lead to a better understanding of subcognitive skills which are inaccessible to introspection. For example, if you are asked by what method you ride a bicycle, you will not be able to provide an adequate answer because that skill has been learned and is executed at a subconscious level. By monitoring performance of a subcognitive skill, we are able to construct a functional description of that skill in the form of symbolic rules. This not only reveals the nature of the skill but also may be used as an aid to training since the student can be explicitly shown what he or she is doing.

Learning control rules by induction provides a new way of building complex control systems quickly and easily. Where these involve safety critical tasks, the "clean-up" effect mentioned in the Discussion holds particular interest. While our experiments have been primarily concerned with flight automation, inductive methods can be applied to wide range of related problems. For example, an anaesthetist can be seen as controlling a patient in an operating theatre in much the same way as a pilot controls an aircraft. The anaesthetist monitors the patient's condition just as a pilot monitors the aircraft's instruments. The anaesthetist changes dosages of drugs and gases to alter the state of a system (the patient) in the same way that a pilot alters thrust and altitude to control the state of a system (the aircraft). A flight plan can be divided into stages where different control strategies are required, for example, take-off, straight and level flight, landing, etc. So, too, the administration of anaesthetics can be divided into stages: putting the patient to sleep, maintaining a steady state during the operation and revival after the procedure has been completed. Process control in safety-critical applications in industry should also be mentioned.

Our current research is aimed at producing a reliable and reproducible method for building controllers. Future work will be directed toward understanding the effects of causality and using structured and constructive induction to help make the control rules more compact and more readable.

Acknowledgments

Jim Kehoe and Peter Horne conducted the human reaction time studies and collected much valuable data. Mark Pendrith performed many of the modifications to the flight simulator. Silicon Graphics Incorporated made the source code of the flight simulator available. This research has been supported by the Australian Research Council and the University of New South Wales.

Note

This chapter first appeared in *Proceedings of the Ninth International Machine Learning Conference (ML '92)*, edited by D. Sleeman and P. Edwards, published by Morgan Kaufmann, San Mateo, CA, 1992, and is reproduced here with permission.

References

Anderson, C. W., and W. T. Miller. (1991). A set of challenging control problems. In Miller, Sutton, and Werbos (eds.), *Neural Networks for Control*. Cambridge, Mass.: MIT Press.

Chambers, R. A., and D. Michie. (1969). Man-machine co-operation on a learning task. In R. Parslow, R. Prowse, and R. Elliott-Green (eds.), *Computer Graphics: Techniques and Applications*. London: Plenum.

Donaldson, P. E. K. (1960). Error decorrelation: A technique for matching a class of functions. In *Proceedings of the Third International Conference on Medical Electronics*, pp. 173–178.

Michie, D., M. Bain, and J. E. Hayes-Michie. (1990). Cognitive models from subcognitive skills. In J. McGhee, M. Grimble, and P. Mowforth (eds.), *Knowledge-Based Systems in Industrial Control*. London: Peter Peregrinus.

Muggleton, S., and W. Buntine. (1988). Machine invention of first-order predicates by inverting resolution. In *Proceedings of the Fifth International Machine Learning Conference*, pp. 339–352. Ann Arbor, Mich. Morgan Kaufmann.

Quinlan, J. R. (1987) Simplifying decision trees. *International Journal of Man-Machine Studies*, 27: 221–234.

Sammut, C., and D. Michie. (1991). Controlling a "black box" simulation of a spacecraft. *AI Magazine*, 12(1): 56–63.

Shapiro, A. D. (1987). *Structured Induction in Expert Systems*. Reading, Mass.: Addison-Wesley.

Widrow, B., and F. W. Smith. (1964). Pattern recognising control systems. In J. T. Tou and R. H. Wilcox (eds.), *Computer and Information Sciences*. London: Clever Hume Press.

8 Imitation of Sequential and Hierarchical Structure in Action: Experimental Studies with Children and Chimpanzees

Andrew Whiten

8.1 Introduction

Until recently, much of the research effort on animal imitation has been devoted to the basic task of discovering, for each species studied, whether some kind of imitation does in fact exist—*do* apes ape? Do monkeys, rats, or pigeons? Establishing which species imitate is important if we wish to elucidate the evolutionary construction process that generated the particular cognitive architecture of our own imitative mind. Unfortunately, the answer to the basic "existence" question is currently controversial for most of the species that have been studied (see, for example, Heyes 1998; Byrne and Russon 1998; and accompanying peer commentaries). Within this literature one finds views as divergent as that imitation has been established only among great apes, or that imitation has been shown in some species of birds and mammals but not yet in nonhuman primates.

There is not scope here for a full review of recent work in this area (see Whiten 2000 on primates and Galef 1998 for a wider perspective), but three possible reasons for the turmoil within it can be highlighted. The first is that some authorities restrict the definition of imitation, excluding the scope others are prepared to accept; for example, some insist the act copied must be "novel," others do not. Second, there is disagreement about the correct interpretation of results emanating from the use of different methodologies; for example, some insist experiments can provide compelling evidence of imitation, which observation of spontaneous behavior cannot. Third is the prospect that the scope of imitation may vary so much among animal taxa that some forms will be difficult to directly compare with others. To be optimistic, it is possible that some of the disagreements in defining imitation are simply reflecting this, so that present disputes and confusions will flower into the clearer, interesting comparative analyses of the future.

So how can we arrive at clearer conclusions that achieve general acceptance? Taking the issue of definition first, nobody is able to legislate on what is "truly" imitation. The best we can hope for is that each writer routinely states what they take imitation to be and by survival of the fittest, some consensual usage will emerge. It is to be hoped that this "technical" usage will map to that in every-day speech, or further confusion can surely be expected. Taking into account also the third issue noted above, about varied *kinds* of imitation, I advocate a relatively broad definition, coupled with recognition that a diversity of processes will be discriminable within this general category. Whiten and Ham (1992, p. 250) defined imitation as a process in which an individual "learns some aspect(s) of the intrinsic form of an act" from another. This defini-tion recognizes that no imitation can be exact, but instead there will be a range of fidelity, which at its lower threshold will repre-sent a "just discriminable match" between the action patterns of imitator and model. This seems to be consistent with both the everyday meaning of imitation and with the ways in which the term is commonly used by the scientific community.

This "threshold" definition can then lead to clear conclusions if coupled with a powerful methodology that has come to be called the "two-action" method in comparative psychology (e.g., Zentall 1996) and "cross-target method" in developmental psychology (e.g., Meltzoff 1996). In these approaches, each subject sees a model perform one of two different action patterns. Consistent with Whiten and Ham's threshold definition, imitation can then be rigorously demonstrated so long as there is *some* measurable bias in one group of subjects' actions relative to the other, in the direc-tion predicted, if some matching is taking place. Of course, the fidelity of an imitation to its model may be greater than this mini-mal requirement, and the two-action approach allows us to mea-sure clearly the extent and scope of the matching achieved. The two-action method appears superior to others that typically com-pare the effect of watching only one type of model with watching no model. In a single-model approach, even if the act modeled has a zero probability of being done by subjects who do *not* see the model, it is unclear just how much of the match shown by a sub-ject is actually a *copy* of the model it has seen. It might be that the model simply draws the attention of the subject to relevant parts of the environment ("stimulus enhancement") and the subject comes to act like the model because this is a good way to tackle the task. The subject might arrive at this by a number of processes ranging from trial and error to more rapid insight. Other possibilities include the subject copying some parts of the task but coming to match others through its own resources; for example, it might learn some elements of the task from observation but organize them sequentially in the same way as the model because it sees this is appropriate to how it understands the task. The two-action method has the potential to disambiguate such possibilities, according to how we design the contrast between the two alternatives. Examples of how we have instantiated this approach using "artificial foods" handled by human and nonhuman primates are described further below.

The power of this approach to offer clear answers about the existence of imitation can be extended to more advanced questions about what *kind* of imitation is occurring. Whiten and Ham (1992) suggested that, in effect, an imitator, B, "has to get the program for the behavior out of A's head"—but exactly what aspects of A's program can B reconstruct? What aspects of the model's acts does the imitator extract, represent, and incorporate into its copy? One can envisage numerous aspects that might, in principle, be independently copied (Whiten and Custance 1996). These include the bodily shape of the act (e.g., type of manual grip used), its laterality (e.g., role of left versus right hands), its extent (e.g., how expansive a gesture is), its speed or tempo (e.g., rate of hammering), its orientation with respect to self (e.g., brushing oneself), orientation to the environment (e.g., targeting of a tool), causal and/or intentional relationships, and sequential and/or hierarchical structure. The beauty of the two-action method is that it can be used systematically to vary models in each of those respects, so as to examine with clarity which of them are represented in subsequent imitation. In the present paper, we consider what young children and chimpanzees acquire when they witness one of two alternative models that differ in the sequential structure of a fixed set of component elements. We then tackle the imitation of hierarchical structure in a similar way.

8.2 Imitation of Sequential Structure

Bruner (1972) proposed that, in great apes at least, imitation might involve "construction of an action pattern by the appropriate sequencing of a set of constituent subroutines to match a model" (p. 695) and he noted that such a hypothesis is amenable to experimental analysis. Whiten and Custance (1996) discussed the merits and pitfalls of two different approaches to this. In one, the modeled sequence would incorporate actions necessary to *enable* the next act to take place. Although this has the merit of emulating the situation often obtaining in the real world, it is weakened by the fact that the experimental condition can only be compared with a no-model control condition, thus suffering the problems of that kind of design outlined earlier. The other approach is to apply the logic of the "two-action" design, offering some subjects a sequence of actions that follows an arbitrarily different order than the one other subjects see. This can offer the most unassailable evidence of sequence-copying, although one must be sensitive to the prospect that negative results might arise if subjects can "see" the arbitrariness of the sequencing. This second approach has been used in a study by Whiten (1998a), the key results of which will next be summarized, before considering the more complex issue of imitating hierarchical structure.

Subjects and Models

Four chimpanzees (two mature and two young adults) were the subjects of this experiment. They were housed in large enclosures, each day experiencing a variety of social interactions among themselves and with their human caretakers. This made it appropriate to use a familiar caretaker as a model to whom subjects were likely to attend closely. This also had the advantage that the actions done by the model could be closely controlled. Whether results similar to those reported below would be obtained if the model were also a chimpanzee is at present not known.

The "Artificial Fruit" Task

The methods we have developed to study imitation experimentally are based upon our own and others' earlier ethological field studies of the foraging behavior of monkeys and apes. Subjects are allowed to watch a model performing a task designed to be an analogue of natural food-processing tasks faced by wild primates—the kinds of tasks they have evolved mechanisms to learn about. "Artificial fruits" (figure 8.1) have been designed that can be processed in different ways, following the logic of the "two-action" method outlined above; differences between the ways observers subsequently approach the task themselves can then show just what they are (or are not) copying.

Figure 8.1 An "artificial fruit." Here, the pin is being spun using an index finger. Above the pin is the handle, which is freed by removing the pin. At the rear are two embedded bolts. When pin, handle, and bolts are moved, the top can be opened to gain access to edible contents.

Whether chimpanzees would imitate sequential structure was studied using an artificial fruit that required the removal of several defenses to extract the edible core. The fruit was essentially a box with a lid that was held in place by the defenses. Defenses included a pair of "bolts," which were passed through rings on both box and lid, linking them together; a "handle" component with a flange holding the lid down; and a pin that held the handle in place. The pin provides the nickname for this fruit—"pin-apple" —distinguishing it from another fruit described later.

In an earlier experiment (Whiten et al. 1996), each subject saw one of two different methods to remove each defense and this was repeated in the present experiment; the bolts were either pulled out with a twisting motion, or poked through with the index finger; the pin was either spun round with one finger, or turned as in winding a clock, before being pulled out; and the handle was either turned so its flange no longer held the lid down, or it was pulled vertically out of the barrel that held it. Whiten and colleagues (1996) found that chimpanzees tended to imitate the method they saw used to remove the bolts, but not the methods used on the other defenses.

In the present experiment, each of four different patterns of removing the defenses was modeled by a human demonstrator in front of a different chimpanzee subject, each ending with lifting the lid:

1. Twist outer bolt—Twist near bolt—Spin pin—Turn handle
2. Poke outer bolt—Poke near bolt—Turn pin—Pull handle
3. Spin pin—Turn handle—Twist outer bolt—Twist near bolt
4. Turn pin—Pull handle—Poke outer bolt—Poke near bolt

Thus, two different sequences of defense removal were used, each sequence being made up of one of the two alternative methods for dealing with each defense. Each subject saw the model three times before its own first attempt; then two further demonstrations were given, each followed by the subject making another attempt.

Results and Discussion

The key result for present purposes was that in the third and final trial, sequence was copied. In fact, the match was perfect for three of the subjects. For the fourth subject, the order in which defenses was removed also matched that of the model, excepting only that he removed the two bolts in a different order, before proceeding to remove the pin and handle, the sequence he had witnessed. This subject also made a tentative approach first to the pin, spinning it once, before turning his attention to removing the bolts, the first defense dealt with by the model he had watched. Taking all four subjects' matching together, these results represent a high and statistically significant level of fidelity to the observed sequential pattern. Imitation of the method of bolt removal was also found (poke versus pull-and-twist), consistent with our earlier study (Whiten et al. 1996). Perhaps surprisingly, this is the first demonstration of imitation of the sequential structure of a series of functional actions by a nonhuman species (Whiten 1998a).

Even for young children, imitation of a sequence of acts has been demonstrated only recently using this approach of showing alternative sequences made up of the same elements (Call and Tomasello 1995). Some other studies have compared young children's imitation of "arbitrary" sequences with imitation of acts that are physically necessary to enable the next one in the sequence. More thorough copying of action patterns of the latter kind was found (e.g., Bauer et al. 1998). However, in these studies the term "arbitrary" does not mean "arbitrarily arranged alternative sequences of the same elements," it refers only to absence of the physically necessary relationships that characterized the other condition. This means there is an inherent ambiguity about what really *is* the sequence and how many elements constitute it, from the subject's perspective. The experimenter may describe a "two-step sequence," but does the subject represent this as two steps, the sequencing of which it copies, or does it in fact represent just one behavior pattern? That may not matter for the research question such studies are designed to answer, but it does mean there is a question about whether the child is performing the sequential pattern because she is copying it, or because she appreciates the order that will be physically necessary. The "mirrored" sequences used in the present experiment (e.g., ABC versus CBA) have the power to offer the strongest evidence that sequential structure is in fact being copied in its own right.

Byrne and Russon (1998) have offered an interesting analysis of possible copying of sequential structure in two phenomena they have studied in the spontaneous behavior of gorillas and orangutans respectively. The first of these concerns feeding skills of wild gorillas that employ several steps, the sequencing of which the authors feel is too difficult for young gorillas to achieve by individual learning. The second concerns orangutans performing acts like those of the humans in the rehabilitation camp they share. The hypothesis that these involve sequence-imitation might be correct, but it seems clear that the evidence needed to test this remains to be collected, as is evident in the peer commentary to Byrne and Russon's (1998) paper. Several commentators (although not all) found the evidence quite compelling that orangutans were copying some actions of humans (including Whiten 1998b), yet none who passed judgment recognized evidence that *sequential order* in the human acts was copied. Likewise, commentators who offered judgment on the gorilla case concluded that evidence is not yet available that would distinguish a hypothesis of social learning from that of individual learning of the sequential patterning evident in adult gorilla feeding. Tomasello and Call (1997) go so far as to list this case as "individual learning" in their comprehensive tabulation of studies referring to social learning (1997, table 9.2). This seems unwarranted (Whiten 2000); the imitation hypothesis has not been disproved, but is instead a plausible scenario to the worker who knows the animals best and surely remains an interesting one to test. Whether this can be done without recourse to experimentation is less clear. In a two-action experiment, any differential copying of *alternative* action-sequences becomes clear. By contrast, young, wild gorillas experience only the efficient, ubiquitously displayed method of their elders, and social and individual learning can be expected to be intimately entangled as the youngsters develop the method themselves over periods of months or even years.

Within the span of the present brief experiment, interesting developmental effects were observed. Sequence-imitation was not immediately apparent but emerged after repeated trials (involving repetitions of both demonstrations and attempts by subjects), suggesting that the underlying representations are built up through repeated processes of revision. These would appear to include overwriting of some of the products of individual learning (since some subjects were originally successful through sequences of action they later abandoned in favor of the one the model used).

This raises a further question as to whether the underlying representation acquired is of a sequence-only program, or one that is hierarchically structured. Either could be capable of generating a sequence like that of the model. A sequential representation might simply specify a chainlike program, of the kind "spin pin, then turn handle, then pull outer bolt, then pull inner bolt," and so on. An alternative would be a set of conditional rules, of the kind "when pin out, pull handle; when handle out, pull outer bolt," and so on, or alternatively and more flexibly, "pull bolt only if handle has been removed," etc. These have yet to be discriminated by experiment, but the first, merely chainlike kind of program seems implausible for animals that are so evidently able to interrupt one goal-directed action temporarily to interleave another. When opening the fruit, our imitating chimpanzees are often temporarily distracted by other events yet, unsurprisingly, do not grind to a halt because a "chain" has been broken. The more flexible kinds of sequencing rules thus offer the most plausible hypotheses for what has been copied.

The alternative of some kind of hierarchical program having been copied arises principally because two of the defenses (the bolts) were similar and were typically removed by the chimpanzees in tandem, as had the model. Might this be because this "nesting" is perceived as part of a hierarchical structure (figure 8.2), or was it the result of pure sequence-following (or even just

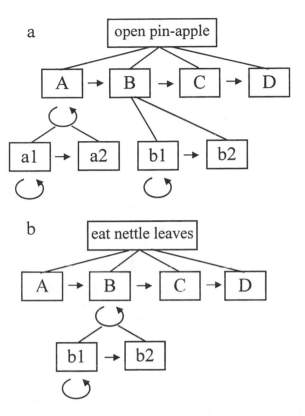

Figure 8.2 Hierarchical structure in (*a*) one set of routines for opening of artificial pin-apple fruit (after Whiten, 1998b, figure 1); A, remove bolts; B, remove pin; C, remove handle; D, open lid; a1, poke bolt; a2, lift from back; b1, spin pin; b2, take out; (*b*) a natural counterpart for comparison—routines for feeding on nettles used by wild gorillas, suggested to be acquired through imitation by Byrne and Russon (1998, after figure 2), A, find patch; B, collect leaves; C, clean (optional); D, fold blades; b1, strip stem; b2, tear off petioles. Curved arrows indicate iteration to a criterion before proceeding to next act to right.

because the bolts are close to each other)? With the artificial fruit used for this experiment, it seems impossible to resolve this question experimentally (Whiten 1998b). Thus, if a model were presented in which instead of the bolts being removed as a nested pair, they were taken out separately (e.g., outer-bolt, pin, handle, inner-bolt), appropriate copying of that model, and appropriate copying of the nested-bolts routine by other subjects who see *that* model, could each be done by learning the observed sequence alone. Clearly, testing for the copying of hierarchical structure requires an inherently more complex experimental design. In the sequence-imitation study, similar elements of action were modeled in different *sequential* orders; now a task is required in which the same set of elements is modeled in different *hierarchical* patterns. To this we now turn.

8.3 Imitation of Hierarchical Structure

Stimulated by Byrne and Russon's (1998) hypothesis that imitation may underlie aspects of the gorilla and orangutan data they discussed, an experimental task to test such a possibility has been constructed. The task is designed to be suitable for both children and chimpanzees. For this reason, it has been kept as simple as possible, but it is necessarily more complex than that used in previous observational learning experiments with apes. Here, we summarize results for 3-year-old children that show both that the method is a good test of hierarchy-copying, and that children of this age respond in instructive ways (Whiten, Brown, and Lee, in preparation, for full details). Testing with chimpanzees remains an aim for the future.

The task is based on another "fruit" in which the model's manipulations of the defenses include actions dealing with sixteen minitasks organized along what we shall call four "rows" and four "columns." The rationale of the approach is that each subject sees either (1) each row dealt with in turn (i.e., the four acts along it done before proceeding to the next row) or alternatively (2) each column dealt with in turn. Thus, two alternative tree-structures are implemented (row-wise versus column-wise priorities), of which each subject sees only one (figure 8.3). There are potentially many different aspects of the hierarchical and sequential structures in the modeled behavior that an observing subject could in principle represent and copy. Thus, they might copy the hierarchical, branching structure, but not any of the sequential order that is indicated by the horizontal arrows in figure 8.3, panels b and c. It could also be that they would copy such sequencing at one level of the tree, but not at another.

Methods

THE TASK
This "fruit" consists of a clear Plexiglas box with a lid that fits over it, held in place by four skewers passing horizontally right through

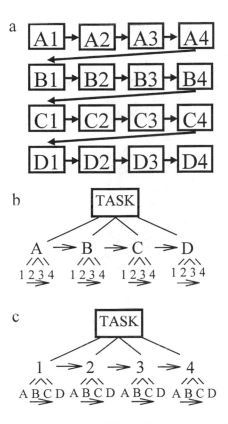

Figure 8.3 Design for study of hierarchy imitation. (*a*) Row-wise execution of 16 items, i.e., each row completed before next row. (*b*) Hierarchical tree structure of row-wise execution. (*c*) Hierarchical tree structure of column-wise execution, i.e., each column completed before next column.

the rim of the lid and the top of the box, from front to back. These skewers have to be removed before the lid can be lifted to obtain the raisins inside. This is difficult because the skewers do not protrude at the back, and at the front they only protrude a little into recesses, each of which is differently shaped and colored. This makes it extremely awkward to attempt to poke out the skewers using the fingers. The way provided to make this job easier is to pick up one of the handle-sticks provided on top of the box, stab it into one of four differently shaped and colored tablets resting at the back of the lid, then use this "key" to poke into the corresponding shape on the front of the lid (figure 8.4), shoving the skewer out at the back where it can be grasped and removed. This needs to be done for each skewer using the appropriate key. For this reason, we have nicknamed this the "key-way" fruit.

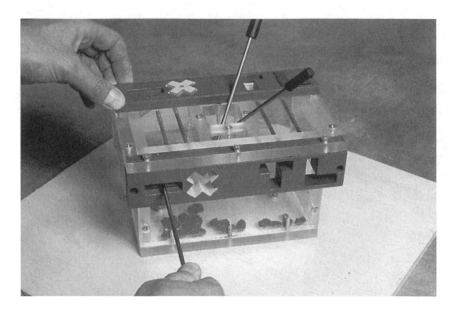

Figure 8.4 "Key-way" fruit. One of the handles has been stabbed into the left-most tablet at the back of the lid (the next, X-shaped tablet can be seen still in place there), to form a tool that is being poked into the appropriately-shaped recess on the front of the lid (the first two steps of a "column-wise" approach). This pushes one of the skewers through so it can be pulled out at the back. The tool is then taken out, completing the fourth act of a "column sequence."

PROCEDURE

There are, of course, two hierarchically different ways to use the keys on the key-way fruit and each of two samples of children saw only one. In the "column" approach, each key was made and used to remove the corresponding skewer, followed by withdrawal and discarding of the key. Half the subjects saw this begin with the left-most column and proceed to the right, half saw the opposite sequence of columns executed (i.e., starting with the right-most). In the alternative "row" method, all the handles were stabbed into the row of tablets; then the tools were each poked in turn into the row of recesses, followed by removal of all the skewers and finally, discarding of all the tools. Again, half the subjects saw the rows executed left-to-right, half saw the opposite sequence.

Each child saw two demonstrations followed by their own attempt. They were not instructed to do what the model had done, but were instead invited to "have their own go." Then, a final demonstration was given and the child was allowed a second attempt.

We anticipated that if some children performed a perfect copy of the sequence they had seen, we still might not know if they were copying the hierarchical structure of what they had seen; they might just have been running through a sequence of 16 items in the observed order. Accordingly, in all demonstrations, the third tablet and corresponding skewer were absent. In the child's second attempt, these items were in place. Our logic was that if the child were merely following the sequence of 12 items they had seen, they would stall at the new, intercalated items, or leave them until last. If, on the other hand, they had extracted the hierarchical structure of what they had seen in a sufficiently abstract way, they would incorporate the new subtask into this pattern.

Results and Discussion

Although there was much individual variation, the statistically reliable tendency among these young children was to copy the hierarchical structure of the version of the actions they had seen. Figure 8.5 portrays this effect for the children's first trial; a similar pattern was obtained in the second trial. This pattern was also obtained for the "test" items added in the second trial—the missing tablet and the associated skewer. This is a clear demonstration of the imitation of hierarchical structure, apparently the first for any primate, including human ones. Developmental psychologists have shown that hierarchical structure in a task can facilitate imitation of it (Bauer and Mandler 1989), and that children develop an increasing facility to copy the structure of actions in a way flexible enough to ignore changes in the props used (Hayne, MacDonald, and Barr 1997), but these findings are not the same as a demonstration that a hierarchical structure of action is itself copied, in the manner shown here.

Whether the sequencing built into the demonstrations (left-right or right-left) was copied is a different matter. In fact, sequence was not copied; at least, at the level of statistical comparisons between the appropriate samples, there was no tendency to follow the sequential order witnessed in any of the four comparisons we can make: sequence within rows, within columns, from row to row, or from column to column. This means that the appropriate representation of what these children had acquired is that illustrated in figure 8.6, which omits the horizontal "sequential" arrows included in figure 8.3, indicating structures that might potentially have been copied. As a group, children copied the hierarchical structure but not the sequential structure in the task. The approxi-

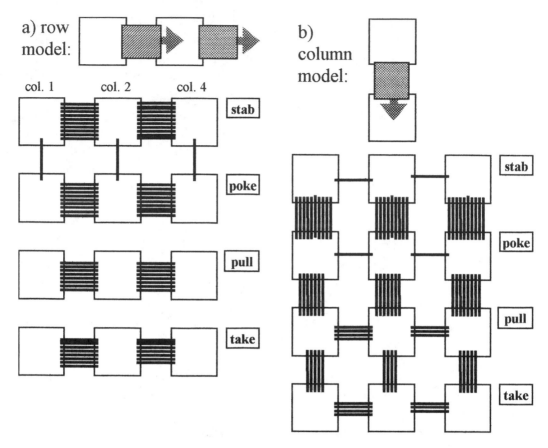

Figure 8.5 Total row-wise and column-wise transitions in trial 1 by children who had seen model use: (*a*) Row method (*n* = 11 children), (*b*) Column method (*n* = 11 children). Each line equals one transition between acts for each child. "Diagonal" transitions involved in moving from one row (or column) to the next are not shown. Note column 3 of the task was missing in this trial. Children showed a clear tendency to follow whichever strategy they had witnessed earlier: those who saw the row model proceeded along rows, making hardly any transitions down columns, in stark contrast to children who saw the column model.

mate content of the imitated part of such a child's approach is suggested in figure 8.7.

However, there were some children who did perform the sequence they saw, at both levels or at only one. Although the group results do not allow us to conclude that these children's efforts are more than chance occurrences, it is also true that they do not allow us to reject the possibility that *some* children are copying sequence as well as hierarchy (whereas others, by contrast, are perhaps exploring alternative routes through the task). Candidate cases of sequence-copying are shown for each of two children in figure 8.6,

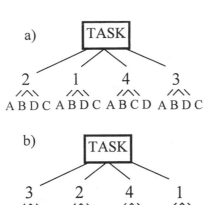

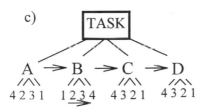

Figure 8.6 What program did children acquire? Utilizing the scheme of figure 8.2, panels show three variations. Hierarchical structure was copied, but omitting sequential ordering where it could vary (logically A must precede B, and B must precede C/D): (*a*) Performance of the "average" child, as implied by the group results, with no matching to sequences observed; (*b*) Performance of child Adam (column condition), showing a match to sequence only at the "lower" level of the hierarchy; (*c*) Performance of child Natalie (row condition), showing a match to sequence at the "upper" level, but absence of matching in all but one of the lower nested sequences.

b and c. That these children incorporated the extra test tablet into the pattern they copied shows they could not *merely* be copying sequence, however. If these children *were* actually copying all of the sequential as well as the hierarchical structure they acted out, the corresponding program content suggested in figure 8.7 would be different. For Adam, it would omit the rule to perform column subroutines in any physically possible order, and instead specify their sequence (as listed in figure 8.7). For Natalie, there would need to be an additional specification, such as amending line 2 to "process_leftmost_column."

Whatever the truth of the hypothesis that *some* children may be copying sequence, the group results show it cannot be regarded as a general characteristic of the "average child" in this study. This may appear to present a paradox, because we have found that

```
┌─────────────────────────────────────────────────────────┐
│  ┌──────────────────────────────┐                        │
│  │ PROCEDURE process_fruit      │                        │
│  ├──────────────────────────────┴─────────────────────┐  │
│  │ {DO process_column UNTIL all_defences_out           │ │
│  │  ┌──────────────────────────────┐                   │ │
│  │  │ PROCEDURE process_column     │                   │ │
│  │  ├──────────────────────────────┴────────────────┐  │ │
│  │  │ {in any physically possible order:             │  │ │
│  │  │ DO pick_handle-stick                           │  │ │
│  │  │ DO stab_tablet UNTIL tablet _fixed (->tool)    │  │ │
│  │  │ DO poke_tool UNTIL right_in                    │  │ │
│  │  │ DO pull_ skewer UNTIL skewer_out               │  │ │
│  │  │ DO take_tool_out_&_discard}                    │  │ │
│  │  └────────────────────────────────────────────────┘  │ │
│  │                                                       │ │
│  │  DO remove_lid UNTIL lid_off                          │ │
│  │  DO harvest_edible-parts UNTIL consumed}              │ │
│  └───────────────────────────────────────────────────────┘ │
└─────────────────────────────────────────────────────────────┘
```

Figure 8.7 "Pseudo-program" consistent with children's imitation, illustrated for column-wise condition. The notation (→ *tool*) is used to indicate that stabbing the tablet creates a keylike tool, that is then used as unit.

young children, tested for sequential imitation in the same manner as for the chimpanzees described earlier, likewise copy the sequence of opening the pin-apple and indeed do so more readily than the chimpanzees (Brown 1996; Whiten and Brown 1999). Speculatively, I suggest that the explanation may lie in the way in which the imitative processes interact with the subjects' other understanding of the world, including, in this case, beliefs about certain aspects of physical causality. To an intelligent adult, close inspection of the key-way fruit could be sufficient to suspect that it really does not matter whether one starts on the left or right. Although the same might be guessed with respect to sequential opening of the pin-apple, this fruit does not have the same obvious symmetry as does the key-way, so subjects (whether child or chimpanzee) may lean to the "imitatively conservative" attitude of copying the sequence of opening manipulations. For all one can see as an observer, this *might* be important to do. Indeed, one cannot *see* that the pin needs pulling before the handle, it is just that the pin does in fact lock the bottom of the handle—similarly, without experimenting, one would not know whether some other internal structure makes the observed sequence of processing the fruit the best order to follow. Understanding how subjects' non-imitative perception and cognition of what they watch interacts with the imitative processes may prove a fruitful target for future research.

8.4   Conclusion

As a result of these experiments, we now have the first evidence of sequence imitation by animals, together with findings about its construction (in chimpanzees) and the first evidence of hierarchy imitation, together with findings about the particular form this takes (in children). Future work should involve establishing more direct child-chimpanzee comparisons with respect to these achievements.

Byrne and Russon (1998) proposed including reference to imitation of both sequential and hierarchical structure in a general concept of "program-level imitation" (PLI). The above results, showing that these two aspects of structure can become dissociated, suggest that we should be wary of any proposal conceptually to roll them together. I therefore prefer to avoid the term PLI in favor of clearer claims for specific achievements that we might more accurately label *sequence-copying* and *hierarchy-copying*. Elsewhere, I discuss some more fundamental problems with the concept of PLI (Whiten 1998b, and in press). Central in these is that PLI is sometimes described as "copying the outline structure" of a task. This is a weak specification that may well apply to much imitation in animals—perhaps all of it, according to Whiten and Ham's (1992) definition cited earlier. At the other extreme, the specification of copying hierarchical structure is a very strong claim, both in the sense that currently no evidence for it exists in animals and that the requirements to demonstrate it are quite severe, as illustrated by the experiment I have described. The reliance of PLI on a variety of criteria, given different emphasis in various attempts to apply them, makes it a confusing notion to pin down empirically.

If we focus instead on specific hypotheses about sequence-copying and hierarchy copying, empirical conclusions may be clearer. As but an ethologist and a psychologist, I would not want to claim that experiments are necessarily the only routes to testing such hypotheses, or indeed to identifying imitation of any kind. However, development of an experimental design for identifying hierarchy-imitation, as described above, may help in working out clearly what is required of any counterpart that could be applied in observation of spontaneous behavior. As the complexity of the experiment described indicates, this is a quite demanding objective!

Acknowledgments

Work reported in this paper was supported by an F. M. Bird Fellowship (Emory University); a Leverhulme Fellowship; a BBSRC Wain Travel Grant, to AW; also NIH grant RR–00165 and NICHHD grant HD06016 to Georgia State University's Language Research Center, directed by D. Rumbaugh and S. Savage-Rumbaugh. I am grateful for the support of the latter in conducting the chimpanzee study. For comments and discussion I thank R. Byrne, J. Call, D. Custance, T. Lee, P. Foldiak, and B. Tiddeman. The contents of this chapter first appeared in *Proceedings of the AISB'99 Symposium on Imitation in Animals and Artifacts*, pp. 38–46, Edinburgh, 1999.

References

Bauer, P. J., L. A. Hertsgaard, P. Dropnik, and B. P. Daly. When even arbitrary order becomes important: Developments in reliable temporal sequencing of arbitrarily ordered events. *Memory* 6: 165–198, 1998.

Bauer, P. J., and J. M. Mandler. One thing follows another: Effects of temporal structure on 1 to 2-year-olds' recall of events. *Developmental Psychology* 25: 197–206, 1989.

Brown, J. D. Imitation, play, and theory of mind in autism: An observational and experimental study. Ph.D. thesis, University of St. Andrews, 1996.

Bruner, J. S. Nature and use of immaturity. *American Psychologist* 27: 687–708, 1972.

Byrne, R. W., and A. E. Russon. Learning by imitation: A hierarchical approach. *Behavioral and Brain Sciences* 21: 667–709, 1998.

Call, J., and M. Tomasello. The use of social information in the problem-solving of orangutans and human children. *Journal of Comparative Psychology* 109: 308–320, 1995.

Galef, B. G. Jr. Recent progress in studies of imitation and social learning in animals. In M. Saborin, F. Craik, and M. Robert, eds., *Advances in Psychological Science: Volume 2. Biological and Cognitive Aspects*, pp. 275–300. Hove, UK: Psychology Press, 1998.

Hayne, H., S. MacDonald, and R. Barr. Developmental changes in the specificity of memory over the second year of life. *Infant Behaviour and Development* 20: 233–245, 1997.

Heyes, C. M. Theory of mind in nonhuman primates. *Behavioral and Brain Sciences* 21: 101–148, 1998.

Meltzoff, A. N. The human infant as imitative generalist: A 20-year progress report on infant imitation with implications for comparative psychology. In C. M. Heyes and B. G. Galef Jr., eds., *Social Learning in Animals: The Roots of Culture*, pp 347–370. London: Academic Press, 1996.

Tomasello, M., and J. Call. *Primate Cognition*. Oxford: Oxford University Press, 1997.

Whiten, A. Imitation of the sequential structure of actions by chimpanzees (*Pan troglodytes*). *Journal of Comparative Psychology* 112: 270–281, 1998a.

Whiten, A. How imitators represent the imitated: The vital experiments. Commentary on Byrne and Russon: "Learning by imitation: A hierarchical approach." *Behavioral and Brain Sciences* 21: 707–708, 1998b.

Whiten, A. Primate culture and social learning. *Cognitive Science* 24: 477–508, 2000.

Whiten, A. The imitator's representation of the imitated: Ape and child. In A. Meltzoff and W. Prinz, eds., *The Imitative Mind*. Cambridge, UK: Cambridge University Press, in press.

Whiten, A., and J. Brown. Imitation and the reading of other minds: Perspectives from the study of autism, normal children, and non-human primates. In S. Braten, ed., *Intersubjective Communication and Emotion in Ontogeny: A Sourcebook*. Cambridge, UK: Cambridge University Press, 1999.

Whiten, A., K. Brown, and T. Lee. Imitation of the hierarchical structure of actions by 3-year-old children. Manuscript, University of St Andrews, in preparation.

Whiten, A., and D. M. Custance. Studies of imitation in chimpanzees and children. In C. M. Heyes, and B. G. Galef Jr., eds., *Social Learning in Animals: The Roots of Culture*, pp. 291–318. London: Academic Press, 1996.

Whiten, A., D. M. Custance, J.-C. Gomez, P. Teixidor, and K. A. Bard. Imitative learning of artificial fruit processing in children (*Homo sapiens*) and chimpanzees (*Pan troglodytes*). *Journal of Comparative Psychology* 110: 3–14, 1996.

Whiten, A., and R. Ham. On the nature and evolution of imitation in the animal kingdom: Reappraisal of a century of research. In P. J. B. Slater, J. S. Rosenblatt, C. Beer, and M. Milinski, eds., *Advances in the Study of Behavior*, 21, pp. 239–283. San Diego: Academic Press, 1992.

Zentall, T. R. An analysis of imitative learning in animals. In C. M. Heyes, and B. G. Galef Jr., eds., *Social Learning in Animals: The Roots of Culture*, pp. 221–243. London: Academic Press, 1996.

9 Three Sources of Information in Social Learning

Josep Call and Malinda Carpenter

9.1 Three Sources of Information in Social Learning

Recent years have seen an unprecedented interest in the topic of social learning in animals. This interest is clearly illustrated by the increasing number of species investigated (e.g., dolphins: Herman, chapter 3 of this volume; parrots: Moore 1996; Pepperberg, chapter 4 of this volume; orangutans: Call and Tomasello 1994a, 1995), the new research methods used (Call and Tomasello 1995; Heyes and Dawson 1990; Whiten et al. 1996), and the new mechanisms that have been described (emulation: Tomasello 1990; goal emulation: Whiten and Ham 1992; program-level imitation: Byrne 1994; string-parsing imitation: Byrne 1999). Different theoretical approaches, from behaviorism to cognitivism, continue to contribute to this fast-growing field.

Although so much research activity is clearly a sign of progress and good health for the field, progress also has its risks. First, some theoretical terms have become too broad or too narrow. For instance, the term *imitation* is used with different meanings by different researchers. While some researchers use it in a general way to denote copying behavior (e.g., Meltzoff and Moore 1989), others prefer to reserve it for those cases in which the organism not only copies behavior but also acquires novel behavior (Thorpe 1956; Zentall 1996). Second, whereas these terms are useful for characterizing the types of social learning mechanisms different species (or children of different ages) tend to use, they are not as helpful when it comes to identifying specific instances of social learning. For example, imitation (with all that the term implies; see below) is assumed when human children reproduce others' behavior, but other mechanisms may be at work in any given instance. Finally, some mechanisms tend to overshadow others, occupying a disproportionate share of research attention. For instance, Matheson and Fragaszy (1998) recently pointed out that too much research attention is devoted to investigating imitation—copying the exact behavioral patterns of a demonstrator—while other mechanisms that may be more relevant to the species' survival are neglected.

One mechanism that, in our opinion, has begun to suffer some of the same problems that have plagued the term *imitation* is emulation. This chapter attempts to remedy this situation to some extent by clarifying the different types of emulation available and by making clear its relation to other social learning mechanisms, especially imitation. We then present a new framework for investigating social learning that is based on focusing on the different types of information that observers are able to extract from models. Finally, we explore the advantages of adopting such a framework for the study of social learning in both animals and artifacts.

9.2 Emulation and Imitation

Traditionally, three main social learning mechanisms have been used to explain an observer's acquisition of some part of the behavioral repertoire of a demonstrator (social learning mechanisms in the sense of Whiten and Ham 1992). These three mechanisms are: stimulus or local enhancement (Spence 1937; Thorpe 1956), observational conditioning (Mineka and Cook 1988), and true imitation (Thorpe 1956). Stimulus enhancement refers to the observer's attention being attracted to a particular aspect of the situation. For instance, when a chimpanzee uses a hammer to crack open a nut, other animals may be attracted to the hammer or the anvil on which the nut was cracked. This attraction, however, does not produce any specific learning; it simply puts observers in an advantageous position to learn individually. Observational conditioning consists of learning about some relation between two stimuli by watching another animal. It is not learning about the response itself, which is already in the behavioral repertoire of the observer. For instance, an observer may learn to avoid snakes upon seeing a conspecific's avoidance responses (Mineka and Cook 1988). Neither of the previous two mechanisms, however, involves learning about the precise behavior of a demonstrator. In contrast, true imitation consists of acquiring a behavior by copying the demonstrator's behavior. The observer acquires the motor movements that are needed to solve a problem. For instance, a child may learn to use the same movements as adults to operate a machine after observing an adult do so.

Tomasello and colleagues (1987; see also Tomasello 1990) added a fourth mechanism called *emulation* to account for some chimpanzee tool use results that could not be accounted for by any of the previous three social learning mechanisms. In this study, three different groups of chimpanzees were presented with three experimental conditions. The first group observed a chimpanzee demonstrator using a stick to retrieve a reward situated on a platform. The second group observed a chimpanzee demonstrator manipulating the tool without the reward being present. The third group did not observe any demonstrator. Chimpanzees that observed the demonstrator using the tool to obtain the reward clearly benefited from this experience because they obtained the reward faster than either of the other two groups of chimpanzees. Yet the successful chimpanzees used a different tool technique from the demonstrator. Thus, chimpanzees learned something from the demonstrator, but did not copy her precise motor patterns (i.e., actions). This was clearly different from either local enhancement or observational conditioning because subjects learned something more specific than the context or the particular stimuli involved, but it did not qualify as true imitation because subjects did not copy the actions of the demonstrator.

Tomasello (1990, 1996) used the term *emulation* to describe this type of social learning and contrasted emulation with imitation on the basis of two main parameters: type of information copied and sensitivity to the demonstrator's intentions. In regard to the information copied, emulation is based on reproducing the results of a demonstrator's actions, whereas imitation is based on copying the actions that brought about those results. In other words, emulation involves reproducing changes in the state of the environment that are a result of the demonstrator's behavior, whereas imitation involves reproducing the actions that produced those changes in the environment. To illustrate, when a demonstrator cracks open a nut with a hammer, emulation would consist of reproducing the cracked-open nut independently of the actions used by the demonstrator, for instance, by biting into it to open it. In contrast, imitation would consist of copying the demonstrator's hammering actions to open the nut.

In regard to the sensitivity to intentions, Tomasello (1990; see also Tomasello, Kruger, and Ratner 1993) argued that reproducing results (i.e., emulation) does not necessarily imply an understanding of what the demonstrator's goals or intentions are. The observer may simply look at the changes that occur in the environment and recreate them with its own skills. In a sense, the observer reinvents the actions that are needed to solve the problem. In contrast,

Tomasello (1990) argued that when imitating, observers copy the actions of a demonstrator because they understand that the demonstrator used those actions with a certain goal in mind. However, Tomasello, Kruger, and Ratner (1993) also distinguished a type of social learning in which observers copy the actions of a demonstrator without understanding the demonstrator's goals: mimicry.

Recent data have blurred the distinction between emulation, imitation, and mimicry in three main ways. First, emulation has been given different meanings. Whereas Tomasello (1990, 1996) argued that emulation was about copying results, Whiten and Ham (1992) coined the term *goal emulation* to indicate reproduction of the end result of a demonstrator's actions *with* an understanding of the demonstrator's goal. As a consequence, one type of emulation implies some sensitivity to intentions in the form of goals whereas the other does not.

Second, in any given instance of social learning, it is difficult to determine which mechanism is being used. For example, Zentall, Sutton, and Sherburne (1996; see also Kaiser, Zentall, and Galef 1997) have presented evidence of pigeons copying a demonstrator's motor patterns in a problem-solving situation, but it is unclear from that instance which mechanism the birds used. If they understood the demonstrator's goal, we can credit the birds with imitation; if not, we should call their behavior mimicry. At this point, it is difficult, if not impossible, to distinguish between imitation and mimicry within a given instance of reproduction of a demonstrator's straightforward, "normal" behavior (although see Carpenter, Nagell, and Tomasello 1998 for an attempt to do this). At the present time, we must use outside evidence of understanding of others' intentions (from experiments that test this understanding directly, e.g., Call and Tomasello 1998; Carpenter, Akhtar, and Tomasello 1998; Meltzoff 1995) to hypothesize about which mechanisms organisms may be using.

Finally, although in the case of mimicry it is possible that reproduction of a demonstrator's actions may not imply understanding of others' goals, the converse is also possible: in some cases, *not* reproducing the demonstrator's actions exactly has been taken as evidence of understanding of intentions. For instance, in a study of imitation of others' unfulfilled intentions, Meltzoff (1995) showed that children do not always copy a demonstrator's actions exactly when they know what the goal is—instead, they reproduce what the adult meant to do. Likewise, Carpenter, Akhtar, and Tomasello

(1998) and Bekkering, Wohlschläger, and Gattis (2000) found that children imitated the motor patterns of a demonstrator or not depending on what they perceived the demonstrator's goal to be.

The danger here is that the terms for the different social learning mechanisms will lose their usefulness since there is not always a clear distinction between imitation, emulation, and mimicry. To remedy this situation, we suggest restricting the use of these terms to developmental or comparative discussions of which mechanisms different-aged children or different species are capable of or tend to use. For considering individual instances of social learning, we propose a new, multidimensional framework that encompasses the different types of information that observers are able to extract from demonstrators.

9.3 A New, Multidimensional Framework

The main idea behind a multidimensional framework is that a demonstrator's model produces several sources of information simultaneously and observers may selectively attend to some of these sources but not others. An analogy will help to clarify this point. When we burn wood, at least three products are released: light, heat, and smoke. Each of these products occurs simultaneously. Similarly, a demonstrator's model releases at least three products: goals, actions, and results (figure 9.1). Goals are the dem-

GOAL   ACTION   RESULT

Figure 9.1 The different sources of information in a social learning situation. In this demonstration, the demonstrator opens a plastic Easter egg and gets the prize that is inside. Note that there are often several hierarchically organized goals (get the prize, open the egg, pull the egg apart), actions (pull on the egg, take the prize), and results (the egg is open, the egg is in two pieces, the prize is available).

onstrator's aim, the final state of affairs that she wants to bring about. Actions are the motor patterns the demonstrator uses to bring about those results. Results are changes in the environment that are a consequence of the demonstrator's actions. These three types of information are hierarchically organized, since goals dictate actions and actions determine the results.

Sources of Information: Independence and Interrelations

It is important to consider all three sources of information—both independently and in relation to each other—in each instance of social learning. By doing so, we can avoid mistakes and explain a greater variety of results. Figure 9.2 presents all the possible combinations of goals, actions, and results, along with the theoretical terms associated with each combination. We hope this figure helps make the following points about the importance of considering the sources of information separately.

First, because the three sources of information are independent of each other, it is important not to use one source as an automatic indication or predictor of another. For instance, copying actions should not be taken as evidence of understanding of goals: observers may copy a demonstrator's actions with or without an understanding of why the demonstrator is performing those actions. Conversely, understanding of goals cannot be used to predict copying actions: observers may be able to infer the goals of a demonstrator but then choose to use their own behavioral repertoire to solve a problem. Moreover, individuals may understand goals but choose not to adopt them, instead copying the actions and reproducing the results for a different goal.[1] In order to figure out which of the sources is being used, the sources should be tested directly, not simply inferred from the presence or absence of other sources of information. Two possible methods of investigating the sources of information used by subjects consist of eliminating some of the sources but not others (e.g., demonstrating only the goal; Meltzoff 1995) or making one of the sources ambiguous and seeing how alternative interpretations of that source affect the others (e.g., demonstrating the same action twice, each time with different goals; Bekkering, Wohlschläger, and Gattis, 2000).

Second, another advantage of focusing on the particular sources of information independently is that false positives can be more

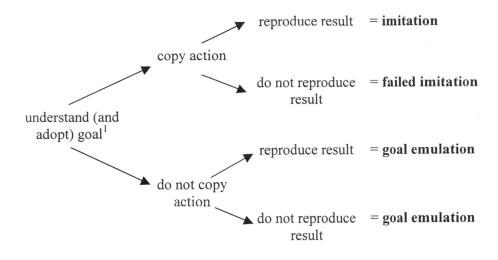

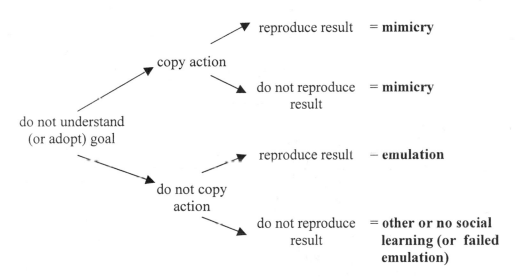

Figure 9.2 The three sources of information with the theoretical terms associated with each combination.

readily detected. For instance, although copying actions is often used as evidence of imitation, it is also possible to copy actions without trying to do so. That is, observers may understand the goal and reproduce the results using the same action as the demonstrator but they could have used the same actions just by convergence since they have similar behavioral repertoires, without attending to the demonstrator's actions at all. Or, observers could copy the demonstrator's actions without intending to reproduce the result but achieve the result anyway. These types of coincidental results are especially probable in studies that use relatively simple problems in the models. Only carefully designed experimental tests that examine each source separately will help avoid these potential problems.

On the other hand, we must also keep in mind the interrelations and interactions among the different sources of information. Often, depending on their interests and population of study, researchers focus on only one of the sources of information, individually, to the relative exclusion of the others. For example, comparative psychologists often focus on whether organisms copy the actions of a demonstrator exactly (e.g., Nagell, Olguin, and Tomasello 1993; Call and Tomasello 1994a, 1995; Whiten et al. 1996; Zentall, Sutton, and Sherburne 1996), without testing whether they understand the goals of the demonstrator. However, focusing on only one of the sources at a time is likely to produce an incomplete and fragmentary picture. For instance, by focusing only on copying actions it would be difficult to explain the findings of several recent studies of infants and young children. First, Meltzoff (1995) found that 18-month-old infants are able to complete unfulfilled actions—actions they have never seen performed in entirety—as easily as they copy fulfilled ones. Second, when accidental (Carpenter, Akhtar, and Tomasello 1998) and incidental (Bekkering, Wohlschläger, and Gattis 2000) actions are included in a demonstration, children differentially disregard those actions and copy only the actions that were performed intentionally or that they consider to be goal related. If children were simply copying the demonstrators' actions, they should have copied the experimenter's failed attempts in Meltzoff's study and the accidental and incidental actions in the Carpenter, Akhtar, and Tomasello and Bekkering, Wohlschläger, and Gattis studies along with the intentional ones. These results can only be explained by considering the interaction of goals and actions.

We know far less about the interaction between different types of information such as goals and results. As discussed above, it is possible to reproduce the results of a demonstrator with or without understanding the demonstrator's goals (goal emulation vs. emulation, respectively). Although most evidence seems to indicate that apes, for example, tend to copy things other than actions from a model (i.e., they use emulation), it is still not clear whether they focus on results (emulation: Call and Tomasello 1994a, 1995; Nagell, Olguin, and Tomasello 1993) or goals (goal emulation: Whiten and Ham 1992). Future research will be needed to resolve this issue. In short, a multidimensional focus is particularly important when attempting to determine what social learning mechanisms are responsible for the acquisition of novel behavior.

Shifting between Sources of Information

Not only do the different sources of information interact, but the emphasis on one or the other (or a combination of them) may shift during a given demonstration. During the course of learning a task, observers may use different types of information from a demonstrator. This is clearly illustrated if we consider the interaction between information acquired through social observation and information acquired through individual practice during problem solving. Strictly speaking, purely observational learning should occur in the first trial without hesitation and producing a complete response. In practice, most of the time even fast learners take a few trials to optimize their behavior to find a solution, during which time the information gathered through observation is constantly combined with the information gathered from practice with the problem.

The problem of the interaction between observational and experiential information is complicated further when we consider that observational information can be of at least three different kinds: goals, actions, and results. With this in mind, it is easy to see that observers may potentially attend to different types of information depending on their previous success or failure, or the information that they gathered from applying their newly acquired information, or both. For example, it is a common experience among adult humans to watch someone achieve some result (e.g., with a new tool, or when learning to play a new sport or musical instrument) and then to attempt to reproduce that result oneself. If one's first

Information attended to   Behavior

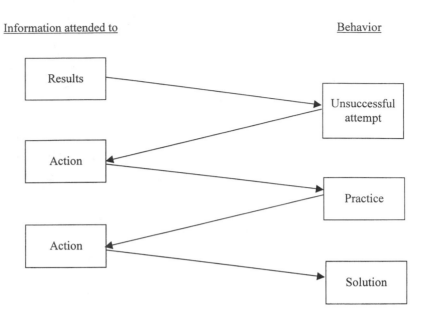

Figure 9.3 Shifting between sources of information in a social learning task.

attempt is unsuccessful, during the next demonstration one might
pay more attention to the demonstrator's actions than to the end
result (figure 9.3). Following such an occurrence, when an observer
first attends to the results of a demonstration, and then on the next
trial attends to the demonstrator's actions, are we justified in
claiming that the observer has learned through emulation or imitation? It seems to us that one solution is to focus on a unit of information that the existing social learning mechanisms, such as
emulation and imitation, do not capture. In other words, emulation
and imitation are tools that are too blunt to do the job. A finer tool
is required, one that breaks down the behavior of the demonstrator
into its constituent pieces: goals, actions, and results.

Developing the Ability to Exploit Various Sources of Information
Human children are capable of using the three types of information (goals: Meltzoff 1995; actions: Nagell, Olguin, and Tomasello
1993; results: Bellagamba and Tomasello 1999). How their predis-
positions change over time and how they come to use each of these
sources are still unanswered questions that will require further research. One possibility we favor is that young infants are primarily
predisposed to attend and to reproduce actions. This idea is sup-

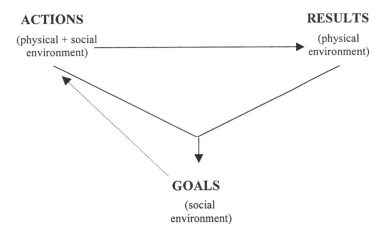

Figure 9.4   Children learn about goals and results from observing others' actions.

ported by the evidence on neonatal imitation and the ease and pleasure with which young infants and children engage in imitative games (Meltzoff 1996). We argue that this tendency to attend to and reproduce the actions of others may contribute significantly to infants' discovery of the two other types of information that emanate from models: results and goals (figure 9.4). In other words, by copying the actions of other people, infants may discover interesting things about both their physical and their social environments. They may learn how objects work, how to produce changes in the environment, and about physical causality by observing and copying the consequences and cause-and-effect of others' actions —the results. In addition, when observing the combination of actions and their results, infants may begin to understand why people behave the way they do—their goals. Particularly useful situations in this regard would include instances in which the demonstrator did not succeed the first time or performed the same action on several occasions, with irrelevant or accidental actions accompanying the intentional action sometimes. Of course, the path of development is not unidirectional: once infants understand others' goals, for example, they can make better sense of their actions (see, e.g., Bekkering, Wohlschläger, and Gattis 2000).

The implications of this account are far reaching because it points to attending to and copying actions as one of the most important components in the cognitive and social development of children. Although using imitation as a key component is not a new idea (Piaget 1962; Meltzoff and Gopnik 1993; Vygotsky 1978), our proposal is innovative for two reasons. First, it helps explain both cognitive and social-cognitive development. Through copying actions, children gain knowledge about both their physical and social worlds. Second, the account provides a comparative and a clinical perspective. In other words, it may help us to understand the differences between humans and apes on the one hand, and between typically developing children and children with autism on the other.

APES

We have distinguished three types of information that can be attended to by observers. Moreover, we have argued that humans are capable of focusing on each of these sources independently, depending on the demands of the situation. One important question is whether other animals can also extract all three different types of information. Of particular interest is whether the great apes are capable of benefiting from all sources of information.

Current evidence on social learning in apes indicates that chimpanzees and orangutans seem to rely primarily on results as their main source of information in problem-solving situations (Call and Tomasello 1994a, 1995; Myowa-Yamakoshi and Matsuzawa 1999; Nagell, Olguin, and Tomasello 1993). These studies indicate that apes are more likely to reproduce results (changes in the environment) than the demonstrator's actions. In fact, evidence of apes copying the actions of a demonstrator independently from its results in a problem solving situation is relatively scarce (but see Whiten et al. 1996). Copying actions from demonstrators is better characterized as a fragile phenomenon at best, one that may be difficult to elicit systematically. Even studies that have specifically trained subjects to reproduce actions on command have met with limited success. For instance, Custance, Whiten, and Bard (1995) found that two juvenile nursery-reared chimpanzees copied less than a third of a set of novel actions after several weeks of training. This study shows that copying actions is not something that chimpanzees do easily or often. Perhaps the apes in this study were attending to other things, like results or goals. To tease apart these different possibilities, other studies along the lines of those by Bekkering, Wohlschläger, and Gattis (2000), Carpenter, Akhtar, and Tomasello (1998), and Meltzoff (1995) are needed.

At present, the general characterization that we favor is one that depicts apes as being biased toward copying results and only rarely copying the actions that bring about those results. In other words, apes may preferentially attend to the changes in the environment rather than to the actions that bring about those changes. This is not to say that apes are incapable of attending to or encoding information about the demonstrator's actions (see Myowa-Yamakoshi 2001, for a discussion) under any circumstances, it is simply that during their normal ontogeny they tend to preferentially focus their attention on results rather than actions.

Interestingly, apes that have been enculturated—that is, raised by humans in the same way as human children—seem to be more adept at copying actions in addition to copying results. Tomasello, Savage-Rumbaugh, and Kruger (1993; see also Hayes and Hayes 1952) found that enculturated bonobos and chimpanzees reproduced a human demonstrator's actions in an object-manipulation task more often than mother-raised apes. The percentage of reproduced actions by enculturated apes in that study was comparable to that of $2\frac{1}{2}$-year-old children presented with the same models and objects. The case for an enhanced ability to focus on actions in enculturated apes is further reinforced by other studies that have shown that enculturated apes outperform mother-reared apes in other domains such as gestural communication (Call and Tomasello 1994b, 1996; Gómez 1996), gaze following (Call, Agnetta, and Tomasello 2000; Itakura and Tanaka 1998), distinguishing accidental from intentional actions (Call and Tomasello 1998), and language acquisition (Savage-Rumbaugh et al. 1986). What all these studies have in common is that they require subjects to focus their attention on the actions performed by humans. At this point, we can only speculate that it is the type of social engagement that apes encounter in their human foster homes that promotes their ability to focus on human actions, not just the results of those actions. In particular, the socialization of attention—that is, the guiding of attention to particular features in the environment—may play a fundamental role in the ability to shift attention from results to actions and vice versa. These suggestive findings may highlight the importance of ontogeny in the development of attention to the various sources of information that emanate from a model and which are the basis for the various social learning mechanisms that we have explored.

INDIVIDUALS WITH AUTISM
Special human populations with developmental delays also constitute an interesting case to study. Particularly interesting is the case of people with autism. Children with autism show some

impairment in their imitative skills (see Rogers 1999; Smith and Bryson 1994 for reviews), although there have been very few studies of imitation in individuals with autism that have addressed the kinds of questions we are concerned with here. Perhaps the most interesting is a recent study by Hobson and Lee (1999). In this study, participants watched as a demonstrator modeled several actions on objects. During each model, the demonstrator performed the action in a particular way—with a particular "style" (e.g., gently or forcefully). Hobson and Lee found that whereas participants reproduced the results of the actions equally as well as control participants with developmental delays but not autism, the participants with autism were less likely than the control participants to reproduce the style the demonstrator used to bring about those results. These findings suggest that individuals with autism may be biased toward attending to and reproducing results rather than actions.

If indeed children with autism (and apes) preferentially pay attention to the results of others' actions instead of the actions themselves, then, following our account of typical development, individuals in these two populations may be missing out on an important way of learning about the social world. That is, whereas the information they gain from focusing on the results of demonstrations may help them learn about the physical world, the information they miss out on by not focusing on actions may hinder their development of an understanding of other individuals. This may help explain the specific pattern of relatively intact physical cognition and relatively impaired social cognition (e.g., skills related to theory of mind) of children with autism and apes, at least as compared with typically developing human children. Of course we realize that the reverse situation could be true too—that an early lack of understanding of or interest in other individuals could account for the tendency to pay attention to results over actions. That is, depending on one's theoretical orientation, these differences in focus on results over actions may be either a cause (e.g., Meltzoff and Gopnik 1993; Rogers and Pennington 1991) or an effect (e.g., Tomasello, Kruger, and Ratner 1993) of difficulties with normal human social-cognitive understanding.

9.4 Conclusion

In this chapter, we propose a new way of looking at social learning: a multidimensional framework that considers each source of information available in a model—goals, actions, and results—separately and in relation to each other. We believe that this framework is more useful than using only the terms already available because it helps us interpret individual instances of social learning and explain new results with more precision. We also think that this framework may be useful theoretically in comparative and clinical perspectives and we hope that it will stimulate research into the different sources of information in a variety of populations.

A final caveat: when considering the different sources of information simultaneously, an effort should be made not to favor one source over the others, or to view the use of one of the sources as more cognitively sophisticated than the others. This situation tends to occur when scholars with different theoretical orientations such as behaviorists and cognitivists tackle the question from different ends of the spectrum. However, it is important to emphasize that attributing a higher cognitive complexity to the use of one or the other source of information is not very useful because the three sources belong to different cognitive dimensions. Whereas understanding goals is sophisticated because it may inform us about what subjects know about others' minds, reproducing results is complex because it entails extracting pieces of information and putting them together to create a novel solution (Call 1999). Each of these two sources is at opposite ends of the spectrum: inferring goals belongs to the domain of social cognition, whereas piecing together results to solve a problem belongs to the domain of physical cognition. Finally, copying actions is in between goals and results because this has both physical and social attributes. On the one hand, it is social because it entails paying attention to social entities, but at the same time, it is closely related to motor and cross-modal skills since visual information must be transformed into kinesthetic information.

Imitation is usually taken to be more complex than emulation. We think this is problematic and we present the following scenario to illustrate this point. Researchers in the field of robotics (e.g., Breazeal and Scassellati, chapter 14 of this volume; Demiris and Hayes, chapter 13 of this volume) are currently working very hard to create robots that can copy others' actions. This is an admirable and useful objective and we are impressed with the results to date (see other chapters in this volume). However, imagine how impressive it would be to create a robot that could *emulate*—that is, observe the achieved change of state in the environment and come up with its own way of reproducing that change of state. We presume that this would be a more serious challenge to programmers than making a robot that uncreatively mimics others' actions. We therefore propose a more egalitarian approach to the study of social learning, with goals, actions, and results—and imitation, emulation, and the other social learning mechanisms—considered equally important and deserving of study.

Acknowledgments

We thank Mike Tomasello for helpful comments on a previous draft. Please address correspondence to: Josep Call, Max Planck Institute for Evolutionary Anthropology, Inselstrasse 22, D-04103 Leipzig, Germany; or call@eva.mpg.de.

Note

1. For instance, in the Easter egg example from figure 9.1, an individual may understand that the goal of a demonstration is to open the egg to get the prize inside. But he may copy the actions and reproduce the results of the demonstrator to achieve a different goal: using half of the egg as a cup to scoop up water.

References

Bekkering, H., A. Wohlschläger, and M. Gattis. Imitation of gestures in children is mediated by goal representation. *Quarterly Journal of Experimental Psychology*, 2000. Vol. 53A. pp. 153–164.

Bellagamba, F., and M. Tomasello. Re-enacting intended acts: Comparing 12- and 18-month-olds. *Infant Behavior and Development*, 1999. Vol. 22, pp. 277–282.

Byrne, R. W. The evolution of intelligence. In P. J. B. Slater and T. R. Halliday (eds.), *Behavior and Evolution* (pp. 223–265). Cambridge, UK: Cambridge University Press, 1994.

Byrne, R. W. Imitation without intentionality: Using string parsing to copy the organization of behaviour. *Animal Cognition* 2: 63–72, 1999.

Call, J. Levels of imitation and cognitive mechanisms in orangutans. In S. T. Parker, R. W. Mitchell, and H. L. Miles (eds.), *Mentalities of Gorillas and Orangutans*, pp. 316–341. New York: Cambridge University Press, 1999.

Call, J., B. Agnetta, and M. Tomasello. Social cues that chimpanzees do and do not use to find hidden objects. *Animal Cognition* 3: 23–34, 2000.

Call, J., and M. Tomasello. The social learning of tool use by orangutans (*Pongo pygmaeus*). *Human Evolution* 9: 297–313, 1994a.

Call, J., and M. Tomasello. Production and comprehension of referential pointing by orangutans (*Pongo pygmaeus*). *Journal of Comparative Psychology* 108: 307–317, 1994b.

Call, J., and M. Tomasello. The use of social information in the problem-solving of orangutans (*Pongo pygmaeus*) and human children (*Homo sapiens*). *Journal of Comparative Psychology* 109(3): 308–320, 1995.

Call, J., and M. Tomasello. The effect of humans on the cognitive development of apes. In A. E. Russon, K. A. Bard, and S. T. Parker (eds.), *Reaching into Thought* (pp. 371–403). New York: Cambridge University Press, 1996.

Call, J., and M. Tomasello. Distinguishing intentional from accidental actions in orang-utans (*Pongo pygmaeus*), chimpanzees (*Pan troglodytes*), and human children (*Homo sapiens*). *Journal of Comparative Psychology* 112: 192–206, 1998.

Carpenter, M., N. Akhtar, and M. Tomasello. Fourteen through 18-month-old infants differentially imitate intentional and accidental actions. *Infant Behavior and Development* 21: 315–330, 1998.

Carpenter, M., K. Nagell, and M. Tomasello. Social cognition, joint attention, and communicative competence from 9 to 15 months of age. *Monographs of the Society for Research in Child Development* 63 (4, serial no. 255), 1998.

Custance, D. M., A. Whiten, and K. A. Bard. Can young chimpanzees (*Pan troglodytes*) imitate arbitrary actions? Hayes and Hayes (1952) revisited. *Behaviour* 132: 837–859, 1995.

Gómez, J. C. Non-human primate theories of (non-human primate) minds: Some issues concerning the origins of mind-reading. In P. Carruthers and P. K. Smith (eds.), *Theories of Theories of Mind* (pp. 330–343). Cambridge, UK: Cambridge University Press, 1996.

Hayes, K. J., and C. Hayes. Imitation in a home-raised chimpanzee. *Journal of Comparative Psychology* 45: 450–459, 1952.

Heyes, C. M., and G. R. Dawson. A demonstration of observational learning in rats using a bidirectional control. *The Quarterly Journal of Experimental Psychology* 42B: 59–71, 1990.

Hobson, R. P., and A. Lee. Imitation and identification in autism. *Journal of Child Psychology and Psychiatry* 40: 649–659, 1999.

Itakura, S., and M. Tanaka. Use of experimenter-given cues during object-choice tasks by chimpanzees (*Pan troglodytes*), an orangutan (*Pongo pygmaeus*), and human infants (*Homo sapiens*). *Journal of Comparative Psychology* 112: 119–126, 1998.

Kaiser, D. H., T. R. Zentall, and B. G. Galef. Can imitation in pigeons be explained by local enhancement together with trial-and-error learning? *Psychological Science* 8: 459–460, 1997.

Matheson, M. D., and D. M. Fragaszy. Imitation is not the "Holy Grail" of comparative cognition. *Behavioral and Brain Sciences* 21: 697–698, 1998.

Meltzoff, A. N. Understanding the intentions of others: Re-enactment of intended acts by 18-month-old children. *Developmental Psychology* 31: 838–050, 1995.

Meltzoff, A. N. The human infant as imitative generalist: A 20-year progress report on infant imitation with implications for comparative psychology. In C. M. Heyes and B. G. Galef Jr. (eds.), *Social Learning in Animals: The Roots of Culture* (pp. 347–370). New York: Academic Press, 1996.

Meltzoff, A. N., and A. Gopnik. The role of imitation in understanding persons and developing a theory of mind. In S. Baron-Cohen, H. Tager-Flusberg, and D. J. Cohen (eds.), *Understanding Other Minds: Perspectives from Autism* (pp. 335–366). New York: Oxford University Press, 1993.

Meltzoff, A. N., and M. K. Moore. Imitation in newborn infants: Exploring the range of gestures imitated and the underlying mechanisms. *Developmental Psychology* 25: 954–962, 1989.

Mineka, S., and M. Cook. Social learning and the acquisition of snake fear in monkeys. In T. R. Zentall and B. G. Galef Jr. (eds.). *Social Learning: Psychological and Biological Perspectives* (pp. 51–73). Hillsdale, N.J.: Lawrence Erlbaum Associates, 1988.

Moore, B. R. The evolution of imitative learning. In C. M. Heyes and B. G. Galef Jr. (eds.) *Social Learning in Animals: The Roots of Culture* (pp. 245–265). New York: Academic Press, 1996.

Myowa-Yamakoshi, M. Evolutionary foundation and development of imitation. In Matsuzawa, T. (ed.), *Primate Origins of Human Cognition and Behavior*, pp. 349–367. Berlin: Springer, 2001.

Myowa-Yamakoshi, M. and T. Matsuzawa. Factors influencing imitation of manipulatory actions in chimpanzees (*Pan troglodytes*). *Journal of Comparative Psychology* 113: 128–136, 1999.

Nagell, K., R. Olguin, and M. Tomasello. Processes of social learning in the tool use of chimpanzees (*Pan troglodytes*) and human children (*Homo sapiens*). *Journal of Comparative Psychology* 107: 174–186, 1993.

Piaget, J. *Play, Dreams, and Imitation in Childhood*. New York: Norton, 1962.

Rogers, S. J. An examination of the imitation deficit in autism. In J. Nadel and G. Butterworth (eds.), *Imitation in infancy* (pp. 254–283). Cambridge, UK: Cambridge University Press, 1999.

Rogers, S. J., and B. F. Pennington. A theoretical approach to the deficits in infantile autism. *Development and Psychopathology* 3: 137–162, 1991.

Savage-Rumbaugh, E. S., K. McDonald, R. A. Sevcik, W. D. Hopkins, and E. Rubert. Spontaneous symbol acquisition and communicative use by pygmy chimpanzees (*Pan paniscus*). *Journal of Experimental Psychology: General* 115: 211–235, 1986.

Smith, I. M., and S. E. Bryson. Imitation and action in autism: A critical review. *Psychological Bulletin* 116: 259–273, 1994.

Spence, K. W. Experimental studies of learning and the mental processes in infra-human primates. *Psychological Bulletin* 34: 806–850, 1937.

Thorpe, W. H. *Learning and Instinct in Animals*. London: Methuen, 1956.

Tomasello, M. Cultural transmission in the tool use and communicatory signaling of chimpanzees? In S. T. Parker and K. R. Gibson (eds.), *"Language" and Intelligence in Monkeys and Apes* (pp. 274–311). Cambridge, UK: Cambridge University Press, 1990.

Tomasello, M. Do apes ape? In C. M. Heyes and B. G. Galef Jr. (eds.), *Social Learning in Animals: The Roots of Culture* (pp. 319–346). New York: Academic Press, 1996.

Tomasello, M., M. Davis-Dasilva, L. Camak, and K. Bard. Observational learning of tool-use by young chimpanzees. *Human Evolution* 2: 175–183, 1987.

Tomasello, M., A. C. Kruger, and H. H. Ratner. Cultural learning. *Behavioral and Brain Sciences* 16: 495–552, 1993.

Tomasello, M., E. S. Savage-Rumbaugh, and A. C. Kruger. Imitative learning of actions on objects by children, chimpanzees, and enculturated chimpanzees. *Child Development* 64: 1688–1705, 1993.

Vygotsky, L. *Mind in Society*. Cambridge, Mass.: Harvard University Press, 1978.

Whiten, A., D. M. Custance, J. C. Gómez, P. Teixidor, and K. A. Bard. Imitative learning of artificial fruit processing in children (*Homo sapiens*) and chimpanzees (*Pan troglodytes*). *Journal of Comparative Psychology* 110: 3–14, 1996.

Whiten, A., and R. Ham. On the nature and evolution of imitation in the animal kingdom: Reappraisal of a century of research. In P. J. B. Slater, J. S. Rosenblatt, C. Beer, and M. Milinsky (eds.), *Advances in the Study of Behavior* (pp. 239–283). New York: Academic Press, 1992.

Zentall, T. R. An analysis of imitative learning in animals. In C. M. Heyes, and B. G. Galef Jr. (eds.), *Social Learning in Animals: The Roots of Culture* (pp. 221–243). New York: Academic Press, 1996.

Zentall, T. R., J. E. Sutton, and L. M. Sherburne. True imitative learning in pigeons. *Psychological Science* 7: 343–346, 1996.

10   The Mirror System, Imitation, and the Evolution of Language

Michael A. Arbib

A Dance Class in Santa Fe, September 25, 1999

The percussion is insistent. Dancers move in rows from the back of
the hall toward the drummers at the front. From time to time, the
mistress of the dance breaks the flow, and twice repeats a sequence
of energetic dance moves. The dancers then move forward again,
repeating her moves, more or less. Some do it well, others not so
well.

Imitation involves, in part, seeing the instructor's dance as a set
of familiar movements of shoulders, arms, hands, belly, and legs.
Many constituents are variants of familiar actions, rather than familiar actions themselves. Thus, one must not only observe actions
and their composition, but also novelties in the constituents and
their variations. One must also perceive the overlapping and
sequencing of all these moves and then remember the "coordinated control program" so constructed. Probably, memory and
perception are intertwined.

As the dancers perform, they both act out the recalled coordinated control program and tune it. By observing other dancers and
synchronizing with their neighbors and the insistent percussion of
the drummers, they achieve a collective representation that tunes
their own, possibly departing from the instructor's original. At the
same time, some dancers seem more or less skilled—some will
omit a movement, or simplify it, others may replace it with their
imagined equivalent. (One example: the instructor alternates
touching her breast and moving her arm outwards. Most dancers
move their arms in and out with no particular target.) Other
changes are matters of motor rather than perceptual or mnemonic
skill—not everyone can lean back as far as the instructor without
losing balance.

These are the ingredients of imitation.

10.1   Introduction

I argue that the ability to imitate is a key innovation in the evolutionary path leading to language in the human and relate this

hypothesis to specific data on brain mechanisms. The starting point is the discovery of the "mirror system" for grasping in monkeys, a region in the monkey brain in which neurons are active when the monkey executes a specific hand action and are also active when the monkey observes another primate (human or monkey) carrying out that same action. In "Language Within Our Grasp," Rizzolatti and Arbib (1998) showed that the mirror system in monkeys is the homologue of Broca's area, a crucial speech area in humans, and argued that this observation provides a neurobiological "missing link" for the long-argued hypothesis that primitive forms of communication based on manual gesture preceded speech in the evolution of language. Their "Mirror System Hypothesis" states that the matching of neural code for execution and observation of hand movements in the monkey is present in the common ancestor of monkey and human, and is the precursor of the crucial language property of parity—namely, that an utterance usually carries similar meaning for speaker and hearer.[1] Here, we refine this hypothesis by suggesting that imitation plays a crucial role in human language acquisition and performance, and that brain mechanisms supporting imitation were crucial to the emergence of *Homo sapiens.*

I stress that imitation—for me at least—involves more than simply observing someone else's movement and responding with a movement that in its entirety is already in one's own repertoire. Instead, I insist that imitation involves "parsing" a complex movement into more or less familiar pieces, and then performing the corresponding composite of (variations on) familiar actions. Note the insistence on "more or less familiar pieces" and "variations." Elsewhere (Arbib 1981), I have introduced the notion of a coordinated control program to show how a new behavior could be composed from an available repertoire of perceptual and motor schemas (the execution of a successful action will, in general, require perceptual constraints on the relevant movements). However, skill acquisition not only involves the formation of new schemas as composites of old ones, it also involves the tuning of these schemas to match a new set of conditions, to the point that the unity of the new schema may override the original identity of the components. For example, if one is acquiring a tennis stroke and a badminton stroke through imitation, the initial coordinated control program may be identical, yet in the end the very different dynamics of the tennis ball and shuttlecock lead to divergent schemas. Conversely, a skill may require attention to details not handled by the constituent schemas of the preliminary coordinated control program. Fractionation may be required, as when the infant progresses from "swiping grasps" at objects to the differentiation of separate schemas for the control of arm and hand movements. Later, the hand movement repertoire becomes expanded as one acquires such novel skills as typing or piano playing, with this extension matched by increased subtlety of eye-arm-hand coordination Thus, we have three mechanisms (at least) to learn completely new actions: forming new constructs (coordinated control programs) based on familiar actions; tuning of these constructs to yield new encapsulated actions; and fractionation of existing actions to yield more adaptive actions as tuned, coordinated control programs of novel schemas.

Imitation, in general, requires the ability to break down a complex performance into a coordinated control program of pieces that approximate the pieces of the performance to be imitated. This then provides the framework in which attention can be shifted to specific components that can then be tuned and/or fractionated appropriately, or better coordinated with other components of the skill. This process is recursive, yielding both the mastery of ever finer details, and the increasing grace and accuracy of the overall performance.

I argue that what marks humans as distinct from their common ancestors with chimpanzees is that whereas the chimpanzee can imitate short novel sequences through repeated exposure, humans can acquire (longer) novel sequences in a single trial if the sequences are not too long and the components are relatively familiar. The very structure of these sequences can serve as the basis for immediate imitation or for the immediate construction of an appropriate response, as well as contributing to the longer-term enrichment of experience. Of course (as our Santa Fe dance example shows), as sequences get longer, or the components become less familiar, more and more practice is required to fully comprehend or imitate the behavior.

Section 10.2 summarizes the basic evidence for the Mirror System Hypothesis for the evolution of language. Section 10.3 will go "Beyond the Mirror" to suggest new considerations that refine the original hypothesis of the 1998 paper. This chapter will take us through seven hypothesized stages of evolution,

1. grasping
2. a mirror system for grasping (i.e., a system that matches observation and execution)
3. a simple imitation system for grasping
4. a complex imitation system for grasping
5. a manual-based communication system
6. speech, which I here characterize as being the open-ended production and perception of sequences of vocal gestures, without implying that these sequences constitute a language
7. language

At each stage, the earlier capabilities are preserved. Moreover, the addition of a new stage may involve enhancement of the repertoire for the primordial behaviors on which it is based.

Three key methodological points:

- We must understand the adaptive value of each of the first six stages without recourse to its role as a platform for later stages.
- We will distinguish between "language" and "language-readiness," stressing that certain biological bases for language may not have evolved to serve language but were selected by other pressures, and then served as the basis for a process of individual discoveries driving cultural evolution—which developed language to the richness we find in all present-day societies, from vast cities to isolated tribes. I will argue that the first six stages involved biological evolution that was completed with the emergence of *Homo sapiens*, but that the richness of language reflects cultural evolution with little if any change in the brain of *Homo sapiens* beyond that required to achieve speech in the limited sense described in stage 6 above.
- We will not restrict language to "that which is expressed in speech, or in writing derived therefrom." By this I mean that language in its fullness may be expressed by an integration of speech, manual gestures, and facial movements to which the written record can do, at best, partial justice.

The argument that follows involves two major sections, "The Mirror System Hypothesis: A New Approach to the Gestural Basis of Language" and "Beyond the Mirror: Further Hypotheses on the Evolution of Language." The first part (section 10.2) reviews neurophysiological and anatomical data on stage 1, grasping, and stage 2, mirror systems for grasping, as well as outlining a computational model, the FARS (Fagg-Arbib-Rizzolatti-Sakata) model, for grasping, named for the modelers Andy Fagg and myself, and for the experimentalists Giacomo Rizzolatti and Hideo Sakata, whose work anchors the model. The model shows how the sight of an object may be processed to yield an appropriate action for grasping it, as well as to explain the shifting patterns of neural activity in a variety of brain regions involved in this visuomotor transformation. We then provide a conceptual analysis of how the brain may indeed use a *mirror system*—that is, one that uses the same neural codes to characterize an action whether it is executed or observed by the agent. A mirror system for grasping in the monkey has been found in area F5 of premotor cortex, while data have been found consistent with the notion of a mirror system for grasping in humans in Broca's area, which is homologous to monkey F5, but in humans is most often thought of as a speech area. After a brief discussion of learning in the mirror system, and a conceptual analysis of the equation "Action = Movement + Goal/Expectation," we use the above data to bridge from action to language with the *Mirror System Hypothesis*—namely, that language evolved from a basic mechanism not originally related to communication: the mirror system for grasping with its capacity to generate and recognize a set of actions.

The second half of the paper (section 10.3) then goes "Beyond the Mirror," offering further hypotheses on the evolution of language, which take us up the hierarchy from elementary actions to the recognition and generation of novel compounds of such actions. The well-known linguist Noam Chomsky (e.g., 1975) has argued that since children acquire language rapidly despite the "poverty of the stimulus," therefore the basic structures of language are encoded in the brain, forming a *Universal Grammar* encoded in the human genome. For example, it is claimed that the Universal Grammar encodes the knowledge that a sentence in a human language could be ordered as subject-verb-object, subject-object-verb, and so on, so that the child simply needs to hear a few sentences of his first language to "set the parameter" for the preferred order of that language. Against this, others have argued that in fact the child does have a rich set of language stimuli, and that there are now far more powerful models of learning than those that Chomsky took into account, allowing us to explain how a child might learn from its social interactions aspects of syntax that Chomsky would see as genetically prespecified. The reader may consult Lieberman (1991) for a number of arguments that counter Chomsky's view. Here, I simply observe that many youngsters today easily acquire the skills of "Web surfing" and video-game playing despite a complete poverty of the stimulus—namely, the inability of their parents to master these skills. I trust that no one would claim that the human genome contains a "Web-surfing gene!" Instead, we know the history of computers, and know that technology has advanced over the last fifty-five years to take us from an interface based on binary coding that only a trained scientist could master to a mouse-and-graphics interface so well adapted to human sensorimotor capabilities that a child can master it. My claim is that languages evolved similarly. Deacon (1997) makes a similar point, but blurs it somewhat in the subtitle of his book *The Symbolic Species: The Co-evolution of Language and the Brain*. I agree that communication (but not of the richness that characterizes all present-day languages) did provide part of the selective pressures that formed the brain of *Homo sapiens*, but I still hold that much of what we regard as the nature of language was formed by a multitude of discoveries that postdated the overall establishment of the human genome.

Note that the argument is over whether or not the "key grammatical structures of all possible human languages" are all preencoded in the human genome, to be selected by parameter setting in early childhood. There is no argument against the view that human evolution yielded genetic specification of some of the structures that *support* language. For example, the human larynx is especially well structured for the clear articulation of vocalization (see Lieberman 1991 for further details), and the human brain provides the necessary control mechanisms for this articulation. However, Lieberman and I reject Chomsky's view that many of the basic alternatives of grammatical structure of the world's current languages are already encoded in the human genome, so that the child's experience merely "sets parameters" to choose among prepackaged alternative grammatical structures. The counterview that I espouse holds that the brain of the first *Homo sapiens* was "language-ready" but that it required many millennia of invention and cultural evolution for human societies to form human languages in the modern sense.

Given the emphasis on the recognition and generation of novel, hierarchically structured compounds of actions as a key to language, we next come to stages 3 and 4, simple and complex imitation systems for grasping. With this, we move to a speculative scenario for how stage 5, a manual-based communication system, broke through the fixed repertoire of primate vocalizations to yield a combinatorially open repertoire, so that stage 6, speech, did not build upon the ancient primate vocalization system, but rather rested on the "invasion" of the vocal apparatus by collaterals from the communication system based on F5/Broca's area. In discussing the transition to *Homo sapiens*, I stress that our predecessors must have had a relatively flexible, open repertoire of vocalizations but this does not mean that they, or the first humans, had language. For stage 7, the transition to language, I offer a scenario for the change from action-object frames to verb-argument structures to syntax and semantics. Finally, I briefly sketch the merest outline of a new approach to neurolinguistics based on these extensions of the Mirror System Hypothesis.

10.2   The Mirror-System Hypothesis: A New Approach to the Gestural Basis of Language

Stage 1:   Grasping

In this section and the next, we will use data on the monkey brain to ground our speculations on what might have been brain structures in the common ancestor of monkey and human that laid the basis for the evolution of a brain that could support imitation and the ability to discover, disseminate, and use language as the basis for new patterns of communication. The task of the present section is to take us through stage 1 (grasping) of our hypothesized stages of evolution, reviewing relevant data and presenting useful grounding concepts provided by the FARS model.

The neurophysiological findings of the Sakata group on parietal cortex (Taira et al. 1990) and the Rizzolatti group on premotor cortex indicate that parietal area AIP (the anterior intraparietal sulcus) and ventral premotor area F5 in the monkey (Rizzolatti et al. 1988) form key elements in a cortical circuit that transforms visual information on intrinsic properties of objects into hand movements that allow the animal to grasp the objects appropriately. See figure 10.1 for the anatomy, and Jeannerod and colleagues (1995) for a review.

Motor information is transferred from F5 to the primary motor cortex (denoted F1 or M1) to which F5 is directly connected, as well as to various subcortical centers for movement execution. For

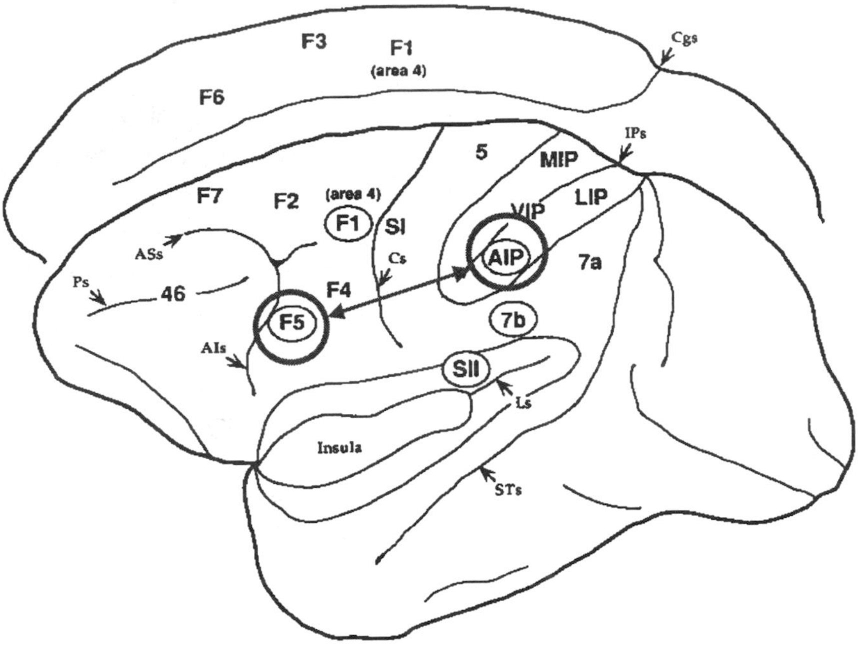

Figure 10.1 A side view of the left hemisphere of the macaque monkey brain dominates the figure, with a glimpse of the medial view of the right hemisphere above it to show certain regions that lie on the inner surface of the hemisphere. The central fissure is the groove separating area SI (primary somatosensory cortex) from F1 (more commonly called MI, primary motor cortex). Frontal cortex is the region in front of (in the figure, to the left of) the central sulcus. Area F5 of premotor cortex (i.e., the area of frontal cortex just in front of primary motor cortex) is implicated in the elaboration of "abstract motor commands" for grasping movements. Parietal cortex is the region behind (in the figure, to the right of) the central sulcus. The groove in the middle of the parietal cortex, the intraparietal sulcus, is shown opened here to reveal various areas. AIP (the anterior region of the intraparietal sulcus) processes visual information relevant to the control of hand movements and is reciprocally connected with F5.

example, neurons located in the rostral part of inferior area 6 (area F5) discharge during active hand and/or mouth movements (di Pellegrino et al. 1992; Rizzolatti et al. 1996a; Gallese et al. 1996). Moreover, discharge in most F5 neurons correlates with an action rather than with the individual movements that form it so that one may classify F5 neurons into various categories corresponding to the action associated with their discharge. The most common are: "grasping-with-the-hand" neurons, "grasping-with-the-hand-and-the-mouth" neurons, "holding" neurons, "manipulating" neurons, and "tearing" neurons. Rizzolatti and colleagues (1988) thus argued that F5 contains a "vocabulary" of motor schemas (Arbib 1981). The situation is in fact more complex, and "grasp execution" involves a variety of loops and a variety of other brain regions in addition to AIP and F5.

The FARS model (Fagg and Arbib 1998) makes clear certain conceptual issues that will be crucial at later stages of the argument. It provides a computational account of what we shall call the canonical system, centered on the AIP → F5 pathway, showing how it can account for basic phenomena of grasping. The highlights of the model are shown in figures 10.2 and 10.3. Our basic view is that AIP cells encode (by a population code whose details are again beyond the present discussion) "affordances" for grasping from the visual stream and sends (neural codes for) these on to area F5—affordances (Gibson 1979) are features of the object relevant to action, in this case to grasping. In other words, vision here provides cues on how to interact with an object, rather than categorizing the object or determining its identity. As figure 10.2 shows, some cells in AIP are driven by feedback from F5 rather than by visual inputs so that AIP can monitor ongoing activity as well as visual affordances. Here, we indicate the case in which the visual input has activated an affordance for a precision pinch, and we show the AIP activity driving an F5 cell pool that controls the execution of a precision pinch. However, what we show is somewhat complicated, because the circuitry is not for a single action, but for a behavior designed by Sakata to probe the time dependence of activity in the monkey brain. In the Sakata paradigm, the monkey is trained to watch a manipulandum until a "go" signal instructs it to reach out and grasp the object. It must then hold the object until another signal instructs it to release the object.

In figure 10.2, cells in AIP instruct the set cells in F5 to prepare for execution of the Sakata protocol using a precision pinch. Activation of each pool of F5 cells not only instructs the motor apparatus to carry out the appropriate activity (these connections are not shown here), but also primes the next pool of F5 neurons (i.e., brings the neurons to just below threshold so they may respond quickly when they receive their own go signal) as well as inhibiting the F5 neurons for the previous stage of activity. Thus, the neurons that control the extension phase of the hand shaping to grasp the object are primed by the set neurons, and they reach threshold when they receive the first go signal, at which time they inhibit the set neurons and prime the flexion neurons. These pass threshold when receiving a signal that the hand has reached its

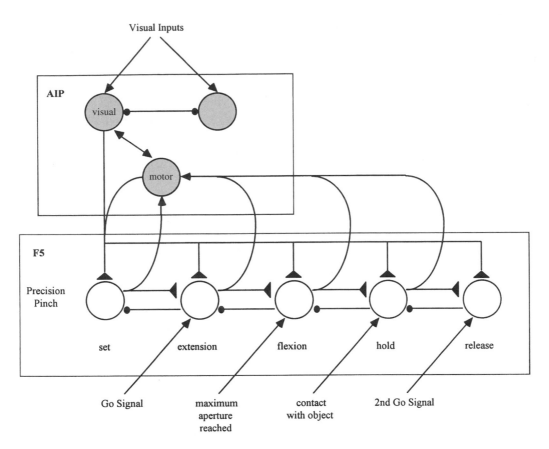

Visual Inputs

AIP

visual

motor

F5

Precision
Pinch

set

extension

flexion

hold

release

Go Signal

maximum
aperture
reached

contact
with object

2nd Go Signal

Figure 10.2 Hypothesized information flow in AIP and F5 in the FARS model during execution of the Sakata paradigm. This neural circuit appears as a rather rigid structure. However, we do not hypothesize that connections implementing the phasic behavior are hardwired in F5. Instead, we posit that sequences are stored in pre-SMA (a part of the supplementary motor area) and administered by the basal ganglia.

maximum aperture; the hold neurons once primed will become active when receiving a signal that contact has been made with the object; and the primed release neurons will command the hand to let go of the object once they receive the code for the second go signal.

Karl Lashley (1951) wrote of "The Problem of Serial Order in Behavior," a critique of stimulus-response approaches to psychology. He noted that it would be impossible to learn a sequence like A, B, A, C as a stimulus-response chain because the association "completing A triggers B" would then be interfered with by the association "completing A triggers C," or would dominate it to yield an infinite repetition of the sequence A, B, A, B,... The gen-

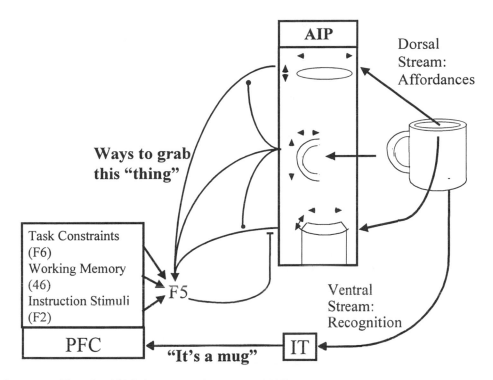

Figure 10.3 The role of IT (inferotemporal cortex) and PFC (prefrontal cortex) in modulating F5's selection of an affordance.

erally adopted solution is to segregate the learning of a sequence from the circuitry that encodes the unit actions, the latter being F5 in the present study. Instead, another area (possibly the part of the supplementary motor area called pre-SMA; Rizzolatti, Luppino, and Matelli 1998) has neurons whose connections encode an "abstract sequence" Q1, Q2, Q3, Q4, with sequence learning then involving learning that activation of Q1 triggers the F5 neurons for A, Q2 triggers B, Q3 triggers A again, and Q4 triggers C. In this way, Lashley's problem is solved. Other studies lead us to postulate that the storage and administration of the sequence (inhibiting extraneous actions while priming imminent actions) is carried out by the portion of the supplementary motor area known as pre-SMA and the basal ganglia, respectively.[2]

Note that the solution offered here is a specific case of a far more general solution to Lashley's problem, based on learning a finite automaton, rather than just a sequence (Arbib 1969; Dominey, Arbib, and Joseph 1995). In the general situation, we have a set X of inputs, a set Y of outputs, and a set Q of states. These are augmented by a state-transition function δ: $Q \times X \to Q$, and an output function β: $Q \to Y$. When in state q, the automaton emits output $\beta(q)$; on receiving input x, it then changes state to $\delta(q, x)$.

We now turn to the crucial role of IT (inferotemporal cortex) and PFC (prefrontal cortex) in modulating F5's selection of an affordance (figure 10.3). Here, the dorsal stream (from primary visual cortex to parietal cortex) carries, among other things, the information needed for AIP to recognize that different parts of the object can be grasped in different ways, thus extracting affordances for the grasp system that (according to the FARS model) are then passed on to F5 where a selection must be made for the actual grasp. The point is that the dorsal stream does not know "what" the object is, it can only see the object as a set of possible affordances. The ventral stream (from primary visual cortex to inferotemporal cortex), by contrast, is able to recognize what the object is. This information is passed to prefrontal cortex, which can then, on the basis of the current goals of the organism and the recognition of the nature of the object, bias F5 to choose the affordance appropriate to the task at hand. In particular, the FARS model represents the way in which F5 may accept signals from areas F6 (pre-SMA), 46 (dorsolateral prefrontal cortex), and F2 (dorsal premotor cortex) to respond to task constraints, working memory, and instruction stimuli, respectively (see Fagg and Arbib 1998 for more details).

Stage 2: Mirror Systems for Grasping

Our task now is to describe neurological data that show that the above "execution system" for grasp in monkeys includes a subset of neurons—the mirror neurons—that form an "observation system," then review preliminary data that there is a homologous system in Broca's area—a language area of humans.

A MIRROR SYSTEM FOR GRASPING IN THE MONKEY
Further study of F5 revealed something unexpected—a class of F5 neurons that discharge not only when the monkey grasped or manipulated objects, but also when the monkey observed the experimenter make a gesture similar to the one that, when actively performed by the monkey, involved activity of the neuron. Neurons with this property are called "mirror neurons" (Gallese et al. 1996). Movements yielding mirror neuron activity when made by

the experimenter include placing objects on or taking objects from a table, grasping food, or manipulating objects. Mirror neurons, in order to be visually triggered, require an interaction between the agent of the action and the object of it. The simple presentation of objects, even when held by hand, does not evoke the neuron discharge. An example of a mirror neuron is shown in figure 10.4. In A, left side, the monkey observes the experimenter grasping a small piece of food. The tray on which the food is placed is then moved toward the monkey and the monkey grasps the food (right side of the figure). The neuron discharges both during grasping observation and during active grasping. B illustrates that when the food is grasped with a tool and not by hand the neuron remains silent. The majority of mirror neurons are selective for one type of action, and for almost all mirror neurons there is a link between the effective observed movement and the effective executed movement. A series of control experiments ruled out interpretations of mirror neurons in terms of a monkey's vision of its own hand, food expectancy, motor preparation for food retrieval, or reward (Gallese et al. 1996).

The response properties of mirror neurons to visual stimuli can be summarized as follows: Mirror neurons do not discharge in response to simple presentation of objects even when held by hand by the experimenter. They require a specific action—whether observed or self-executed—to be triggered. The majority of them respond selectively in relation to one type of action (e.g., grasping). This congruence can be extremely strict—that is, the effective motor action (e.g., precision grip) coincides with the action that, when seen, triggers the neuron (e.g., again precision grip). For other neurons the congruence is broader. For them, the motor requirement (e.g., precision grip) is usually stricter than the visual (any type of hand grasping, but not other actions). All mirror neurons show visual generalization. They fire when the instrument of the observed action (usually a hand) is large or small, far from or close to the monkey. They also fire even when the action instrument has shapes as different as those of a human or monkey hand. A few neurons respond even when the object is grasped by the mouth. The actions most represented are: grasp, manipulate, tear, put an object on a plate. Mirror neurons also have (by definition) motor properties. However, not all F5 neurons respond to action observation. We thus distinguish mirror neurons, which are active both when the monkey performs certain actions and when the monkey

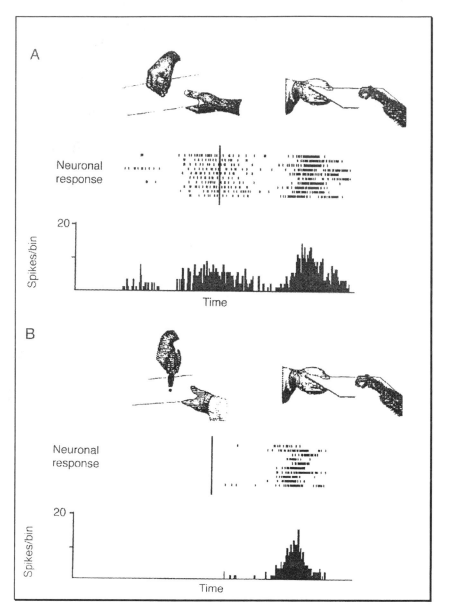

Figure 10.4 Example of a mirror neuron. Upper part of each panel: behavioral situations. Lower part: neuron's responses. The firing pattern of the neuron on each of a series of consecutive trials is shown above the histogram which sums the response from each trial. (*A*, left) The experimenter grasps a piece of food with his hand, then moves it toward the monkey, who (*A*, right) at the end of the trial, grasps it. The neuron discharges during observation of the experimenter's grasp, ceases to fire when the food is given to the monkey and discharges again when the monkey grasps it. (*B*, left) When the experimenter grasps the food with an unfamiliar tool, the neuron does not respond, but the neuron again discharges when the monkey grasps the food. The rasters are aligned with the moment when the food is grasped (vertical line). Each small vertical line in the rasters corresponds to a spike. Histogram bin width: 20 ms. Ordinates, spikes/bin; abscissae, time.

observes them performed by others, from canonical neurons in F5, which are active when the monkey performs certain actions but not when the monkey observes actions performed by others. Mirror neurons receive input from the PF region of parietal cortex encoding observations of arm and hand movements. This is in contrast with the canonical F5 neurons, which receive object-related input from AIP. It is the canonical neurons, with their input from AIP, that are modeled in the FARS model.

The monkey may have a limited "hardwired" repertoire of basic grasps, such as the precision pinch and the power grasp. These capabilities may then be extended through learning:

1. Developing a further set of useful grasps (extending the repertoire of actions for canonical F5 neurons);
2. Learning to associate view of one's hand with grasp and object and matching this to views of others grasping (linking F5 mirror neurons with the appropriate visual preprocessing and F5 canonical neurons to match the representations of self-generated actions with similarly goal-oriented actions executed by others). An interesting anecdote from the Rizzolatti laboratory (unpublished) is suggestive for further analysis: when a monkey first sees the experimenter grasp a raisin using a pair of pliers, his mirror neurons will not fire. However, after many such experiences, the monkey's mirror neurons encoding precision grip will fire when he sees the pliers used to grasp a raisin—the initially novel performance has been characterized as a familiar action.

In summary, the properties of mirror neurons suggest that area F5 is endowed with an observation/execution matching system: when the monkey observes a motor act that resembles one in its movement repertoire, a neural code for this action is automatically retrieved. This code consists in the activation of a subset, the mirror neurons, of the F5 neurons that discharge when the observed act is executed by the monkey itself.

A MIRROR SYSTEM FOR GRASPING IN HUMANS

The notion that a mirror system might exist in humans was tested by two PET[3] experiments (Rizzolatti et al. 1996; Grafton et al. 1996). The two experiments differed in many aspects, but both compared brain activation when subjects observed the experimenter grasping a 3-D object against activation when subjects simply observed the object. Grasp observation significantly activated the superior temporal sulcus (STS), the inferior parietal lobule, and the inferior frontal gyrus (area 45). All activations were in the left hemisphere. The last area is of especial interest—areas 44 and 45 in left hemisphere of the human constitute Broca's area, a major component of the human brain's language mechanisms. Although there is no data set yet that shows the same activated voxels for grasping execution and grasping observation in Broca's area, such data certainly contribute to the growing body of indirect evidence that there is a mirror system for grasping in Broca's area. F5 in monkeys is generally considered (Rizzolatti and Arbib 1998) to be the homologue of Broca's area in humans—that is, it can be argued that these areas of monkey and human brain are related to the same region of the common ancestor. Thus, the cortical areas active during action observation in humans and monkeys correspond very well. Taken together, human and monkey data indicate that in primates there is a fundamental mechanism for action recognition: we argue that individuals recognize actions made by others because the neural pattern elicited in their premotor areas (in a broad sense) during action observation is similar to a part of that internally generated to produce that action. This mechanism in humans is circumscribed to the left hemisphere.

Primate Vocalization

Monkeys exhibit a primate call system (a limited set of species-specific calls) and an orofacial (mouth and hand) gesture system (a limited set of gestures expressive of emotion and related social indicators), as shown in figure 10.5, which includes a linkage be-

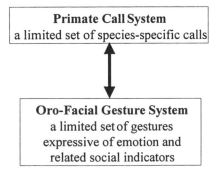

Figure 10.5 The communication system for the monkey is based on a finite set of calls ("vocal gestures") and orofacial gestures.

tween the two systems to stress that communication is inherently multimodal. (Body posture also plays a role in social communication, not emphasized here.) This communication system is *closed* in the sense that it is restricted to a specific repertoire. This is to be contrasted with human languages, which are *open* in two senses: (i) the language is generative, or productive, being made up of words and grammatical markers that can be combined in diverse ways to yield an essentially unbounded stock of sentences (you are able to comprehend this sentence even though you have neither seen nor heard it before); and (ii) new words (such as "computer" and "subsidiarity") may always be added to expand the scope of the language.[4]

What is to be stressed here is that:

1. Combinatorial properties for the openness (productivity) of utterances are virtually absent in basic primate calls and orofacial communication, even though individual calls may be graded.
2. The neural substrate for primate calls is in a region of cingulate cortex distinct from F5, which we have seen to be the monkey homologue of human Broca's area.

Our challenge in charting the evolution of human language, which for most humans is so heavily intertwined with speech, is thus to understand why it is F5, rather than the cingulate area already involved in monkey vocalization, that is homologous to Broca's area's substrate for language. But before proceeding to stage 3, we need to discuss in more detail the nature of the mirror system in monkeys, which, we presume, carries over into the mirror systems of chimpanzees and humans, but which receives further refinements in these species.

Action = Movement + Goal/Expectation

What makes a movement into an action is that (1) it is associated with a goal, and (2) initiation of the movement is accompanied by the creation of an expectation that the goal will be met. To the extent that the unfolding of the movement departs from that expectation, an error will be detected and the movement modified. In other words, an individual performing an action is able to predict its consequences and, therefore, the action representation and its consequences are associated. Thus a "grasp" involves not only a specific cortical activation pattern for the preshape and enclose movements, but also expectations concerning making appropriate contact with a specific object. Elsewhere (Arbib and Rizzolatti 1997), we have asserted that "an individual making an action 'knows' what action he is performing to the extent that he predicts the consequences of his pattern of movement" but we must be very careful to distinguish "knowledge of action" in the sense of "has a neural representation of Movement + Goal/Expectation" from "has a representation that corresponds to a human's conscious awareness of what she or he is doing." Indeed, the FARS model contains mechanisms for creating and monitoring expectations even though it only models canonical F5 neurons, not mirror neurons. However, the creation of an expectation associated with one's own action is quite distinct from inferring the action of another from a glimpse of the movement involved.

The data presented earlier show that a major evolutionary development has been established in primates: the individual can recognize ("understand") the actions made by others in the sense that the neural pattern elicited by those actions is similar to that generated by him in doing the action. We suggest that the evolution of mirror neurons extended "knowing" from the individual to the social. Further evolution was required for such a system to mediate imitation. In later sections, we will discuss the importance of imitation not only in and for itself, but also as a crucial step toward the skills needed to mediate language (evolving a "language-ready brain").

It is probably the case that "understanding" involves the cooperation of many brain systems, and cannot be reduced to just the activity in a subset of the monkey's F5 neurons. Similarly for imitation. To say that firing of neurons in the monkey's mirror system is "predictive" means that it "creates a neural representation of a potential future state." Again, while mirror activity may be the key to "understanding," that activity in isolation from other brain systems encodes the ability "to match an external (unknown) event to an internal (known) event." I am not saying that the monkey has no awareness of the results of its actions or is incapable of knowing what another monkey is doing (though I would argue that human language and other cognitive abilities make our awareness very different from that of monkeys; Arbib 2001), only that F5 activity in isolation is insufficient to mediate that awareness.

Many authors have suggested that language and understanding are inseparable, but our experience of scenery and sunsets and songs and seductions makes clear that we humans understand

more than we can express in words. Some aspects of such awareness and understanding, then, may certainly be available to animals who do not possess language. Of course, this does not deny
the crucial point that our development, as "modern" humans, that
is, as individuals within a language-based society, greatly extends
our understanding beyond that possible for nonhumans or for
humans raised apart from a language community. Conversely, of
course, other species are aware of aspects of their environment and
society that we humans can at best dimly comprehend.

Two caveats should be noted:

1. There is no claim that this mirroring is limited to primates. It is
   likely that an analogue of mirror systems exists in other mammals,
   especially those with a rich and flexible social organization. Moreover, the evolution of the imitation system for learning songs by
   male songbirds is divergent from mammalian evolution, but for the
   neuroscientist there are intriguing challenges in plotting the similarities and differences in the neural mechanisms underlying
   human language and birdsong.

2. The recognition of consequences may extend to actions beyond the
   animal's own repertoire, and may in some such cases involve
   mechanisms not much more complex than classical conditioning,
   rather than invoking a mirror system. For example, dogs can recognize the consequences of a human's use of a can opener (the
   sound of the can opener becomes associated with the subsequent
   presentation of the dog food from the can) without having a motor
   program for opening cans, let alone mirror neurons for such a program.

Figure 10.6 presents a conceptual framework for analysis of the
role of F5 in grasping. This combines mechanisms for (1) grasping
a seen object (the right hand path from "view of object" to "grasp
of object"); and (2) imitating observed gestures[5] in such a way as to
create expectations that not only play a role in "social learning"
but also enable the visual feedback loop to eventually serve for
(delayed) error correction during, for example, reaching toward a
target (the loop on the left of the figure). (A more detailed model,
with explicit learning rules, is currently being developed [Oztop
and Arbib 2001].)

The Expectation Neural Network (ENN) is the "direct model" of
Command $\rightarrow$ Response, which transforms the command into a
code for the response. When the animal gives a command (i.e.,

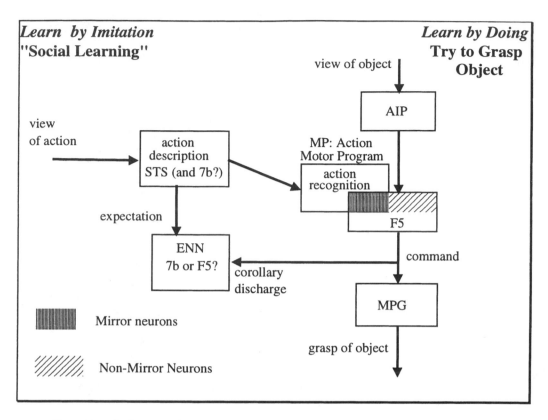

Figure 10.6 An integrated conceptual framework for analysis of the role of F5 in grasping. The right hand, vertical, path is the *execution system* from "view of object" via AIP and F5 to the motor pattern generator (MPG) for grasping a (seen) object. The loop on the left of the figure provides mechanisms for imitating observed actions in such a way as to create expectations which enable the visual feedback loop to serve both for "social learning" (i.e., learning an action through imitation of the actions of others) and also for (delayed) error correction during, e.g., reaching towards a target. It combines the *observation matching system* from "view of action" via action description (STS) and action recognition (mirror neurons in F5 and possibly 7b) to a representation of the "command" for such an action, and the *expectation system* from an F5 command via the expectation neural network ENN to MP, the motor program for generating a given action. The latter path may mediate a comparison between "expected action" and "observed action" in the case of the monkey's self-generated movement.

brain regions issue the neural signals that initiate a movement), ENN generates the expected neural code for the visual signal generated by the resulting gesture. This is different from the FARS model (Fagg and Arbib 1998), which creates sensory expectations of the result of the movement, such as "the feel of the object when grasped," which are "private" to the animal. Here, we look at "public" symptoms of the ongoing movement. The key to the mirror system is that it brings those symptoms for self-movement together with those for other-movement in generating, we claim, a code for "action" (movement + goal) and not just for movement alone. However, there is a subsidiary problem here—namely, recognizing which "symptoms" of self-movement correspond to which symptoms of other-movement, since the retinal display for, say, the hand movement of one's self or another is radically different. In any case, we explicitly label the input to ENN, a copy of the motor command, as a corollary discharge. By contrast, the Motor Program (MP) provides an "inverse model" of Command → Response, going from a desired response to a command that can generate it.

Where are the various stages forming the imitation loop? Here are two, admittedly speculative, possibilities. The first is that the various model stages are located in different anatomical areas. In this case, the inverse model that converts the view of an action to a corresponding command could be located along the path leading from STS to F5 (possibly via 7b). The reciprocal path from F5 to superior temporal sulcus would provide the direct model, ENN. It is equally probable, however, that both ENN and MP are located in F5 and the interplay between stages occurs entirely within F5. If the latter interpretation is accepted, the role of STS areas would be that of giving a merely "pictorial," though highly elaborated description, of actions—with the observation/execution system entirely located in the frontal lobe.

The integrated model of figure 10.6 thus relates the "grasp an object" system to the "view an action" system. The expectation network is driven by F5 irrespective of whether the motor command is "object-driven" (via AIP) or "action-driven." It thus creates expectations both for what a hand movement will look like when "object-driven" (an instrumental action directed toward a goal) or "action-driven" (a "social action" aimed at making a self-generated movement approximate—by some criterion that does not match body-centered localization—an observed movement).

The right-hand path of figure 10.6 exemplifies "learning by doing," refining a crude "innate grasp"—possibly by a process of reinforcement learning, in which the success/failure of the grasp acts as positive/negative reinforcement. The left-hand path of figure 10.6 exemplifies another mode of learning (the two may be sequential or contemporary), which creates expectations about actions as well as exemplifying "social learning" based on imitation of actions made by others.

Bridging from Action to Language: The Mirror-System Hypothesis

Before proceeding further, we must distinguish "pragmatic action" in which the hands are used to interact physically with objects or other creatures, and "gestures" (both manual and vocal), whose purpose is communication. Our assumption is that monkeys use hand movements only for pragmatic actions. The mirror system allows other monkeys to understand these actions and act on the basis of this understanding. Similarly, the monkey's orofacial gestures register emotional state, and primate vocalizations can also communicate something of the current situation of the monkey. The monkey exhibits what might be called "involuntary communication" of its current internal state or situation either through its observable actions or through a fixed species-specific repertoire of orofacial gestures and vocal gestures. We will develop the hypothesis that the mirror system made possible (but in no sense guaranteed) the evolution of the displacement of hand movements from pragmatic action to gestures that can be controlled "voluntarily."

Hewes (1973), Corballis (1991, 1992), Kimura (1993), and Armstrong, Stokoe, and Wilcox (1995) are among those who have long argued that communication based on manual gesture played a crucial role in human language evolution, preceding communication by speech. In this regard, we stress that the "openness" or "generativity," which some see as the hallmark of language (i.e., its openness to new constructions, as distinct from having a fixed repertoire like that of monkey vocalizations), is present in manual behavior, which can thus supply the evolutionary substrate for its appearance in language. Kimura (1993) argues that the left hemisphere is specialized not for language, but for complex motor programming functions, which are, in particular, essential for language production. However, it is not clear whether (1) hominid evolution yielded circuitry used for all forms of complex motor control, so that whether or not specific neurons are involved in control of language behavior is purely a result of experience-based learning; or (2) evolution at some stage duplicated the circuitry used for complex motor control, with one copy then becoming specialized for the type of motor sequencing mechanisms needed for language (e.g., those involving the coordinated control of larynx, hands, and facial expression) while the other copy remained available for other forms of coordinated behavior. If, in case (ii), the two circuits remained adjacent or even overlapping, it would make lesions that dissociate language performance from other forms of motor control very rare.

With our understanding that the mirror system in monkeys is the homologue of Broca's area in humans, we can now appreciate the central hypothesis of "Language Within Our Grasp" (Rizzolatti and Arbib 1998)—namely, that this homology provides a neurobiological "missing link" for the long-argued hypothesis that gestural communication (based on manual gesture) preceded speech in the evolution of language. Rizzolatti and Arbib's novel tenet is that the parity requirement for language in humans—what counts for the speaker must count for the hearer—is met because of:

THE MIRROR SYSTEM HYPOTHESIS
Language evolved from a basic mechanism *not* originally related to communication—the *mirror system for grasping* with its capacity to generate *and* recognize a set of actions.[0]

However, it is important to be quite clear as to what the Mirror System Hypothesis does not say:

1. It does not say that having a mirror system is equivalent to having language. Monkeys have mirror systems but do not have language, and we expect that many species have mirror systems for varied socially relevant behaviors.

2. It is unclear whether the mirror system for grasping is sufficient for the copying of actions. It is one thing to recognize an action using the mirror system, it is another thing to use that representation as a basis for repeating the action. In an earlier version of this paper, I stated that "monkeys seldom if ever repeat an action, but the mirror system helps them recognize the actions of others as a basis for social cooperation and competition." However, Judy Cameron (personal communication) offers the following observation from

the Oregon Regional Primate Research Center: "Researchers at the Center had laboriously taught monkeys to run on a treadmill as a basis for tests they wished to conduct. It took five months to train the first batch of monkeys in this task. But they then found that if they allowed other monkeys to observe the trained monkeys running on a treadmill, then the naive monkeys would run successfully the first time they were placed on a treadmill." This is not evidence that the monkey mirror system for grasping is part of a system for imitation of hand movements, but does render this likely. We need new experiments to test this possibility and determine to what extent other brain regions besides F5 are required to exploit "mirroring" for the purpose of imitation.

However, I stress again that the ability to copy *single* actions is just the first step toward imitation, since we have earlier insisted that imitation involves "parsing" a complex movement into more or less familiar pieces, and then performing the corresponding composite of (variations on) familiar actions. The subtleties in going from "recognizing a familiar action" to "imitating a complex behavior based on an interweaving of variations on familiar actions" were illustrated in the opening description of a dance class in Santa Fe, and it is such observations that challenge us to go "beyond the mirror," that is, beyond the recognition of single actions by the mirror system, in later sections of this paper. Note, too, the observation that the synchronization of movements in a group of dancers is enhanced by the rhythm of the music shows that imitation requires the ability for multimodal associative learning, in this case matching rhythmic auditory and locomotor patterns.

3. It does not say that language evolution can be studied in isolation from cognitive evolution more generally. In using language, we make use of, for example, negation, counterfactuals, and verb tenses. But each of these linguistic structures is of no value unless we can understand that the facts contradict an utterance, and we can recall past events and imagine future possibilities.

10.3   Beyond the Mirror: Further Hypotheses on the Evolution of Language

Having established the basic Mirror System Hypothesis, we now go "beyond the mirror" to discuss possible stages in the evolution from a monkeylike mirror system to the human capacity for language. We first distinguish language readiness from "language hard-wired into the brain," and then examine the next four stages of posited biological evolution—3 and 4, a simple and complex imitation system for grasping; 5, a manual-based communication system, and 6, speech (in the sense of the ability to produce and comprehend sequences of vocal gestures; I distinguish this from the capacity for spoken language in the modern sense)—which, I claim, provided *Homo sapiens* with a language-ready brain. The argument in part parallels, in part extends, that of Rizzolatti and Arbib (1998). However, I shall also argue that stage 7, the emergence of language, required many millennia of cultural evolution for our ancestors to extend earlier forms of hominid vocal communication into the complex communication systems that we recognize as human languages.

Language Readiness

Ease of acquisition of a skill does not imply genetic encoding of the skill per se: the human genome does not encode strategies for exploring the Internet or playing video games, but computer technology has evolved to match the preadaptations of the human brain and body.

The human brain and body evolved in such a way that we have hand, larynx, and facial mobility suited for generating gestures that can be used in language, and the brain mechanisms needed to produce and perceive rapidly generated sequences of such gestures. In this sense, the human brain and body are *language ready*.

We thus reframe the old question: "How did language evolve?" as two questions:

1. What really evolved by natural selection? Brains "equipped" with language, or language readiness?
2. How do we move beyond the mirror system to map changes in the evolutionary tree of primates and hominids in a *variety* of brain structures relevant to language readiness and cognition?

(A third question, beyond the scope of this article, addresses the dynamics of language on multiple time scales: How can the study of language acquisition and of historical linguistics help tease apart biological and cultural contributions to the mastery of language by present-day humans?)

To proceed, we list several criteria for a set of "utterances" to constitute a language in the sense of a present-day human language.

This list will help guide our understanding of what it means for the human brain to "have language" or "be language ready." Note that nothing in this list rests on the medium of exchange of the language, applying to spoken language, sign language, or written language, for example.[7]

Naming: the ability to associate an arbitrary symbol with a class of events, objects, and actions, etc.

Parity (mirror property): what counts for the speaker (or producer) must count for the listener (or hearer)

Hierarchical structuring: production and recognition of constituents with subparts

Temporal ordering: temporal activity coding these hierarchical structures[8]

Recursivity: the ability to build utterances using recursive rules—for example, "a noun phrase is still a noun phrase if you insert an (or another) adjective," in which the generic construct appears as a term in its own definition

Beyond the here-and-now: verb tenses (or other language constructs for representing past events or future possibilities) demand neural machinery (language readiness) to recall past events or imagine future ones

Lexicon, syntax, and semantics: "Language proper"—successfully matching syntactic structures to semantic structures

Learnability: to qualify as a human language, a set of symbolic structures must be learnable by most human children

Our quest to explore the hypothesis that the mirror system provided the basis for the evolution of human language (readiness) will next lead us to argue that "imitation" takes us beyond the "basic" mirror system for grasping, and that the ability to "acquire novel sequences if the sequences are not too long and the components are relatively familiar" takes us a step further. This leads us to the questions:

· What were the further biological changes supporting language readiness?

· What were the cultural changes extending the utility of language as a socially transmitted vehicle for communication and representation?

· How did biological and cultural change interact "in a spiral" prior to the emergence of *Homo sapiens*?

Our approach to these issues builds, as I have said, on the hypothesis (Rizzolatti and Arbib 1998) that the homology of the mirror system in monkeys with Broca's area in humans provides a neurobiological "missing link" for the long-argued hypothesis that communication based on manual gesture preceded speech in the evolution of language. It is important here to distinguish "communication using hand gestures" from "sign language." The former can take the primitive form that preceded the evolution of speech; the latter is the use of manual gestures (as distinct from the vocal gestures of spoken language) in a fully expressive human language. My hypothesis is that a sign language exploits many of the same brain mechanisms as does a spoken language, and that the subtlety of modern sign languages rests on a long process of cultural coevolution with spoken languages across many millennia following the biological emergence of *Homo sapiens*.

In this regard, let me briefly note the issue of nonhuman use of "sign language." The most impressive example for an ape is the case of the bonobo (pygmy chimpanzee) Kanzi. Savage-Rumbaugh, Shanker, and Taylor (1998) report that Kanzi and a $2\frac{1}{2}$-year-old girl were tested on their comprehension of 660 sentences phrased as simple requests (presented once). Kanzi was able to carry out the request correctly 72% of the time, whereas the girl scored 66% on the same sentences and task. Two observations: (1) No nonhuman primate has exhibited any of the richness of human language that distinguishes the adult human from the two-year-old, suggesting a biological difference in the brain's "language readiness" between humans and other primates (in addition to the fact that the human brain and larynx together support voluntary control of vocal articulations that the bonobo's cannot—thus the use of signing or other manual-based symbols). (2) No bonobo or other nonhuman primate has been seen "in the wild" to use symbols in the way that Kanzi has learned to use them. It is Kanzi's exposure to human culture that lets him learn to use signing to communicate, but what he acquires is but a small fragment of the full richness of the sign language of an adult human signer.

Stages 3 and 4: Simple and Complex Imitation Systems for Grasping

Figure 10.7 shows two key branch points in primate evolution. Twenty million years separate monkeys and humans from their common ancestor, while five million years separate chimps and

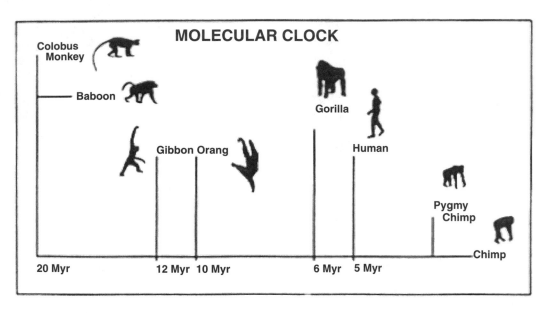

Figure 10.7 The timetable for hominid evolution inferred from the molecular clock. The crucial dates are 20 million years ago (divergence of monkeys from the line that led to humans and apes), and 5 million years ago (divergence of the hominid line from the line that led to modern apes). The pygmy chimp is also known as the bonobo, a quite different species from chimpanzee. (Adapted from Gamble, 1994, figure 4.2)

humans from their common ancestor. We remind the reader again that language played no role in the evolution of monkey or chimp or the common ancestors we share with them. Any changes we chart prior to the hominid line should be shown to be adaptive in their own right, rather than as precursors of language. Overall, the weight of evidence suggests that apes imitate far more than do monkeys. This leads to the following:

IMITATION HYPOTHESIS
Extension of the mirror system from *recognizing* single actions to *being able to copy* compound actions was the key innovation in the brains of human, chimp, and the common ancestor (as compared to the monkey-human common ancestor) relevant to language.

There is no hard and fast distinction between simple and compound actions. An apparently complex behavior may, with sufficient practice, become available as a unitary behavior from which yet more complex behaviors can be compounded. An action is compound relative to the current stock of unitary actions if it may be put together in some way (as a sequence, or some more subtle interleaving) from that stock. In this sense, we would hypothesize that the F5 mirror system would at any time bridge between the execution and observation of the unitary actions currently in the animal's repertoire but that it would require a superordinate system to perceive or execute the relationships between these units that define a compound action. In view of the earlier observations from the Oregon Regional Primate Research Center, it is clear that much more field work needs to be done to more formally characterize the capacities of monkey (and these may well vary from species to species of monkey) and chimpanzee. In any case, we need to do much more to characterize the relevant monkey neurophysiology and relate it to brain imaging in monkey, chimpanzee, and human.

It was noted in the Introduction that imitation generally requires the ability to break down a complex performance into a coordinated control program of pieces that approximate the pieces of the performance to be imitated. This then provides the framework in which attention can be shifted to specific components that can then be tuned and/or fractionated appropriately, or better coordinated with other components of the skill. This process is recursive, yielding both the mastery of ever finer details, and the increasing grace and accuracy of the overall performance. Given this framework, I argued that

1. monkey and, even more so, chimpanzee (and, presumably, the common ancestor of human and chimpanzee) has "simple imitation": they can imitate short novel sequences through repeated exposure, whereas
2. the human has "complex imitation": she or he can acquire (longer) novel sequences in a single trial

Important evidence for imitation in chimpanzees is that they use and make tools. Different tool traditions are apparent in geographically isolated groups of chimpanzees: Different types of tools are used for termite fishing at the Gombe in Tanzania and at sites in Senegal. Boesch and Boesch (1983) have observed chimpanzees in Tai National Park, Ivory Coast, using stone tools to crack nuts open, although Goodall has never seen chimpanzees in the Gombe do this. The nut-cracking technique is not mastered until adulthood. Mothers overtly correct and instruct their infants from the time they first attempt to crack nuts, at 3 years of age, and at least four years of practice are necessary before any benefits are obtained. To open soft-shelled nuts, chimps use thick sticks as hand hammers, with wood anvils. They crack harder-shelled nuts with stone hammers and stone anvils. The Tai chimpanzees live in a dense forest where suitable stones are hard to find. The stone anvils are stored in particular locations to which the chimpanzees continually return. Chimpanzees also use stones and other objects as projectiles with intent to do harm (Goodall 1986).

Note that the form of imitation reported here for chimpanzees is a long and laborious process compared to the rapidity with which humans can acquire novel sequences. As long as the sequences are not too complex, their very structure can serve for humans as the basis for immediate imitation or for the immediate construction of an appropriate response, as well as contributing to the longer-term enrichment of experience. Of course (as our Santa Fe dance example shows), as sequences get longer, or the components become less familiar, more and more practice is required to fully comprehend or imitate the behavior.

Figure 10.6 focused on the generation and observation of a single hand action. We will need to extend this to handle the imitation of compound sequences in a way that meets criteria abstracted from the dance class example. Arbib (1981) showed how to describe perceptual structures and distributed motor control in terms of functional units called schemas that may be combined to form new schemas as coordinated control programs linking simpler (perceptual and motor) schemas. Jeannerod and colleagues (1995) provide a recent application of schema theory to the study of neural mechanisms of grasping. This raises points to be explicitly addressed in detailed modeling (not provided in this chapter; see Bischoff-Grethe and Arbib 2001, for a nonadaptive model of nonmirror aspects of this).

We hypothesize that the plan of an action (whether observed or "intended") is encoded in the brain. We have to be a little subtle here. In some cases, a whole set of actions is overlearned and encoded in stable neural connectivity. In other cases, the whole set of actions is planned in advance based on knowledge of the current situation. In yet other cases, dynamic planning is involved, with the plan being updated and extended as new observations become available. Consider, for example, how one's plan for driving to work may be modified both trivially—changing lanes to avoid slower cars, stopping for pedestrians—and drastically—as when changing traffic conditions force one to take a detour. We earlier spoke of generalizing a sequence to an automaton with a set X of inputs, a set Y of outputs, and a set Q of states, augmented by a state-transition function $\delta\colon Q \times X \to Q$, and an output function $\beta\colon Q \to Y$. This formalism is broad enough to encompass the above range from overlearned to dynamic plans, but it is still an open question as to how best to distribute the encoding of the various components of the automaton between stable synapses, rapidly changing synapses, and neural firing patterns.

In general, this "automaton" will be event driven, rather than operating on a fixed clock—different subbehaviors take different lengths of time, and may be terminated either because of an external stimulus, or by some internal encoding of completion. Neural activity may then encode the current state q as well as priming the code for $\delta(q, x)$ for a small set of "expected" events x. When one of these, say x_1 occurs, the brain then brings $\delta(q, x_1)$ above threshold —thus releasing output $\beta[\delta(q, x_1)]$, which will be emitted for as long as the neural code for $\delta(q, x_1)$ is sufficiently active—and inhibits q and the other primed states, while priming a small set of candidate successor states. However, if the actual input when in state q is unexpected, say x_2, then $\delta(q, x_2)$ will be unprimed and thus the transition to the new state, and thus new output, will be delayed.

At a basic level, then, we might characterize imitation in terms of ability to "infer automata," recognizing the set of relevant outputs Y (the task of the mirror system) and overt transition signals X, and "inferring" a set of states Q and a set of "covert inputs" X' that allow one to mimic the observed behavior. However, a crucial observation of Arbib (1981) is that complex behaviors may be expressed as coordinated control programs, which are built up from assemblages of simpler schemas. In the corresponding formalism, we thus replace simple automaton inference by concurrent computation in a schema assemblage modeled as a network of port automata (Arbib 1990; Steenstrup, Arbib, and Manes 1983). The task then becomes to recognize that portions of a novel behavior can be assimilated to existing schemas. Imitation involves, then, the ability to decompose behaviors into constituent schemas and then rapidly encode an assemblage of schemas that yields an approximation of the overall behavior. Further learning can then act both at the level of "assemblage code" (see Arbib 1990), and at the level of parametric tuning of both the constituent schemas and of the linkages between them. For example, as noted earlier, if one is acquiring a tennis stroke and a badminton stroke through imitation, the initial coordinated control program may be identical, yet in the end the very different dynamics of the tennis ball and shuttlecock lead to divergent schemas.

Stage 5: A Manual-Based Communication System

We have now got to the stage in evolution in which a creature (the postulated common ancestor of human and chimpanzee) had the ability to imitate simple manual performances, and we have suggested that the early stages of hominid evolution yielded the perceptual and motor ability to imitate performances of increasing complexity. I now want to discuss how further hominid evolution might have yielded a manual-based communication system (stage 5). I will suggest below how this might have led to the further evolution of brain and body mechanisms supporting speech and then will return to the idea that this evolutionary process did not yield, in the first *Homo sapiens*, creatures that already had language in the sense shared by modern human languages. Rather, I shall argue that early *Homo sapiens* was "language ready," and suggest the sort of cultural evolution that might have then led to the diversity of modern languages.

The story of hominid evolution is briefly summarized in figure 10.8. Imprints in the cranial cavity of endocasts indicate that "speech areas" were already present in early hominids such as *Homo habilis* long before the larynx reached the modern "speech-optimal" configuration, but there is a debate over whether such areas were already present in australopithecines. This leads us to a related hypothesis: The transition from australopithecines to early *Homo* coincided with the transition from a mirror system used only for action recognition and imitation to a humanlike mirror system used for intentional communication.

The function of mirror neurons has been advanced to be that their firing "represents" an action internally (Rizzolatti et al. 1996a; Gallese et al. 1996; Jeannerod 1994) as a basis for understanding actions. Here, understanding means the capacity that individuals have to recognize that another individual is performing an action, to differentiate the observed action from other actions, and to use this information in order to act appropriately. According to this view, mirror neurons represent the link between

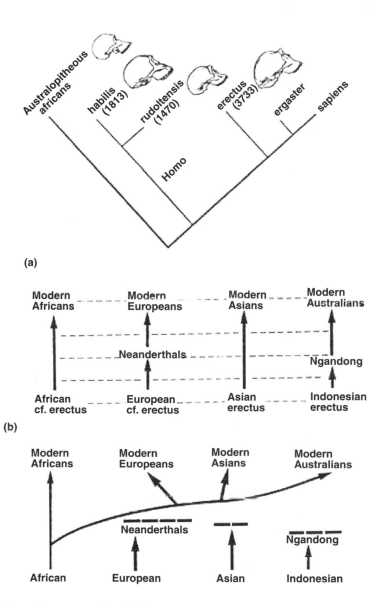

Figure 10.8   Five million years of hominid evolution. (Adapted from Gamble 1994) (*a*) A family tree for hominids, with the common ancestor of humans, *Homo sapiens*, and australopithecines preceding that for *Homo sapiens* and *Homo habilis* which in turn precedes the common ancestor of *Homo sapiens* and *Homo erectus*. (*b*) It is widely agreed that *Homo erectus* evolved in Africa, and expanded from there to Europe and Asia. We reject the view (top panel) that erectus evolved independently into *Homo sapiens* in Africa, Europe and Asia, and instead adopt the view (bottom panel) that *Homo sapiens* evolved in Africa, and formed a second expansion out of Africa.

sender and receiver that Liberman (1993; Liberman and Mattingly 1985, 1989) postulated as the necessary prerequisite for any type of communication.

We agree, then, with Liberman's "motor theory of perception"— that the basic mechanism appears to be that of matching the neural activity resulting from observation of a gesture with that underlying its execution. However, there are cases of children learning to recognize spoken language without being able to produce it (Giuseppe Cossu, personal communication). In terms of figure 10.6, we explain this by noting that the Expectation Neural Network (ENN) is tuned by corollary discharge from F5, and that this may still be available when F5 cannot control appropriate motor pattern generators. Nonetheless, the system can be tuned—for a child motivated enough to pay attention—by matching expectation of what will be said to what actually is said in an overheard conversation or in a classroom setting.

Our hypothetical sequence leading to manual gesture and beyond is then:

1. Pragmatic action directed toward a goal object.
2. Imitation of such actions.
3. Pantomime in which similar actions are produced in the absence of any goal object. In terms of observable behavior, imitation of an action and pantomime of an action may appear the same. However, imitation is the generic attempt to reproduce movements performed by another, whether to master a skill or simply as part of a social interaction. By contrast, pantomime is performed with the intention of getting the observer to think of a specific action or event. It is essentially communicative in its nature. The imitator observes; the panto-mimic intends to be the observed.
4. Abstract gestures divorced from their pragmatic origins (if such existed): in pantomime it might be hard to distinguish a grasping movement signifying "grasping" from one meaning "a [graspable] raisin," thus providing an "incentive" for coming up with an arbitrary gesture to distinguish the two meanings. This suggests that the emergence of symbols occured when the communicative capacities of pantomiming were exhausted.
5. The use of such abstract gestures for the formation of compounds that can be paired with meanings in more or less arbitrary fashion.

My current hypothesis is that stages (3) and (4) and a rudimentary (presyntactic) form of (5) were present in prehuman hominids, but that the "explosive" development of (5), which we know as language, depended on "cultural evolution" well after biological evolution had formed modern *Homo sapiens*. This remains speculative, and one should note that biological evolution may have continued to reshape the human genome for the brain even after the skeletal form of *Homo sapiens* was essentially stabilized, as it certainly has done for skin pigmentation and other physical characteristics. However, the fact that people can master any language equally well, irrespective of their genetic community, shows that these changes are not causal with respect to the structure of language.

Stage 6: Speech

We earlier noted that the neural substrate for primate calls is in a region of cingulate cortex distinct from F5, which latter is the monkey homologue of human Broca's area. We thus need to explain why F5, rather than the a priori more likely "primate call area," provided the evolutionary substrate for speech and language. Rizzolatti and Arbib (1998) answer this by suggesting three evolutionary stages going beyond the capacities of figure 10.5:

1. A *distinct* manuobrachial (hand-arm) communication system evolved to complement the primate calls/orofacial communication system.
2. The "speech" area of early hominids (i.e., the area presumably homologous to monkey F5 and human Broca's area) mediated orofacial and manuobrachial communication but not speech.
3. The manual-orofacial symbolic system then "recruited" vocalization. Association of vocalization with manual gestures allowed them to assume a more open referential character, and exploit the capacity for imitation of the underlying brachiomanual system.

Thus, we answer the question "Why did F5, rather than the primate call area provide the evolutionary substrate for speech?" by saying that the primate call area could not of itself access the combinatorial properties inherent in the manuo-brachial system.

The claim, then, is that the biological evolution of hominids yielded a mirror system embedded in a far larger system for execution, observation, and imitation of compound behaviors composed from orofacial, manual, and vocal gestures. I also accept that this system supported communication in *Homo erectus*—since otherwise it is hard to see what selective pressure could have brought about the lowering of the larynx, which, as Lieberman (1991) observes, makes humans able to articulate more precisely than other primates, but with an increased likelihood of choking.[9] Clearly, some level of language readiness and vocal communication preceded this—a core of protospeech was needed to provide pressures for larynx evolution. However, I do not accept that this means that the earliest *H. sapiens* was endowed with language in anything like its modern human richness. Rather, biological evolution equipped early humans with "language-ready brains" that proved rich enough to support the cultural evolution of human languages in all their commonalities and diversities.[10]

I have schematized the result of the above three evolutionary stages in figure 10.9. A key question for later analysis is whether we should consider the manual gesture system as a primitive system atop which evolved the "advanced" speech system, or whether we should view these two as actually different aspects of one multimodal controller, depending upon which efferent system we focus. (Note that we are here talking of speech as being the open-ended production and perception of sequences of vocal gestures, without implying that these sequences constitute a language.)

Perception systems are not shown in the figure. The mirror system is thus implicit. Extending the Mirror System Hypothesis, we

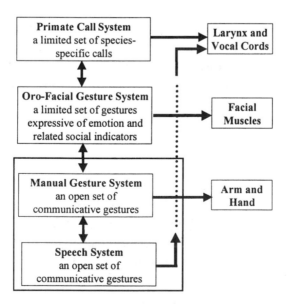

Figure 10.9 A production view of the evolved speech system of early humans. (Perception systems are not shown.)

must show how the ability to comprehend and create utterances via their underlying syntactico-semantic hierarchical structure can build upon the observation/execution of single actions. Here I stress, as Rizzolatti and Arbib did not, that the transition to language readiness, with the necessary openness to the creation of compound expressions, required imitation in the sense defined earlier: not just simply observing someone else's movement and responding with a movement that in its entirety is already in one's own repertoire, but rather "parsing" a complex movement into more or less familiar pieces, and then performing the corresponding composite of (variations on) familiar actions.

Having shown why speech did not evolve "simply" by extending the classic primate vocalization system, we must note that the language and vocalization systems are nonetheless linked. Lesions centered in the anterior cingulate cortex and supplementary motor areas of the brain can also cause mutism in humans, similar to the effects produced in muting monkey vocalizations. Conversely, a patient with a Broca's area lesion may nonetheless swear when provoked. But note that "emitting an imprecation" is more like a monkey vocalization than like the syntactically structured use of language. Lieberman (1991) suggests that the primate call made by an infant separated from its mother not only survives in the human infant, but, in humans, develops into the breath group—that is, the pattern of breathing in and breathing out that is shaped to provide the contour for each continuous sequence of an utterance. I thus hypothesize that the evolution of speech yielded the pathways for cooperative computation between cingulate cortex and Broca's area, with cingulate cortex involved in breath groups and emotional shading, and Broca's area providing the motor control for rapid production and interweaving of elements of an utterance.

Rizzolatti and Arbib (1998) state that "This new use of vocalization necessitated its skillful control, a requirement that could not be fulfilled by the ancient emotional vocalization centers. This new situation was most likely the 'cause' of the emergence of human Broca's area." I would now rather say that *Homo habilis* and even more so *Homo erectus* had a "proto-Broca's area" based on an F5-like precursor mediating communication by manual and oro-facial gesture. This made possible a process of collateralization whereby this "proto" Broca's area gained primitive control of the vocal machinery, thus yielding increased skill and openness in vocalization, moving from the fixed repertoire of primate vocalizations to the unlimited (open) range of vocalizations exploited in speech. Larynx and brain regions could then coevolve to yield the configuration seen in modern *Homo sapiens*.

Noting that the specific communication system based on primate calling was not the precursor of language, some people (e.g., Bickerton 1995) have claimed that communication could not have been a causal factor in the evolution of language readiness. They then argue that it was the advantage of being able to represent a complex world that favored language evolution. However, we should not be constrained by such either/or thinking. Rather, the coevolution of communication and representation was essential for the emergence of human language. Both representation within the individual and communication between individuals could provide selection pressures for the biological evolution of language readiness and the further cultural evolution of language, with advances in the one triggering advances in the other.

The Transition to *Homo sapiens*

If we look at figure 10.1, we can see that the cerebral cortex of the monkey can be divided into many different regions. Moreover, the extent of these regions can vary drastically in different primate species. Different species may not only have nuclei (groups of neurons) and cortical regions of different sizes, but may actually have nuclei lacking in other species, or may have nuclei present in other species specialized for quite different functions. How can this be? Butler and Hodos (1996) show that the course of brain evolution among vertebrates has been determined by:

1. Formation of multiple new nuclei through elaboration or duplication of nuclei present in the ancestral species.
2. Regionally specific increases in cell proliferation in different parts of the brain can vary the relative size of a given region across species.
3. Gain of some new connections and loss of some established connections may change the inputs and outputs of a region, thus changing its computations and their impact on brain and behavior.

These phenomena (and others described by Butler and Hodos 1996) can be influenced by relatively simple mutational events that can thus become established in a population as the result of random variation. Selective pressures determine whether the behavioral phenotypic expressions of central nervous system organization produced by these random mutations increase their proportional representation within the population and eventually become established as the normal condition.

Let me list here a few contrasts between monkey and human brains. There is no space here to go into details; rather, I want to offer a corrective to any false impression I might have created that "turning F5 into Broca's area" is the one key neural correlate of human evolution. The differences between monkey and human not only include many bodily changes (including upright gait, a lowered larynx, and increased manual dexterity) but also changes in many neural systems related to new motor and cognitive abilities as well as dramatic extensions of "cognitive reach." Among the changes to be noted are:

1. Enlargement of the prefrontal lobe (which uses motivation to evaluate future courses of action) to provide sophisticated memory structures (coupled, e.g., to hippocampus with its key role in episodic memory) to extend "cognitive comprehension" in space and time
2. Extension of the number, sophistication, and coordination of parietal-frontal perceptuo-motor systems
3. Enlargement of the POT (parieto-occipito-temporal cortex) as a semantic storehouse
4. Adding prefrontal circuitry with refinements of the basal ganglia and cerebellum keeping pace
5. An increased ratio of premotor cortex to motor cortex

How did evolution couple the separate parietal ↔ frontal subsystems into an "integrated state of knowledge?" Fuster (1995) sees prefrontal cortex as evolving to increase working memory capacity. Petrides (1985) argues that we need prefrontal cortex to go beyond single items to keeping multiple objects or events in order. We note again the challenge of embedding the mirror system in a system for handling sequential structure, and hierarchical structure more generally. The detailed consideration of these brain regions and the attendant claims is beyond the scope of this article. Here we note that, irrespective of whether or not they possessed language, all primates possess the ability for visual (and multimodal) scene perception—perceiving the changing spatial relationships between a number of objects and organisms in the environment, and attending to the key events relevant for ongoing behavior. Events—not objects—are primary in our story, keeping action at the center.

A Multimodal System

Our use of writing as a record of spoken language has long since created the mistaken impression that language is a speech-based system. However, McNeill (1992) has used videotape analysis to show the crucial use that people make of gestures synchronized with speech. Even blind people use manual gestures when speaking. As deaf people have always known, but linguists only much later discovered (Klima and Bellugi 1979), sign languages are full human languages, rich in lexicon, syntax, and semantics. Moreover, not only deaf people use sign language. So do some aboriginal Australian tribes, and some native populations in North America. Thus, language is more than "that part of speech that can be captured in writing."

Thus, where Rizzolatti and Arbib (1998) state that "Manual gestures progressively lost their dominance, while in contrast, vocalization acquired autonomy, until the relation between gestural and vocal communication inverted and speech took off," I would now downplay the autonomy: the above considerations suggest that we locate language in a speech-manual-orofacial gesture complex and that during language acquisition, a normal person shifts the major information load of language—but by no means all of it—into the speech domain, whereas for a deaf person the major information load is removed from speech and taken over by hand and orofacial gestures. On this basis, I answer the question following figure 10.9 by saying that "the vote is in: one box replaces three," as shown in figure 10.10. A warning: although we claim that there is but one communication system we stress that it involves many brain regions, each with its own evolutionary story. Neither figure 10.9 nor figure 10.10 shows the neuroanatomy of these mechanisms.

Language Evolving from Action-Object Frame to Verb-Argument Structure to Syntax and Semantics

The divergence of the Romance languages took about 1,000 years. The divergence of the Indo-European languages to form the immense diversity of Hindi, German, Italian, English, and so on, took about 6,000 years. How can we imagine what has changed since the emergence of *Homo sapiens* some 200,000 years ago? Or in 5,000,000 years of prior hominid evolution?

I claim that the first humans were language ready but did not have language in the modern sense. We have already seen that

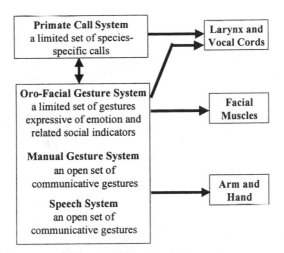

Figure 10.10 The fruit of evolution: Not three separate communication systems, but a single system operating in at least three motor modalities and at least two sensory modalities.

some form of communication, first manual then an integration of oral, manual, and facial communication, must have arisen in hominid evolution. What, then, might be the nature of such communication if it does not yet constitute the use of language as humans know it today? A basic component of modern human languages is the verb-argument structure, expressing an "action-object frame" like look(Mary, John) with a sentence such as "Mary looks at John," with "look" the verb, and "Mary" and "John" the arguments. My suggestion is that the first *Homo sapiens* would have been able to perceive that one individual was looking at another, and might even have had the ability to form a distinctive vocalization to draw this event to the attention of another tribe member, but that the vocalization used would be arbitrary, rather than being decomposable into something that would be understood as part of a general class of "something like verbs" and two somethings that would be understood as part of a general class of "something like nouns." In other words, I hypothesize that (1) the ability for visual scene perception that must underlie the present human ability to employ verb-argument structures—the perception of action-object frames in which an actor, an action, and related role players can be perceived in relationship—was well established in the primate line; (2) the ability to communicate a fair number of such frames was established in the hominid line prior to the emergence of *Homo sapiens*; but that (3) these "communicative signals" lacked (almost all) syntactic structure and the extraction of semantic structure therefrom.

Our starting point for the biological basis of language readiness is then that "it is innate to know there are things and events." Again, we recognize an evolutionary progression:

1. Acting on objects.

2. Recognizing acting on objects: an "action-object frame." Here we extend the mirror system concept to include recognition not only of the action (mediated by F5) but also of the object (mediated by IT [inferotemporal cortex]; see figure 10.3). This reflects a crucial understanding gained from figure 10.3 that is often missing in the study of the mirror system: the canonical activity of F5 already exhibits a congruence between the affordances of an object (mediated by the dorsal stream) and the nature of the object (as recognized by IT and elaborated upon [in a process of "action-oriented perception"] in prefrontal cortex, PFC). In the same way, the activity of mirror neurons does not rest solely upon the parietal recognition (in an area called PF not shown in figure 10.3) of the hand motion and the object's affordances (AIP) but also (I here postulate) on the "semantics" of the object as extracted by IT and relayed to F5 via PFC.[11] It is this matching of actions with "object semantics" and "goals," rather than just with affordances, that makes possible the transition to:

3. Creating symbols linked to specific action-object frames. Here I must reiterate the subtle point that the original communicative signal for an action-object frame need not have involved separate lexical entries for the action or the objects. Thus, *griffle* might mean "grasp a peanut with a precision pinch," while *tromfok* means "grasp a daisy stem with a precision pinch." Nothing said so far demands a lexical decomposition of these structures. However, the ability to symbolize more and more situations required the creation of a "symbol toolkit" of meaningless elements from which an open-ended class of symbols could be generated. The distinction I have in mind here relates to the earlier point that in pantomime, it might be hard to distinguish a grasping movement signifying "grasping" from one meaning "a [graspable] raisin," thus providing an "incentive" for coming up with an arbitrary gesture to distinguish the two meanings. However, it can also be argued that the passage from pantomime did not occur originally in the brachio-manual system, but occurred as speech evolved

"atop" manual gesture with the two systems evolving into one integrated system for communication: in this scenario, the ability to create novel sounds to imitate manual gestures in the vocal domain (for example, rising pitch might represent an upward movement of the hand), coupled with a coevolved ability to imitate novel sound patterns yielding vocal gestures through onomatopoeia that were not linked to manual gestures, created the divorce of gesture from meaning required to create an open-ended vocabulary.

In any case, it is a distinct step in language evolution to proceed from stage 3 to the ability, for example, to invoke the same word(s) for "grasp with a precision pinch" irrespective of the specific type of object that is grasped:

4. Naming objects and actions. This involves the creation of symbols (whether vocal or manual) that allow the communicative signal for an action-object frame to become an explicit compound, a verb-argument structure in which a specific action can be denoted by (some variant of) a specific verb no matter what the context, and specific arguments are represented by specific nouns. (Of course, the nouns may themselves be single lexical items, or themselves phrases, but this takes us beyond the present basic evolutionary scenario.)

Stage 4 is then the crucial step in the transition from communication in general to human language as we know it: abstract symbols are grounded (but more and more indirectly) in action-oriented perception; members of a community may acquire the use of these new symbols (the crucial distinction here is with the fixed repertoire of primate calls) by imitating their use by others; and, crucially, these symbols can be compounded in novel combinations to communicate about novel situations for which no agreed-upon unitary communicative symbol exists.

In our example, the ability to differentially signal "grasping" from "a [graspable] raisin" could then have laid the basis for replacing a "unitary symbol" for a verb-argument structure into a compound of two components of what we would now recognize as precursors of a verb and a noun. This could have, in turn, formed the basis for the abstraction and compounding of more generic verb-argument structures. Again, much of this would at first have been based on a limited yet useful set of templates, variations on a few basic themes. It might have taken many, many millennia for people to discover syntax and semantics in the sense of gaining immense expressive power by "going recursive" with a relatively limited set of strategies for compounding and marking utterances, based on a vocabulary that expanded with the kinship structures and technologies of the different tribes, these cultural products themselves enhanced by the increased effectiveness of transmission from generation to generation that the growing power of language made possible. Consistent with the earlier distinction between "language readiness" and "having language," we need more research to determine what it is about a brain that makes it possible to "go recursive." The hypothesis is that whatever is involved is completely distinct from the encoding of specific recursive rules of syntax within a Universal Grammar.

The cultural evolution of *Homo sapiens* may then have involved an increased ability to name actions and objects to create a rapidly growing set of verb-argument structures, and the ability to compound those structures in diverse ways. I would suggest that many ways of expressing these relationships were the discovery of *Homo sapiens*. That is, many grammatical structures like adjectives, conjunctions such as *but*, *and*, *or* and *that*, *unless*, *because* might well have been "postbiological" in their origin. The spread of these innovations rested on the ability of other humans not only to imitate the new actions and compounds of actions demonstrated by the innovators, but also to do so in a way that related increasingly general classes of symbolic behavior to the classes, events, behaviors, and relationships that they were to represent. Indeed, consideration of the spatial basis for "prepositions" may help show how visuomotor coordination underlies some aspects of language, while the immense variation in the use of corresponding prepositions even in closely related languages like English and Spanish shows how the basic functionally grounded semantic-syntactic correspondences have been overlaid by a multitude of later innovations and borrowings. We still have much work to do to understand how the needs of human biology and the constraints of the human brain shaped these basic discoveries, their dissemination, and their stabilization.

10.4 Conclusion

With this, I conclude my argument that the ability to imitate is a key innovation in the evolutionary path leading to language in the human. However, much has to be done to complete the linkage of this hypothesis to specific data on brain mechanisms. We have taken this argument through seven hypothesized stages of evolution:

1. grasping
2. a mirror system for grasping (i.e., a system that matches observation and execution)
3. a simple imitation system for grasping
4. a complex imitation system for grasping
5. a manual-based communication system
6. speech
7. language

Certainly, stages 1 and 2 are firmly grounded in neurophysiological data for the monkey, these data have been modeled in detail for stage 1 and are now being analyzed by careful modeling of stage 2. At the other end, stage 7, we have neurological data on localization of mechanisms related to both spoken and sign language in the human brain. The data on the intermediate stages are still limited. Neurophysiology of the chimpanzee is no longer permitted, but we can hope that advances in the refinement of techniques for noninvasive brain imaging, such as the PET and fMRI studies of humans conducted at present, will help us fill the gap as we seek to link comparative brain imaging studies of a variety of primates with detailed neurophysiological and neuroanatomical studies where available. Computational models of the biological circuitry underlying both simple and complex imitation will play a crucial role, as will the use of mathematical techniques (such as the Synthetic PET technique of Arbib et al. 1994) that link models of circuitry to predictions of relative regional activation in brain imaging studies. However, there is a paucity of satisfactory neurolinguistic modeling that sheds light on the stage 6 imaging data by tracing the cooperative computation of these regions during language performance.

It is my hope that "Mirror Neurolinguistics" will build on the hypotheses presented above to respond to the challenge of constructing a computational neurolinguistics issued more than 20 years ago (Arbib and Caplan 1979). The rest of this section offers an early response to this challenge, but the reader will easily see how much more needs to be done. Our evolutionary theory suggests a progression from action to pantomime to (proto)language:

1. object $\rightarrow$ AIP $\rightarrow$ F5$_{\text{canonical}}$: pragmatics
2. action $\rightarrow$ PF $\rightarrow$ F5$_{\text{mirror}}$: action understanding
3. scene $\rightarrow$ Wernicke's $\rightarrow$ Broca's: utterance

Goodale, Milner, Jakobson, and Carey (1991) studied a patient (DF) who developed a profound visual form of agnosia following carbon monoxide poisoning in which most of the damage to cortical visual areas was apparent in areas 18 and 19, but not area 17 (V1)—still allowing signals to flow from V1 toward PP but not from V1 to IT. When asked to indicate the width of a single block by means of her index finger and thumb, her finger separation bore no relationship to the dimensions of the object and showed considerable trial-to-trial variability. Yet when she was asked simply to reach out and pick up the block, the peak aperture (well before contact with the object) between her index finger and thumb changed systematically with the width of the object, as in normal controls. A similar dissociation was seen in her responses to the orientation of stimuli. In other words, DF could preshape accurately, even though she appeared to have no conscious appreciation (expressible either verbally or in pantomime) of the visual parameters that guided the preshape.

Castiello, Paulignan, and Jeannerod (1991) report a study of impairment of grasping in a patient (AT) with a lesion of the visual pathway that left PP, IT, and the pathway V $\rightarrow$ IT relatively intact, but grossly impaired the pathway V $\rightarrow$ PP. This patient is the "opposite" of DF—she can use her hand to pantomime the size of a cylinder, but cannot preshape appropriately when asked to grasp it. Instead of an adaptive preshape, she will open her hand to its fullest, and only begin to close her hand when the cylinder hits the "web" between index finger and thumb. But there was a surprise! When the stimulus used for the grasp was not a cylinder (for which the "semantics" contains no information about expected size), but rather a familiar object—such as a reel of thread, or a lipstick—for which the "usual" size is part of the subject's knowledge, AT showed a relatively adaptive preshape.

The "zero order" model of AT and DF data is:

4. Parietal "affordances" $\rightarrow$ preshape
5. IT "perception of object" $\rightarrow$ pantomime or verbally describe size

which leads to the inference that one cannot pantomime or verbalize an affordance; but rather one needs a "unified view of the

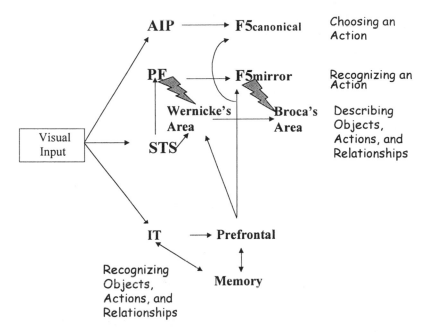

Figure 10.11 Extending the FARS model to include the mirror system for grasping and the language system evolved "atop" this. Note that this simple figure neither asserts nor denies that the extended mirror system for grasping and the language-supporting system are anatomically separable, nor does it address issues of lateralization.

object" (IT) to which attributes can be attributed before one can express them. The problem with this is that the "language" path as shown in (5) is completely independent of the parietal → F5 system, and so the data seem to contradict our view in (3).

To resolve this apparent paradox, we must return to the view of the FARS model given in figure 10.2, and stress the crucial role of IT and PFC in modulating F5's selection of an affordance, leading us to include paths from prefrontal cortex to F5 (canonical and mirror) and Broca's area in figure 10.11. This figure provides a first speculative attempt to extend the FARS model conceptually to include not only the mirror system for grasping but also the language system evolved "atop" this. The crucial point is that all three paths defined above:

1. object → AIP → $F5_{canonical}$: pragmatics
2. action → PF → $F5_{mirror}$: action understanding
3. scene → Wernicke's → Broca's: utterance

are now enriched by the prefrontal system for "scene perception," which combines current IT-input with memory structures combining objects, actions, and relationships. The "lightning bolts" link "grasp boxes" to "language boxes" and are completely speculative.

Much more must be done to take us up the hierarchy from elementary actions to the recognition and generation of novel compounds of such actions. Nonetheless, the above preliminary account strengthens the case that no Universal Grammar need have been encoded in the brain of the first *Homo sapiens*. Rather, it was the imitation-enriched mirror system that enabled human societies, across many millennia of invention and cultural evolution, to achieve human languages in the modern sense.

Acknowledgments

I recall with pleasure my sabbatical visit to the University of Western Australia in February, March, and April of 1999 and the conversations with Robyn Owens and other colleagues there which laid the basis for the present article, as well as the many discussions with Giacomo Rizzolatti and Giuseppe Cossu, which helped shape the article's further development while I continued my sabbatical in Rizzolatti's Institute in Parma, Italy, in May, June, and July of 1999. I thank Aude Billard and the editors for their constructive comments on recent drafts.

Notes

1. Since we will be concerned in what follows with sign language as well as spoken language, I ask the reader to understand that "speaker" and "hearer" may actually entail using hand gestures rather than vocal gestures for communication. The claim will be that communication using hand gestures provided the scaffolding for converting a vocal repertoire comprising a limited set of species-specific calls into the open-ended production and perception of sequences of vocal gestures necessary for speech. In other words, speech did not evolve directly within the vocal-auditory domain, but rather was supported by the evolution of a system of manual gestures for communication.

2. Here a caveat is in order. Analysis in neuroscience often goes to the extreme of focusing on one circuit or brain region and trumpeting it as "the" circuit implementing some specific function X, just as if we were to claim that Broca's area is "the" region for language. The other extreme is "holism," stressing that X may involve dynamic activity integrating all areas of the brain. Holism may be correct, but seems to me useless as a guide to understanding. My preferred approach is a compromise. I stress that any "schema" or function X involves the cooperative computation of many neural circuits (see chapter 3 of Arbib, Érdi, and Szentágothai 1998), but then proceed by using a survey of the literature to single out a few regions for which good data are available correlating neural activity with the performance of function X. I then seek the best model available (from the literature, by research in my own group, or by a combination of both) that can yield a causally complete neural model that approximates both the patterns of behavior seen in

animals performing X and the neural activity observed during these performances. As time goes by, the model may yield more and more insight into the data on X (some of which may be new data whose collection was prompted by the modeling), whether by conducting new analyses of the model, increasing the granularity of description of certain brain regions, or in extending the model to include representations of more brain regions. Other challenges come from integrating separate models developed to explain distinct functions X, Y, and Z and integrating them to derive a single model of interacting brain regions able to serve all these functions. Thus, the above paragraph should not be interpreted as saying "the only parts of the brain relevant to modeling sequential behavior are pre-SMA and the related portions of basal ganglia," but rather that as we extend our F5-based model of sequences of hand movements, our current targets for detailed modeling are pre-SMA and basal ganglia (Bischoff-Grethe and Arbib 2001). As we come to understand more fully the roles of these brain regions, we can then turn to more extensive models. However, I fear that if we try to model "everything all at once" we will understand nothing, since the map would then be coextensive with the whole territory (Borges 1975).

3. PET (positron emission tomography) and fMRI (functional magnetic resonance imaging) are two methods that allow one to measure regional cerebral blood flow (rCBF) in the brain. Since rCBF is correlated with some aspects of neural activity, both methods can be used as the basis of statistical procedures that generate maps showing which brain regions are significantly more active when a human is performing task A rather than task B.

4. Although each human language is open as to, for example, nouns and verbs, it is (almost) closed with respect to the stock of prepositions and grammatical markers.

5. The present discussion is preliminary. A full discussion of imitation involves the recognition that a novel action can be approximated by a composite of variations of familiar actions, and with the improvement of that approximation through practice (recall the Santa Fe dance example). I ask the reader to recognize here that much more work needs to be done to tease apart the neural mechanisms serving for recognition in this extended sense.

6. The orofacial mirror neurons seem to be irrelevant here because our argument is that it is the manual system that provides the combinatorial richness (consider the endless possibilities of grooming, feeding, and other forms of manipulation) that leads us toward language in a way in which isolated orofacial gestures and primate vocal calls do not.

7. However, it is only in the case of written language that the boundaries that separate one "word" from another are clearly represented. Even here, the division is somewhat arbitrary, for example, "can not" versus "cannot" versus "can't."

8. "Parsing" is the problem of inferring from a linear string of words the hierarchical structure it represents—e.g., determining which words go together to form the subject of the sentence. Ambiguity arises when parsing does not yield a unique structure, as well as when constituent words have multiple meanings. Ambiguity is the enemy of parity. I believe that the structure of each language reflects, among many other things, the results of an attempt to balance efficiency (getting a message across in as few words as possible) with avoidance of ambiguity *within the context of the current communication*.

9. The Perth psychologist Colin McLeod (personal communication) quips that "The human vocal tract evolved so that we could cry out 'Help, I'm choking!'"

10. The reader should be warned of the dangerous methodology that I employ here. My work is anchored in a rigorous knowledge of modern neuroscience, including detailed modeling of many neural systems, and informed by a reasonable knowledge of psychology, linguistics, and evolutionary theory. On the other hand, my knowledge of anthropology and human evolution is limited, compounding the severe limitations on the database on the evolution of language—after all, we have no record of writing that is more than 6,000 years old. Thus, when I assert that *H. sapiens* was not originally endowed with language in anything like its modern human richness, I am not appealing to hard data, but rather forwarding a hypothesis based on, but in no sense implied by, a variety of evidence. However, I do not (nor should the reader) accept my hypotheses uncritically. Rather,

each new hypothesis is confronted with new data and competing hypotheses as my reading progresses. The hypotheses presented in this article have thus survived a great deal of "cross-examination," and have been refined in the process. For example, although my reading of historical linguistics impressed me with the rapidity with which languages change (and I view human language as the sum of human languages, not as some abstract entity above and beyond these biocultural products) and thus led me to distinguish the notion of a "language-ready" brain from a "language-equipped" brain, further reading and reflection leads me to accept that the dichotomy here is not as sharp as I may have believed earlier.

11. This suggests the hypothesis that inactivation of IT that does not disturb AIP will disrupt mirror activity in F5, but not canonical activity in F5.

References

Arbib, M. A. Memory limitations of stimulus-response models. *Psychological Review* 76: 507–510, 1969.

Arbib, M. A. Perceptual structures and distributed motor control. In V. B. Brooks, ed., *Handbook of Physiology*, section 2: The nervous system, vol. II, Motor control, part 1, pp. 1449–1480. American Physiological Society, 1981.

Arbib, M. A. Programs, schemas, and neural networks for control of hand movements: Beyond the RS framework. In M. Jeannerod, ed., *Attention and Performance XIII. Motor Representation and Control*, pp. 111–138. Hillsdale, N.J.: Erlbaum, 1990.

Arbib, M. A. Co-evolution of human consciousness and language. In P. C. Maijuan (ed.), *Cajal and Consciousness: Scientific Approaches to Consciousness on the Centennial of Ramón y Cajal's Textura. Annals of the New York Academy of Sciences* 929: 195–220, 2001.

Arbib, M. A., and D. Caplan. Neurolinguistics must be computational. *Behavioral and Brain Sciences* 2: 449–483, 1979.

Arbib, M. A., A. Bischoff, A. H. Fagg, and S. T. Grafton. Synthetic PET: Analyzing large-scale properties of neural networks. *Human Brain Mapping* 2: 225–233, 1994.

Arbib, M. A., P. Érdi, and J. Szentágothai. *Neural Organization: Structure, Function, and Dynamics*. Cambridge, Mass.: MIT Press, 1998.

Arbib, M. A., and G. Rizzolatti. Neural expectations: A possible evolutionary path from manual skills to language. *Communication and Cognition* 29: 393–424, 1997.

Armstrong, D., W. Stokoe, and S. Wilcox. *Gesture and the Nature of Language*. Cambridge, UK: Cambridge University Press, 1995.

Bickerton, D. *Language and Human Behavior*. Seattle: University of Washington Press, 1995.

Bischoff-Grethe, A., and M. A. Arbib. *Sequential Movements: A Computational Model of the Roles of the Basal Ganglia and Supplementary Motor Area*. (to appear), 2001.

Boesch, C., and H. Boesch. Optimization of nut-cracking with natural hammers by wild chimpanzees. *Behavior* 83: 265–286, 1983.

Borges, J. L. Of exactitude in science. In *A Universal History of Infamy*, p. 131. New York: Penguin Books, 1975.

Butler, A. B., and W. Hodos. *Comparative Vertebrate Neuroanatomy: Evolution and Adaptation*. New York: Wiley, 1996.

Castiello, U., Y. Paulignan, and M. Jeannerod. Temporal dissociation of motor responses and subjective awareness: A study in normal subjects. *Brain* 114: 2639–2655, 1991.

Chomsky, N. *Reflections on Language*. New York: Pantheon, 1975.

Corballis, M. C. *The Lopsided Ape: Evolution of the Generative Mind*. New York: Oxford University Press, 1991.

Corballis, M. C. On the evolution of language and generativity. *Cognition* 44: 197–226, 1992.

Deacon, T. W. *The Symbolic Species: The Co-evolution of Language and the Brain*. New York: Norton, 1997.

di Pellegrino, G., L. Fadiga, L. Fogassi, V. Gallese, and G. Rizzolatti. Understanding motor events: A neurophysiological study. *Experimental Brain Research* 91: 176–180, 1992.

Dominey, P. F., M. A. Arbib, and J.-P. Joseph. A model of corticostriatal plasticity for learning associations and sequences, *Journal of Cognitive Neuroscience* 7: 311–336, 1995.

Fadiga, L., L. Fogassi, G. Pavesi, and G. Rizzolatti. Motor facilitation during action observation: A magnetic stimulation study. *Journal of Neurophysiology* 73: 2608–2611, 1995.

Fagg, A. H., and M. A. Arbib. Modeling parietal-premotor interactions in primate control of grasping. *Neural Networks* 11: 1277–1303, 1998.

Fuster, J. M. Memory in the cerebral cortex: An empirical approach to neural networks in the human and nonhuman primate. Cambridge, Mass.: MIT Press, 1995.

Gallese, V., L. Fadiga, L. Fogassi, and G. Rizzolatti. Action recognition in the premotor cortex. *Brain* 119: 593–609, 1996.

Gamble, C. *Timewalkers: The Prehistory of Global Colonization.* Cambridge, Mass.: Harvard University Press, 1994.

Gibson, J. J. *The Ecological Approach to Visual Perception.* Boston: Houghton Mifflin, 1979.

Goodale, M. A., A. D. Milner, L. S. Jakobson, and D. P. Carey. A neurological dissociation between perceiving objects and grasping them. *Nature* 349: 154–156, 1991.

Goodall, J. *The Chimpanzees of Gombe: Patterns of Behavior.* Cambridge, Mass.: Harvard University Press, 1986.

Grafton, S. T., M. A. Arbib, L. Fadiga, and G. Rizzolatti. Localization of grasp representations in humans by PET: 2. Observation compared with imagination. *Experimental Brain Research* 112: 103–111, 1996.

Hewes, G. Primate communication and the gestural origin of language. *Current Anthropology* 14: 5–24, 1973.

Jeannerod, M. The representing brain: Neural correlates of motor intention and imagery. *Behavioral and Brain Sciences* 17: 187–245, 1994.

Jeannerod, M., M. A. Arbib, G. Rizzolatti, and H. Sakata. Grasping objects: The cortical mechanisms of visuomotor transformation. *Trends in Neurosciences* 18: 314–320, 1995.

Kimura, D. *Neuromotor Mechanisms in Human Communication* (Oxford Psychology Series no. 20). Oxford University Press/Clarendon Press, Oxford, New York, 1993.

Klima, E. S., and U. Bellugi. *The Signs of Language,* Cambridge, Mass.: Harvard University Press, 1979.

Lashley, K. S. The problem of serial order in behavior. In L. A. Jeffress, ed., *Cerebral Mechanisms in Behavior: The Hixon Symposium.* New York: Wiley, 1951.

Liberman, A. M. *Haskins Laboratories Status Report on Speech Research.* 113: 1–32, 1993.

Liberman, A. M., and I. G. Mattingly. The motor theory of speech perception revised. *Cognition* 21: 1–36, 1985.

Liberman, A. M., and I. G. Mattingly. A Specialization for Speech Perception. *Science* 243: 489–494, 1989.

Lieberman, P. *Uniquely Human: The Evolution of Speech, Thought, and Selfless Behavior.* Cambridge, Mass.: Harvard University Press, 1991.

McNeill, D. *Hand and Mind: What Gestures Reveal about Thought.* Chicago: University of Chicago Press, 1992.

Oztop, E., and M. A. Arbib. Schema design and implementation of the grasp-related mirror neuron system. (to appear), 2001.

Petrides, M. Deficits in conditional associative-learning tasks after frontal and temporal lesions in man. *Neuropsychologia* 23: 601–614, 1985.

Rizzolatti, G., and M. A. Arbib. Language within our grasp. *Trends in Neurosciences* 21(5): 188–194, 1998.

Rizzolatti, G., R. Camarda, L. Fogassi, M. Gentilucci, G. Luppino, and M. Matelli. Functional organization of inferior area 6 in the macaque monkey. II. Area F5 and the control of distal movements. *Experimental Brain Research* 71: 491–507, 1988.

Rizzolatti, G., L. Fadiga, V. Gallese, and L. Fogassi. Premotor cortex and the recognition of motor actions. *Cognitive Brain Research* 3: 131–141, 1996a.

Rizzolatti, G., L. Fadiga, M. Matelli, V. Bettinardi, D. Perani, and F. Fazio. Localization of grasp representations in humans by positron emission tomography: 1. Observation versus execution. *Experimental Brain Research* 111: 246–252, 1996b.

Rizzolatti, G., G. Luppino, and M. Matelli. The organization of the cortical motor system: New concepts. *Electroencephalography and Clinical Neurophysiology* 106: 283–296, 1998.

Savage-Rumbaugh, S., S. G. Shanker, and T. T. Taylor. *Apes, Language, and the Human Mind.* New York: Oxford University Press, 1998.

Steenstrup, M., M. A. Arbib, and E. G. Manes. Port automata and the algebra of concurrent processes. *Journal of Computer and System Sciences* 27: 29–50, 1983.

Taira, M., S. Mine, A. P. Georgopoulos, A. Murata, and H. Sakata. Parietal cortex neurons of the monkey related to the visual guidance of hand movement. *Experimental Brain Research* 83: 29–36, 1990.

11 Imitation: A Means to Enhance Learning of a Synthetic Protolanguage in Autonomous Robots

Aude Billard

11.1 Introduction

This chapter addresses the role of imitation as a means to enhance the learning of communication skills in autonomous robots. A series of robotic experiments are presented in which autonomous mobile robots are taught a synthetic protolanguage. Learning of the language occurs through an imitative scenario where the robot replicates the teacher's movements. Imitation is used here as an implicit attentional mechanism that allows the robot imitator to share a similar set of proprio- and exteroceptions[1] with the teacher. The robot grounds its understanding of the teacher's "words," which describe the teacher's current observations, upon its own perceptions, which are similar to those of the teacher. Learning of the robot is based on a dynamical recurrent associative memory architecture (DRAMA).

Learning is unsupervised and results from the self-organization of the robot's connectionist architecture. Results show that the imitative behavior greatly improves the efficiency and speed of the learning. Moreover, without imitation, learning of symbolic expressions to describe the robot's proprioceptions was shown not to be possible.

These experiments illustrate the following proposal: *the sharing of a similar perceptual context between imitator and imitatee creates a meaningful social context onto which language—that is, the development of a common means of symbolic communication—can develop.* This work follows a nonnativist approach to language development (Garton 1992; Nadel et al. 1999; Trevarthen, Kokkinaki, and Famenghi 1999) that stresses the importance of social cues, such as coordinated behavior and imitation, as the precursor to language development in infants. Furthermore, these experiments show that association of arbitrary symbols to meaning is possible in embodied agents other than humans, and that it can be done by a simple, in comparison to that of animals, neural architecture. In particular, the results establish that the word-meaning association is strongly dependent on constraining the temporal uncertainty of the association. This is achieved by creating a spatio-temporal bonding between the teacher-learner agents through the imitative strategy.

11.2   Robotic Models of Imitation

Psychologists, ethologists, and roboticists find a common interest in the study of high-level social skills for robots, which can be used for gaining a better understanding of the mechanisms behind skills in animals (Brooks et al. 1998; Dautenhahn 1997; Matarić 1997a) or for improving the robot's performance in interaction with humans or robots (Dautenhahn 1995; Klingspor, Demiris, and Kaiser 1997; Kuniyoshi 1994; Matarić 1997b; Pfeifer 1998). Relevant to this chapter are studies that investigate the use of imitation[2] through human-robot or robot-robot interactions. While there is still some debate as to what observed behavior the term "imitation" refers to, there is also a need for clarification as to how many different cognitive processes studies on animal and human imitation refer to. The work of roboticists can shed light on the different cognitive processes by implementing separate models for each of them and commenting on the emergent behaviors each model leads to. From a programming point of view, the ability to imitate amounts to solving at least three problems: (1) how to get the agent to observe the example—that is, how to constrain the agent's attention to observing only the relevant stimuli (Scassellati 1999); (2) how to get the agent to reproduce the observed action pattern, which amounts to defining a mapping process from the agent's sensory stimuli (observation of the other actions) to the agent's actuators (Demiris 1999; Demiris and Matarić 1998; Nehaniv and Dautenhahn 1998; Nehaniv and Dautenhahn 1999); (3) what to learn from the reproduction/imitation process—for example, learning action-sequence patterns (Billard and Hayes 1999a; Hayes and Demiris 1994; Kuniyoshi 1995; Schaal 1997) or patterns of perception-action sequences (Billard 1999; Demiris and Hayes 1996; Dautenhahn 1995; Gaussier et al. 1998).

There is an intricate relationship between learning and imitating. One might better separate between them if one thinks separately of the three following concepts: the ability of imitating, that of learning to imitate, and that of learning by imitation (Hayes and Demiris 1994; Nehaniv and Dautenhahn 1999). Biologically inspired models of the ability to imitate have been developed

(Demiris and Hayes, chapter 13 of this volume; Kuniyoshi 1994) and applied to experiments in which the robot could mirror both head and arm movements of a human. Learning to imitate, for example, how to instantiate a sensory-motor mapping, was addressed to some extent by Demiris (1999) and Schaal (1999), who proposed algorithms for comparing and choosing among a set of predictors of visual patterns (recognition of visual primitives) that were already connected to motor patterns. The work presented in this chapter is concerned with learning by imitation. In particular, it addresses the role of imitation as a means to enhance the learning of communication skills in autonomous robots. Here, the ability of imitating is built-in.

Imitation as a Means to Direct Attention

Learning by imitation has been used in different experiments for teaching robots new motor skills (Billard and Hayes 1997; Dautenhahn 1995; Demiris and Hayes 1996; Gaussier et al. 1998; Cooke et al. 1997; Kuniyoshi and Inoue 1994; Schaal 1997). While the robot replicates the demonstrator's movements, it learns to adjust its own motor parameters and perceptuo-motor mapping to match as closely as possible the actions of the demonstrator. An important advantage (to roboticists) of such an approach is that it alleviates the programmer's tedious work of tuning the robot's motor control parameters.

A key idea underlying such work is that imitation can be an indirect and efficient means of directing the robot's actions. Having the robot replicate the demonstrator's actions leads the robot to make similar proprioception (of movements), which further enables the robot to learn new motor skills without explicit (symbolic or internally prespecified) teaching. I want to stress this point further: imitation allows the imitator and imitatee to share similar sets of both proprio- and exteroceptions. For example, in the following scenario with two mobile robots, described later in this chapter (Billard and Dautenhahn 1997), the imitator experiences similar proprioceptions, not only of movement, but also of other factors, for example, of inclination and of relative energy consumption. Moreover, the imitator also has similar exteroceptions to that of the imitatee, as both agents share simultaneously the same physical space. Note, however, that the similarity can never be perfect, as two physical agents, whether robotics or humans, are never the same; noise in sensor perception makes their simultaneous sensor information different, and they never share exactly the same "view" of the environment.

This chapter and the experiments that I present illustrate the proposal that the sharing of a similar perceptual context between imitator and imitatee creates a meaningful social context onto which language—that is, the development of a common means of symbolic communication, can develop. The idea that social cues, such as coordinated behavior (which is used in the experiments on learning by imitation described in this chapter), can be the precursor to language development in infants is not new to psycholinguistics, and will be presented in more detail in section 11.3.

The rest of this chapter presents a series of robotic experiments in which autonomous mobile robots are taught a protolanguage; *proto* relates to the fact that the robot is taught a symbolic communication system that shares only some of the features associated with human language. In these experiments, a robot learns a lexicon to name its proprio- and exteroceptions and it learns to make protosentences to describe its own actions as well as those of the teacher. Learning of the language occurs through an imitative scenario wherein the robot replicates the teacher's movements.

The behavioral and learning abilities of the robot are enabled by a single connectionist architecture, a Dynamical Recurrent Associative Memory Architecture (DRAMA) (Billard and Hayes 1999a). It is a general mechanism whose computation capacity for fast and robust learning of time series and of spatio-temporal regularities has been demonstrated theoretically (Billard and Hayes 1999a; Billard 1998) and through experimental work (Billard and Dautenhahn 1998; Billard and Dautenhahn 2000). Section 11.4 describes the DRAMA architecture in detail, and section 11.5 summarizes the different sets of robotic experiments. Section 11.6 discusses the experiments' results and their contribution to the above proposal (that social biases create a meaningful perceptual context that can enhance the development of a symbolic form of communication). Section 11.7 concludes the discussion by proposing further robotics experiments to pursue this approach and to investigate outstanding questions not addressed by this study.

11.3 The Role of Imitation in Language Learning

Learning of a language is perceived by many and, in particular, by linguists as a demonstration of the highly complex cognitive capabilities of humans. It is often thought that this is one of the main characteristics that distinguishes us from other animals.[3] Language is very complex because of its high number of grammatical rules, its large vocabulary, its verb conjugations, and so on. It is therefore astonishing that infants master it so quickly (that is, too quickly for it to be the result of pure association across all perceptual cues), given the low redundancy of single utterances and the high variability of other perceptions. To answer this problem, two main approaches have often been contrasted.

The first approach, by Chomsky (1968), is nativist. It argues for innate cognitive capacities for understanding and producing a language. In particular, it postulates the existence of an innate universal grammar underlying all human languages. Learning of a language consists then of acquiring a lexicon[4] and then instantiating the parameters of the sets of built-in syntactical rules. The second, nonnativist approach favors the idea that infants' language development results from complex learning skills, applied to general cognition including that of language. These skills are the product of evolution (Deacon 1997; Armstrong, Stokoe, and Wilcox 1995; Arbib and Hill 1988) and of development (Garton 1992; Piaget 1962; Trevarthen 1979). This approach assumes that humans are given general learning abilities for combinatorial association, which are then applied to map words and meanings and to produce combinations of words such as to satisfy any grammatical rules (rather than only a universal one) (Deacon 1997; Harnad 1993; Pulvermuller 1999).

The two above approaches give only a cognitivist account of language development. However, cognitive functions of associativity are not sufficient for learning a language. In order to account for the ease with which children learn a language, a behaviorist[5] approach has been proposed that looks for additional, socially driven attentional processes that would shorten the time required for the associative process to converge by reducing the number of considered perceptions. It is interesting to note that the query of how language is learned can be traced back to Saint Augustine, who viewed learning of words as an association of sound input with visual cues, driven by two social cues—namely, gaze tracking and pointing (see quotation in Messer 1994, p. 59). Closer to our time, Vygotsky's behaviorist position (followed later by Trevarthen[6]) has often been contrasted to Piaget's cognitivist position (see Trevarthen 1979). In opposition to Piaget, who concentrates on the infants' internal and asocial cognitive processes, Vygotsky stressed the importance of social interactions alongside the infants' cognitive development.

In short, I see two views to language development. The first one—nativist—assumes it to be the results of biologically predefined language-specific abilities and is not just by-product of more general cognitive abilities. The second one—nonnativist—views language development as part of the neurological and cognitive development as a whole. In this case, two variations can be distinguished: Piaget's approach, which considers the infant's (asocial, egocentric) interactions with the world as the main source of language development (Piaget 1967); and Vygotsky's approach, which views the infant's social interactions with other humans as a key factor for language development (Vygotsky 1962). Similar to Dautenhahn and Billard (1999), the approach taken in this chapter can be considered close to Vygostky's approach. In the following, I summarize what I think are the key aspects in social interactions underlying language development.

Social Interactions behind Language Development

Imitation has been attributed three different roles in infants' language development: in the motor control of speech, in the infants' internal cognitive development, and in the infant social interactions. In the latter, imitation is a social factor that guides the infant in cognitive development.

Vocal and verbal imitation is the process whereby the infant repeats part of the speech output produced by the caregiver (partial reproduction of the sound pattern in the case of vocalization and of words or sentences in the case of verbal imitation). Practicing vocal utterances is thought to be a means of reinforcing the network responsible for the sequential activation of articulation muscles (Speidel 1989).

An infant's ability for imitating others is thought to play a role in the infant's cognitive development. Vocal imitation, as a rehearsal of sound utterances, might reinforce the process of meaning-sound matching (Speidel 1989; Speidel and Herreshoff 1989). Deferred imitation—that is, the ability to reproduce the observed actions following a long delay (hours, days) after their presentation—requires the ability for internalizing the observation of a situation. The ability for deferred imitation is a first step toward symbolic representation and therefore might be a precursor to language (Meltzoff and Gopnik 1989).

Gestural and behavioral imitation, displayed in activities other than speech, has a social function (Nadel et al. 1999). It is a means to coordinate one's behavior with that of conspecifics, which can be used for engaging in body communication with peers (Garton 1992; Nadel et al. 1999; Trevarthen, Kokkinaki, and Famenghi 1999). This last role of imitation in language learning is particularly relevant to the study presented in this chapter. In the following, I expand the ideas underlying this approach.

Turn Taking as a Precursor to Verbal Communication

"Social communication is fundamental to the development of language and cognition, permitting the establishment of a partnership within which communication takes place" (Garton 1992). This partnership consists of being an active participant in a turn-taking game. Indeed, verbal communication would suffer if one would not respect the social rule of turn taking in speech (Messer 1994). Therefore, alongside learning of a language, the child should also learn certain social rules. Moreover, learning of these social rules might play a role in the actual development of the infant's understanding of language. By learning the rhythm of speech patterns (conversation), the infant might build up expectancies for certain forms of speech, which would simplify its learning of speech-meaning associations, where the meaning is given by the perceptual context.

The joint activity of the mother (or other caretaker) and the child participates in the scaffolding process of learning a language. Scaffolding relates to a step-by-step teaching process that directs the child's learning process. "This process is local, task-directed and focuses the child's attention on relevant aspects of the task" (Lock 1978). The child must first learn to communicate, that is, to correctly respond in a turn-taking game. This implies understanding the specificity of speech patterns (interrogative, imperative, declarative speech) and learning to produce appropriate responses. The child's prelinguistic understanding of these communication patterns is described by Bremner and Gavin (1997, 1988), who observed that children develop an ability for "synchrony of movements with adult speech patterns, imitation of facial expressions and selective attention to aspects of speech" (Bremner and Gavin 1988). Further, the child develops the ability to synchronize his visual attention to that of the mother by following the mother's direction of gaze and to produce vocalizations in synchrony to the mother's speech. Jacqueline Nadel and others (1999) study the development of infants' ability for turn-taking games, from being the imitator to being the imitatee. They observe that this developmental step is a marker for the child's development of a more-complex form of verbal communication exchanges.

Imitation as a Means to Coordinate Behavior

The synchrony of activity between the child and his mother results in their shared attention to specific visual and auditive patterns. The child develops his understanding of the mother's speech by associating a meaning to the mother's utterance in terms of his visual perceptions. The importance of a "co-ordination of joint activities involving mutual direction of attention" (Bruner and Watson 1983) between the mother and child for the grounding of the child's understanding of language was first pointed out by Lock (1978) and then further expanded by diverse authors (see Bruner and Watson 1983; Harley 1994; Nadel et al. 1999). In summary: "to be effective early language learning must take place in a social setting [where] turn taking, mutual gaze and pointing are social devices [used for] establishing a joint attention [between speaker and listener] that creates a meaningful social setting necessary for the development of language" (Harley 1994).

11.4 Robotic Experiments

This work seeks to contribute to a nonnativist approach that favors social scaffolding behind language learning. It presents robotics experiments in which the robot's ability to imitate another robot or a human teacher enhances the efficiency with which the robot learns a protolanguage. Experiments are carried out with two types of robots—wheeled (vehicle-like) mobile robots and a doll-shaped robot. (For a technical description of the robots' hardware, see Billard and Hayes 1999a; Billard, Dautenhahn, and Hayes 1998.) The robot's imitative behavior consists, in the first case, of the ability to follow another robot and, in the second case, of the ability to mirror the movements of a human instructor. The imitative behavior and the learning of the robot are controlled by a single artificial neural network architecture DRAMA. A complete mathematical description of DRAMA can be found in Billard and Hayes (1999a). Below is a short summary of DRAMA's functioning.

The Robot's Controller

The robot's controller in the experiments is composed of two parts: a set of event recognition modules for detecting variations in the robot's sensor-actuator state and a learning module, the DRAMA architecture, which associates the temporal changes across all the sensor-actuator modalities of the robot. At each processing cycle, the sensor-actuator vector state is measured. When a variation (i.e., more than one bit change) in one sensor or actuator input has been measured, the new information is forwarded to the associative architecture (DRAMA) to be correlated with all simultaneous and previously recorded events in other sensor-actuator systems.

DRAMA is a fully connected recurrent neural network, without hidden units.[7] The self-connections on the units provide a short-term memory of the units' activation. Consequently, sensor and actuator information (i.e., their corresponding network units' activation) is memorized for a fixed duration; the memory duration is determined by the decay rate of unit activation along the self-connection on the unit (see equation 11.1). This allows association to be made between time-delayed presentations of two inputs, hence learning of time series. In the experiments, the robot learns sequences of actions (dance patterns)—that is, consecutive activation of different actuator states. It also learns words (which are themselves experienced as perceptions) to label its perceptions—that is, it associates labels (radio signal or a combination of typed keys on a keyboard) with other consecutive, simultaneous, or precedent perceptions. Finally, it learns to combine sequentially the labels to form protosentences and to associate these combinations with a meaning in terms of other perceptual inputs.

Figure 11.1 shows a schematic representation of the robot's controller with three sensor systems as inputs. The number of sensors and actuators used in the experiments vary from 10 (for the vehicle robots, which have 2 bumpers, 2 infrared sensors, 2 light detectors, 1 compass, 1 radio transceiver and 2 motors) to 19 (for the doll robot, which has an 8-key keyboard, 6 touch switches on the body, 4 pairs of infrared emitter-receptors and 3 motors). The number of nodes in DRAMA varies consequently from 18 up to 169, each sensor being represented by a different number of nodes depending on the granularity of its encoding. Nodes in DRAMA are artificial neural nodes that have activation values y_i at node i. Output $y_i(t)$ of unit i at time t is a function of its input $x_i(t)$ at time t, its output $y_i(t-1)$ at time $t-1$ and the outputs $y_j(t-1)$ at time $t-1$

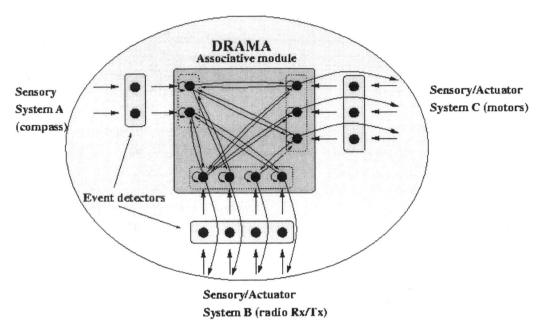

Figure 11.1 Schema of the connectionist architecture DRAMA which controls the imitative and learning skills of the robot.

of all other units j (equation 11.1). It is a real number with a value between 0 and 1. Long-term memory of consecutive activation of two units in DRAMA consists of updating the parameters of the connection linking these two units following pseudo-Hebbian rules (equations 11.3 and 11.4). Similar to time-delay neural networks (Day and Davenport 1993), each connection in the DRAMA network has two associated parameters: a time parameter (τ) and a confidence factor (w). Time parameters and confidence factors are positive numbers; they record respectively the time delay between two units' activations and the frequency of their coactivations.

Unit Activation Function

$$y_i(t) = F\left(x_i(t) + \tau_{ii} \cdot y_i(t-1) + \sum_{j \neq i} G(\tau_{ji}, w_{ji}, y_j(t-1))\right) \tag{11.1}$$

F, the transfer function, is the identity function for input values less than 1 and saturates to 1 for input values greater than 1 ($F(x) = x$ if $x \leq 1$ and $F(x) = 1$ otherwise) and G is the retrieving function whose definition is given below in equation 11.2. The variable x_i is the activation of the input to the node i. The indices notation used in the equations should be interpreted as follows: w_{ji} is the confidence factor of the connection leading from unit j to unit i. In short, the output y_i of a unit i in the network takes values between 0 and 1: $y_i(t) = 1$ when (1) an event has just been detected ($x_i(t) = 1$) or (2) when the sum of activation provided by the other units is sufficient to pass the two thresholds of time and confidence factor, represented by the G function. A value inferior to 1 represents the memory of a past full activation (value 1).

$$G(\tau_{ji}, w_{ji}, y_j(t-1)) = A(\tau_{ji}, y_j(t-1)) \cdot B(w_{ji}, y_j(t-1))$$

$$A(\tau_{ji}, y_j(t-1)) = 1 - \theta(|y_j(t-1) - \tau_{ji}|, e) \tag{11.2}$$

$$B(w_{ji}, y_j(t-1)) = \theta\left(w_{ji}, \frac{\max_{y_k>0}(w_{ki})}{T}\right)$$

$\max_{y_k>0}(w_{ki})$ is the maximal value of confidence factor of all the connections from all activated units k to the fixed unit i, which satisfy the temporal condition encoded in the term $A(\tau_{ki})$. The variable e specifies the error margin on the time delay within which the temporal condition is satisfied. The function $\theta(x, H)$ is a threshold function that outputs 1 when $x \geq H$ and 0 otherwise. The threshold T is a fixed positive number that determines the minimal value of confidence factor required to satisfy the θ threshold function.

Training Rules

$$w_{ji}(t) = w_{ji}(t-1) + a \tag{11.3}$$

$$\tau_{ji}(t) = \frac{\tau_{ji}(t-1) \cdot \dfrac{w_{ji}}{a} + \dfrac{y_j(t)}{y_i(t)}}{\dfrac{w_{ji}}{a} + 1} \tag{11.4}$$

The variable a is a fixed positive number by which the weights are incremented during learning.

The DRAMA network has general capacities for learning of spatio-temporal regularities and time series. A formal analysis of these properties can be found in Billard (1998) and Billard and Hayes (1999). The network can learn series of the type (1) ABA, cyclic sequence; (2) ABCDE and HJCKAE, crossing sequences on states C and A; and (3) ABCDEFCDG, sequence with a loop on states CD and divergence on state D. These properties are very relevant to the learning of a language, which is made of multiple combinations of the same primary items (words) and where sentences are often recursive combinations of the same instances. For example, ABCDEFCDG could represent the sentence "I think that you should recognize that you are wrong" and ABA could represent "(To be) (or not) (to be)." ABCDE and HJCKAE could be "My parents work at home," "I will work at home." In short, the network can learn sequences with several loops on the same subpatterns. The only limitation is that the patterns or subgroup of patterns on which the sequences loop should not occur at the beginning of the sequences, as a pattern previous to the loop is necessary to determine the activation of the correct subsequent pattern.

DRAMA's property for extracting spatiotemporal invariance is exploited in the experiments of section Experiments 1, where vehicle robots learn word-meaning pairings. Learning of time series is used in the experiments of section Experiments 2, where the doll robot is taught sequences of actions and protosentences (combinations of words of the lexicon).

Built-in behaviors can easily be defined by presetting particular sensor-actuator connections. In the experiments, the robot's imitative behavior of following (section Experiments 1) and of mirroring (section Experiments 2) the teacher agent's movements result from the presetting of particular connections between light sensors (sensitive to visual and infrared light) and the robot's motors. The recall of the DRAMA units' outputs (following equation 11.1) is used to direct the robot's movements (retrieval of the predefined sensor-motor connectivity). Results of the learning can then be immediately exploited.

For instance, in section Experiments 1, the recall of learning of the motor sequences results in the robot's immediate repetition of the sequence. Similarly, the recall of the word-perception associations (section Experiments 2) results in the robot emitting the correct word or combination of words given a particular combination of perceptions. Note that no special memory module exists in the architecture—rather, recall emerges from the connectivity and parameter values in the DRAMA architectures in the course of experience.

Figure 11.2 The experiments are based on an imitative scenario, namely, following behavior (left) and mirroring of arm and head movements (right), whereby the learner robot replicates the movements of the teacher.

11.5 Experiments

Two main sets of experiments were carried out. In the first set (section Experiments 1), a learner robot is taught by a teacher robot a lexicon to describe its proprio- and exteroceptions. In the second set (section Experiments 2), a doll robot is taught by a human experimenter. It learns a lexicon and how to combine the words of the lexicon to produce protosentences in order to describe its interactions with a human teacher.

In the following, I briefly summarize the main results of these experiments. I refer in places to detailed reports of each of these experiments.

Imitative Setup

The experiments are based on an imitative scenario whereby the learner robot replicates the movements of the teacher agent. The robot's ability to imitate is built-in and serves as scaffolding for learning. In the first set of experiments (section Experiments 1), the learner robot closely follows the teacher robot and, therefore, implicitly replicates the teacher's movements in the plane (see figure 11.2, left). Following proceeds from mutual phototaxis of the two agents. Because tracking is mutual, it results in a smooth binding between the two agents. The agents seldom lose sight of each other, because if the learner runs slower, the teacher waits for it.

In the second set of experiments (section Experiments 2), the doll robot mirrors the demonstrator's movements of the arms (up and down lifts) and of the head (left and right turns). The robot's mirroring behavior results from a predefined coupling between motors and infrared sensors (IRs). The coupling is done by presetting the DRAMA's internal connections between IRs inputs and motor commands. A pair of IRs is attached to the robot's ears and detects the demonstrator's head movements by measuring the reflection of the two IR emitters on the demonstrator's glasses (figure 11.2, right). A second pair of IRs placed on the robot's chest detects the demonstrator's hand movements by measuring the IR emission of the sensors the demonstrator holds in her hands.

Experiments 1: Learning of a Lexicon

Four experiments were carried out in which a learner robot was taught by a teacher robot a small vocabulary (composed of four to eight words). Two types of wheeled robots were used (Fischer-Technik and Lego-based robots), with different sensors and different morphologies. Learning of the vocabulary consists of the robot learning to correctly associate radio signals (the labels) with different sensory inputs. While following the teacher robot, the learner robot picks up radio signals emitted by the teacher robot. These signals are labels for either the teacher's external perceptions (observation of a box or a light bulb; Billard and Dautenhahn 1998) or of its internal perceptions of movement (move, stop, turn left or right; Billard and Hayes 1999b), of inclination (up, down, plane; Billard and Dautenhahn 1997), and of orientation (north, south, west, east; Billard and Hayes 1999a).

The robot learns the meaning of the teacher's signals by associating them with its owns perceptions. While they are bonded by the following process, learner and teacher agents are set in a position from which they share a common context of both external (facing the same direction) and internal (performing the same movement, traveling the same distance and over the same ground) perceptions. This implicit similarity between the two agents' perceptions is what enables the learner to make sense of the teacher's words, as the teacher talks only of what it senses, unaware of the learner's actual perceptions. It is thus an unsupervised teaching strategy. Learning of word-observation pairs results from the statistical associative process provided by the DRAMA architecture.

Signal and meaning are usually not perceived simultaneously. Because of the spatial displacement between the two robots while following each other, the learner robot's perception of, for example, inclination and of actions would become similar to that of the teacher only after a delay—the time to reach the same spatial position (for the inclination) and the time to react to the observation of a change in the travel direction of the teacher (for the actions). There is thus an important temporal uncertainty in the presentation of the signal-meaning pattern. Moreover, in addition to the radio signal and the relevant sensor input (the word's meaning), the robot perceives several other irrelevant stimuli (provided by its other sensors). The robot learns the correct word-meaning pairs by extracting the correct spatiotemporal invariance in the continuous pattern of sensor-actuator state. Incorrect associations, which arise from a mismatch between the agents' observations, are discarded compared to correct ones by a process of statistical elimination depending on their relative frequency of occurrence (see section 11.4) . In the experiments, the robot faced up to 30% and 50% imprecision, respectively, in the temporal and spatial dimensions of its perceptual information. Under these conditions, learning was shown to be successful.

Figure 11.3 left shows an example of the robot's neural activity resulting from the sensor-actuator activation. These data are the results of experiments in which the robot was taught four words to describe the four directions of compass (north/south/west/east)[8] (see Billard and Hayes 1999a). The three lines starting from the bottom show the receptions of the teacher's radio signals and the consecutive measurements of compass variations. In order to correctly associate the radio and compass stimuli, the robot has to discard the activity of its other sensors (namely, the two light and infrared sensors) and actuators (the two motors), which bear no direct correlations with the radio signals.

Figure 11.3 right shows the progress of the robot's learning alongside teaching of the words "south," "north" and "object," which had to be attached to corresponding compass and infrared values. Data are the variations (between two teaching episodes) of the time parameters of the three concerned radio-sensor connections. The figure shows strong fluctuations of the parameter values at the beginning of the run for the first third (about 60 steps) of the teaching. This corresponds to the learning phase; that is, the time during which the robot adjusts the time parameters to fit the training data.

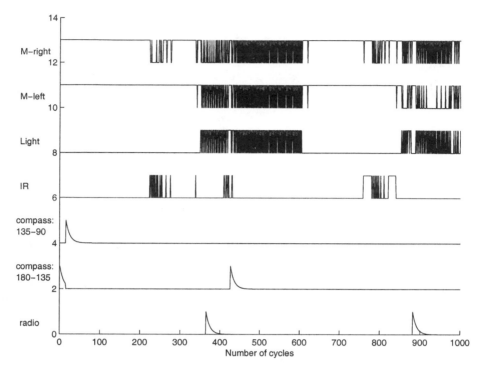

Figure 11.3 (Left) Robot's neural activity resulting from the sensor-actuator activation during a run. (Right) Variation of the time parameter values for each correct connection signal-object.

The curve then stabilizes around the zero value, which means that the robot's network has converged to the correct time parameter values. Small fluctuations remain at times 140 and 180, which are due to the imperfect traveling of the robots and consequently the irregular travel timing.

The Importance of the Imitative Skills

Simulations were carried out to investigate scaling up of the teacher-learner scenario to transmit a vocabulary among a group of robots, from a teacher robot to a group of learner robots (Billard and Dautenhahn 2000). Simulations were used to validate the model, the learning architecture, and the imitative teaching scenario, by generating statistically significant data. The main advantage of simulations over physical experiments is that they are repeatable, faster (simulating a 1-hour experiment takes about 5 minutes), and do not suffer unexpected hardware breakdown. The

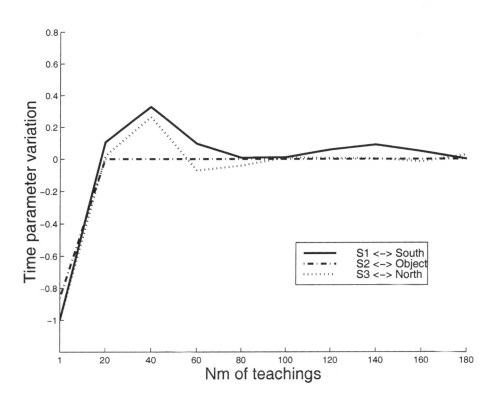

Figure 11.3 (continued)

disadvantages in terms of model faithfulness are, of course, well known (for a more complete discussion of this see Torrance 1992).

In order to determine the importance of the imitative/following strategy for the success of learning, simulations were carried out with two types of learner agents, some with and some without the ability of following. The agents had to learn three different types of vocabularies: (1) a vocabulary to describe nine objects (colored patches) in the environment, (2) a vocabulary to label scaled values of polar coordinates referring to the objects' locations, and (3) a vocabulary for the four quadrants of a compass, which measured the robot's individual orientation. Follower, nonfollower, and teacher agents were all present at the same time. That is, we did not study follower and nonfollower behaviors separately. Table 11.1 shows the mean value of the ratio (number of correctly learned words over total vocabulary) over the ten runs for each experiment and for each learner robot.

Results showed that the nonfollower agents are less successful on average and slower at learning the vocabulary concerning global variables, such as names of objects and the measure of the

Table 11.1 Comparison of learning success of follower and nonfollower agent

	OBJECTS		POLAR COORDINATES		ORIENTATION	
	Follower	*Nonfollower*	*Follower*	*Nonfollower*	*Follower*	*Nonfollower*
Number of correctly learned words/total vocabulary	100% ± 20%	60% ± 20%	50% ± 10%	50% ± 20%	60% ± 10%	0% ± 10%

objects' location in global coordinates. However, the nonfollower agents were in all cases unsuccessful at learning the vocabulary concerning the agent's relative perception of orientation (relative to its compass). In this experiment, the capacity of following the other is particularly important when the word to be learned concerns the agent's proprioceptions—for example, of orientation—because it allows the two agents to share a similar internal perception of it, as they point in the same direction.

Experiments 2: Learning of Protosentences

The second set of experiments was carried out with a small doll-shaped robot called Robota (see Billard 1998; Billard 1999 for a complete report). As mentioned in section 11.4, the robot can imitate (mirror) the arm and head movements of a demonstrator (figure 11.2, right). In an experiment, the robot was taught to perform different sequences of actions (consecutive movements of arms and head) by replicating those performed by the human demonstrator and to label these action sequences with different "names." In these experiments, rather than radio signals, a name consisted of a combination of keys typed on a keyboard connected to the robot (the eight keys of the keyboard are interpreted by the DRAMA controller as another set of switch inputs, in addition to that on the robot's body). In a second experiment, the robot was taught combinations of words (combinations of keys, where one key is one word) that formed English protosentences (e.g., "I touch left arm," "You move head right"), to describe its actions and perceptions of touch on different parts of its body. Exploratory tests were also done with children 5 and 6 years old, who taught the robot words

Table 11.2 Results of teaching of dance patterns and sentences

EXPERIMENT TYPE	TIME (MIN)	NO. OF TRIALS	NO. OF PATTERNS
Action sequences	15 ± 4	1.2 ± 0.5	8 ± 0
Word sequences	12 ± 10	2 ± 1.5	6 ± 2

to label different parts of its body and simple action sequences (Billard, Dautenhahn, and Hayes 1998). Children took a real pleasure in having the robot respond to their interaction. These tests suggest that the imitative and communicative behaviors of Robota make it an interesting toy for children.

Table 11.2 shows the results of the experiments on teaching sequences of movements (first line) or "dances" and on teaching protosentences (second line). Each experiment was carried out by five different experimenters. Data are mean value and standard deviation of time until learning, the number of trials per taught pattern (until learning), and the number of taught patterns. In the first experiment, the robot was taught eight action patterns, which consisted of different sequences of head and arm movements. The experimenter was free to choose the number of movements of each dance he wanted to teach. As a result, none of the teaching was similar (there were dance patterns common to two teaching episodes but the complete sets of dance patterns were different). In addition, as each experimenter would move at a different speed, one could evaluate the performance of the DRAMA network in adapting to variation in the input timing.

In order to teach the robot in this experiment, the demonstrator first performs the dance herself, moving her arms and head sequentially, which the robot immediately imitates in response to the infrared reception of the emitters attached to the glasses of the demonstrator and those the demonstrator holds in her hands. At the end of the dance, the demonstrator presses a key on the keyboard. The robot associates the pressing of the key (which activates the corresponding sensor unit) with the complete sequence of actions it has memorized. It updates the parameters of the connections linking the sensor unit, corresponding to the key, to the actuator units, which have been activated by the different actions of the dance. The demonstrator repeats the same process for each key, teaching a different dance pattern each time. During the training, the demonstrator verifies if the robot has correctly learned the dance patterns by pressing the keys again. This activates retrieval of the associated action sequence by reading backwards the DRAMA connections from the keyboard switches' inputs to the robot's actuator outputs. Note that because the time delay between each action is recorded in the network's time parameters, each action of the sequence is retrieved after the time delay as observed during the demonstration.

In the second experiment, the robot was taught four to eight different sentences to describe its actions and its perceptions of touch on the body. The experimenter was free to choose the eight-word combination (one word per keyboard key) he or she wanted to use in the sentences. The words were written on stickers, which the demonstrator put in front of each key of the keyboard, to help him or her remember the meaning of each key during the training. Examples of taught protosentences are *I move right arm, I turn head left, You touch mouth, You touch left/right foot.* In order to teach the robot, the demonstrator first pressed the relevant switch or activated the robot's arm or head by moving the corresponding sensors, and then pressed the corresponding keys on the keyboard, one after the other, so as to preserve the sequential order. During training, the demonstrator verified whether the robot learned the sequence, by pressing the switch again or activating the robot's arm or head. This prompted the robot to retrieve the key sequence, by reading backwards the DRAMA connections from the sensor-actuator inputs to the keyboard switches' inputs, which resulted in the sequential activation of the light bulbs placed above each of the keys on the mini-keyboard.

Table 11.3 shows the progress of the robot's learning alongside one of the different trainings. There, the robot was taught five complete sentences (middle column) for describing its different motions and touch perceptions (left column). It learned the meaning of each word from extracting the invariances across all teachings (e.g., the word "arm" in line 3, the word combination "you touch" and the word "foot" in line 6, and the adjective "right" in line 7; see table 11.3). The robot learns also the position of each word relative to one another in a sentence by extracting temporal invariance in the words' consecutive occurrences. Finally, the robot can use its learning to infer the correct combination of words

Table 11.3 Example of sentence teaching

ACTIVATED SENSOR	TAUGHT SENTENCE	RETRIEVED SENTENCE
Move right arm	*I move right arm*	
Touch left arm	*You touch left arm*	
Move right arm + touch left arm		*arm*
Touch right foot	*You touch right foot*	
Touch left foot	*You touch left foot*	
Touch right foot + left foot		*You touch foot*
Move right arm + touch right foot		*right*
Touch left arm + left foot		*You touch left*
Touch mouth	*You touch head*	
Touch right arm		*You touch right arm*

for describing a touch on the right arm (line 10 of the example), for which it had not yet been taught a sentence.

These experiments demonstrated that the DRAMA architecture could allow learning of a basic "protolanguage," which shares some properties with natural language: (1) each word (key in our experiment) can carry a specific meaning; (2) words can be combined, and the combination can be given a different meaning while not losing the meaning of each word taken separately; (3) different combinations of the same words can be given different meanings, the meaning of each combination being determined by the order of appearance of each word in the combination; (4) conceptual meanings of each word can be learned implicitly by only presenting them as part of complete sentences, which can then be used to infer new word combinations; (5) precedence between word appearance in the combination is learned and can be used to infer the correct order when constructing a new word combination.

In summary: these experiments allowed us (1) to verify the computational ability of the DRAMA architecture for learning redundant combinations and sequences of inputs, such as to form the basis of a protolanguage; (2) to show that a mode of interaction with a robot, which is based on imitation and synthetic communication, could be acceptable to humans (to both infants and adults who participated in the experiments); and (3) that it could be an easy means of teaching a robot (within the capabilities of young children).

Note that only simple sentence examples were used so far, in which the words could easily be tied to the taught concepts. Moreover, the "language" the robot was to learn was regular; that is, the robot's learning task was to recognize temporal regularities in the words' ordering across the taught sentences and to correlate the words' usage with its sensors' and actuators' activity. As such, these experiments were a first step toward demonstrating the validity of the system (the learning architecture and the imitative strategy) for teaching a robot a symbolic communication system.

The fact that the DRAMA architecture is comparable in function to a Hidden Markov model or other recurrent neural networks (Billard 1998), which are models currently used in techniques of Natural Language Processing (NLP), suggests that the model could scale up successfully to learning an arbitrary regular language (see, e.g., Howie 1991). However, it remains to be shown how the system could scale up to learning a complete natural language with grammatical structure and irregularities.

A second doll has now been constructed, which uses a more powerful microcontroller. The sensor abilities of the doll have been increased. The keyboard has been replaced by a commercial speech processor. The doll is provided with a colored CCD (closed-circuit digital) camera and pyroelectric sensor for detecting the demonstrator's movements. Current experiments are testing the system for learning more complex speech patterns, as made possible by the speech-recognizer system. Updates on this work's progress can be found at ⟨http://www-slab.usc.edu/billard/doll.html⟩.

11.6 Discussion

This chapter reviewed a series of experiments in which a robot was taught basic elements of a synthetic protolanguage. The robot grounded a lexicon concerning its perceptions and learned to combine the words of the lexicon to describe situations. The experiments were based on an unsupervised learning strategy wherein the robot grounded meaning into another agent's utterances in terms of its own perception. The teacher agent had no access to the robot's internal state and, thus, did not direct its teaching depending on the robot's performance. The learning of the robot was, however, implicitly guided by the teacher, as the robot's movements and perceptual attention were coordinated to that of the teacher. This coordination resulted from the robot's ability to imitate the teacher's movements. Results showed that the imitative behavior greatly improves the efficiency and speed of the learning. Moreover, without imitation, learning of symbolic expressions to describe the robot's proprioceptions was not possible.

Contribution to Robotics

The work presented in this chapter does not follow directly from any previous studies of robotics. Indeed, little work has yet been done in teaching a physical robot a synthetic form of communication. The most closely related studies are those of Yanco and Stein (1993) and Steels and Vogt (1997), in which a robot learns a lexicon to describe sets of actions and perceptions respectively. The present study differs from those works in two main aspects: (1) The learning and behavioral capacities of the robots result from a single connectionist architecture, which has general ability for extracting spatiotemporal regularities in a dynamic environment; (2) the language the robot is taught is not restricted only to a lexicon, where each word of the lexicon relates to a single specific perception, as in the two compared studies.

I am conscious, however, that these experiments are somewhat simple in terms of the number of words and combinations learned. The experiments so far were mainly aimed at illustrating the general capacities of DRAMA together with the imitative strategy for the learning of a simple protolanguage. Further experiments are currently carried out with the aim to study the learning of more complex patterns of sensory inputs with more sophisticated robots (such as the second doll robot).

Contribution to Computational Linguistics

The success of the experiments reported here validated the proposed unsupervised imitative learning strategy for transmitting a basic synthetic mode of symbolic communication across heterogeneous agents. Moreover, these experiments showed that association of arbitrary symbols to meaning is possible in embodied agents other than humans; and that it can be done by a simple (in comparison to that of animals) neural architecture. In particular, the results show that the word-meaning association is strongly dependent on constraining the temporal uncertainty of the association. Language learning occurs in a highly noisy and sensory rich environment. The experiments simulated only very partially some of this complexity, but as such it was already an important step compared to previous work in the domain.

In the robotics studies on grounding of a lexicon, which were cited earlier (Yanco and Stein 1993; Steels and Vogt 1997), the spatial and temporal variability of the word-meaning pattern is almost nonexistent. Learning occurs between only the relevant (to the learning) sensory channels, which reduces strongly the possibility of incorrect signal-sensory input associations. There is no temporal ambiguity in the associations, as the experiments are static.

The embodied aspect of grounding of meaning has also been neglected by simulated studies of language evolution (e.g., Arita and Koyama 1998; Kirby and Hurford 1997; MacLennan 1991; Di Paolo 1998; Steels 1997). In these studies, grounding of communication is regarded as a computational problem that can be solved solely by means of combinatorial analysis. For these authors, categorization of sensor perceptions into concepts results from a process of statistical elimination among all possible meaning-object pairs, where the most likely pairs—that is, the most frequently observed—are chosen.

In my opinion, combinatorial analysis is not sufficient: it becomes quickly intractable when the number of dimensions in the sensory space is high and when temporal delays are taken in consideration (as they should be in any physical implementation). In this case, additional attentional mechanisms would be required to reduce the uncertainty on the spatial and temporal dimensions of the sensory inputs. The introduction and section 11.2 of this chapter stressed the importance of social interactions as an external attentional mechanism. I referred to studies of psycholinguistics, which pointed out several social mechanisms that are possible attentional mechanisms. These are provided either by the speaker/teacher (pointing, increasing the tone of voice, linguistic deixis) and/or by the listener/learner (focus of gaze in the direction of the speaker's gaze or the direction pointed by the speaker's finger). These attentional mechanisms act as a cognitive process that restricts the number of observations before any combinatorial analysis. However, there is more to this than just a single cognitive process. There is an interactive process between the two communicative agents, which requires a behavioral coordination between the two agents. In the experiments reported in this chapter, this behavioral coordination between teacher and learner agents is achieved by creating a spatiotemporal bonding between the agents' behaviors through an imitative strategy.

In summary, this work brings a novel contribution to current research concerned with the modeling of language learning, as it addresses both the behavioral (agent-environment interaction) and cognitive aspects of the symbol-grounding problem (Harnad 1990). In particular, it suggests that providing a robot with primary social abilities might enhance its development of more complex social skills. As such, this study is a first step toward the development and application of complex social skills for robots.

11.7 Conclusion

This chapter presented a series of robotic experiments in which autonomous mobile robots were taught a basic synthetic proto-language. The robots grounded a lexicon concerning their percep-tions and learned to combine the words of the lexicon to describe their interactions with the teacher. Learning of the robots was unsupervised and resulted from the self-organization of the robots' connectionist architecture. The success of the experiments vali-dated the proposed unsupervised imitative learning strategy for transmitting a basic synthetic mode of symbolic communication across heterogeneous agents.

This work wished to contribute to a nonnativist approach, which sees social biases behind language learning. It was argued that ad-ditional, socially driven, attentional processes are required along-side associative processes for the grounding of word meaning. The robot experiments reinforced this claim by showing that imitative behavior, which implicitly constrains the robot's perceptions, could improve the robot's performance at learning a protolan-guage. In particular, results showed that imitative behavior was necessary for grounding the robot's proprioceptions, such as nam-ing its relative orientation and inclination.

This work is a first step toward studies of the development of complex social skills for robots. It opens the way to further im-plementation of the connectionist models, such as DRAMA, in experiments on teaching a robot a complete language, which includes a syntax and other grammatical rules (with the limita-tion that handling of irregularities and ambiguities might not be possible). Moreover, it suggests that providing a robot with primary social abilities might enhance its development of more complex social skills. Developing more complex imitative scenarios would allow transmitting more complex systems of communication. This could, for instance, be the development of the robot's capability for imitating facial expressions (as currently investigated by Breazeal and Scassellati 2000), used then for transmitting symbolic expressions to label human emotional states. Further, the robot's ability at replicating complex action sequences and learning long perception-action sequences could be used to teach the robot more complex conceptual notions for describing its behavior. In this case, the robot's internal state would be more complex than simply the robot's sensor and actuator state (e.g., it would also include the value of different motivational factors) and, therefore, higher-level conceptual information (e.g., concerning goals, rewards) could be transmitted through the language. The latter direction is currently under investigation by the author.

Acknowledgments

I want to thank very warmly Kerstin Dautenhahn and Gillian Hayes for their precious comments and guidance all along this project. Many thanks to Chrystopher Nehaniv and Michael Arbib for constructive comments on the writing of this paper. An enormous thanks to all the technicians of the Department of Artificial Intelligence at the University of Edinburgh, whose precious help made this work possible. Facilities were provided by the Department of Artificial Intelligence at the University of Edinburgh. Aude Billard was supported by personal grants from the L. and H. Mouttet Foundation and the Swiss National Science Foundation.

Notes

1. The terms *proprio-* and *exteroception* relate, respectively, to internal and external perceptions of the agent.
2. I follow Davis's general definition of the term *imitation*. He refers to a behavior skill that leads to "some sort of similarity in behavior among two or more individuals" (Davis 1973).
3. This is a very controversial subject. For instance, people argue that some species of apes might be capable of simple forms of language. Their argumentation is based, for example, on the successful experiment of Savage-Rumbaugh (1993) at teaching chimpanzees a basic lexicon, on the studies of parrots' amazing ability to reproduce human speech (Moore 1992), and that of dolphins' and whales' complicated songs (Herman and Uyeyama 1999;

Helweg et al. 1992). (For some insight into this debate, see, e.g., Bickerton 1990; Deacon 1997; Wilson 1980.)

4. Note that the acquisition of a lexicon may well make use of all kinds of learning, including social mechanisms for sharing meaning. The acquisition of lexicon is not an area where there is disagreement between nativists and nonnativists. Generally, the disagreements are on the role of innate factors in the acquisition of grammar.

5. Cognitive and behavioral capabilities are here distinguished. The former relate to the agent's internal computational processes and the latter relate to the interaction of these internal processes' outputs and inputs—the agent's actions and perceptions—with the environmental dynamics.

6. There are several other approaches to the idea of social bias behind language development, see Messer 1994 for a review.

7. The reader can refer to Hertz, Krogh, and Palmer 1991 for a general introduction to artificial neural networks and to Pearlmutter 1995 for a detailed presentation of recurrent neural network models.

8. An on-line animated demonstration of this experiment can be found at ⟨http://www-slab.usc.edu/billard/Drama.html⟩.

References

Arbib, M. A., and J. C. Hill. Language acquisition: Schemas replace universal grammar. In J. A. Hawkins, ed., *Explaining Language Universals*, pp. 56–72. Basil: Blackwell, 1988.

Arita, T., and Y. Koyama. Evolution of linguistic diversity in a simple communication system. *Artificial Life* 4: 1, 9–17, 1998.

Armstrong, D., W. C. Stokoe, and S. E. Wilcox. *Gesture and the Nature of Language*. Cambridge, UK: Cambridge University Press, 1995.

Bickerton, D. *Language and Species*. Chicago: University of Chicago Press, 1990.

Billard, A. DRAMA, a connectionist model for robot learning: Experiments on grounding communication through imitation in autonomous robots. Doctoral dissertation, Dept. of Artificial Intelligence, University of Edinburgh, UK, 1998.

Billard, A. DRAMA, a connectionist architecture for on-line learning and control of autonomous robots: Experiments on learning of a synthetic proto-language with a doll robot. *Industrial Robots* 26: 1, 59–66, 1999.

Billard, A., and K. Dautenhahn. Grounding communication in situated, social robots. In *Proceedings of TIMR 97, Towards Intelligent Mobile Robots Conference*, Manchester. Tech. Rep. Series, Dept. of Computer Science, Manchester University, ISSN 1361–6161. Report no. UMCS-97-9-1, 1997.

Billard, A., and K. Dautenhahn. Grounding communication in autonomous robots: An experimental study. *Robotics and Autonomous Systems*, special issue on scientific methods in mobile robotics 24: 1–2, 71–81, 1998.

Billard, A., and K. Dautenhahn. Experiments in social robotics: Grounding and use of communication in autonomous agents. *Adaptive Behavior*, special issue on simulation models of social agents, 7(3/4): 415–438, 2000.

Billard, A., K. Dautenhahn, and G. Hayes. Experiments on human-robot communication with Robota, an imitative learning and communicating doll robot. In *Proceedings of Socially Situated Intelligence Workshop, Zurich CH*, as part of the Fifth Conference of the Society of Adaptive Behavior. Centre for Policy Modelling technical report series: no. CPM-98-38, 1998.

Billard, A., and G. Hayes. Learning to communicate through imitation in autonomous robots. In *Proceedings of ICANN97, Seventh International Conference on Artificial Neural Networks*, pp. 763–768, 1997.

Billard, A., and G. Hayes. DRAMA, a connectionist architecture for control and learning in autonomous robots. *Adaptive Behavior* 7(1): 35–64, 1999a.

Billard, A., and G. Hayes. Transmitting communication skills through imitation in autonomous robots. In A. Birk and J. Demiris (eds.), *Learning Robots*: 79–95. LNAI Series, Springer-Verlag, 1999b.

Breazeal, C., and B. Scassellati. Infant-like social interactions between a robot and a human caretaker. *Adaptive Behavior* 8(1): 49–74, 2000.

Bremner, J. G. *Infancy*. Oxford: Basil Blackwell, 1988.

Bremner, J. G., A. Slater, and G. Butterworth. *Infant Development: Recent Advances*. Hove: Psychology Press, 1997.

Brooks, R., C. Ferrell, R. Irie, C. C. Kemp, M. Marjanovic, B. Scassellatti, and M. Williamson. Alternative essences of intelligence: Lessons from embodied AI. In *AAAI-98 AAAI Conference*, pp. 961–967, Menlo Park, Calif.: AAAI Press, 1998.

Bruner, J. S., and R. Watson. Child's Talk: Learning to Use Language. Oxford: Oxford University Press, 1983.

Chomsky, N. *Language and Mind*. Harcourt Brace Jovanovich, 1968.

Cooke, S. R., B. Kitts, R. Sekuler, and M. J. Matarić. Delayed and real-time imitation of complex visual gestures. In *Proceedings of the International Conference on Vision, Recognition, Action: Neural Models of Mind and Machine*, Boston University, 1997.

Dautenhahn, K. Getting to know each other—Artificial social intelligence for autonomous robots. *Robotics and Autonomous Systems* 16: 333–356, 1995.

Dautenhahn, K. I could be you—The phenomenological dimension of social understanding. *Cybernetics and Systems*, special issue on epistemological aspects of embodied AI 28(5): 417–453, 1997.

Dautenhahn, K., and A. Billard. Bringing up robots or—The psychology of socially intelligent robots: From theory to implementation. In *Proceedings of Autonomous Agents (Agents '99) Conference*, Seattle, Washington, pp. 366–367. ACM, 1999.

Davis, J. M. Imitation: A review and critique. In P. Klopfer (ed.), *Perspectives in Ethology*, vol. 1, pp. 43–72. New York: Plenum, 1973.

Day, S. P., and M. R. Davenport. Continuous-time temporal back-propagation with adaptive time delay. *IEEE Transaction on Neural Networks* 4: 348–354, 1993.

Deacon, T. *Symbolic Species: The Co-evolution of Language and the Human Brain*. General Science, 1997.

Demiris, J. Movement imitation mechanisms in robots and humans. Doctoral dissertation, Dept. of Artificial Intelligence, University of Edinburgh, 1999.

Demiris, J., and G. Hayes. Imitative learning mechanisms in robots and humans. In *Proceedings of the 5th European Workshop on Learning Robots*, Bari, Italy, pp. 9–16, 1996. Also as Research Paper no. 814 at the Dept. of Artificial Intelligence at the University of Edinburgh.

Demiris, J., and M. Matarić. Perceptuo-motor primitives in imitation. *Working Notes, Autonomous Agents '98 Workshop on Agents in Interaction—Acquiring Competence Through Imitation*. Minneapolis/St. Paul, 1998.

Di Paolo, E. An investigation into the evolution of communication. *Adaptive Behavior* 6(2): 285–324, 1998.

Garton, A. F. Social interaction and the development of language and cognition. In *Essays in Developmental Psychology*. Hillsdale, N.J.: Erlbaum, 1992.

Gaussier, P., S. Moga, J. Banquet, and M. Quoy. From perception-action loop to imitation processes: A bottom-up approach of learning by imitation. *Applied Artificial Intelligence* 7(1): 701–727, 1998.

Harley, T. *The Psychology of Language: From Data to Theory*. Erlbaum, UK: Taylor and Francis, 1994.

Harnad, S. The symbol grounding problem. *Physica* D 42: 335–346, 1990.

Harnad, S. Grounding symbols in the analog world with neural nets. *Think*, special issue on connectionism versus symbolism 2(1): 12–78, 1993.

Hayes, G., and J. Demiris. A robot controller using learning by imitation. In *Proceedings of the Second International Symposium on Intelligent Robotic Systems*, Grenoble, France, pp. 198–204, 1994.

Helweg, D. A., A. S. Frankel, J. R. Mobley, and L. M. Herman. Humpback whale song: Our current understanding. In J. R. Thomas, R. A. Kastelein, A. Ya. Supin, eds., *Sensory Processes of Marine Mammals* 459–483. New York: Plenum, 1992.

Herman, L. M., and R. Uyeyama. The dolphin's grammatical competency; Comments on Kako (1999). *Animal Learning and Behavior* 27: 18–23, 1999.

Hertz, J., A. Krogh, and R. Palmer. *An Introduction to the Theory of Neural Computation.* Reading, Mass.: Addison-Wesley, 1991.

Howie, J. M. *Automata and Languages.* Oxford: Clarendon Press, 1991.

Kirby, S., and J. Hurford. Learning, culture, and evolution in the origin of linguistic constraints. In *Proceedings of the Fourth European Conference on Artificial Life, ECAL97.* Cambridge, MA: MIT Press, 1997.

Klingspor, V., J. Demiris, and M. Kaiser. Human-robot-communication and machine learning. *Applied Artificial Intelligence Journal* 11: 719–746, 1997.

Kuniyoshi, Y. M. The science of imitation—Towards physically and socially grounded intelligence. *RWC Joint Symposium*, 1994.

Kuniyoshi, Y. M. Behavior matching by observation for multi-robot cooperation. In *International Symposium of Robotics Research, ISRR'95*, 1995.

Kuniyoshi, Y. M., and I. Inoue. Learning by watching: Extracting reusable task knowledge from visual observation of human performance. *IEEE Transactions on Robotics and Automation* 10(6): 799–822, 1994.

Lock, E. *Action, Gesture, and Symbols: The Emergence of Language.* New York: Academic Press, Harcourt Brace Jovanovich, 1978.

MacLennan, B. Synthetic ethology: An approach to the study of communication. In *Proceedings of the Second Artificial Life Workshop*, pp. 631–658, 1991.

Matarić, M. J. Studying the role of embodiment in cognition. *Cybernetics and Systems*, special issue on epistemological aspects of embodied AI 2(6): 457–470, 1997a.

Matarić, M. J. Learning social behavior. *Robotics and Autonomous Systems* 20: 191–204, 1997b.

Meltzoff, M. A., and A. Gopnik. On linking nonverbal imitation, representation and language: Learning in the first two years of life. In G. E. Speidel and K. E. Nelson, eds., *The Many Faces of Imitation in Language Learning*, pp. 23–52. Berlin: Springer Verlag, 1989.

Messer, D. J. *The Development of Communication: From Social Interaction to Language.* New York: Wiley, 1994.

Moore, B. R. Avian movement imitation and a new form of mimicry: Tracing the evolution of a complex form of learning. *Behavior* 122: 614–623, 1992.

Nadel, J., C. Guerini, A. Peze, and C. Rivet. The evolving nature of imitation as a format for communication. In J. Nadel and G. Butterworth (eds.), *Imitation in Infancy*, 209–234. Cambridge, UK: Cambridge University Press, 1999.

Nehaniv, C., and K. Dautenhahn. Mapping between dissimilar bodies: Affordances and the algebraic foundations of imitation. In *Proceedings of EWLR97, Seventh European Workshop on Learning Robots*, Edinburgh, 1998.

Nehaniv, C., and K. Dautenhahn. Of hummingbirds and helicopters: An algebraic framework for interdisciplinary studies of imitation and its applications. In J. Demiris and A. Birk (eds.), *Interdisciplinary Approaches to Robot Learning.* World Scientific Press, 1999. Series in Robotic and Intelligent Systems, vol 24 pp. 136–161.

Pearlmutter, B. A. (1995). Gradient calculations for dynamic recurrent neural networks: A survey. *IEEE Transactions on Neural Networks* 6: 1212–1228, 1995.

Pfeifer, R. Embodied system life. In *Proceedings of the International Symposium on System Life*, Tokyo, 1998.

Piaget, J. *Play, Dreams, and Imitation in Childhood.* New York: Norton, 1962.

Piaget, J. *The Language and the Thought of the Child.* London: Routledge and Kegan Paul, 1967.

Pulvermuller, F. Words in the brain's language. *Behavioral and Brain Sciences* 22(2): 253–279, 1999.

Savage-Rumbaugh, E. S. *Language Comprehension in Ape and Child.* Chicago: University of Chicago Press, 1993.

Scassellati, B. Imitation and mechanisms of joint attention: A developmental structure for building social skills on a humanoid robot. In C. Nehaniv (ed.), *Computation for Metaphors, Analogy, and Agents*, Lecture Notes in Artificial Intelligence, 1562 pp. 176–195. Springer Verlag, 1999.

Schaal, S. Learning from demonstration. *Advances in Neural Information Processing Systems* 9: 1040–1046, 1997.

Schaal, S. Nonparametric regression for learning nonlinear transformations. In H. Ritter and O. Holland (eds.), *Prerational Intelligence in Strategies, High-Level Processes and Collective Behavior*. Kluwer Academic Press, 1999.

Speidel, G. E. Imitation: A bootstrap for learning to speak. In G. E. Speidel and K. E. Nelson (eds.), *The Many Faces of Imitation in Language Learning*, pp. 151–180. New York: Springer Verlag, 1989.

Speidel, G. E., and M. Herreshoff. Imitation and the construction of long utterances. In G. E. Speidel and K. E. Nelson (eds.), *The Many Faces of Imitation in Language Learning*, pp. 181–198. New York: Springer Verlag, 1989.

Steels, L. The spontaneous self-organization of an adaptive language. In Muggleton, S., ed., *Machine Intelligence 15*. Oxford: Oxford University Press, 1997.

Steels, L., and P. Vogt. Grounding adaptive language games in robotic agents. In *Proceedings of the Fourth European Conference on Artificial Life, ECAL97*, pp. 473–484. Cambridge, MA: MIT Press, 1997.

Torrance, M. C. The case for a realistic mobile robot simulator. In *Working Notes of the AAAI Fall Symposium on Applications of Artificial Intelligence to Real-World Autonomous Mobile Robots*, October. Cambridge, MA: 1992.

Trevarthen, C. Communication and cooperation in early infancy: A description fo primary intersubjectivity. In M. Bullowa (ed.), *Before Speech*. Cambridge, UK: Cambridge University Press, 1979.

Trevarthen, C., T. Kokkinaki, and G. A. Famenghi Jr. What infants' imitations communicate: With mothers, with fathers, and with peers. In J. Nadel and G. Butterworth (eds.), *Imitation in Infancy*, pp. 127–185. Cambridge, UK: Cambridge University Press, 1999.

Vygotsky, L. S. *Thought and Language*. Cambridge, MA: MIT Press, 1962.

Wilson, E. O. *Sociobiology: The New Synthesis*, 2d ed. Social Sciences. Abridged ed. Cambridge, Mass.: Belknap Press of Harvard University Press, 1980.

Yanco, H., and L. A. Stein. An adaptive communication protocol for cooperating mobile robots. In *From Animals to Animats 2: Proceedings of the Second International Conference on the Simulation of Adaptive Behavior*, pp. 478–485. Cambridge, MA: MIT Press, 1993.

12 Rethinking the Language Bottleneck: Why Don't Animals Learn to Communicate?

Michael Oliphant

12.1 Introduction

While most work on the evolution of language has been centered on the evolution of syntax, my focus in this chapter is instead on more basic features that separate human communication from the systems of communication used by other animals. In particular, I argue that human language is the only existing system of learned arbitrary reference. While innate communication systems are, by definition, directly transmitted genetically, the transmission of a learned system must be indirect. Learners must acquire the system by being exposed to its use in the community. Although it is reasonable that a learner has access to the utterances that are produced, it is less clear how accessible the meaning is that the utterance is intended to convey. This is particularly problematic if the system of communication is symbolic—where form and meaning are linked in a purely conventional way. Given this, I propose that the ability to transmit a learned symbolic system of communication from one generation to the next represents a key milestone in the evolution of language.

12.2 Features of Human Language

To theorize about the evolution of human language is to theorize about how human communication differs from the communication systems used by other species, and what biological basis underlies these differences. The features of human language that I suggest we need to account for are as follows:

- *Syntax:* Human language is compositional, conveying structured meanings through the use of structured forms.
- *Learning:* Human language is passed on from one generation to the next via cultural transmission.
- *Symbolic reference:* The mapping between basic lexical elements and their meanings is arbitrary and conventional.

In distinguishing human language from other forms of communication, the attention has largely been focused on the evolution of syntax (Bickerton 1990; Pinker and Bloom 1990; Newmeyer 1991). This is unsurprising, as syntactic structure is certainly the most salient feature of human language. Because other species seem to have no means of combining simple signals with each other to form more complex meanings, the prime objective of most research on the evolution of language has been to explain how such an ability arose in humans.

In this chapter, I will instead focus on the other, perhaps more basic, features of human language that make it unique—learning and symbolic reference. Although there are other forms of communication that are *learned*, and there are other forms of communication that are *symbolic*, I will argue that human language is the only existing system of communication that is both learned *and* symbolic. Moving from a simple (nonsyntactic) innate system of communication to an equally simple learned system is nontrivial. Making such a transition is particularly difficult if the mapping between forms and meanings is an arbitrary convention.

12.3 Innateness and Symbolic Reference

Because I am putting aside the issue of syntax, the systems of communication that I am concerned with are what Lewis (1969) termed *signaling systems*—systems that map between unstructured signals and unanalyzed meanings. Lewis gives as an example a communication system used in Boston during the American Revolution. In this system, immortalized in the phrase "one if by land, two if by sea," lanterns were used to signal the existence and nature of an impending British attack. One lantern was lit to signal that Paul Revere should warn of a land attack, two lanterns were lit to warn of an attack across the Charles River, and no lanterns indicated that there was no attack coming. This signaling system is diagrammed in figure 12.1.

I will refer to each bidirectional association between a signal (such as displaying two lanterns) and the meaning it denotes ("attack by sea") as a *sign*, after de Saussure (1959). In classifying a system of communication, I will ask two questions about the signs that compose it. First, are the signs innate or learned? An innate sign is an association that is specified genetically and passed on from one generation to the next through reproduction. A learned sign, on the other hand, is established experientially through the use of some learning mechanism. Rather than being passed on ge-

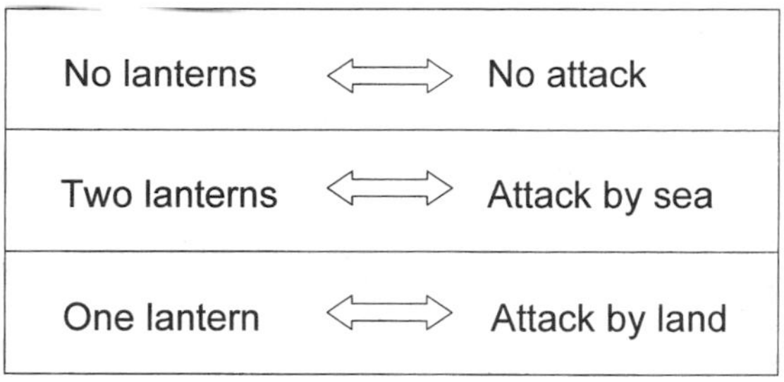

No lanterns	$\Longleftrightarrow$	No attack
Two lanterns	$\Longleftrightarrow$	Attack by sea
One lantern	$\Longleftrightarrow$	Attack by land

Figure 12.1 A simple signaling system, consisting of a set of signals and their associated meanings.

netically, if a learned sign is to be perpetuated it must be culturally transmitted from one generation to the next.

The second question that I want to ask is whether or not the signs are *symbolic*. Peirce (1932) defines a symbol as "a sign which refers to the Object that it denotes by virtue of a law, usually an association of general ideas, which operates to cause the Symbol to be interpreted as referring to that Object" (p. 276). A symbol, then, is linked with its referent by convention. Symbols are arbitrary, bearing no inherent relationship to that which they denote. There is no sense, for example, in which the word "dog" has any "dog-ness" in it, in either its spoken or written form. One might object that any particular individual's use of the word "dog" is in fact *not* arbitrary—an individual's use of any particular word is deter-mined by the way that word is used in the language community. This objection makes it clear that in stating that a sign is arbitrary, we must state exactly what it is arbitrary with respect to. We can thus clarify the definition of a symbol in the following way: *A symbol is a sign that refers to the object that it denotes in a way that is arbitrary with respect to the process of conventionalization that established it.* In the case of learned signs, then, we would say that they are symbolic if they are arbitrary with respect to the rele-vant learning mechanism. A child's use of the word "dog" is sym-bolic because this use simply reflects the convention used by the language community. We can evaluate the signs used in innate animal communication systems in a similar way. Although it may seem strange to talk of innate symbols, it is completely consistent with the definition of what it is to be symbolic. In the case of in-nate communication, the process of conventionalization is natural selection. Animal signaling behavior is symbolic if it is arbitrary with respect to the process of natural selection.

	Non-Symbolic	Symbolic
Innate	Threat displays Bee dance Facial expressions	Most alarm calls
Learned	Chimpanzee gestures Road signs	Human language

Figure 12.2 Classifying communicative behavior with respect to innateness and symbolic reference.

12.4 Classifying Communicative Behavior

The distinctions made in the previous section give us the means to classify systems of communication based on whether they are innate or learned, and whether they are symbolic or not. Figure 12.2 shows the four possible combinations under this classification. In the following sections, I will look at each of these classes of communication in turn.

Innate Nonsymbolic Systems

One way in which reference can be nonsymbolic is for the sign to be what Peirce calls *iconic*. An icon refers by virtue of resemblance, such as the way a road sign indicates that a road is slippery by using wavy lines. In the realm of animal communication, iconic signaling often occurs in threat-display behavior, where aggressive intent is conveyed by such actions as the lowering of antlers or the revealing of teeth—actions that perceptually resemble the preparatory motions associated with an aggressive attack. Another example of iconic communication is the dance done by honeybees to convey information about the location of food sources to other bees in the hive. The bee "language," decoded by von Frisch (1974), is used by a bee that has discovered a source of food to inform others of its approximate angle and distance from the hive. A bee, upon returning to the hive, performs a tail-wagging dance in the shape of a figure eight. The amount of time it takes the bee to traverse the straight, central portion of the dance indicates the distance to the food source, while the angle of this traversal gives the angle of the source using the position of sun as a reference. The degree of vigorousness of the dances indicates the quality of food at the source.

Communicative behavior need not be iconic to be nonsymbolic. Many animal signals derive from intention movements through a process of ritualization (Tinbergen 1952). Consider the problem faced by flocks of birds that take flight as a group. If one bird is preparing to fly, the others need to recognize this and prepare to fly as well. To accomplish this, natural selection can tune the behavior of the birds such that the preparatory motions of other birds trigger the initiating of flight. In Peirce's terms, this form of reference is *indexical*—the preparatory motions signal a bird's intent to take flight by virtue of being part of the same causal chain of events.

Innate Symbolic Systems
Humans are not the only species that have a symbolic system of communication (contrary to Deacon [1997], who uses the term "symbol" in an unorthodox way). Many nonhuman animals have innate symbolic systems of communication—arbitrary systems of reference that have been tuned by natural selection. The process by which natural selection can tune such systems is well understood, both mathematically (Warneryd 1993; Blume, Kim, and Sobel 1993; Kim and Sobel 1995; Skyrms 1996) and computationally (see, for example, Oliphant 1997).

Perhaps the most commonly cited example of an innate system of arbitrary reference is the alarm call behavior of the vervet monkey (Strusaker 1967; Seyfarth, Cheney, and Marlor 1980a; Seyfarth, Cheney, and Marler 1980b). Vervets use a system of alarm calls that distinguishes the different kinds of danger posed by various species of their predators. When a vervet sees an eagle, it gives an alarm call that sounds like a cough. When a large cat such as a leopard is seen, a barking sound is made. When a vervet sees a snake, it utters a chuttering sound. Each of these alarms calls causes other vervets that hear them to engage in evasive behavior appropriate to the predator: in response to the eagle call, the monkeys look up or run into bushes, the calls given in response to large cats cause vervets to run into trees, and the snake call causes the monkeys to stand up and look in the grass. That the monkeys are responding to the alarm calls, and not to the predators themselves is indicated by the results of playback studies. Seyfarth, Cheney, and Marler (1980b) have shown that vervets make the appropriate response to recorded calls in the absence of an actual predator.

The vervet system is symbolic because there is no sense in which the acoustic properties of the alarm calls are intrinsically related to either the predators they correspond to, or the appropriate evasive behavior. In fact, it is difficult to imagine what iconic alarm call would be like, unless it imitated some sound that the predator made.

While the vervet alarm call system involves a learned component, it is best thought of as an innate system of communication. Comparisons of recordings of spontaneous calls given by immature animals to alarm calls given by adults indicates that learning is relatively unimportant in determining the acoustic properties of calling behavior (Seyfarth and Cheney 1986; Hauser 1996). The set of alarm calls appears to be innately constrained. Vervets do, however, learn to fine-tune the use of alarm calls through experience. Seyfarth and Cheney (1986), in analyzing the use of the eagle alarm call, have found that it initially is used by infants and juveniles in response to perceptually similar nonpredatory species such as vultures. Only later in life does it get narrowed to be a response to the eagles that prey on the vervets. While learning plays a role in tuning the specificity of an alarm call, it seems that the general danger categories such as "airbone eagle-like predator" are determined innately (Hauser 1996). Because adult vervets generally ignore false-alarm calls by infants, it seems likely that these categories get narrowed through selective reinforcement; only in the case of a true predator will an infant's alarm call generate a response from others.

A schematic diagram of this view of the vervet call system is shown in figure 12.3. Solid lines represent associations that are innate, while dashed lines represent learned associations. The association between a given danger category (such as "airborne predator") and the corresponding alarm call (a coughing sound) is innately specified. The association between a danger category and the precise nature of the perceptual stimulus that represents it is learned. The plasticity in the system involves perception, rather than communication. What is the reason for this plasticity? It may give some flexibility in the class of predators an alarm call can refer to. Perhaps more likely, however, is the possibility that the plasticity only exists because it isn't feasible to genetically encode the precise perceptual description of a predator.

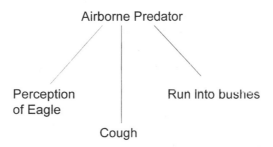

Figure 12.3 Innate and learned components of the vervet alarm call system. The top diagram represents the system as a whole, while the diagram on the bottom shows the alarm call behavior in response to eagles. Solid lines represent innate associations, while dashed lines represent associations that are learned.

Learned Nonsymbolic Systems

Learned systems of communication are extremely rare. By far, the more common case is for communication to involve an innate mapping between signal and meaning. One of the few cases where we do find evidence of learned communication is, perhaps unsurprisingly, in the apes. Chimpanzees use a wide variety of gestural signals to mediate social interaction, using them in situations such as play, caregiving, and aggressive and sexual interactions. At least some aspects of this gestural communication appear to be learned. Evidence that this is the case comes both from observation of the animals in their natural habitat (Goodall 1986), and from observational studies of gesturing in captive chimpanzees placed in a physical and social setting designed to resemble that which exists in the wild (Tomasello et al. 1985; Tomasello, Gust, and Frost 1989; Tomasello et al. 1994). The communicative behavior shows variation across groups and individuals, and also changes ontogenetically, apparently adapting to the changing social environment as the animal grows from infant to adult (Tomasello, Gust, and Frost 1989).

Although the animals do seem to learn to use gestures, this communicative behavior is of a specific and limited kind. The gestures tend to be simple, ritualized shortcuts, where a component of a behavior is used as a signal for the entire sequence of action. An example is an infant touching its mother's arm as a nursing request. This signal is a ritualized version of an action that initially involved the infant moving its mother's arm to get access to the nipple (Tomasello 1990). Tomasello (1996) calls this process *ontogenetic ritualization*. As the name suggests, this process can be seen as a learning equivalent of the ritualization of innate behaviors described in section 12.3.

Chimpanzee gestural communication, then, is indexical rather than symbolic, with the signal being related causally to the meaning it represents. Because of the derived nature of the signals that are used, the ritualization process limits what meanings can be referred to. Communication involving more arbitrary relationships between signal and meaning would be much more difficult to establish through such ritualization.

Learned Symbolic Systems

Although, as the previous several sections have shown, there are a variety of nonhuman communication systems that are either learned or symbolic, human language seems to be the only system that is both. I would argue that this is true despite the results of a large number of studies demonstrating the ability of a variety of species to learn to use symbolic systems of communication (Hayes and Hayes 1951; Gardener and Gardener 1969; Premack 1971; Herman, Richards, and Wolz 1984; Pepperberg 1987). The key issue here is what it means to say that a system of communication is learned. In the cases cited above, the system was designed by the researchers and explicitly taught to the animals using a reinforcement-based training program. These studies do not constitute evidence that the species in question are capable of supporting a learned symbolic system of communication because there is no evidence that the system would perpetuate in a population of animals without human intervention.

Work done by Savage-Rumbaugh and colleagues with bonobo chimpanzees comes close to providing such evidence. The observation that an infant bonobo showed evidence of having learned a communication task that not he, but his mother was being trained in indicated that perhaps explicit reinforcement was not required (Savage-Rumbaugh et al. 1986). Although this kind of study is exactly what is needed to refine our understanding of the differences (and similarities) between humans and other apes, it has not yet demonstrated learned symbolic communication among bonobos. Instead, it has shown that, under the right conditions, bonobos can learn a symbolic system of communication from humans. We still have no evidence that bonobos can use and maintain such a system over time, passing it from one generation to the next. The fact that we do not see such systems in the wild would seem to indicate there must be *some* reason for their absence.[1]

12.5 Why Is Learning Hard?

If we accept that human language is the only existing system of learned symbolic communication, the next step is to come up with an explanation as to why this might be the case. What is it that makes a simple learned system more problematic than an equally simple innate system? One possible answer to this question lies in differences in how innate and learned systems are transmitted.

For a system of communication to persist in a population, it must be heritable from one generation to the next. In the case of an innate system, such heritability is trivial. If the innate system has been tuned by natural selection, it is simply transmitted genetically (figure 12.4). In the case of learned communication, however, the system cannot be passed on directly from one individual to another. Instead, transmission must be mediated by the communicative behavior itself (figure 12.5). The extent to which such transmission is possible will be determined by how difficult it is to learn a communication system by being exposed to its use by others.

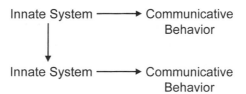

Figure 12.4 Transmission of an innate communication system. The representation of the system is passed on genetically.

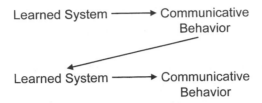

Figure 12.5 Transmission of a learned communication system. The representation of the system cannot be passed on directly, but must be mediated by the production of and exposure to communicative behavior.

The results of computational simulation work have given us a good understanding of what is required for a population of individuals to establish and maintain a learned system of communication. This simulation work can be separated into two forms of learning: those that use some form of reinforcement learning (Yanco and Stein 1993; Hutchins and Hazelhurst 1995; Steels 1996; Murciano and Millan 1996), and those that use a purely observational model (Oliphant and Batali 1997; Oliphant 1997). Reinforcement learning makes use of some form of error signal (generally, whether or not an attempt at communicating was successful) to allow individuals to adapt their communicative behavior. In a purely observational learning paradigm, a communication system is learned solely on the basis of observing the communicative behavior of others.

The value of these simulation studies is that they give us information about what is computationally required of a learner, and what they tell us is quite startling. Very simple learning mechanisms seem to be sufficient. In fact, Hebbian learning, perhaps the simplest form of learning one could imagine, has been found to be sufficiently powerful to establish and sustain a learned system of communication in a population of observational learners (Oliphant 1997).

This result would seem to indicate that making a transition from innate to learned systems of communication should not be particularly difficult. How are we to reconcile this with the fact that learned communication is so rare? The answer, I think, lies in the assumptions that are made by the simulation studies with regard to what information a learner has access to. In the case of reinforcement learning, it is assumed that there is a reliable error signal that tells learners whether they are communicating appropriately or not. It is not clear, however, that such an error signal exists. In the case of human language, for example, it is argued that children do not get sufficient reinforcement from their parents (Wexler and Culicover 1980; Crain 1991).

In the case of observational learning, what has been assumed is that learners have access to the communicative behavior of others in the form of signal/meaning pairs. Having access to the signals that others are producing seems reasonable, but how is a learner to have reliable access to the meanings that others are intending to convey?[2]

12.6 The Problem of Observing Meaning

Understanding the problem a learner faces in determining the meaning a signal is intended to convey is central, I think, to explaining the rarity of learned communication. In the case of innate communication, the problem does not exist—simply for the reason that learning is not required for the system to be transmitted from one generation to the next.

The difficulty of observing meaning also accounts for why learned symbolic communication is so rare. In an innate system, transmission of an arbitrary sign is no more difficult than transmitting an iconic one—such distinctions are unimportant to the process of biological reproduction. This is not the case with respect to the transmission of a learned system. Iconic or indexical signs refer by resemblance and causal relationship, respectively. In both cases, the signal gives direct information about the meaning it refers to. In contrast, a symbol will, by definition, bear no discernible relationship to the meaning to which it refers—the association is purely conventional.

Learned symbolic systems of communication are rare, then, because it is in the case of symbols that the problem of observing meaning is most difficult. Humans seem to be the only species that have managed to find a way to cope with this difficulty. Children are able to learn to use words because they are adept at determining their meaning from the context in which they appear. They seem to simplify the task of deciding what a word denotes through knowledge of the existence of taxonomic categories (Markman 1989), awareness of the pragmatic context (Tomasello 1995), and reading the intent of the speaker (Bloom 1997). In addition, human adults seem, at least to some degree, to make the meaning of their utterances more salient to the child. When talking to young children, adults modify their speech along a number of dimensions, and this may aid the child in acquisition (Snow 1977).

12.7 Discussion

I have argued in this chapter that human language is the only existing system of learned symbolic communication. While other species use innate symbolic systems, or learned nonsymbolic systems, cultural transmission of arbitrary reference seems to exist only in humans. This uniqueness can be explained by looking at how the problem of transmission is different in the case of learned communication, even if the communication system itself is no more complex. While innate systems can simply be transmitted genetically, learned systems must be acquired ontogenetically. Learned systems cannot be transmitted directly, but must instead involve acquisition of the behavior produced by others.

Although simulation work has shown that very simple learning mechanisms are sufficient to support this process of acquisition, this has been based on the assumption that a learner has easy access to the meaning that a signal is intended to convey. Getting such access is likely to be a nontrivial process, particularly in the case of symbolic reference, where the signal and meaning are linked purely by convention.

Given this, I propose that a key milestone in the evolution of language is the ability to transmit a learned symbolic system of communication from one generation to the next. It is only when this ability is in place that the stage is set for the development of linguistic complexity. At this point, perhaps the addition of syntactic structure will require additional biological change. It is possible that the ability to communicate by combining sequences of signals requires cognitive skill that other animals do not have.

It is also possible, however, that the problem of transmitting a learned symbolic system is the primary factor limiting the evolution of language ability. Perhaps, the achievement of syntactic communication is an extension that is comparatively less difficult. That this might be true is supported by evidence of the use of syntactic forms in nonhuman animals (Greenfield and Savage-Rumbaugh 1990), and computational work showing that syntactic structure can emerge on a cultural, rather than evolutionary time scale (Batali 1997; Hutchins and Hazelhurst, forthcoming; Kirby, to appear; Hurford, to appear). In any case, we should not be preoccupied with the evolution of syntax, and should give careful examination to more basic features that may separate the communicative ability of humans from that of other animals.

Acknowledgments

I would like to thank Simon Kirby, Jim Hurford, and Robbins Burling for helpful discussion on the ideas presented in this chapter. This research was funded by ESRC grant R000237551 and a research fellowship at the Collegium Budapest Institute for Advanced Study.

Notes

1. This assumes, of course, that we have an accurate picture of what the animals are doing in the wild. While it is possible that learned symbolic systems exist that we are unaware of, and we must be open to this possibility, it seems best to theorize based on what evidence we currently have available to us.
2. [Editorial note: Work of A. Billard, K. Dautenhahn, J. Demiris, and G. Hayes addresses the learning of meaning of symbols in simulations and robotics experiments via imitation games *without access to "intended meaning."* The learner follows a teacher that emits arbitrary signals (symbols) associated to its perceptions. By following the teacher and observing this use of symbols, the learner—which may have a *different* body, sensors, and effectors than the teacher—comes to associate its own perceptions with these signals, allowing it to learn at least a small symbolic vocabulary. "Observing meaning" in these studies is thus grounded in shared similar (but not identical) experience resulting as a consequence of following the teacher while perceiving the symbols it uses. Subtleties include the important fact that there is a *delay* in the follower's experiencing stimuli similar to those experienced by the teacher as compared to its reception of the signal. (See chapter 11 by Aude Billard in this volume and references cited there.)—CJN]

References

Batali, J. Computational simulations of the emergence of grammar. In J. Hurford, C. Knight, and M. Studdert-Kennedy (eds.), *Evolution of Language: Social and Cognitive Bases for the Emergence of Phonology and Syntax.* Cambridge, UK: Cambridge University Press, 1997.

Bickerton, D. *Language and Species.* Chicago: Chicago University Press, 1990.

Bloom, P. Intentionality and word learning. *Trends in Cognitive Sciences* 1(1): 9–12, 1997.

Blume, A., Y. Kim, and J. Sobel. Evolutionary stability in games of communication. *Games and Economic Behavior* 5: 547–575, 1993.

Crain, S. Language acquistion in the absence of experience. *Behavioral and Brain Sciences* 14: 597–611, 1991.

Deacon, T. *The Symbolic Species: The Co-evolution of Language and the Brain.* New York: W. W. Norton, 1997.

de Saussure, F. *Course in General Linguistics.* New York: McGraw-Hill, 1959.

Gardener, B., and P. Gardener. Teaching sign language to a chimpanzee. *Science* 165: 664–672, 1969.

Goodall, J. *The Chimpanzees of Gombe*. Cambridge, Mass.: Harvard University Press, 1986.

Greenfield, P., and E. Savage-Rumbaugh. Grammatical combination in *Pan paniscus*: Processes of learning and invention in the evolution and development of language. In S. Parker and K. Gibson (eds.), *"Language" and Intelligence in Monkeys and Apes*, pp. 540–578. Cambridge, UK: Cambridge University Press, 1990.

Hauser, M. *The Evolution of Communication*. Cambridge, Mass.: MIT Press, 1996.

Hayes, K., and C. Hayes. The intellectual development of a home-raised chimpanzee. *Proceedings of the American Philosophical Society* 95: 105, 1951.

Herman, L., D. Richards, and J. Wolz. Comprehension of sentences by bottlenosed dolphins. *Cognition* 16: 129–219, 1984.

Hurford, J. Social interaction favours linguistic generalization. In C. Knight, M. Studdert-Kennedy, and J. Hurford (eds.), *The Emergence of Language*. London, to appear.

Hutchins, E., and B. Hazelhurst. How to invent a lexicon: The development of shared symbols in interaction. In N. Gilbert and R. Conte (eds.), *Artificial Societies: The Computer Simulation of Social Life*. London: UCL Press, 1995.

Hutchins, E., and B. Hazelhurst. The emergence of propositions from the coordination of talk and action in a shared world. Forthcoming.

Kim, Y., and J. Sobel. An evolutionary approach to pre-play communication. *Econometrica* 65(5): 1181–1193, 1995.

Kirby, S. Syntax without natural selection: How compositionality emerges from vocabulary in a population of learners. In C. Knight, M. Studdert-Kennedy, and J. Hurford (eds.), *The Emergence of Language*. London, to appear.

Knight, C., M. Studdert-Kennedy, and J. Hurford (eds.), *The Emergence of Language*. London, to appear.

Lewis, D. *Convention: A Philosophical Study*. Cambridge, Mass.: Harvard University Press, 1969.

Markman, E. *Categorization and Naming in Children: Problems of Induction*. Cambridge, Mass.: MIT Press, 1989.

Murciano, A., and J. Millan. Learning and signaling behaviors and specialization in cooperative agents. *Adaptive Behavior* 5(1): 5–28, 1996.

Newmeyer, F. J. Functional explanation in lingusitics and the origins of language. *Language and Communication* 11: 3–28, 1991.

Oliphant, M. *Formal Approaches to Innate and Learned Communication: Laying the Foundation for Language*. Ph.D. thesis, University of California, San Diego, 1997.

Oliphant, M., and J. Batali. Learning and the emergence of coordinated communication. *Center for Research on Language Newsletter* 11(1): 1997.

Peirce, C. *Collected Papers of Charles Saunders Peirce*. Vol. 2, *Elements of Logic*. Cambridge, Mass.: Harvard University Press, 1932.

Pepperberg, I. Evidence for conceptual quantitative abilities in the African parrot: Labeling of cardinal sets. *Ethology* 75: 37–61, 1987.

Pinker, S., and P. Bloom. Natural language and natural selection. *Behavioral and Brain Sciences* 13: 707–784, 1990.

Premack, D. Language in chimpanzee? *Science* 172: 808–822, 1971.

Savage-Rumbaugh, E., K. McDonald, R. Sevcik, W. Hopkins, and E. Rubert. Spontaneous symbol acquisition and communicative use by pygmy chipmanzees (*Pan paniscus*). *Journal of Experimental Psychology: General* 115: 211–235, 1986.

Seyfarth, R., and D. Cheney. Vocal development in vervet monkeys. *Animal Behavior* 34: 1640–1658, 1986.

Seyfarth, R., D. Cheney, and P. Marler. Monkey responses to three different alarm calls: Evidence for predator classification and semantic communication. *Science* 210: 801–803, 1980a.

Seyfarth, R., D. Cheney, and P. Marler. Vervet monkey alarm calls: Semantic communication in a free-ranging environment. *Animal Behavior* 28: 1070–1094, 1980b.

Skyrms, B. *Evolution of the Social Contract*. Cambridge, UK: Cambridge University Press, 1996.

Snow, C. Mothers' speech research: From input to interaction. In C. Snow and C. Ferguson (eds.), *Talking to Children: Language Input and Acquisition*, pp. 31–49. Chicago: University of Chicago Press, 1977.

Steels, L. Self-organizing vocabularies. In *Preproceedings of the Fifth Artificial Life Workshop on the Synthesis and Simulation of Living Systems*, Nara, Japan. Also in C. G. Langton and K. Shimohara (eds.), *Artificial Life V*, pp. 179–184, Cambridge, Mass.: MIT Press (1997), 1996.

Strusaker, T. Auditory communication among vervet monkeys (*Ceropithecus aethiops*). In S. Altmann and K. Gibson (eds.), *Social Communication among Primates*, pp. 281–324. Chicago: University of Chicago Press, 1967.

Tinbergen, N. Derived activities: Their causation, biological significance, origin, and emancipation during evolution. *Quaterly Review of Biology* 27: 1–32, 1952.

Tomasello, M. Cultural transmission in the tool use and communicatory signaling of chimpanzees? In S. Parker and K. Gibson (eds.), *Language and Intelligence in Monkeys and Apes: Comparative Developmental Perspectives*. Cambridge, UK: Cambridge University Press, 1990.

Tomasello, M. Pragmatic contexts for early verb learning. In M. Tomasello and W. Merriman (eds.), *Beyond Names for Things: Young Children's Acquisition of Verbs*. Hillsdale, N.J.: Erlbaum, 1995.

Tomasello, M. Do apes ape? In C. Heyes and B. Galef (eds.), *Social Learning in Animals: The Roots of Culture*, pp. 319–436. San Diego: Academic Press, 1996.

Tomasello, M., J. Call, K. Nagell, R. Olguin, and M. Carpenter. The learning and use of gestural signals by young chimpanzees: A trans-generational study. *Primates* 35: 137–154, 1994.

Tomasello, M., B. George, A. Kruger, J. Farrar, and E. Evans. The development of gestural communication in young chimpanzees. *Journal of Human Evolution* 14: 175–186, 1985.

Tomasello, M., D. Gust, and T. Frost. A longitudinal investigation of gestural communication in young chimpanzees. *Primates* 30: 35–50, 1989.

von Frisch, K. Decoding the language of the bee. *Science* 185: 663–668, 1974.

Warneryd, K. Cheap talk, coordination, and evolutionary stability. *Games and Economic Behavior* 5: 532–546, 1993.

Wexler, K., and P. Culicover. *Formal Principles of Language Acquisition*. Cambridge, Mass.: MIT Press, 1980.

Yanco, H., and L. Stein. An adaptive communication protocol for cooperating mobile robots. In J. Meyer, H. Roitblat, and S. Wilson (eds.), *From Animals to Animats 2: Proceedings of the Second International Conference on Simulation of Adaptive Behavior*. Cambridge, Mass.: MIT Press, 1993.

13 Imitation as a Dual-Route Process Featuring Predictive and Learning Components: A Biologically Plausible Computational Model

John Demiris and Gillian Hayes

13.1 Introduction

We do not exist alone. Humans and most other animal species live in societies where the behavior of an individual influences and is influenced by other members of the society. Within societies, an individual learns not only on its own, through classical conditioning and reinforcement, but to a large extent through its conspecifics, by observation and imitation. Species from rats to birds to humans have been observed to turn to their conspecifics for efficient learning of useful knowledge. One of the most important mechanisms for the transmission of this knowledge is imitation.

At the heart of the ability to imitate lies a mechanism that matches perceived external behaviors with equivalent internal behaviors of its own, recruiting information from the perceptual, motor, and memory systems. This mechanism has been shown to be present even in newborn infants, which have been observed to imitate the facial gestures of their caretakers. In humans, malfunctions of this mechanism, surfaced as an inability to imitate, have been used as detectors of pathological disorders including autism and some forms of apraxia. This chapter presents a computational model of this mechanism.

Why is this an interesting problem? From an engineering perspective, designing an architecture that equips robots with the ability to imitate will allow the possibility for learning through demonstration.

A human demonstrator can show an example of the task and the robot can learn by imitating the human. This will give people unfamiliar with robot programming the ability to teach robots to perform tasks. From a scientific perspective, research on imitation spans several disciplines including neurophysiology, psychology, psychophysics, and pathology. The available data are often found at completely different levels of description, from neural recordings to behavioral data from human neuropathological examinations (for reviews, see Carey, Perrett, and Oram 1997; Schaal 1999). Computational modeling has the potential to integrate data from several disciplines in a common platform. The need for very precise descriptions so that mechanisms can be implementable on computational and robotic platforms illuminates gaps in theories, and allows research to focus on filling these gaps. Even more important, computational modeling enables the development of predictions, which can be an important tool for directing further experiments.

In brief, this chapter offers the following contributions:

- It introduces a distinction between passive and active imitation, to distinguish between approaches where the imitator goes through a "perceive-recognize-reproduce" cycle (passive imitation) and the motor systems are involved only during the "reproduce" phase, and the approaches where the imitator's motor systems are actively involved even during the perception process (active imitation).
- It develops a computational architecture inspired by Meltzoff's Active Intermodal Matching (AIM) mechanism (Meltzoff and Moore 1997), hypothesized to underlie *infant* imitation. The architecture (which belongs to the "passive" category) is capable of imitating and acquiring any demonstrated movement that is within the capabilities of the imitator, but its "passive" characteristics do not correlate well with some of the biological data available for *adult* imitation.
- To overcome the disadvantages of the passive architecture above, a novel, distributed imitation architecture with "active" properties is developed. The novelty of this architecture lies in that the same motor structures that are responsible for the *generation* of a movement are recruited in order to perform movement *perception*. Imitation becomes an active, predictive process: instead of going through a passive "perceive-recognize-reproduce" cycle, the imitator actively generates possible behaviors in parallel, executes them on internal forward models (internal simulators, or predictors) and selects among them based on the quality of the predictions they offer with respect to the states of the ongoing demonstration. However, the disadvantage of this route is that it is not capable of imitating demonstrated movements not already present in the imitator's repertoire.
- In order to get the best of both worlds, the two architectures above are combined into the final dual-route architecture: known movements are imitated through the active route; if the movement is novel, evident from the fact that all internal behaviors have failed

to predict adequately well, control is passed to the passive route, which is able to imitate and acquire the demonstrated movement.

- Computational experiments are performed that demonstrate the ability of the architecture to imitate, as well as acquire, a variety of movements, including unknown, partially known, and fully known sequences of movements. They also reveal the inability of the architecture to match demonstrated movements with existing equivalent ones of its own, when they are demonstrated at speeds unattainable by the imitator.

- Finally, the developed architecture is proposed as a model of primate movement imitation mechanisms. A comparison is performed between the characteristics of the architecture and biological data on human and monkey imitation mechanisms. It is shown that they correlate well, thus offering possible explanations for the biological data. Perhaps more important, the computational experiments offer *testable* predictions regarding the behavior of the biological mechanisms.

13.2   On Passive Imitation

The potential of imitation to ease the robot programming process was recognized by robotics researchers who realized that instead of going through lengthy and complex programming, robots could learn how to perform various tasks by observing a human demonstrator. Research by Ikeuchi and Suehiro (1992), Suehiro and Ikeuchi (1992), Kuniyoshi, Inaba, and Inoue (1994), Hovland, Sikka, and McCarragher (1996), Kaiser and Dillmann (1996), Kang and Ikeuchi (1997), and Yeasin and Chaudhuri (1997) has successfully used human demonstration to program robots to perform assembly tasks. The techniques that have been utilized to achieve this differ, but the philosophy is essentially the same—the imitation process proceeds serially through three stages: perception (visual systems), recognition (memory systems), and reproduction (motor systems). There is no substantial interaction between the three stages, and the motor systems are only involved at the final reproduction stage.

Approaches by Hayes and Demiris (1994), Dautenhahn (1995), Demiris and Hayes (1996), and Billard (1999) in the mobile robotics domain have attempted to follow a different approach by trying to devise imitation mechanisms that will work directly *without* a recognition stage. This line of work is relatively new, but it makes an important distinction: the imitator is not imitating because it is understanding what the demonstrator is showing, rather, it is understanding it *because* it is imitating. Imitation is used as a mechanism for bootstrapping further learning and understanding.

The distinction between the two approaches is new in the field of robotics but not in psychology. Researchers studying imitation in infants have made a similar distinction while formulating hypotheses regarding the mechanisms underlying early infant imitation. Meltzoff and Moore (1977) first reported young infants, between 12 and 21 days old in the original report, being able to imitate both facial and manual gestures, including tongue protrusion, mouth opening, and lip protrusion. The experimenters suggested that the infants are able to represent visual and proprioceptive information in a form common to both modalities. These results were against the popular belief of the time, that infants are only capable of imitation after 8 to 12 months from birth, and that imitation abilities are a result of the infant's cognitive development. Various hypotheses regarding the mechanisms underlying this phenomenon were compared by Meltzoff and Moore (1989), including the "innate release mechanism (IRM) model," which postulates that the demonstrator's behavior simply triggers and releases equivalent fixed-action-patterns (FAPs) by the infant. The IRM model relies on the existence of a set of FAPs, but there isn't a precise specification of what this set is (Meltzoff and Moore 1989). IRM was judged to be an unlikely candidate for two reasons:

- The range of actions imitated was wide, which would mean that the infant would have to have a large number of FAPs in its repertoire.
- The fact that the infants attempt to and succeed in improving the quality of the imitated act (Meltzoff 1981).

Meltzoff and Moore (1983, 1989) put forward the "Active Intermodal Mapping" (AIM) hypothesis, which postulates that the infants use the demonstrator's states, perceived visually, as a target against which to direct their own body states, perceived proprioceptively. This hypothesis is particularly attractive in the case of facial or head movements for which the infant has no other way of knowing the state of its own body other than proprioception. The existence of a mechanism that matches stimuli between different modalities has also been advocated by Maurer (1993), but while

Meltzoff's AIM mechanism appears to be activated as a choice made by the infant, Maurer argues that the infant's intermodal matching of stimuli is a by-product of what was termed neonatal "synesthesia": the infant *confuses* input from the different senses. The infant, it is argued, does not register the modality that the stimuli appeared in, but rather it responds to changes in the stimulation's intensity summed over all of the undifferentiated sensory modalities. Synesthesia is hypothesized to be a normal stage of early infant development: it is argued that the primary sensory cortex is not very specialized in infants, but with development it becomes so, the senses become more differentiated, and "true" intermodal matching develops. Whatever the exact mechanism is, the ability of the infant to match stimuli between modalities is well documented, and has been demonstrated between other modalities in addition to the visual/proprioceptive cases mentioned earlier, for example, tactual/visual intermodal matching (Meltzoff 1981, 1993).

At this stage, it is useful to draw parallels between this work and the assembly and mobile robot imitation work mentioned earlier. There are a lot of commonalities between the passive imitation model in assembly robots and the IRM model in infants. Both rely on the existence of a set of predefined action patterns, which are triggered after the perception and classification of the visual input. This set, at least in the robot work, is fixed and frequently tuned to the requirements of the task in hand.

The mobile robot imitation work (Hayes and Demiris 1994; Dautenhahn 1995) is closer to the AIM hypothesis model, since the robots do not attempt to recognize the type of action performed by the demonstrator, but imitate directly. However, there is a difference between AIM and the approach followed by the mobile robot researchers: the robot imitators do not attempt to match the demonstrator's state with their own (as AIM suggests), but usually achieve it by trying to maintain a quantity constant. For example, in Hayes and Demiris (1994), where a robot learns how to negotiate a maze by imitating the movements of another robot, the imitator robot simply tries to maintain the distance between itself and the demonstrator robot constant.

Demiris and Hayes (1996) presented a computational architecture that follows the AIM model more closely, and demonstrated it in the context of imitation of head movements by a robotic head (Demiris et al. 1997). The details of this architecture have been

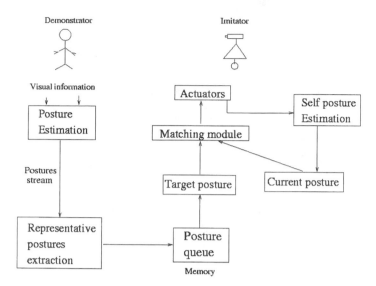

Figure 13.1 The passive imitation architecture.

presented elsewhere (Demiris and Hayes 1996; Demiris et al. 1997), but the essential parts are shown in figure 13.1.

The visual stimuli from the visual perception modules are fed into the posture estimation module, which at each iteration estimates and outputs the current postural state of the demonstrator (posture is defined here as the set of angles between all connected body parts of the agent). This posture stream is stored in memory after being filtered so only the "representative postures" (the postures that are sufficient to define the movement sequence to be reproduced) are retained. The postures are then fed into the movement-matching module, which outputs the motor commands needed to match these postures with equivalent postures by the imitator, perceived proprioceptively.

Experiments performed utilizing this architecture on a robot head in the context of imitation of head movements performed by a human demonstrator have shown (Demiris et al. 1997) that the architecture is capable of imitating any kind of demonstrated movement that the hardware of the imitator system can afford. It does so by having very low requirements on needed information: the postures of the demonstrator, perceived visually, and those of the imitator, perceived proprioceptively. The choice of posture as the unit of representation is not arbitrary. The postures of the demonstrator and imitator are always well defined and computable. In addition, postures have a high biological significance: animals frequently use them for communicative purposes (Bruce and Green 1990; Groothuis 1993)—for example, threat, appeasement, and mating postures, and human body language. Their biological significance might even have led to the development of specialized feature detectors that respond selectively to postures. Indeed, work by Perrett and his colleagues has shown the existence of cells in the superior temporal sulcus (STS) area of the monkey's brain that respond when a demonstrator assumes certain postures—for example, cells that are responsive to specific head views (Perrett et al. 1990, 1991). Cells selective to other body parts have also been reported (Tanaka 1993; see also Carey, Perrett, and Oram 1997 for an overview).

Similarly, as Helms Tillery, Soechting, and Ebner (1996) point out, physiological studies throughout the somatosensory system have revealed discharges related to self static limb postures: unit activity is usually monotonically related to changes in joint angle. The degree of accuracy of a proprioception-based estimate of the static posture is not completely determined, and it has been shown that it improves when visual information about the state of the body part is also available (Desmurget et al. 1995), or is even being partially substituted by it when proprioception is not available in deafferented patients (Ghez and Sainburg 1994). Scott and Kalaska (1995) demonstrated that cell activity in the monkey motor cortex is highly sensitive to changes in arm posture even if the resulting hand trajectory remains similar.

Finally, evidence that at least some type of movements are controlled on the basis of a joint angular error has been provided by Desmurget and Prablanc (1997), who have shown that three-dimensional upper-limb movements are controlled via a mechanism that is comparing an estimate of the current postural state with a target value.

By relying on information known to exist in the human brain and requiring only an intermodal matching mechanism that is known to be within the capabilities of infants, the passive architecture above manifests itself as an attractive model for the infant imitation abilities. Could it be a universal model for movement imitation for later ages too? There are two issues that are against this. First, by virtue of its design, there is no concept of known and novel movements: all demonstrations are processed and imitated through the same mechanism. In addition, there is a clear separation between perception and action: the motor system is involved only at the late stages of imitation. Both these aspects have been challenged by recent biological data—particularly human brain activation data—that indicate that actions are processed differently if they are known to the imitator than if they are novel, and that the motor system is already actively involved during the perception phase of the imitation. In the next section, a different type of architecture will be introduced that tackles these issues and explains these biological data better. However, it would be premature to dismiss the "passive" architecture as invalid. Later on in this chapter, this architecture will be combined with the "active" architecture of the next section: it will be used as a learning component in what will be the final dual-route active-passive imitation architecture.

13.3 Active Imitation

Having seen the advantages and disadvantages of the passive imitation approach, this section will describe work toward the development of an architecture that tightly couples the perception and the generation of an action. The concept of internal forward models will be introduced, and the imitation architecture will subsequently be developed as a parallel set of behaviors paired with forward models. Using a dynamics simulator of a thirteen-degrees-of-freedom robot, it will be demonstrated how such an architecture can be used to generate an action as well as perceiving it when generated by others.

Definitions

The architecture that will be described makes extensive use of the concepts of behaviors and of forward models. A forward model of a controlled object (a "plant" as it is known in the control literature) is a function that, given the current state of the plant and a control command to be applied on it, outputs the predicted next state. Also, for the purposes of this work, a behavior is defined as a function that, given the current state of the plant and the target goal(s), outputs the control commands that are needed in order to achieve or maintain the goal(s). Target goals might be implicit or need to be made explicit. For example, for a pick-object behavior, the target object to be picked up must be stated explicitly and fed to the behavior, while for a head-nodding-yes behavior, the target goal (i.e., moving the head downward) is already defined implicitly and the current state is enough to determine the motor commands needed to execute this behavior. A behavior is similar to what is known in the control literature as an "inverse model"; however, contrary to behaviors, inverse models do not usually utilize feedback about the current state, but output commands in a feed-forward manner. The boundary between behavior and inverse model however, is not a rigid one since, as Wolpert and Kawato (1998) pointed out, "even control strategies, such as feedback control, which do not explicitly invoke an inverse model can be thought of as implicitly constructing an inverse model."

Combinations of forward and inverse models have been used for various applications such as arm trajectory formation (Wada and Kawato 1993) and supervised learning (Jordan and Rumelhart 1992), among others. Internal forward and inverse models have also been hypothesized to exist in the human brain (Wolpert, Miall, and Kawato 1998), where they are utilized for a variety of tasks including sensorimotor integration (Wolpert, Ghahramani, and Jordan 1995), and motor control (Miall and Wolpert 1996; Wolpert and Kawato 1998).

The Architecture

The fundamental structure of the architecture is a behavior paired with a forward model (figure 13.2). In order to execute a behavior within this structure, the behavior module receives information about the current state (and, optionally, of the target goal[s]), and outputs the motor commands it believes are necessary to achieve or maintain the implicit or explicit target goal(s). The forward

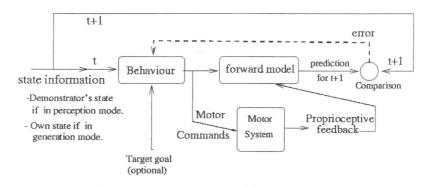

Figure 13.2 The architecture's basic building block, a behavior paired with a forward model.

model provides an estimate of the next state (for time $t + 1$), which is fed back to the behavior, allowing it to adjust any parameters of the behavior (an example of this, as will be shown in the next section [implementation], is adapting the gains of the PID controller used to implement a behavior in order to achieve different movement speeds).

More important, the same structure can be used in order to match a visually perceived demonstrated behavior with the imitator's equivalent motor one. This is done by feeding the demonstrator's current state as perceived by the imitator to the behavior modules and having it generate the motor commands that it would output *if it was in that state and wanted to execute this particular behavior*. The motor commands are inhibited from being sent to the motor system. The forward model outputs an estimated next state, which is a prediction of what the demonstrator's next state will be. This prediction is compared with the actual demonstrator's state at the next time step.

This comparison results in an error signal that can be used to increase or decrease the behavior's confidence value, which is an indicator of how confident the particular imitator's behavior is that it can match the demonstrated behavior.

Figure 13.3 shows the complete architecture, which consists of several of the structures that were described above, operating in parallel. When the demonstrator executes a behavior, the perceived states are fed into the imitator's available behaviors, which generate motor commands that are sent to the forward models. The forward models generate predictions about the demonstrator's next state, which are compared with the actual demonstrator's state at the next time step, and the error signal resulting from this comparison affects the confidence values of the behaviors. At the end of the demonstration (or earlier if required) the behavior with the highest confidence value—that is, the one that is the closest match to the demonstrator's—is selected.

Implementation of the Architecture

This section presents and analyzes the results of implementing the architecture above on a dynamics simulator of a thirteen-degrees-of-freedom robot. The results show that the architecture is capable of correctly selecting the appropriate behavior even when the demonstrator and the imitator have different dynamics. As behav-

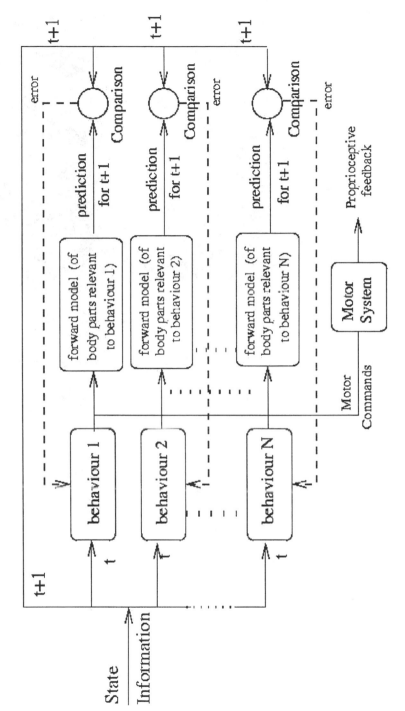

Figure 13.3 The complete active architecture, with multiple behaviors-forward models operating in parallel.

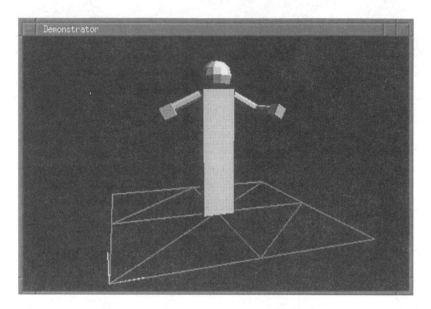

Figure 13.4 Bouncer, the 13 degrees-of-freedom simulated robot.

iors, we implemented various movements involving moving both arms from the rest position to various positions. To allow for easy comparison, compact description, and graph display of the results, we used an "alphabet," the postures of the international standard semaphore code (ISSC), as the final positions that the arms reach (implementing here a total of 26 behaviors). For example, in figure 13.5, the eight windows are a snapshot of behaviors that currently show movement toward letters E, N, L, K, I, E, T, and E, respectively. The experiments involved single movements ("letters") and sequences of movements ("words").

A thirteen-degrees-of-freedom simulated robot was constructed and its dynamics simulated using the DynaMechs dynamical simulation library (McMillan, Orin, and McGhee 1995). "Bouncer" (figure 13.4) has three degrees of freedom at the neck joint, three at each shoulder, one at each elbow, and one at each wrist.

Bouncer operates under the effect of gravity, so if no forces are applied to a joint, the connected body part moves toward the ground. Movement is also subject to friction at the joints. The full experimental platform (figure 13.5) consists of two simulated robots, a demonstrator and an imitator, with similar body structure. In some of the experiments that were conducted, the dynamics of the two robots were the same, while in others they were different. The imitator is allowed to read the demonstrator's postural states

Figure 13.5 The complete experimental platform includes a demonstrator and an imitator (top left and right), and windows for displaying the behaviors that the imitator is currently considering.

(joint angles) in a crude simulation of visual capabilities. To account for the fact that in the case of the imitator, real vision and proprioception never result in perfectly correct values of the visually perceived demonstrator states and proprioceptively perceived imitator states, uniformly distributed random noise is added to both of them before they become available to the imitator.

Behaviors were implemented as sets of representative body postures, coupled with proportional-integral-derivative (PID) controllers (Astrom and Hagglund 1996), that drive the controlled body part(s) through these key postures that constitute the behavior. The PID controllers, one for each of the thirteen controlled joints, output torque values that are calculated by summing three terms: the proportional, integral, and derivative terms, respectively, all of which are based on the error between the current state and the target state. If we take $e(t)$, the error at time t, to be the difference between the target state and the plant's state at time t, then the formula is as follows (for more details see Demiris 1999):

$$T(t) = k_P e(t) + k_i \int^t e(t) \, dt + k_d \frac{de(t)}{dt}$$

where k_p, k_i, k_d are gains coefficients that were determined experimentally and are allowed to adapt (within limits) in order to cope with different movement speeds.

An important issue to note is that the PID controllers perform best within a specific range of gain values; if they are not tuned within this range, they perform suboptimally or might even lead to a destabilization of the controlled plant. The gain parameters k_p, k_i, k_d of all behaviors start having their optimal settings, but are allowed to adapt in order to reduce the prediction error between the anticipated states produced from internally executed behaviors and perceived demonstrator states. A simple adaptation mechanism was implemented for this: at each iteration, if the prediction for a joint angle value proves to be different from the actual value, the corresponding gains for the PID controller that controls that joint angle are increased or reduced (depending on whether the prediction underestimated or overestimated the actual value) by a small constant amount. However, although the gain parameters are allowed to fluctuate, (experimentally determined) upper and lower bounds are imposed in order to prevent the controller from outputting very high torque values and destabilizing the plant. As will be demonstrated later, this renders the perception of particular instances of some behaviors impossible.

The DynaMechs simulation package (McMillan, Orin, and McGhee 1995) includes libraries for simulating rigid body dynamics, and these were used in order to implement the forward models. The procedure involves four steps:

1. Applying the forces supplied by the behavior, taking into account the current state (joint positions and velocities) of the robot.
2. Calculating all the forces exerted (including joint friction and gravity) and the inertias that are present in each joint.
3. Calculating the resulting accelerations recursively for each body part starting from the torso and moving toward the wrist.
4. Calculating the new state (joint positions and velocities).

Although in the experiments reported here the forward models are directly coded in, they can also be learned by randomly generating motor commands, and using the resulting actual state as the target output state for the forward model, in what is sometimes called "motor babbling" (Bullock, Grossberg, and Guenther 1993; Jordan and Rumelhart 1992), which is considered an important stage in the development of infants (Meltzoff and Moore 1997; Meer, Weel, and Lee 1995).

Experimental Results

The first set of experiments reported here consists of the demonstrator performing a behavior that was composed of a single action and the imitator observing it having a set of behaviors in its repertoire. The number of behaviors is not important since the behaviors run in parallel and they are independent of each other (only their confidences need to be compared, a simple computation performed at the end of the demonstration). Experiments with six behaviors are shown for graph clarity reasons.

Figure 13.6 shows an example confidence graph for an experiment where the demonstrator was executing the behavior [R], while the imitator had in its repertoire behaviors [A, B, C, D, E, R]: the imitator's behaviors start initially by having the same confidence, zero, and end up having a confidence correlated with their similarity to the demonstrated behavior. Since the demonstrator is demonstrating the movement toward reaching the letter [R], the imitator's [R] behavior gets the highest confidence, well above zero. All the other behaviors end up well below zero. Since all the behaviors in the first iteration assume the posture of the demonstrator, initially, and for several iterations, they all receive positive reinforcement, because they all look plausible at the onset of the movement. It is only after a few iterations (i.e., after the demonstrated movement has advanced) that some of the behaviors look less plausible (i.e., their predictions are very different from the actual demonstrated states), and their confidence levels begin to reflect that.

Similar results were obtained with a variety of different demonstrator and imitator dynamics, and with behaviors implementing sequences of movements ("words"). (The full set of experimental results can be found in Demiris 1999.)

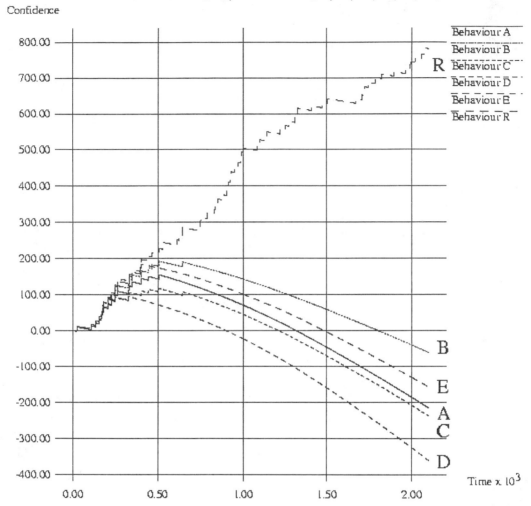

Figure 13.6 Confidences of imitator's internal behaviors [A, B, C, D, E, R] when demonstrator executes behavior [R].

The architecture described in this section only considered the cases where the demonstrated action or sequence of actions were already in the imitator's repertoire. If the demonstrated action is not in the imitator's set of known actions, it will neither be recognized nor imitated. In the next section we deal with these cases, by blending the active imitation architecture of this section with the passive one of the previous section—with the final dual-route architecture able to imitate and learn novel behaviors.a

13.4 Combining Active and Passive Imitation Routes

In the experiments described in the previous section, the demonstrator does not perform any movements that are not already in the imitator's repertoire. One of the imitator's behaviors always ends up having positive confidence and is selected as the one to be imitated. However, if the demonstrator performs a behavior that the imitator does not know, all behaviors end up with negative or zero confidence and none of them is judged as suitable for imitation. This can be used as a trigger condition in order to attempt to learn the demonstrated behavior. Note that in the work reported here, learning is the process of acquiring a behavior—either its trajectory specifications or the motor commands needed to achieve it. Learning as used here does not imply generalization or adaptation to different circumstances or any other processes as used in the field of machine learning (Shavlik and Dietterich 1990).

The solution that is proposed in this section is to use the passive architecture of section 13.2 in order to imitate any movements not already in the imitator's repertoire. Figure 13.7 demonstrates this from a high-level perspective.

The representative postures that are extracted while the unknown behavior is demonstrated are stored and, together with a PID controller, form new behaviors that are added to the imitator's set.

Figure 13.8 shows the confidences plot of the imitator's behaviors [A–F] while the demonstrator executes [R]. All of the imitator's behaviors end up with a negative confidence value; concurrently with the internal execution of candidate behaviors, the passive route was extracting the representative postures of the demonstrated movement. Since none of the behaviors performed adequately during the demonstration, the extracted representative

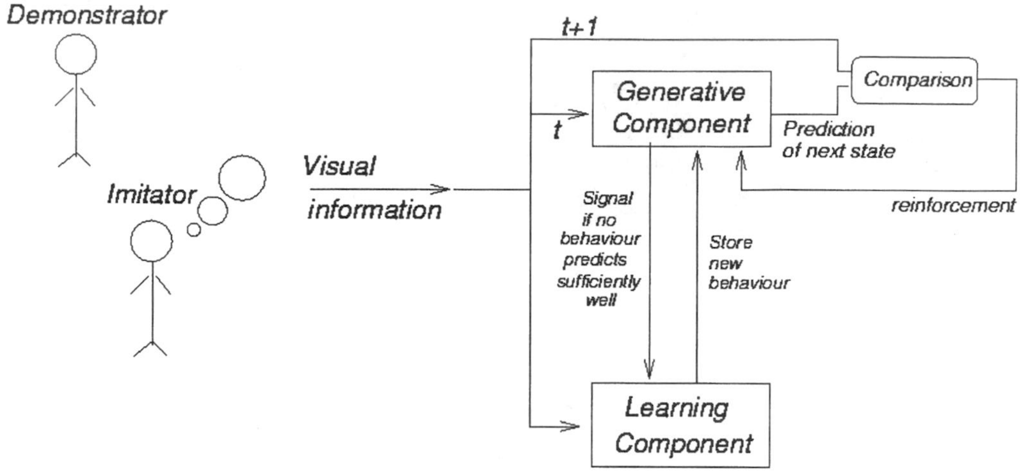

Figure 13.7 The complete dual-route architecture featuring generative-predictive and learning components.

postures, together with a PID controller, formed a new behavior ([learned-R]), which was added to the imitator's repertoire.

The experiment is now repeated with the imitator equipped with the [learned-R] behavior. Figure 13.9 shows the confidences plot of the imitator's internal behaviors while the demonstrator executes [R], where [learned-R] does end up with positive confidence. This demonstrates the ability of the architecture to learn new behaviors through the passive route and utilize them through the active one.

Experiments were also done with sequences of movements, covering the cases where all or some of the demonstrated components of the sequence are known, and the learning of the sequence is required, with equally favorable results (Demiris 1999).

13.5 A Model of Primate Imitation Mechanisms

In the previous sections, two imitation architectures were presented, a passive and an active one, and a combination of them was subsequently developed. In this section, the biological plausibility of the combined dual-route architecture will be examined by proposing it as a model of primate action imitation mechanisms. First, a set of criteria that a model must meet in order to be useful will be presented, followed by an analysis of the model based on these criteria.

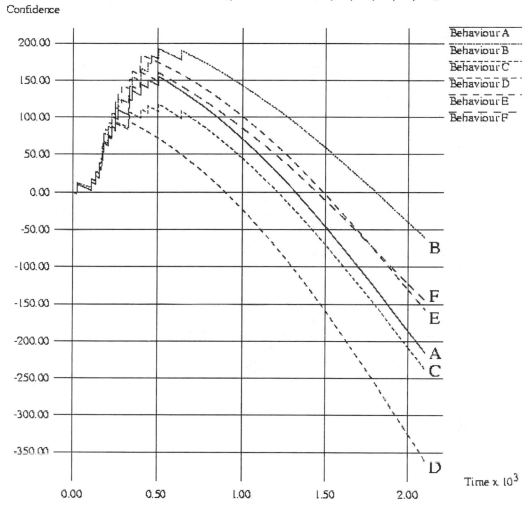

Figure 13.8 Confidences of imitator's internal behaviors [A, B, C, D, E, F] when demonstrator executes behavior [R].

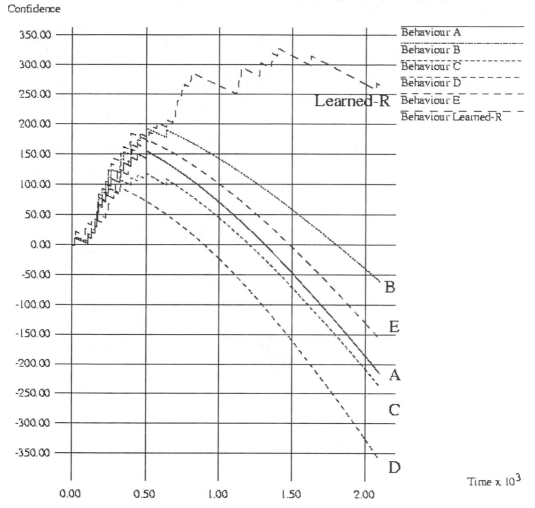

Figure 13.9 Confidences of imitator's internal behaviors [A, B, C, D, E, Learned-R] when demonstrator executes behavior [R].

On Criteria for Useful Models

Despite extensive use of the word "model" in artificial intelligence, cognitive science, and artificial life, there are surprisingly few attempts to develop a set of criteria with respect to what a proper and useful model should be like (notable exceptions, frequently from scientists in other fields, include Lehman 1977; Rothenberg 1989; Webb 1993). By considering programs as the computational embodiments of a theory of how the modeled system might work, a substantial amount of theoretical work from the philosophy of science literature (Popper 1972) on the possible criteria concerning the adequacy and proper form of a theory can be useful here. Having as a primary target the development of useful models, the following criteria were set for use in this work:

- A model should be clear on what it is a model *of*. This allows the incorporation of a number of pieces of evidence regarding the structure and behavior of the modeled system as test sets for the plausibility of the model. A model should be accurate with respect to this evidence. The degree of accuracy, and the range of evidence that it agrees with can be used as a measure of the generality of the model.
- By virtue of being designed as an analog of the modeled system, a model should provide possible explanations for the data available about the modeled system.
- A model should be able to generate testable predictions. This is considered important in order to establish the scientific usefulness of the model, and demarcate it from useless exercises in computer programming.

The Architecture as a Model of Primate Imitation Mechanisms

The first of the above criteria requires an explicit statement on what the architecture is a model *of*. The aim of this section is to propose the dual-route architecture described in section 13.4 as a model of primate imitation mechanisms, and describe evidence from imitation research in primates that can be used as test sets for the plausibility of the model. Why specifically target primates? The main reason is that, in contrast to "lower" animals where the majority of research has concentrated on whether a certain animal is capable of imitation or not, there is a sufficient amount of data with respect to the underlying mechanisms of primate imitation to make a computational model possible.

The Validation Data

This section presents neurophysiological, psychological, and brain activation data pertaining to issues important to the approach adopted in this work. First, human brain activation data are presented, followed by neurophysiological data on "mirror neurons" found in the premotor areas of the monkey brain. The interplay between observing, imagining, performing, and imitating a movement is the unifying theme of the psychophysical data presented subsequently, and the presentation of the validation data is concluded with the examination of data available on human imitation capabilities following brain damage, focusing on resulting apraxia disorders.

ACTIVATION OF BRAIN STRUCTURES IN HUMANS

In humans, several experiments have investigated the interplay between action generation and action perception. Fadiga and colleagues (1995) stimulated the motor cortex of human observers and recorded the motor evoked potentials (MEPs) from hand muscles, utilizing the assumption that if action observation activates the premotor cortex (as it does in monkeys), this activation should induce an increase of the motor evoked potentials elicited by the magnetic stimulation of the motor cortex. They found a significant increase of the MEPs when subjects observed movements, and additionally the pattern of muscle activation was very similar to the pattern of muscle contraction present during the execution of the same action—that is, the increase was present only in those muscles that were active when the human subjects executed these actions.

A different set of experiments with human subjects used positron emission tomography (PET) brain scanning as a way of mapping the brain regions whose activations are associated with the observation of hand actions (Decety et al. 1997), as well as mental rehearsal (Decety et al. 1994) (similar to what was termed "internal generation" in the architecture of section 13.3).

In Decety and colleagues (1994), normal subjects were asked to either passively observe movements of a virtual hand grasping objects or to imagine their own hand grasping objects, presented through a virtual reality system. Their brain activity during these conditions was mapped. The results demonstrated that cortical and subcortical motor structures were activated both during movement observation and movement imagery. It was concluded that consciously representing an action involved a pattern of cortical and subcortical activation that resembles the one observed during an intentionally executed action. It is important to note that during the observation condition, subjects were instructed to watch the movements of the virtual hand "as if it were their own hand" (this is similar to the first step taken by the behaviors in the active imitation route—that is, internally assuming the observed state of the demonstrator). The importance of the observer's intentions during observation was further examined in Decety and colleagues (1997), where subjects observed actions with the aim of either recognizing them or imitating them later. The results showed that the pattern of activation was different between the two conditions, suggesting that the motivations and intent of the observer during the demonstration determine (or at least influence) which brain structures will be activated to process the incoming stimuli. Decety and colleagues (1997) also examined the effect that the meaning of the observed actions has on the patterns of brain activation during observation. The results were striking: different brain structures were activated when the actions demonstrated were meaningless to the observer than those activated when the actions were known to the observer. This is very interesting since it indicates that knowing or not knowing the action demonstrated has an influence on the way this action will be processed in order to be imitated.

MIRROR NEURONS IN MONKEYS

Neurophysiological experiments with macaque monkeys have revealed an important class of neurons in area F5 of the monkey's premotor cortex, which were termed "mirror neurons" (Gallese et al. 1996; di Pellegrino et al. 1992). These neurons were found to become active both when the monkey executes goal-oriented movements and when it observes the demonstration of similar movements executed by another monkey or a human demonstrator. A variety of mirror neurons were discovered: grasping, tearing, manipulating, and placing objects neurons, among others. Some of the neurons were active only during the demonstration while some others remained active for a while after the end of the demonstrated action. The majority of the mirror neurons are active selectively when the monkey is observing a particular type of action (e.g., grasping), and some of them are highly selective not only to the type of action, but also to the particular way that the action is executed (e.g., grasping with the index finger and the thumb). The distance of the demonstrator from the monkey does not affect the responses of the mirror neurons, and control experiments have ruled out the possibility that the neurons are active simply as a response to particular visual configurations (for example, either of the demonstrator's hand or of the monkey's own hand) since most of them are also active when the monkey executes the action in darkness. Nonbiological stimuli (for example, observing a set of pliers grasping the object) do not activate the neurons.

OBSERVATION, IMAGERY, ACTUAL PERFORMANCE, AND IMITATION

Of relevance to the work presented in this chapter are also psychophysical experiments investigating the differences between observing an action, imagining an action, and executing that action. Vogt (1995) performed a series of studies wherein subjects learned to reproduce a sequence of cyclical arm movements, either through repeatedly observing the sequence on a monitor or through mentally or physically rehearsing the sequence. The results were very interesting since they demonstrated that observation or mental or physical rehearsal led to similar improvement in temporal consistency when the subject was later asked to reproduce the observations. Some further experiments (Vogt 1996) with a short-term memory paradigm, where subjects were allowed to observe the model movement only once, showed that timing imitation did not benefit from any further intermediate imitation (imaginary or physical) in the interval between the presentation of the model movement and the point where the subjects were asked to reproduce it. Related results were obtained in "mental chronometry" experiments by Decety (1996). Subjects were asked to perform a task either mentally or physically. The movement times required to execute the task were very similar irrespective of the modality of execution (mental or physical). In related sets of experiments (Decety et al. 1991; Wang and Morgan 1992; Wuyam et al. 1995), subjects were asked to mentally perform tasks that would require different physical effort and found that autonomic responses (cardiac and respiratory activity) during motor imagery paralleled the autonomic responses to physically performing the task.

BRAIN AND COGNITIVE DISORDERS AND IMITATION ABILITIES
Since imitation is a complex task involving the integration of information from multiple brain systems including perception, memory, and motor systems, it has been used as a reference task for identifying and assessing various brain and cognitive disorders. In particular (and most relevant to this chapter) it has been used to identify and assess the various forms of *apraxia*, a "neurological disorder of learned purposive movement skills that is not explained by deficits of elemental motor or sensory systems" (Gonzalez-Rothi and Heilman 1997). Apraxia usually results from brain damage (usually in the left hemisphere) and its symptoms vary, giving rise to the various forms of apraxia, which are identified through a series of tests that involve performance of actions on verbal command, imitation of meaningful and meaningless gestures, and gesture recognition and naming. A type of apraxia of particular relevance here is *visuo-imitative apraxia* (Mehler 1987). Patients suffering from this apraxia are able to perform meaningful gestures when they are described verbally, or when they are asked to imitate them after a demonstration, but are unable to imitate meaningless gestures (Goldenberg and Hagmann 1997; Merians et al. 1997). The nature of the demonstrated act, and in particular whether the act is known or not to the imitator, appears to be very important and determines whether or not the patient will be able to imitate it. This correlates well with the brain activation data described earlier, which show that different brain areas are activated depending on the nature of the demonstrated act, and its meaning to the observer (Decety et al. 1997).

Two additional disorders are also of interest here: *autism* and *imitation behavior*. Autism is a syndrome that includes abnormalities of social and communicative development, partially characterized by an inability to comprehend the viewpoints of other people (Baron-Cohen, Tager-Flusberg, and Cohen 1993). People suffering from autism display severe deficits in imitation and pantomime tasks (Smith and Bryson 1994), which cannot be attributed to visual recognition memory, motor initiation, and basic motor coordination deficits (Rogers et al. 1996). Furthermore, autistic children show deficiencies in empathy and joint attention tasks, as well as an inability to engage in pretend play (Charman et al. 1997). On the other side of the spectrum are patients that suffer from frontal-lobe damage, and display a pathological behavior that has been termed "imitation behavior" (Lhermitte, Pillon, and Serdaru 1986). These patients imitate the demonstrator's gesture although they were not instructed to do so, and some times even when told *not* to do so (de Renzi, Cavalleri, and Facchini 1996). An explicit, direct command from the doctor to the patient would stop the imitation behavior but a simple distraction to a different subject was sufficient to see imitation reappearing, despite the patient remembering what he or she had been told.

Explanations

INVOLVEMENT OF MOTOR SYSTEMS DURING PERCEPTION

The human brain and mirror-neuron activation data suggest that there is a motor system involvement during observation of movement. The explanation offered for these data by this work (Demiris 1999) is that the motor system is activated in order to generate and internally simulate candidate behaviors and to offer predictions regarding the incoming perceptual data from the demonstrator. On a more specific note, the fact that some mirror neurons cease to be active when the demonstration is complete while others continue to be active for a while after the end of the demonstration can be explained if viewed within the composite nature of the organization of the behaviors: more complex ones can be composed from elementary ones. Upon completion, a behavior X ceases to be active; however, a behavior X*, which incorporates X as its initial step, will continue to be active, since it is still capable of offering further predictions about the demonstrator's future states until X* completes its remaining steps. This suggests that the mirror neurons that cease to be active when the demonstrated action finishes represent that action specifically, while the other class of neurons, which remain active, represent sequences of actions that incorporate the demonstrated action as their first part.

The active route of the architecture understands an action by internally generating it. The observer does imitate the demonstrated movement internally, even when it does not do so externally. This feature of the architecture could explain why physically imitating a set of demonstrated movements does not aid their later recall (Zimmer and Engelkamp 1996), as well as why physical rehearsal of a demonstrated behavior does not lead to any significant differences in the levels of performance improvement from mental rehearsal or mere observation (Vogt 1995). Since observation, imagery, and imitation are done using mostly the same structures (behavioral modules and forward models) the same laws should govern their operation, which explains the mental chronometry data by Decety (1996), which indicate that it takes roughly the same time to perform a task mentally or physically.

INFLUENCE OF CONTENT OF THE DEMONSTRATED ACTION
The human brain activation data described by Decety and colleagues (1997) indicate that different brain structures are activated during the observation of an action depending on whether the action is known to the observer or not. This is explained by the dual-route nature of the architecture: if the demonstrated act is known to the imitator, then the corresponding behavior in the active imitation route will be activated. If the demonstrated act is not known to the imitator, then the passive route will be activated in order to extract the representative postures and acquire the demonstrated behavior. Currently, there are no brain activation data to correlate with the behavior of the architecture for the cases where the demonstration consisted of sequences of actions, and, in particular, partially known sequences.

If the passive route is destroyed, the architecture will no longer be able to imitate any novel behaviors—although, with the active route intact, behaviors that are already known will be successfully imitated. This correlates favorably with the neuropathological data for patients suffering with visuo-imitative apraxia (Mehler 1987).

Predictions
The computational studies of Demiris (1999) revealed limits to what the architecture can perceive, particularly with respect to movement speeds. For example, in figure 13.10, the demonstrator is executing a behavior that the imitator does have in its repertoire ([cooler]); however, this time the imitator is 400% heavier than the demonstrator, so it is not capable of executing the demonstrated behavior at the demonstrator's speed levels. As a result, all the behaviors end up with very low (below zero) confidence values.

D: [Cooler]; I: [Cool], [Cook], [Cookie], [Cooker],[Coot], [Cooler]

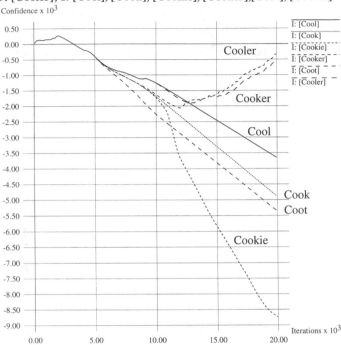

Figure 13.10 Confidences of imitator's internal behaviors [Cool, Cook, Cookie, Cooker, Coot, Cooler] when demonstrator executes behavior [Cooler] at speeds unattainable by the imitator.

So, if the demonstration is performed at speeds that cannot be attained by the imitator, the demonstrated actions will not be understood, even if they are in the imitator's repertoire. By projecting this behavior to that of the mirror neurons described earlier, the architecture offers a testable prediction: a mirror neuron that is active during the demonstration of an action should not be active (or possibly be less active) if the demonstration is done at speeds unattainable by the monkey. A further prediction with respect to mirror neurons has already been hinted at earlier in the explanation section. Mirror neurons that remain active for a period of time after the end of the demonstration are encoding more complex sequences that incorporate the demonstration as their first part. Further investigation through manipulation of the demonstration (adding further actions to it, while retaining the first part) should reveal the exact sequence that the neuron is encoding. Two less easily testable predictions regarding the mirror neurons are: (a) the existence of other goal-directed mirror neurons and (b) the train-ability of new mirror neurons. The first one predicts that there exist mirror neurons for other goal-directed actions: since perception and generation of an action is so tightly coupled, it can be expected that at least the most important actions in the monkey's repertoire (body postures that convey messages—for example, threat postures, facial expressions, among others) should have mirror neurons associated with them. The second one predicts that, since the passive route provides the active route with new behaviors after their demonstration, it should be possible to create new mirror neurons by training the monkey to imitate a demon-strated action.

Discussion

The architecture, if viewed as a model, suggests that when humans and other primates observe a movement with the intent to imitate, they "put themselves in the place of the demonstrator," and do what they would do if they were in the demonstrator's place. Understanding a demonstrated movement comes from internally generating alternatives and selecting among those, based on the quality of their predictions. But why predict? Why not wait until the demonstration has finished and classify the result? From an evolutionary perspective, the ability to predict and its adoption during observation might have prevailed since it allows the animal to act/respond to an action of a conspecific before that (potentially nonbeneficial to the observer) action has been completed.

The initial step taken by the observer, of putting herself in the position of the demonstrator, seems to be important too. Autistic children who suffer from an inability to do so, as witnessed by their poor performance in empathy, joint attention, and pretend play tests, are unable to imitate. Normal children observing a human experimenter demonstrating an act but failing at it (for example, trying to pull apart a dumbbell, but failing due to finger slippage), do imitate the intended action of the human success-fully, but do not do so when they see a mechanical device trying to do the same act but failing (Meltzoff 1995). An explanation for this could be that the children did manage to imagine themselves in the place of the demonstrator when the demonstrator was hu-man but not when it was of a nonbiological nature. As mentioned earlier, mirror neurons also do not respond when the action (e.g., grasping) is done with pliers, and not by a human arm (Gallese et al. 1996).

The dual-route nature of the architecture is interesting too. It was discussed in the explanations section earlier that damaging the passive route leads to behavior similar to that of visuo-imitative apraxic patients. What about the reverse condition? There is currently no evidence for the reverse dissociation—that is, having the active route destroyed while retaining the passive one intact. This condition would be hard to detect, since known behaviors can still be imitated through the passive route as being novel. However, it is important to note that, essentially, the active route maps the observed movements to the imitator's internal ones—that is, it serves as a recognition process. Any internal representations associated with these behaviors (including symbolic ones; for example, the name of the behavior, or emotional significance, intentions, or any other attributes) can be retrieved through this route (note that it has been suggested in Gallese and Goldman 1998 that the role of the mirror neurons is to facilitate the detection of the mental states of observed conspecifics by adopting their perspective). There are cases reported related to a disruption to this process: Gonzalez-Rothi, Mack, and Heilman (1986) reported two patients who could imitate demonstrated pantomimes but could not recognize (or discriminate among) them in what is termed as "pantomime agnosia."

In the experiments reported in this chapter, all behaviors that are present in the imitator's repertoire are activated in order to generate alternatives and offer predictions as to what comes next. For efficiency reasons, it is conceivable that context can be used in order to select, among all the available actions, the ones that are applicable or at least relevant to the current situation. Although it is still early to speculate about the exact nature of this process, experiments with humans and monkeys have shown that actions applicable to a certain context are retrieved even if no action is required on behalf of the subject. Rizzolati and colleagues (1988) and Murata and colleagues (1997) have shown that there are neurons in the area F5 (the same area with the mirror neurons) of the monkey's premotor cortex that are active during grasping movements, but are also active when the monkey views a graspable object. The interpretation favored by the experimenters was that the responses of the F5 neurons represented the description of the presented object in motor terms—that is, the visual features of the object are automatically translated into a potential motor action (regardless of whether the monkey intended to move or not). In humans, experiments with positron emission tomography have shown (Grafton et al. 1997) that observation of tools activated the premotor areas in the absence of any overt motor demand (it is interesting to note that the additional task of silent tool naming did not result in any additional activation of the premotor cortex, but tool-use naming did). These data indicate that the brain might indeed be using context to reduce the amount of behaviors that will be tried out.

Currently, a single presentation is enough for the architecture to acquire a new behavior. It is not clear how this relates to primate behavior, but the architecture could be modified so that only frequently occurring behaviors get acquired, or possibly the most biologically important to the imitator. Then the passive route would essentially act as a short-term memory that would filter the behaviors, letting only some of them through to the long-term memory of the active route.

13.6 Epilogue

In this chapter, a computational architecture for equipping robots with the capability to imitate was proposed, and subsequently proposed as a model of primate imitation mechanisms. The architecture has an active and a passive route: within the active route, the imitator mentally places itself in the place of the demonstrator and internally executes ("imagines") candidate behaviors, eventually selecting among them based on the accuracy of their predictions regarding the demonstrator's incoming states as they are being perceived as the demonstration unfolds. If there are no behaviors that can predict sufficiently well, the passive imitation route learns the demonstrated behavior, and adds it in the imitator's behavioral repertoire.

Computational experiments were performed instantiating this architecture using a dynamics simulator of a thirteen-degrees-of-freedom robot, and showed the architecture to be able to imitate known behaviors, as well as acquiring new ones and successfully utilizing them later. The architecture was also proposed as a model of primate imitation mechanisms and its characteristics, as explored by the computational experiments, were correlated with data on biological imitation generating a number of explanations and predictions. Completely understanding the underlying mechanisms of imitation is still a distant goal, and utilizing computational and robotic architectures as models of real neural systems is a difficult and relatively new endeavor, but the biological data that are available indicate that the behavior displayed by this architecture points in the right direction.

References

Astrom, K. J., and T. Hagglund. PID Control. In *The Control Handbook*, pp. 198–209, W. S. Levine (ed.). IEEE Press, 1996.

Baron-Cohen, S., H. Tager-Flusberg, and D. J. Cohen. *Understanding Other Minds: Perspectives from Autism*. Oxford, UK: Oxford University Press, 1993.

Billard, A. DRAMA: A connectionist model for robot learning: Experiments on grounding communication through imitation in autonomous robots. Ph.D. thesis, University of Edinburgh, Scotland, UK, 1999.

Bruce, V., and P. Green. *Visual Perception: Physiology, Psychology, and Ecology*. Hove and London, UK: Lawrence Erlbraum Associates, 1990.

Bullock, D., S. Grossberg, and F. H. Guenther. A self-organising neural model of motor equivalent reaching and tool use by a multijoint arm. *Journal of Cognitive Neuroscience* 5(4): 408–435, 1993.

Carey, D. P., D. I. Perrett, and M. W. Oram. Recognizing, understanding, and reproducing action. In *Handbook of Neuropsychology*, 11, pp. 111–129, F. Boller and J. Graftman (eds.). Elsevier Science, 1997.

Charman, T., J. Swettenham, S. Baron-Cohen, A. Cox, G. Baird, and A. Drew. Infants with autism: An investigation of empathy, pretend play, joint attention, and imitation. *Developmental Psychology* 33(5): 781–789, 1997.

Dautenhahn, K. Getting to know each other—Artificial social intelligence for autonomous robots. *Robotics and Autonomous Systems* 16: 333–356, 1995.

Decety, J. Do imagined and executed actions share the same neural substrate? *Cognitive Brain Research* 3: 87–93, 1996.

Decety, J., M. Jeannerod, M. Germain, and J. Pastene. Vegetative response during imagined movement is proportional to mental effort. *Behavioural Brain Research* 42: 1–5, 1991.

Decety, J., D. Perani, M. Jeannerod, V. Bettinardi, B. Tadary, R. Woods, J. C. Mazziota, and F. Fazio. Mapping motor representations with positron emission tomography. *Nature* 371: 600–602, 1994.

Decety, J., J. Grezes, N. Costes, D. Perani, M. Jeannerod, E. Procyk, F. Grassi, and F. Fazio. Brain activity during observation of actions: Influence of action content and subject's strategy. *Brain* 120: 1763–1777, 1997.

Demiris, J. Movement imitation mechanisms in robots and humans. Ph.D. thesis, University of Edinburgh, Scotland, UK, 1999.

Demiris, J., and G. M. Hayes. Imitative learning mechanisms in robots and humans. *Proceedings of the 5th European Workshop on Learning Robots*, pp. 9–16, Bari, Italy, 1996.

Demiris, J., S. Rougeaux, G. M. Hayes, L. Berthouze, and Y. Kuniyoshi. Deferred imitation of human head movements by an active stereo vision head. *Proceedings of the 6th IEEE International Workshop on Robot Human Communication*, pp. 88–93, Sendai, Japan: IEEE Press, 1997.

Desmurget, M., and C. Prablanc. Postural control of three-dimensional prehension movements. *Journal of Neurophysiology* 77: 452–464, 1997.

Desmurget, M., Y. Rosselli, C. Prablanc, G. E. Stelmach, and M. Jeannerod. Representation of hand position prior to movement and motor variability. *Canadian Journal of Physiology and Pharmacology*, 73: 262–272, 1995.

Fadiga, L., L. Fogassi, G. Pavesi, and G. Rizzolatti. Motor facilitation during action observation: A magnetic stimulation study. *Journal of Neurophysiology* 73(6): 2608–2611, 1995.

Gallese, V., and A. Goldman. Mirror neurons and the simulation theory of mind-reading. *Trends in Cognitive Sciences* 2(12): 493–501, 1998.

Gallese, V., L. Fadiga, L. Fogassi, and G. Rizzolatti. Action recognition in the premotor cortex. *Brain* 119: 593–609, 1996.

Ghez, C., and R. Sainburg. Proprioceptive control of interjoint coordination. *Canadian Journal of Physiology and Pharmacology* 73: 273–284, 1994.

Goldenberg, G., and S. Hagmann. The meaning of meaningless gestures: A study of visuoimitative apraxia. *Neuropsychologia* 35(3): 333–341, 1997.

Gonzalez-Rothi, L. J., and K. M. Heilman. *Apraxia: The Neuropsychology of Action*. East Sussex, UK: Psychology Press, 1997.

Gonzalez-Rothi, L. J., L. Mack, and K. M. Heilman. Pantomime agnosia. *Journal of Neurology, Neurosurgery, and Psychiatry* 49: 451–454, 1986.

Grafton, S. T., L. Fadiga, M. A. Arbib, and G. Rizzolatti. Premotor cortex activation during observation and naming of familiar tools. *Neuroimage* 6: 231–236, 1997.

Groothuis, T. G. G. The ontogeny of social displays: Form development, form fixation, and change in context. *Advances in the Study of Behavior* 22: 269–322, 1993.

Hayes, G. M., and J. Demiris. A robot controller using learning by imitation. *Proceedings of the Second International Symposium on Intelligent Robotic Systems*, Grenoble, France, pp. 198–204, 1994.

Hovland, Sikka, and McCarragher. Skill acquisition from human demonstration using a hidden markov model. *Proceedings of the 1996 IEEE International Conference on Robotics and Automation*, Minn. pp. 2706–2711. IEEE Press, 1996.

Ikeuchi, K., and T. Suehiro. Towards an assembly plan from observation—Part I: Assembly task recognition using face-contact relations (polyhedral objects). *Proceedings of the IEEE International Conference on Robotics and Automation*, Nice, France, pp. 2171–2177. IEEE Press, 1992.

Jordan, M., and D. Rumelhart. Forward models: Supervised learning with a distal teacher. *Cognitive Science* 16: 307–354, 1992.

Kaiser, M., and R. Dillmann. Building elementary robot skills from human demonstration. *Proceedings of the IEEE International Conference on Robotics and Automation*, Minn. IEEE Press, 1996.

Kang, S. B., and K. Ikeuchi. Toward automatic robot instruction from perception—Mapping human grasps to manipulator grasps. *IEEE Transactions on Robotics and Automation* 13(1): 81–95, 1997.

Kuniyoshi, Y., M. Inaba, and H. Inoue. Learning by watching: Extracting reusable task knowledge from visual observation of human performance. *IEEE Transactions on Robotics and Automation* 10(6): 799–822, 1994.

Lehman, R. S. *Computer Simulation and Modelling: An Introduction*. Hillsdale, N.J.: Erlbaum, 1977.

Lhermitte, F., B. Pillon, and M. Serdaru. Human autonomy and the frontal lobes. Part I: Imitation and utilization behavior: A neuropsychological study of 75 patients. *Annals of Neurology* 19(4): 326–334, 1986.

Maurer, D. Neonatal synesthesia: Implications for the processing of speech and faces. In *Developmental Neurocognition: Speech and Face Processing in the First Year of Life*, pp. 109–124, B. de Boysson-Bardies et al. (eds.). Kluwer Academic, 1993.

McMillan, S., D. E. Orin, and R. B. McGhee. DynaMechs: An object oriented software package for efficient dynamic simulation of underwater robotic vehicles. In *Underwater Robotic Vehicles: Design and Control*, pp. 73–98, J. Yuh (ed.). TSI Press, 1995.

Meer, A. L. H. van der, F. R. van der Weel, and D. N. Lee. The functional significance of arm movements in neonates. *Science* 267: 693–695, 1995.

Mehler, M. F. Visuo-imitative apraxia. *Neurology* 37: 129, 1987.

Meltzoff, A. N. Imitation, intermodal coordination, and representation in early infancy. In *Infancy and Epistemology: An Evaluation of Piaget's Theory*, pp. 85–114, G. Butterworth (ed.). Harvester Press, 1981.

Meltzoff, A. N. Molyneux babies: cross-modal perception, imitation, and the mind of the preverbal infant. In N. Eilan, R. McCarthy, B. Brewer (eds.), *Spatial Representation*, pp. 219–235. Oxford, UK: Blackwell, 1993.

Meltzoff, A. Understanding the intentions of others: Re-enactment of intended acts by 18-month-old children. *Developmental Psychology* 31(5): 838–850, 1995.

Meltzoff, A. N., and M. K. Moore. Imitation of facial and manual gestures by human neonates. *Science* 198: 75–78, 1977.

Meltzoff, A. N., and M. K. Moore. Newborn infants imitate facial gestures. *Child Development* 54: 702–709, 1983.

Meltzoff, A. N., and M. K. Moore. Imitation in newborn infants: Exploring the range of gestures imitated and the underlying mechanisms. *Developmental Psychology* 25(6): 954–962, 1989.

Meltzoff, A., and M. K. Moore. Explaining facial imitation: A theoretical model. *Early Development and Parenting* 6(2): 179–192, 1997.

Merians, A. S., M. Clark, H. Poizner, B. Macauley, L. J. G. Rothi, and K. M. Heilman. Visual-imitative dissociation apraxia. *Neuropsychologia* 35(11): 1483–1490, 1997.

Miall, R. C., and D. M. Wolpert. Forward models for physiological motor control. *Neural Networks* 9(8): 1265–1279, 1996.

Murata, A., L. Fadiga, L. Fogassi, V. Gallese, V. Raos, and G. Rizzolatti. Object representation in the ventral premotor cortex (area F5) of the monkey. *Journal of Neurophysiology* 78: 2226–2230, 1997.

Pellegrino, G. di, L. Fadiga, L. Fogassi, V. Gallese, and G. Rizzolatti. Understanding motor events: A neurophysiological study. *Experimental Brain Research* 91: 176–180, 1992.

Perrett, D. I., M. H. Harries, A. J. Mistlin, J. K. Hietanen, P. J. Benson, R. Bevan, S. Thomas, M. W. Oram, J. Ortega, and K. Brierley. Social signals analysed at the single cell level: Someone is looking at me, something touched me, something moved! *International Journal of Comparative Psychology* 4(1): 25–55, 1990.

Perrett, D. I., M. W. Oram, M. H. Harries, R. Bevan, J. K. Hietanen, P. J. Benson, and S. Thomas. Viewer-centred and object-centred coding of heads in the macaque temporal cortex. *Experimental Brain Research* 86: 159–173, 1991.

Popper, K. R. *The Logic of Scientific Discovery*. Hutchinson, London.

Renzi, E. de, F. Cavalleri, and S. Facchini. Imitation and utilisation behaviour. *Journal of Neurology, Neurosurgery, and Psychiatry* 61: 396–400, 1972.

Rizzolatti, G., R. Camarda, L. Fogassi, M. Gentilucci, G. Luppino, and M. Matelli. Functional organisation of inferior area 6 in the macaque monkey—Part II: Area F5 and the control of distal movements. *Experimental Brain Research* 71: 491–507, 1988.

Rogers, S. J., L. Bennetto, R. McEvoy, and B. F. Pennington. Imitation and pantomime in high functioning adolescents with autism spectrum disorders. *Child Development* 67(5): 2060–2073, 1996.

Rothenberg, J. The nature of modelling. In L. E. Widman, K. A. Loparo, and N. R. Nielsen (eds.), *Artificial Intelligence, Simulation, and Modeling*, pp. 75–92. New York: Wiley, 1989.

Schaal, S. Is imitation learning the way to humanoid robots? *Trends in Cognitive Sciences* 3(6): 233–242, 1999.

Scott, S. H., and J. F. Kalaska. Changes in motor cortex activity during reaching movements with similar hand paths but different arm postures. *Journal of Neurophysiology* 73: 2563–2567, 1995.

Shavlik, J. W., and T. G. Dietterich. *Readings in Machine Learning*. San Mateo, Calif.: Morgan Kaufmann, 1990.

Smith, I. M., and S. E. Bryson. Imitation and action in autism: A critical review. *Psychological Bulletin* 116(2): 259–273, 1994.

Suehiro, T., and K. Ikeuchi. Towards an assembly plan from observation—Part II: Correction of motion parameters based on fact contact constraints. *Proceedings of the*

IEEE/RSJ International Conference on Intelligent Robots and Systems, Raleigh, N.C., pp. 2095–2102. IEEE Press, 1992.

Tanaka, K. Neuronal mechanisms of object recognition. *Science* 262: 685–688, 1993.

Helms Tillery, S. I., J. F. Soechting, and T. J. Ebner. Somatosensory cortical activity in relation to arm posture: Nonuniform spatial tuning. *Journal of Neurophysiology* 76(4): 2423–2438, 1996.

Vogt, S. On relations between perceiving, imagining, and performing in the learning of cyclical movement sequences. *British Journal of Psychology* 86: 191–216, 1995.

Vogt, S. Imagery and perception-action mediation in imitative actions. *Cognitive Brain Research* 3: 79–86, 1996.

Wada, Y., and M. Kawato. A neural network model for arm trajectory formation using forward and inverse dynamics models. *Neural Networks* 6: 919–932, 1993.

Wang, Y., and W. P. Morgan. The effect of imagery perspectives on the psychophysical responses to imagined exercise. *Behaviour Brain Research* 52: 167–174, 1992.

Webb, B. H. Perception in real and artificial insects: A robotic investigation of cricket phonotaxis. Ph.D. thesis, University of Edinburgh, Scotland, UK, 1993.

Widman, L. E., K. A. Loparo, and N. R. Nielsen (eds.). *Artificial Intelligence, Simulation and Modeling*, pp. 75–92. New York: Wiley, 1989.

Wolpert, D., Z. Ghahramani, and M. Jordan. An internal model for sensorimotor integration. *Science* 269: 1880–1882, 1995.

Wolpert, D. M., and M. Kawato. Multiple paired forward and inverse models for motor control. *Neural Networks* 11: 1317–1329, 1998.

Wolpert, D. M., R. C. Miall, and M. Kawato. Internal models in the cerebellum. *Trends in Cognitive Sciences* 2(9): 338–347, 1998.

Wuyam, B., S. Moosavi, J. Decety, L. Adams, R. Lansing, and A. Guz. Imagination of dynamic exercise produced ventilatory responses which were more apparent in competitive sportsmen. *Journal of Physiology* 482: 713–724, 1995.

Yeasin, M., and S. Chaudhuri. Automatic robot programming by visual demonstration of task execution. *Proceedings of the International Conference on Advanced Robotics (ICAR)*, Monterey, Calif., pp. 913–918. IEEE Press, 1997.

Zimmer, H. D., and J. Engelkamp. Routes to actions and their efficacy for remembering. *Memory* 4(1): 59–78, 1996.

Cynthia Breazeal and Brian Scassellati

14.1 Introduction

Humans (and some other animals) acquire new skills socially through direct tutelage, observational conditioning, goal emulation, imitation, and other methods (Galef 1988; Hauser 1996). These social learning skills provide a powerful mechanism for an observer to acquire behaviors and knowledge from a skilled individual (the model). In particular, imitation is an extremely powerful mechanism for social learning that has received a great deal of interest from researchers in the fields of animal behavior and child development.

Similarly, social interaction can be a powerful way for transferring important skills, tasks, and information to a robot. A socially competent robot could take advantage of the same sorts of social learning and teaching scenarios that humans readily use. From an engineering perspective, a robot that could imitate the actions of a human would provide a simple and effective means for the human to specify a task to the robot and for the robot to acquire new skills without any additional programming. From a computer science perspective, imitation provides a means for biasing interaction and constraining the search space for learning. From a developmental psychology perspective, building systems that learn through imitation allows us to investigate a minimal set of competencies necessary for social learning. We can further speculate that constructing an artificial system may provide useful information about the nature of imitative skills in humans (or other animals).

Initial studies of social learning in robotics focused on allowing one robot to follow a second robot using simple perception (proximity and infrared sensors) through mazes (Hayes and Demiris 1994) or an unknown landscape (Dautenhahn 1995). Other work in social learning for autonomous robots addressed learning interpersonal communication protocols between similar robots (Steels 1996) and between robots with similar morphology but that differed in scale (Billard and Dautenhahn 1998). Robotics research has also focused on how sequences of known behaviors can be

chained together based on input from a model. Matarić, Williamson, Demiris, and Mohan (1998) used a simulated humanoid to
learn a sequence of gestures from a set of joint angles recorded
from a human performing those same gestures, and Gaussier,
Moga, Banquet, and Quoy (1998) used a neural network architecture to allow a robot to sequence motor primitives in order to follow the trajectory of a teacher robot. One research program has
addressed how perceptual states can be categorized by matching
against models of known behaviors; Demiris and Hayes (1999)
implemented an architecture for the imitation of movement on a
simulated humanoid by predictively matching observed sequences
to known behaviors. Finally, a variety of research programs have
aimed at training robots to perform single tasks by observing a
human demonstrator. Schaal (1997) used a robot arm to learn a
pendulum-balancing task from constrained visual feedback, and
Kuniyoshi, Inaba, and Inoue (1994) discussed a methodology for
allowing a robot in a highly constrained environment to replicate a
block-stacking task performed by a human but in a different part of
the workspace.

Traditionally in robot social learning, the model is indifferent to
the attempts of the observer to imitate it. In general, learning in
adversarial or indifferent conditions is a very difficult problem that
requires the observer to decide who to imitate, what to imitate,
how to imitate, and when imitation is successful. To make the
problem tractable in an indifferent environment, researchers have
vastly simplified one or more aspects of the environment and the
behaviors of the observer and the model. Many have simplified the
problem by using only simple perceptions, which are matched to
relevant aspects of the task, such as Kuniyoshi, Inaba, and Inoue's
(1994) use of white objects on a black background without any
distractors, or Matarić, Williamson, Demiris, and Mohan's (1998)
placement of reflective markers on the human's joints and use of
multiple calibrated infrared cameras. Others have assumed the
presence of a single model, which is always detectable in the scene
and is always performing the task that the observer is programmed
to learn, such as Gaussier, Moga, Banquet, and Quoy (1998), and
Schaal (1997). Many have simplified the problem of action selection by having limited observable behaviors and limited responses
(such as Steels 1996 and Demiris and Hayes 1999), by assuming
that it is always an appropriate time and place to imitate (such as
Dautenhahn 1995), and by fixing the mapping between observed

behaviors and response actions (such as Billard and Dautenhahn 1998). Few have addressed the issue of evaluating the success of an imitative response; most systems use a single, fixed success criteria that can only be used to learn a strictly specified task with no hope for error recovery (although see Nehaniv and Dautenhahn 1998 for one treatment of evaluation and body mapping).

Our approach is to constrain the learning scenario in a different manner—we assume that the model is motivated to help the observer learn the task. A good teacher is very perceptive to the limitations of the learner and sets the complexity of the instruction and task accordingly. As the learner's performance improves, the instructor incrementally increases the complexity of the task. In this way, the learner is always competent but slightly challenged— a condition amenable for successful learning. This assumption allows us to build useful implementations on our robots, but limits the applicability of these results to less-constrained learning environments (such as having an indifferent model). However, we believe that the problems that must be addressed in building systems with the assumption of an active instructor are also applicable to robotics programs that use other assumptions and to investigations of social learning in natural systems.

We will use the word *imitate* to imply that the observer is not merely replicating the actions of the model but rather is attempting to achieve the goal of the model's action by performing a novel action similar to that observed in the model. Although we focus on this relatively strong definition, more basic forms of social learning share many of the same challenges. Simpler mechanisms such as stimulus enhancement, emulation, and mimicry must also address challenges such as determining what actions are relevant in the scene and finding conspecifics, while other challenges (such as determining the goal behind an action) are specific to this definition of imitation. It is an open question as to whether or not inferring intent is necessary to explain particular behaviors (Byrne 1999). However, for a robot to fulfill the expectations of a human instructor, the robot must have a deeper understanding of the goal and intent of the task it is learning to perform.

In this chapter, we outline four hard problems in building robots that imitate people and discuss how the social cues that humans naturally and intuitively provide could be used by a robot to solve these difficult problems. By attempting to build systems that imitate, we are forced to address issues that are not currently discussed in developmental psychology, animal behavior, or other research domains. However, we believe that these issues must be addressed by any creature or artifact that learns through imitation, and the study of these issues will yield greater insight into natural systems. We will present our progress toward implementing a set of critical social skills on two anthropomorphic robots, and discuss initial experiments that use these skills to benefit the imitative learning process.

14.2 Hard Problems in Robot Imitation

The ability to imitate relies upon many perceptual, cognitive, and motor capabilities. Many of these requirements are precursor skills that are necessary before attempting any task of this complexity, but are not directly related to the act of imitation. For example, the robot will require systems for basic visual-motor behaviors (such as smooth pursuit tracking and vergence); perceptual abilities for detecting motion, color, and scene segmentation; postural control; manipulative abilities (such as reaching for a visual target or controlled-force grasping); social skills (such as turn taking and recognition of emotional states); as well as an intuitive physics (including object permanence, support relations, and the ability to predict outcomes before attempting an action).

Even if we were to construct a system that had all of the requisite precursor skills, the act of imitation also presents its own unique set of research questions. Each of these questions is a complex research problem that the robotics community has only begun to address. In this chapter, we focus on four of these questions:

- How does the robot know when to imitate?
- How does the robot know what to imitate?
- How does the robot map observed actions onto behavioral responses?
- How does the robot evaluate its actions, correct errors, and recognize when it has achieved its goal?

To investigate these questions, consider the following example: The robot is observing a model opening a glass jar. The model approaches the robot and places the jar on a table near the robot. The model rubs his hands together and then sets himself to removing the lid from the jar. He grasps the glass jar in one hand and the lid in the other and begins to unscrew the lid. While he is opening the jar, he pauses to wipe his brow, and glances at the robot to see what it is doing. He then resumes opening the jar. The robot then attempts to imitate the action.

How Does the Robot Know When to Imitate?

A socially intelligent robot should be able to use imitation for the variety of purposes that humans do. Human children use imitation not only to acquire new skills, but also to acquire new goals from their parents. By inferring the intention behind the observed actions, children can gain an understanding of the goals of an individual. Children also use imitation to acquire knowledge about socializing, including the social conventions of their culture and the acceptable dynamics necessary for social communication. Imitation can be a mechanism for developing social attachments through imitative play and for gaining an understanding of people. Just as infants learn about physical objects by acting on them, infants learn about people by interacting with them. As Meltzoff and Moore (1994) wrote, "Imitation is to understanding people as physical manipulation is to understanding things." Imitation can also be used to explore and expand the range of possible actions in the child's repertoire—learning new ways of manipulating objects or new motor patterns that the child might not otherwise discover. Finally, imitation can be a mechanism for establishing personal identity and discovering distinctions between self and other. Meltzoff and Moore (1994) have proposed that deferred imitation may serve to establish the identity of a previously encountered individual.

A social robot should selectively use imitation to achieve many of these goals. However, the robot must not merely be a "puppet on a string."[1] The robot must decide whether or not it is appropriate to engage in imitative behavior based on the current social context, the availability of a good model, and the robot's internal goals and motivations. For example, the robot may need to choose between attending to a learning opportunity or fulfilling another goal, such as recharging its batteries. This decision will be based upon the social environment, how likely the robot is to have another opportunity to engage in that particular learning opportunity, the current level of necessity for charging the batteries, the quality of the instruction, and other competing motivations and goals. Furthermore, the robot should also recognize when

imitation is a viable solution and act to bring about the social context in which it can learn by observation, perhaps by seeking out
an instructor or motivating the instructor to perform a certain task.

How Does the Robot Know What to Imitate?

Faced with an incoming stream of sensory data, the robot must
make a number of decisions to determine what actions in the
world are appropriate to imitate. The robot must first determine
which agents in the scene are good models (and be able to avoid
bad models). The robot must not only be able to distinguish the
class of stimuli (including humans and perhaps other robots) that
might be a good model but also determine if the current actions of
that agent are worthy of imitation. Not all humans at all times will
be good models, and imitation may only be appropriate under certain circumstances.

Once a model has been selected, how does the robot determine
which of the model's actions are relevant to the task—which may
be part of the social/instructional process—and which are circum-
stantial? In the example above, the robot must segment the scene
into salient objects (such as the instructor's hand, the lid, and the
jar) and actions (the instructor's moving hand twisting the cap and
the instructor's head turning toward the robot). The robot must determine which of these objects and events are necessary to the task
at hand (such as the jar and the movement of the instructor's
elbow), which events and actions are important to the instructional
process but not to the task itself (such as the movement of the
instructor's head), and which are inconsequential (such as the instructor wiping his brow). The robot must also determine to what
extent each action must be imitated. For example, in removing the
lid from a jar, the movement of the instructor's hand is a critical
part of the task while the instructor's posture is not. The robot
must also recognize the important aspects of the objects being
manipulated so that the learned action will be applied to only appropriate objects of the same class (Scassellati 1999b).

How Does the Robot Map Observed Actions onto Behavioral Responses?

Once the robot has identified salient aspects of the scene, how
does it determine what actions it should take? When the robot
observes a model opening a jar, how does the robot convert that

perception into a sequence of motor actions that will bring its arm to achieve the same result? Mapping from one body to another involves not only determining which body parts have similar structure but also transforming the observed movements into motions that the robot is capable of performing. For example, if the instructor is unscrewing the lid of the jar, the robot must first identify that the motion of the arm and hand are relevant to the task and determine that its own hand and arm are capable of performing this action. The robot must then observe the movements of the instructor's hand and arm and map those movements onto the motor coordinates of its own body.

How Does the Robot Evaluate Its Actions, Correct Errors, and Recognize Success?

Once a robot can observe an action and attempt to imitate it, how can the robot determine whether or not it has been successful? In order to compare its actions with respect to those of the model, the robot must be able to identify the desired outcome and to judge how similar its own actions were to that outcome. If the robot is attempting to unscrew the lid of a jar, has the robot been successful if it merely mimics the model and rotates the lid but leaves the lid on the jar? Is the robot successful if it removes the lid by pulling instead of twisting? Is the robot successful if it smashes the jar in order to open it? In the absence of internal motivations that provide feedback on the success of the action, the evaluation will depend on an understanding of the goals and intentions of the model. Further, if the robot has been unsuccessful, how does it determine which parts of its performance were inadequate? The robot must be able to diagnose its own errors in order to incrementally improve performance.

14.3 Approach

Our approach to building systems that address the problems of determining saliency and relevance, mapping observed actions onto behavioral responses, and implementing incremental refinement focuses on three keystones. First, *saliency results from a combination of inherent object qualities, contextual influences, and the model's attention.* This provides the basis for building perceptual systems that can respond to complex social situations. Second, our robots utilize *similar physical morphologies* to simplify the task of body mapping and recognizing success. By building humanlike robots we can vastly simplify the problems of mapping perceived actions to behavioral responses while providing an interface that is intuitive and easy to correct. Third, our systems *exploit the structure of social interactions*. By recognizing the social context and the stereotypical social actions made by the model, our robots can recognize saliency. By engaging in those same types of stereotypical social actions, the dynamics between the robot and the model provide a simplified means for recognizing success and diagnosing failures.

Saliency Results from a Combination of Inherent Object Qualities, Contextual Influences, and the Model's Attention

Knowing what to imitate is fundamentally a problem of determining saliency. Objects can gain saliency (that is, they become the target of attention) through a variety of means. At times, objects are salient because of their inherent properties; objects that move quickly, objects that have bright colors, and objects that are shaped like faces are all likely to attract attention. (We call these properties *inherent* rather than *intrinsic* because they are perceptual properties, and thus are observer dependent and not strictly a quality of an external object.) Objects can also become salient through contextual effects. The current motivational state, emotional state, and knowledge of the observer can impact saliency. For example, when the observer is hungry, images of food will have higher saliency than they otherwise would. Objects can also become salient if they are the focus of the model's attention. For example, if the model is staring intently at a glass jar, the jar may become a salient part of the scene even if it is otherwise uninteresting. Fundamental social cues (such as gaze direction) can also be used by the observer to determine the important features of a task.[2] People naturally attend to the key aspects of a task while performing that task. For example, when opening the jar, the model will naturally look at the lid as he grasps it and at his own hand while twisting off the lid. By directing its own attention to the object of the model's attention, the observer will automatically attend to the critical aspects of the task. In the case of social instruction, the observer's gaze direction can also serve as an important feedback signal for the instructor. For example, if the observer is not attending to the jar, then the instructor can actively direct the observer's attention by increasing the jar's saliency, perhaps by pointing to it or tapping on it.

Utilize Similar Physical Morphologies

Three of the problems outlined above can be simplified by assuming a similar physical morphology between the model and the observer. If the observer and the model have a similar shape, the perceptual task of determining saliency can be constrained by the possible actions of the observer. If the observer witnesses an ambiguous motion of the model's arm, the observer can postulate that the perception must have been one of the actions that it could possibly perform in that situation and eliminate any other possible perceptual interpretations.

The mapping problem can also be simplified by having similar physical morphologies. If the observer can identify that it is the model's arm that is moving, it need not initially try to match that motion with an action that it is capable of performing only with its mouth or legs. Additionally, the position of the model's arm serves as a guideline for an initial configuration for the observer's arm. A different morphology would imply the need to solve an inverse kinematics problem in order to arrive at a starting position or the more complicated problem of mapping unlike body parts between model and observer (for example, see chapter 3 of this volume by Herman for imitation between dolphins and humans). In general, this transformation has many solutions, and it is difficult to add other constraints that may be important (e.g., reducing loading or avoiding obstacles). By constraining the space of possible mappings, the computational complexity of the task is reduced.

Similar physical morphology also allows for a more accurate evaluation. If the observer's morphology is similar to the model's, then the observer is likely to have similar failure modes. This potentially allows the observer to characterize its own failures by observing the failures of the model. If the observer watches the model having difficulty opening the jar when his elbows are close together, the observer may be able to extrapolate that it too will fail without sufficient leverage. In situations where the model is taking an active role in instructing the observer, a similar morphology also allows the model to more easily identify and correct errors from the observer. If the observer's arms are too close together when attempting to open the jar, the model's knowledge about his own body will assist him in evaluating the failure mode and in providing an appropriate solution.

Exploit the Structure of Social Interactions

Social interactions have structure that can be exploited to simplify the problems of imitation. By recognizing the appropriate social context, the observer can limit the number of possible perceptual states and determine whether the attention state of the model is an appropriate saliency signal. When the model is performing a manipulative task, the focus of attention is often very relevant. However, when engaged in some social contexts, the focus of attention is not necessarily important. For example, it is customary in many cultures to avert eye contact while taking one's turn in a conversation and to establish eye contact when ending a turn. Exploiting these rules of social conduct can help the observer to recognize the possible value of the attention state of the model (thus simplifying the saliency problem).

The structure of social interactions can also be used to provide feedback in order to recognize success and correct failures. In the case of social instruction, the difficulty of obtaining success criteria can be simplified by exploiting the natural structure of social interactions. As the observer acts, the facial expressions (smiles or frowns), vocalizations, gestures (nodding or shaking of the head), and other actions of the model all provide feedback that will allow the observer to determine whether or not it has achieved the desired goal. The structure of instructional situations is iterative; the instructor demonstrates, the student performs, and then the instructor demonstrates again, often exaggerating or focusing on aspects of the task that were not performed successfully. The instructor continually modifies the way he performs the task, perhaps exaggerating those aspects that the student performed inadequately, in an effort to refine the student's subsequent performance. By repeatedly responding to the same social cues that initially allowed the observer to understand and identify which salient aspects of the scene to imitate, the observer can incrementally refine its approximation of the actions of the instructor.

Monitoring the structure of the social interaction can assist the instructor in maintaining an appropriate environment for learning. Expressive cues such as facial expressions or vocalizations can regulate the rate and quality of instruction. The instructor modifies both the speed and the content of the demonstration based on feedback from the student. By appearing confused, the student causes the instructor to slow down and simplify the demonstration.

Recognizing the appropriate social context can be an important cue in knowing when imitation is an appropriate solution to a problem. Internal motivations will serve as a primary mechanism for determining when to search for an appropriate model and when an attempt to perform an imitative act is appropriate. However, opportunistic use of good models in the environment can also be important in learning new skills. By recognizing which social contexts are likely to produce a good model behavior, the robot can exploit learning opportunities when they arise.

14.4 Robotic Implementations

For the past four years, our group at the MIT Artificial Intelligence Laboratory has been attempting to build anthropomorphic robots that respond socially (Brooks et al. 1998). Building a system that can imitate requires the integration of many different social, perceptual, cognitive, and motor skills. To date, we have constructed some modules that will be useful components of a social learning mechanism. We still require many additional components, and we have yet to meet the challenge of integrating all of these components into a system that can learn from a human instructor.

In this section, we will describe some of the components that have already been implemented to address a few of the problems of social interaction, including a perceptual system for *finding the model using face-detection and skin-color detection*, a *context-sensitive attention system*, a system for producing *expressive displays through facial expressions and body posture*, and a system for *regulating social exchanges* to optimize the learning environment. Each of these components has been evaluated individually using traditional engineering techniques. In some cases, it is appropriate to compare the performance of a module with humans or animal data. Once all of the necessary components are integrated, we can ultimately evaluate the complete system using the same techniques that are used to characterize human behavior. Because the robot is embodied in the world, it can be evaluated side-by-side against a human in the same physical environment and in the same social context (using the same instructor and the same task). We begin with a description of the two robot platforms.

Robot Platforms

Our work with imitation has focused on two robot platforms: an upper-torso humanoid robot called Cog and an active vision system enhanced with facial features called Kismet (figure 14.1). A basic repertoire of perceptual capabilities and sensorimotor skills have been implemented on these robots (see Brooks et al. 1999 for a review).

Cog approximates a human being from the waist up with twenty-two degrees of freedom (DOF) and a variety of sensory systems. The physical structure of the robot, with movable torso, arms, neck, and eyes gives it humanlike motion, while the sensory systems (visual, auditory, vestibular, and proprioceptive) provide rich information about the robot and its immediate environment. The robot Kismet is based on the same active vision system used on Cog. Kismet has an additional fifteen degrees of freedom in facial expressions, including eyebrows that lift and arch, ears that lift and rotate, eyelids, lips, and a mouth. The robot is able to show a wide variety of facial expressions and displays that it uses to engage a human in face-to-face exchanges (Breazeal and Scassellati 1999a).

By focusing on robotic platforms that are anthropomorphic, we simplify the problems of social interaction in three ways. First, it allows for a simple and natural means of interaction. People already know how to provide the robot with appropriate feedback, how to attract its attention, and can guess what capabilities it might possess. Second, the responses of the robot can be easily identified and interpreted by a naive observer. Third, by having a similar body structure, the problem of mapping observed actions onto the robot's own body is simplified.

Finding a Good Model Using Face Detection and Skin-Color Detection

For our robots, one of the first tasks that must be performed is locating an appropriate model. Because we assume that a good model will attempt to assist the robot and because human instructors attend to their students throughout the instructional process, the robot should be most interested in human faces that are ori-

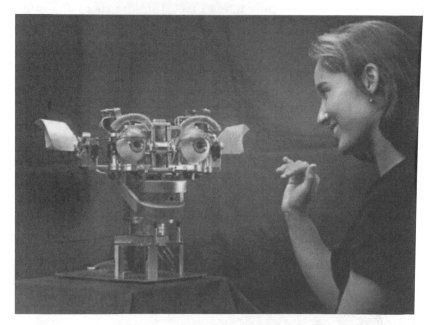

Figure 14.1   Cog (top) and Kismet (bottom), our two anthropomorphic robot platforms.

ented toward it. Difficulties with occlusion and multiple-viewpoint recognition can be avoided because a helpful instructor will position himself in face-to-face contact with the robot.

Our face-detection techniques are designed to identify locations that are likely to contain a face, not to verify with certainty that a face is present in the image. The face detector is based on the ratio-template technique developed by Sinha (1996), and has been previously reported by Scassellati (1998). The ratio template algorithm has been evaluated on Turk and Pentland's (1991) database of frontal views of faces under different lighting and orientations, and has been shown to be reasonably invariant to changes in illumination and rotation (see Scassellati 1998 for further evaluation of this technique). The algorithm can operate on each level of an image pyramid in order to detect faces at multiple scales. In the current implementation, due to limited processing capability, we elected to process only a few image scales for faces. A 14×16 ratio template applied to a 128×128 image finds faces in a range of approximately 6 to 15 feet from the robot and applied to a 64×64 image finds faces in a range of 3 to 6 feet from the robot. This range was suitable for our current investigations of face-to-face social interactions, and could easily be expanded with additional processors. The implemented face detector operates at approximately 20 Hz. In combination with this template-based method, we also use a filter that selects skin-color regions from the image by selecting pixel locations that fall within a prespecified range in the color space. These two techniques allow us to recognize the location of potential models (figure 14.2).

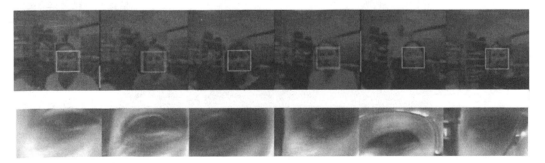

Figure 14.2 Examples of successful face and eye detections. The system locates faces in the peripheral camera, saccades to that position (shown at top), and then extracts an image of the eye (bottom). The position of the eye is inexact, in part because the human subjects are not motionless.

A Context-Dependant Attention System for Determining Saliency

To recognize salient objects, we have been constructing attention and perception systems that combine information on visual motion and innate perceptual classifiers (such as face detectors, color saliency, depth segmentation, and auditory information) with a habituation mechanism and a motivational and behavioral model. This attention system allows the robot to selectively direct computational resources and exploratory behaviors toward objects in the environment that have inherent or contextual saliency.

From infancy, people show a preference for stimuli that exhibit certain low-level feature properties. For example, a four-month-old infant is more likely to look at a moving object than a static one, or a facelike object than one that has similar, but jumbled, features (Fagan 1988). Both Cog and Kismet use a perceptual system that combines basic feature detectors including face detectors, motion detectors, skin-color filters, and color-saliency analysis. Low-level perceptual inputs are combined with high-level influences from motivations, behaviors, and habituation effects (figure 14.3). This system is based upon models of adult human visual search and attention (Wolfe 1994) and has been reported previously (Breazeal and Scassellati 1999b). The attention process constructs a linear combination of the input feature detectors and a time-decayed Gaussian field that represents habituation effects. High areas of activation in this composite generate a saccade to that location and compensatory neck movement. The weights of the feature detectors can be influenced by the motivational and behavioral state of the robot to preferentially bias certain stimuli (figure 14.4). For example, if the robot is searching for a playmate, the weight of the face detector can be increased to cause the robot to show a preference for attending to faces. The addition of saliency cues based on the model's focus of attention can easily be incorporated into this model of attention, but the perceptual abilities needed to obtain the focus of attention have yet to be fully developed.

Expressive Displays: Facial Expressions and Body Posture

By identifying the emotional states of the instructor and responding with its own emotional displays, our robots will have additional information to help determine what to imitate, evaluate success, and provide a natural interface. We have developed robots with the

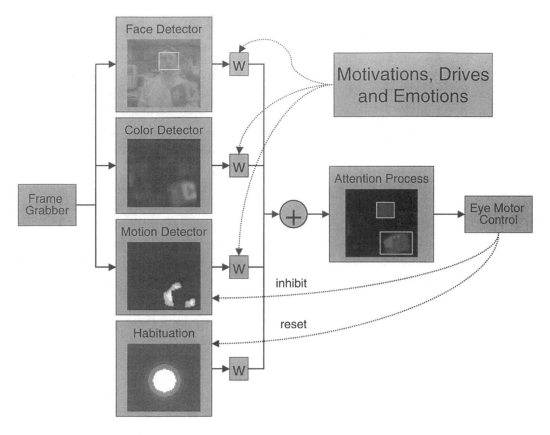

Figure 14.3 Overview of the attention system. A variety of visual feature detectors (color, motion, and face detectors) combine with a habituation function to produce an attention activation map. The attention process influences eye control and the robot's internal motivational and behavioral state, which in turn influence the weighted combination of the feature maps. Displayed images were captured during a behavioral trial session.

ability to display facial expressions (figure 14.5) and have developed emotional models that drive them based upon environmental stimuli, behavioral state, and internal motivations (Breazeal and Scassellati 1999a).

The robot's emotional responses are implemented though a variety of affective circuits, each of which implements one of the six basic emotions hypothesized to be innate in humans—anger, disgust, fear, joy, sadness, and surprise (Ekman and Davidson 1994). The activation of an emotional response depends upon the affective contributions that each circuit receives from drives, behaviors, and perceptual stimuli. Collectively, these influences can be represented as a point in a three dimensional space that has axes corre-

Figure 14.4 Preferential looking based on habituation and top-down influences. When presented with two salient stimuli (a face and a brightly colored toy), the robot prefers to look at the stimulus that has behavioral relevance to the currently active goal (shown at top). Habituation causes the robot to also spend time looking at the nonpreferred stimulus.

Figure 14.5 Kismet displaying expressions of contentment, disgust, sadness, and surprise.

sponding to arousal (high, neutral, or low), valence (positive, neutral, or negative), and stance (approach, neutral, or withdraw). To generate the facial expression of the robot, each dimension of this space has a characteristic facial posture and body posture (the basis set). The resulting facial expression is an average of these basis postures weighted by the location of the affective state within this space. For example, more negatively valenced values result in having the robot frown more. The basis set of face and body postures are chosen so that each generated expression is reminiscent of the corresponding facial expression and body posture in humans when in an analogous affective state. An initial web-based study demonstrated that both valence and arousal in the robot's expression were included in subjects' descriptions of photos of the robot, while the robot's stance was present less often in subjects' descriptions (Breazeal and Foerst 1999).

Regulating Social Exchanges

To learn efficiently, the robot must be capable of regulating the rate and intensity of instruction to match its current understanding and capabilities. Expressive displays combine with knowledge of social processes (such as turn taking) to allow the robot to regulate the interaction to optimize its own learning. For example, if the instructor is moving too quickly, the robot will have a difficult time maintaining the interaction and will respond with a frustrated and angry expression. In our informal observations, these behaviors are readily interpreted even by naive instructors.

With Kismet, we implemented a system that engages in a mutually regulatory interaction with a human while distinguishing between stimuli that can be influenced socially (facelike stimuli) and those that cannot (motion stimuli) (Breazeal and Scassellati 2000). A human interacts with the robot through direct face-to-face interaction by waving a hand at the robot or by using a toy to play with the robot. The perceptual system classifies these interactions in terms of their nature (engaging faces or playing with toys) and their quality (low intensity, good intensity, and overwhelming). These stimuli are used by the robot to satiate its drives, each of which represents a basic "need" of the robot. (i.e., a need to be with people, a need to be played with, and a need for rest). Each drive contributes to the selection of the active behavior, which will act to either reestablish or to maintain that drive within homeostatic balance. The drives influence the affective state of the robot (contributing to a state of distress when a drive approaches a homeostatic limit or to a state of contentment as long as the drives remain within bounds). This mechanism is designed to activate emotional responses (such as fleeing to avoid a threatening stimulus) appropriate for the regulatory process.

In addition, the robot's facial expression and body posture are external signs of the robot's internal state. Our informal observation is that naive subjects given no instructions will adapt their behavior to maintain a happy and interested expression on the robot's face. Figure 14.6 shows one example of how the robot's

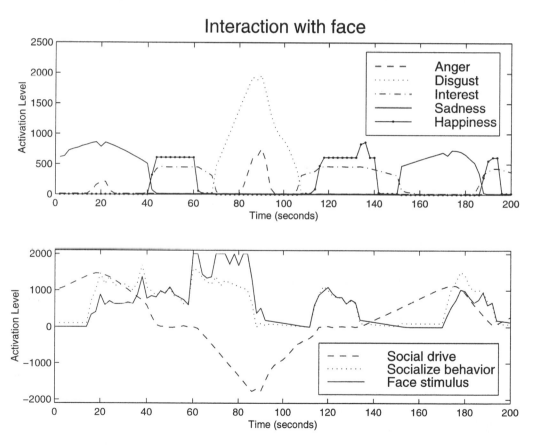

Figure 14.6 This is a trace of Kismet's perceptual, behavioral, and motivational state while interacting with a person. When the face stimulus is absent, the social drive rises away from the homeostatic point causing the robot to display a sad expression, which encourages the human to engage the robot, thereby restoring the drive. When the stimulus becomes too intense, the social drive drops away from the homeostatic point causing an expression of fear, which encourages the human to stop the interaction, thereby restoring the drive.

emotive cues are used to regulate the nature and intensity of social interaction, and how the nature of the interaction influences the robot's social drives and behavior.

14.5 Ongoing Work

Our current work on building systems that are capable of social learning focuses on three areas: the *recognition of vocal affect and communicative intent* as a feedback signal for determining success, the use of *joint reference* skills to identify salient objects and to diagnose and correct errors, and the use of *imitative games* to distinguish between self and other, to distinguish between social and nonsocial stimuli, and to model human infant facial expression imitation.

Recognizing Vocal Affect and Communicative Intent

We are currently implementing an auditory system to enable our robots to recognize vocal affirmation, prohibition, and attentional bids while interacting with a human. By doing so, the robot will obtain natural social feedback on which of its actions have been successfully executed and which have not. Our approach is inspired by the findings of Fernald (1989), who has studied how parents convey both affective and communicative intent to infants through prosodic patterns of speech (including pitch, tempo, and tone of voice). These prosodic patterns may be universal, as infants have demonstrated the ability to recognize praise, prohibition, and attentional bids even in unfamiliar languages. Similar to the work of Slaney and McRoberts (1998), we have used a multidimensional Gaussian mixture-model and simple acoustic measures such as pitch, energy, and cepstral coefficients to discriminate between these states on a database of infant-directed utterances. Ongoing work focuses on developing a real-time version of this system and integrating the system into social learning (Breazeal and Velasquez 1998).

Joint Reference

While our current attention systems integrate perceptual and context-dependent saliency information, we are also constructing systems to utilize the model's focus of attention as a means of determining which actions and objects are relevant. Locating the model's focus of attention is also relevant for allowing incremental improvement. By observing the model's focus of attention while attempting a behavior, the student can gain valuable feedback on the expected action, on the possible outcomes of that action, and on possible corrective actions when an error occurs.

We have already constructed perceptual systems that allow us to detect faces, orient to the detected face, and obtain a high-resolution image of the model's eyes (Scassellati 1998). We are currently working on utilizing information on the location of the pupil, the angle of gaze, the orientation of the head, and body posture to determine the object of the model's attention. This emphasis on joint reference is part of a larger project to build a "theory of mind" for the robot, which would allow it to attribute beliefs, desires, and intentions to the model and to imitate the *goal* of an action instead of the explicit action being performed (Scassellati 1999a). Our models of joint reference are taken from developmental psychology, from animal behavior, and from studies of autism (Baron-Cohen 1995).

Imitative Games

Imitative games can serve as a powerful motivator for young children. Our most recent work focuses on using the social context of an imitative game to allow the robot to perform two difficult perceptual tasks: distinguishing between stimuli that are socially responsive and stimuli that are unresponsive, and distinguishing between perceptual stimuli that are a result of the robot's own body and stimuli that correspond to other agents in the world. During an imitative game, the robot takes on two roles. As the *leader*, the robot performs an action and looks for objects in the scene that perform a similar action soon thereafter. As the *follower*, the robot attempts to imitate the actions of a particular object in the world. Stimuli that respond socially and play an imitative game with the robot will allow it to be both a good follower (by performing a variety of actions that the robot can imitate) and a good leader (by imitating the robot). Static objects, such as a bookcase, will be poor followers and poor leaders; they will neither imitate the robot's actions nor perform actions the robot can imitate. Objects that are good leaders but poor followers might be objects that are always unresponsive (such as a tree branch moving in the wind or a television), or people that are not interested in engaging the robot at the current time. Objects that are good followers but poor leaders are likely to be self-motion (either reflections or direct perceptions of itself); a mirror image or a shadow never acts on its own, but is always a perfect follower. In this way, we can begin to see a means for classifying stimuli based on their similarity to the robot.

One difficulty in this approach is determining a matching between observed actions and the robot's own behaviors (the mapping problem). For actions like facial expressions, the robot is not capable of observing its own motor behaviors directly, and thus the mapping must either be innate or learned using an external reinforcement source. We have proposed an implementation of Meltzoff and Moore's AIM model (1997) of human infant imitation of facial expressions and an implementation that allows the robot to learn a body mapping by observing its own reflections in a mirror (Breazeal 1999a). This work is motivated by a belief that imitative games may play a functional role in developing an understanding of people and the development of social skills (Meltzoff and Moore 1994; Dautenhahn 1994).

14.6 Challenges in Building Imitative Robots

Researchers in robotics will recognize that there are many open and unsolved problems in our discussions. In this short section, we hope to provide researchers outside robotics with some insight into where the difficulties in building these robots exist. From a practical perspective, building a robot is an enormous investment of time, engineering, money, and effort. Maintaining these systems can also be a frustrating and time-consuming process. Furthermore, to build all of these systems to operate in real time requires an enormous dedication to building computational architectures and optimized software.

Constructing the perceptual, motor, and cognitive skills that are necessary to begin to address the specific problems of imitation is extremely difficult. Figure 14.7 shows a system architecture under development for our humanoid robots. We are currently expanding this architecture to support imitative learning. Many of the skills to support the challenges of imitative learning are listed within the architecture, but certainly there are many skills that we have not yet begun to address. Most of the listed skills represent the work of

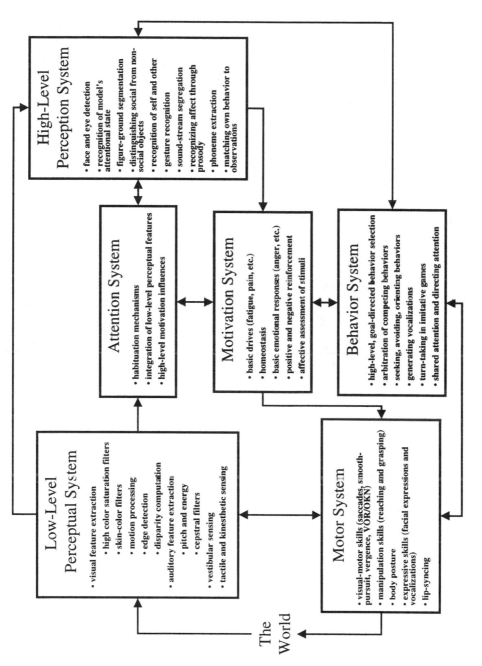

Figure 14.7 A generic control architecture under development for use on our humanoid robots Cog and Kismet. Under each large system, we have listed components that have either been implemented or are currently under development. There are also many skills that reside in the interfaces between these modules, such as learning visual-motor skills and regulating attention preferences based on motivational state. Machine learning techniques are an integral part of each of these individua systems, but are not listed individually here.

large communities of researchers, with individual books, journals, and conferences dedicated to each. The integration of each of these components is also a challenging topic by itself. For example, representing the dynamic interaction between different behaviors or understanding the compromises involved in using many different perceptual filters presents new sets of challenges. To begin to address the specific problems of imitation, each robotics research team must make some simplifying assumptions and trade-offs. Simplifications in the hardware design, the computational architecture, the perceptual systems, the behavioral repertoire, and cognitive abilities allow a research team to address the more complex issues without implementing complete solutions to other problems. Each research team must be very careful to describe the assumptions that are made and the potential implications of these assumptions on the generality of their results. While these simplifications at one level are unavoidable, it is important to keep the big picture in mind.

Evaluating complex robotic systems presents another level of challenges. Most individual components can be evaluated as stand-alone modules using traditional engineering performance measures, such as comparisons against standardized data sets or considerations of optimization and efficiency. Evaluating the behavior of an integrated system using standard techniques from ethology and behavioral psychology is difficult for many reasons. First, before the complete behavior can be evaluated, all of the required system components must be implemented and integrated together. Second, the particular assumptions used in constructing the systems may limit the types of interactions in which the robot can be evaluated. For example, limits to perception may restrict the robot to only certain limited classes of stimuli, or to stimuli that are marked in certain ways. Similarly, simplified sets of motor responses can limit the types of behavior that we can expect to observe. Third, long-term studies of behavior are difficult because the hardware systems are fragile and constantly changing. Simply maintaining a robot at a given level of functionality requires full-time support, and few robotic systems are designed to operate for extended periods of time without human intervention. Furthermore, because of the expenses of building a robot, each research robot is often supporting a variety of research studies, many of which are constantly altering the hardware platform. Fourth, comparing results between robots is difficult because of differences in

the underlying assumptions and differences in the hardware platforms. Despite these difficulties, we believe that the application of
behavioral measurement techniques will be a critical step in the
development of future robots. It is the goal of our research to
achieve a level of functionality with our robots that would permit
such an evaluation.

14.7 Summary

Imitation and social learning are studied by researchers in many
different fields, and each field raises different questions about
social learning. In this article, we have outlined some of the questions that robotics poses when considering imitation. If a robot is
to learn through imitation, in addition to a variety of perceptual,
cognitive, and motor capabilities that must be constructed, there
are unique research issues that must be addressed. The robot must
locate a good model, and then determine which of the model's
actions are relevant to the task at hand. Those observed actions
must then be mapped onto behavioral responses that the robot is
capable of performing. Finally, the robot must have some mechanism for recognizing when it has succeeded and for correcting
errors when they occur. To begin to address these issues, we have
proposed a methodology that exploits the structure of social interactions, utilizes similar physical morphology to simplify the mapping problem, and constructs saliency from a combination of
inherent object qualities, contextual influences, and the model's
focus of attention. Using two anthropomorphic robots, we have
begun to build systems that have the necessary skills to enable
social learning, including finding models based on face detection
and skin color, combining saliency through a context-sensitive
attention system, producing expressive displays, and regulating
social exchanges. We believe that the problems of implementing
social learning systems on a robot force us to address questions
that are applicable to biological systems, but which are not currently under investigation.

Acknowledgments

The work presented in this paper has been funded in part by
DARPA/ITO under contract DABT 63-99-1-0012, and by ONR
under contract N00014-95-1-0600, ''A Trainable Modular Vision

System." The authors would like to acknowledge the contributions of the humanoid robotics group at the MIT AI lab, as well as Kerstin Dautenhahn for her collaborations on discriminating self from other through the use of imitative games. Interval Research graciously permitted the use of a database of infant-directed speech for training auditory systems. We would also like to thank Kerstin Dautenhahn and one anonymous reviewer for their comments and suggestions throughout the writing of this chapter.

Notes

1. Our thanks to Kerstin Dautenhahn for pointing out this colorful analogy.
2. Note that detecting these social cues (such as gaze direction) is a mechanistic process that does not require an understanding of the model's intentional state. However, it has been hypothesized that these mechanistic processes are critical precursors to an understanding of intentionality (Baron-Cohen 1995).

References

Baron-Cohen, S. *Mindblindness*. Cambridge, Mass.: MIT Press, 1995.

Billard, A., and K. Dautenhahn. Grounding communication in autonomous robots: An experimental study. *Robotics and Autonomous Systems* 24(1–2): 71–81, 1998.

Breazeal, C. Imitation as social exchange between humans and robots. In *Proceedings of the AISB'99 Symposium on Imitation in Animals and Artifacts (Edinburgh, 7–9 April)*, pp. 96–104. Brighton, U.K.: Society for the Study of Artificial Intelligence and Simulation of Behaviour, 1999a.

Breazeal, C. Robot in society: Friend or appliance? In *Proceedings of the 1999 Autonomous Agents Workshop on Emotion-Based Agent Architectures*, Seattle, pp. 18–26. 1999b.

Breazeal, C., and A. Foerst. Schmoozing with robots: Exploring the boundary of the original wireless network. In *Proceedings of the Third International Cognitive Technology Conference (CT-99)*, San Francisco, pp. 375–390. M.I.N.D. Lab, Michigan State University, 1999.

Breazeal, C., and B. Scassellati. How to build robots that make friends and influence people. In *Proceedings of the 1999 IEEE/RSJ International Conference on Intelligent Robots and Systems (IROS-99)*, Kyongju, Korea, pp. 858–863. 1999a.

Breazeal, C., and B. Scassellati. A context-dependent attention system for a social robot. In *Proceedings of the Sixteenth International Joint Conference on Artificial Intelligence (IJCAI-99)*, Stockholm, Sweden, pp. 1146–1151. San Francisco: Morgan Kaufmann, 1999b.

Breazeal, C., and B. Scassellati. Infant-like social interactions between a robot and a human caretaker. *Adaptive Behavior* 8(1): 49–74, 2000.

Breazeal, C., and J. Velasquez. Toward teaching a robot "infant" using emotive communication acts. In *Proceedings of the 1998 SAB Workshop on Socially Situated Intelligence*, Zurich, Switzerland, pp. 25–40. 1998.

Brooks, R., C. Breazeal (Ferrell), R. Irie, C. Kemp, M. Marjanovic, B. Scassellati, and M. Williamson. Alternative essences of intelligence. In *Proceedings of the Fifteenth National Conference on Artificial Intelligence (AAAI-98)*, Madison, WI, pp. 961–967. Menlo Park, Calif.: AAAI Press, 1998.

Brooks, R., C. Breazeal (Ferrell), M. Marjanovic, B. Scassellati, and M. Williamson. The Cog project: Building a humanoid robot. In C. Nehaniv, ed., *Computation for Metaphors, Analogy, and Agents*. Lecture Notes in Artificial Intelligence 1562. Berlin: Springer-Verlag, 1999.

Byrne, R. W. Imitation without intentionality. Using string parsing to copy the organization of behavior. *Animal Cognition* 2: 63–72, 1999.

Dautenhahn, K. Trying to imitate—A step towards releasing robots from social isolation. In *Proceedings of the From Perception to Action Conference*, Lausanne, Switzerland, pp. 290–301. Los Alamitos Calif.: IEEE Computer Society Press, 7–9 September 1994.

Dautenhahn, K. Getting to know each other—Artificial social intelligence for autonomous robots. *Robotics and Autonomous Systems* 16(2–4): 333–356, 1995.

Demiris, J., and G. Hayes. Active and passive routes to imitation. In *Proceedings of the AISB'99 Symposium on Imitation in Animals and Artifacts (Edinburgh, 7–9 April)*, pp. 81–87. Brighton, U.K.: Society of the Study of Artificial Intelligence and Simulation of Behaviour, 1999.

Ekman, P., and R. Davidson. *The Nature of Emotion: Fundamental Questions*. New York: Oxford University Press, 1994.

Fagan, J. Infants' recognition of invariant features of faces. *Child Development* 47: 627–638, 1988.

Fernald, A. Intonation and communicative intent in mother's speech to infants: Is the melody the message? *Child Development* 60: 1497–1510, 1989.

Galef, B. G. Imitation in animals: History, definitions, and interpretation of data from the psychological laboratory. In T. Zentall and B. G. Galef, eds., *Social Learning: Psychological and Biological Perspectives*. Hillsdale, N.J.: Erlbaum, 1988.

Gaussier, P., S. Moga, J. P. Banquet, and M. Quoy. From perception-action loops to imitation processes: A bottom-up approach of learning by imitation. *Applied Artificial Intelligence Journal*, special issue on socially intelligent agents 12(7–8): 701–729, 1998.

Hauser, M. *The Evolution of Communication*. Cambridge, Mass.: MIT Press, 1996.

Hayes, G. M., and J. Demiris. A robot controller using learning by imitation. In *Proceedings of the Second International Symposium of Intelligent Robotic Systems*, Grenoble, France, pp. 198–204. 1994.

Kuniyoshi, Y., M. Inaba, and H. Inoue. Learning by watching: Extracting reusable task knowledge from visual observation of human performance. *IEEE Transactions on Robotics and Automation* 10, no. 6: 799–822, 1994.

Matarić, M., M. Williamson, J. Demiris, and A. Mohan. Behaviour-based primitives for articulated control. In *Proceedings of the Fifth International Conference on Simulation of Adaptive Behavior*, pp. 165–170. Cambridge, Mass.: MIT Press, 1998.

Meltzoff, A., and K. Moore. Imitation, memory, and the representation of persons. *Infant Behavior and Development* 17: 83–99, 1994.

Meltzoff, A., and K. Moore. Explaining facial imitation: A theoretical model. *Early Development and Parenting* 6: 179–192, 1997.

Nehaniv, C. L., and K. Dautenhahn. Of hummingbirds and helicopters: An algebraic framework for interdisciplinary studies of imitation and its applications. In J. Demiris and A. Birk, eds., *Interdisciplinary Approaches to Robot Learning*, vol. 24, pp. 136–161. World Scientific Press, 1998.

Scassellati, B. Finding eyes and faces with a foveated vision system. In *Proceedings of the Fifteenth National Conference on Artificial Intelligence (AAAI-98)*, Madison, WI, pp. 969–976. Menlo Park, Calif.: AAAI Press, 1998.

Scassellati, B. Imitation and mechanisms of joint attention: A developmental structure for building social skills on a humanoid robot. In C. Nehaniv, ed., *Computation for Metaphors, Analogy, and Agents*. Lecture Notes in Artificial Intelligence 1562. Berlin: Springer-Verlag, 1999a.

Scassellati, B. Knowing what to imitate and knowing when you succeed. In *Proceedings of the AISB'99 Symposium on Imitation in Animals and Artifacts (Edinburgh, 7–9 April)*, pp. 105–113. Brighton, U.K.: Society of the Study of Artificial Intelligence and Simulation of Behaviour, 1999b.

Schaal, S. Robot learning from demonstration. In D. H. Fisher Jr., ed., *International Conference on Machine Learning (ICML-97)*, pp. 12–20. San Francisco: Morgan Kaufmann, 1997.

Sinha, P. Perceiving and recognizing three-dimensional forms. Ph.D. thesis, Massachusetts Institute of Technology, 1996.

Slaney, M., and G. McRoberts. Baby ears: A recognition system for affective vocalizations. In *Proceedings of the 1998 International Conference on Acoustics, Speech, and Signal Processing (ICASSP-98)*, Seattle, pp. 12–15. IEEE, 1998.

Steels, L. Emergent adaptive lexicons. In *Proceedings of the Fourth International Conference on Simulation of Adaptive Behavior*, Cape Cod, pp. 562–567. Cambridge, Mass.: MIT Press, 1996.

Turk, M., and A. Pentland. Eigenfaces for recognition. *Journal of Cognitive Neuroscience* 3(1): 71–86, 1991.

Wolfe, J. Guided search 2.0: A revised model of visual search. *Psychonomic Bulletin and Review* 192: 202–238, 1994.

15 Sensory-Motor Primitives as a Basis for Imitation: Linking Perception to Action and Biology to Robotics

Maja J. Matarić

15.1 Introduction

Imitation is a powerful means of skill acquisition, social interaction, and cultural transfer. Although popular notions of "monkeying" and "parroting" make the phenomenon appear ubiquitous, the more formal definition of "true imitation" limits it to very few species, as it requires the ability to acquire arbitrary new skills from observation (Tomasello, Kruger, and Rather 1993; Byrne and Russon 1998). The difficulty in teasing true imitation apart from related phenomena, including stimulus enhancement, social facilitation, emulation, and priming, indicates that the underlying mechanism for imitation likely involves a complex interaction of learning mechanisms. We consider imitation to be a broad capability based on a spectrum of behavior and learning systems of increasing complexity, only the most sophisticated of which correspond to the definition of true imitation.

In our work, we view imitation as the capability to acquire new skills by observation, based on the imitator's existing behavioral repertoire, which may be simple or sophisticated. Specifically, we focus on motor behaviors, and on their underlying mechanisms. In this chapter, we present a model of imitation that results from an incrementally evolved capability based on an evolutionarily old motor control structure (motor primitives), utilized by a mechanism for movement understanding and simple mimicry (mirror neurons), driven by a specialized attentional mechanism. The entire system is based on the notion of primitives, structures that directly link the visual and motor systems in the context of complete generalized movements. The capacity for mimicry is based on this direct mapping mechanism, and itself serves as a basis for more complex, less direct forms of imitation and social learning. Thus, *primitives* are the fundamental substrate for a powerful system that couples visual perception and motor execution, and unifies recognition, classification, and learning of movement skills.

A "primitive" can refer to something that is old in an evolutionary sense, such as structures that organize the underlying mechanisms of movement, including spinal fields (Bizzi, Mussa-Ivaldi, and Giszter 1991) and central pattern generators (Stein 1997). In a computational sense, primitives can be viewed as a basis set of motor programs that are sufficient, through combination operators, for generating the entire movement repertoire. Our imitation model combines the two interpretations; it involves a system that is innately primed with a set of primitives sufficient for a large movement repertoire, and is capable of learning arbitrary new skills that can, in a hierarchical fashion, be used as new compositional elements.

Our model is inspired and constrained by the following lines of evidence from psychophysics and neuroscience:

1. The existence of mirror neurons, which map observed movements onto executable ones, thus performing sensory-motor integration and transformation. The mechanism in the model is driven by the features from the attentional mechanism and maps onto the corresponding motor primitive(s), discussed in section 15.3.
2. The existence of a selective attention mechanism for extracting biological movement information from the visual stream. The mechanism in our model is based on data from attentional studies and our own eye-tracking work, described in section 15.4.
3. The existence of motor primitives for structuring movement, constituting a motor vocabulary composable into a broad movement repertoire. In the model, the primitives are the general basis for movement, invoked by the mirror neurons as a part of the direct mimicry system underlying imitation, as discussed in section 15.5.
4. The existence of a classification-based learning system. In the model, this system encodes new motor skills by using sequencing and superposition of motor primitives, as described in section 15.6.

We bring these four lines of evidence together in a general imitation model involving movement perception, learning, and reproduction. The model is based on a direct mapping between the sensory and motor systems, organized in terms of primitives. We do not model the involved mirror and motor structures at the neural level. Instead, we propose an information-processing model based on key structural and organizational constraints arising from neuroscience and psychophysical evidence. This level of modeling allows us to experiment with various specific implementations to validate our theories and test their practical applications. As our goal is to gain insight into imitation in natural systems and enable it in artificial ones, we relate the components of our model to relevant work in neuroscience, cognitive science, and robotics.

The rest of the chapter is organized as follows. We begin in section 15.2 with the motivation for this work, which bridges the fields of cognitive science and neuroscience to robotics. Next, in section 15.3, we survey the evidence from neuroscience, focusing on mirror neurons, and touch on relevant inspiration from cognitive science and developmental psychology. In section 15.4, we review work on movement perception, and describe the results of our eye-tracking study that serve as the basis for the attentional mechanism in our model. In section 15.5, we discuss motor control in biology and robotics, focusing on motor primitives. Section 15.6 brings together the discussed components of the model into a unified framework. Section 15.7 describes our experimental methods and test beds, and summarizes some of the experimental results. Section 15.8 gives an overview of other imitation work in robotics. Section 15.9 summarizes the chapter and discusses continuing work.

15.2 Motivation

Before describing how we model imitation, we first address our dual motivation for pursuing it. Imitation is a challenge for both natural and artificial systems, as it involves the integration of multiple cognitive/computational systems—namely, perception, memory, action, and learning. Thus, both analysis and synthesis of imitation are difficult, and any insights gained are likely to be relevant to both biology and robotics.

Historically, the majority of work on imitation in nature emphasized precise classification of the phenomenon into distinct types and stages (Piaget 1962; Davis 1973; Tomasello, Kruger, and Rather 1993) and addressing its role in social behavior (Bandura and Walters 1963; Bandura 1977; Meltzoff and Moore 1994). More recently, the evolution of imitation and its relation to other forms of learning are being explored (Moore 1996, 1992). Our work bears on the evolutionary history of imitation in that it outlines a potentially phylogenetically old mechanism as the core of the phenomenon.

Imitation is not only a powerful learning mechanism, but it is also thought to be a keystone in the evolution of communication and language (Arbib and Rizzolatti 1996; Rizzolatti et al. 1996b;

Jeannerod et al. 1995; Donald 1993; chapter 10, this volume). Thus, it "vertically" integrates cognitive systems from the lowest levels of perception and motor control to the highest levels of cognition. The notion of vertical integration is a foundational principle of behavior-based robotics, a branch of robotics and artificial intelligence that aims at developing autonomous, adaptive, embodied systems that exist in the physical world and cope with the demands in the "here and now" (Brooks 1986, 1991; Matarić 1997; Arkin 1998). Unlike traditional robotics, where thinking (computation) takes more time than does action, behavior-based robotics focuses on fully integrated systems that act in real time in their environment.

Imitation presents a potentially powerful mechanism for automated programming and control of robots. In the past, the idea of "teaching by showing" or "learning by demonstration" was limited to reproducing the goal or output state of the activity, but not the complete process that achieved it, or the underlying mechanism. In contrast, current efforts focus on modeling the imitation mechanism itself, in order to develop a general tool for improved robot control and more natural interaction with robots. Section 15.8 provides a more detailed overview of relevant work on imitation in robotics. In addition to programming robots more directly and efficiently, a functional model of imitation has a variety of other pragmatic applications for more natural human-machine interaction. An important one is aiding skill (re)learning in children, athletes, the handicapped, and those recovering from stroke or injury. Thus, the motivation for studying imitation comes from the challenge of understanding this complex and powerful natural phenomenon, as well as applying it for programming of artificial systems toward a more natural human-machine interaction.

15.3 Inspiration

A strong connection between perception and action is a key component of our imitation model, and is inspired by evidence from neuroscience, cognitive science, and developmental psychology. Decety (1996) and Jeannerod and Decety (1995) demonstrated that a shared neural substrate is used both in imagined and executed movements. Subjects involved in imagination and visualization of motor tasks demonstrated activation of motor pathways similar to that during execution of movement. Similarly, increased activity in the motor cortex was measured during observation of movement, both in humans watching another human (Jeannerod et al. 1995; Fadiga et al. 1995) and in monkeys watching a human (di Pellegrino et al. 1992).

The direct connection between movement perception and its execution is supplied by the so-called mirror neurons found in area F5 of the monkey premotor cortex (Rizzolatti et al. 1996b). These neurons fire when the monkey observes a specific movement as well as when it executes the same movement. Since their discovery, mirror neurons have become a subject of intense study, as they are a natural candidate for neural theories of imitation. It is reasonable to postulate that the function these neurons perform, the connection between observed and performed behavior, is the substrate for imitative capability. The mirror system likely enables mimicry in monkeys, who are not thought capable of "true imitation." The presence of mirror neurons in other species has not yet been tested extensively. However, similar facility was found in the left Broca's area (area 45) and the dorsal premotor area 6 of the human brain (Iacoboni et al. 1999; Rizzolatti et al. 1996a). It is currently not known what movements are represented by the mirror system (besides the few that were tested directly), and whether the movements are learned or innate.

The neuroscience evidence discussed so far has addressed the connection between sensory and motor systems. Psychophysical experiments addressing the cognitive aspect of this connection provide complementary evidence. Vogt (1995) tested human subjects for the existence of an intermediate coding level between perception and action during an imitation task consisting of copying drawings with closed eyes. Subjects showed no improvement after immediate rehearsal, and no effect from distractions, possibly due to a lack of intermediate coding and the existence of a generative perception module that automatically prepares for action. Similarly, Pelisson, Goodale, and Prablanc (1978) showed that adjustments of hand pointing to visual targets do not require visual information about the moving arm, implying the existence of internal models of movement that transform visual information into motor representations.

Further evidence supporting sensory-motor integration and generative perception can be found in lesion studies (Goodale et al. 1994), studies of athletic performance (Abernethy 1990; Elkins 1996; Savelsvertgh and Bootsma 1994), and in developmental psychology (Bertenthal 1996). Developmental psychology work in infant imitation also supports sensory-motor integration as the basis of imitation. Meltzoff and Moore argue that imitation is a fundamental human capability, found in newborns and based on an innate link between perceptual and motor systems (Meltzoff and Moore 1988, 1994), enabling young children to imitate facial expressions and hand movements without visual feedback. They hypothesize an imitation mechanism involving innate, integrated, supramodal representations of human movements and postures (Meltzoff and Moore 1995, 1997).

The above biological evidence serves as powerful inspiration for our philosophy and approach to modeling imitation. We postulate that imitation is based on a simpler mimicry system encoded through mirror neurons and involving direct mappings between observed and executable movements. The executable movements are encoded using the phylogenetically older system of motor primitives. Thus, mimicry involves mapping observed movements to an existing motor primitive repertoire. Imitation, in contrast, involves a more complex process capable of creating arbitrary new motor skills by composing complex hierarchical combinations of primitives and other already learned skills.

Our imitation model thus employs a series of cognitive systems that build upon each other in precisely the incremental fashion one would expect from an evolved capacity. The complete system utilizes four key components: (1) movement perception through a specialized selective attention system, (2) direct sensory-motor mapping between the perceived and executable movement, (3) movement generation through a structured system of composable motor primitives, and (4) learning of new movements and skills by building on the existing repertoire of primitives, through classification and combination. Each of these components is now addressed in detail.

15.4 Movement Perception

We postulate that imitative capability takes advantage of a specialized attentional system attuned to biological movement. This system predates imitation, and possibly evolved for social interaction with conspecifics. Its ability to recognize biological movement and, given a complex visual input, selectively attend to the areas containing task-related information, is a key aspect of imitation.

We will propose that this specialized movement perception and attention system is not only driven by external visual input, but also by the motor primitives, which serve as predictors of what movement will occur next. To explain and support this claim, we overview relevant evidence from neuroscience, and then describe an eye-tracking study we conducted with the goal of addressing precisely the question of selective attention in imitation.

Neuroscience Evidence

Johansson (1973) demonstrated the human capability to recognize biological motion from a small number of structured visual cues such as light dots in key locations on the limbs. This well-known experiment points toward a specialized mechanism for body-motion detection. Perrett and coauthors performed a series of studies of movement perception in the macaque monkey. The results support the existence of specialized neural detectors and predictors for specific postures, movements, and goal-oriented behaviors. Perrett and colleagues (1985) show macaque neurons that selectively respond to specific movement types and stimulus forms, such as particular movements of the whole body or body parts. Perrett and colleagues (1989a) demonstrate similar, view-independent results, implying the potential for viewer-centered and goal-centered descriptions of the movement. Perrett and colleagues (1989b) describe a population of neurons involved in the recognition of specific actions of others, and Perrett and colleagues (1990) show that expectation of movement indirectly correlates with the amount of resulting neural firing. Taken together, this evidence supports the existence of a specialized biological movement detection system also capable of prediction.

Eye-Tracking Evidence

Little is known about visual attention involved specifically in imitation. Based on our interest in visuomotor integration theories of imitation, we conducted a set of eye-tracking experiments aimed at addressing the following questions:

1. Is there a difference between watching a movement with the intention to imitate and just watching?
2. When watching with the intention to imitate, what features are fixated on?

In a standard cognitive model of perception and motor control, one would expect the answer to the first question to be positive, denoting different processing involved in observation alone compared to observation combined with or followed by motor planning. However, if we adopt a strong sensory-motor integration assumption, which postulates a direct mapping between movement observation and reproduction, we would expect to see no difference in fixation patterns between the imitation and no-imitation conditions. The expectation would be that, in both cases, the sensory-motor system maps the observed movement to the executable motor programs; in the former condition the execution of the movements results in imitation, while in the latter, movement is inhibited.

The second question was aimed at gaining insight into the attentional mechanism, and its relation to the underlying motor control system. Given that subjects have limited attentional resources and are thus forced to fixate selectively, we were interested in finding out what they would attend to and how the visual information fixated on would serve as a basis for subsequent imitation.

In the experiment, fixation patterns of 40 subjects were recorded while being shown 25 three-second-long videos of different types of unfamiliar finger, hand, and arm movements on a computer screen. Before each set of videos, the subjects were told whether they would subsequently imitate each video after viewing it. The computer screen was black between the stimuli and during the imitation phase. In the imitation condition, the subject's right arm was extended and imitation took place without visual feedback.

Regardless of the type and size of presented stimulus, and regardless of whether the subjects intended to subsequently imitate, they attended to the hand most frequently and for the longest time periods; fixation frequency and duration were both maximized at the hand. The only difference between the subjects' behavior between the imitation and no-imitation conditions was in pupil dilation. In the imitation condition, dilation was significantly larger, while the fixation behavior remained the same in both conditions. Finally, in spite of focusing overt attention mostly on the hand, subjects were effective at imitating the presented movements. (For a detailed description of the experiments, analysis, and results, see Matarić and Pomplun 1998.)

These data provide a decisive negative answer to the first question, testing for the existence of any difference between observation with and without intention to imitate. Thus, the results add overt fixation behavior measured through eye tracking to data from other modalities that all support the direct sensory-motor mapping theory. The results are consistent with the neuroscience and developmental psychology work discussed above, all supporting generative perception of movement as a general property of visuo-motor processing, and thus of imitation.

The data also allow some interesting interpretations for the second question above, asking what the location of fixation tells us about the underlying motor control mechanism. The results demonstrating consistent selective attention on the hand allow for several hypotheses that impact imitation:

1. Perception of biological motion focuses overt attention at the end-effector; this insight can be used to greatly simplify models of attention.
2. Internal models, possibly in the form of motor primitives, are used to fill in the motor control details, which are not directly observed.
3. Those internal models also in influence the attentional mechanism by providing movement prediction or expectation.
4. An efficient transformation between the visual (extrinsic) and motor (intrinsic) representations and coordinate frames converts the observed end-effector information into executable movement.

The results of this study, in conjunction with other evidence we overviewed, serve as the basis for the attentional mechanism of our imitation model, described in section 15.6. The data also support our primitives-based framework, described in the next section.

15.5 Motor Control and Motor Primitives

Our model postulates that the motor system is organized into a collection of primitives—motor programs that encode complete stereotypical movements. These can be executed sequentially or concurrently (through parameterized superposition), to create a large movement repertoire. This general organization of the motor system is then used by the mirror system (which is phylogenetically newer) to instantiate direct sensory-motor mappings onto executable motor programs. In this section, we describe the neuroscience inspiration for the motor primitives aspect of our model.

Understanding the modular organization of biological movement and implementing it in artificial systems are outstanding challenges in biology and robotics. The theory of motor primitives has served as an inspiration for work both in behavior-based control in general and in robot models of imitation in specific. Mussa-Ivaldi and Giszter (1992) and Giszter, Mussa-Ivaldi, and Bizzi (1993) suggested the existence of spinal force-field motor primitives that converge to single equilibrium points and produce high-level behaviors such as reaching and wiping. In experiments with spinalized frogs and rats, when the spine is stimulated with an electrode, a particular field is activated, causing the leg to execute a complete behavior and come to rest at the field's equilibrium point. When two or more fields are stimulated at the same time, either a linear superposition of the fields is obtained, or one dominates (Mussa-Ivaldi, Giszter, and Bizzi 1994). In either case, a meaningful movement of the leg results. Only a small number of such distinct fields was found in the frog's spine; thus only a dozen primitives may be sufficient for coding the frog's entire motor repertoire, through sequencing and superposition of supraspinal inputs through descending pathways (Bizzi, Mussa-Ivaldi, and Giszter 1991).

This suggests elegant and modular organization for motor control, in which entire behaviors are coded with primitives whose composition results in more complex motor outputs. Our previous work (Matarić and Marjanović 1993; Matarić 1995, 1997) used this organization to structure motor control of single and multiple mobile robots into a collection of basis behaviors that fit the notion of primitives directly into the modular behavior-based control paradigm (Arkin 1998). The approach was demonstrated to be effective for various individual and group behaviors, including navigation, foraging, following, flocking, and homing. Arkin (1987) applied schema theory (Arbib 1992) to behavior-based mobile robots and employed a similar notion of composable behaviors, also stemming from neuroscience foundations (Arbib 1981).

The idea of using primitives for motor control has also been studied in articulated, humanoid robotics. Williamson (1996) and Marjanović, Scassellati, and Williamson (1996) developed a 6-DOF (degrees of freedom) robot arm controller. In contrast to biological and mobile robotics movement primitives, theirs coded for four static postures, three for reaching and one for resting. Interpolation was applied to reach any desired end-point position within the 3-D space encompassed by the primitives. Schaal and Sternad (1998) used nonlinear attractor dynamics to create two types of motor primitives, and demonstrate them on a rhythmic drumming task with a 7-DOF robot arm.

Our own previous work on articulated humanoid control (Matarić, Zordan, and Williamson 1999) applied to the control of 7-DOF arms of a physics-based 20-DOF humanoid simulation and implemented two versions of the force-field primitives. One closely modeled the frog data described above, using an intrinsic, joint-space representation. The other used another biologically inspired approach, impedance control (Hogan 1985), which operates in the extrinsic end-point (hand) coordinate frame. Both were shown to provide an effective substrate for control of a complicated sequential motor task, but each had limitations in terms of ease of control for certain types of movements. We proposed a combination approach, employed in our current model and discussed in the next section.

The issue of coordinate frame choice is just one of the many that must be resolved in order to practically apply the primitives-based approach to motor control. While an expressive and composable vocabulary of motor primitives is an appealing idea, what the primitives in such a vocabulary should be remains a difficult problem. In the next section we discuss this issue, describe our choice of primitives, and their role in the imitation model.

15.6 Our Model

Attempts to endow robots with biologically inspired imitation capabilities are recent, and those aimed at studying biological imitation through robotics are few. Our effort brings together insights and methods from these two fields into a testable model of imitation with practical applications. We combine the discussed biological inspirations into the following model components:

1. A selective attentional mechanism for extracting salient movement information from the visual stream by focusing on the effectors (hands or tools). We assume that this mechanism is based on an evolutionarily old capacity to recognize kin and conspecifics (Parr and de Waal 1999) and interpret their actions and situation-specific intentions (Cheney and Seyfarth 1990).

2. A mirrorlike sensory-motor mapping system as a means of representational integration and transformation from visual input into executable motor programs. This mechanism performs the functions

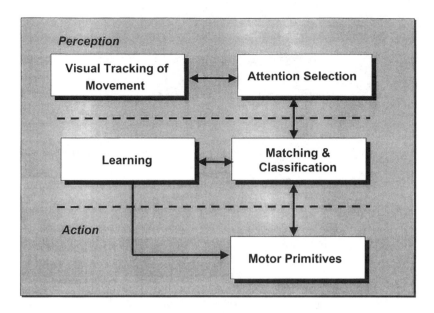

Figure 15.1 The information processing flow in our imitation model.

variously referred to as direct matching, mirroring, or resonance (Iacoboni et al. 1999; Rizzolatti et al. 1996b), found in the monkey and human.

3. A motor control system consisting of primitives that constitute the basic motor vocabulary composable into a broad movement repertoire through sequencing and superposition. These can be thought to perform the function of spinal force-field primitives (Bizzi, Mussa-Ivaldi, and Giszter 1991) as well as cortical central pattern generators (Brooks 1981; Stein 1997).

4. A classification-based learning mechanism that learns from the match between the observed and executable movements and is biased toward parameterized reuse of the existing motor programs through hierarchical composition. Figure 15.1 shows the model, with the information processing flow indicated among its main components. We now describe each of the model components in turn.

Attention in Movement Tracking

Deciding what to pay attention to for subsequent imitation is a difficult problem. Based on the literature on visual attention (Pashler 1999) and on our own eye-tracking results (Matarić and Pomplun 1998), we assume that the focus of attention is not driven directly by the intention to imitate. Instead, in our model, we postulate an attentional mechanism that takes into consideration both intrinsic bottom-up image features (such as velocity changes and the position of the end-point) and extrinsic, top-down task goals (imitation or otherwise) in selecting what to attend to.

Our attentional mechanism performs a segmentation of the retinal space, then evaluates the current interest level of each feature, and finally displaces the center of attention accordingly. We transform all of the features into an egocentric coordinate frame (Stein 1992; Flanders, Helms Tillery, and Soechting 1992; Flanders and Soechting 1995) suitable for subsequent higher-level processing. The frame is initially anchored on a fixed feature (e.g., the head) or on a visual landmark, if one is observed. The retinal segmentation is fovea based, using a log-polar grid (Hubel and Wiesel 1977). As the distance between a feature and the center of attention increases, the resolution of the feature decreases.

The evaluation of the current interest level for a feature is based on three factors: retinal movement, captivation, and task-level bias. Retinal movement is the amount a feature has recently moved in the retinal image. Captivation is based on the recent interest level of the feature, and on the overall level of "boredom," inversely proportional to the novelty of the image. A feature loses interest when it is given attention and produces little or no newly occupied cells in the retina. Finally, task-level bias is any preference for specific features (e.g., the feet for learning dance steps). The three factors are normalized and weighted so that retinal movement is the basic driver of attention, sufficient captivation supersedes it, and task-level bias, when present, overrides both.

Retinal movement, captivation, and task-level bias represent dimensions in feature-interest space. Each is represented as a point in that space, with its magnitude corresponding to its interest level. Displacement of the center of attention is based on the computed and thresholded interest levels of the features and their distance, in interest space, from the current center of attention. The feature with the most interest captures the focus of attention and inhibits the others. If no features meet the criteria, attention de-focuses on either the entire body or a subset of recently interesting features. Figure 15.2 illustrates the attentional system. More detail about the attentional part of the model can be found in Jenkins (2000).

The selected features serve as the basis for movement classification into primitives.

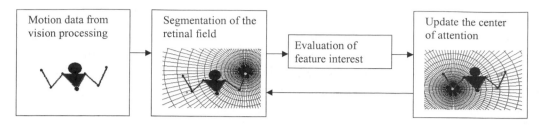

Figure 15.2 The attentional system.

Primitive-Based Sensory-Motor Integration

Combining perceptual and motor properties into a unified representation is a key challenge of the direct mapping hypothesis that drives our work. The motor primitives in this model, much like the basis behaviors in our previous work (Matarić 1995; Matarić and Marjanović 1993), are derived from a combination of top-down and bottom-up constraints, reflecting evolutionary interaction between morphology and behavior. The bottom-up constraints stem from the physical properties of the motor system, its kinematics and dynamics. The top-down constraints are shaped by the motor behaviors the system performs, based both on the evolutionary bias for a given species and by the specific skills learned during a lifetime.

At the perceptual end, primitives are shaped by the structure of the visual system and the inputs it receives. In general, this input is underconstrained and defies classification into a parsimonious set of task-independent categories. Fortunately, the mirror system is specialized for mapping observations of biological movements, particularly those from systems with similar morphology—that is, conspecifics. As a result, the driving forces that shape the primitive matching system from both the perceptual and motor sides are consistent.

Our approach does not involve a detailed model of the mirror system, as insufficient neuroscience data is currently available. Instead, we focus on the selection of the motor primitives, and the way in which they fundamentally shape movement perception, discussed in the following sections.

What Type of Primitives?

Research in motor control typically addresses either discrete or oscillatory movements, but rarely both within a unified framework.

A primitive-based motor control system must account for both types and provide an efficient means of encoding both.

We have proposed three types of primitives: (1) discrete, consisting of unobstructed straight-line movements based on reaching; (2) oscillatory, consisting of repetitive movements based on central pattern generators; and (3) postural, involving large subsets or whole-body arrangements of joints (Demiris and Matarić 1998). Assuming this division, we implemented each primitive in the most "natural" frame of reference—that is, one that minimized coordinate transformation computations. We used intrinsic (joint) space representations for postural and oscillatory movements, and extrinsic (Cartesian) space for discrete ones (Matarić, Zordan, and Williamson 1999). We have also explored various representations, including convergent vector fields in both joint and Cartesian space, impedance control (well suited for discrete movements), interpolated joint-space control, and central pattern generators (CPGs). To address the problem of self-collisions, we introduced an avoidance primitive, which was superimposed with any currently executing primitive (Matarić, Zordan, and Mason 1998). These primitives were validated in a task of executing a dance (Matarić, Zordan, and Williamson 1999).

The discrete and oscillatory primitives are both driven by the end-effector movement(s) of the demonstrator, while postures require task-based bias to draw attention to the specific body parts. We postulate that, from an evolutionary perspective, imitation of postures is less useful than imitation of end-effector behaviors, which include the use of tools and gesture-based communication. Since these convey a selective advantage, they could have resulted in the adaptation of the mirror system, the mechanism that performs the direct mapping between the observed and executed end-effector movements.

One of the issues we are exploring with this work concerns the extent to which end-point trajectories are sufficient for movement imitation, given that the attentional mechanism provides that information with highest fidelity. In extensions of the above work, we are exploring the encoding of movement ranging from end-point only, end-point with added postural constraints, and finally adding the wrist and elbow positions. The last presents a higher-dimensional problem and an added challenge for an invariant primitive representation. We are currently exploring encodings involving wavelets and principal components analysis (PCA) methods for reducing the dimensionality of the movement data and developing a more general representation. Human planar discrete movements have been shown to reduce to a small number of principal components (Sanger 2000); we are pursuing the question of how that property scales to free movements (in 3-D) and to movement reconstruction.

The motor primitives in our model are a set of parametric motor controllers capable of generating stereotypical discrete, oscillatory, and postural movements. We first address the issue of parameterization, and then the more overarching question of what constitutes a "stereotypical" movement—that is, what and how many primitives should there be.

Parameterizing Primitives

The parameters in the motor primitive representation represent the invariants in the perceptuo-motor mapping: in order to keep the primitives general, we make them invariant to exact Cartesian position, rate of motion, size, and perspective. However, in order to produce an accurate imitation, these values must be correctly reconstructed. Thus, they are provided directly to the motor primitives from the perceptual system as parameters, but are not stored within the primitive representation. As a result, the primitives determine the high-level, generic description and parameterization of an observed movement; the specific parameter values are used to instantiate the generic primitive description into a specific executable trajectory.

The generic encoding of parametric primitives provides a parsimonious representation for control. From a robotics perspective, the notion of endowing a system with a collection of behavioral primitives and thus avoiding on-line run-time trajectory planning is very appealing, and is gaining popularity (Matarić, Zordan, and Williamson 1999; Schaal and Sternad 1998). Our past work has addressed the process of designing primitives, or basis behaviors, for a specific system and set of tasks in the domain of mobile robotics (Matarić 1995) and humanoid articulated control (Matarić, Zordan, and Williamson 1999). Such "innate" primitives are effective but are determined by the designer; we next discuss how they can be automatically generated.

Learning Primitives from Movement Data

To study the question of what the primitives should be in a bottom-up fashion, we are using three types of human movement data: (1) visual data of torso movement, (2) 3-D marker data of the human arm, and (3) joint angle data from the full body (each described in more detail in section 15.7, Experimental Validation). These data are given as input into statistical clustering methods, in order to explore any natural groupings contained therein. We are currently exploring two different clustering approaches. In one, we bias our clusters by psychophysical evidence about known movement properties. Thus, discrete and oscillatory movements are separated by directly selecting reaching-type invariants in the data. In the second approach, we explore the means for converting the spatio-temporal movement data into a more abstract, symbolic form, and apply string-matching algorithms to find patters therein. A key challenge of this approach is the reduction of the high dimensionality of the continuous movement data into an abstract form.

We postulate that given sufficient data, most of the clustering techniques should extract similar movement classes, based on the inherent kinematics and dynamic properties of the underlying movements. Once the primitive groupings are extracted, we apply generalization methods to create the desired higher-level, parametric representations for them, in order to use them as the basis set for observed movement classification.

Classification

Instead of assuming a one-to-one mapping between observed and executed movements (which greatly limits the imitative ability of a system), we favor a small set of additive basis primitives as a substrate. The classification mechanism finds the best fit between the observed behavior and any combination of the primitives, resulting in a richer mapping. Through learning, new skills are created that then serve as primitives.

In the most basic version of the model, which corresponds to a simple interpretation of the mirror system, a small set of primitives is built in, and used to map a subset of observed behaviors in a one-to-one fashion. Reaching for objects, observed in the monkey mirror system (Rizzolatti et al. 1996b), for example, is a likely primitive in such a model, and one we use in our system. In a more general version of our model, one we have experimented with so far, the observed movements are mapped to a basis set of three primitives: discrete, oscillatory, and postural, and are parameterized and sequenced to represent more complex movements. We present results from implementations of this model in section 15.7. The most general version of the model involves two extensions. The first is the superposition of primitives; so far, we have only used superposition of the avoidance primitive with other behaviors. We are currently exploring representations for primitives that facilitate superposition. The second extension is learning new primitives and using them as part of a continually expanded basis for classification and imitation, as described in the next section.

New Skill Learning

In our model, learning is a part of the comparison and classification processes that map the observed onto the known. A simple and direct match that generates a close approximation of the observed behavior results in the reinforcement of an existing skill, already encoded in the form of a parameterized combination of the primitives. On the other hand, a novel match that generates a significant performance error requires rehearsal and training. This organization leads us to the following specific expectations, consistent with the general performance of human skill acquisition:

1. The more similar skills are learned, the easier learning becomes, as the probability of a match to an existing motor program is higher.
2. Observation and learning of a skill similar to one that is known is faster than that of a completely new skill.
3. Refinement of a skill that is similar to an already known one is slower due to interference.

Thus, the process of skill learning by imitation in our model occurs during classification as well as during and after performance, based on the feedback through proprioception and external observation (by the learner and a teacher, if present). This type of learning lends itself to modeling with reinforcement-based methods (Kaelbling, Littman, and Moore 1996; Sutton and Barto 1998). The interaction of the classification and rehearsal learning systems is an important part of our research.

When sufficient training is provided, a novel pattern becomes stereotyped and encoded as part of the composable building blocks. This results in a hierarchical structure allowing classification to be done at a high level, if a similar skill already exists, or at a lower, more basic level, for novel observations. Such a hierarchy of increasingly more abstract representations allows for simpler and more compact coding of behaviors, and their use not only for motor execution but also for communication. This structure also facilitates symbol grounding, a key problem in artificial intelligence and robotics, involving the challenge of connecting high-level symbolic representations with low-level sensory and motor control (Harnad 1990).

15.7 Experimental Validation

We are validating our imitation model using a large body of input movement data, applied to a collection of experimental test beds, in a series of imitation learning tasks, described next.

Human Movement Data

We briefly overview the methods we use for movement data gathering. We have developed a motion-tracking system for extracting features from a video stream (Weber 2000). This system is simple and can easily be replaced by more sophisticated commercial versions, but is capable of selecting a collection of features from the moving image, based on a constrained (unoccluded and unambiguous) initial position and kinematics model of the object/body being imitated. Our work so far assumes that a human is being imitated, and the kinematics model used is that of a generic adult human. However, the system is general and can use any kinematics model. This greatly simplifies establishing the initial match between the features in the visual image and the underlying body. The match enables tracking of the body over time, using a planar rectangle representation of the limbs. This allows for fast computation and updating of limb position, and for simple prediction of future positions, which is in turn used to speed up recognition. Input from the motor primitives could provide further predictive capability, but we have yet to properly explore it.

We have also gathered a large body of data of human arm movements using the Fast Trak system, which provides 3-D Cartesian positions of the markers. These data were gathered in a collaborative experiment conducted at the National Institutes of Health Resource for the Study of Neural Models of Behavior, at the University of Rochester. Similar to our eye-tracking experiment (section 15.4), subjects watched and imitated short videos of arm movements, but were, in this case, also fitted with a set of markers on their imitation arm. Four markers were used, located near the shoulder, elbow, wrist, and middle finger joint. In addition to the subject data, marker data are also available for the demonstrator. These data are used for validation of the automatic primitive generation and primitives-based classification systems, as well as for testing implementations of the model and comparing its performance to that of human subjects on the same tasks.

Finally, we are also using full-body human movement data captured by the Sarcos SenSuit, a flexible exoskeleton that simultaneously measures 35 degrees of freedom, including the shoulder, elbow, wrist, hip, knee, waist, and ankle joints.

Experimental Test Beds

We are using several distinct experimental test beds to validate various implementations of our imitation model.

PHYSICS-BASED HUMANOID SIMULATION

Adonis, a physics-based humanoid simulation,[1] is actuated from the waist up, and has 20 degrees of freedom (DOF): 3 in the neck, 3 in the waist, and 7 in each arm (3 in the shoulder and wrist, and one in the elbow). Adonis uses external sensing (such as vision input), and internal joint-angle-state sensors. This test bed was used for our past motor control work and continues to be the closest test bed to human body control. Figure 15.3 shows a snapshot of Adonis.

HUMANOID AVATARS

Two COSIMIR[2] humanoid avatars are fully actuated and consist of 37 body DOF and 14 hand DOF in actuated fingers. Various models of the dynamics, muscles, and control can be applied. All sensing is external. Figure 15.4 shows a snapshot of the two avatars.

ROBOT DOG

Laika, an Aibo[3] dog robot, has 18 degrees of freedom: 2 in the neck and 4 in each leg. It also has passively compliant paws. Its sensors

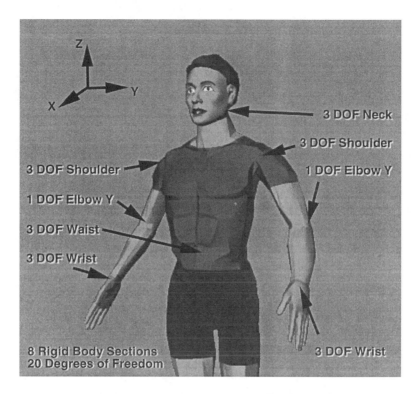

Figure 15.3 The Adonis 20 degrees-of-freedom physics-based dynamic simulation.

Figure 15.4 The two COSIMIR humanoid avatars.

Figure 15.5 The Sony Aibo robot dog.

include a color CCD camera, stereo microphones, joint encoders in the legs, and touch sensors on the paws and the head. The motivation for using Laika is to study imitation between different body morphologies and kinematics. Laika will be used to test our imitation model on imitating a human. Additionally, Laika's movements will be used as input to the other experimental test beds. Figure 15.5 shows a snapshot of Laika.

WHEELED MOBILE ROBOTS

Increasing numbers (currently 9) of Pioneer[4] mobile robots, equipped with pan and tilt color cameras, front and rear ultrasound sensors, and differentially steered bases, are used for group robotics research in our laboratory. Although these robots are too different from any biological system to be used for studying the direct mechanisms of true imitation, they are convenient for addressing task-level imitation, which is a challenging problem in its own right, given the limitations of robot sensors and effectors. Figure 15.6 shows a collection of our mobile robots.

FULL-BODY HUMANOID ROBOT

Our future plans include implementation and evaluation of the model on the Sarcos full-body humanoid robot, through collabora-

Figure 15.6   Our mobile robot family.

tion with the Kawato Dynamic Brain Project at the ATR Human Information Processing Labs in Kyoto, Japan. The humanoid has 30 DOF: 3 in the neck, 7 in each arm, 3 in the trunk, 3 in each leg, and 2 in each eye.

The purpose behind using such a broad variety of test beds is to validate the generality of our model, as well as to put it to practical use on various complex agents and robots with potential real-world programming and control applications.

Experimental Validation of the Model

Our experiments to date have demonstrated several aspects of the model. As described earlier (section 15.6), we have experimentally validated and compared several types of movement primitives along different evaluation criteria (Matarić, Zordan, and Williamson 1999).

In Weber, Matarić, and Jenkins (2000), we report on using a small set of three primitives (discrete straight and curved movements and oscillatory closed-curve movements) as a basis for recognition and reconstruction of various human upper-body movements,

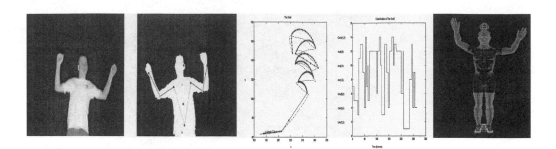

Figure 15.7 An implementation of the imitation system.

including dance (e.g., aerobics) and athletics (e.g., throwing a base-ball) on the 20 DOF humanoid simulation. The particular primitives were chosen because they cover the space of possible observed end-point trajectories. To provide spatiotemporal invariance for the end-point data, we used a sliding horizon window of normalized movement gradients rather than absolute end-point positions. Each instance of the window is a high-dimensional vector classified into one of the three primitives based on a Euclidean distance metric. Temporally consecutive windows are grouped based on classification results and produce a sequence of parameterized primitives; the parameters are extracted directly from the movement data. In the imitation phase, the hand of the humanoid executes the sequence of primitives using impedance control (Hogan 1985) in a similar fashion as demonstrated in our previous work (Matarić, Zordan, and Williamson 1999). The motor controller is provided with the 3D Cartesian end-point position and a default upper-arm orientation, resulting in a natural-looking trajectory reconstruction for all of the various types of movements. Figure 15.7 overviews the implementation. Details of the primitives, segmentation, and videos of the imitation can be found at ⟨http://www-robotics.usc.edu/~agents/Links/Research/imitation.html⟩.

Besides demonstrating sequencing of primitives, we have experimented with superposing primitives as well. We combined an avoidance primitive with reaching and postural primitives in order to produce collision-free hand trajectories around the torso and head of the Adonis simulation performing the Macarena dance (Matarić, Zordan, and Mason 1998). Details and videos can be found at ⟨http://www-robotics.usc.edu/~agents/Links/Research/macarena.html⟩.

We have also implemented a connectionist version of the imitation model, using central pattern generators as primitives for arm and leg movements, and a recurrent neural network architecture as the mechanism for learning novel behavior sequences (Billard and Matarić 2000b). The implementation was validated on the pair of COSIMIR avatars imitating various arm and finger movements from visual motion tracking (Billard and Matarić 2000b), as well as on the dog robot imitating a visually tracked wooden puppet (Billard and Matarić 2000a).

15.8 Imitation in Robotics

To relate our approach to others, we now provide a brief survey of related work on modeling imitation in physical robotic systems. We begin with an overview of various methods for visual perception and understanding of human movement, as it is a critical aspect of imitation as well as a major research challenge in machine vision.

Computational theories and implementations of movement perception have largely dealt with classifying movement by employing tools from time-series analysis. Hidden Markov models (HMMs) (Rabiner and Juang 1986), originally used to automatically segment and recognize speech (Rabiner 1989), are the most popular modeling tools used for analyzing visual data of human and robot movement. Pook and Ballard (1993) used HMMs to analyze a video of a robot flipping a plastic fried egg. Brand, Oliver, and Pentland (1997) used a coupled HMM for recognizing and analyzing time-extended behaviors such as object assembly. Lee and Xu (1996) used a similar HMM-based approach to recognize several hand-shaped letters. Yang, Xu, and Chen (1997) applied the HMM representation to human skill learning by observation and skill transfer to articulated robot arms applied to recognition and copying of written digits and parts replacement by tele-operation. Finally, our own work has used a simplified form of HMMs to capture the dynamics of robot interactions over time as models of basis behavior execution patterns (Goldberg and Matarić 1999, 2000). The field of human-computer interfaces and its various relatives has addressed movement perception and greatly broadened the spectrum of approaches being studied. People-tracking and gesture recognition from video are two major applications of interest. A detailed survey of movement perception is beyond the scope of this chapter (for more information see Essa 1999).

The earliest robotics work to address imitation was focused on achieving assembly tasks from observation. Typically, a series of still visual images of a human performing simple object moving/ stacking tasks was recorded, segmented, interpreted, and then repeated by a robotic arm (Ikeuchi et al. 1990; Ikeuchi, Kawade, and Suehiro 1993; Kuniyoshi, Inaba, and Inoue 1994; Hovland, Sikka, and McCarragher 1996; Kaiser 1997). The work was aimed at task-level imitation (Byrne and Russon 1998), achieving the final outcome of the observed behavior, not at imitating the process that brought the result about. Motor control consisted of applying a conventional trajectory planner to reach each extracted subgoal (e.g., pick up block1, put on top of block2). Recent efforts, including our own (Matarić 1994), have been increasingly oriented toward analyzing the underlying mechanisms of imitation in natural systems and modeling those on artificial ones. Schaal (1997) used imitation for "priming" a model-based reinforcement learning system in the task of balancing a pole by a 7 DOF robot arm observed from a brief human demonstration. Demiris and colleagues (1997) demonstrated a robot head with a pair of cameras that observed and imitated a small set of head movements of a human demonstrator, by using a built-in system that directly mapped a set of possible observed head movements to the robot's own movements. Using a mobile robot, Hayes and Demiris (1994) employed a similar direct-mapping imitation mechanism to learn maze navigation. The strategy of following a demonstrator robot was also used by Dautenhahn (1994, 1995), who investigated the social dimension of learning by imitation. Demiris (1999) describes a model related to ours, which also employs classification-biased recognition and prediction, as a part of a dual-route active-passive system. Haruno, Wolpert, and Kawato (1999) and their related work (Haruno, Wolpert, and Kawato 1998; Kawato 1995) describe a more general bidirectional approach to human motor control and learning, based on multiple pairs of forward (predictive) and inverse (controller) models, organized hierarchically. Experienced movement is segmented into predictive forward models, and the learning process is based on the error in the prediction. This is similar to our model, where segmentation is done at the level of primitives and known skills, which drive the classification and prediction.

Unlike the above, we assume a smaller set of internal models—that is, primitives.

15.9 Summary and Continuing Work

We have presented a model of imitation based on phylogenetically old mechanisms of mirror neurons and motor primitives. Combining evidence from neuroscience and cognitive science, we have postulated that imitation uses selective visual attention driven by end-point movement, a mirrorlike matching and classification system for mapping the observed movement onto a set of motor primitives, a basis movement vocabulary consisting of those primitives, and a learning mechanism for creating novel sequences and superpositions of the primitives into a continually expanding movement repertoire. We then briefly described several experimental validations of our model and related it to other robotic imitation implementations.

We continue to develop and validate this imitation model on a variety of robotic test beds, and hope to provide both novel insights into biological imitation and novel techniques for controlling and interacting with robots.

Acknowledgments

The National Science Foundation Career Award IRI 9624237 supports the work described here. The author is grateful to the anonymous reviewers, to her imitation research group (Aude Billard, Chad Jenkins, and Ajo Fod), and especially to Richard Roberts, for invaluable comments on earlier drafts of this chapter.

Notes

1. Developed in the animation Lab at Georgia Institute of Technology, using S/D Fast.
2. Developed at the University of Dortmund, described in Romann (1999).
3. Developed and distributed by Sony.
4. Distributed by ActivMedia.

References

Abernethy, B. Expertise, visual search, and information pick-up in squash. *Perception* 19: 63–78, 1990.

Arbib, M. Perceptual structures and distributed motor control. In V. B. Brooks, ed., *Handbook of Physiology: Motor Control*, pp. 809–813, Cambridge, Mass.: MIT Press, 1981.

Arbib, M. Schema theory. In S. Shapiro, ed., *The Encyclopedia of Artificial Intelligence*, 2d ed., pp. 1427–1443. New York: Wiley-Interscience, 1992.

Arbib, M., and G. Rizzolatti. Neural expectations: A possible evolutionary path from manual skills to language. *Communication and Cognition* 29(2–4): 393–424, 1996.

Arkin, R. C. Motor schema based navigation for a mobile robot: An approach to programming by behavior. In *IEEE International Conference on Robotics and Automation*, Raleigh, NC, pp. 264–271, IEEE Press, 1987.

Arkin, R. C. *Behavior-Based Robotics*. Cambridge, Mass.: MIT Press, 1998.

Bandura, A. *Social Learning Theory*. Englewood Cliffs, N.J.: Prentice-Hall, 1977.

Bandura, A., and R. H. Walters. *Social Learning and Personality Development*. New York: Holt, Rinehart, and Winston, 1963.

Bertenthal, B. I. Origins and early development of perception, action, and representation. *Annual Review of Psychology* 47: 431–459, 1996.

Billard, A., and M. J. Matarić. Betty: Robot, play with me! Robot: O. K. How do we play? Betty: You watch me and do like I do. Look! In *Proceedings, Workshop on Interactive Robotics and Entertainment (WIRE-2000)*, Pittsburgh. 2000a.

Billard, A., and M. J. Matarić. A biologically inspired robotic model for learning by imitation. In *Proceedings, The Fourth International Conference on Autonomous Agents (Agents 2000)*, Barcelona, Spain, pp. 373–380. ACM Press, 2000b.

Bizzi, E., F. A. Mussa-Ivaldi, and S. Giszter. Computations underlying the execution of movement: A biological perspective. *Science* 253: 287–291, 1991.

Brand, M., N. Oliver, and A. Pentland. Coupled hidden Markov models for complex action recognition. In *Proceedings, CVPR*, pp. 994–999. IEEE Press, 1997.

Brooks, R. A. A robust layered control system for a mobile robot. *IEEE Journal of Robotics and Automation* RA-2: 14–23, 1986.

Brooks, R. A. Intelligence without reason. In *Proceedings, IJCAI-91*, pp. 569–595. Sydney, Australia: Morgan Kaufmann, 1991.

Brooks, V. B. *Handbook of Physiology: Motor Control*. Cambridge, Mass.: MIT Press, 1981.

Byrne, R. W., and A. E. Russon. Learning by imitation: A hierarchical approach. *Journal of Behavioral and Brain Sciences* 16: 3, 1998.

Cheney, D. L., and R. M. Seyfarth. *How Monkeys See the World*. Chicago: University of Chicago Press, 1990.

Dautenhahn, K. Trying to imitate—A step towards releasing robots from social isolation. In *Proceedings of Perception to Action*, pp. 290–301. Lausanne, Switzerland: IEEE Computer Society Press, 1994.

Dautenhahn, K., Getting to know each other—Artificial social intelligence for autonomous robots. *Robotics and Autonomous Systems* 16: 333–356, 1995.

Davis, J. M. Imitation: A review and critique. In Bateson and Klopfer, eds., *Perspectives in Ethology*, 1, pp. 43–72. New York: Plenum Press, 1973.

Decety, J. Do imagined and executed actions share the same neural substrate? *Cognitive Brain Research* 3: 87–93, 1996.

Demiris, J. Active and passive routes to imitation. In K. Dautenhahn and C. Nehaniv, eds., *Proceedings of the AISB'99 Symposium on Imitation in Animals and Artifacts (Edinburgh)*. pp. 81–87. Brighton, U.K.: The Society for the Study of Artificial Intelligence and Simulation of Behaviour, 1999.

Demiris, J., and M. J. Matarić. Perceptuo-motor primitives in imitation. In K. Dautenhahn and G. M. Hayes, eds., *Proceedings of the Autonomous Agents 98 Workshop on "Agents in Interaction: Acquiring Competence through Imitation,"* Minneapolis/St. Paul. 1998.

Demiris, J., S. Rougeaux, G. M. Hayes, L. Berthouze, and Y. Kuniyoshi. Deferred imitation of human head movements by an active stereo vision head. In *Proceedings of the Sixth IEEE International Workshop on Robot Human Communication (RoMan97)*. Sendai, Japan: IEEE Press, 1997.

di Pellegrino, G., L. Fadiga, L. Fogassi, and G. Rizzolatti. Understanding motor events: A neurophysiological study. *Experimental Brain Research* 91: 176–180, 1992.

Donald, M. Précis of origins of the modern mind: Three stages in the evolution of culture and cognition. *Journal of Behavioral and Brain Sciences* 16: 737–791, 1993.

Elkins, J. *The Object Stares Back: On the Nature of Seeing*. New York: Simon and Schuster, 1996.

Essa, I. A. Computers seeing people. *AI Magazine* 20(2): 69–82, 1999.

Fadiga, L., L. Fogassi, G. Pavesi, and G. Rizzolatti. Motor facilitation during action observation: A magnetic stimulation study. *Journal of Neurophysiology* 73(6): 2608–2611, 1995.

Flanders, M., and J. F. Soechting. Frames of Reference for Hand Orientation. *Journal of Cognitive Neuroscience* 7(2): 182–195, 1995.

Flanders, M., S. I. Helms Tillery, and J. F. Soechting. Early stages in a sensorimotor transformation. *Behavioral and Brain Sciences* 15: 309–362, 1992.

Giszter, S. F., F. A. Mussa-Ivaldi, and E. Bizzi. Convergent force fields organized in the frog's spinal cord. *Journal of Neuroscience* 13(2): 467–491, 1993.

Goldberg, D., and M. J. Matarić. Coordinating mobile robot group behavior using a model of interaction dynamics. In O. Etzioni, J. P. Muller, and J. M. Bradshaw, eds., *Proceedings, the Third International Conference on Autonomous Agents (Agents '99)*, pp. 100–107. Seattle: ACM Press, 1999.

Goldberg, D., and M. J. Matarić. Reward maximization in a non-stationary mobile robot environment. In *Proceedings, the Fourth International Conference on Autonomous Agents (Agents 2000)*, Barcelona, Spain, pp. 92–99. ACM, 2000.

Goodale, M. A., L. S. Jakobson, A. D. Milner, D. I. Perrett, P. J. Benson, and J. K. Hietanen. The nature and limits of orientation and pattern processing supporting visuomotor control in a visual form agnosia. *Journal of Cognitive Neuroscience* 6(1): 46–56, 1994.

Harnad, S. The symbol grounding problem. *Physica D* 42: 335–346, 1990.

Haruno, M., D. M. Wolpert, and M. Kawato. Multiple paired forward-inverse models in the cerebellum. In *Proceedings of the Fifth International Conference on Neural Information Processing (ICONIP '98)*, 13, pp. 1177–1180. 1998.

Haruno, M., D. M. Wolpert, and M. Kawato. Multiple forward-inverse models for human motor learning and control. In M. S. Kearns, S. A. Solla, and D. A. Cohn (eds.), *Advances in Neural Information Processing Systems 11*, pp. 31–37. Cambridge, Mass.: MIT Press, 1999.

Hayes, G., and J. Demiris. A robot controller using learning by imitation. In A. Borkowski and J. L. Crowley, eds., *Proceedings of the International Symposium on Intelligent Robotic Systems*, Grenoble, France: LIFIA-IMAG, pp. 198–204. 1994.

Hogan, N. Impedance control: An approach to manipulation. *Journal of Dynamic Systems, Measurement, and Control* 107: 1–24, 1985.

Hovland, G. E., P. Sikka, and B. J. McCarragher. Skill acquisition from human demonstration using a hidden Markov model. In A. Borkowski, J. Crowley, *Proceedings, IEEE International Conference on Robotics and Automation*, Minneapolis, pp. 2706–2711. 1996.

Hubel, D., and T. Wiesel. Functional architecture of macaque monkey cortex. *Proceedings of the Royal Society of London* 198: 1–59, 1977.

Iacoboni, M., R. P. Woods, M. Brass, H. Bekkering, J. C. Mazziotta, and G. Rizzolatti. Cortical mechanisms of human imitation. *Science* 286: 2526–2528, 1999.

Ikeuchi, K., M. Kawade, and T. Suehiro. Assembly task recognition with planar, curved, and mechanical contacts. In *Proceedings of IEEE International Conference on Robotics and Automation*, Atlanta. IEEE Press, 1993.

Ikeuchi, K., T. Suehiro, P. Tanguy, and M. Wheeler. Assembly plan from observation. Technical report, Carnegie Mellon Univeristy Robotics Institute Annual Research Review, 1990.

Jeannerod, M., and J. Decety. Mental motor imagery: A window into the representational stages of action. *Current Opinion in Neurobiology* 5: 727–732, 1995.

Jeannerod, M., M. A. Arbib, G. Rizzolatti, and H. Sakata. Grasping objects: The cortical mechanisms of visuomotor transformation. *Trends in Neurosciences* 18: 314–320, 1995.

Jenkins O. C. An attention selection mechanism for moving human figures. Technical report IRIS-00-381, University of Southern California, Institute for Robotics and Intelligent Systems, 2000.

Johansson, G. Visual perception of biological motion and a model for its analysis. *Perception and Psychophysics* 14: 201–211, 1973.

Kaelbling, L. P., M. L. Littman, and A. W. Moore. Reinforcement learning: A survey. *Journal of Artificial Intelligence Research* 4: 237–285, 1996.

Kaiser, M. Transfer of elementary skills via human-robot interaction. *Adaptive Behavior* 5(3–4): 249–280, 1997.

Kawato, M. Unidirectional versus bi-directional theory for trajectory planning and control. In T. Hida, ed., *Mathematical Approach to Fluctuations: Complexity and Nonlinearity*, pp. 144–180. Singapore: World Scientific, 1995.

Kuniyoshi, Y., M. Inaba, and H. Inoue. Learning by watching: Extracting reusable task knowledge from visual observation of human performance. *IEEE Transactions on Robotics and Automation* 10(6): 799–822, 1994.

Lee, C., and Y. Xu. Online, interactive learning of gestures for human/robot interfaces. In *Proceedings, IEEE International Conference on Robotics and Automation*, vol. 4, Minneapolis, pp. 2982–2987. 1996.

Marjanović, M., B. Scassellati, and M. Williamson. Self-taught visually-guided pointing for a humanoid robot. In P. Maes, M. Matarić, J.-A. Meyer, J. Pollack, and S. Wilson, eds. *Proceedings Fourth International Conference on Simulation of Adaptive Behavior*, Cape Cod, pp. 35–44. Cambridge, Mass.: MIT Press, 1996.

Matarić, M. J. Learning motor skills by imitation. In *Proceedings, AAAI Spring Symposium Toward Physical Interaction and Manipulation*, Stanford University. Menlo Park, Calif.: AAAI Press, 1994.

Matarić, M. J. Designing and understanding adaptive group behavior. *Adaptive Behavior* 4(1): 50–81, 1995.

Matarić, M. J. Behavior-based control: Examples from navigation, learning, and group behavior. *Journal of Experimental and Theoretical Artificial Intelligence* 9(2–3): 323–336, 1997.

Matarić, M. J., and M. J. Marjanović. Synthesizing complex behaviors by composing simple primitives. In *Self Organization and Life: From Simple Rules to Global Complexity, European Conference on Artificial Life (ECAL-93)*, Brussels, Belgium, pp. 698–707. 1993.

Matarić, M. J., and M. Pomplun. Fixation behavior in observation and imitation of human movement. *Cognitive Brain Research* 7(2): 191–202, 1998.

Matarić, M. J., V. B. Zordan, and Z. Mason. Movement control methods for complex, dynamically simulated agents: Adonis dances the macarena. In W. L. Johnson (ed.), *Proc. Second International Conference on Autonomous Agents*, pp. 317–324. Minneapolis/St. Paul: ACM Press, 1998.

Matarić, M. J., V. B. Zordan, and M. Williamson. Making complex articulated agents dance: An analysis of control methods drawn from robotics, animation, and biology. *Autonomous Agents and Multi-Agent Systems* 2(1): 23–44, 1999.

Meltzoff, M. A., and M. K. Moore. Imitation of facial and manual gestures by human neonates. *Science* 198: 75–78, 1988.

Meltzoff, M. A., and M. K. Moore. Imitation, memory, and the representation of persons. *Infant Behavior and Development* 17: 83–99, 1994.

Meltzoff, M. A., and M. K. Moore. Infants' understanding of people and things: From body imitation to folk psychology. In J. L. Bermudez, A. Marcel, and N. Eilan, eds., *The Body and the Self*, pp. 44–69. Cambridge, Mass.: MIT Press, 1995.

Meltzoff, M. A., and M. K. Moore. Explaining facial imitation: A theoretical model. *Early Development and Parenting* 6(2): 179–192, 1997.

Moore, B. R. Avian movement imitation and a new form of mimicry: Tracing the evolution of a complex form of learning. *Behavior* 122: 614–623, 1992.

Moore, B. R. The evolution of imitative learning. In C. M. Heyes and B. G. Galef, eds., *Social Learning in Animals: The Roots of Culture*, pp. 245–265. New York: Academic Press, 1996.

Mussa-Ivaldi, F. A., and S. F. Giszter. Vector field approximation: A computational paradigm for motor control and learning. *Biological Cybernetics* 67: 491–500, 1992.

Mussa-Ivaldi, F. A., S. F. Giszter, and E. Bizzi. Linear combinations of primitives in vertebrate motor control. *Proceedings of the National Academy of Sciences* 91: 7534–7538, 1994.

Parr, L. A., and F. B. M. de Waal. Visual kin recognition in chimpanzees. *Nature* 399: 647–648, 1999.

Pashler, H. E. *The Psychology of Attention.* Cambridge, Mass.: MIT Press, 1999.

Pelisson, D., M. A. Goodale, and C. Prablanc. Adjustments of hand pointings to visual targets do not need visual reassurance from the moving limb. In J. K. O'Regan and A. Levy-Schoen, eds., *Eye Movements, From Physiology to Cognition: Selected/ Edited Proceedings of the Third European Conference on Eye Movements,* pp. 115–121, 1978.

Perrett, D. I., M. H. Harries, R. Bevan, S. Thomas, P. J. Benson, A. J. Mistlin, A. J. Chitty, J. K. Hietanen, and J. E. Ortega. Frameworks of analysis for the neural representation of animate objects and actions. *Journal of Experimental Biology* 146: 87–113, 1989a.

Perrett, D. I., M. H. Harries, A. J. Mistlin, and A. J. Chitty. Recognition of objects and actions: Frameworks for neuronal computation and perceptual experience. In O. Guthrie, ed., *Higher Order Sensory Processing.* Manchester University Press, 1989b.

Perrett, D. I., M. H. Harries, A. J. Mistlin, J. K. Hietanen, P. J. Benson, R. Bevan, S. Thomas, M. W. Oram, J. Ortega, and K. Brierley. Social signals analyzed at the single cell level: Someone is looking at me, something touched me, something moved! *International Journal of Comparative Psychology* 4(1): 25–55, 1990.

Perrett, D. I., P. A. J. Smith, A. J. Mistlin, A. J. Chitty, A. S. Head, D. D. Potter, R. Broennimann, A. D. Milner, and M. A. Jeeves. Visual analysis of body movements by neurones in the temporal cortex of the macaque monkey: A preliminary report. *Behavioral Brain Research* 16: 153–170, 1985.

Piaget, J. *Play, Dreams, and Imitation in Children.* New York: W. W. Norton, 1962.

Pook, P. K., and D. H. Ballard. Recognizing teleoperated manipulations. In *Proceedings of IEEE International Conference on Robotics and Automation,* vol. 2, Atlanta, pp. 578–585. 1993.

Rabiner, L. R. A tutorial on hidden Markov models and selected applications in speech recognition. *Proceedings of the IEEE* 77(2): 257–286, 1989.

Rabiner, L. R., and B. H. Juang. Introduction to hidden Markov models. *IEEE ASSP Magazine* 3: 4–16, 1986.

Rizzolatti, G., L. Fadiga, M. Matelli, V. Bettinardi, D. Perani, and F. Fazio. Localization of grasp representations in humans by positron emission tomography: 1. Observation versus execution. *Experimental Brain Research* 111: 246–252, 1996a.

Rizzolatti, G., L. Fadiga, V. Gallese, and L. Fogassi. Premotor cortex and the recognition of motor actions. *Cognitive Brain Research* 3: 131–141, 1996b.

Romann, J. F. E. Projective virtual reality: Bridging the gap between virtual reality and robotics. *IEEE Transaction on Robotics and Automation; Special Section on Virtual Reality in Robotics and Automation* 15(3): 411–422, 1999.

Sanger, T. D. Human arm movements described by a low-dimensional superposition of principal components. *Journal of Neuroscience* 20(3): 1066–1072, 2000.

Savelsvertgh, G. J. P., and R. J. Bootsma. Perception-action coupling in hitting and catching. *International Journal of Sport Psychology* 25: 331–343, 1994.

Schaal, S. Learning from demonstration. In M. Mozer, M. Jordan, and T. Petsche, eds., *Advances in Neural Information Processing Systems 9,* pp. 1040–1046. Cambridge, Mass.: MIT Press, 1997.

Schaal, S., and D. Sternad. Programmable pattern generators. In *Proceedings, Third International Conference on Computational Intelligence in Neuroscience,* Research Triangle Park, NC, pp. 48–51. 1998.

Stein, J. F. The representation of egocentric space in the posterior parietal cortex. *Behavioral and Brain Sciences* 15: 691–700, 1992.

Stein, P. S. G., D. G. Stuart, and A. I. Selverston (eds.). *Neurons, Networks, and Motor Behavior.* Cambridge, Mass.: MIT Press, 1997.

Sutton, R. S., and A. G. Barto. *Reinforcement Learning*. Cambridge, Mass.: MIT Press, 1998.

Tomasello, M., A. C. Kruger, and H. H. Rather. Cultural learning. *Journal of Behavioral and Brain Sciences* 16(3): 495–552, 1993.

Vogt, S. Imagery and perception-action mediation in imitative actions. *Cognitive Brain Research* 3: 79–86, 1995.

Weber, S. Simple human torso tracking from video. Technical report IRIS-00-380, University of Southern California, Institute for Robotics and Intelligent Systems, 2000.

Weber, S., M. J. Matarić, and O. C. Jenkins. Experiments in imitation using perceptuomotor primitives. In C. Sierra, M. Gini, J. S. Rosenschein (eds.), *Proc. Fourth International Conference on Autonomous Agents*, ACM Press, Barcelona, Spain, 2000.

Williamson, M. Postural primitives: Interactive behavior for a humanoid robot arm. In P. Maes, M. Matarić, J.-A. Meyer, J. Pollack, and S. Wilson, eds., *Proceedings Fourth International Conference on Simulation of Adaptive Behavior*, Cape Cod, pp. 124–131. Cambridge, MA: MIT Press, 1996.

Yang, J., Y. Xu, and C. S. Chen. Human action learning via hidden Markov model. *IEEE Transactions on Systems, Man, and Cybernetics-Part A: Systems and Humans* 27(1): 34–44, 1997.

16 Imitation or Something Simpler? Modeling Simple Mechanisms for Social Information Processing

Jason Noble and Peter M. Todd

16.1 Introduction

In the pine forests of Israel, black rats (*Rattus rattus*) have hit upon a novel feeding technique. They strip the scales from pinecones to obtain the nutritious seeds inside (Terkel 1996). The behavior seems to be socially learned in some way, rather than genetically inherited: Terkel has shown that rat pups will learn to strip cones if they are born to a naive mother but then fostered to an experienced one. What mechanism is implicated in the transmission of this behavior? It could be that rat pups are genuinely imitating their mothers, but this would mean that they are solving a complex correspondence problem in translating novel visual input—from observations of cone manipulation—into appropriate motor outputs. Might a simpler mechanism be involved?

The social transmission of pinecone-stripping behavior is only one example of the general strategy of gaining information from the behavior of one's conspecifics. Every animal is constantly facing the problem of what to do next: given the various cues that it can detect in its environment at any one time, what behavior is most likely to further its ultimate goals of survival and reproduction? In all but the most solitary of species, the cues available from the environment will include information about the behavior of other animals.

Investigation of the general question as to how animals might learn from or be otherwise influenced by the behavior of their conspecifics has often been overshadowed by a focus on the specific issue of imitation. This emphasis has been around for some time: Galef (1988), in a historical review, points out that the debate over whether nonhuman animals are capable of imitation dates back at least to the dispute between Darwin and Wallace over whether the human mind is of evolved or divine origin. One product of this long controversy has been a plethora of definitions of imitation (see Zentall and Galef 1988; Heyes and Galef 1996), which we lack the space here to adequately review. For the purposes of our argument, we will simply take true imitation to be the goal-directed copying of another's behavior. As Tomasello (1996) notes in his discussion of "imitative learning" (p. 324), successful imitation— in the sense we are interested in—requires not only perceiving and reproducing the bodily movements of another, but understanding the changes in the environment caused by the other's behavior, and finally being able to grasp the "intentional relations" between these—that is, knowing how and why the behavior is supposed to bring about the goal. We realize that in stipulating such a definition of imitation, we are setting the bar quite high. Our aim is not to define imitation away, but to offer an explicit definition and thereby focus attention on the issue of mechanism. We feel that "imitation," with its connotations of intelligent, purposeful action, has been used in the past as a vague, catch-all term to cover instances of social learning for which the underlying mechanisms were very poorly understood.

Many authors have focused on imitative learning because it seems likely to be implicated in the origin of culture (e.g., Tomasello, Kruger, and Ratner 1993). The existence and the title of this book are themselves testaments to the abiding interest that psychologists, biologists, and cognitive scientists have had in imitation. Nevertheless, our contention in this chapter is that the power of simpler social information processing mechanisms has been underestimated. In this we are not alone: several phenomena that were once seen as clearly imitative, such as the opening of milk bottles by birds (Fisher and Hinde 1949) and the washing of food by monkeys (Kawamura 1959; Kawai 1965), have since been questioned (Galef 1976; Sherry and Galef 1984; Galef 1988; Cheney and Seyfarth 1990; Byrne 1995). We will argue that individual-based simulation modeling, already a popular technique in the field of adaptive behavior, is an excellent tool for exploring how animals can be successful using simple mechanisms. We will also review the literature on social learning, and identify mechanisms that provide parsimonious explanations for many apparently imitative phenomena.

A Cautionary Tale

Human observers of animal and robot behavior have a propensity to invoke mechanisms that are more complex than those strictly needed to explain the observable facts. Braitenberg (1984) demonstrates this nicely in his book *Vehicles* by asking us to imagine a

Sensors

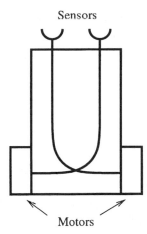

Motors

Figure 16.1 Braitenberg's (1984) Vehicle 2b—crossed connections between light sensors and motors produce apparently purposeful pursuit of a light source.

robot that appears to behave aggressively in the presence of light sources. This robot turns to face any light source within the range of its sensors and accelerates toward it, eventually smashing into it at high speed. If the source moves, the robot will pursue it accordingly. Braitenberg suggests that we will find it difficult to avoid attributing a *dislike* of the light source to the robot (for empirical support of this point see Bumby and Dautenhahn 1999). An observer—let's say a cognitive psychologist—asked to speculate about the internal workings of the robot might guess that it contains some sort of light-detection mechanism, which invokes an attack response, passing information to a central processor that in turn sets off the motor movements needed to bring the robot closer to the light. In fact, the robot is very simply constructed. Figure 16.1 shows that wires from two light sensors at the front of the machine are cross-connected to two motors at the back. This is all that is required to bring about the behavior described.

Once you know how the robot works, it is clear that the given design will get the job done. But it is very difficult to correctly deduce the robot's internal workings from its behavior alone. Braitenberg refers to this phenomenon as the "law of uphill analysis and downhill invention." We want to apply two lessons from Braitenberg's fable to our review of social learning. First, the mechanism that produces a given behavior may be a great deal simpler than appearances suggest—quite possibly this has something to do with the human tendency to interpret the world from an "intentional stance" (Dennett 1987). Second, the best way to understand the mechanisms necessary for a certain behavior may be to build an artificial system that performs that behavior (see also Simon 1995, in this regard).

Why and How Questions

The idea that animals are influenced by the behavior of others poses both why and how questions—that is, questions of evolved function and questions of mechanism. In recent years there has been some progress toward understanding the function of social learning. Models of cultural transmission (Cavalli-Sforza and Feldman 1981; Boyd and Richerson 1985), highly horizontal (within-generation) transmission (Laland, Richerson, and Boyd 1993, 1996), and what economists call herding behavior (Banerjee 1992; Bikhchandani, Hirshleifer, and Welch 1998) help to delineate the conditions under which it will be advantageous for individuals to learn from others rather than finding things out for themselves. However, these models tend to result in rather general conclusions. For example, Laland, Richerson, and Boyd (1996, p. 140) summarize the results of work on cultural transmission thus:

When environments change very slowly, all information should be transmitted genetically, since the modest demands for updating are easily met by the genetic system responding to selection. When environmental change is very rapid, tracking by pure individual learning is favored. At intermediate rates of change, social learning is an advantage.

Results like these are useful, but to get a complete picture of any one instance of social learning we also need to understand the mechanism involved—something that is less often attempted. Terkel's (1996) black rats, for instance, clearly gain a selective advantage if they learn to strip pine cones, because there is little alternative food available in their environment. But *how* do they do it? What process allows the rat to take in sensory information relating to pine cones and the feeding habits of conspecifics, and from this acquire the behavior? In asking these questions we seek an explanation at the cognitive level; we want to know what behavioral program or algorithm underlies the rats' performance. Another way of considering the problem is to suppose that we wanted to construct a simulated or robotic rat. Assuming we had given our construction sensory and motor capabilities that matched those of the real animals, what would be the minimal set of instructions we could give it that would allow it to mimic real *behavior*?

Much of the work that professes to be about mechanisms of social learning does not really confront this challenge. For example, Bandura (1969) discusses the process of "identification," whereby a human observer comes to adopt the attitudes and behaviors of a model. Tomasello, Kruger, and Ratner (1993) talk about "perspective taking" as being central to the ability to truly imitate another. In neither of these cases do the authors go any further than labeling the phenomenon; we are left in the dark as to just how identification or perspective taking might be achieved. This is a deficiency we believe could be redressed through the use of simulation modeling.

Modeling Simple Mechanisms

As observers of animal behavior, we are in a similar position to the observer of Braitenberg's hypothetical vehicle. We can see the outward behavior, but the underlying mechanism is hidden from our view. What's more, in the animal case there is no indulgent designer who will take the cover off and show us how it works. How, then, are we to avoid ascribing mechanisms of spurious complexity to the animals whose social behavior we study? We believe that one answer lies in the "downhill invention" part of Braitenberg's law—that is, in model building.

A number of authors (Judson 1994; Miller 1995; Di Paolo 1996; Todd 1996) have recently made a case for individual-based simulation modeling as a way of making progress in areas like social learning, in which the empirical data are often insufficient to distinguish between competing theories. In such simulations, individual organisms interact in a shared environment—although both the organisms and the environment may be very simple. Sometimes the behavioral strategies of the organisms, as well as other model parameters, are set by the designer. Alternatively, many of these simulations incorporate an evolutionary process, in which organisms that are more successful have a greater likelihood of passing on their strategy to the next generation: this kind of artificial selection can be employed either as a general tool for optimization, or as a way of looking explicitly at evolutionary dynamics.

The method is inspired by work in the field of artificial life and the simulation of adaptive behavior (for introductory reviews, see Langton 1989 and Meyer 1994, respectively). Simulation is not new as a research tool in biology, but conventional biological simulations tend to model whole populations, abstracting away from the individual organism, and they tend to be extensions of simple game-theoretic models, thus incorporating radical simplifying assumptions such as random mating and the absence of a spatial distribution. Social learning and social information processing in general are self-evidently about interactions between individuals mediated by an environment, and we believe that individual-based simulations can be useful tools in their investigation, much as they have been for studying the evolution of individual learning (e.g., Todd and Miller 1991; Belew and Mitchell 1996). It has long been recognized within fields like artificial life that complex global phenomena can arise from simple local rules, and this is precisely what we will suggest is happening in many social information processing contexts: individuals follow a simple rule (e.g., "stay close to your mother") and, in combination with some form of learning, the overall pattern of behavior that arises makes human observers suspect complex imitative abilities.

Previous work on behavioral simulation has certainly considered social dynamics in such contexts as communication, dominance and territorial behavior, and flocking or schooling. However, as yet relatively few models have addressed the specific topic of social information processing. Some simulations have modeled stigmergic communication, a process by which one individual influences another via alterations in the environment (Theraulaz and Bonabeau 1999). For example, Deneubourg, Theraulaz, an Beckers (1992) and Bonabeau and colleagues (1994) looked at the kinds of nest structures that could be built if a group of simulated wasps could not perceive each other, but only each other's construction work. These models capture an indirect form of social influence. A more clear-cut example is the work of Toquenaga, Kajitani, and Hoshino (1994); the authors constructed a simulation of foraging and nesting behavior in egrets. They used their model to demonstrate that a tendency to approach others (see Stimulus Enhancement section below) is more likely to evolve when food resources are patchy rather than evenly distributed; when food comes in discrete patches, approaching others often equates to approaching food. Furthermore, the overall pattern of behavior that occurs when all of the birds exhibit this approach tendency strongly resembles flock foraging and colonial roosting.

We see simulations like that of Toquenaga, Kajitani, and Hoshino as suggestive of a productive feedback cycle between evolutionary simulation models and empirical research on mechanisms of social learning. The model shows that a complex pattern of foraging and roosting *could* emerge from something as simple as a tendency to approach conspecifics. This idea now stands as a kind of null hypothesis; we only have to change our ideas about egrets if someone can demonstrate that the real animals behave in a way that cannot be accounted for by this simple rule. Toquenaga and colleagues' simulation could also be used to generate predictions of interest to field biologists: for example, what happens if the food distribution suddenly or periodically changes from patchy to even? How does this compare with parallel real-world cases? Through this kind of interaction between the model and the world, we can build our confidence that a certain process not only could explain the observed results, but is in fact the real mechanism involved. In a field such as social learning and imitation, where the data are relatively clear but their interpretations hotly contested, this would be no small achievement.

16.2 Some Simple Mechanisms

Once we are focused on *how* social information can affect the behavior of individuals, a variety of simple mechanisms become candidates for the production of imitative or imitation-like behavior. In this section, we present a selection of such social information processing mechanisms; we owe much to review articles by Galef (1988) and Zentall (1996). We claim that these mechanisms are *simpler* than true imitation; by this we mean roughly that the algorithms involved can be specified using fewer bits of information. We do not anticipate serious resistance to this idea. True imitation, as we have defined it in section 16.1, necessarily involves multiple processes dealing with behavior recognition and matching, noticing the effects of behavior on the environment, and imputing goals to others. Even if a clever short cut could be demonstrated for each subtask, the overall algorithm for true imitation would remain relatively complex because of the number of steps involved.

Observers tend to suspect imitation when they see one animal perform a behavior X, and then see another animal doing X shortly afterward. Perhaps the simplest way for such behavioral matching to occur is for two animals to independently choose the same action because they are faced with similar environmental stimuli and have similar inherited or learned behavioral priorities. For example, Brockmann (1995) looked at mating in horseshoe crabs: unattached males congregate around certain copulating pairs but not others. This behavior could have been due to mate-choice copying by the males (see Dugatkin 1996) but Brockmann established that it is in fact the result of common preferences for certain characteristics in females. Tooby and Cosmides (1992, pp. 115–116) describe a thought experiment that makes the same point: if all the people on Earth were replaced with jukeboxes, and if each jukebox was equipped with a clock and a location sensor that determined the song it would play, then at any one time, all the jukeboxes in Rio de Janeiro would play one song, and all those in Beijing would play another. The result might be suggestive of cultural transmission or social learning, but appearances would be deceptive.

Social Facilitation

One very simple kind of social influence involves behaving differently depending on the presence of conspecifics. Imagine a species that follows the behavioral rule "Don't do anything unless others are nearby." Suppose that two animals are hungry and alone, and then come into contact with each other: now they can begin to eat. An observer might declare that one animal was imitating the other, but of course it is doing no such thing. This is approximately the logic of social facilitation (Zajonc 1965), although Zajonc's original theory is more detailed, and is intended to explain the effects of an audience on human performances. Clayton (1978) suggests that social facilitation in animals could be due to the reduction of isolation-induced fear, and this makes intuitive sense: a rule like "Don't do anything except watch for predators unless others are nearby" could clearly be adaptive, and observations that birds will spend less time on vigilance when feeding with others (e.g., Sullivan 1984; Bekoff 1995) support the idea. Hemelrijk's (1999) simulation of dominance interactions among primates offers a synthetic example of social facilitation. Her simulated organisms simply turn on the spot when alone, but if a conspecific comes within detection range, their behavior switches accordingly: the two will approach each other (and possibly fight), but neither organism is truly imitating the other.

Contagious Behavior

Contagious behavior is exemplified by a rule such as "If others are fleeing, flee also." The idea is that the stimuli produced by the performance of a particular behavior serve as triggers for others to behave in the same way. For instance, consider a robot that has a direct connection from its auditory sensors to its motors, such that the characteristic sound of another robot moving rapidly causes it to do likewise. In a group of these robots, any stimulus that causes one of them to flee will lead to a chain reaction of rapid movements. Possible examples of contagious behavior include flight responses, movement in flocks or schools, and chorusing by birds and dogs (Galef 1988). Laughing and yawning are excellent examples of contagious behavior in humans (Provine 1996).

Zentall (1996) stresses that contagious behavior must have a genetic basis—that is, it must involve the triggering of an instinctive response. Zentall wants to prevent the term from being used to explain too broad a range of phenomena, and clearly there is a distinction to be made between mere contagious behavior and the purposeful copying of an act novel to the observer. However, the capacity for simple associative learning is virtually universal in animals, and behavioral contagion combined with learning may result in more than the sum of the parts. Continuing with our robotic example, suppose that these robots have the ability to build associative links between stimuli—that is, to learn—perhaps through the operation of a Hebbian neural network. Let us further suppose that one of the robots has developed a "fear" of the color green. When a green stimulus is presented, the focal robot flees, precipitating a wave of contagious flight by the others. But the other robots learn, and if this sequence is repeated several times they will develop an association between the previously neutral green stimulus and their own flight response—that is, they will come to fear green as well. In other words, contagious behavior plus learning could lead to something like cultural transmission.

Stimulus Enhancement

Stimulus enhancement (also called local enhancement) is what happens when animals obey a rule like "Follow someone older than you, and then learn from whatever happens." Galef's (1988, p. 15) description is apt:

A tendency on the part of naive individuals to approach conspecifics, alterations conspecifics have made in the environment, or objects they have contacted, can increase a naive individual's probability of exposure to one set of stimuli rather than others. Enhanced exposure can lead to habituation, familiarity, perceptual learning, latent learning, increased probability of manipulation of one portion of the environment, and so forth.

For example, if you follow your parents everywhere, and your parents sometimes eat chocolate, we do not need to postulate a capacity for genuine imitation to explain the fact that you develop a liking for chocolate. Perhaps you sample chocolate pieces dropped by your parents; you then learn that chocolate-eating is good. Again, a simple behavioral tendency—in this case, following a conspecific—combines with the capacity for learning to result in the potential transmission of acquired behaviors.

Stimulus enhancement explains the acquisition of pinecone-stripping behavior in Terkel's (1996) work on black rats. Terkel and his colleagues found that although naive rats never learned to strip cones unaided, the animals were capable of learning the trick if partially stripped cones were provided, and especially so if they were exposed to cones with progressively fewer rows of scales removed. Furthermore, the investigators noticed that young rats pay close attention to whatever their mother is eating, and often manage to steal partially eaten cones from her. Thus, we can explain the transmission of the feeding technique by supposing that the pups are programmed to "watch whatever mother is eating," that this results in them being exposed to cones at various stages of stripping, and that individual learning then does the rest.

Cecconi and colleagues (1996) describe an instance of stimulus enhancement in simulation: young organisms are carried around for a time on the shoulders of their parents, and are thus able to learn effective foraging strategies before striking out on their own. The authors use this result to argue that delayed maturation in species like our own may be due to the benefits of this type of social learning while young. Billard and Dautenhahn (1998) employed stimulus enhancement in getting a robot to learn a simple vocabulary: a learning robot followed a teacher and thereby gained an adequate perceptual context for acquiring new word meanings through simple associative learning. The model of roosting and foraging in egrets (Toquenaga, Kajitani, and Hoshino 1994) described in Modeling Simple Mechanisms (in section 16.1) is also an example of stimulus enhancement.

Observational Learning

If we add slightly more sophisticated learning abilities to stimulus enhancement, we get observational learning. The algorithm involved is approximately "Pay attention to what others are doing or experiencing, and if the results *for them* appear to be good or bad then learn from this." Mineka and Cook's (1988) work on fear acquisition in monkeys illustrates the idea: the authors took naive, lab-raised rhesus monkeys and allowed them to observe an experienced conspecific reacting fearfully to the presence of a snake. The observers, previously indifferent to snakes, rapidly acquired a persistent fear of them. Mineka and Cook argue that the sight of a fearful conspecific is therefore an unconditioned stimulus for a fearful response. It is easy to see that in the wild, this sort of learning could result in the transmission of acquired fears, and would appear to be imitative. All that needs to be assumed is that the monkeys have evolved both an innate ability to recognize the cues associated with fear on the part of a conspecific (such as grimacing and retreating), and the tendency to learn to fear a co-occurrent stimulus (i.e., the snake).

Observational learning can also exist in a simpler form: explicit evaluation of the conspecific's experience as good or bad may be omitted. For example, Norway rats will develop a marked preference for a novel food that they smell on the breath of a conspecific (Galef 1996). We might say that the first rat, the observer, learns that the new food is good because it observes positive consequences for the second rat, the demonstrator. That is, the observer notes that the demonstrator is still alive to tell the tale after eating a new and potentially toxic substance. It turns out, however, that the rats are not sensitive to the consequences of eating poisonous foods: they do not learn that a food is bad if the demonstrator has become ill after eating it; in fact they develop a preference as usual. So the rats' heuristic is simply "Pay attention to what others are eating and do likewise." Tuci, Noble, and Todd (1999) simulated this phenomenon, and showed that given certain assumptions about the rats' environment (e.g., the lethality of poison and the behavior of sick animals) their failure to evaluate the demonstrator's health is not a mistake, but is actually an adaptive strategy.

Matarić (1994) put both kinds of observational learning to work in engineering cooperative robots that could carry out tasks as a group. Each learning robot had three sources of feedback: information about its own performance, information on the reinforcement of other group members (i.e., knowing whether the other robots were being rewarded or punished for their behavior), and reinforcement for simply performing the same behavior as other group members (i.e., a reward for conformity). The second and third sources of feedback correspond to observational learning with and without evaluation of the conspecific's experience. Of course, Matarić's work does not establish that observational learning is the equal of true imitation in fostering robot culture; we mention it only in order to show that observational learning can be effectively implemented in a real system.

Matched-Dependent Behavior

We know from laboratory work on animal learning that such species as rats and pigeons can readily be trained to discriminate; for example, to press one bar when a red light is on and to press another for a green light. Miller and Dollard (1941) showed that this sort of learning was equally possible when the behavior of another animal served as the discriminative stimulus; they trained rats to follow a leader left or right at a maze junction. Thus, simple reinforcement learning can result in social learning if the contingencies are right. There is no implication that the follower understands the leader's intentions, nor even that the follower is aware of the match between the leader's behavior and its own. The only rule we need to postulate is along the lines of "Given the perceived situation, do something that has previously resulted in a positive outcome."

Along similar lines, Skinner (1953) suggested that a wild pigeon could learn through trial and error that scratching in a field was likely to be rewarding (i.e., likely to result in ingesting food) if other pigeons could be seen scratching there. In fact, the pigeon need not even observe others feeding: learning a correspondence between hidden food and the evidence of feeding, such as scratch marks, would amount to the same thing. The general point is that contagious behavior may sometimes be learned. Suppose that one of the hypothetical robots discussed earlier was to be deprived of its contagious flight response, perhaps by severing the direct connection between its auditory sensor and its motor output. The robot would be able to reacquire the behavior by learning that a certain noise—the sound of others fleeing—was associated with an imminent negative experience that could only be avoided by activating a certain behavior—that is, flight.

Cross-Modal Matching

Vocal mimicry on the part of birds occupies a special place in discussions of social learning. It is often argued that because the original stimulus and the animal's response are in the same sensory modality—that is, because birds can hear their own sounds in the same way that they hear sounds made by others—a relatively simple pattern-matching mechanism could account for the phenomenon. In contrast, copying the movements of another animal requires cross-modal matching; the observer must be able to translate the visual input associated with another's movements into appropriate motor outputs. Consider that there is no trivial link between the sight of watching someone else scratch their nose, and the experience of scratching your own nose (see Heyes, chapter 19 of this volume).

None of the simple mechanisms discussed so far requires an ability to perform cross-modal matching. Even though processes like contagious behavior or learned copying could mean that the sight of one animal doing X was a sufficient stimulus for another animal to do X, there is no suggestion of a systematic ability to copy movements. However, imagine an animal that was able to identify the movements of others, and map them to movements of its own muscles. If such an ability was combined with observational learning, we would get the behavioral rule "If someone else moves their head (or forelimb or tail, etc.) thus or so, make the same movement yourself." (As with observational learning, the rule might be conditional on positive outcomes for the observed animal.) Admittedly, this is a reasonably complicated rule, and it is not easy to see how such a mapping would be achieved. Some authors would claim that this rule is indeed the ability to imitate, but Heyes (1993) makes the point that cross-modal matching can explain quite sophisticated social learning without postulating the kind of intentional perspective taking and sensitivity to goals that Tomasello, Kruger, and Ratner (1993) find to be characteristic of human imitation. Work on "mirror neurons" in monkeys (Gallese and Goldman 1998) and humans (Iacoboni et al. 1999) is highly suggestive that, at least in primates, direct mappings may exist between movements seen and movements performed. Meltzoff's (1996) findings on the imitative powers of very young infants also point to an innate ability to perform cross-modal matching in humans. Finally, the qualified success of the COG project in getting a humanoid robot to mimic behaviors such as head nodding (Scassellati 1999) shows that cross-modal matching may result in apparent imitation without requiring the ability to attribute intentions.

16.3 Conclusion

The implications of our emphasis on the explanatory possibilities of simple mechanisms are different depending on one's goals. For scientists interested in explaining animal behavior, the recognition that some simpler mechanism could be responsible for apparently imitative behavior is not the end of the story. In particular, computer modeling helps investigators to pose the right empirical questions, first by acting as an "intuition pump," and second by allowing exploration of the range of parameters for which a particular mechanism could be effective and evolutionarily stable. On the other hand, if one is an engineer, and interested in the idea that robots with the ability to imitate would be useful artifacts, then the message is that simpler mechanisms such as stimulus enhancement or contagious behavior may give rise to the desired effects. Of course, it may be the case that adding true imitation learning to a group of artificial agents can greatly enhance their ability to adapt to a novel environment, much as theoretically taboo Lamarckian inheritance can greatly speed up technologically pragmatic evolutionary systems (see Ackley and Littman 1994). Nevertheless, building a truly imitative system is unlikely to be easy. To the extent that we want to build artificial systems that mimic nature, or want to use artificial systems to understand nature, copying the preferences of most researchers in the adaptive behavior field for simple mechanisms is the better place to start.

References

Ackley, D. H., and M. L. Littman. A case for Lamarckian evolution. In C. G. Langton, ed., *Artificial Life III*, pp. 487–509. Reading, Mass.: Addison-Wesley, 1994.

Bandura, A. Social learning theory of identificatory processes. In D. A. Goslin, ed., *Handbook of Socialization Theory and Research*, pp. 213–262. Chicago: Rand-McNally, 1969.

Banerjee, A. V. A simple model of herd behavior. *Quarterly Journal of Economics* 107: 797–817, 1992.

Bekoff, M. Vigilance, flock size, and flock geometry: Information gathering by western evening grosbeaks (Aves, Fringillidae). *Ethology* 99: 150–161, 1995.

Belew, R., and M. Mitchell, eds. *Adaptive Individuals in Evolving Populations: Models and Algorithms*. Reading, Mass.: Addison-Wesley, 1996.

Bikhchandani, S., D. Hirshleifer, and I. Welch. Learning from the behavior of others: Conformity, fads, and informational cascades. *Journal of Economic Perspectives* 12(3): 151–170, 1998.

Billard, A., and K. Dautenhahn. Grounding communication in autonomous robots: An experimental study. *Robotics and Autonomous Systems* 24: 71–79, 1998.

Bonabeau, E., G. Theraulaz, E. Arpin, and E. Sardet. The building behavior of lattice swarms. In R. A. Brooks and P. Maes, eds., *Artificial Life IV*, pp. 307–312. Cambridge, Mass.: MIT Press, 1994.

Boyd, R., and P. J. Richerson. *Culture and the Evolutionary Process*. Chicago: University of Chicago Press, 1985.

Braitenberg, V. *Vehicles: Experiments in Synthetic Psychology*. Cambridge, Mass.: MIT Press, 1984.

Brockmann, H. J. Satellite male groups in horseshoe crabs. *Limulus polyphemus*. *Ethology* 102(1): 1–21, 1995.

Bumby, K. E., and K. Dautenhahn. Investigating children's attitudes towards robots: A case study. In K. Cox, B. Gorayska, and J. Marsh, eds., *Proceedings of the Third Cognitive Technology Conference, CT'99*, pp. 391–410. M.I.N.D. Lab, Michigan State University, East Lansing, MI, 1999.

Byrne, R. W. *The Thinking Ape: Evolutionary Origins of Intelligence*. Oxford: Oxford University Press, 1995.

Cavalli-Sforza, L. L., and M. W. Feldman. *Cultural Transmission and Evolution: A Quantitative Approach*. Princeton: Princeton University Press, 1981.

Cecconi, F., F. Menczer, and R. K. Belew. Maturation and the evolution of imitative learning in artificial organisms. *Adaptive Behavior* 4(1): 27–48, 1996.

Cheney, D. L., and R. M. Seyfarth. *How Monkeys See the World*. Chicago: University of Chicago Press, 1990.

Clayton, D. A. Socially facilitated behavior. *Quarterly Review of Biology* 53: 373–391, 1978.

Deneubourg, J.-L., G. Theraulaz, and R. Beckers. Swarm-made architectures. In F. J. Varela and P. Bourgine, eds., *Toward a Practice of Autonomous Systems: Proceedings of the First European Conference on Artificial Life*, pp. 123–133. Cambridge, Mass.: MIT Press, 1992.

Dennett, D. C. *The Intentional Stance*. MIT Press/Bradford Books, Cambridge, MA, 1987.

Di Paolo, E. A. Some false starts in the construction of a research methodology for artificial life. In J. Noble and S. R. Parsowith, eds., *The Ninth White House Papers: Graduate Research in the Cognitive and Computing Sciences at Sussex*. Cognitive science research paper 440, School of Cognitive and Computing Sciences. Brighton, U.K.: University of Sussex, 1996.

Dugatkin, L. A. Copying and mate choice. In Heyes and Galef (1996), pp. 85–105.

Fisher, J., and R. A. Hinde. The opening of milk bottles by birds. *British Birds* 42: 347–357, 1949.

Galef, B. G. Jr. Social transmission of acquired behavior: A discussion of tradition and social learning in vertebrates. *Advances in the Study of Behavior* 5: 77–100, 1976.

Galef, B. G. Jr. Imitation in animals: History, definition, and interpretation of data from the psychological laboratory. In Zentall and Galef (1988), pp. 3–28.

Galef, B. G. Jr. Social enhancement of food preferences in Norway rats: A brief review. In Heyes and Galef (1996), pp. 49–64.

Gallese, V., and A. Goldman. Mirror neurons and the simulation theory of mind-reading. *Trends in Cognitive Sciences* 2(12): 493–501, 1998.

Hemelrijk, C. K. An individual-orientated model of the emergence of despotic and egalitarian societies. *Proceedings of the Royal Society of London. Biological Sciences* 266: 361–369, 1999.

Heyes, C. M. Imitation, culture, and cognition. *Animal Behaviour* 46: 999–1010, 1993.

Heyes, C. M., and B. G. Galef Jr., eds. *Social Learning in Animals: The Roots of Culture.* San Diego: Academic Press, 1996.

Iacoboni, M., R. P. Woods, M. Brass, H. Bekkering, J. C. Mazziotta, and G. Rizzolatti. Cortical mechanisms of human imitation. *Science* 286: 2526–2528, 1999.

Judson, O. P. The rise of the individual-based model in ecology. *Trends in Ecology and Evolution* 9: 9–14, 1994.

Kawai, M. Newly acquired pre-cultural behavior of the natural troop of Japanese monkeys on Koshima Inlet. *Primates* 6: 1–30, 1965.

Kawamura, S. The process of sub-culture propagation among Japanese macaques. *Primates* 2: 43–60, 1959.

Laland, K. N., P. J. Richerson, and R. Boyd. Animal social learning: Toward a new theoretical approach. In P. P. Klopfer, P. P. Bateson, and N. Thomson, eds., *Perspectives in Ethology*, pp. 249–276. New York: Plenum Press, 1993.

Laland, K. N., P. J. Richerson, and R. Boyd. Developing a theory of animal social learning. In Heyes and Galef (1996), pp. 129–154.

Langton, C. G. Artificial life. In C. G. Langton, ed., *Proceedings of the Interdisciplinary Workshop on the Synthesis and Simulation of Living Systems (ALIFE '87)*, pp. 1–48. Redwood City, Calif.: Addison-Wesley, 1989.

Matarić, M. J. Learning to behave socially. In D. Cliff, P. Husbands, J.-A. Meyer, and S. W. Wilson, eds., *From Animals to Animats 3: Proceedings of the Third International Conference on Simulation of Adaptive Behavior*, pp. 453–462. Cambridge, Mass.: MIT Press, 1994.

Meltzoff, A. N. The human infant as imitative generalist: A 20-year progress report on infant imitation with implications for cognitive psychology. In Heyes and Galef (1996), pp. 347–370.

Meyer, J.-A. The animat approach to cognitive science. In H. Roitblat and J.-A. Meyer, eds., *Comparative Approaches to Cognitive Science.* Cambridge, Mass.: MIT Press, 1994.

Miller, G. F. Artificial life as theoretical biology: How to do real science with computer simulation. Cognitive Science Research Paper 378, School of Cognitive and Computing Sciences, University of Sussex, Brighton, UK, 1995.

Miller, N. E., and J. Dollard. *Social Learning and Imitation.* New Haven: Yale University Press, 1941.

Mineka, S., and M. Cook. Social learning and the acquisition of snake fear in monkeys. In Zentall and Galef (1988), pp. 51–73.

Provine, R. R. Contagious yawning and laughter. In Heyes and Galef (1996), pp. 179–208.

Scassellati, B. Imitation and mechanisms of joint attention: A developmental structure for building social skills on a humanoid robot. In C. L. Nehaniv, ed., *Computation for Metaphors, Analogy, and Agents*, vol. 1562 of Lecture Notes in Artificial Intelligence, pp. 176–195. Berlin: Springer, 1999.

Sherry, D. F., and B. G. Galef Jr. Cultural transmission without imitation: Milk bottle opening by birds. *Animal Behaviour* 32: 937–938, 1984.

Simon, H. A. Artificial intelligence: An empirical science. *Artificial Intelligence* 77: 95–127, 1995.

Skinner, B. F. *Science and Human Behavior.* New York: Macmillan, 1953.

Sullivan, K. A. The advantages of social foraging in downy woodpeckers. *Animal Behaviour* 32: 16–21, 1984.

Terkel, J. Cultural transmission of feeding behaviour in the black rat (*Rattus rattus*). In Heyes and Galef (1996), pp. 17–47.

Theraulaz, G., and E. Bonabeau. A brief history of stigmergy. *Artificial Life* 5(2): 97–116, 1999.

Todd, P. M. The causes and effects of evolutionary simulation in the behavioral sciences. In Belew and Mitchell (1996), pp. 211–224.

Todd, P. M., and G. F. Miller. Exploring adaptive agency II: Simulating the evolution of associative learning. In J.-A. Meyer and S. W. Wilson, eds., *From Animals to Animats: Proceedings of the First International Conference on Simulation of Adaptive Behavior*, pp. 306–315. Cambridge, Mass.: MIT Press, 1991.

Tomasello, M. Do apes ape? In Heyes and Galef (1996), pp. 319–346.

Tomasello, M., A. C. Kruger, and H. H. Ratner. Cultural learning. *Behavioral and Brain Sciences* 16: 495–552, 1993.

Tooby, J., and L. Cosmides. The psychological foundations of culture. In J. H. Barkow, L. Cosmides, and J. Tooby, eds., *The Adapted Mind: Evolutionary Psychology and the Generation of Culture*, pp. 19–136. New York: Oxford University Press, 1992.

Toquenaga, Y., I. Kajitani, and T. Hoshino. Egrets of a feather flock together. *Artificial Life* 1(4): 391–411, 1994.

Tuci, E., J. Noble, and P. M. Todd. I'll have what she's having: A simulation analysis of the copying of food preferences in Norway rats. In K. Dautenhahn and C. L. Nehaniv, eds., *Proceedings of the AISB'99 Symposium on Imitation in Animals and Artifacts*, pp. 74–79. Brighton U.K.: Society for the Study of Artificial Intelligence and Simulation of Behaviour, 1999.

Zajonc, R. B. Social facilitation. *Science* 149: 269–274, 1965.

Zentall, T. R. An analysis of imitative learning in animals. In Heyes and Galef (1996), pp. 221–243.

Zentall, T. R., and B. G. Galef Jr., eds. *Social Learning: Psychological and Biological Perspectives*. Hillsdale, N.J.: Erlbaum, 1988.

17 Imitation as a Perceptual Process

Robert W. Mitchell

17.1 Imitation: Overview and Definition

Anyone attempting a review of all the different things researchers have called imitation is in a difficult position, because imitation has had many different connotations and implications through the last hundred years or so of its psychological investigation (Whiten and Ham 1992). In this chapter, I present a definition of imitation and a view of its development. Following this presentation, I examine evidence for a type of imitation—imitation based on matching between kinesthesis and vision—that has wide-ranging implications for human (and some nonhuman) cognition.

In a preliminary attempt to come to grips with the similarity present among different forms of imitation, I provided a definition (Mitchell 1987) that I hoped included the range of phenomena that so many authors had felt reasonable to name "imitation." I offered the following:

Imitation occurs when

1. something C (the copy) is produced by an organism and/or machine, where
2. C is similar to something else M (the model),
3. registration (or perception) of M is necessary for the production of C, and
4. C is designed to be similar to M.

Thus, a photocopied reproduction is just as much an imitation as babbling, pretending to be mommy, or a portrait painting. The definition was not intended to be prescriptive, to say what "true" imitation is, of all the varied forms. The definition tells how speakers and writers use the word, and does not focus attention on any particular type.

Some researchers have suggested that this definition is too inclusive or liberal, and have designated, with conflicting definitions, what "true" imitation is. So, for example, Galef (1988) focuses on the similarity between the motor patterns of the model and the copy as necessary for "true" imitation, whereas Thorpe (1956) and others (e.g., Visalberghi and Fragaszy 1990) require that the copy be a novel action for the animal, even if not precisely similar to the model. Other definitions combine both ideas, requiring that the imitator "learn ... some part of the form of a behavior" from the model (Whiten and Ham 1992, p. 247). By some of these definitions, reproduction of another's facial gestures by infants using familiar actions (discussed below) cannot be imitations, as these are not novel or learned behaviors; by others, replication of a caregiver's eyeblink by an orangutan using its finger to push down its eyelid (discussed below) cannot be imitation as the same motor patterns are not used; yet both are so obviously imitations that something must be wrong with these definitions. From what I can see, calling something "true" imitation depends more upon what you are interested in focusing on than on any accuracy or "truth" in the label. What counts as a match depends upon the concerns of the observer (Nehaniv and Dautenhahn, 2000). In addition, the significance of imitation—what imitation is taken to indicate—as well as how its existence is determined varies within different traditions (Russon et al. 1998). So, for example, in studies of ape language, the chimpanzee (*Pan troglodytes*) Nim was considered to be "merely" imitating gestures, and thus not understanding their meaning (Terrace 1979); whereas in child language studies, children are viewed as coming to understand the meaning of gestures and words through imitating them (Speidel and Nelson 1989). In child language, imitation is "smart"; in ape language, imitation is "dumb" (Mitchell 1994b). Descriptions of the different sorts of evidence for and implications of imitation in different areas of scientific inquiry are presented in table 17.1.

Interpreting reproductions of actions or sounds as imitations hinges on the "design" component of imitation, that the copy is "designed" to be similar to the model. The fact that something A resembles something B is usually not enough evidence that A is designed to resemble B. Design is a usefully ambiguous word, in that it can refer to the copy having the biological *function* of being similar to the model, or to the copy having been *entrained* to resemble the model, or to the copy being *intentionally* made similar to the model. (A biological function is "designed" by evolution and selection, a metaphorical holdover from the natural theologians' idea that adaptation results from a designer—God.) In general, "designing" as a process refers to a selection among alternatives toward some end that is beneficial or good (from the per-

Table 17.1 The diverse concerns and sources of evidence used in different areas of scientific study

AREA OF STUDY	SOURCES OF EVIDENCE	CONCERN
Child language	Immediate repetition of word/sign	Language learning
Ape language	Immediate repetition of sign	Meaningfulness of signs
Animal learning	Savings in learning	Existence of animal imitation
Animal cognition		
Natural	Immediate repetition	Imitative propensity
Acquired	Two-choice task	Capacity for imitation
Acquired	"Do same" task	Capacity for generalized imitation
Animal culture	Repetition of another's novel action	Capacity for culture
Birdsong	Later repetition of novel sounds	Plasticity of learning
Mirror-self-recognition	Mark test; self-exploration	Kinesthetic-visual matching
Child development		
Infant facial imitation	Repetition of another's familiar bodily or facial actions	Representational capacity
Deferred imitation	Repetition of another's bodily and facial actions	Representational capacity

spective of adaptation, learning, a conscious being, etc.). In the case of imitation, matching is usually beneficial for an end that the matching serves.

In many imitations of animals' own actions or sounds, a design criterion is evident in the action or sound being used for deception: the reproduction of their own actions or sounds outside their (presumed) "normal" context benefits the imitator when others respond to the actions as they would under "normal" circumstances. Most, if not all, instances of deception in animals are minimally based on reproducing one's own kinesthetically (or viscerally) experienced movements, or one's own kinesthetically or acoustically experienced sounds (see Mitchell 1994a). These deceptions are forms of self-imitation (Baldwin 1894/1903; Guillaume 1926/1971) in which the model is the organism's own actions, which are perceived by the organism, and the copy is the reinstatement of the actions via the reproduction of the previous perceptual experience.

In some cases, the "design" aspect of an imitation is supported by the extensiveness of the match between model and copy, and on the copier's general ability to produce similar matches. Such support is especially true for vocal imitation in parrots (*Psittacus erithacus*) and human children, who reproduce distinctive human speech and other sounds with relative ease and precision (Speidel and Nelson 1989; Pepperberg, Brese, and Harris 1991). Although copies can be similar to models in several ways (Knowlton 1966), here I will focus on perceptual similarities between model and copy—do they sound the same, or look the same, or feel the same, for example, or does one look like what the other feels like?

17.2 Imitation and Development

A definition of imitation is helpful as a beginning, but from a psychological standpoint, some imitations appear more complex than others. Around the turn of the last century, the different forms of imitation, from simple to complex, came to be of interest to developmental and evolutionary theorists such as Morgan (1896/1973), Baldwin (1894/1903), Guillaume (1926/1971), and Piaget (1945/1962). These theorists depicted imitation as progressing through a variety of stages that would be present, to some degree, in human development, nonhuman development, and evolutionary changes. For these theorists, the development of imitation is based on the transformation of something like "programs" (or schemas). A program is "a set of coded instructions for insertion into a machine, in accordance with which the machine performs a desired sequence of operations" (*American Heritage Dictionary*), so the term is used metaphorically to refer to biological or psychological "instructions" in organisms. Transformation occurs through modification of biological and/or psychological capacities (programs) to create more advanced or more complex capacities. Application of this framework provides an outline of the development of imitation applicable across species and machines, in which various programs internal or external to organisms or machines lead to different forms of imitation (Mitchell 1987; see table 17.2).

The first type (or level) of design process, design by evolution and morphogenesis, produces genetic programming in animals that results in mimicry, including such things as looking like something inconspicuous to avoid detection. The second type requires coordination of perception and action, such that the imitator perceives (or registers) something, and has programs that induce it to imitate upon perception or to reproduce previous perceptual experiences (as in some circular reactions). Neonatal imitation is

Table 17.2 Types of designing processes leading to imitations of various types, and the types of "programs" that are created

DESIGNING PROCESS	EARLY NAMES	PROGRAM
Evolution and morphogenesis	Mimicry (Morgan) Stage 1 imitation (Piaget)	Always look like M Do M repeatedly
Coordination of perception and action	Simple imitation (Baldwin) Instinctive imitation (Morgan) Imitative suggestion (Guillaume) Stages 2 and 3 imitation (Piaget) Neonatal imitation	Do C when you perceive M
Learning and memory	Persistent imitation (Baldwin) Intelligent imitation (Morgan) Trial-and-error imitation (Guillaume) Stages 4 and 5 imitation (Piaget) Neonatal imitation showing improvement?	Make C more like M
Pretense and planning (prior intention)	Internal persistent imitation (Baldwin) Reflective imitation (Morgan) Symbolic imitation (Guillaume) Deferred/stage 6 imitation (Piaget)	Transform C in relation to M
Interpersonal interaction	Non-natural meaning (Grice) Interpersonal imitation, satire Metacommunication (Bateson)	Use match between C and M to communicate
Externalization	Representational art, artifacts	Create C, an image of M
Mechanization	Invent Xerox machines, audiotapes	Create machine Y, which can produce C, an image of M

an example: after observing facial gestures, infants reproduce them soon after. At this level of imitation, the information can be retained in memory, but there is no attempt to make the copy more like the model. (Note that each type of designing process depends on earlier ones, such that evolution and morphogenesis are presumed for coordination of perception and action, and so on—see Mitchell 1987.) The third type is designed by processes of learning and memory, and has a program that recognizes resemblances and disparities between copy and model and induces more accurate reproductions of the model by diminishing disparities and accenting resemblances. Learning to pronounce a foreign language shows such a program in operation, as might the childhood game of "Simon says," and some neonates may evince such a program in trying to perfect their imitation of facial gestures (Kugiumutzakis

1999; Meltzoff and Moore 1999; compare Mitchell 2002). The fourth type of imitation is designed by the entity itself, in relation to a plan of action. In this case, the organism can program its own actions for its own purposes. Pretend play is a good example, in that the child reproduces some aspects of others' behavior according to his or her own plans. At this point, the designing process is initiated by the organism itself, which designs its own imitations.

Analogically, machines can show similar design processes, although humans are their ultimate designers, not evolution and morphogenesis. A machine analogy for imitation by perception and action is a tape recorder that copies sounds, rewinds, and plays them back, or a photocopier that registers shades of light and dark and reproduces them on a page. An imitation via learning and memory might be a missile that is set to hit a moving target and corrects any deviations from the direct line to the target; in essence, the missile imitates the direction of or change in movement of the target (presuming that direction of or change in movement is what the missile registers). The closest machine example for planned imitation is of a robot programmed to follow another robot through a maze, such that it can later go through the maze by itself (discussed in Nehaniv and Dautenhahn 2000). Although in this instance the machine did not originally program itself to imitate, it contains a program that allows it to reprogram itself based on its registrations. The machine examples tend to provide much less complex imitations than do the biological examples.

Subsequent types of imitation are unlikely to be present in machines. The fifth type of imitation is designed to communicate, calling attention to the fact of imitation to communicate something. Someone might pantomime actions to indicate something, or exaggerate actions to indicate imitation as in satire or caricature (see Mitchell 1994a). Children often simply imitate other children as a means of communicating mutual interest (Nadel et al. 1999), and sometimes even imitate each other to insult (personal observation). For this type, the body is used to imitate, either by visual or auditory means. (Some authors have even suggested that human communication developed from exaggeratedly imitating an involuntary "natural" action to communicate voluntarily—so-called "nonnatural" meaning; see Bateson 1956; Grice 1982; Mitchell 1991.) The sixth type (externalization) is also designed to communicate by imitation, but here an artifact—a painting, a sculpture, a pictogram—is created that imitates something. And the seventh type (mechanization) produces imitations via the creation of a machine that imitates.

17.3   Imitation and Perceptual Matching

Although most early theorists presumed that developments in imitation were similar across perceptual domains, they also believed that organisms can develop imitative skills with variation across these domains. For example, Baldwin and Guillaume viewed imitation via different perceptual modalities as initially distinct processes that intercoordinate in development, and Piaget drew attention, in his idea of *décalage*, to the fact that the schemas associated with different perceptual modalities develop at different rates. So, for example, a child may understand well how to imitate motor activities before the child understands well how to imitate vocal sounds (or vice versa). This idea of different developments in different modalities, with the same overarching developmental sequence, was picked up by researchers studying nonhuman primates, who noted that auditory imitation either is not found in nonhuman primates or is not as developed as it is in humans, whereas in apes but not monkeys imitation of visually perceived actions seems to follow the same course as that in human development (Chevalier-Skolnikoff 1977; Parker 1977). More recent research shows that imitation of others' gestures and vocalizations are possible at birth for both human and chimpanzee infants (Bard and Russell 1999; Butterworth 1999; Meltzoff and Moore 1999; Trevarthen, Kokkinaki, and Fiamenghi 1999), but that (for human infants) imitation of others' gestures is more common (Kugiumutzakis 1999) and follows a different course than vocal imitation (Užgiris 1999).

Perceptual matching requirements seem fairly obvious for many imitations: imitation of one's own bodily movements requires the know-how to produce a kinesthetic bodily match to a prior kinesthetic perception; imitation of another's bodily movements requires the know-how to produce a kinesthetic bodily match to a prior visual perception; vocal imitation of another's vocalizations requires the know-how to produce matching between auditions; and vocal imitation of one's own vocalizations requires either or both of these matchings. As noted above, the most distinctive evidence for self-imitation of audition and movement are deceptions (Mitchell 1994a), and these are apparently most prevalent in primates (Whiten and Byrne 1988). Auditory imitations of others are most prevalent in parrots (*Psittacus erithacus*; Pepperberg, Brese, and Harris 1991; Moore 1992) and bottlenose dolphins (*Tursiops truncatus*; Reiss and McCowan 1993; Herman, chapter 3 of this volume). It is interesting to note that at least one parrot has learned to use his imitations of another's words to communicate (Pepperberg, Brese, and Harris 1991; Pepperberg 1999, and chapter 4 of this volume), indicating a sophisticated use of imitation (Mitchell 1987).

Although the perceptual requirements for imitation seem obvious, it is unclear what exactly needs to be perceived or registered for imitation to occur. Copies may be made through several different processes (Stein and Meredith 1993; Bahrick and Pickens 1994; Lewkowicz 1994; Rose 1994; Smith 1994; Streri and Molina 1994; Walker-Andrews 1994): amodal recognition of perceived invariants, as when an infant matches its body rhythm with the rhythm in its parent's speech (Trevarthen, Kokkinaki, and Fiamenghi 1999), or when an infant matches its parent's facial expression (Meltzoff and Moore 1999; Kugiumutzakis 1999); modality-specific experiences, as when an infant matches a sound from its parent's speech (Kugiumutzakis 1999); or extraction/abstraction of similar aspects across modality-specific experiences (as in kinesthetic-visual matching discussed below). In fact, all these processes can be involved in imitation, and one method may lead to developments in another, as Lewkowicz (1994, p. 193) imagines for infant development in auditory-visual matching: "once infants become adept at responding to a given intersensory temporal attribute (e.g., synchrony), they then can rely on that attribute to 'discover' the next and more complex temporal attribute" (see also Bahrick and Pickens 1994).

The focus on perceptual matchings as the basis for imitation influenced me to see if humans can recognize matches between different perceptual modalities, presumably the basis for human imitative skills. My colleague and I (Mitchell and Gallaher 2001) asked a dancer to produce dances congruent with three musical pieces. We then asked just under 400 subjects to match the congruent music and dance when these were temporally separated, and answer questions about how they did it: half listened to a piece of music and then selected from among 3 dances, and the other half watched a dance and then selected from among 3 pieces of music (all were suitably counterbalanced). In support of the idea that people can match between diverse perceptual modalities, subjects selected the appropriate piece of music or the appropriate dance at greater than chance levels. More relevant is that most people acknowledged matching auditory musical images in memory to their visual experiences of dance, and visual dance images in memory to auditory musical experiences, suggesting cross-modal matching. But for some music/dance combinations, people also noticed the similar rhythm and tempo between music and dance, similarities in emotion, and similarities in style (e.g., African quality, fluidity). What appears to be cross-modal matching may be just that, or it may rely on amodal recognition of equivalence between modalities, without any distinct matching between perceptions, or it may utilize both amodal and cross-modal skills.

17.4 Kinesthetic-Visual Matching

My initial awareness of the importance of perceptual modalities for understanding imitation occurred when trying to come up with an explanation for mirror-self-recognition. I realized (as had Guillaume 1926/1971) that the same kind of capacity that allowed for mirror-self-recognition is also likely to be present in elaborate bodily and facial imitation, and in recognizing that you are being imitated: the organism had to match between kinesthetic and visual modalities (Mitchell 1993a,b, 1994a, 1997a,b).

Less well studied than vision, kinesthesis is a complicated perceptual system that informs about the position and movement of parts of the body; consequently, experiencing kinesthesis often requires movement of the body, implicating a motor component as part of the perception. (Indeed, the motor component is so much a part of the perception that Gibson [1966] denied that kinesthesis is a perceptual modality.) Another part of kinesthesis is somasthesis, the feeling of the outline of the body. It is interesting to note that people (and other animals) still feel this outline even if they are born without a body part, or have had it amputated—so-called phantom limbs (von Fieandt 1966; Melzack 1989, 1992). In addition, somasthesis maps to prostheses attached to the body, supplying feeling to them and mapping to their visual outline (Melzack 1989, 1992). Kinesthetic-visual matching may initially derive from experience of multiple invariants between kinesthetic feelings of one's body (including somasthetic feelings) and visual experiences of it.

The only cross-modal match similar to kinesthetic-visual matching in the "exactness" of the match is present in echolocating animals, who appear to have very close matchings between vision and echolocation, such that when an object is perceived by echolocation, almost all of its visual properties are known (Herman, Pack, and Hoffmann-Kuhnt 1998). Of course, all visual properties of something are not knowable through echolocation, but shape and texture apparently are; similarly, all visual properties of the body are not knowable through kinesthesis, but the outline of the body and the position and movements of its parts are.

Kinesthetic-visual matching as I imagine it requires some kinesthetic involvement in visual experiences of bodies, including one's own and those of others. The idea of kinesthetic-visual matching can perhaps be made most salient by discussing its presence in "prism experiments," in which one's own kinesthetic feelings seem to be present where one's hand visually appears to be, rather than where it really is. In these studies, humans wear prisms that distort the visual field (Harris 1965). When they see their arm dislocated through a prism, people actually have kinesthetic feeling in a new location (where they *see* their arm); that is, they maintain the match between kinesthesis and vision even when they know that the match is nonsensical. When subjects looking through a prism *continuously* observe their displaced hand pointing toward various locations over several trials (such that the hand becomes adapted to the deviation) and are then asked after the prism is removed to point to an object with each hand separately, they tend to misjudge their point with their adapted hand (the one they used while the prism was on), but to point accurately with their nonadapted hand (if they had misjudged with this hand, it would be indicative of transfer of adaptation). However, when subjects are allowed to observe only their *completed* point over several trials (called terminal exposure) and are then asked after the prism is removed to point to an object with each hand separately, they tend to misjudge their points with either hand, indicating transfer of the pointing error to the nonadapted hand (Cohen 1967; Kornheiser 1976, p. 793).

It seems the explanation for these differences has to do with which sensory modality subjects take as veridical. If the visual modality is taken as veridical (as it would be in the continuous observation task, as vision is the most salient perception), subjects map their kinesthetic sensations to the visual (and therefore do not transfer to the other hand). However, if the kinesthetic modality is taken as veridical (as it would be in the terminal exposure task, as kinesthesis is the only perception the subject experiences for most of the task), subjects map the visual sensations to the felt kinesthetic sensations (and therefore transfer to the other nonadapted hand: kinesthetic perceptions are apparently not as easily separable into parts as visual perceptions are). Kinesthetic-visual matching is rarely brought to one's attention, as the visual and kinesthetic images of one's self are so finely attuned.

An interesting difference is observed in autistic children. By contrast with normal children and adults, when autistic children wear a prism that distorts their vision in the continuous observation task and are tested after removal of the prism, they appear to extend the translocation of kinesthetic feelings to the arm they had not viewed with the prism: they make errors with the nonadapted (as well as the adapted) hand, and thereby show transfer, when they have continuously observed their other hand point to a location over several trials (Masterton and Biederman 1983). This unique transfer shows kinesthetic-visual matching, but seems to indicate that autistic children accept kinesthesis as more veridical than vision.

My realization of the importance of kinesthetic-visual matching was dependent upon a rereading of Guillaume's (1926/1971) work on imitation. (A similar realization by Sue Parker [1991] depended upon thinking through Piaget's work on imitation and understanding causality.) Guillaume (1926/1971) initially posited that the human infant's recognition of the similarity between its own actions and those of others (which would lead to flexible bodily imitation) derives from an infant's initially attempting to recreate the objective effects of another's actions on objects, and only later trying to reproduce the movements that led to the effects. Gradually, through imitation of effects, in which the visually experienced actions of the model become a cue for the production of the same visually experienced act by the child, the kinesthetic subjective feeling of the child's act is associated with the model's act; the ability to imitate others' bodily actions results. In Guillaume's model, visual-visual matching leads to the kinesthetic-visual matching present in generalized imitation—the ability to duplicate to some degree myriad actions of another. Guillaume recognized that the same kinesthetic-visual matching that allowed for imitating another's actions also allowed the child to recognize his or her own image in a mirror. More recent theorists, such as Meltzoff and Moore (1999), argue that infants are born with an ability for matching their own and others' behavior at a supramodal level that ignores modality-specific information, and that actual cross-modal matches (evinced in imitation after a long delay and self-recognition) develop from this ability.

The ideas that kinesthetic-visual matching is responsible for self-recognition and for mature forms of bodily and facial imitation, and that imitation can be based on matching between or within perceptual modalities, focuses attention on research related to kinesthetic-visual matching. Research supports the theory that a match between kinesthesis and vision is essential for skills such as self-recognition, generalized imitation of another's behavior, pretend play, and even recognition of being imitated by another, especially for human children (Meltzoff 1990; Asendorpf and Baudonnière 1993; Mitchell 1993a,b, 1994a, 1997a,b; Parker, Mitchell, and Boccia 1994; Asendorpf, Warkentin, and Baudonnière 1996). Minimally, the evidence supports the conclusion that the first two skills at least (generalized imitation and self-recognition) develop in humans, great apes, and perhaps dolphins. The evidence also suggests that one particular perceptual match—that between kinesthesis and vision—leads organisms to more developed imitative abilities, from bodily and facial imitation based on the coordination of perception and action—type 2—through to imitation in interpersonal interaction—type 5 (see discussion of humans below). What follows is my take on evidence *suggestive* of kinesthetic-visual matching in humans and animals, most of which is based on simpler processes, such as visual-visual matching, amodal matching, or even (in some cases) no matching at all.

17.5   Evidence of Kinesthetic-Visual Matching

Human Neonates and Infants

Neonatal human infants, whether normal or with Down's syndrome, can imitate a variety of actions of others, which seem based on kinesthetic-visual matching, including tongue protrusion, mouth opening, eyeblinks, and vocalizations, suggesting non-reflexive flexible intentional matching (Heimann and Ullstadius 1999; Kugiumutzakis 1999; Meltzoff and Moore 1999; Trevarthen, Kokkinaki, and Fiamenghi 1999). But how important perceptual experiences as such are for neonatal facial and gestural imitation is unclear (Mitchell 2002). Infant visual acuity is limited (Trevarthen, Kokkinaki, and Fiamenghi 1999, p. 145)—at best 20/660 vision at birth and still only 20/100 vision by 6 months (Courage and Adams 1990)—which seems likely to make observation of the fine details of a human face difficult (Meltzoff and Moore 1999, p. 23). Most of the researchers studying neonatal facial and gestural imitation argue for amodal representation of visual and kinesthetic experiences, in which the infant recognizes invariances in "supramodal" representation of acts (coded independent of modality-specific information). Similarly, a common rhythm observed visually in an infant's movements, felt by that infant in his or her movements, and discerned by that infant in his or her parents' speech (Condon and Sander 1974; Trevarthen, Kokkinaki, and Fiamenghi 1999) could be recognized amodally, such that the infant need not be matching vision to kinesthesis to audition, but rather could simply be detecting an invariant aspect (sharp abrupt movements are associated with sharp abrupt tones) common to all three perceptions (as might an adult at times). Neonatal imitations seem to follow the rule "do C when you perceive (or register) M," in that actions and vocalizations of another cause some infants to reproduce some aspect of those actions. (Note, though, that not all infants imitate, and infants vary in what they imitate.)

Although there is some evidence that infants try to perfect their imitations (Meltzoff and Moore 1999), some infants also appear to decrease the similarity between their imitation and the model (Kugiumutzakis 1999), which suggests either that there is individual variability in neonates' ability or desire to perfect their imitation, or that the increase in accuracy in some infants' reproductions is in the eye of the beholder, rather than in the gesture of the infant. By 9 months (Meltzoff and Moore 1999), or perhaps later (Nadel et al. 1999), some infants can test the imitative quality of another's behavior by modeling a new action following another's imitation of the infant to see if the other imitates the new action, suggesting the beginnings of kinesthetic-visual matching. This testing behavior, which can also be observed toward the mirror image (see Parker, Mitchell, and Miles 1994), seems to indicate imitation of the third type—that based on learning and memory.

Children After the First Year

Normal human children show developing evidence of kinesthetic-visual matching (using fourth-level skills) in planning (deferred imitation) by 9 months, in generalized bodily and facial imitation, pretense and recognition of being imitated by 14 months of age (see Meltzoff 1990; Meltzoff and Moore 1999; Mitchell 1993a,b, 1994a; Hart and Fegley 1994; Užgiris 1999), and self-recognition in mirrors usually begins at 15 months (Lewis and Brooks-Gunn 1979). Indeed, children's social imitations of gestures begin to develop elaborately just prior to self-recognition (Asendorpf and Baudonnière 1993; Hart and Fegley 1994; Asendorpf, Warkentin, and Baudonnière 1996). These gestural imitations seem to have a communicative role, in that they instigate children to test that they are being imitated, and to initiate modeling of actions in turns (Nadel et al. 1999), suggesting fifth-level skills. By the end of the second year, children frequently enact strange imitations with familiar objects (pretending to be drinking from a shoe), something they avoided a year earlier when they avidly imitated familiar actions with objects (pretending to be drinking from a cup) (Užgiris 1999). Retarded children also recognize themselves in mirrors (Hill and Tomlin 1981; Loveland 1987), and can learn to imitate bodily and facial imitations (Baer, Peterson, and Sherman 1971).

Autistic Children

Autistic children are an interesting test of the idea that kinesthetic-visual matching is the basis for self-recognition, imitation, and recognizing that one is being imitated, in that they are generally impaired in imitation of action (Smith and Bryson 1994; Heimann and Ullstadius 1999; Nadel et al. 1999; Rogers 1999). Yet the majority nevertheless reproduce a variety of actions they observe, and most show self-recognition (see Mitchell 1997a). Most autistic children can imitate another person's (or a doll's) body movements, hand or arm gestures (with or without objects), and non-symbolic actions. About 33 to 40% of autistic children tested could perform unfamiliar actions and invisible facial gestures, and some were able to perform generalized imitation on command.

Most autistic children tested show deferred imitation (reproducing an action after it is no longer visible), which indicates that they develop plans for their own actions. Relatively young autistic children (4–6 years of age) recognize when they are being imitated in that they gaze longer at an adult who imitates their actions on objects than they do to an adult who simply uses the same object as the child or an adult who acts with an object unrelated to the child (Tiegerman and Primavera 1984). Autistic children can also produce, in relation to someone who is imitating them, actions for the other to model (Nadel et al. 1999).

The bodily imitations of autistic children can often be "odd" by comparison with those of other children. When autistic children are asked to imitate with their hand actions in which the palm of the model faces the child, they sometimes (3 of 16 tested) invert their hand so that the palm of their own hand faces themselves (Ohta 1987). When these same subjects were asked to perform bimanual tasks, the incidence of such "inverted" ("partial") imitations is more common (7–8 of 16 autistic children tested): for example, when shown two hands making a T, such that the back of one of the model's hands faces the child and covers (to some degree) the model's other hand, some autistic children showed a bimanual T in which the hand representing the top of the 'T' had the palm facing the model, and the hand representing the base of the T was in front of the other hand (and therefore visible to the model) (Ohta 1987). (At least 12 out of 44 normal 3- to $3\frac{1}{2}$-year old children also showed partial imitations like those of autistic children.) Similar "inversion" of hand or hands was observed in a study of 19 autistic children asked to imitate eight unimanual and eight bimanual actions after delay, after no delay, and when unable to observe their hands visually: 11 autistic children made two or more "visual matches" between the model's and their own hands, and 8 made one or none (Smith 1995). (By contrast, out of 19 language-impaired and 19 normal children, 16 and 14, respectively, made zero or one visual matches.) These visual matches suggest that visual-visual matching (which is relatively easily learned—Piaget 1945/1962; Rose 1994), rather than kinesthetic-visual matching, is used as a default at times in imitation by autistic children (Smith 1995). Note, however, that these children provided a match even when they did not see their own hands (indicating kinesthetic-visual matching), and the gesture itself, though not its relation to one's body, is apparently retained in such visual matches: specifically, the T shape itself is maintained, even though the T in relation to the body is inverted. Thus, kinesthetic-visual matching is at least partly responsible for the imitated form. In addition, it is unclear that the autistic children (or the normal children showing the same pattern) understood the task to be one of perfect mirroring of the entire bodily posture. As the hand and arm were the most salient part of the body that moved when the child was asked to imitate it, perhaps the autistic child thought that only that part of the body should be imitated, in which case the use of the rest of the body as a reference point is possible but unnecessary.

Another hypothesis to explain partial imitations is that the autistic child produced an image that was congruent with the model's perception, indicating visual perspective taking. Many of the activities that kinesthetic-visual matching leads to (e.g., mirror-self-recognition, recognition of being imitated) provide a child with a different perspective on him or herself—a visual perspective. Thus, it seems possible that the idea of alternative visual perspectives would arise from experience with activities developed from kinesthetic-visual matching, such that a child who had used kinesthetic-visual matching in activities would recognize, to some degree, that divergent visual perspectives exist, and that another might (literally) feel similarly to the child him- or herself (see Mitchell 1993a,b). And, indeed, autistic children do well on visual perspective-taking tasks (moving an object to show another person various requested facets of it), as well as on some cognitive perspective-taking tasks (telling about what another feels or perceives), although their perspectival skills are generally below normal (Hobson 1984; Baron-Cohen 1989; Reed and Peterson 1990; Reed 1994). It may be that the partial imitations observed by Ohta (1987) and Smith (1995) are attempts by the autistic child to maintain the model's perspective in the reproduction of the model's action.

Relevant Brain Area in Humans

Kinesthetic-visual matching appears to be localized in the parietal area of the left hemisphere of the brain. Adult humans with parts of their parietal region destroyed show ideomotor apraxia in which they are incapable of imitating gestures; the parietal area is presumed to contain "visuokinesthetic motor engrams, where motor acts may be programmed" (Heilman, Rothi, and Valenstein 1982, p. 342). When people with ideomotor apraxia and left brain damage were asked to imitate meaningless gestures of a hand toward a face on themselves or on a mannikin, they generally failed on both tasks, indicating a generic incapacity to imitate bodily gestures (Goldenberg 1995). The opposite occurs when patients have lesions in the areas of the frontal lobe, which normally inhibit the parietal lobes: these patients cannot help but imitate the actions of others (Lhermitte, Pillon, and Serdaru 1986).

Great Apes (and Lesser Apes)

The only species of great apes that have been evaluated extensively for imitation based on kinesthetic-visual matching are orangutans (*Pongo pygmaeus*) and chimpanzees. The orangutan Chantek was taught to imitate the sounds, effects, and motor patterns of his caregivers upon their gesturally signed request to *do the-same-thing*, and imitated a variety of actions (many nonvisible), including patting the top of his head, touching his tongue with his finger, blinking his eye, and jumping (Miles, Mitchell, and Harper 1996). In some of these imitations, Chantek produced the bodily or facial movement via a different means because he was unable to perform the activity: in imitating blinking his eye, he pushed his eyelid down with his finger (apparently not having voluntary control over his eyelids), and in imitating jumping he lifted his feet off the ground while holding himself up with his hands (apparently not being able to jump). Chantek engaged in his first instances of simultaneous gestural imitation (in relation to nonvisible parts of his body) at 16 months, of pretense at 20 months, self-recognition at 25 months, and delayed imitation of a gestural sign at 35 months. These "first" instances may not actually be the first time the animal displayed a skill (because he was not observed 24 hours a day or from birth, and someone could have failed to notice an instance), but the trajectory of Chantek's development suggests that kinesthetic-visual matching is necessary to exhibit most of these skills. Other orangutans, rehabilitants being returned to the wild in Borneo, imitated a variety of activities, some of which indicate kinesthetic-visual matching: brushing teeth, applying insect repellent on head and appendages, and holding a burning stick to a cigarette held with lips (Russon and Galdikas 1993). Although neither of these studies proves that orangutans can imitate novel actions in that the actions the animals used may, in other contexts, have been familiar to them, the generalizability of the imitative ability to novel actions seems a reasonable expectation (see discussion by Russon and Galdikas 1993; Miles, Mitchell, and Harper 1996; Bard and Russell 1999; Butterworth 1999).

Many early observational and experimental studies of chimpanzees (discussed in Whiten and Ham 1992; Mitchell 1994a; Custance, Whiten, and Bard 1995) indicate that chimpanzees could model a human's behavior rather specifically, and more recent experiments indicate that chimpanzees produce arbitrary (and nonvisible) actions based on kinesthetic-visual matching, including closing eyes, protruding lips, touching the nose, puffing out cheeks, and touching an ear (Custance, Whiten, and Bard 1995). Although gorillas (*Gorilla g. gorilla*) apparently can imitate novel bodily, facial, and manual actions on the first trial and after a delay (Chevalier-Skolnikoff 1977, p. 169), only one specific action is described: touching the ear (p. 179), and this by a gorilla who also recognizes herself in a mirror (Patterson and Cohn 1994). Similarly, one bonobo (*Pan paniscus*) has shown behavioral evidence of spontaneous imitation of other's gestures and actions (Savage-Rumbaugh and Lewin 1994). At least some members of all great ape species show self-recognition (Parker, Mitchell, and Miles 1994; Mitchell 1997b; Swartz, Sarauw, and Evans 1999), and recent evidence suggests that some lesser apes—gibbons (*Hylobates sp.*)—also show self-recognition (Ujhelyi et al. 2000).

Macaques

Only three observations of imitation suggesting kinesthetic-visual matching are found for macaques, two of which are *Macaca mulatta*. One instance is based upon animals producing a strange behavior like that of another animal: when a rhesus macaque with a distinctive tic of touching its forehead with its hand was placed among 32 other laboratory rhesus, within 3 months another monkey was making similar movements, and within $1\frac{1}{2}$ years three additional monkeys were also making the same movements (Rivers et al. 1983, p. 8). Another instance shows a concurrent matching by one rhesus of another: one free-ranging female rhesus monkey holding half of a coconut shell followed behind a mother carrying her own infant; the following female held the coconut shell in the same position the mother held her infant, and when the mother moved the infant and held it in a different way, the female moved her coconut shell to conform to the position of the infant on the mother (Breuggeman 1973, p. 196). The last instance suggests delayed imitation by an unidentified species of macaque: one juvenile monkey watched another subadult monkey look up and down a road, place its hand over its eyes, and "jauntily amble ... in a curious three-legged stride down the road"; the juvenile then moved to where the subadult had been, covered its eyes, and followed the subadult with the same "odd gait" (Burton 1992, p. 39). Only one study has attempted to test a macaque for imitation: a long-tailed macaque was conditioned to scratch when a human model scratched, but failed to learn to scratch where the model scratched (Mitchell and Anderson 1993). The three observations of spontaneous imitation are difficult to interpret: perhaps only very few macaques show a limited ability for kinesthetic-visual matching, or perhaps the few instances mentioned are happenstance. Imitation in other monkey species is apparently nonexistent (Visalberghi and Fragaszy, chapter 18 of this volume). Successful self-recognition by a few macaques is controversial (see Parker, Mitchell, and Miles 1994; Mitchell 1997a).

Bottlenosed Dolphins

Indian Ocean bottlenosed dolphins (*Tursiops aduncus*) in captivity imitated a variety of different postures and behaviors of seals and humans (Tayler and Saayman 1973) in a manner suggestive of kinesthetic-visual matching. The dolphins imitated the sleeping, grooming, and swimming patterns of a cape fur seal, and the actions of humans cleaning the windows of the dolphins' tank (including putting the flipper against the window frame while cleaning the window with an object, much as human divers put their hand against it while cleaning). These actions are extremely atypical for a dolphin, and clearly support kinesthetic-visual matching as an explanation. An attempt to train two *T. truncatus* to imitate actions upon a command failed with novel actions, but worked with familiar actions (Bauer and Johnson 1994; see also Herman, chapter 3 of this volume). *T. truncatus* appear to self-recognize (Marten and Psarakos 1994, 1995; Reiss and Marino 2001).

Parrots and Other Birds

Perhaps the most surprising evidence of imitation based on kinesthetic-visual matching comes from an African Grey parrot named
Okíchoro (Moore 1992). The parrot, when alone, showed behaviors
similar to those of his caregiver, and said a verbal label associated
with the behaviors. These verbal "labels" were used only with
particular movement patterns (p. 253). Kinesthetic-visual matching
is implicated for some behaviors: waving wings or foot when saying
"Ciao," moving its foot up (like the model holding up food) when
saying "Peanut," opening its beak when saying "Look at my
tongue," shaking its head left and right when saying "Shake," and
moving its head up and down when saying "Nod." Not all of these
movement-sound combinations need to have derived from kinesthetic-visual matching, however. For example, moving a foot up
when saying "Peanut" may have derived from the parrot's own
activity of grabbing a peanut when offered, and simply saying
"Look at my tongue" may, with some of the parrot's vocal variations, have produced an open mouth. In addition, the movement of
foot and wings while saying "ciao" may have derived from the
parrot's own movements as well: when I worked with the parrot
Alex studied by Pepperberg (1999), some common reactions of
Alex to someone's leaving (and to many stressful events) were to
lift up his foot or wave his wings; Okíchoro may have produced
a similar response upon another's leave-taking, and associated
"Ciao" with that event. Unfortunately, no reliability measures are
presented; given the difficulty in providing reliable discriminations
between avian behaviors using the same appendage (Galef, Manzig,
and Field 1986, pp. 194–95), reliability would surely help in
ascertaining that the "Ciao" waving and "Peanut" foot-lifting, or
"Shake" head shakes and "Nod" head nods, were indeed different
behaviors. With all of these problems, the evidence that African
Grey parrots can imitate human actions based on kinesthetic-visual
matching is not convincing. However, the evidence is suggestive,
and the claims deserve experimental replication.

More recent work provides evidence of behavioral imitation in
pigeons (sp. unspecified) and Japanese quail (*Coturnix japonica*)
(Akins and Zentall 1996; Zentall, Sutton, and Sherburne 1996;
Akins and Zentall 1998). In one set of studies, these birds observed
a demonstrator who either stepped on or pecked a treadle to receive food, and were then placed in the same situation in which

the demonstrator had been. Birds tended to reproduce the behaviors they had observed the demonstrator perform, but only when the demonstrator had been rewarded. The imitative effect was evident for birds who had observed treadle pecking, but was not statistically significant for treadle stepping; still, some birds who had observed treadle stepping when tested showed treadle stepping only or preferentially, which indicates some imitation of treadle stepping. A generalized imitation capacity is inadequately supported by this research, however, in that in the best case only one behavior was imitated by each bird. Although the data are suggestive as evidence of at least a limited ability for kinesthetic-visual matching, one surprising aspect of the research is that the observer birds' behaviors while observing the demonstrator birds' demonstrations were apparently never recorded. What do pigeons and quail do when forced to be next to a conspecific who is hopping at them (treadle stepping) or pecking at food (treadle pecking)? One imagines that they most likely hop back at or away from them, or peck for potential food, respectively, which suggests that the imitative response may be based on normal social responses that are not imitative per se, but are rewarded vicariously.

Similar research (Galef, Manzig, and Field 1986) evaluated whether budgerigar (*Melopsittacus undulatus*) observers could imitate the same motor patterns as budgerigar demonstrators. In this study, demonstrators either pulled part of a machine with their beak or tipped part of a similar looking machine with their foot in order to obtain food. Imitation was discerned if the observer used the same appendage toward the machine. (Observer birds were tested on a machine like those of demonstrators, which worked by either pulling or tipping.) Imitation of only one motor pattern was tested for each bird, and birds tended initially to use the same appendage as the demonstrator, but this imitation disappeared after the second trial. Although use of a similar motor pattern suggests kinesthetic-visual matching, it is questionable whether seeing another bird perform the act was even necessary for imitation. Perhaps the birds would have responded with the same appendage if they had simply observed the machine dispensing food after moving by itself in a particular way: pulling may seem to afford using a beak to a bird, and tipping to afford using a foot. Indeed, demonstrator birds all spontaneously used beaks on the machine that required pulling, and feet on the one that required tipping.

Rats, Marmosets, and Tamarins

Kinesthetic-visual matching is implicated by researchers studying imitations in rats (*Rattus norvegicus*). Observer rats watched demonstrator rats push a joystick consistently in a given direction in relation to a background to receive a food reward, and then were allowed in the observer's area with the joystick and background in the same or a perpendicular location. The observer rats significantly more than chance pushed the joystick in the same direction as had the demonstrator rat. The researchers suggest that "observer rats tend to push the joystick in the same direction relative to their own bodies as did their demonstrator" (Heyes, Dawson, and Nokes 1992, p. 236), even "when the joystick moves through a plane perpendicular to that in which it was moved by the demonstrators" (p. 238). The idea that rats push in a direction relative to their own body, after having visually observed the demonstrator, suggests kinesthetic-visual matching. However, rats are very good at spatial knowledge, and could instead have learned to "push the joystick *that way* in relation to the mesh or background closest to the joystick" (Mitchell 1997a). Recent evidence indicates that even this level of matching is not used by rats, who are influenced to push in a given direction by odor cues left by demonstrators on the side of the joystick they pushed: when researchers turned the joystick itself 180 degrees, rats more frequently pushed it in the direction opposite to that of the demonstrator rat (Mitchell, Heyes, and Gardner 1999).

Marmosets (*Callithrix jacchus*) show imitation in a similar situation: after observing a modeler marmoset pull the door of a box outward to retrieve food, three of five observer marmosets placed in the same situation also pulled the door outward more often than they pushed the door inward, whereas the other two did the opposite (Bugnyar and Huber 1997). Of 6 control marmosets who did not observe the modeler, one was more likely to pull the door, whereas the other five were more likely to push. As with the rats, the marmosets may not have used kinesthetic-visual matching, as they could have observed that food was obtained when the door moved "that way" in relation to the wall of the box (a visual-visual match). However, two of the imitating observers opened the door in a manner similar to that of the modeler—suggestive of kinesthetic-visual matching: inserting the claws of their left hand into either the door's hook on the right, or into space on the right between the door and the wall of the box. Unfortunately, no test for the marmosets' handedness was performed prior to the study, so it is unclear whether or not the similarity in handedness results because the left was their preferred hand.

More recent evidence of marmoset imitation (Voelkl and Huber 2000) is also suggestive as evidence of kinesthetic-visual matching: observer marmosets tended to open a film canister to obtain food using the same body configuration (via hand vs. via mouth) that the observed marmoset had used. Specifically, after observing another marmoset open film canisters using its mouth, four of six observer marmosets opened at least one canister (actually, 2, 6, 11, and 13) out of 14 to 15 with its mouth (which is infrequent among marmosets); by contrast, after observing another marmoset open film canisters using its hands, all five observer marmosets used only their hands to open the canisters. While suggestive, imitation may not even be present. Based on the pictorial depictions of both actions presented in Voelkl and Huber's article (p. 197), the method of opening by mouth suggests that the marmoset is attacking the lid of the canister, whereas the method of opening by hand suggests that the marmoset is exploring what's inside the canister. Thus, it may be that marmosets did not "imitate" the specific action of opening used by the observed marmoset, but rather responded in an identical attitude toward the objects. Similarly, chimpanzees tended to react aggressively or with exploration toward a hidden object when another chimpanzee who had seen the object acted aggressively or with exploration (Menzel 1973), and no one has suggested that imitation occurred in these instances. (Note, however, that imitation of the second type may be present in the actions described for both marmosets and chimpanzees, which seem unintentionally designed to be like those of the model.)

Kinesthetic-visual matching is also suggested in the mirror-self-recognition claimed for two cotton-top tamarins (*Saguinus oedipus*) who looked in the mirror at body parts not visible without the mirror (Hauser et al. 1995), but there are reasons for skepticism about this interpretation of their behavior (Anderson and Gallup 1997; compare Hauser and Kralik 1997). Because the observational evidence for self-exploration was ambiguous and baseline measures of mark-directed behaviors without the mirror present were not recorded, it is unclear how it was discerned that the tamarins were using the mirror to look at their normally visually inaccessible body parts. Although suggestive, more evidence is needed to support kinesthetic-visual matching in marmosets and tamarins.

17.6   Speculation and Conclusion

In this overview, I have argued that perceptual matching is a significant factor in imitation, and that one particular form of perceptual matching—kinesthetic-visual matching—is essential for generalized bodily (including facial) imitation and self-recognition, and likely for pretense and recognizing that another is imitating you as well. It will be interesting to see if animals other than great apes and dolphins show any extensive propensity for generalized bodily imitation, which I expect to be congruent with a capacity for self-recognition. I suspect that the kinesthetic-visual matching necessary for generalized bodily imitation is what initially allows people and other animals to ascribe internal experiences to both themselves and others (Mitchell 1997a,b, 2000), in that kinesthetic-visual matching is a structure or schema that is "relatively transferable from one sensory domain to the other in the case of my own body, just as it could be transferred to the domain of the other" (Merleau-Ponty 1960/1964, p. 118). More specifically, Merleau-Ponty argues that "I can perceive, across the visual image of the other, that the other is an organism, that that organism is inhabited by a 'psyche,' because the visual image of the other is interpreted by the notion I myself have of my own body and thus appears as the visible envelopment of another 'corporeal schema'" (p. 118). The "corporeal schema" Merleau-Ponty describes as ascribable to both self and other seems to imply an ability to match kinesthetic/somasthetic experience of one's body to visual experiences of one's body (in the mirror) and of others' bodies (in imitation). I expect that those species who have kinesthetic-visual matching could, at some point in their development, exhibit some of the more complex imitations based on pretense and interpersonal interaction described in table 17.2. It may be the case that those species that match others' sounds can also exhibit these complex forms of imitation, which may also lead to understanding other minds. Recognition of matching between, and imitation of, diverse perceptual modalities seems to be the basis for social psychological development, which itself seems unlikely in nonbiological entities. Programming a machine shaped like a human to position its limbs similarly to the positions of a human's limbs, or even to recognize a match between itself and its mirror image is not hard to imagine, but programming or inducing something similar to kinesthetic-visual matching into a machine may be limited by more than our imagination.

References

Akins, C. K., and T. R. Zentall. Imitative learning in male Japanese quail (*Coturnix japonica*) using the two-action method. *Journal of Comparative Psychology* 110: 316–320, 1996.

Akins, C. K., and T. R. Zentall. Imitation in Japanese quail: The role of reinforcement of demonstrator responding. *Psychonomic Bulletin and Review* 5: 694–697, 1998.

Anderson, J., and G. G. Gallup Jr. Self-recognition in *Saguinus*? A critical essay. *Animal Behaviour* 54: 1563–1567, 1997.

Asendorpf, J. B., and P. M. Baudonnière. Self-awareness and other-awareness: Mirror self-recognition and synchronic imitation among unfamiliar peers. *Developmental Psychology* 29: 88–95, 1993.

Asendorpf, J. B., V. Warkentin, and P. M. Baudonnière. Self-awareness and other-awareness II: Mirror self-recognition, social contingency awareness, and synchronic imitation. *Developmental Psychology* 32: 313–321, 1996.

Baer, D. M., R. F. Peterson, and J. A. Sherman. The development of imitation by reinforcing behavioral similarity to a model. In A. Bandura, ed., *Psychological Modeling: Conflicting Theories*. Chicago: Aldine/Atherton, 1971.

Bahrick, L. E., and J. N. Pickens. Amodal relations: The basis for intermodal perception and learning in infancy. In D. J. Lewkowicz and R. Lickliter, eds., *The Development of Intersensory Perception*. Hillsdale, N.J.: Erlbaum, 1994.

Baldwin, J. M. *Mental Development in the Child and the Race*. New York: Macmillan, 1894/1903.

Bard, K. A., and C. L. Russell. Evolutionary foundations of imitation: Social cognitive and developmental aspects of imitative processes in non-human primates. In J. Nadel and G. Butterworth, eds., *Imitation in Infancy*. Cambridge, UK: Cambridge University Press, 1999.

Baron-Cohen, S. Perceptual role taking and protodeclarative pointing in autism. *British Journal of Developmental Psychology* 7: 113–127, 1989.

Bateson, G. The message "This is play." In B. Schaffner, ed., *Group Processes: Transactions of the Second Conference*. Madison, N.J.: Josiah Macy Jr. Foundation, 1956.

Bauer, G. B., and C. M. Johnson. Trained motor imitation by bottlenose dolphins (*Tursiops truncatus*). *Perceptual and Motor Skills* 79: 1307–1315, 1994.

Breuggeman, J. A. Parental care in a group of free-ranging rhesus monkeys. *Folia Primatologica* 20: 170–210, 1973.

Bugnyar, T., and L. Huber. Push or pull: An experimental study on imitation in marmosets. *Animal Behaviour* 54: 817–831, 1997.

Burton, F. D. The social group as information unit: Cognitive behaviour, cultural processes. In F. D. Burton, ed., *Social Processes and Mental Abilities in Non-Human Primates*. Lewiston, Pa.: Edwin Mellen Press, 1992.

Butterworth, G. Neonatal imitation: Existence, mechanisms, and motives. In J. Nadel and G. Butterworth, eds., *Imitation in Infancy*. Cambridge, UK: Cambridge University Press, 1999.

Chevalier-Skolnikoff, S. A Piagetian model for describing and comparing socialization in monkey, ape, and human infants. In S. Chevalier-Skolnikoff and F. E. Poirier, eds., *Primate Biosocial Development*. New York: Garland Publishers, 1977.

Cohen, M. M. Continuous versus terminal visual feedback in prism aftereffects. *Perceptual and Motor Skills* 24: 1295–1302, 1967.

Condon, W. S., and L. W. Sander. Synchrony demonstrated between movements of the neonate and adult speech. *Child Development* 43: 456–462, 1974.

Courage, M. L., and R. J. Adams. The early development of visual acuity in the binocular and monocular peripheral fields. *Infant Behavior and Development* 13: 123–128, 1990.

Custance, D. M., A. Whiten, and K. A. Bard. Can young chimpanzees (*Pan troglodytes*) imitate arbitrary actions? Hayes and Hayes (1952) revisited. *Behaviour* 132: 837–859, 1995.

Galef, B. G. Jr. Imitation in animals: History, definition, and interpretation of data from the psychological laboratory. In T. A. Zentall and B. G. Galef, eds., *Social Learning in Animals*. Hillsdale, N.J.: Erlbaum, 1988.

Galef, B. G. Jr., L. A. Manzig, and R. M. Field. Imitation learning in budgerigars: Dawson and Foss (1965) revisited. *Behavioural Processes* 13: 191–202, 1986.

Gibson, J. J. *The Senses Considered as Perceptual Systems*. Boston: Houghton-Mifflin, 1966.

Goldenberg, G. Imitating gestures and manipulating a mannikin—The representation of the human body in ideomotor apraxia. *Neuropsychologia* 33: 63–72, 1995.

Grice, H. P. Meaning revisited. In N. V. Smith, ed., *Mutual knowledge*. London: Academic Press, 1982.

Guillaume, P. *Imitation in Children*, 2d ed. Chicago: University of Chicago Press, 1926/1971.

Harris, C. S. Perceptual adaptation to inverted, reversed, and displaced vision. *Psychological Review* 72: 419–444, 1965.

Hart, D., and S. Fegley. Social imitation and the emergence of a mental model of self. In S. T. Parker, R. W. Mitchell, and M. L. Biocca, eds., *Self-awareness in Animals and Humans*. Cambridge, UK: Cambridge University Press, 1994.

Hauser, M. D., and J. Kralik. Life beyond the mirror: A reply to Anderson and Gallup. *Animal Behaviour* 54: 1568–1571, 1997.

Hauser, M. D., J. Kralik, C. Botto-Mahan, M. Garrett, and J. Oser. Self-recognition in primates: Phylogeny and the salience of species-typical traits. *Proceedings of the National Academy of Sciences* 92: 10811–10814, 1995.

Heilman, K. M., L. J. Rothi, and E. Valenstein. Two forms of ideomotor apraxia. *Neurology* 32: 342–346, 1982.

Heimann, M., and E. Ullstadius. Neonatal imitation and imitation among children with autism and Down's syndrome. In J. Nadel and G. Butterworth, eds., *Imitation in Infancy*. Cambridge, UK: Cambridge University Press, 1999.

Herman, L. M., A. A. Pack, and M. Hoffmann-Kuhnt. Seeing through sound: Dolphins (*Tursiops truncatus*) perceive the spatial structure of objects through echolocation. *Journal of Comparative Psychology* 112: 292–305, 1998.

Heyes, C. M., G. R. Dawson, and T. Nokes. Imitation in rats: Initial responding and transfer evidence. *Quarterly Journal of Experimental Psychology* 45B: 229–240, 1992.

Hill, S. D., and C. Tomlin. Self-Recognition in retarded children. *Child Development* 52: 145–150, 1981.

Hobson, R. P. Early childhood autism and the question of egocentrism. *Journal of Autism and Developmental Disorders* 14: 85–104, 1984.

Knowlton, J. Q. On the definition of "picture." *Audio-Visual Communication Review* 14: 157–182, 1966.

Kornheiser, A. S. Adaptation for laterally displaced vision: A review. *Psychological Bulletin* 83: 783–816, 1976.

Kugiumutzakis, G. Genesis and development of early infant mimesis to facial and vocal models. In J. Nadel and G. Butterworth, eds., *Imitation in Infancy*. Cambridge, UK: Cambridge University Press, 1999.

Lewis, M., and J. Brooks-Gunn. *Social Cognition and the Acquisition of Self*. New York: Plenum Press, 1979.

Lewkowicz, D. J. Development of intersensory perception in human infants. In D. J. Lewkowicz and R. Lickliter, eds., *The Development of Intersensory Perception*. Hillsdale, N.J.: Erlbaum, 1994.

Lhermitte, F., B. Pillon, and M. Serdaru. Human autonomy and the frontal lobes, Part 1: Imitation and utilization behavior: A neuropsychological study of 75 patients. *Annals of Neurology* 19: 326–334, 1986.

Loveland, K. A. Behavior of young children with Down syndrome before the mirror: Finding things reflected. *Child Development* 58: 928–936, 1987.

Marten, K., and S. Psarakos. Evidence of self-awareness in the bottlenose dolphin (*Tursiops truncatus*). In S. T. Parker, R. W. Mitchell, and M. L. Biocca, eds., *Self-Awareness in Animals and Humans*. Cambridge, UK: Cambridge University Press, 1994.

Marten, K., and S. Psarakos. Using self-view television to distinguish between self-examination and social behavior in the bottlenose dolphin (*Tursiops truncatus*). *Consciousness and Cognition* 4: 205–224, 1995.

Masterton, B. A., and G. B. Biederman. Proprioceptive versus visual control in autistic children. *Journal of Autism and Developmental Disorders* 13: 141–152, 1983.

Meltzoff, M. A. Foundations for developing a concept of self: The role of imitation in relating self to other and the value of social mirroring, social modeling, and self practice in infancy. In D. Cicchetti and M. Beeghly, eds., *The Self in Transition: Infancy to Childhood*. Chicago: University of Chicago Press, 1990.

Meltzoff, M. A., and M. K. Moore. Persons and representation: Why infant imitation is important for theories of human development. In J. Nadel and G. Butterworth, eds., *Imitation in Infancy*. Cambridge, UK: Cambridge University Press, 1999.

Melzack, R. Phantom limbs, the self, and the brain. *Canadian Psychology* 30: 1–16, 1989.

Melzack, R. Phantom limbs. *Scientific American* 266: 120–126, 1992.

Menzel, E. W. Jr. Leadership and communication in young chimpanzees. In E. W. Menzel Jr., ed., *Precultural Primate Behavior*. Basel: S. Karger, 1973.

Merleau-Ponty, M. The child's relations with others. In J. M. Edie, ed., *The Primacy of Perception and Other Essays on Phenomenological Psychology, the Philosophy of Art, History and Politics*. Evanston, Ill.: Northwestern University Press, 1960/1964.

Miles, H. L., R. W. Mitchell, and S. Harper. Simon says: The development of imitation in an enculturated orangutan. In A. Russon, K. Bard, and S. T. Parker, eds., *Reaching into Thought: The Minds of the Great Apes*. Cambridge, UK: Cambridge University Press, 1996.

Mitchell, C. J., C. M. Heyes, and M. R. Gardner. Limitations of a bidirectional control procedure for the investigation of imitation in rats: Odour cues on the manipulandum. *Quarterly Journal of Experimental Psychology* 52B: 193–202, 1999.

Mitchell, R. W. A comparative-developmental approach to understanding imitation. In P. P. G. Bateson and P. H. Klopfer, eds., *Perspectives in Ethology*. Vol. 7, *Alternatives*. New York: Plenum Press, 1987.

Mitchell, R. W. Bateson's concept of "metacommunication" in play. *New Ideas in Psychology* 9: 73–87, 1991.

Mitchell, R. W. Mental models of mirror-self-recognition: Two theories. *New Ideas in Psychology* 11: 295–325, 1993a.

Mitchell, R. W. Recognizing one's self in a mirror? A reply to Gallup and Povinelli, de Lannoy, Anderson, and Byrne. *New Ideas in Psychology* 11: 351–377, 1993b.

Mitchell, R. W. The evolution of primate cognition: Simulation, self-knowledge, and knowledge of other minds. In D. Quiatt and J. Itani, eds., *Hominid Culture in Primate Perspective*. Boulder: University Press of Colorado, 1994a.

Mitchell, R. W. Imitation in theory and elsewhere: It's more pervasive than you think. Symposium organized by B. G. Galef and C. Heyes on *Social Learning and Tradition in Animals*. Cambridge, UK, 1994b.

Mitchell, R. W. A comparison of the self-awareness and kinesthetic-visual matching theories of self-recognition: Autistic children and others. *New York Academy of Sciences* 818: 39–62, 1997a.

Mitchell, R. W. Kinesthetic-visual matching and the self-concept as explanations of mirror-self-recognition. *Journal for the Theory of Social Behavior* 27: 101–123, 1997b.

Mitchell, R. W. A proposal for the development of a mental vocabulary, with special reference to pretense and false belief. In K. Riggs and P. Mitchell, eds., *Children's Reasoning and the Mind*. Hove, UK: Psychology Press, 2000.

Mitchell, R. W. Review of *Imitation in Infancy*. *British Journal of Developmental Psychology*, 20: 150–151, 2002.

Mitchell, R. W., and J. Anderson. Discrimination learning of scratching, but failure to obtain imitation and self-recognition in a long-tailed macaque. *Primates* 34: 301–309, 1993.

Mitchell, R. W., and M. Gallaher. Embodying music: Matching music and dance in memory. *Music Perception*, 19: 65–85, 2001.

Moore, B. R. Avian movement imitation and a new form of mimicry: Tracing the evolution of a complex form of learning. *Behaviour* 122: 231–263, 1992.

Morgan, C. L. *Habit and Instinct.* New York: Arno Press, 1896/1973.

Nadel, J., C. Guérini, A. Pezé, and C. Rivet. The evolving nature of imitation as a format for communication. In J. Nadel and G. Butterworth, eds., *Imitation in Infancy.* Cambridge, UK: Cambridge University Press, 1999.

Nehaniv, C. L., and K. Dautenhahn. Of hummingbirds and helicopters: An algebraic framework for interdisciplinary studies of imitation and its applications. In J. Demiris and A. Birk, eds., *Interdisciplinary Approaches to Robot Learning*, pp. 136–161. World Scientific Press, 2000.

Ohta, M. Cognitive disorders of infantile autism: A study employing the WISC, spatial relationship conceptualization, and gesture imitations. *Journal of Autism and Developmental Disorders* 17: 45–62, 1987.

Parker, S. T. Piaget's sensorimotor period in an infant macaque. In S. Chevalier-Skolnikoff and F. E. Poirier, eds., *Primate Biosocial Development.* New York: Garland Publishers, 1977.

Parker, S. T. A developmental approach to the origins of self-recognition in great apes. *Human Evolution* 6: 435–449, 1991.

Parker, S. T., R. W. Mitchell, and M. L. Biocca, eds., *Self-Awareness in Animals and Humans.* New York: Cambridge University Press, 1994.

Patterson, F. G. P., and R. H. Cohn. Self-recognition and self-awareness in lowland gorillas. In S. T. Parker, R. W. Mitchell, and M. L. Biocca, eds., *Self-Awareness in Animals and Humans.* New York: Cambridge University Press, 1994.

Pepperberg, I. M. *The Alex Studies: Cognitive and Communicative Abilities of Grey Parrots.* Cambridge, Mass.: Harvard University Press, 1999.

Pepperberg, I. M., K. J. Brese, and B. J. Harris. Solitary sound play during acquisition of English vocalizations by an African Grey parrot (*Psittacus erithacus*): Possible parallels with children's monologue speech. *Applied Psycholinguistics* 12: 151–178, 1991.

Piaget, J. *Play, Dreams, and Imitation in Childhood.* New York: W. W. Norton, 1945/1962.

Reed, T. Performance of autistic and control subjects on three cognitive perspective-taking tasks. *Journal of Autism and Developmental Disorders* 24: 53–66, 1994.

Reed, T., and C. Peterson. A comparative study of autistic subjects' performance at two levels of visual and cognitive perspective taking. *Journal of Autism and Developmental Disorders* 20: 555–567, 1990.

Reiss, D., and B. McCowan. Spontaneous vocal mimicry and production by bottlenose dolphins (*Tursiops truncatus*): Evidence for vocal learning. *Journal of Comparative Psychology* 107: 301–312, 1993.

Reiss, D., and L. Marino. Mirror self-recognition in the bottlenose dolphin: A case of cognitive convergence. *Proceedings of the National Academy of Sciences* 98: 5937–5942, 2001.

Rivers, A., U. Bartecku, J. V. Brown, and G. Ettlinger. An unexpected "epidemic" of a rare stereotypy: Unidentified stress or imitation? *Laboratory Primate Newsletter* 22: 5–7, 1983.

Rogers, S. J. An examination of the imitation deficit in autism. In J. Nadel and G. Butterworth, eds., *Imitation in Infancy.* Cambridge, UK: Cambridge University Press, 1999.

Rose, S. A. From hand to eye: Findings and issues in infant cross-modal transfer. In D. J. Lewkowicz and R. Lickliter, eds., *The Development of Intersensory Perception.* Hillsdale, N.J.: Erlbaum, 1994.

Russon, A. E., and B. Galdikas. Imitation in free-ranging rehabilitant orangutans. *Journal of Comparative Psychology* 107: 147–160, 1993.

Russon, A. E., R. W. Mitchell, L. Lefebvre, and E. Abravanal. The comparative evolution of imitation. In J. Langer and M. Killen, eds., *Piaget, Evolution, and Development.* Hillsdale, N.J.: Erlbaum, 1998.

Savage-Rumbaugh, S., and R. Lewin. *Kanzi: The Ape at the Brink of the Human Mind.* New York: Wiley, 1994.

Smith, I. M. Imitation and gestural representation in autism. Poster presented at meeting of the Society for Research in Child Development, Indianapolis, Indiana, 1995.

Smith, I. M., and S. E. Bryson. Imitation and action in autism: A critical review. *Psychological Bulletin* 116: 259–273, 1994.

Smith, L. B. Foreword. In D. J. Lewkowicz and R. Lickliter, eds., *The Development of Intersensory Perception*. Hillsdale, N.J.: Erlbaum, 1994.

Speidel, G. E., and K. E. Nelson, eds., *The Many Faces of Imitation in Language Learning*. New York: Springer-Verlag, 1989.

Stein, B. E., and M. A. Meredith. *The Merging of the Senses*. Cambridge, MA: MIT Press, 1993.

Streri, A., and M. Molina. Constraints on intermodal transfer between touch and vision in infancy. In D. J. Lewkowicz and R. Lickliter, eds., *The Development of Intersensory Perception*. Hillsdale, N.J.: Erlbaum, 1994.

Swartz, K. B., D. Sarauw, and S. Evans. Comparative aspects of mirror self-recognition in great apes. In S. T. Parker, R. W. Mitchell, and H. L. Miles, eds., *The Mentalities of Gorillas and Orangutans*. Cambridge, UK: Cambridge University Press, 1999.

Tayler, C. K., and G. S. Saayman. Imitative behaviour by Indian Ocean bottlenose dolphins (*Tursiops aduncus*) in captivity. *Behaviour* 44: 286–298, 1973.

Terrace, H. S. *Nim: A Chimpanzee Who Learned Sign Language*. New York: Knopf, 1979.

Thorpe, W. H. *Learning and Instinct in Animals*, 2d ed. Cambridge, Mass.: Harvard University Press, 1956/1966.

Tiegerman, E., and L. H. Primavera. Imitating the autistic child: Facilitating communicative gaze behavior. *Journal of Autism and Developmental Disorders* 14: 27–38, 1984.

Trevarthen, C., T. Kokkinaki, and G. A. Fiamenghi Jr. What infants' imitations communicate: With mothers, with fathers, and with peers. In J. Nadel and G. Butterworth, eds., *Imitation in Infancy*, pp. 127–185. Cambridge, UK: Cambridge University Press, 1999.

Ujhelyi, M., P. Buk, B. Merker, and T. Geissmann. Observations on the behavior of gibbons (*Hylobates leucogenys, H. gabriellae*, and *H. lar*) in the presence of mirrors. *Journal of Comparative Psychology* 114: 253–262, 2000.

Užgiris, I. Imitation as activity: Its developmental aspects. In J. Nadel and G. Butterworth, eds., *Imitation in Infancy*. Cambridge, UK: Cambridge University Press, 1999.

Visalberghi, E., and D. Fragaszy. Do monkeys ape? In S. T. Parker and K. Gibson, eds., *"Language" and Intelligence in Monkeys and Apes: Comparative Developmental Perspectives*. Cambridge, UK: Cambridge University Press, 1990.

Voelkl, B., and L. Huber. True imitation in marmosets. *Animal Behaviour* 60(2): 195–202, 2000.

von Fieandt, K. *The World of Perception*. Homewood, Ill.: Dorsey Press, 1966.

Walker-Andrews, A. Taxonomy for intermodal relations. In D. J. Lewkowicz and R. Lickliter, eds., *The Development of Intersensory Perception*. Hillsdale, N.J.: Erlbaum, 1994.

Whiten, A., and R. W. Byrne. Tactical deception in primates. *Behavioral and Brain Sciences* 11: 233–244, 1988.

Whiten, A., and R. Ham. On the nature and evolution of imitation in the animal kingdom: Reappraisal of a century of research. *Advances in the Study of Behavior* 21: 239–283, 1992.

Zentall, T. R., J. E. Sutton, and L. M. Sherburne. True imitative learning in pigeons. *Psychological Science* 7: 343–346, 1996.

18 "Do Monkeys Ape?"—Ten Years After

Elisabetta Visalberghi and Dorothy Fragaszy

18.1 Introduction

In 1990 we published a chapter entitled "Do Monkeys Ape?" included in a volume edited by Sue Parker and Kathleen Gibson (Visalberghi and Fragaszy 1990a). In our chapter, we noted that the view that monkeys are able to learn by imitation was widespread among laymen belonging to different cultures as well as among scientists (e.g., Romanes 1884/1977). However, in our review of the scanty empirical evidence supporting that view, we noted that it came from anecdotal observations that were anthropomorphically interpreted, or from studies lacking the necessary control procedures to rule out alternative, equally plausible, explanations. For example, the spread of the food-washing behavior in Japanese macaques can be accounted for by learning processes other than imitation (Galef 1990, 1992; see also Visalberghi and Fragaszy 1990a,b). Finally, we presented evidence from several studies carried out in our own laboratories with tufted capuchin monkeys (*Cebus apella*) to argue that monkeys did not learn novel behaviors by imitation.

During these past ten years, social learning processes in animals, and in nonhuman primates in particular, have been the subject of much additional research and discussion (e.g., Heyes and Galef 1996; Tomasello and Call 1997). The definition of imitative learning, whether it exists in nonhumans, and if so, in what animals and under what circumstances, all remain points of controversy; for example, we have seen titles such as "Do apes ape?" (Tomasello 1996) and "Do rats ape?" (Byrne and Tomasello 1995), and many other detailed treatments focused on imitation (e.g., Whiten and Ham 1992; Byrne and Russon 1998). We have also continued our investigations of social learning in capuchin monkeys in the controlled (but socially and physically enriched) settings of our laboratories and we have tested capuchins and other species (common chimpanzees and young children) in the same tasks (e.g., Bard, Fragaszy, and Visalberghi 1996; Perucchini et al. 1997; Modena and Visalberghi 1998). Overall, our data highlight the huge difference in the ways in which children learn new skills (where imitation can make substantive contributions) and the ways in which monkeys (and to a lesser extent apes, see Call and Carpenter, chapter 9 of this volume; Whiten, chapter 8 of this volume) learn new skills. In both the latter taxa, imitation makes a feeble contribution, or none at all, although other forms of social learning still make substantial contributions.

Most broadly defined, social learning occurs when an individual acquires information about the environment through direct observation of, or interaction with, another individual; or indirectly, through encountering the products of another individual's activity. In essence, social learning requires the use of information produced in some form by another individual ("public information"; Giraldeau 1997), rather than solely self-discovered information. Social learning is socially mediated learning, not learning about social matters; the word "social" in the phrase "social learning" concerns the manner, not the content, of the learning. Social learning has the potential to save the learner time, effort, and risk, and to increase the rate of behavioral change within a group relative to strictly individualistic learning processes (Giraldeau 1997). Social learning is therefore of likely (and occasionally demonstrated) importance to the behavioral biology of social animals in natural circumstances; it is not a form of learning bound to the laboratory (Terkel 1996; Laland, Odling-Smee, and Feldman 2000; Box and Gibson 1999).

Social learning can occur via local enhancement, stimulus enhancement, and social facilitation (Spence 1937; Thorpe 1956; Galef 1988), as well as by imitation. In the former processes, the observer's attention is channeled toward locations, stimuli, or activities that foster the acquisition of a new skill, but no particular motor action is learned from observing the partner. For certain sorts of learning (procedural knowledge; how to do things with the body, or how to act on objects in the environment), imitation provides a more powerful mechanism than these other forms for rapid and effective learning. Imitation is particularly useful when opportunities for practice are limited, when the cost of errors is high, or when learning by individual experience would be a very slow process.

The tricky part, from the point of view of identifying distinctive learning mechanisms, is to distinguish imitation from other forms of social learning. In common parlance, imitation simply means reproduction of an observed action. It is not restricted to a learning context; when an adult repeats an infant's "peekaboo" actions, we call it imitation; and when the infant repeats the adult's actions, we likewise call that imitation too, with no implication that learning is involved for either party. We also use the same term, *imitation*, when something *is* learned (such as how to use an object). Unfortunately, there are many things that we simply accept in humans that have not, in fact, been tightly demonstrated in experimental terms, and many accepted examples of learning by imitation are among these. (For example, do we really learn to tie shoelaces by imitation? The complexity of the action belies the idea.) Imitation is often a default explanation for how an individual learned to do something that we consider somewhat unlikely to have been discovered individually. But we cannot be this casual with other species, and indeed, it would be useful to examine our own species' behavior more critically. Probably many kinds of behavior where social partners influence learning rely on learning mechanisms other than, or in addition to, imitation.

To identify what kinds of evidence are needed to claim imitative learning (as distinct from other forms of social learning), we provided a definition of imitative learning (Visalberghi and Fragaszy 1990a) using Mitchell's (1987) definition as a starting point. This definition distinguishes imitation from social facilitation and stimulus or local enhancement (for a definition of these terms see Spence 1937; Thorpe 1956). We said that imitative learning occurs when and only when:

1. something C (the copy of the behavior) is produced by an organism
2. where C is similar to something else M (the model's behavior)
3. observation of M is necessary for the production of C (above baseline levels of C occurring spontaneously)
4. C is designed to be similar to M
5. the behavior C must be a *novel behavior*, not already organized in that precise way in the organism's repertoire

Several of these features are difficult to obtain with experimental rigor. For example, point 4 must be inferred; we can not observe "design" directly. The clearest demonstration will involve the most unlikely behaviors (so that characteristics 2–5 can be evaluated most clearly as present). Even so, determining what constitutes a "behavior," and what aspects constitute "novelty" are controversial (see Visalberghi and Fragaszy 1990a). However, this

Figure 18.1 Tufted capuchin monkeys (*Cebus apella*) are usually very interested in what conspecifics are doing.

definition does capture the essence of what *learning by imitation* is about.

Capuchin monkeys (from South and Central America) possess several characteristics that make them particularly suited for studying how they might use information provided by others to learn a novel behavior. Capuchin monkeys are generally tolerant to other members of their groups, especially to immature individuals, and young animals in particular are persistently interested in others' activities (Fragaszy, Feuerstein, and Mitra 1997) (figure 18.1). Capuchin monkeys of all ages devote considerable time and energy to manipulating objects, and they spontaneously display many innovations in their manipulative activity, including the use of tools (Fragaszy and Adams-Curtis 1991; Visalberghi 1987; Fragaszy and Visalberghi 1989). Indeed, capuchins are the most versatile tool users among monkeys (Visalberghi 1990; Anderson 2000; Tomasello and Call 1997). Occasionally, capuchin monkeys living in the wild and in seminatural conditions have been seen to use tools as well (e.g., Fernandes 1991; Boinski 1988; Boinski, Quatrone, and Swarts, submitted), indicating that their prowess with tools in the laboratory is not solely an artifact of captivity. If prevalence of social learning is related to potential opportunities for, and benefits of, learning socially, if manipulative propensity is indicative of an underlying cognitive sophistication, and/or if learning abilities are modular in some sense, one could reasonably predict that capuchins should possess stronger social learning propensities than other primate species that do not display equivalent tolerance, interest in each others' activities, and innovations in manual activity. Perhaps for these reasons, capuchins have been regarded as strong (and perhaps the best) candidates for elaborated social learning abilities among monkeys.

In contrast to their noteworthy status in social and instrumental domains, capuchins are comparable to other species of monkeys in their achievements in tasks commonly used to assess memorial, attentional, and conceptual abilities (e.g., Piagetian sensorimotor tasks, various discrimination, matching, and conceptual learning tasks, and social cognition tasks; D'Amato and Salmon 1984; Adams-Curtis 1990; Antinucci 1989; Anderson 1996; De Lillo; see Tomasello and Call 1997 for comparative review). If one adopts a domain-general model of cognitive organization (e.g., Case 1994) that posits core attentional, memorial, and relational characteristics constrain individual performance, one would predict that capuchins should present monkey-typical social learning abilities. That is, what they learn socially ought to be consistent with what they learn in individual contexts. In this chapter, we discuss the results of many recent studies carried out with capuchin monkeys by us and by others that support the domain-general view of their social learning abilities, and that argue against a capacity to imitate in a strong sense. Capuchins are unusual among monkeys in some ways, but not in their abilities to match actions. Taxa from other orders in addition to primates, including many mammals, birds, and fishes, also exhibit extensive social learning, and some exhibit sophisticated imitative abilities (i.e., dolphins, *Tursiops truncatus*, Mercado et al. 1998; and Herman, chapter 3 of this volume; and parrots, *Psittacus erithacus*, Moore 1992, 1996; see Box and Gibson 1999 for general review). The argument for modular social learning abilities may be better supported in these other groups; this is an open question in our minds. However, these matters are beyond

the scope of our chapter. Here we restrict our discussion to capuchin monkeys for the purposes of highlighting one (rather unusual)
taxon's social learning propensities.

For capuchin monkeys, learning to use an object as a tool is possible when the task is fairly simple (as in pushing something with
a stick), but it is unlikely in any given short period of time. In the
past, we have experimentally investigated the capacities of capuchin monkeys to learn to use different tools (and to perform other
innovative behaviors) with and without conspecific models as proficient demonstrators (Visalberghi and Fragaszy 1990a; Fragaszy
and Visalberghi 1989, 1990). In our tasks, both model and learner
worked with apparatus that contained or delivered a highly
desired food item, and the task involved simple actions well within the capabilities of the subjects. We concluded that although
social influences on behavior were clearly evident and supporting
of learning to solve the tasks, there was no evidence for imitative
learning per se. For example, Visalberghi (1993) reported lack of
imitation in a task requiring the use of a stick tool to push a reward
out of a horizontal transparent tube (figure 18.2). In this experiment, unsuccessful adult and juvenile capuchins were exposed to
proficient conspecifics (models) repeatedly solving the tube task.
The results showed that although the capuchin observers had
ample opportunity to watch the model(s) solving the task, none of
them acquired tool use by imitation, nor did they improve the orientation of the tool toward the tube after exposure to the models.
Furthermore, data also showed that the visual attention of capuchin observers was not selectively focused on the events relevant
for learning (e.g., insertion of the stick in the tube, pushing the reward vs. holding the stick, eating the reward). In short, the potential learners did not behave as if they regarded the model's actions
as relevant to their own activities.

Modena and Visalberghi (1998) conducted a cross-sectional
study with children using the same tube task as was presented to
the monkeys. Sixty-five children of 12, 15, 18, 21, and 24 months
of age were tested (figure 18.3). Children were first presented with
a three-minute pretrial of the tube task and the 44 children who
were not successful were randomly assigned to the control group
(no model) or to the model group and received two trials with the
tube task. The children in the model group witnessed the model
solving the task twice; after each solution they were invited to get
the reward themselves. In the control group children were invited

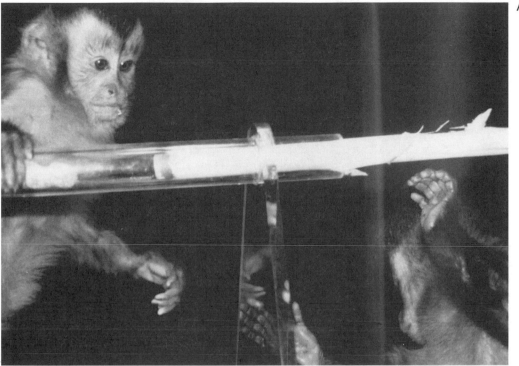

Figure 18.2 (a) The capuchin monkey on the left, who does not know how to use a stick to push the peanut out of the tube, attentively observes a group member solve the task. (b) Despite having observed many solutions, the observer makes awkward attempts to obtain the peanut and does not succeed.

3-MIN PRE-TRIAL

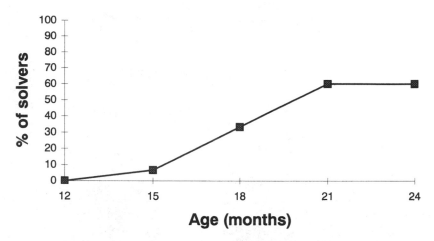

Figure 18.3 Percentages of infants who spontaneously solved the tube task during the first 3-min trial. The infants tested were $N = 10$ at 12 and 24 months of age and $N = 15$ at 15, 18 and 21 months of age.

by the experimenter to try to get the reward out of the tube by themselves. Watching the model solve the task twice did not improve the performance of 12-month-old children compared to that of children in the control group (in fact, there were no solvers in both cases). Watching the model significantly improved the performance of 15-, 18- and 21-month-old children, compared to that of the children in the control groups (figure 18.4). All the 24-month-old children became successful regardless of whether they were in the model or in the control condition; at this age, exposure to the task without a model improved performance as effectively as watching a model solving the task. In short, whereas capuchin monkeys did not learn how to solve the tube task by watching a model, 15- to 21-month-old children did; however, very young children, for whom the task is not within their grasp through other modes of experience, are not able to benefit from watching the model.

18.2 New Data from Capuchin Monkeys about Repeating Familiar Actions and Matching Novel Actions

Given the generally unpromising results concerning capuchins' abilities to learn how to use a tool from observing conspecifics, we decided to change the focus of our efforts to assess their social

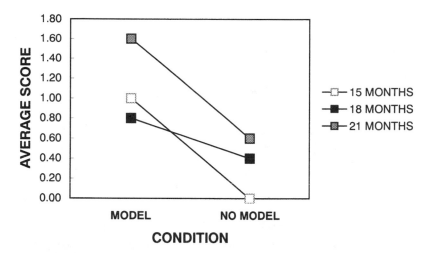

Figure 18.4 Average score obtained in the tube task by 15-, 18-, and 21 month old infants in the Model and Control conditions (No Model). An infant who solves the tube task in the first trial (in the Model condition this means in the trial after 1 demonstration) gets a score of 2; an infant who solves the tube task in the second trial (in the Model condition this means after 2 demonstrations) gets a score of 1; an infant who does not solve the tube task gets a score of 0.

learning abilities. We chose something that we expected they would be more likely to achieve: replicating a behavior that is already in their repertoire when they observe a model (a conspecific or a human model) performing it (imitation, in the sense of Meltzoff).

Imitation, in the sense of Meltzoff consists of:

1. something C (the copy of the behavior) is produced by an organism
2. where C is similar to something else M (the model behavior)
3. observation of M is *not* necessary for the production of C, but it makes C more frequent than in the baseline activity
4. C is designed to be similar to M [since there is no obvious goal, it cannot be assessed]
5. the behavior C is *not novel*

In essence, all that is required is that the organism produce C where C is like M.

Early Imitation

This paradigm has been used very successfully by Meltzoff and others to examine imitative learning in human infants. Meltzoff and Moore (1977, 1983) reported that human newborns are able to perform some facial movements they have just witnessed a person doing in front of them. From birth and for the next several weeks, a full-term infant sometimes protrudes its tongue when it sees the model doing so, opens its mouth when the model does so, and so on. According to these authors, infants reliably imitated the behavior they witnessed (rather than making some other facial movement not witnessed). However, in these experiments no learning is evident because the infant is already able to perform those different actions. The infant just performs the same behavior it saw the model performing; the infant matches the model's behavior. Although in an extensive review and reanalysis of neonatal imitation data Anisfeld (1996) argues that of the several behaviors listed by Meltzoff and Moore (1977), only mouth opening is reliably imitated across experimental studies—in any case, the phenomenon of imitation in children at later ages is more than robust (Meltzoff 1996).

An experiment similar to that of Meltzoff and Moore (1977) has been carried out by Myowa (1996), with one nursery-reared infant chimpanzee from week 5 to week 15. In Myowa's study, the experimenter made three different facial movements (mouth protrusion, lips protrusion, and mouth opening) or presented a still face to the neonate. Her results show that the chimpanzee was able to imitate tongue protrusion between the fifth and the tenth week of age and mouth opening between the fifth and the eleventh week of age (but see Bard and Russell 1999, for an extensive review of imitation of facial expressions and movements in infant chimpanzees). Matching by neonatal chimpanzees is fragile and to some extent context dependent, but it is present. The same is true for humans.

On a few occasions, we have tried to elicit matching of these kinds of facial movements in neonatal infant capuchin monkeys; however, we have not been successful. Given the difference in the scale and morphology of the human face and the capuchin face, this is perhaps not surprising. However, neonatal capuchins, like neonatal chimpanzees and neonatal humans, do turn their heads toward the human voice and do visually track the human face (Fragaszy and Bard 1997).

Repetition of Familiar Actions and Matching of Novel Actions

CONSPECIFICS AS MODELS
Let us see what older capuchin monkeys spontaneously do when they are allowed to perform the same action(s) they see a monkey

model perform. Some years ago Perucchini and colleagues (1997) replicated with capuchin monkeys an experiment previously carried out by Camaioni, Baumgartner, and Pascucci (1988) with 12–24-month-old children. Children were tested in pairs in a room in which two sets of identical toys and opportunities for play were available to them. The authors scored the frequency of various types of spontaneous imitative actions in the children (facial imitation, vocal imitation, linguistic imitation, and imitation of exploratory, manipulative activities with objects). Imitation was scored when all three of the following conditions were met: (1) the observer watched the model before performing the behavior; (2) the observer performed the behavior right after having watched it; (3) the behavior was not probable in that context. Imitation might occur on the same object or the other one like it.

Perucchini and colleagues (1997) followed as much as possible the same procedure and presented one pair of juvenile capuchins and one pair of adult capuchins with sets of identical objects for six sessions of 5 min each. They scored the occurrence of interactions with objects for both subjects. They focused on (1) the frequencies of imitation (the requirements for imitation were the same as for children, see above); (2) the frequencies of replication of routine actions (social facilitation); and (3) the frequencies of activity by one monkey toward an object followed by the partner contacting the same (or the corresponding) object (social enhancement). Note that these latter two categories were not scored for children because these behaviors were too frequent.

By comparing the results of these two experiments, striking differences emerge. The frequencies of imitation of actions with objects in 12-month-old children and 24-month-old children were 0.44 and 0.40 per min, respectively, whereas no imitation of this kind was ever observed in the capuchin pairs. Juvenile and adult capuchins performed replications of common actions (social facilitation) 0.16 times per min and 0.12 times per min, respectively; and stimulus enhancement was scored 0.51 times per minute for juveniles and 0.17 for adults. Like children, monkeys were interested in the objects and played and explored with them. But in contrast to children, monkeys did not watch each other very much and did not spontaneously match each other's activities, including nonroutine actions. Capuchins do attend to each other intently and perform mutual gaze for extended periods of time in other circumstances, however, such as during social play and most especially during courtship.

A rather different paradigm for studying imitation was developed by Heyes and Dawson (1990). In this paradigm, one rat observed a "demonstrator" rat from a face-on position while the demonstrator moved a lever to one side. Then the observer was placed in the demonstrator's place, and the direction the observer pushed the lever was noted. Recently, Gardner, Visalberghi, and Heyes (submitted; see also Gardner 1997) have tested capuchins in a task designed to be similar to that used by Heyes and Dawson (1990) with rats. Two subjects (members of two different groups) were trained to slide to the right or to the left a transparent Plexiglas panel in order to get access to a food reward. A hole, the rim of which was painted black, in the panel afforded the monkey a grasp of the panel and facilitated the sliding action. The training of the "demonstrators" required only a few minutes of behavioral shaping. These monkeys served as "demonstrators" for 10 "observer" capuchins (five in each group). The apparatus was positioned in a connecting opening between two adjacent concrete cages.

In phase 1, the demonstrator and the observers were in the two adjacent cages. Five "observer" monkeys observed through the transparent panel their "demonstrator" sliding the ring to the left and getting the reward; five other observer monkeys saw their demonstrator sliding the ring to the right and getting the reward. Immediately after having observed the demonstrator, each subject spent 10 min in the cage where their demonstrator had been, so that they now had access to the panel. For the observers, success was possible by sliding the panel in either direction. In phase 1, each observer subject had two such sessions. The experimenters scored whether the subject had acquired the technique for getting the reward (which consisted of grasping the panel ring and sliding it) and whether it moved the panel in accord with its own egocentric axis (i.e., the demonstrator moved the panel on its own left; therefore, since it faced the demonstrator, the subject saw the panel moving to its own right; then, when the subject moved to the adjacent cage, it subsequently moved the panel to its own right), or alternatively, whether it moved the panel in accord with the allocentric axis of the space in which the object moved (i.e., the subject saw the panel moving toward the left corner of the test cage, and subsequently moved the panel toward the same corner of the cage). Only two of the ten observer monkeys succeeded in phase 1; these solvers saw the demonstrator moving the panel to its own right (i.e., to the observer's left) and, when given access to the panel, both observers tended to move the ring to their egocentric left direction.

The other eight subjects entered phase 2. In this phase the observers were in the same cage with their demonstrator for 10 min and then the demonstrator was removed. It should be noted that in phase 2 the demonstrator and the observers were in the same cage and the observers had continuous visual and manual access to the panel while the demonstrator slid the ring and got the reward, and that allocentric and egocentric axes matched. In this phase, when the demonstrator was removed, seven of eight subjects slid the panel toward the left and obtained the reward. Only one of these eight subjects slid the panel in the opposite direction of its demonstrator. Overall, across both phases, eight of nine solvers moved the panel in accord with their own egocentric observation of the most recently observed solutions. These results do not provide evidence of imitation; instead they provide some evidence of object movement reenactment (i.e., that the capuchins reproduced the direction in which they saw an object moved; see Custance, Whiten, and Fredman 1999 and below for further details). This form of matching is the only aspect of matching detected in the human-reared monkeys studied by Custance, Whiten, and Fredman (1999) and Fragaszy and colleagues (unpublished) using two other testing paradigms (see below).

HUMANS AS MODELS

Recent studies have investigated whether monkeys will match actions they see a human "demonstrator" perform. For example, Deputte and colleagues have conducted studies with capuchin monkeys participating in the "programme d'aide simienne aux *tétraplégiques*" of Kerpape-Lorient (France); this program was aimed at evaluating the feasibility of using monkeys as helpers for quadriplegic human beings. Given this goal, scientists were interested in finding the most effective and efficient way to teach the subject to perform specific behaviors and sequences of behaviors relevant to assisting the handicapped person. Social learning is an obvious possibility in this effort. In a first study, Hervé and Deputte (1993) report how the manipulative behavior of an 8-month-old infant capuchin monkey was affected by the trainer showing simple actions on objects. They found that the monkey contacted more objects and manipulated them more after the trainer had designated them; however, the monkey never matched the action the trainer performed on objects.

In a second study (Hemery, Fragaszy, and Deputte 1998; Fragaszy et al., unpublished), three young ($4\frac{1}{2}$-year-old) capuchins raised in human homes were tested in a version of the Hayes and Hayes (1952) "Do as I do" paradigm, in a partial replication and extension of Custance, Whiten, and Bard's (1995) study with chimpanzees. The capuchins were trained to match the demonstrator's actions by rewarding them for performing familiar actions upon objects or species-typical actions upon their bodies following their demonstration by a familiar human. For the actions including an object, the human demonstrator handled one object from a set of eight on a tray in a distinctive way (for example, unzipping a zipper, or opening a hinged wooden "book"), or combining one object with another (for example, placing a stick into a hollow cylinder). The sessions were videotaped. Several forms of data were collected by an observer familiar with the testing protocol from the videotapes. The extent of visual attention to the demonstrator and the degree to which the performed action matched the demonstrated action were rated using a 4-point scale. For actions, a score of 0 indicated that the subject did not act after the demonstration, or did an action completely different from the one demonstrated, and on a different object; a score of 3 indicated that the subject unambiguously performed the full action on the correct object. For visual attention, a score of 0 indicated that the subject did not watch the demonstration at all; a score of 3 indicated the subject maintained visual attention during the demonstration for 3 or more seconds. We also noted what object(s) the monkey contacted. Two capuchins contacted the same object(s) contacted by the human following 60% of demonstrations; and the third monkey in 30% of demonstrations. However, they unambiguously matched the *action* in only a small percentage (20%, 11%, and 4.3%, respectively) of all the actions. For the two better subjects, level of matching was better when they were more attentive to the demonstration, and was better for those actions that involved contacting an object (e.g., open a book) and combining an object with another object or surface (e.g., put a stick into a cylinder) than for an action on the body (e.g., touch the arm).

Only the best performer entered the second phase of the experiment in which novel actions were interspersed with familiar ones in a one-to-four ratio. The familiar observer again coded the data for degree of match and visual attentiveness. In this phase, scores for visual attention and performance of the familiar actions were maintained at the rates evident at the end of the training sessions. The rate of contacting the objects that the demonstrator had contacted was also similar as in the previous phase. However, although the subject responded as quickly to demonstrations of novel actions as of familiar actions, and performed some action on nearly all trials (88%), 3/4 of the demonstrations (36 out of 48) of novel actions were followed by an action that was judged to be unrelated to the one demonstrated. In the remaining 12 trials, the monkey contacted the same object, but only partially performed the demonstrated action.

Videotapes from this phase were also scored using a double-blind procedure. First, naive scorers independently noted what actions the monkey performed at each trial, using agreed-upon descriptors of the common actions and the experimental objects. They produced identical descriptions on 68% of trials, descriptions that varied by the addition of one other action by one observer on 19% of trials, and on 13% of trials they produced different descriptions, or one scored no action while the other scored an action. These data indicate that naive observers could identify the monkey's actions and the objects it contacted with acceptable reliability. Next, the scorers were given a list of the demonstrated actions. They then reviewed the tapes a second time to judge whether the subject's action on a given trial matched any item in the demonstrated repertoire. The observers agreed 100% on which trials the subject produced a demonstrated behavior, and agreed on which action it was on 90% of these trials. Finally, the two scorers were given the ordered list of demonstrated actions. Of the 96 familiar actions demonstrated in the experimental phase, the scorers judged that the subject matched the demonstrated action on 24% of the trials, replicating the results of the first scoring. Of the 24 novel actions demonstrated, the subject was judged to have matched the action on three trials (12.5%). The matched actions included turning a screw with a screwdriver, putting one notched block across another matching notched block in an X pattern, and turning a crank handle. These actions the first scorer had considered imperfect matches, because the objects were not fully aligned (blocks), or the subject did not move the crank or the screw the same distance or number of rotations as the demonstrator. The rate of matching the novel actions (that all involved repositioning an object) is half that of familiar actions, which was already a modest rate, but it is above zero.

To establish that this rate differed from chance, we would need to provide the same objects to monkeys without a demonstrator, to determine a baseline rate of these particular forms of repositioning. Although they are not a fully adequate comparison, we do have some relevant data on this point. In a previous study with a different aim (Fragaszy et al., unpublished), a series of objects like the crank and the screw were provided to untrained group-housed monkeys for several half-hour sessions. We saw some exploratory contacts with these objects, including some that produced motion in the crank (1/4 turn or less) very like that seen in the study under discussion here. Thus, capuchin monkeys have some low probability of repositioning an object in the same ways the human demonstrated through independent exploratory activity. However, in this study, the subject had only a short time to act, many other objects to contact, and many other things it could have done with the object used by the demonstrator. Thus, it seems unlikely that the subject produced even three partial matches fully by chance. Fragaszy and colleagues conclude that capuchin monkeys predictably contact objects that have been acted upon by the demonstrator, as found also by Hervé and Deputte (1993), and (with a much lower probability) they will move an object to achieve (or toward) a demonstrated movement or new position of the object. However, except in this circumstance, capuchins do not match the *actions* performed by others.

These findings are similar in substance to those reported by Custance, Whiten, and Fredman (1999) with a larger number of capuchin monkeys similarly in training to become helpers for quadriplegic humans in Israel. These investigators used a two-action design, in which two distinctive actions on an object are shown and each group of subjects is exposed to one of the two actions. They examined whether the monkeys would perform more frequently the actions they had seen performed by a human demonstrator than the actions they had not seen. The task consisted of opening a transparent box containing a food reward; the box was closed by a "barrel latch," or by a "bolt latch." Each latch could be opened with two techniques. Each technique consisted of two related actions. Eleven subjects saw their familiar caretaker acting on the latches to open the box. In the "barrel-latch" task, half the subjects saw a pin at the front of the box being *turned* several times and then a handle *turned*; the other half saw the pin being *spun* and then the handle *pulled*. In the "bolt-latch" task, half the subjects saw two rods at the top of the box being *poked* and *pushed*; the other half saw the rods being *twisted* and *pulled*. Custance, Whiten, and Fredman (1999) assessed for each type of latch whether the monkeys used the particular opening actions they witnessed more than the alternative ones. Two scorers, who knew what actions were demonstrated but were naive as to which actions each monkey had observed, viewed videotapes of the experimental sessions. They were asked to: (1) make a decision about which of the two demonstrations each subject had seen and then rate the confidence about that decision, and (2) count the number of each of the two actions (e.g., poking vs. twisting, pushing vs. pulling, etc., and other related subcategories) each subject performed.

Results showed that in the "barrel" latch, the monkey subjects did not reproduce the demonstrated technique at different frequencies than the nondemonstrated one. Nor were the human scorers able to infer reliably which technique the monkeys saw demonstrated. Similarly, in the "bolt" latch, the monkey subjects did not reproduce the demonstrated technique at different frequencies than the nondemonstrated one. However, the human scorers were able to infer reliably which technique the monkeys saw demonstrated. Therefore, for this latch, in addition to the modeled technique (*poke-push* vs. *twist-pull*), Custance, Whiten, and Fredman (1999) paid attention to the location (front vs. back of the box) where the monkeys acted and they analyzed the directions in which the rod was acted upon and from where it was removed (back vs. front, respectively). They found that their experimental groups differed in the frequencies with which they (a) pulled the rod from the front or the back side of the box, (b) pushed the rod from the front side of the box (but not from the back side), and (c) removed the rod from the front or from the back side of the box. It should be noted that pulling or pushing, followed by removing, constitute behavioral sequences in which actions are dependent on one another. For example, if a monkey pushes the rod from the front of the box, it is likely to pull it and remove it from the back of the box. The spatial features of the monkeys' actions (i.e., whether they occurred in the front or the back of the box) appear likely to have been the cues that allowed the naive scorers to discriminate between the experimental groups. For example, the scorers could have discriminated between groups on the basis of the side of the box from which the rods were removed.

Custance, Whiten, and Fredman (1999) label the phenomenon of reproducing the direction of the rods' movement as "object movement re-enactment." They suggest that either this interpretation or "perhaps simple imitation" (p. 21) of the modeled familiar acts may account for their results and that they cannot be distinguished in their study. However, because the frequencies of the specific modeled techniques were not affected by their demonstrations for either latch, we conclude that imitation (as we define it) is not a possible interpretation of their data. Instead, the notion that the monkeys acted to move an object at the front or at the back of the box (the side where they saw it move) is plausible.

The foraging actions of capuchins incorporate many forms of poking, pushing, or pulling, and attending to the spatial relations of an object in relation to substrate (such as front vs. back) in such situations seems potentially very useful. This form of social influence is like the one seen in the Fragaszy and colleagues (unpublished) study reviewed above (see also Gardner, Visalberghi, and Heyes, submitted), in which capuchins acted to bring together objects that the experimenter had handled and brought together, and (at least a few times) to move an object to reproduce its movement or a new position. Capuchins that are attentive to human demonstrators seem able to capture some of the spatial relations about objects from the human's actions with those objects.

In collaboration with Custance, we have also attempted to test our socially housed capuchins in both of these paradigms ("Do as I do" and with a two-action task, with human demonstrators). Informally, we have also tried several times with different subjects, apparatus, and reinforcement procedures to shape or elicit matching behaviors in capuchins with human demonstrators. All these efforts have come to naught. We thought that attention to the human demonstrator (or rather, lack of it) in group-housed monkeys might have been responsible for the monkeys' poor performance. In retrospect, we can see that intensive and prolonged interaction with humans (during early life, and in the course of extended training to respond to verbal commands issued by humans) does affect capuchins' visual attention to humans, and enhances their interest in objects a human touches, and these perceptual tendencies may enhance the monkeys' probability of matching object movements. However, such experience does not seem to lead to enhanced ability to match *action*, the signature feature of imitation.

It is interesting to note that the two young chimpanzees in Custance, Whiten, and Bard's (1995) study were able to match to a moderate degree a considerable proportion (38%) of novel actions involving only the body (e.g., touching the nose, or clapping hands) or acting on a substrate (e.g., slap the floor), whereas capuchin monkeys had the most trouble with these actions. Custance and colleagues did not include actions with objects in their list of modeled acts. Recently, however, that has been done by Myowa-Yamakoshi and Matsuzawa (1999), working with chimpanzees, in a study designed to investigate whether chimpanzees were better able to match certain kinds of manipulative actions than others. These authors report that chimpanzees were better able to match a novel action if the action involved orienting an object toward something else (another object, the substrate, or the subject's own body) than if it involved manipulating the single object alone. They concluded that directionality of the object's movement was a more salient cue for their subjects than the demonstrator's bodily movements. Thus, it seems that both capuchin monkeys and chimpanzees share a perceptual bias to notice directional movement of objects, more so than movement of a conspecific's arms or hands. It remains to be seen if this is true of humans as well, although Whiten and Custance's (1996) findings with children suggest that it is not true of 2- to 4-year-old children. In any case, incorporating this bias to notice and remember direction of object movement might be a useful starting point for a digital model of a "novice imitator" that can, with practice, expand its ability to notice action as well. In at least some situations, objects stay in their new positions for a longer duration than the movements that put them there, affording more time to see and remember them in the new location. Perhaps this temporal property supports the capuchins' and chimpanzees' better abilities to match direction of object movement and object positions than movements of an animate actor.

Byrne's (1999) description of a new theory to explain imitation by string-parsing algorithms seems compatible with this idea. According to Byrne's theory, an individual detects, over repeated encounters, the unvarying or highly probable sequence of actions leading to a goal. The learner eventually perceives the regularity of action, the organization of activity, and can reproduce it in its own action. This view has much in common with Gibsonian theory (Gibson 1966, 1979), which also emphasizes the perceiver's improving detection of environmental regularities as a core element in learning.

To summarize all the laboratory studies to date on capuchins' matching of acts they have observed:

1. They can match familiar actions with objects, but this requires overt training. They have greater difficulty matching a familiar action on the body. (Mitchell and Anderson 1993 report that a long-tailed macaque learned to produce scratching on cue, but it was not easily learned.)
2. They do not match novel actions.
3. They can reproduce positions of objects somewhat.
4. Neonatal capuchins do not match human facial expressions.

In comparison, under similar circumstances, chimpanzees can match objects on the body, can match novel actions, are better at reproducing object position than movement, and exhibit a fragile ability as neonates to match human facial actions (tongue protrusion and mouth opening). Overall, it seems clear, chimpanzees are somewhat better than capuchin monkeys at noticing and reproducing humans' actions and movements of objects. Presumably, these characteristics contribute to behavior in natural circumstances, and it is thus not surprising that stronger evidence of traditions in natural circumstances (but not imitation, in the strict sense of our 1990a definition) is available for chimpanzees than for capuchins (Boesch and Tomasello 1998; Whiten et al. 1999).

The negative findings about capuchins' abilities to match actions do not mean that social influences are unimportant to capuchins' behavior, in the laboratory or in nature. Instead, they suggest we should look for different kinds of social learning processes than imitation in the sense of Visalberghi and Fragaszy (1990a), imitation in the sense of Meltzoff and Moore (1977, 1983), imitation in the sense of Camaioni, Baumgartner, and Pascucci (1988), imitation in the sense of Heyes and Dawson (1990), and the repetition of familiar actions or the matching of novel actions. Therefore, we have looked to feeding behavior for contexts where social influences could be expected to impact behavior.

18.3 Social Influences on Feeding

It has often been argued that social learning might be of great advantage in learning when, how, and what to feed upon (e.g., Giraldeau 1997). Dietary convergence in wild groups is often interpreted as due to social learning and the common view is that most primates, being social animals, learn to identify the foods they eat from watching conspecifics eating (e.g., King 1994; Byrne 1999; for a critical review, see Visalberghi 1994). We know that humans can be socially influenced both to initiate and to continue food consumption and to choose certain foods that are eaten by others (Rozin 1988; Birch and Fisher 1996). For example, De Castro (1990) has shown that the presence of others affects the onset of a meal, and increases the amount of food eaten and duration of time spent eating. Our studies, which are in the same vein as those with humans, investigated whether in capuchin monkeys the initiation, the consumption, and the selection of foods are affected by the feeding activity and by the food choices of a conspecific.

Visalberghi and Fragaszy (1995) found that the presence of group mates (and possibly the fact that they were eating) does not increase consumption of familiar foods but does increase consumption of novel foods when encountered for the first time. Do these results mean that homogeneity of diet within a group of monkeys is aided by social influences on acceptance of novel foods? To explore this, Visalberghi, Valente, and Fragaszy (1998) carried out an experiment that looked at consumption of novel foods when these foods are repeatedly encountered by individuals only when alone, or when encountered *only* in the presence of group mates. The results showed that during the first several encounters, eating is socially facilitated—that is, monkeys eat more of unfamiliar foods when in the presence of their conspecifics. After five to six encounters, the difference in the amount of time spent feeding by the monkeys who encountered the unfamiliar foods in a group versus those who encountered the unfamiliar foods alone disappeared.

At this point it becomes important to understand better the manner in which the presence or activity of conspecifics affect consumption. Galloway (submitted) investigated the effects of a conspecific A eating a particular food on the feeding behavior of an individual B. She tested four pairs of male *Cebus apella*. Each pair was housed together, constituting a long-term and compatible social unit. Within each pair, one individual was the facilitator and the other was the observer for a given procedure, and then roles were reversed. The question was whether observers choose to eat the same food the facilitator is eating. The food presented was applesauce, a desirable and familiar food to all the monkeys. The appearance of the applesauce was the independent variable. The addition of red or yellow food colors produced two different experimental foods. Capuchins were shown to able to discriminate these colors. For half the subjects, the facilitator had red applesauce; the other half had yellow applesauce when they served as facilitators. All observers had applesauce of the two colors from which to choose. The results show that the observers ate red and yellow applesauce equally often, regardless of the color of the food eaten by the facilitator, and that the experimental subjects' first choices of food were evenly distributed between red and yellow. In short, "what" the facilitator was eating did not affect the food choices of the observer.

Galloway (submitted) also showed that *whether* animals in any pair were feeding did affect the likelihood that animals in any other pair in the same room would eat. In this experiment, the monkeys were observed a few hours after the morning meal had been given. All pairs had a quantity of the primary diet (pellets of commercial monkey chow) remaining in the cage. One experimenter gave one pair (the facilitator pair) additional fruit, and another monitored the feeding behavior of the other pairs. Social facilitation of eating (familiar) foods was evident: the nonsupplemented pairs ate more of their leftover chow in this setting than they did in the control condition, when the experimenter stood in front of the facilitator pair's cage but did not give them supplemental foods.

On the basis of these results, we may look again at the results of our experiments that suggested social facilitation increased consumption of novel or unfamiliar foods. It is possible that consumption of novel food is greater in the presence of familiar conspecifics than when alone because the absence of the familiar companions induces stress, or alternatively, because their presence reduces the neophobic response (Greenberg 1990), or because their presence increases the perceived "value" of the food (as a function of perceived competition). It is also possible that the facilitatory effect in the novel food condition might have been related to a nonspecific facilitation of eating more when others were eating, regardless of the exact type of food the other monkey(s) were feeding upon. The simple facilitation of eating can result in an individual accepting and consuming more of a novel food if that novel food is what the observer has available. The results of a recent experiment by Visalberghi and Addessi (2000) fully supports this last hypothesis; they demonstrated that when group members were present and eating a familiar food, there was a significant increase in the acceptance of novel foods. Therefore, they argued that social facilitation of eating may indeed be a quicker way to overcome neophobia than encountering food alone. However, social facilitation is not necessarily a safe way to learn about a potential new food's palatability unless it works selectively and attention is paid to what the others are eating.

18.4 Conclusions

Social learning in animals can be described as socially biased individual learning (Galef 1995), and as learning about the environment from information provided by others. Experiments with tufted capuchin monkeys afford insight into the strength and specificity of social bias affecting the manipulation of objects, the replication of familiar action, the matching of novel actions, the initiation feeding, and food choice. Capuchins can be taken either as representative of monkeys in general (in line with cognitive abilities), and thus could be expected to illustrate monkey-typical social learning, or they can be taken as probable candidates for elaborated social learning, and more specifically, for imitative ability (on the basis of social and instrumental proclivities) (see section 18.1, Introduction). We have found that social partners do affect many aspects of behavior in capuchins, in line with their social proclivities. However, they do not imitate or learn unlikely behaviors from one another. The domain-specific hypothesis that imitative ability co-varies with manipulative ability is not supported. As capuchins do not imitate, we have no strong grounds at present for expecting that any other species of monkey will be able to do so. In fact, despite the many efforts to find imitative learning in other monkey species, the recent data supporting it are few and, like the earlier studies cited in our original "Do Monkeys Ape?" chapter in 1990, open to alternative interpretations. For example, Tanaka (1995) reported on the basis of extremely detailed field recordings that techniques of allogrooming were shared among members of the same low-ranking matriline. Although fascinating findings in their own right, these are correlative data that do not permit one to infer any particular basis for the similarity in actions. In another recent report, Bugnyar and Huber (1997) tested marmosets with a dual-action task. In their study, the experimental monkeys observed a trained demonstrator pulling a door open on a test apparatus and then the observers could act on the door themselves either by pulling or by pushing. Control subjects encountered the apparatus without having seen the demonstrator acting on it. Three of five subjects that watched the demonstrator pull the door initially pulled it more than pushed it when they began to interact with the apparatus, and they persisted in the same form of action for somewhat longer bouts than the other two monkeys or the control (naive) monkeys. The other two monkeys in the experimental group did not show these biases. Naive monkeys were equally likely to push or pull when they first encountered the apparatus, and to alternate among these actions rapidly. Although the researchers claim some support for imitative learning from these data, in our view the results are not clear enough to draw any strong conclusions. Moreover, a better explanation for the findings is a weak tendency to match the direction of object movement, as we have argued occurs in capuchins as well. In both taxa, the phenomenon appears to be rather weak, and in the case of marmosets, further study is required to confirm its existence.

Many years ago, the English biologist George Romanes (1884/ 1977, p. 477) wrote that "it is proverbial that monkeys carry the principle of imitation ... they are animals that imitate for the mere sake of imitating." Although his words are eloquent, we think Romanes dramatically overstated the case. On the basis of both older and newer studies, for capuchin monkeys (and other monkey species too), imitation has yet to be demonstrated. Instead, others' actions influence whether or not the capuchin observer eats (but not what it eats), and channels its interest in particular objects, and perhaps where objects are moved (but not the details of what the other does with those objects). Under natural circumstances, these influences are sufficient to support the development of group-homogeneous patterns of food choice and to synchronize feeding activities, and probably many other kinds of behavioral coordination among members of a group. We think this characterization of susceptibility to social influence in action fits other non-human primates well, including the apes, which admittedly have expressed greater likelihood of reproducing object movements, and even of reproducing actions (as in Myowa's 1996 study with neonatal chimpanzees reproducing facial movements) than have monkeys. Nothing in our findings suggests specialized abilities in social learning that are not evident in other domains; a domain-general view of cognition seems to work better.

Social learning continues to fascinate us, as well as many others in the fields of comparative psychology and evolutionary biology (e.g., Laland, Odling-Smee, and Feldman, 2000). Perhaps it is good to remind ourselves that dichotomous approaches to social learning ("can they or can't they") are misguided *because* the paths through which knowledge is acquired are redundant: an individual, and even more so an individual in a social situation, may learn the same thing by more than one process. This means that the same behavior can be learned through different processes by different individuals and/or that the same individual may learn similar tasks (e.g., different types of tool use) through different processes, and that several processes can contribute to learning the same behavior by one individual. However, in all cases, social learning should lead to faster dissemination of a learned behavior in a group than individual learning, as social learning depends on "public information" from behavior and each new proficient individual provides such information to those around itself when it performs the learned behavior (Giraldeau 1997).

Finally, a new puzzle has recently appeared for primatologists, like us, and neurologists as well, to solve. Neuroscientists have identified neurons in a particular area of premotor cortex of macaques that fire selectively in response to both an *executed* grasping action, and an *observed* grasping action performed by another individual, monkey or human (di Pellegrino et al. 1992; see also Rizzolatti et al. 1996; Arbib, chapter 10 of this volume). The researchers who discovered these neurons designated them as "mirror neurons" and they proposed that these neurons' activity constitutes a system for matching observation and execution of motor actions. Perhaps these neurons provide a neural substrate for segmenting a stream of action into discrete elements matching those in the observer's repertoire, as Byrne (1999) has suggested in connection with his string-parsing theory of imitation. It is tempting to think that these neurons may provide us with insight into how the brain achieves matching of observed movement to produced movement. Many puzzles must be solved to know if they can meet this expectation. The first puzzle is whether neural "mirror" responsiveness contributes to monkeys' abilities to produce object movements and positions, in addition to detecting them. If they are involved in production, a second puzzle is to identify those additional processes that allow humans to match actions, in addition to object movements and positions, and so afford humans an imitative "edge."

References

Adams-Curtis, L. A. Conceptual learning in capuchin monkeys. *Folia Primatologica* 54: 129–137, 1990.

Anderson, J. R. Chimpanzees and capuchin monkeys: Comparative cognition. In A. E. Russon, K. A. Bard, S. T. Parker, eds., *Reaching into Thought: The Minds of the Great Apes*, pp. 23–56. Cambridge, UK: Cambridge University Press, 1996.

Anderson, J. R. Tool-use, manipulation, and cognition in capuchin monkeys (*Cebus*). In C. Harcourt, ed., *New Perspectives in Primate Evolution and Behaviour*, pp. 91–110. Otley, UK: Westbury Publishing, 2000.

Anisfeld, M. Only tongue protrusion modeling is matched by neonates. *Developmental Review* 16: 149–161, 1996.

Antinucci, F., ed. *Cognitive Structures and Development in Nonhuman Primates*. Hillsdale, N.J.: Erlbaum, 1989.

Bard, K. A., D. Fragaszy, and E. Visalberghi. Acquisition and comprehension of a tool-using behavior by young chimpanzees (*Pan troglodytes*): Effects of age and modeling. *International Journal of Comparative Psychology* 8: 47–68, 1996.

Bard, K. A., and C. L. Russell. Evolutionary foundations of imitation: Social, cognitive, and developmental aspects of imitative processes in non-human primates. In J. Nadel and G. Butterworth, eds., *Imitation in Infancy*, pp. 89–123. Cambridge, UK: Cambridge University Press, 1999.

Birch, L. L., and J. A. Fisher. The role of experience in the development of children's eating behavior. In E. D. Capaldi, ed., *Why We Eat What We Eat. The Psychology of Eating*. Washington, DC: American Psychological Association, 1996.

Boesch, C., and M. Tomasello. Chimpanzee and human cultures. *Current Anthropology* 39(5): 591–614, 1998.

Boinski, S. Use of a club by a wild white-faced capuchin (*Cebus capucinus*) to attack a venomous snake (*Bothrops asper*). *American Journal of Primatology* 14: 177–179, 1988.

Boinski, S., R. Quatrone, and H. Swarts. Substrate and tool use by brown capuchins in Suriname: Ecological contexts and cognitive bases (submitted).

Box, H., and K. Gibson. *Social Learning in Mammals*. Cambridge, UK: Cambridge University Press, 1999.

Bugnyar, T., and L. Huber. Push or pull: An experimental study on imitation in marmosets. *Animal Behaviour* 54: 817–831, 1997.

Byrne, R. W. Imitation without intentionality. Using a string parsing to copy the organization of behaviour. *Animal Cognition* 2: 63–72, 1999.

Byrne, R. W., and M. Tomasello, Do rats ape? *Animal Behavior* 50: 1417–1420, 1995.

Byrne, R. W., and A. E. Russon, Learning by imitation: A hierarchical approach. *Behavioral Brain Sciences* 21: 667–721, 1998.

Camaioni, L., E. Baumgartner, and M. Pascucci. Interazioni imitative e complementari tra bambini nel secondo anno di vita. *Età Evolutiva* 29: 37–45, 1988.

Case, R. *The Mind's Staircase: Exploring the Conceptual Underpinnings of Children's Thought and Knowledge*. Hillsdale, N.J.: Erlbaum, 1994.

Custance, D. M., A. Whiten, and K. A. Bard. Can young chimpanzees (*Pan troglodytes*) imitate arbitrary actions? Hayes and Hayes (1952) revisited. *Behaviour* 132: 837–859, 1995.

Custance, D. M., A. Whiten, and T. Fredman. Social learning of artificial fruit task in capuchin monkeys (*Cebus apella*). *Journal of Comparative Psychology* 113: 13–23, 1999.

D'Amato, M. R., and D. P. Salmon. Cognitive processes in cebus monkeys. In H. L. Roitblat, T. G. Bever, and H. S. Terrace, eds., *Animal Cognition*, pp. 149–168. Hillsdale, N.J.: Erlbaum, 1984.

De Castro, J. M. Social facilitation of duration and size but not rate of the spontaneous meal intake in humans. *Physiology and Behavior* 47: 1129–1135, 1990.

De Lillo, C., and E. Visalberghi. Transfer index and mediational learning in tufted capuchin monkeys (*Cebus apella*). *International Journal of Primatology* 15: 275–287, 1994.

di Pellegrino, G., L. Fadiga, L. Fogassi, V. Gallese, and G. Rizzolatti. Understanding motor events: A neurophysiological study. *Experimental Brain Research* 91: 176–180, 1992.

Fernandes, E. B. M. Tool use and predation of oysters (*Crassostrea rhizophorae*) by the tufted capuchin, *Cebus apella apella*, in brackish water mangrove swamp. *Primates* 32(4): 529–531, 1991.

Fragaszy, D. M., and L. E. Adams-Curtis. Generative aspects of manipulation in tufted capuchin monkeys (*Cebus apella*). *Journal of Comparative Psychology* 105: 387–397, 1991.

Fragaszy, D. M., and E. Visalberghi. Social influences on the acquisition of tool-using behaviors in tufted capuchin monkeys (*Cebus apella*). *Journal of Comparative Psychology* 103: 159–170, 1989.

Fragaszy, D. M., and E. Visalberghi. Social processes affecting the appearance of innovative behaviors in capuchin monkeys. *Folia Primatologica* 54: 155–165, 1990.

Fragaszy, D. M., A. F. Vitale, and B. Ritchie. Variation among juvenile capuchins in social influences on exploration. *American Journal of Primatology* 32: 249–260, 1994.

Fragaszy, D. M., J. M. Feuerstein, and D. Mitra. Transfer of foods from adults to infants in tufted capuchins (*Cebus apella*). *Journal of Comparative Psychology* 111: 194–200, 1997.

Fragaszy, D. M., and K. Bard. Comparison of life history in *Pan* and *Cebus*. *International Journal of Primatology* 18: 683–701, 1997.

Fragaszy, D. M., B. L. Deputte, C. Hemery, and E. Johnson. Human-socialized capuchins can match familiar but not novel actions (unpublished).

Galef, B. G. Jr. Imitation in animals: history, definition, and interpretation of data from the psychological laboratory. In T. R. Zentall, and B. G. Galef, Jr., eds., *Social Learning. Psychological and Biological Perspectives*, pp. 1–28. London: Erlbaum, 1988.

Galef, B. G. Jr. Traditions in animals: Field observations and laboratory analyses. In M. Bekoff and D. Jamieson, eds., *Methods, Inference, Interpretation, and Explanation in the Study of Behavior*, pp. 74–95. Boulder: Westview Press, 1990.

Galef, B. G. Jr. The question of animal culture. *Human Nature* 3: 157–178, 1992.

Galef, B. G. Jr. Why behaviour patterns animals learn socially are locally adaptive. *Animal Behavior* 49: 1325–1334, 1995.

Galloway, A. T. Social inducement of feeding and food preferences in pair-housed capuchin monkeys, *Cebus apella* (submitted).

Gardner, M. R. Imitation: The methodological adequacy of directional control tests. Ph.D. thesis, University College of London, 1997.

Gardner, M. R., E. Visalberghi, and C. Heyes. Suggestive evidence of object movement reenactment but not imitation in capuchin monkeys (*Cebus apella*). *Journal of Comparative Psychology* (submitted).

Gibson, J. J. *The Senses Considered as Perceptual Systems*. Boston: Houghton Mifflin, 1966.

Gibson, J. J. *The Ecological Approach to Visual Perception*. Boston: Houghton Mifflin, 1979.

Giraldeau, L. A. The ecology of information use. In J. Krebs and N. Davies, eds., In *Behavioral Ecology*, 4th ed., pp. 42–68. Oxford: Blackwell Science, 1997.

Greenberg, R. Ecological plasticity, neophobia, and resource use in birds. *Studies in Avian Biology* 13: 431–437, 1990.

Hayes, J. K., and C. Hayes. Imitation in a home-raised chimpanzee. *Journal of Comparative Psychology* 45: 450–459, 1952.

Hemery, C., D. M. Fragaszy, and B. L. Deputte. Human-socialized capuchins match objects but not actions. Paper presented at the XVII Congress of the International Primatological Society, Antananarivo, Madagascar, 10–14 August, 1998.

Hervé, N., and B. L. Deputte. Social influence in manipulations of a capuchin monkey raised in a human environment: A preliminary case study. *Primates* 34(2): 227–232, 1993.

Heyes, C. M., and G. R. Dawson. A demonstration of observational learning in rats using a bidirectional control. *Quarterly Journal of Experimental Psychology* 42B: 59–71, 1990.

Heyes, C. M., and B. G. Galef Jr., eds. *Social Learning in Animals. The Roots of Culture.* London: Academic Press, 1996.

King, B. J. *The Information Continuum.* Santa Fe: SAR Press, 1994.

Laland, K. N., J. Odling-Smee, and M. W. Feldman. Niche construction, biological evolution, and cultural change. *Behavioral and Brain Sciences* 23: 131–146, 2000.

Meltzoff, M. A. The human infant as imitative generalist: A 20-year progress report on infant imitation with implications for comparative psychology. In C. M. Heyes and B. G. Galef Jr., eds., *Social Learning in Animals. The Roots of Culture*, pp. 347–370. London: Academic Press, 1996.

Meltzoff, M. A., and M. K. Moore. Imitation of facial and manual gestures by human neonates. *Science* 198: 75–78, 1977.

Meltzoff, M. A., and M. K. Moore. Newborn infants imitate adult facial gestures. *Child Development* 54: 702–709, 1983.

Mercado, E. III, S. O. Murray, R. K. Uyeyama, A. A. Pack, and L. M. Herman. Memory for recent action in the bottlenosed dolphin (*Tursiops truncatus*): Repetition of arbitrary behaviors using an abstract rule. *Animal Learning and Behavior* 26: 210–218, 1998.

Mitchell, R. W. A comparative-developmental approach to understanding imitation. In P. G. Klopfer, and P. H. Bateson, eds., *Perspectives in Ethology*, vol. 7, pp. 183–215. New York: Plenum, 1987.

Mitchell, R. W., and J. R. Anderson. Discrimination learning of scratching, but failure to obtain imitation and self-recognition in a long-tailed macaque. *Primates* 34: 301–309, 1993.

Modena, I., and E. Visalberghi. Imitazione e uso di strumenti in bambini nel secondo anno di vita. Comparazione con altre specie di primati non-umani. *Età Evolutiva* 59: 11–20, 1998.

Moore, B. R. Avian movement imitation and a new form of mimicry: Tracing the evolution of a complex form of learning. *Behaviour* 122: 231–263, 1992.

Moore, B. R. The evolution of imitative learning. In C. M. Heyes and B. G. Galef Jr., eds., *Social Learning in Animals. The Roots of Culture*, pp. 245–265. London: Academic Press, 1996.

Myowa, M. Imitation of facial gestures by an infant chimpanzee. *Primates* 37(2): 207–213, 1996.

Myowa-Yamakoshi, M., and T. Matsuzawa. Factors influencing imitation of manipulatory actions in chimpanzees (*Pan troglodytes*). *Journal of Comparative Psychology* 113: 128–136, 1999.

Perucchini, P., F. Bellagamba, E. Visalberghi, and L. Camaioni. Influenza del comportamento di un conspecifico sulla manipolazione nel cebo. *Età Evolutiva* 58: 50–58, 1997.

Rizzolatti, G., L. Fadiga, V. Gallese, and L. Fogassi. Premotor cortex and the recognition of motor actions. *Cognitive Brain Research* 3: 131–141, 1996.

Romanes, G. J. *Mental Evolution in Animals.* New York: AMS Press, 1884/1977.

Rozin, P. Social learning about food by humans. In T. R. Zentall and B. G. Galef Jr, eds., *Social Learning. Psychological and Biological Perspectives*, pp. 165–187. London: Lea, 1988.

Spence, K. W. Experimental studies of learning and higher mental processes in infrahuman primates. *Psychological Bulletin* 34: 806–850, 1937.

Tanaka, I. Matrilinear distribution of louse egg-handling techniques during grooming in free-ranging Japanese macaques. *American Journal of Physical Anthropology* 98: 197–201, 1995.

Terkel, J. Cultural transmission of feeding behavior in the black rat (*Rattus rattus*). In C. M. Heyes and B. G. Galef Jr., eds., *Social Learning in Animals. The Roots of Culture*, pp. 17–64. San Diego: Academic Press, 1996.

Thorpe, W. H. *Learning and Instinct in Animals*. Methuen, London, 1956.

Tomasello, M. Do apes ape? In C. M. Heyes and B. G. Galef Jr., eds., *Social Learning in Animals. The Roots of Culture*, pp. 319–346. San Diego: Academic Press, 1996.

Tomasello, M., and J. Call. *Primate Cognition*. New York: Oxford University Press, 1997.

Visalberghi, E. Acquisition of nut-cracking behavior by 2 capuchin monkeys (*Cebus apella*). *Folia Primatologica* 49: 168–181, 1987.

Visalberghi, E., Influences of aversive processes on innovative behaviors in primates. In P. Brain, S. Parmigiani, R. J. Blanchard, and D. Mainardi, eds., *Fear and Defence*, pp. 309–328. Chur, Switzerland: Harwood Academic Publishers, 1990.

Visalberghi, E. Capuchin monkeys. A window into tool use activities by apes and humans. In K. Gibson and T. Ingold, eds., *Tools, Language and Cognition in Human Evolution*, pp. 138–150. Cambridge, UK: Cambridge University Press, 1993.

Visalberghi, E. Learning process and feeding behavior in monkeys. In B. J. Galef, M. Mainardi, and P. Valsecchi, eds., *Behavioral Aspects of Feeding. Basic and Applied Research on Mammals*, pp. 257–270. Chur, Switzerland: Harwood Academic Publishers, 1994.

Visalberghi, E., and D. M. Fragaszy. Do monkeys ape? In S. T. Parker and K. R. Gibson, eds., *"Language" and Intelligence in Monkeys and Apes*, pp. 247–273. Cambridge, UK: Cambridge University Press, 1990a.

Visalberghi, E., and D. M. Fragaszy. Food-washing behaviour in tufted capuchin monkeys (*Cebus apella*) and crab-eating macaques (*Macaca fascicularis*). *Animal Behaviour* 40: 829–836, 1990b.

Visalberghi, E., and D. M. Fragaszy. The behaviour of capuchin monkeys (*Cebus apella*) with novel food: The role of social context. *Animal Behaviour* 49: 1089–1095, 1995.

Visalberghi, E., M. Valente, and D. M. Fragaszy. Social context and consumption of unfamiliar foods by capuchin monkeys (*Cebus apella*) over repeated encounters. *American Journal of Primatology* 45: 367–380, 1998.

Visalberghi, E., and E. Addessi. Seeing group members eating a familiar food enhances the acceptance of novel foods in capuchin monkeys. *Animal Behaviour* 60: 69–76, 2000.

Whiten, A., and R. Ham. On the nature and evolution of imitation in the animal kingdom: A reappraisal of a century of research. In P. J. B. Slater, C. Rosenblatt, and M. Milinski, eds., *Advances in the Study of Behavior*, pp. 239–283. New York: Academic Press, 1992.

Whiten, A., and D. Custance. Studies on imitation in chimpanzees and children. In C. M. Heyes and B. G. Galef Jr., eds., *Social Learning in Animals. The Roots of Culture*. London: Academic Press, 1996.

Whiten, A., J. Goodall, W. C. McGrew, T. Nishida, V. Reynolds, Y. Sugiyama, C. E. G. Tutin, R. W. Wrangham, and C. Boesch. Cultures in chimpanzees. *Nature* 399: 682–685, 1999.

19 Transformational and Associative Theories of Imitation

Cecilia Heyes

19.1 Introduction

The interests of those who investigate imitation in animals and artifacts converge on questions of proximate mechanism. The ethologists and psychologists who study imitation in animals may be more preoccupied than artificial intelligence and robotics specialists with questions about the evolutionary origins and adaptive functions of imitation, and "artifact people" may be more concerned than "animal people" with the potential technological uses of imitation, but both groups seek to understand the processes mediating imitation. It is important for all of us to apprehend how observation of another system's body movements (rather than the effects of those movements on objects) can cause the observing system, not merely to become more active or to direct activity to certain objects, but to execute similar body movements.

This chapter surveys a range of existing theories of the proximate psychological mechanisms of imitation and, in the final section, outlines a new "associative sequence learning" (ASL) theory. In this context, a "psychological mechanism" is a process with properties analogous to those of a physical machine, which intervenes in the causation of behavior between sensation and peripheral motor control (Heyes, in press). It is assumed that psychological mechanisms are implemented in the central nervous system, but not that they are necessarily reducible or identifiable with known neurobiological mechanisms.

The present survey of theories of the psychological mechanisms of imitation is very far from comprehensive (see Heyes, forthcoming, for a more complete review). It focuses on hypotheses that seek to explain how agents produce or acquire the information necessary to copy body movements that are in some sense "novel"— that were not part of the observer's repertoire prior to imitative execution. Consequently, the survey excludes hypotheses about the motivation (rather than the ability) to imitate, theories that do not distinguish reproduction of object movements from reproduction of body movements, and those that are concerned with cognitive processing of observed action but not with the observation-action transition—that is, the way in which information from action observation is translated into matching behavior (e.g., Byrne 1999). Many of the excluded theories are of considerable interest in their own right, but they do not tackle the obstinate and intriguing problem that motivates the present discussion: the problem of "perceptual opacity."

After a brief outline of this problem, I will review clear examples of each of the two principal types of theory of imitation distinguished by Heyes and Ray (2000), "transformational" and "associative."[1] Broadly speaking, associative theories claim that the information required to produce an imitative match between the behavior of an observer and that of its demonstrator (or model) is derived from experience. They suggest that the capacity to imitate a given action, X, now, derives from experience of simultaneously observing and executing X in the past. In contrast, transformational theories assert that a substantial portion of the information necessary to produce a behavioral match is internally generated by complex cognitive processes. These processes transform the sensory input from the demonstrator's action into a representation containing the information necessary to guide execution of matching behavior by the observer. This chapter gives more coverage to the associative theories because they are less well known and, in their original presentations, more difficult for the nonspecialist to penetrate. They are also more direct precursors of associative sequence learning theory.

Perceptual Opacity

The focal challenge for any theory of the mechanisms of imitation is to explain how an observer can imitate an action that is similar to the model's only from a third party perspective. In other words, it is especially difficult to explain the imitation of actions, such as facial expressions, that give rise to very different sensory inputs to the observer when they are performed by the observer and when they are performed by a model. I shall refer to actions of this sort, including "invisible" actions (Piaget 1951), as "perceptually opaque," and to actions that yield relatively similar sensory inputs when observed and executed as "perceptually transparent."

As an example of a perceptually transparent action, imagine what I would see if I looked at my right arm as I extended it forward and turned my wrist so that the palm of my hand was facing inward. My retinae would receive much the same pattern of stimulation, and my visual system would construct much the same image, as they would if I were looking over the shoulder of another person executing the same movement. In the latter case, I would not be able to feel the action, it would not give rise to any kinesthetic, proprioceptive or tactile stimulation, and the viewing angle would be slightly different, but the visual percept would be similar. Likewise, if I hum a snatch of Gershwin's "But Not for Me," the resonance of the typanic membranes in my ears, and my auditory percept, will resemble that which occurs when I listen to someone else humming the same tune.

In contrast, perceptually opaque actions naturally give rise to very different patterns of sensory stimulation when observed and executed. For example, when I watch another person curtsy, I have a frontal view of a whole body, with arms extended laterally, the top of the head clearly visible, and the legs bending such that the torso moves downward. In contrast, when I curtsy, with my head bowed and eyes open, I see my chest in the foreground, one of my feet sticking out below, and a knee appear briefly above the foot.

Imitation of perceptually opaque actions is more difficult to explain than imitation of perceptually transparent behavior because in the former case one cannot assume that the observer detects the similarity between its own behavior and that of the model via some relatively simple process of sensory matching. It seems that the observer could not detect the similarity by comparing directly sensory input from the model and sensory feedback from the observer's own action.

19.2 Transformational Theories

Two transformational accounts of imitation will be discussed in this section: Bandura's (1986) "social cognitive theory" and Meltzoff and Moore's (e.g., 1977, 1999) "active intermodal matching" (AIM) theory. Aronfreed's (1969) template theory and, more recently, Whiten and Byrne's (1991) and Tomasello's (in press; Tomasello and Call 1997) intentional accounts of imitation are also primarily transformational models. Although they have substantial merits, these models are less representative of transformation theory because they either contain associative components (Aronfreed 1969) or seek to explain the motivation to imitate rather than the origins of the information required for imitation.

Social Cognitive Theory

According to Bandura's (1986) social cognitive theory, imitation is governed by four sets of constituent processes:

Attentional processes *regulate exploration and perception of modeled activities; through* retentional processes, *transitory experiences are converted into symbolic conceptions that serve as internal models for response production and standards for response correction;* production processes *govern the organisation of constituent subskills into new response patterns; and* motivational processes *determine whether or not observationally acquired competencies will be put to use.* (p. 51, emphasis added)

In other words, to imitate, an observer must (1) attend to a model's action, (2) store information about the action in the form of some sort of "symbolic conception" that can be used to generate and select behavioral variants, and (3) execute behavior derived from the symbolic conception when (4) motivated to do so.

This theory has three notable features. First, in contrast with some associative theories, it denies that observation of the model's behavior must be accompanied by reinforcement. Bandura insists that attention to the model's behavior is sufficient; neither direct nor vicarious reinforcement is required for the formation of a mental representation of the model's action. Second, it ascribes to the mental representation formed by observation a generative as well as a selective role in the production of imitative behavior. In other transformational models (e.g., Aronfreed 1969), the mental representation formed through observation does not increase the probability that the observer will generate a behavioral variant resembling the observed behavior. It merely functions to increase the likelihood that such a variant will be repeated or retained if it is generated by chance or through some independent process. In contrast, Bandura's theory claims that the mental representation derived from observation can both generate "a rough approximation of the action" it represents, and act as a guide in a subsequent selection process. This process corrects the behavior until it matches that of the model.

The conceptual representation provides the internal model for response production and the standard for response correction. Behavioral production primarily involves a conception-matching process in which the incoming sensory feedback from enactments is compared to the conception. The behavior is then modified on the basis of comparative information to achieve progressively closer correspondence between conception and action (Bandura 1986, p. 64).

Finally, social cognitive theory denies that the production and maintenance of imitative behavior depends on reinforcement. It assumes that imitative performance is regulated by "incentives," rather than reinforcement, and that the incentives can be "self-produced" as well as direct and/or vicarious. Thus, observers will produce and persist in producing imitative behavior to the extent that they anticipate that such performance will have emotionally positive effects on them—either directly, via similar effects on others (vicarious incentive), or via "self-evaluation" or "self-efficacy" judgments. For example, a city slicker may want to imitate a method of baiting a fishing line because she expects it to give her the pleasure of fish for tea, a nice feeling when her tutor is satisfied with her skills, and/or a sense that she is good person because she can hack it with rustics and sportsmen.

The primary problem with social cognitive theory is one of underspecification. It claims that imitation is mediated by a powerful kind of mental entity, a "symbolic" or "conceptual" representation, but says little about the nature of this entity or how it does its work. To say that information is "symbolically" coded implies only that it is *not* represented in a modality-specific sensory code, but what would be needed to understand imitation within Bandura's framework, particularly imitation of perceptually opaque actions, is a positive characterization of the content and coding of "conceptual" representations.

As a consequence of its underspecification, social cognitive theory makes few testable predictions about the conditions in which imitation will and will not occur. Because it does not specify functions mapping sensory information from the model onto information coded in the conceptual representation, or information in the conceptual representation onto motor programs, social cognitive theory does not imply any central constraints on imitative competence. In principle, a system with the architecture of social cognitive theory can imitate any action, regardless of novelty and complexity, provided that it has attended to the model and has adequate peripheral motor control. The theory imposes constraints at the level of performance rather than competence in saying that imitative behavior depends on anticipation by the observer of direct, vicarious, or self-produced rewards. However, since a reward may be anticipated when it will not, in fact, occur, and since anticipation of self-produced rewards is difficult to measure, even these predictions, which have no bearing on the central mysteries of imitation, are very hard to test.

Active Intermodal Matching

Meltzoff and Moore (e.g., 1977, 1999) have developed a theory of imitation based on their own evidence of facial gesture imitation in human neonates. Unlike any other, active intermodal matching (AIM) theory focuses exclusively on the imitation of perceptually opaque actions, and it is stark, consisting of three basic claims: (1) "supramodal" representations of action are formed during observation; (2) these representations are used actively or deliberately to generate imitative performance; (3) the capacity to form and make active use of supramodal representations to generate imitative performance of perceptually opaque actions is innate. Thus, AIM denies that the representations mediating imitation are either sensory or motor, but beyond this it does not indicate how they are formed or the code in which they represent information. In this respect, it shares the weakness of underspecification inherent in Bandura's theory. In claiming that imitation is active, AIM postulates that the observer is in some sense striving to match the model's behavior. With respect to the third of its claims, AIM is a "starting state" rather than a "modular" nativist theory. It suggests that the capacity to imitate is present at birth, and is not subject to significant change in the course of ontogeny.

Other nativist theories have suggested that execution of a behavior already in an observer's repertoire can, by virtue of an innate releasing mechanism, be triggered by the sight of the same behavior executed by a model. It is important to distinguish this view from AIM, which postulates that the capacity to imitate novel actions is innate, and that the innate mechanism is not merely a reflex, but a process that recognizes and represents the equivalence of perceptually disparate modeled and observed actions.

19.3 Associative Theories

Historically, associative theories have been of two kinds. "Contiguity" theories assume that the associations underlying imitation are formed through simultaneous or temporally contiguous occurrence of stimuli and responses, while "reinforcement" theories claim that the stimulus and response must be followed by reward in order to become associated. In both cases, the focal stimuli typically consist of demonstrator behavior and the responses of observer behavior.

Contiguity

In the 1920s and 1930s, several psychologists (e.g., Allport 1924; Guthrie 1935; Holt 1931; Humphrey 1921) provided analyses of imitation based on what was then believed about the process of conditioning. These are known as contiguity or "early associative" theories of imitation (Bandura 1986). Holt (1931) was alone among the early associationists in trying to explain imitation of novel, perceptually opaque actions. He focused on the example of a child confronting an adult when the adult demonstrates a gesture that is new to the child. Under these circumstances, Holt believed that the child would "almost infallibly" imitate the gesture, and that this is due to generalization following a conditioning process in which movements of the child's body are paired with movements of its eyes as it tracks the performance of an imitating adult:

It is common knowledge that in all animals whose eyes are mobile, the eyes will follow any moving object; this is adience of the eyes. Now in the progress of our game [in which the adult copied the child] when the child moved, say, his right arm out to the right, his eyes were led to follow the movement (vis-à-vis) of the older person's left arm out to the child's right: similarly for movements to the child's left, and up, and down. Thus the proprioceptive afferent impulses ... after any movement of the child's eyes (right, left, up, or down) will get motor outlet into muscles that carry the child's hand or leg in the same direction (right, left, up, or down). But these are the four components of any movement that a person standing vis-à-vis to the child can make in that right-left plane in which each sees the other. Hereafter the child will tend to imitate any movement in this plane which he sees another person execute. (pp. 118–19)

Thus, according to Holt, when an adult imitates a child's body movement, the child has an opportunity to associate proprioceptive feedback from the eye movements involved in tracking the adult's action with the stimuli (nature unspecified) that provoked the child's performance of the adult-imitated body movement. For example, when the child and adult are facing one another, movement of the child's eyes to the child's right (tracking a movement, to the child's right, of the adult's left arm) is paired with the stimuli that made the child move its own right arm to the child's right in the first place. Once feedback from eye movements and stimuli for body movements have been paired in this way across a range of body movements, *any* movement by the adult in the right-left plane has the potential to elicit a mirror image movement in the child. That is, for any adult movement in this plane, the feel of the observer's eyes tracking the model's movement "will get motor outlet into muscles that carry the child's hand or leg in the same direction" (Holt 1931).

Holt's theory of imitation has a number of notable features. First, and most obviously, it predicts that an individual will not acquire the capacity to imitate unless and until they are themselves imitated. Second, Holt's theory presupposes the occurrence of backward conditioning. When an adult imitates a child, the onset of stimulation from the child's tracking eye movements will occur after the onset of stimuli that elicit the child's body movement, and yet Holt assumes that the feedback from eye movements will become a conditioned stimulus for that body movement. Third, Holt assumed, or predicted, mirror imitation but not transposition imitation—that is, imitation in which the observer's limbs move in the same direction *relative to the actor's body* as those of the model. The mechanism that he postulated might generate transposition imitation if, while the model was imitating the observer, the observer viewed the model from behind. However, this arrangement is unlikely to be common in nature because, with his or her back turned to the observer, the model would be unlikely to see, and therefore to imitate, the observer's body movements.

Three other characteristics of Holt's theory are more clearly weaknesses: (1) it does not address imitation of actions in which the model's body moves toward the observer, or indeed in any plane other those running parallel to the observer's ventral surface; (2) Holt presented his theory as an explanation for the imitation of novel actions, but he did not make clear whether, by novel, he meant actions not previously in the observer's repertoire, or actions that the observer has performed in the past but that have never been imitated by a model; (3) like transformational theories, Holt's contiguity theory is vague about its key mechanism; it does not say *how* "proprioceptive afferent impulses ... get motor outlet into muscles" (1931).

In spite of these limitations, one cannot help admiring Holt for going against the grain of early associative theories. While others ignored the possibility of imitation of novel, perceptually opaque actions, Holt's firm belief in its educational potential led him not only to denounce any teacher who neglected imitation as "a fool, and the dupe of his own brutishness" (1931, p. 118), but to attempt to explain in terms of conditioning principles the most challenging examples of imitation.

Reinforcement

J. B. Watson, one of the earliest and most influential promoters of reinforcement (or "behaviorist") theories of learning, showed signs of psychic conflict about imitation. In *Psychology from the Standpoint of the Behaviorist* (1919) he attributed all imitation to instinct, and, just a few years later (Watson 1925), insisted that it was all due to learning. Furthermore, in the latter phase, this stern advocate of the Law of Effect accepted a continuity account of the origins of imitative behavior!

Two other major reinforcement theorists, Edward Thorndike and Clark Hull, also failed to offer an account of imitation. Thorndike (1898) successfully fractionated the phenomena commonly known as "imitation" into scientifically useful categories, but he said little about the psychological processes involved in "true imitation." However, two of Hull's students, Miller and Dollard (1941), published two theories of imitation ("matched-dependent behavior" and "copying"), and Skinner (1953) gave the subject some attention.[2]

Matched Dependent Behavior

Miller and Dollard (1941) argued that all imitation arises from stimulus-response (S-R) habit formation in which either the behavior of the model, or the relationship between the model's and the observer's behavior, is the stimulus component of the habit. They called instances of the former type "matched-dependent behavior," and in discussing this phenomenon formulated the first of several reinforcement theories of imitation that claim that an observer will reliably perform the same behavior as a model, without knowing that its behavior is similar to that of the model, if and only if the observer has been rewarded for doing so in the past. These theories cast the model's behavior as a discriminative stimulus (S^D) (Miller and Dollard 1941) or occasion setter (Skinner 1953) for the same behavior by the observer.

Miller and Dollard (1941) illustrated their matched-dependent behavior theory with experiments showing that when observer rats are rewarded for running down the same arm of a Y maze as a model or leader rat, they develop a reliable tendency to follow the leader, but when they are rewarded for taking the opposite turn, they develop an equally reliable tendency *not* to follow the leader. Similarly, when children are allowed on several successive occasions to open one of two boxes, they learn to open the box that they have seen another child opening if that is the one in which they have found sweets in the past, and to open the other box if the sweets were consistently found in the box the model child did not open. In these examples, there is no more than a gross resemblance between the actions of the observers and the models; they turn in the same direction in space and act on the same object. But Miller and Dollard (1941), and Skinner (1953) believed that cases in which there is a topographic match between the perceptually opaque actions of observer and model could be explained in exactly the same way. Indeed, Skinner illustrated his reinforcement theory using the examples of actors imitating attitudes and facial expressions, and dancers matching precise sequences of steps.

Thus, like continuity theories of imitation, reinforcement theories did not attempt to explain how a body movement can be learned through observation of its execution by a model. They denied that this could happen, insisting that, like all other behavior, responses that *seem* to be learned by observation, have in fact been acquired through a reinforcement process. Skinner tried to explain why imitation seems to involve observational learning through a componential analysis of behavior, while Miller and Dollard (1941) attempted to do so with reference to generalization.

Skinner's (1953) componential analysis assumed that a behavior can only be imitated if it has already occurred by chance, and has been reinforced, in the presence of the same behavior by the model. He saw imitation, like all learning, as involving what he called a "three term relationship," between an occasion-setting stimulus, a response, and a reinforcer. Skinner argued that the belief that body movements can be learned by observation alone (which he equated with belief in magic), arises from the fact that people tend to acquire rich, or closely packed, imitative repertoires in particular behavioral domains.

Imitative repertoires are often developed in relatively discrete sets of responses. In learning to dance, a set of more or less stereotyped responses is acquired by virtue of which a step executed by the instructor is duplicated by the pupil. The good dancer possesses a large imitative repertoire of dance steps. When this repertoire is faulty, the imitation is poor, and the novice finds it difficult to match a complicated step. In dancing, as in singing by ear, the imitative ability of a good performer seems almost magical to the untutored. (Skinner 1953, p. 120)

In this passage, Skinner implies that a "single" dance step is composed of a large number of small behavioral units, and that a skilled dancer can duplicate a model's performance of the step, without having executed the step before, only because the dancer has learned to imitate, via the three-term relationship, all of the component units.

Thus, Skinner's theory suggests that observation of a model can trigger execution of a behavior that is novel in the sense that the observer has not previously performed its components in the same order, and that the triggering function of model observation does not constitute learning. A problem with this analysis is that it does not explain why an observer would execute action components in the same order as the model, and, if it did, it would probably have to concede that some of the learning contributing to imitation is "behaviorally silent" (Dickinson 1980). Matching of serial order would imply that *something* has been learned by observation alone; not the topography of individual components, but the sequence in which they occur.

Miller and Dollard (1941) used the concept of generalization in their attempt to show that imitation does not involve behaviorally silent learning. They conceded that a matching behavior, X^1, can occur in response to a model's behavior, X, when X^1 has not previously been exhibited and reinforced in the presence of X. However, they argued that in these cases the matching behavior is still due to reinforcement history. Specifically, they claimed that it is a product of past experience in which either X^1 was reinforced in the presence of a cue, Y, that is similar to X (stimulus generalization), or Y^1, a response similar to X^1, was reinforced in the presence of X (response generalization).

Illustrating the principle of stimulus generalization, Miller and Dollard (1941) showed that observer rats that had been rewarded for following white rats in a maze, subsequently followed black rats more reliably than did observer rats previously rewarded for not following white rats. In Miller and Dollard's demonstration of response generalization, children that had been rewarded for moving a handle with the same action (depression or rotation) as a model, were more likely—than children that had been rewarded for using a different technique than a model—to choose to open the same box as the model when given a choice between two boxes to search for sweets.

Miller and Dollard's appeal to the principle of generalization goes some way toward explaining why it may not always be obvious that apparent imitation is due to the observer's history of reinforcement. However, it did not make their analysis of matched-dependent behavior a satisfactorily testable theory of imitation because they did not indicate conditions in which generalization will and will not occur. The mere suggestion that generalization will occur to "similar" stimuli or responses is not enough. In which respects must they be similar, and why? Referring to the example of response generalization given above, what does handle rotation have in common with opening box A, that is not common to handle depression and opening box A?

In addition to being difficult to test, reinforcement theories that portray the model's behavior as a conditional cue are implausible for cases of imitation in which there is a precise topographic match between the observer's and the model's behavior, and the observer's behavior is relatively unconstrained. When, as in Miller and Dollard's (1941) experiments, the observer has only a few, crudely defined response options, there is a fair probability that natural contingencies of reinforcement would reward the learner only for selecting the same option as the model, and that initially random behavior would swiftly converge on this option without the learner detecting the relationship between its own response and that of the model. However, when conditions allow an observer to make a wide range of responses, it is unlikely that natural contingencies of reinforcement would be such that the observer was rewarded only when it happened to make exactly the same response as the model, or that, under such contingencies, the matching response would become established in a reasonable time without the observer seeking or detecting the match.

Copying

Acknowledging that matched-dependent behavior could not be responsible for all imitative performance, Miller and Dollard (1941) advanced a second reinforcement theory of imitation, involving the concept of "copying." According to this theory, when an observer copies a model, it is the relationship between the model's behavior and the observer's behavior, not the model's behavior alone, that constitutes a discriminative stimulus or conditional cue. For example, when a model sings a note, and an observer sings a lower note, the dissonant product sound, or the disparity between the two notes, may act as a "difference cue" eliciting the response of a higher, matching note from the observer.

Miller and Dollard's copying theory was designed to explain the acquisition of what Skinner (1953) called imitative repertoires. Using the example of a person being taught to sing, it offered an account of how this observer comes to be able to match any note, or sequence of notes, sung by another person. In stage 1 of training to match a single note, say C, the teacher detects sameness and difference cues and the observer responds to them randomly. Thus, when the observer voices a note higher or lower than C, the teacher says "No" or "That's wrong," this makes the observer feel anxious, and initiates random variation in the note he is producing. When the observer finally hits upon C, the teacher says "Yes" or "Good," and the learner feels relieved. In stage 2, the teacher says "Too high" or "Too low" when the observer is producing the wrong note, and the observer responds directionally, by producing a higher or lower note.

In stages 3 and 4, the observer becomes able to detect the sameness and difference cues himself. When the trainer says "No," "Yes," "Too high," or "Too low," the observer repeats these words to himself and then experiences the twinge of anxiety or feeling of relief originally provoked by the trainer's utterance. The learner's repetition of the words is close to reinforcement (an increase or decrease in anxiety) and therefore, according to Hullian learning theory, these responses become "anticipatory"; they begin to occur in direct response to the sameness and difference cues. After some practice guided by direct detection of the sameness and difference cues, the learner will be able to match a C reliably at first attempt, and he can then move on to other notes. Miller and Dollard said that it would be easier for the learner to match each successive note tackled in training, because the sameness and difference cues would have something in common with those of previous notes in the sequence, and therefore generalization would occur.

Having learned to copy every single musical note in stage 5, in stage 6 the observer learns, through the processes described for stages 1 to 5, to copy sequences of notes. Stage 6 learning is facilitated, via generalization, by prior training to match single notes, and after learning to match a range of sequences, Miller and Dollard claimed that the one-time novice would be an expert, capable of copying without practice novel sequences of notes.

Miller and Dollard's (1941) copying theory overcomes the problem of behavioral variants encountered by their matched-dependent behavior theory and other reinforcement theories that construe the model's behavior as a conditional cue. In effect, copying theory concedes that, when there are many behavioral options available to an observer, there is just one kind of situation in which naturally occurring contingencies of reinforcement are likely to reward the observer only for performing exactly the same behavior as a model—namely, situations in which the model or a third party deliberately sets up those contingencies and thereby teaches the observer to imitate. Therefore, in dealing with the problem of behavioral variants, copying theory makes the prediction that precise imitation will be possible only in those domains of action in which the observer has been explicitly trained to imitate.

A second virtue of copying theory is that it accommodates the fact that people often report an intention to imitate, and an appreciation of the degree to which their behavior matches that of a model. Copying theory accounts for this "verbal behavior" in terms of an "acquired drive to imitate" and the detection of sameness and difference cues, while other reinforcement theories are at best silent about its origins, and at worst incompatible with such reports.

In spite of these virtues, copying theory has two significant weaknesses, one distinctive and one in common with other reinforcement theories. The distinctive weakness relates to the claim that, at stage 3 in learning to copy, the observer's behavior comes under the direct control of sameness and difference cues via repetition of the model's (or "critic's") instructions by the observer (or "copier"):

the copier gradually became able to reach the correct note more rapidly and to respond independently to the cues of sameness and difference. Previously he had been saying "No" to himself and responding with a twinge of anxiety after each "No" from the critic. He had also been saying "Yes" to himself, relaxing, and feeling pleased after each "Yes" from the critic. Gradually these responses began to become anticipatory, so that [for example] the cue of dissonance (plus perhaps the cue of "higher than" or "lower than") tended to elicit anxiety responses and to cause the subject to vary the pitch of his note even before the critic said "No." (Miller and Dollard 1941, p. 156)

This implies that before an observer can learn to copy any other actions, they must be able to copy, albeit implicitly, models' instructions, the responses through which models communicate whether a putative imitation is right or wrong. But if this is the case, how do observers achieve this initial feat of imitation; how do they come to be able to copy the instructions themselves? Miller and Dollard do not address this question.

The second problem with copying theory is that it assigns a critical role to generalization without specifying dimensions of generalization, and thereby making it plausible that generalization could fulfill this role. This problem is concealed in Miller and Dollard's copying theory because their exposition deals almost exclusively with imitative singing of musical notes. Actions in this domain, for example, "singing C," "singing D," have two unusual properties: They are defined, differentiated one from another, in terms of their sensory consequences, rather than the effectors involved, and the sensory consequences that define the actions can be ordered on a known scale. These features of singing are important because, in combination, they make it plausible that generalization would, for example, make it easier to learn to copy a D than an E note after learning to copy a C. It is possible to specify the psychophysical dimensions on which the sameness cue DD is more like CC than is EE, and on which the difference cue DB is more like CB than is EB. However, actions in most domains cannot be ordered on a scale (or, at least, we do not know the scale on which they can be ordered) and therefore, for most actions, the claim that there is generalization of learning to copy could be tested only on the basis of ancilliary hypotheses about generalization gradients, and at present these would be very difficult to formulate.

Consider, for example, a person who has been trained to copy a curling movement of their left index finger and is now learning to copy a curling motion of the left ring finger. Will this person's prior training help them, via generalization, more or less than if it had involved imitation of a curling movement of the right ring finger, a curling movement of the third toe on either foot, or a rigid, up-and-down movement of the left ring finger? We don't know, and we have no firm basis for making a prediction because the action "curling a finger" is not part of a known scale.

19.4 Associative Sequence Learning

ASL theory (Heyes and Ray 2000) is an associative model that includes elements of Holt's (1931) contiguity theory and of Skinner's (1953) and Miller and Dollard's (1941) reinforcement theories. However, unlike behaviorist accounts, it postulates that a significant proportion of the information underlying imitation is acquired by observational learning—that is, learning that is behaviorally silent. In this sense, it could be said to be a cognitive, as well as an associative, theory.

Although rudimentary, ASL theory makes testable predictions (see Heyes and Ray 2000). Its primary purpose is to stimulate the development of other testable models of imitation, associative and transformational, to guide analytic experiments.

Action Units

ASL theory is schematically represented in figure 19.1. It assumes that, rather than being unitary, the vast majority of actions comprise sequences of component actions or "action units." Thus, while it is conventional to think and speak of "an action" being imitated, ASL assumes that it is always a sequence of action units that is imitated. The hand icons at the top of figure 19.1 represent a sequence of hand movements: pointing, followed by splaying the fingers, followed by a victory sign. This action sequence will be used for illustrative purposes, but two considerations should be borne in mind. First, the action units involved in any given case of imitation may be smaller (e.g., closing one finger toward the palm) or larger (e.g., incorporating pointing and splaying). Second, ASL theory applies to relatively perceptually opaque actions such as

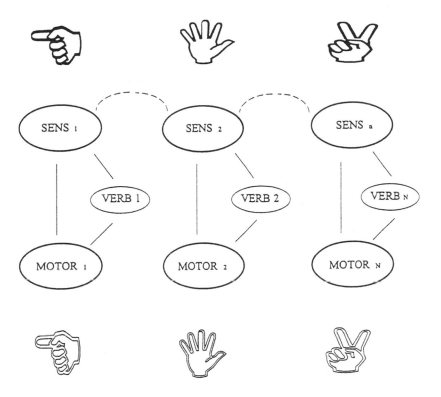

Figure 19.1   Associative sequence learning (ASL) theory of imitation.

facial expressions, as well as to relatively perceptually transparent actions such as hand movements.

Horizontal Processes

Suppose that an observer sees this set of hand movements in this order (point, splay, victory) for the first time—that is, the *sequence* is novel. ASL theory suggests that two sets of associative processes, resulting in "horizontal" and "vertical" links, determine whether and to what extent the observer will be able to imitate the sequence. Through the horizontal processes, associations are formed that link sensory, in this case visual, representations of the action units in the sequence ($\text{SENS}_{1...n}$). These visual representations may be associated with one another in a chain, such that, for example, activation of SENS_1 activates SENS_2 directly, but studies of list learning in humans have shown that such chaining models seldom apply (Henson et al. 1996). It is more likely that the horizontal processes conform to a context-based model (see Brown

1997 for review), in which sensory representations of successive action units become associated with successive states of a time-varying context or control signal, such as the output of an internal clock. This distinction, between chaining and context-based horizontal association, is not crucial for the present purposes, but the lines connecting sensory representations in figure 19.1 are dashed and curved to signify that context-based association is more likely to occur.

Through the horizontal processes, the observer could be said to learn what the action sequence "looks like"; the observer learns a stimulus sequence. For example, if the observer were given a jumbled set of cards each showing an action component (Carroll and Bandura 1982), they would be able to pick out the components that appeared in the sequence and put those cards in the appropriate order. However, the horizontal processes are not unique to imitation (formation of visual representations, and their association with one another, proceeds as in other cases where the individual learns a sequence of visual stimuli) and they are not sufficient to enable the observer to reproduce the novel action sequence. For imitation of the observed action sequence, the vertical processes are also necessary.

Vertical Processes

The vertical processes typically operate before the novel sequence is observed, and result in a sensory representation of each action component (e.g., $SENS_1$), formed through action observation, becoming associated with a motor representation of the same component (e.g., $MOTOR_1$). In accordance with recent neurophysiological evidence that action representations combine somatosensory information with motor commands (e.g., Jeannerod et al. 1995), ASL theory assumes that motor representations encode kinesthetic feedback from performance of the action unit and/or a motor program. What is important is that ASL assumes that a motor representation of an action unit can be formed only through performance of that unit, and therefore that the functioning of the vertical processes is such that the accuracy of imitative performance is directly related to the proportion of the components in an action sequence executed prior to sequence observation.

Vertical processes can result in sensory (formed through action observation) and motor (formed through action execution) representations becoming associated directly or indirectly. Direct associations are formed when an action unit is contiguously observed and executed, seen and done. There are three major sources of such experience: self-observation, mirrors, and synchronous action. Self-observation provides the kind of contiguous experience that will support imitation only for relatively perceptually transparent actions. For example, when an observer looks at her hand while moving her fingers, she receives contiguous experience of seeing and doing the finger movements. Mirrors and synchronous action (i.e., performing the same action at the same time as another individual) provide contiguous experience of observing and executing perceptually opaque as well as perceptually transparent actions. Behavioral synchrony may result from imitation of the observer by the model, or simultaneous responding to a common environmental stimulus.

Indirect links between sensory and motor representations of the same action unit are formed when a second stimulus, distinct from sensory input arising from observation of the action unit itself, is consistently paired on some occasions with sensory input from the action unit, and on other occasions with performance of that unit. This is the "acquired equivalence" route (Hall 1996) to imitation, and in humans the second stimulus is usually a word or phrase ($VERB_{1...n}$).

Summary of ASL Theory

ASL theory suggests that imitation consists of the reproduction of a succession of action units, the sequence of which is novel—that is, that prior to imitative performance, the observer has not executed the action units in the modeled order. It postulates that two sets of associative, contiguity-based processes are necessary for imitation. The horizontal processes operate during observation of the novel action sequence and do not require any overt action on the part of the observer. Hence, this is an associative, but not a behaviorist theory. The horizontal processes (which also operate when information is acquired about the serial order of nonaction stimuli) mediate observational (i.e., behaviorally silent; Dickinson 1980) learning of what the sequence "looks like," but are not sufficient to support imitation.[3] Reproduction of the action sequence will be possible to the extent that sensory representations of the sequence components have become associated, via vertical processes, with motor representations of the same components. Associations of this kind are formed when, in the course of self-observation, mirror exposure, and/or synchronous action, the observer contiguously observes and executes an action unit, or through acquired equivalence training—that is, experience in which observation and execution of an action unit have each been paired with a common stimulus such as a word or phrase. To the extent that such vertical links have been formed, exposure to the novel action sequence, or recollection of that sequence mediated by the horizontal processes, will activate motor representations in the order appropriate for sequence reproduction—that is, imitation. This activation gives the learner the potential to imitate the observed action sequence (represented by the bottom row of icons in figure 19.1), the information necessary to reproduce the action sequence.

It is beyond the scope of this article to survey evidence relating to ASL theory (see Heyes and Ray 2000), but one exception may help to illustrate its claims: ASL theory implies that "canonical neurons" in area F5 of monkey premotor cortex (i.e., neurons that are active only when the animal is executing one type of action) become "mirror neurons" (i.e., acquire the property of being activated by both observation and execution of this type of action) through vertical processes, and specifically through contiguous experience of observing and executing the action (Rizzolatti et al. 1988). For example, certain mirror neurons have been found to respond when a monkey grasps an object and when it observes a human grasping an object, but not when a mechanical claw effects object displacement. If the ASL hypothesis is correct, these neurons would begin to respond to all three categories of input if the monkey were allowed repeatedly to grasp the object just after watching the mechanical claw operate, and they would cease to respond during observation of grasping by a human if the monkey was systematically prevented from grasping the object after watching a human do so.

Learning and Performance

It is important to note that ASL theory is a theory of imitative learning or competence, not of imitative performance. It specifies inputs and processes that result in an observer being able to imitate a novel sequence of action units, but just because the observer *can* imitate, it does not necessarily mean that it *will* imitate. Performance will be governed by additional, motivational processes. However, just as there is no reason to suppose that distinctive perceptual and attentional mechanisms operate on sensory input from body-movement stimuli, there is no reason to assume that imitative performance is regulated by special motivational processes. Some of the nonimitative behavior of people and animals is reflexive or habitual, while other nonimitative behavior is goal directed (see Dickinson 1994, for discussion), and it is likely that imitative behavior represents a similar combination. Thus, in some species and circumstances, if the processes specified by ASL have taken place, exposure to a novel action sequence may be sufficient to elicit imitation of that sequence. In other taxa and conditions, imitative performance (but not imitative learning) may depend on a representation of the consequences of the observed action, or even on a "metarepresentation" (Whiten and Byrne 1991)—that is, a representation of the demonstrator's representation of the consequences of the action. Thus, ASL theory is not necessarily inconsistent with research emphasizing the goal directedness or intentionality of imitation (e.g., Tomasello and Call 1997; Whiten and Byrne 1991). This research is concerned primarily with the motivation to imitate, not, as in ASL theory, with the origins of the information necessary to achieve behavior matching.

19.5   Conclusion

Contemporary empirical research on imitation in human infants and nonhuman animals is concerned almost exclusively with demonstrating imitative capacity. It is hoped that the foregoing survey of theories will assist animal and artifact researchers in adjusting this focus by formulating testable hypotheses about the mechanisms of imitative learning, and subjecting them to analytic experiments.

Notes

1. Strictly speaking, it is psychological mechanisms, rather than theories, that are either transformational or associative. However, a theory may be classified as, for example, transformational, if all or the majority of the mechanisms that it postulates are transformational. Clear examples of each type of theory are those that postulate only one of the two kinds of mechanism.

2. Mowrer's (1960) associative theory of imitation combines contiguity- and reinforcement-based processes. Although it provides a promising account of vocal imitation and imitation of other perceptually transparent actions, Mowrer's model was not chosen as an

example of an associative theory because it contains transformational elements and, more important, clearly does not apply to perceptually opaque actions.

3. Within the framework of ASL theory, Byrne's (1999) string-parsing theory of imitation is concerned exclusively with horizontal processes, sequential analysis of observed action, and does not propose a mechanism fulfilling the function of the vertical processes—that is, effecting performance of the observed action.

References

Allport, F. H. *Social Psychology*. Cambridge, MA: Riverside, 1924.

Aronfreed, J. The problem of imitation. *Advances in Child Development and Behavior* 4: 209–319, 1969.

Bandura, A. *Social Foundations of Thought and Action: A Social Cognitive Theory*. Englewood Cliffs, NJ: Prentice Hall, 1986.

Brown, G. D. A. Formal models of memory for serial order. In M. A. Conway, ed., *Cognitive Models of Memory*. Psychology Press, 1997.

Byrne, R. W. Imitation without intentionality: Using string passing to copy the organization of behaviour. *Animal Cognition* 2: 43–72, 1999.

Carroll, W. R., and A. Bandura. The role of visual monitoring in observational learning of action patterns: Making the unobservable observable. *Journal of Motor Behavior* 14: 153–167, 1982.

Dickinson, A. *Contemporary Animal Learning Theory*. Cambridge, UK: Cambridge University Press, 1980.

Dickinson, A. Instrumental conditioning. In N. J. Mackintosh, ed., *Handbook of Perception and Cognition (Second Edition): Animal Learning and Cognition*. San Diego: Academic Press, 1994.

Guthrie, E. R. *The Psychology of Learning*. New York: Harper, 1935.

Hall, G. Learning about associatively activated stimulus representations: Implications for acquired equivalence and perceptual learning. *Animal Learning and Behavior* 24: 233–255, 1996.

Henson, R. N. A., D. G. Norris, M. P. A. Page, and A. D. Baddeley. Unchained memory: Error patterns rule out chaining models of immediate serial recall. *Quarterly Journal of Experimental Psychology* 19: 80–115, 1996.

Heyes, C. M. *Imitation*. Book manuscript in preparation for Oxford University Press, 1999.

Heyes, C. M. Evolutionary psychology in the round. In C. M. Heyes and L. Huber, eds., *Evolution of Cognition*. MIT Press (in press).

Heyes, C. M. and E. D. Ray. What is the significance of imitation in animals? *Advances in the Study of Behavior* 29: 215–245, 2000.

Holt, E. B. *Animal Drive and the Learning Process* (vol. 1). New York: Holt, 1931.

Humphrey, G. Imitation and the conditioned reflex. *Pediatric Seminar* 28: 1–21, 1921.

Jeannerod, M., M. A. Arbib, G. Rizzolatti, and H. Sakata. Grasping objects: The cortical mechanisms of visuomotor transformation. *Trends in Neurosciences* 18: 314–320, 1995.

Meltzoff, A. N., and M. K. Moore. Imitation of facial and manual gestures by human neonates. *Science* 198: 75–78, 1977.

Meltzoff, A. N., and M. K. Moore. Persons and representations: Why infant imitation is important for theories of human development. In J. Nadel and G. Butterworth, eds., *Imitation in Infancy*. Cambridge, UK: Cambridge University Press, 1999.

Miller, N. E., and J. Dollard. *Social Learning and Imitation*. New Haven: Yale University Press, 1941.

Mowrer, O. H. *Learning Theory and the Symbolic Processes*. New York: Wiley, 1960.

Piaget, J. *Play, Dreams and Imitation in Childhood*. New York: Norton, 1951.

Rizzolatti, G., R. Camarda, L. Fogassi, M. Gentilucci, G. Luppino, and M. Matelli. Functional organization of inferior area 6 in the macaque monkey. II: Area F5 and the control of distal movements. *Experimental Brain Research* 71: 491–507, 1988.

Skinner, B. F. *Science and Human Behavior*. New York: Free Press, 1953.

Thorndike, E. L. Animal intelligence. *Psychological Review Monographs* 2, no. 8, 1898.

Tomasello, M. Two hypotheses about primate cognition. In C. M. Heyes and L. Huber, eds., *Evolution of Cognition*. Cambridge, MA: MIT Press (in press).

Tomasello, M., and J. Call. *Primate Cognition*. Oxford: Oxford University Press, 1997.

Watson, J. B. *Psychology from the Standpoint of a Behaviorist*. Philadelphia: Lippincott, 1919.

Watson, J. B. *Behaviorism*. New York: Norton, 1925.

Whiten, A., and R. W. Byrne. The emergence of metarepresentation in human ontogeny and primate phylogeny. In A. Whiten and R. W. Byrne, eds., *Natural Theories of Mind*. Basil Blackwell, 1991.

20 Dimensions of Imitative Perception-Action Mediation

Stefan Vogt

20.1 Introduction

Imitating the actions of others is often seen as a basic, primary mode of behavior. Newborns cannot do much, but the facial expressions they can make they can also imitate (Meltzoff and Moore 1997). When frontal lobe damage "liberates" parietal lobe activity, patients become strongly dependent on external stimuli, and, unlike normal subjects, they tend to imitate an examiner's gestures (Lhermitte, Pillon, and Serdaru 1986), as if a primitive mode of behavior is unlocked through loss of prefrontal lobe inhibition. Eidelberg (1929) demonstrated that when normal subjects are given verbal commands that conflict with simultaneous, irrelevant gestural displays (e.g., "point to your nose," and experimenter pointing to a lamp), they often follow the irrelevant gesture—that is, they imitate, rather than do what they are told. In his recent survey, Kinsbourne (in press) summarized: "Imitation is inherent in the organization of the central nervous system and may have to be restrained for nonimitative responses to occur." Particularly when perception is seen as enactive—that is, coupled to the observer's motor repertoire—imitating the actions of others seems to follow naturally from perceiving them, as if imitation is just "uninhibited perception" (Kinsbourne, in press).

These examples lead us to expect a close linkage between perceiving and producing action, and possibly a dedicated mechanism of imitative perception-action mediation. Still, imitation is neither ubiquitous nor necessarily easy. It is surprisingly sparse in animals (Köhler 1924; Visalberghi and Fragaszy, chapter 18 of this volume), despite its demonstration in certain cases. Infant imitation is not compulsory (Meltzoff and Moore 1997), provoking interference effects from action displays requires subtle experimental setups, and everybody knows that the mastery of sports or musical skills can take years rather than seconds—despite ample opportunities to watch expert performers. Finally, sustained imitation in social interaction would be, well, pretty boring.

Thus, how direct or basic imitation is depends very much on the context in which it is considered. In this chapter, I seek to make this context explicit through describing a number of dimensions along which imitative behaviors can be distinguished descriptively and theoretically. It will become clear that the term *imitation* embraces a multiplicity of phenomena, and that different perceptual and motor mechanisms may operate in each case. Without a detailed knowledge of the particular mechanisms involved, generalizations about imitation per se appear premature.

Nevertheless, times are exciting for imitation researchers. The widely known discovery of "mirror neurons" by Rizzolatti and colleagues (Rizzolatti et al. 1996a; Arbib, chapter 10 of this volume) has indicated that motor cortical areas are not only involved in preparing one's own movements but also when observing the actions of others. Once motor processes are involved in observation, the step toward reproducing the observed action appears small. Accordingly, the "mirror system" has been suggested to form the neural substrate for imitation and observational learning (Jeannerod 1994, 1997). Does reproducing a seen action just require a full activation of the motor representations that were already primed during observation? We will see that such a view is likely to be incomplete.

The question of how action is informed by perception (*perception-action mediation* for short) is a core issue for cognitive-psychological imitation research. The demonstration of the mirror system in monkeys and humans has highlighted the possibility that this mediation may occur at a very early stage and not only during preparation of the imitative response, as was implicitly assumed in a number of theories of imitation and observational learning. This issue of *early versus late mediation* is a central theme in this chapter and is pursued in each of the following sections. In section 20.2, I discuss three major descriptive distinctions of different forms of imitation: observational learning versus reproducing familiar actions, on-line versus deferred imitation, and levels of display complexity. In section 20.3, I focus on two theoretical distinctions: sensory and motor representations, and semantic and visuomotor mediation. Throughout the chapter I refer to experimental work, which is mainly used to illustrate the distinctions made and not meant to provide an exhaustive review. I also seek to make plausible the somewhat moderate ambitions of current cognitive-psychological research on imitation, which is predominantly concerned with rather simple displays and imitative responses, including our present work. In section 20.4, I turn to neurophysiological findings about the involvement of motor processes in action observation and discuss their significance for understanding imitation on the background developed. Despite the multifaceted character of imitation, I hope to show that important steps in our understanding of certain forms of imitation have been made, and point out where further research is most needed and promising.

20.2 Dimensions of Imitative Actions

Observational Learning of Novel Actions versus Reproducing Familiar Actions

The distinction between novel and familiar actions is so consequential that in certain branches of imitation research, the reproduction of familiar actions is excluded from the definition of imitation, that is, novelty is used as a defining feature (Byrne and Russon 1998). In the psychological and neuropsychological literature, normally a wider definition of imitation is used, which can refer to novel *and* familiar actions, and the term *observational learning* is reserved for imitative skill acquisition. Clearly, learning skills from observing others is a powerful factor in skill acquisition and development, and understanding the cognitive processes involved here is possibly the ultimate challenge in imitation research. It is not an easy one to tackle, however.

Our initial research on observational learning has shown that the model display is normally only one among a large number of factors that have an impact on imitative performance. When participants were asked to repeatedly reproduce a sequence of large and small cursor oscillations using a hand-held lever (figure 20.1, left panel), we were initially surprised about the precise match in the temporal structure of model and subjects' reproductions (Vogt, Stadler, and Kruse 1988). In the second experiment, we therefore altered the temporal structure of the model pattern toward isochrony (same duration for large and small cycles). Subjects' reproductions still showed the same covariation of amplitude and cycle duration as in the first study. That is, they now systematically deviated from the model pattern, and did so even after more than 100 demonstrations/reproductions. Whereas the precise match we

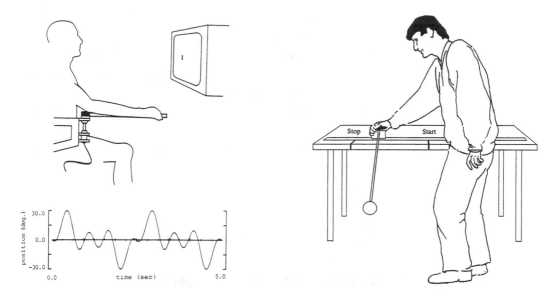

Figure 20.1 Two tasks used in studies on observational learning. (Left) A sequence of horizontal cursor movements with different amplitudes is shown on a monitor (example position-time plot in lower left panel). Using a hand-held lever, the sequence either reproduced in direct succession or after a number of demonstrations (Vogt et al., 1988; Vogt, 1995). (Right) A pendulum is to be moved quickly from start to stop with minimal swing remaining at the stop position (Vogt, 1996a). Observing a skilled performer for 60 trials produced similar improvements as physical practice.

had observed before could have been interpreted as a result of copying, the second experiment uncovered that the covariation of amplitude and cycle duration was simply a natural way of performing the task (an organismic constraint), which subjects produce irrespective of its presence in the display.[1] Thus, possible *shared organismic constraints* between model and imitator, and not the display alone, must be taken into account when deciding if a particular aspect of imitative performance is based on a representation of the model. Another class of constraints that affect imitative performance besides the model are *environmental constraints*— that is, objects and surfaces in the environment to which our actions are attuned (for the concept of constraints see Newell 1985, 1991). For example, when I try to imitate a badminton smash, I may base my performance on a representation of the model's action, but I must also process information about the approaching shuttle, as well as information about my position in the court. A good part of mastery in a skill depends on how such environmental information is used to control action, and this is not transparent from merely observing a model. Thus, many constraints impinge on imitative performance, not just on the model display.

Further, providing demonstrations in sports training schemes is normally accompanied by a host of other methods such as verbal instructions, physical practice, and various forms of feedback (McCullagh, Weiss, and Ross 1989; Schmidt and Lee 1999). In studies that compared individual training methods, demonstrations alone have sometimes been shown to be no more effective than discovery learning (e.g., Vereijken and Whiting 1990). Vereijken and Whiting suggested that the availability of a model when exploring a new apparatus (a ski simulator in their study) may actually distract subjects from focusing on exploring the dynamics of the task (i.e., required forces), since only the kinematics are conveyed through observation. To say the least, effects of observational learning are task specific. In two studies where we compared the effects of pure observational periods with other types of practice, results were more encouraging.

In the first study (Vogt 1995a), subjects were repeatedly shown a similar sequential pattern as we used before, and were either allowed to reproduce the pattern after each trial, to imagine it, or to count backwards in steps of three. To our surprise, the latter, "pure" observational practice condition produced similar effects on posttest performance as the other conditions. This was not only so for global measures of pattern similarity, but also for temporal consistency—a more fine-grained measure of motor output that is normally seen to increase only with physical practice. A further experiment confirmed the equivalence of observational, mental, and physical practice in this task by demonstrating superior performance of these practice groups over a control group that watched an irrelevant pattern. We concluded that motor processes may not only be involved during mental or physical practice, but also during repeated observation of a—at least partially—familiar pattern. In some observational trials, subjects briefly closed their eyes during the display period, only to see if their motor plan of the pattern was still correct when they opened their eyes again. This further supported the notion that model observation is an active process that involves predictive representations on the side of the observer.

In the second learning study (Vogt 1996a), we were interested to see if effects of observational practice could also be found in a task that requires an exploration of task characteristics to a greater extent than the learning of sequential movements. Neisser (1983) had argued that exploring the "medium" of a skill (e.g., the relevant physical properties of a tennis racket) cannot be done in mental practice, and we reckoned that a similar limitation may exist for observational learning. In our task, subjects had to move the pivot of a pendulum along a linear track so that the pendulum stood still again when the target position was reached (figure 20.1, right panel). Mastery of this task requires a biphasic movement that is precisely attuned to the pendulum's inertia and swing duration. We found that a group that just observed a skilled model for 60 trials showed improvements in posttest performance (28.8%), similar to that of a physical practice group (without model observation, 29.5%). In contrast, no improvements were observed in a control group (−6%). Two principles may explain this exploratory effect of observational learning—*visuomotor couplings* and *gradual correction*. As in the earlier study, it is likely that subjects activated their own motor repertoire when observing the model, which allowed for the formation of an appropriate motor plan. Furthermore, observers should then be able to detect divergencies between their plan and the model, and use these for gradual corrections either in the current trial or when preparing the next (overt or covert) performance. Similarly, Meltzoff and Moore (1997) stress that infants' imitations are seldom perfect from the start; moreover, they gradually correct their imitative attempts in a series of ordered steps. Adult imitation may involve an internalization of this process and may thus act as a shortcut in exploring unfamiliar tasks.

These examples indicate that effects of pure observational practice can be shown under controlled conditions in a range of tasks. The observation that effects extend to variables such as consistency of motor output, which have previously been seen to depend largely on overt physical practice, was interpreted as evidence for an early perception-action mediation that occurs already during model observation. In addition, the examples demonstrate that observational learning is not an effortless one-off operation but includes complex, covert correction processes, which are only gradually different from trial-and-error learning. The presence of a model "improves the situation" (Koffka 1925), but there is still a lot left to be done. It is presently not known to what extent motor structures are involved in the initial stage of observational skill acquisition when the displayed action is largely unfamiliar, but when at least segments of the pattern are familiar, we have good reason to believe that motor structures become involved and then benefit from repeated model observation.

In our current research (see section 20.4), we have moved away from observational learning to focus on the imitation of simple actions that are already in the behavioral repertoire of the observer. A similar focus on the "here and now" can also be found in other recent cognitive-psychological research on imitation (e.g., Bekkering and Prinz, chapter 21 of this volume; Prinz, in press). One reason for this may be that learning studies imply a rather long delay (of minutes or even hours) between the process of interest (display observation) and assessing its effects in posttest performance. For a microanalysis of the cognitive mechanisms of perception-action mediation, a more direct probing of the stages involved in reproducing a single action display is desirable. Furthermore, one may well ask how we should be able to understand the coding of novel actions when we have not yet fully understood how a single, familiar action is perceived and reproduced. Finally, the process of skill learning, of which observational learning is only one part, is per se less well understood than processes of preparation and execution of highly practiced actions such as prehension (see Jeannerod 1997). It would seem logical to expect that we are in a better position for understanding model-based skill acquisition once imitation of familiar actions is better understood (see discussion in Whiting, Vogt, and Vereiken 1992).

On-Line versus Deferred Imitation

When the interval between display and reproduction is short, model and imitator move in near synchrony (on-line imitation), or with only a brief delay in between (short-term deferred imitation). In other experiments, even a week-long delay has been used between demonstration and reproduction (Meltzoff 1988). Although it is more likely to find on-line imitation with familiar actions, and deferred imitation in the context of observational learning, specific aspects of a skill may well be learned during synchronous performance (e.g., in dance or skiing), and deferred imitation can, of course, include familiar actions.

Different intervals impose different constraints on perception-action mediation. Whereas on-line imitation requires an immediate perception-action coupling on the side of the observer, in deferred imitation there is, by definition, no need for an immediate response. For deferred imitation, it is therefore possible to assume temporally distinct stages of perceptual processing and a later "translation" of the resulting (verbal or iconic) representation into action (e.g., Carroll and Bandura 1990; Keele 1986). The theoretical alternative that, also in deferred imitation, a motor representation is already formed during observation, has been neglected in a good part of imitation research up to the early 1990s. One way of deciding between these alternatives is to examine possible performance advantages when subjects are explicitly asked to form a motor representation in the interval between display and reproduction. In a deferred imitation paradigm (Vogt 1996b), subjects reproduced, either immediately or after a brief delay, the relative timing of a two-cycle movement, which was displayed on a monitor and could vary between 1:1 and 2.5:1 (setup as in figure 20.1, left panel). The main finding from this study was that timing imitation did not benefit from any intermediate imaginal or physical rehearsal in the interval between presentation and reproduction. Although this result is well in line with the idea that motor processes were already involved during observation (and did not require additional rehearsal), it is also open to other interpretations. Specifically, perception-action mediation in timing tasks may be achieved via a dedicated, amodal timing mechanism rather than via a direct sensorimotor link. The idea of an isolable timing mechanism that can be employed by different motor and perceptual systems has been supported in a series of studies by Keele and colleagues (Ivry and Keele 1989; see also Ivry and Hazeltine 1995). Further, in tests with a range of neurological patients, Ivry and Keele (1989) found that only patients with cerebellar lesions were significantly impaired on perceptual and motor tasks, and suggested that the timing mechanism is likely to involve a loop between cortex and cerebellum.

To summarize, our deferred imitation study has confirmed the possibility of an early perception-action mediation to some extent. The results can, however, also be explained by a dedicated timing mechanism (T) that is shared between perceptual (P) and motor (M) tasks. This can be expressed as (P-T) for observation and (T-M) for reproduction, whereas direct sensorimotor links would imply (P-M) for observation and (M) or (P-M) for reproduction. More generally speaking, imitation tasks that involve delays between display and reproduction often give rise to more than one account of perception-action mediation (see also Sensory and Motor Representations in section 20.3). In contrast, on-line imitation paradigms allow a more clear-cut interpretation regarding any motor involvement during perception, since this involvement is forced and directly observable in overt behavior.

Three Levels of Display Complexity

Regarding the displays used in research on action perception and imitation, at least three levels of complexity can be distinguished: (1) *sequences of actions*, (2) *individual actions*, and (3) *parameters of a given action*. Typical for the latter case are experiments where only, for example, the target of pointing action or the orientation of a grasping hand are varied from trial to trial. In contrast, when a pointing action is shown in one trial and a grasping action in another trial, the imitator has to select between different actions (level 2). Sequences of actions (1) are the most complex display type. Let us consider the control and imitation of such actions in greater detail.

Byrne and Russon (1998) have recently proposed a new look on the issue of whether an animal can imitate, which is grounded in their analyses of complex sequential behavior in great apes. Building on earlier work on the hierarchical organization of human behavior (Lashley 1951; Miller, Galanter, and Pribram 1960; see Rosenbaum 1991), they demonstrate that food preparation techniques of mountain gorillas show evidence of hierarchical organization, where behavior is controlled by a modifiable structure of goals and subgoals rather than by the linear association of elementary actions (see also Whiten, chapter 8 of this volume). From comparing the food preparation techniques within and between different populations, Byrne and Russon conclude that the propagation of a particular technique within a population likely relies on imitation, but that it is primarily the organization of goals and subgoals—that is, the hierarchcal structure—that is copied ("program-level imitation"), rather than a linear chain of actions or the precise details of the individual manual actions. Although the authors suspect that great apes are also capable of imitating at the latter level ("action-level imitation"), the idiosyncrasies found in the details of the individual actions of each animal make it likely that these were acquired by trial and error. The line between program- and action-level imitation is not an easy one to draw, however, since a perfect copy of kinematic details, or even muscle twitches, is never achieved, and since also action-level imitation may rely on structural organization (Vogt and Carey 1998). Already, in his discussion of lower-level imitation, Koffka (1925) pointed out that "even here, if one compares the movement imitated with its imitation, it is the integrated movement-melody of each which stands forth as being the common element. A photographic reproduction of the separate movements involved is never found" (p. 308 f.).

Also, work with human subjects indicates that hierarchically organized behavior can be learned through observation (e.g., Howard, Mutter, and Howard 1992; Kohl and Shea 1992; see Vogt 1995a). In the sequencing experiments described above, we repeatedly showed the same display. This resembles situations in formation dancing or musical performance, where the serial order of events is part of the task. However, a learner may also be confronted with sequences of actions that are not identical from trial to trial but that show flexibility regarding certain elements but not others. It would be interesting to study if this variability across demonstrations makes observational learning more difficult, or if it even facilitates the identification of mandatory and optional states to be achieved (see figure 5 in Byrne and Russon 1998).

There are at least two ways in which motor processes can be involved in observational learning of action sequences: parsing for elements, and genuine sequence learning. When an observer has the elementary actions within an observed sequence already in her or his behavioral repertoire, it is only their organization that needs to be learned. Still, also in program-level imitation, parsing the stream of behavior in the display for constituent elements is a prerequisite for reconstructing their serial order. Linking the observed behavior with the observer's own action capabilities should facilitate this parsing. As yet, however, little is known about the involvement of motor processes in parsing, since mainly displays of individual and predictable actions were used in the available neurophysiological studies (see section 20.4). Second, making predictions about the next element(s) in a sequence, as subjects reported in our sequence-learning study (Vogt 1995a), can be seen as generative involvement on a higher level and is an integral part of sequence learning.

The perceptual processing of elementary actions, as apparent in parsing, can also be studied in isolation, namely when displays of *individual actions* are shown (level 2). Surprisingly little cognitive-psychological research has been done where subjects are asked to directly copy a single action without prior knowledge about which action will be shown. In the study of object-guided actions, Rumiati and Humphreys (1998, discussed below) have developed an experimental paradigm wherein subjects are shown pictures of various individual objects and are to make the appropriate gesture of how this object is normally used. Similar experiments, but involving action displays, would provide valuable insights about imitative actions, both with and without employment of brain-imaging techniques.

Displays that vary only regarding certain *parameters* may be located at the lower end of display complexity (level 3). Here, the imitator has advance knowledge about the type of action shown in the next trial, and is required to adjust only certain aspects of his performance, such as target location or hand orientation, to the display. Accordingly, the imitator can engage in partial motor preparation even before the display is shown, whereas this is normally not possible when different individual actions are shown. The way in which parametric variations of action displays have an impact on motor control has been studied in a number of recent behavioral experiments, which are described in the next section.

20.3 Theoretical Issues

Sensory and Motor Representations

An observed action can be represented in the form of a dynamic visual image of model and/or observer. Representations of dynamic (i.e., temporally extended) events can also be formed for other sensory modalities (auditory, proprioceptive), but I will mainly consider visual processing here. An observed action can also be represented in a purely motor format—that is, in terms of the motor commands the observer needs to generate in order to match the model's action (see Jeannerod 1994, for the distinction between visual and motor representations). As noted above, in most theories of imitation and observational learning up to the early 1990s, sensory or more abstract cognitive representations have been explicitly or implicitly favored over motor representations (e.g., Carroll and Bandura 1990; Keele 1986; Meltzoff 1988).

Further, these authors have assumed that these representations are "translated" into action only when the observer is going to physically reproduce the displayed action. I have referred to this view as *late mediation* between perception and action, whereas the discovery of mirror neurons, and the behavioral evidence reported above, have recently given credit to *early mediation* accounts (see also Vogt, in press).

Early and late mediation need not be seen as mutually exclusive. That is, evidence for the (early) involvement of motor structures in action observation does not exclude the possibility that nonmotor representations continue to play a role during the (later) imitative performance. As noted by Adams (1987, p. 63), cognitive representations have been assigned a dual role in Bandura's (1986) theory, namely, (1) to *guide* the observer's imitative behavior, and (2) to serve as a *standard of correctness* for the detection of deviations between imitative performance and the represented model. Indeed, Meltzoff and Moore's (1997) observations of gradual corrections in infant imitation are difficult to explain without assuming some form of memory of the observed act that is distinct from the preparatory and executive motor processes on the side of the imitator. Also, the first role of cognitive representations, namely, to be causally involved in the concurrent guidance of performance, may be a viable characterization of certain imitation tasks. That is, a visual image of an observed action may be sufficient to guide the observer's reproduction at a later point in time. However, such cognitive guidance appears unnecessary when the motor system of the observer is already fully informed about the desired action, for which the most likely cases are on-line and briefly deferred imitation.

Thus, sensory and motor representations may well coexist, and their roles may be different depending on the interval between demonstration and reproduction, the familiarity of the action, or the complexity of the display. Nevertheless, it should be possible to precisely identify these roles for a given task. Steps in this direction have recently been undertaken in a series of studies by Bekkering, Prinz, and coworkers.

The studies by Brass, Bekkering, and Prinz (in press), and by Stürmer, Aschersleben, and Prinz (2000) employed interference paradigms similar to the study by Eidelberg (1929) mentioned above, known *as stimulus-response compatibility* (SRC) paradigms (e.g., Hommel and Prinz 1997). In Stürmer, Aschersleben, and Prinz's experiments (2000), subjects were instructed to open or close the fingers of their right hand depending on the color of a stimulus shown on a monitor. This stimulus was a hand that either performed the same movement as was signaled by the color (compatible trials), or the opposite movement (incompatible trials). The hand movement was to be ignored by the subjects. A common trick in compatibility experiments is to use imperative stimuli (here: color) that are only linked arbitrarily to the response. They are often processed relatively slowly (for color, see Pisella, Arzi, and Rossetti 1998). In contrast, the irrelevant stimulus dimension (here: movement of the hand) is typically more closely related to the required response, and is often processed more quickly. As may be expected then, in Stürmer's study, subject's latency in responding to the color of the display was modulated by the irrelevant hand movement shown. For example, opening the hand was initiated faster when an opening hand was shown. Further, when only static pictures of the end positions of the irrelevant stimulus were displayed (opened or closed hand) in a subsequent experiment, effects were at least as pronounced as with the moving hand display. One explanation of the latter finding is that more clear-cut information (though irrelevant) was available earlier in time; another is that action planning may involve anticipated end postures (Rosenbaum et al. 1995), and that the static stimuli have thus specifically interfered with this aspect of action planning.

But why does a task-irrelevant display of a moving or static hand at all affect the performance of similar hand movements by the observer, when she or he is instructed to ignore the seen hand and only to attend to its color? Prinz's (in press) general explanation is that identical representational structures are involved in perception and action (see also Bekkering and Prinz, chapter 21 of this volume; Prinz 1997). With reference to Greenwald's (1970) ideomotor principle, he further suggests that action planning generally sets off from an anticipation of the desired sensory effects, which is associated with motor commands that have produced these effects in the past. Accordingly, when subjects are to choose between hand opening and closing, they first need to translate the relevant stimulus dimension (e.g., blue color) into a desired sensory effect (e.g., image of open hand), which then automatically activates the associated motor commands. When, in such a situation, external stimuli are shown that share features with one of the expected sensory effects, responses are biased toward producing effects that match the external stimuli.

There are at least two ways in which this may occur, *stimulus competition* and *response competition*: It is possible that the irrelevant stimuli compete (respectively, unite) with the internal formation of anticipated effects, but it is also possible that both the internally anticipated and the external stimulus are linked directly to response selection. The latter would produce competition at the response-selection stage. Similar to late and early mediation, these possibilities do not exclude each other. Whereas interference in response selection has been favored in most previous approaches to S-R compatibility, Brass and colleagues (in press) seem to interpret their effects in terms of stimulus competition. Different from Stürmer's task, Brass, Bekkering, and Prinz's (in press) subjects always executed the same finger movement (e.g., lifting) in a block of trials. The imperative stimulus was the movement onset of one finger of a displayed hand, and the irrelevant stimulus dimension was, for example, if this finger moved up or down. Even in this simple-response task, they observed marked compatibility effects. In clever subsequent experiments, this effect could be decomposed into a directional component (up vs. down) and a movement-type component (lifting vs. tapping). Brass, Bekkering, and Prinz conclude that the latter component "can be best described as a match between the event perceived and the representation of what one intends to do, that is, an anticipation of the sensory consequences of the planned action" (in press). Nevertheless, an explanation in terms of response competition would accommodate their results equally well and without implicating anticipated effects in the control of simple response tasks. Clearly, more work is needed in order to decide between stimulus and response competition explanations of these findings.

What do these considerations tell us about the cognitive processes involved in imitative actions? The latter differ from the described interference tasks in at least two respects. First, attentional demands are radically different. In interference tasks, subjects try to ignore what they attend to in imitation tasks. Thus, although interference effects are powerful demonstrations of involuntary perception-action mediation, it is likely that imitation tasks exhibit a wider range of couplings than detectable in interference tasks. For example, whereas subjects may well be able to imitate a movement's temporal structure, timing-specific interference effects may be hard to find. Second, the response alternatives in interference tasks are highly restricted, normally to one or two. This should strongly direct both motor preparation and visual processing—the latter possibly in the sense of reentrant visual selectivity (Craighero et al. 1999). In contrast, this degree of motor directedness is not typical for imitation, where the displayed action is normally not predictable for the observer. Whereas in imitation an early motor involvement in action observation would clearly originate from visual processing (and likely contribute to it), an early motor involvement in interference tasks should, first of all, reflect the restrictedness of the task itself. The latter allows subjects to set up a highly selective visuomotor control system that may be radically different from the openness required in most imitation tasks. Nevertheless, it is possible that anticipated effects play a role in imitation tasks, but this requires further, specific empirical investigation and cannot be concluded from the available interference studies. Conclusions from interference tasks to action imitation are, indeed, difficult to draw.

In summary, sensory and motor representations can play different, overlapping, and similar roles in imitation tasks. Sensory representations are possibly unique in providing a standard of correctness. The other role of sensory or cognitive representations, namely, to guide concurrent imitative behavior ("late mediation"), is less clearcut. For example, it is difficult to see how fast sequential actions, as in musical performance, should be guided by sensory representations. It is also not clear why sensory representations should take a guiding role when a motor representation of the observed action is already in place, as assumed in early mediation accounts.

Semantic and Visuomotor Mediation

Up to this point, I have not used the concepts of "meaning" and "goal-directed imitation," except in the discussion of Byrne and Russon's work. Already Koffka (1925) made the distinction between imitation of a movement or of a series of movements versus imitation of a purposive action to meet the same result, and pointed out the fallacy of ignoring the second type: "For a long time animal-psychologists have looked only for the first of these types (*imitation of a movement, SV*), and when they failed to find it, have concluded that there can be no general capacity for imitation" (p. 308). He then criticizes Thorndike's (1911, p. 89) argument against imitation, namely, the example of a cat that, after observing another cat pulling a loop with the teeth, pulled it with the paws. Pulling the loop appears to be the single objective of imitation here, regardless of the organ used to perform this act. Clearly, Byrne and Russon (1998) have done a good job of defending and elaborating this possibility of higher-level imitation that is focused on the achievement of goals and subgoals rather than the—ultimately impossible—reproduction of muscle twitches. Also, in the domain of robotics, the abstraction from kinematic details in favor of to-be-achieved end states is now recognized as a crucial challenge to be met in models of robot imitation (see Nehaniv and Dautenhahn, 2000, and related chapters in this volume). In psychology, the idea that actions are goal directed and preceded by a representation of what is intended has already been put forward by Lotze (1852) and James (1890) (see Bekkering and Prinz chapter 21 of this volume). Let us consider the possible role of goals for the different types of imitation as distinguished in section 20.2.

Particularly in observational learning, taking insight into the goal of the observed action can be a crucial step toward successful reproduction and may imply a restructuring of the organization of the observer's action. Unfortunately, it is not easy to find unambiguous behavioral equivalents of this process, although developments in dynamical systems theory and synergetics make this a more tangible enterprise than ever before (e.g., Kelso 1995; Newell 1991; Vogt 1998).

When imitating familiar actions, a successful imitation may well involve understanding, but it doesn't have to. The latter possibility has first been demonstrated in neuropsychological studies with apraxic and pantomime agnosic patients. Rothi, Mack, and Heilman (1986) reported patients who, despite being unable to comprehend or discriminate gestures, could nevertheless imitate these gestures—possibly as if these were a series of meaningless movements. Rothi, Ochipa, and Heilman (1997) suggested that these patients bypassed an impaired lexical (i.e., semantic) mediation route and instead used a nonlexical, possibly iconic route that is normally only used for the imitation of meaningless gestures and may be spared in those patients with ideomotor apraxia who show improvements in imitation tasks. A similar argument for a direct, nonsemantic route from vision to motor control was made by Goldenberg and Hagmann (1997), based on a selective deficit of imitation of meaningless gestures found in two apraxic patients, which indicated a selective impairment of this route.

As pointed out before, the imitation of different actions in normal subjects is still one of the blind spots of psychological imitation research. At least, the work by Rumiati and Humphreys (1998) on object-guided actions provides a promising framework for such research. Their subjects had to either quickly name or make a suitable gesture to pictures of a variety of objects. The authors found that the number of visual errors in gesturing (e.g., making a hammering gesture when the picture of a razor was shown) was higher as compared to the naming condition, whereas semantic errors (e.g., a hammering gesture made in response to the picture of a saw) were lower in gesturing. In accordance with their earlier neuropsychological work (e.g., Riddoch and Humphreys 1987), the authors concluded that stored structural descriptions (visual representations) of objects are directly associated with stored action patterns, without requiring access to semantic knowledge ("direct visual route" vs. "semantic route"). They also discuss the possibility that the processing of crucial parts of an object, without recognition of the whole object, may have been sufficient to select an appropriate action in their task. Both interpretations (full or partial descriptions) can explain their results. Similar, yet untested, hypotheses for the imitation of different actions can be put forward, namely, (1) that individual properties of an observed action specify the response in an elementary manner, (2) that a compound visual representation of a displayed gesture directly activates an appropriate action, and (3) that perception and action are mediated via semantic representations.

Whereas the study by Rumiati and Humphreys (1998) is inspiring for work on the on-line imitation of different *actions*, the study by Tucker and Ellis (1998) indicates priming effects of seen objects on the level of motor *parameters*. As did Rumiati and Humphreys, Tucker and Ellis also presented pictures of objects, but they used a compatibility paradigm. In one experimental setup, the relevant stimulus was the upright or inverted presentation of the objects, to which subjects had to respond with a right- or left-hand keypress. The irrelevant stimulus dimension was the horizontal orientation of the object, which afforded either a right- or left-hand grasp. As expected, response times were affected in the sense that right-hand keypresses were faster when the displayed object afforded a right-hand grasp. The authors conclude that seen objects automatically "potentiate" components (respectively, parameters) of the actions they afford. They further suggest that action goals may operate on already existing (partial) motor representations of the possible actions in a visual scene.

When extrapolating from such object-guided to model-guided actions, we might expect that also parametric aspects of an observed action (e.g., its direction or speed) can have an impact on motor preparation independent of, and possibly prior to, intentional goal formation. Indeed, the above-mentioned studies by Brass and colleagues (in press) and Stürmer and colleagues (2000) on model-guided actions have demonstrated such effects, and can be seen as close counterparts to Tucker and Ellis's (1998) work on object-guided actions. In both lines of research, compatibility paradigms were used, and interference effects from irrelevant model or object displays were found. Model- and object-guided actions certainly differ in that the former achieve similarity between observed and performed action, whereas the latter achieve complementarity between object and action. Thus, a challenging task for future research is to identify potential differences between both classes of interference effects and to uncover to what extent the same mechanisms are involved.

From the work described so far, it appears plausible to expect that also in imitation proper, semantic mediation is not the only pathway from perception to action. Given that semantic mediation is possibly the least controversial form of mediation, the primary interest in our present research is to elucidate more direct forms of visuomotor coupling in imitation tasks (Vogt, in press). So far, we have explored the possibility of such visuomotor couplings in two tasks.

In the first study (Vogt 1995b), the timing imitation task as used by Vogt (1996b; see also section 20.2) was extended by two further conditions. In the *naming condition*, subjects had to name the relative timing shown using percentage values between 100% and 250%. In the *production condition*, a percentage value was read to the subjects, and they had to produce the corresponding movement. Both tasks were well practiced before we compared subjects' performance on these two tasks with imitation. If, in the imitation condition, subjects were converting the displayed pattern into a percentage value and then used this symbolic representation to guide their reproduction, errors in imitative performance should derive from the combined error scores in naming and production. This symbolic mediation or "concatenation model" could be rejected. Both on a total error and a residual variable error measure, subjects' imitation performance was significantly more accurate than predicted from the concatenation model. Further, immediate imitation was found to be more accurate than production on verbal command on the residual error score. Correlations between naming and both production and imitation were not significant, whereas the residual error for imitation correlated both with the residual error for production ($r = .59$) and with the combined residual error score ($r = .59$), the latter likely due to the large production component in the combined score. These results indicate that imitative performance did not, or at least not exclusively, rely on verbal/symbolic mediation and thus point toward the involvement of a more direct form of mediation. Sternberg and Knoll (1984) had reached a similar conclusion from a series of tapping studies. Thus, in timing imitation tasks, perception-action mediation does not just rely on verbal labels, even if these are well associated with the visual and motor pattern, but it relies on a more precise sensory, motor, or dedicated timing representation (see discussion in section 20.2).

In the second study, we developed an on-line imitation paradigm in which subjects were asked to imitate the direction of a reaching movement displayed by a model facing the subject (Vogt 1999; Vogt, in preparation; see figure 20.2). Experimenter and subject began to reach out for an object in near synchrony, which allowed us to assess the minimal time in which subjects could respond to an unexpected shift in the model's reach direction for another object (called "perturbation"). A 120 Hz/3-D optical tracking system (MacReflex, Qualisys Incorporated) was used to record the trajectories of the subject's and model's thumb, index, and wrist. The perturbation technique has been used extensively in the study of object-oriented actions, and has shown that subjects can respond to shifts in object location within 110 and 275 milliseconds, depending on the particular method used (Paulignan et al. 1991; see also Brenner and Smeets 1997). This brief delay, and the fact that responses can occur without, or at least substantially before, conscious awareness (Jeannerod 1997, chapter 3.5), indicate that these responses are mediated by a direct visuomotor coupling. Its cortical substrate are connections between parietal

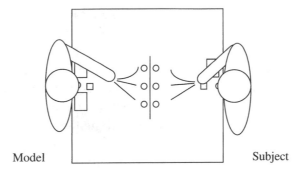

Model   Subject

Figure 20.2 The on-line imitation paradigm developed by Vogt (in prep.). The model reaches initially for the middle of three dowels. In 25% of trials, illumination of this dowel is shifted to the right or left dowel (invisible to the subjects), and the model redirects his reach. The imitating subjects begin to reach for the middle of another set of three dowels when they see the model starting to move. They are instructed to respond to the model's shift of direction by redirecting their own reach to the dowel next to the model's aimed-for dowel. Visuomotor latencies were found to be similarly short in model- and object-guided performance.

and premotor cortical areas devoted to specific sensorimotor transformations (Rizzolatti, Luppino, and Matelli 1998), also known as *dorsal* cortical pathway (Milner and Goodale 1995).

The first main finding was that subjects' responses to perturbation of the model's reach direction were equally fast as their responses to shifts in object location (approximately 240 ms and 225 ms, respectively). We hypothesize that also in the imitation task, the fast dorsal stream was involved. In contrast, when subjects had to respond to a shift in the color of the objects, response latencies were significantly longer (approximately 380 ms). Also, Pisella, Arzi, and Rossetti (1998) found longer latencies in a color-cueing condition and explained this by the involvement of the slower, *ventral* cortical pathway. Nevertheless, our conclusions about dorsal and ventral stream involvement are indirect and more direct support via brain-imaging techniques would be desirable. In any case, we can conclude that directionally compatible, but not arbitrary, visual cues have fast access to response selection, and that the former include displays of human hands.

The second question addressed in this study was similar to the one posed by Bekkering, Wohlschläger, and Gattis (2000), namely, can subjects imitate more than one feature in the display? In their ear-grip task (see also Bekkering and Prinz, chapter 21 of this volume), children's imitations showed a clear selectivity when displays varied in more than one parameter. Instead of varying ears touched and hands used, our model modulated, in 1/3 of the unperturbed trials, the speed, height of transport, or grip aperture of his reaching movement. If subjects' motor preparation was automatically coupled also to these display properties, we should expect that their movements would reflect these modulations, even though this was not part of the instruction. Preliminary analyses indicate that subjects were largely "immune" against these task-irrelevant modulations. That is, although they fully attended to the model's hand and redirected their reach very quickly when the model did so, they did not copy other aspects of the model's action. Thus, with variations in more than one display dimension, a similar high selectivity has been uncovered both in this study and in Bekkering, Wohlschläger, and Gattis's experiments, despite different tasks, displays, and time constraints. This selectivity is an important finding, since it shows that imitation is not just replicating what is "out there," but is driven and constrained by knowledge about task-relevant aspects of the display. The fact that we find this selectivity also in an on-line imitation task with very brief delays between display change and response, makes it unlikely that on-line goal reconstruction is the only mechanism capable of producing such selectivity. The place of goals is not necessarily in concurrent perception-action mediation but, more likely, in the preparatory attentional and motor processes that occur before stimuli are shown and responses are made.

To summarize, direct visuomotor couplings between seen and performed actions do indeed exist, which supports the more general notion of early perception-action mediation. However, by far, not all aspects of the observed movement are imitated spontaneously, which points toward a high selectivity of imitative visuomotor processing. Although these simple tasks are miles away from the learning of complex skills, sport scientists emphasize that for successful training schemes that involve modeling, attentional focusing to specific aspects of the display is essential.

20.4 Neurophysiological Aspects

As mentioned in section 20.1, the discovery of "mirror neurons" in the premotor cortex of macaque monkeys by Rizzolatti and colleagues (Rizzolatti et al. 1996a) has provided a potential physiological underpinning for early mediation accounts of imitative actions. Mirror neurons, located in premotor area F5, tend to discharge when a monkey observes another individual performing an action, as well as when the monkey performs this or a related action himself. The discharge during action observation does not manifest itself in overt behavior, and is also found when the observing monkey is restrained from performing the action. Importantly, F5 neurons seem to code primarily the meaning of the observed or performed action, rather than kinematic details, such as movement direction or speed. Consequently, Rizzolatti and colleagues (1996a) have interpreted this early involvement of motor structures primarily as contributing to the *understanding* of the observed action, and not necessarily to imitation. Their (adult) monkeys simply did not imitate. Similarly, Gallese and Goldman (1998) have interpreted the monkey's mirror system as a rudimentary form of "mind-reading," in the sense that the actor's intentions are reconstructed from the display by referring to the observer's intentions when performing such actions ("When I perform this action, I normally seek to achieve X"). Such mind-reading could subserve anticipating the conspecific's imminent physical or communicative actions (Rizzolatti and Arbib 1998), as well as forming more enduring representations of the minds of others. This interpretation of the mirror system as operating somewhat "detached" from instantaneous behavior is also in agreement with Byrne and Russon's (1998) concept of program-level imitation, where it is mainly the organization of elementary actions that is copied, and not the kinematic details of the actions. As pointed out in section 20.2, the identification of individual actions is a prerequisite for reconstructing their sequential organization, and mirror neurons may well subserve this parsing function.

The described characteristics of mirror neurons leave us with two main questions: First, does a similar perception-action matching system exist in humans? Second, should we expect this system to form the neural substrate for such different activities as imitating kinematic details and imitating different kinds of actions? The answer to the first question is a "yes, but more research is needed"; the answer to the second question will be addressed in the form of two predictions.

The relevant brain imaging studies have indeed indicated the existence of a mirror system in humans. Also, the described "detached," high-level operation of mirror neurons seems to be shared between monkey and man. In the majority of studies (Decety et al. 1997; Grafton et al. 1996; Grezes, Costes, and Decety 1998; Hari et al. 1998; Iacoboni et al. 1999; Rizzolatti et al. 1996b), motor preparatory areas were found to be involved in action observation per se. Conditions that required immediate overt imitation were, however, not often used for comparison. In the first imaging study that included such a condition (Krams et al. 1998), on-line imitation did not involve premotor cortical activity to the same extent as motor imagery-related instructions. Also, in Fadiga, Fogassi, Pavesi, and Rizzolatti's (1995) study, a deferred imitation condition did not produce a stronger motor facilitation than an observe-to-recognize condition. Further, in Grezes, Costes, and Decety's (1998) study, Brodmann areas 44/45 (the possible human equivalent of F5 mirror neurons, see Rizzolatti and Arbib 1998) were only involved in the observation of meaningful actions without purposeful observation, and not when subjects were instructed to watch the actions with the intention to imitate them after the scanning. In the latter condition, however, other motor areas were found activated, namely, the right cerebellum and lateral premotor cortex, and additionally the supplementary motor area (SMA) and orbitofrontal cortex when meaningful actions were displayed. This is currently the only evidence from neurophysiological studies for motor areas as subserving (deferred) imitation of different actions.

Whereas these studies do not indicate a role of frontal areas in imitation that goes beyond pure action observation, the recent fMRI study by Iacoboni and colleagues (1999) indicates this possibility in a direct comparison between observation and imitation conditions. Both the left frontal operculum (area 44) and the right anterior parietal cortex were found to be activated during pure observation and during observation/imitation of a finger movement. Further, the imitation task produced a stronger activation in these areas than observation alone. Unfortunately, a comparison between imitative execution and performing a movement different from the one displayed was not included in Iacoboni and colleagues' study. Thus, it is unclear if the enhanced activation during imitation did just reflect the cumulative activity found during observation and nonimitative execution of a finger movement (as demonstrated in additional conditions), or if it reflected a movement-specific perception-action matching, as claimed by the authors.

To summarize, we have at least some evidence that motor structures are involved not only in action observation per se but also in the observational stage of imitative behavior. However, it appears implausible that this involvement of motor structures during action observation can form a motor representation of the observed action that is sufficiently detailed to allow a reproduction with high spatiotemporal fidelity. From Bekkering, Wohlschläger, and Gattis's (2000) and Vogt's (in preparation) studies, we have begun to see the high selectivity of imitative behavior, which demonstrates that the brain does not just mirror the (social) environment but creates task-specific representations. Accordingly, future neurophysiological research may uncover further differences in brain activation between pure observation, observing-to-imitate, and motor preparation of the imitative response, rather than just identical patterns. The study by Grezes et al. (1998) has already nicely shown that different (meaningful vs. meaningless) displays may be reflected in different or widely overlapping cortical activation patterns, depending on whether the task is just to observe, or to observe with the intention to imitate.

Nevertheless, the available studies clearly indicate that observing actions is not purely contemplative. Mirror neurons support imitative actions to some extent, even if additional motor preparatory processes are likely to be required. From the discussions in the previous sections, we can make two predictions about the neural substrate involved in imitative actions. The first prediction is that this should be *task-specific*. Neurons in areas 44/45 are likely to subserve the imitation of certain, particularly manual actions, but, for example, the cerebellum may be involved in tasks with a strong timing component, and the SMA in sequential tasks.

The second prediction is that the imitation of *parametric* variations of an action should be largely supported by dorsal stream processing, whereas the imitation of *different actions* should further involve ventral stream processing. The dorsal cortical stream extends from occipital to parietal and further to premotor areas and provides specific sensorimotor transformations, for which the fast responses to shifts in the position of an aimed-for object were given earlier as just one example. Accordingly, the dorsal stream has been characterized as "how"-pathway (Milner and Goodale 1995). In addition to controlling object-oriented actions, the dorsal stream may also subserve certain model-guided behaviors. Tasks such as imitation of movement direction, as used in my reaching study, are prime candidates for dorsally mediated imitation (Vogt, in press). This proposal is well in line with Rizzolatti, Fadiga, Fogassi, and Gallese's (in press) concept of a "low level resonance mechanism" that mediates imitative behavior even in the absence of a recognized goal.

Finally, our suggestion that the ventral cortical stream, or "what"-pathway, should be involved in the imitation of different actions derives from the work by Perrett et al. (1989; see also Carey, Perrett, and Oram 1997). These authors have shown that a variety of meaningful, observed actions (such as pick, tear, or manipulate) are coded in the monkey's superior temporal sulcus (STS), which is part of the ventral stream. These neurons exhibit many aspects of generalization typical for ventral stream processing, which allows the detection of a given action from various viewpoints and distances and regardless of variations in motor details. Also, Grafton et al. (1996), Grezes et al. (1998), and Rizzolatti et al. (1996b) found the ventral pathway activated when subjects observed meaningful actions. The fact that this ventral involvement ceased when the subjects in Grezes et al.'s study later watched the same actions with the intention to imitate is at variance with my suggestion, but this outcome may be due to specificities of this study (e.g., habituation effects, focus on accurate reproduction) rather than reflect a general absence of ventral stream processing in imitation tasks where meaning matters.

Given the high-level properties of the monkey's area F5 (and areas 44/45 as their possible human equivalent), these areas are the likely frontal target areas for the imitation of meaningful actions ("high level resonance mechanism," Rizzolatti et al., in press). The issue of to what extent the frontal target areas of both forms of imitation—of parametric details and of meaningful actions—coincide needs further investigation, as does the general proposal of dorsally and ventrally mediated imitation. It is also likely that both streams interact in certain observation/imitation tasks. After all, to achieve certain motor details may well become an action goal (e.g., in musical performance), and the goal of an observed action needs to be reconstructed from the elementary movements in the display. Nevertheless, further imaging studies that directly contrast the imitation of motor details with the imitation of different actions are highly desirable in order to dissociate the two proposed mechanisms.

20.5 Conclusion

This chapter set out with apparently contradictory observations about imitative actions. On the one hand, they look primitive, direct, and almost inescapable, on the other hand we know how difficult it can be to imitate skilled musicians or athletes. Both are true, and I hope to have shown that which view is favored depends on the particular type of imitation in question. Also, the answers about which type of representation and mediation is used depend at least in part on the task. Behavioral, neuropsychological and neurophysiological evidence for an early involvement of motor structures, namely during action observation, has been discussed, but this does not preclude that visual representations or images can play a role in guiding and correcting imitative actions.

The proposed distinction between imitation of parametric details and imitation of different actions may be suited to clarify some of the apparent contradictions. Individual aspects of the model's behavior can indeed be incorporated in the observer's action with remarkable speed (dorsal stream), but this form of imitation appears to be highly selective and focused on specific aspects of the display. When different actions (or sequences of actions) are imitated, this normally relies at least in part on stored knowledge about these actions (ventral stream), which also includes the observer's own motor repertoire. In a sense, then, neither in parameter imitation nor in action imitation is the reproduction guided by a detailed representation derived from the model. In action imitation, the imitator's own action prototype is accessed on a high level of coding, and in parameter imitation, only specific aspects of performance are "opened" to visual guidance. Thus, it appears that the richness of human imitative behavior emerges from the "eye of the needle" of a rather limited capacity for on-line coupling.

Acknowledgments

I wish to thank Kerstin Dautenhahn, Brian Hopkins, and an anonymous reviewer for their comments on an earlier draft of this chapter.

Note

1. Stronger deviations from a natural temporal structure can, however, be learned to some extent through observation, particularly when combined with physical practice and feedback (see Blandin, Lhuisset, and Proteau 1999).

References

Adams, J. A. Historical review and appraisal of research on the learning, retention, and transfer of human motor skills. *Psychological Bulletin* 101: 41–74, 1987.

Bandura, A. *Social Foundations of Thought and Action: A Social Cognitive Theory.* Englewood Cliffs, N.J.: Prentice-Hall, 1986.

Bekkering, H., Wohlschläger, A., and Gattis, M. Imitation of gestures in children is goal-directed. *Quarterly Journal of Experimental Psychology, Section A: Human Experimental Psychology* 53A: 153–164, 2000.

Blandin, Y., Lhuisset, L., and Proteau, L. Cognitive processes underlying observational learning of motor skills. *Quarterly Journal of Experimental Psychology, Section A: Human Experimental Psychology* 52A: 957–979, 1999.

Brass, M., Bekkering, H., and Prinz, W. Movement observation affects movement execution in a simple response task. *Acta Psychologica* (in press).

Brenner, E., and Smeets, J. B. J. Fast responses of the human hand to changes in target position. *Journal of Motor Behavior* 29: 297–310, 1997.

Byrne, R. W., and Russon, A. E. Learning by imitation: A hierarchical approach. *Behavioral and Brain Sciences* 21: 667–721, 1998.

Carey, D. P., Perrett, D. I., and Oram, M. W. Recognizing, understanding, and reproducing action. In F. Boller, J. Grafman (series eds.), and M. Jeannerod (vol. ed.), *Handbook of Neuropsychology, Vol. 11, Section 16: Action and Cognition* (pp. 111–129). Amsterdam: Elsevier, 1997.

Carroll, W. R., and Bandura, A. Representational guidance of action production in observational learning: A causal analysis. *Journal of Motor Behavior* 22: 85–97, 1990.

Craighero, L., Fadiga, L., Rizzolatti, G., and Umiltà, C. Action for perception: A motor-visual attentional effect. *Journal of Experimental Psychology: Human Perception and Performance* 25: 1673–1692, 1999.

Decety, J., Grezes, J., Costes, N., Perani, D., Jeannerod, M., Procyk, E., Grassi, F., and Fazio, F. Brain activity during observation of actions: Influence of action content and subject's strategy. *Brain* 120: 1763–1777, 1997.

Eidelberg, L. Experimenteller Beitrag zum Mechanismus der Imitationsbewegung. *Jahroo büchei für Psychiatrie und Neurologie* 46: 170–173, 1929.

Fadiga, L., Fogassi, L., Pavesi, G., and Rizzolatti, G. Motor facilitation during action observation: A magnetic stimulation study. *Journal of Neurophysiology* 73: 2608–2611, 1995.

Gallese, V., and Goldman, A. Mirror neurons and the simulation theory of mind-reading. *Trends in Cognitive Sciences* 2: 493–501, 1998.

Goldenberg, G., and Hagmann, S. The meaning of meaningless gestures: A study of visuo-imitative apraxia. *Neuropsychologia* 35: 333–341, 1997.

Grafton, S. T., Arbib, M. A., Fadiga, L., and Rizzolatti, G. Localization of grasp representations in humans by positron emission tomography: 2. Observation compared with imagination. *Experimental Brain Research* 112: 103–111, 1996.

Grezes, J., Costes, N., and Decety, J. Top-down effect of strategy on the perception of human biological motion: A PET investigation. *Cognitive Neuropsychology* 15: 553–582, 1998.

Greenwald, A. G. Sensory feedback mechanisms in performance control: With special reference to the ideo-motor mechanism. *Psychological Review* 77: 73–99, 1970.

Hari, R., Forss, N., Avikainen, S., Kirveskari, E., Salenius, S., and Rizzolatti, G. Activation of human primary motor cortex during action observation: A neuromagnetic study. *Proceedings of the National Academy of Sciences* 95: 15061–15065, 1998.

Hommel, B., and Prinz, W., eds. *Theoretical Issues in Stimulus-Response Compatibility.* Amsterdam: Elsevier, 1997.

Howard, J. H. Jr., Mutter, S. A., and Howard, D. V. Serial pattern learning by event observation. *Journal of Experimental Psychology: Learning, Memory, and Cognition* 18: 1029–1039, 1992.

Iacoboni, M., Woods, R. P., Brass, M., Bekkering, H., Mazziotta, J. C., and Rizzolatti, G. Cortical mechanisms of human imitation. *Science* 286: 2526–2528, 1999.

Ivry, R. B., and Hazeltine, R. E. Perception and production of temporal intervals across a range of durations: Evidence for a common timing mechanism. *Journal of Experimental Psychology: Human Perception and Performance* 21: 3–18, 1995.

Ivry, R. B., and Keele, S. W. Timing functions of the cerebellum. *Journal of Cognitive Neuroscience* 1: 136–152, 1989.

James, W. *The Principles of Psychology*. Cambridge, Mass.: Harvard University Press, 1890/1983.

Jeannerod, M. The representing brain: Neural correlates of motor intention and imagery. *Behavioral and Brain Sciences* 17: 187–245, 1994.

Jeannerod, M. *The Cognitive Neuroscience of Action*. Oxford: Blackwell, 1997.

Keele, S. W. Motor control. In K. R. Boff, L. Kaufman and J. P. Thomas (eds.), *Handbook of Perception and Human Performance, Vol. 2: Motor Control* (pp. 30, 1–60). Wiley: New York, 1986.

Kelso, J. A. S. *Dynamic Patterns: The Self-Organization of Brain and Behavior*. Cambridge, MA: MIT Press, 1995.

Kinsbourne, M. The role of imitation in body ownership and mental growth. In A. N. Meltzoff and W. Prinz (eds.), *The Imitative Mind: Development, Evolution, and Brain Bases*. Cambridge, MA: Cambridge University Press (in press).

Koffka, K. *Growth of the Mind*. New Brunswick, NJ: Transaction Books, 1925/1980.

Kohl, R. M., and Shea, C. H. Pew (1966) revisited: Acquisition of hierarchical control as a function of observational practice. *Journal of Motor Behavior* 24: 247–260, 1992.

Köhler, W. *The Mentality of Apes*. New York: Harcourt, Brace, 1924.

Krams, M., Rushworth, M. F. S., Deiber, M.-P., Frackowiak, R. S. J., and Passingham, R. E. The preparation, execution, and suppression of copied movements in the human brain. *Experimental Brain Research* 120: 386–398, 1998.

Lashley, K. S. The problem of serial order in behavior. In L. A. Jeffress (ed.), *Cerebral Mechanisms in Behavior: The Hixon Symposium* (pp. 112–146). New York: Wiley, 1951.

Lhermitte, F., Pillon, B., and Serdaru, M. D. Human autonomy and the frontal lobes. Part I: Imitation and utilization behaviour. A neuro-psychological study with 75 patients. *Annals of Neurology* 19: 335–343, 1986.

Lotze, H. (1852). *Medicinische Psychologie oder Physiologie der Seele*. Leipzig: Weidmannsche Buchhandlung, 1852.

McCullagh, P., Weiss, M. R., and Ross, D. Modeling considerations in motor skill acquisition and performance: An integrated approach. *Exercise and Sport Sciences Reviews* 17: 475–513, 1989.

Meltzoff, A. N. Infant imitation after a 1-week delay: Long-term memory for novel acts and multiple stimuli. *Developmental Psychology* 24: 470–476, 1988.

Meltzoff, A. N. Understanding the intentions of others: Re-enactment of intended acts by 18-month-old children. *Developmental Psychology* 31: 838–850, 1995.

Meltzoff, A. N., and Moore, M. K. Explaining facial imitation: A theoretical model. *Early Development and Parenting* 6: 179–192, 1997.

Miller, G. A., Galanter, E., and Pribram, K. H. *Plans and the Structure of Behavior*. New York: Holt, Rinehart, and Winston, 1960.

Milner, A. D., and Goodale, M. A. *The Visual Brain in Action*. Oxford: Oxford University Press, 1995.

Nehaniv, C. L., and Dautenhahn, K. Of hummingbirds and helicopters: An algebraic framework for interdisciplinary studies of imitation and its applications. In J. Demiris and A. Birk (eds.), *Interdisciplinary Approaches to Robot Learning*, pp. 136–161. World Scientific Press, 2000.

Neisser, U. Towards a skillful psychology. In D. Rogers and J. A. Sloboda (eds.), *The Acquisition of Symbolic Skills* (pp. 1–17). New York: Plenum Press, 1983.

Newell, K. M. Coordination, control, and skill. In D. Goodman, R. B. Wilberg, and I. M. Franks (eds.), *Differing Perspectives in Motor Learning, Memory, and Control* (pp. 295–317). Amsterdam: North-Holland, 1985.

Newell, K. M. Motor skill acquisition. *Annual Review of Psychology* 42: 213–237, 1991.

Pauhgnan, Y., MacKenzie, C., Marteniuk, R., and Jeannerod, M. Selective perturbation of visual input during prehension movements: I. The effects of changing object position. *Experimental Brain Research* 83: 502–512, 1991.

Perrett, D. I., Harries, M. H., Bevan, R., Thomas, S., Benson, P. J., Mistlin, A. J., Chitty, A. J., Hietanen, J. K., and Ortega, J. E. Frameworks of analysis for the neural representation of animate objects and actions. *Journal of Experimental Biology* 146: 87–113, 1989.

Pisella, L., Arzi, M., and Rossetti, Y. The timing of color and location processing in the motor context. *Experimental Brain Research* 121: 270–276, 1998.

Prinz, W. Why don't we perceive our brain states? *European Journal of Cognitive Psychology* 4: 1–20, 1992.

Prinz, W. Perception and action planning. *European Journal of Cognitive Psychology* 9: 129–154, 1997.

Prinz, W. Experimental approaches to imitation. In A. N. Meltzoff and W. Prinz (eds.), *The Imitative Mind: Development, Evolution, and Brain Bases.* Cambridge University Press (in press).

Riddoch, M. J., and Humphreys, G. W. Visual object processing in a case of optic aphasia: A case of semantic access agnosia. *Cognitive Neuropsychology* 4: 131–185, 1987.

Rizzolatti, G. Nonconscious motor images (Commentary on a target article by M. Jeannerod). *Behavioral and Brain Sciences* 17: 220, 1994.

Rizzolatti, G., and Arbib, M. A. Language within our grasp. *Trends in Neurosciences* 21: 188–194, 1998.

Rizzolatti, G., Fadiga, L., Fogassi, L., and Gallese, V. From mirror neurons to imitation: Facts and speculations. In A. N. Meltzoff and W. Prinz (eds.), *The Imitative Mind: Development, Evolution and Brain Bases.* Cambridge, Mass.: Cambridge University Press, in press.

Rizzolatti, G., Fadiga, L., Gallese, V., and Fogassi, L. Premotor cortex and the recognition of motor actions. *Cognitive Brain Research* 3: 131–141, 1996a.

Rizzolatti, G., Fadiga, L., Matelli, M., Bettinardi, V., Paulesu, E., Perani, D., and Fazio, F. Localization of grasp representations in humans by PET: 1. Observation versus execution. *Experimental Brain Research* 111: 246–252, 1996b.

Rizzolatti, G., Luppino, G., and Matelli, M. The organization of the motor cortical system: New concepts. *Electroencephalography and Clinical Neurophysiology* 106: 283–296, 1998.

Rosenbaum, D. A. *Human Motor Control.* New York: Academic Press, 1991.

Rosenbaum, D. A., Loukopoulos, L. D., Meulenbroek, R. J., Vaughan, J., and Engelbrecht, S. E. Planning reaches by evaluating stored postures. *Psychological Review* 102: 28–67, 1995.

Rothi, L. J. G., Mack, L., and Heilman, K. M. Pantomime agnosia. *Journal of Neurology, Neurosurgery, and Psychiatry* 49: 451–454, 1986.

Rothi, L. J. G., Ochipa, C., and Heilman, K. M. A cognitive neuropsychological model of limp praxis. In L. J. G. Rothi and K. M. Heilman (eds.), *Apraxia: The Neuropsychology of Action* (pp. 29–49). Hove, UK: Psychology Press, 1997 [originally published 1991 in *Cognitive Neuropsychology* 8: 443–458].

Rumiati, R. I., and Humphreys, G. W. Recognition by action: Dissociating visual and semantic routes to action in normal observers. *Journal of Experimental Psychology: Human Perception and Performance* 24: 631–647, 1998.

Schmidt, R. A., and Lee, T. D. *Motor Control and Learning: A Behavioral Emphasis.* Champaign, IL: Human Kinetics, 1999.

Sternberg, S., and Knoll, R. L. Perception, production, and imitation of time ratios by skilled musicians. In J. Gibbon and L. Allan (eds.), *Timing and Time Perception. Annals of the New York Academy of Sciences*, vol. 423 (pp. 429–441). New York: New York Academy of Sciences, 1984.

Stürmer, B., Aschersleben, G., and Prinz, W. *Correspondence Effects with Manual Gestures and Postures: A Study of Imitation.* Journal of Experimental Psychology: Human Perception and Performance, 26, pp. 1746–1759, 2000.

Thorndike, E. L. *Animal Intelligence: Experimental Studies.* New York: Macmillan, 1911.

Tucker, M., and Ellis, R. On the relations between seen objects and components of potential actions. *Journal of Experimental Psychology: Human Perception and Performance* 24: 830–846, 1998.

Vereijken, B., and Whiting, H. T. A. In defence of discovery learning. *Canadian Journal of Sports Sciences* 15: 99–106, 1990.

Vogt, S. On relations between perceiving, imagining, and performing in the learning of cyclical movement sequences. *British Journal of Psychology* 86: 191–216, 1995a.

Vogt, S. Imitation of rhythmical patterns: Symbolic and "direct" mediation between perception and action. Paper presented at the Eighth International Conference on Perception and Action. Marseille, July 1995b.

Vogt, S. The concept of event generation in movement imitation—Neural and behavioural aspects. *Corpus, Psyche, et Societas* 3: 119–132, 1996a.

Vogt, S. Imagery and perception-action mediation in imitative actions. *Cognitive Brain Research* 3: 79–86, 1996b.

Vogt, S. Beiträge und Perspektiven der ökologischen Psychologie zum Neulernen motorischer Fertigkeiten. In M. Fikus, and L. Müller (eds.), *Sich-Bewegen—Wie Neues Entsteht* (pp. 39–60). Hamburg: Czwalina, 1998.

Vogt, S. Constraints in human imitative behaviour. In K. Dautenhahn, and C. L. Nehaniv (eds.), *Proceedings of the AISB '99 Symposium on Imitation in Animals and Artifacts* (pp. 17–19). Brighton, UK: Society for the Study of Artificial Intelligence and Simulation of Behaviour, 1999.

Vogt, S. Visuomotor couplings in object-oriented and imitative actions. In A. N. Meltzoff and W. Prinz (eds.), *The Imitative Mind: Development, Evolution, and Brain Bases.* Cambridge, Mass.: Cambridge University Press (in press).

Vogt, S. *Chronometry of Imitative Prehensile Actions: Effects of Directional Perturbation and Task-Irrelevant Modulations.* Manuscript in preparation.

Vogt, S., and Carey, D. Toward a microanalysis of imitative actions (Commentary on a target article by Byrne and Russon). *Behavioral and Brain Sciences* 21: 705–706, 1998.

Vogt, S., Stadler, M., and Kruse, P. Self-organization aspects in the temporal formation of movement gestalts. *Human Movement Science* 7: 365–406, 1988.

Whiting, H. T. A., Vogt, S., and Vereijken, B. Human skill and motor control: Some aspects of the motor control-motor learning relation. In J. J. Summers (ed.), *Approaches to the Study of Motor Control and Learning* (pp. 81–111). Amsterdam: North-Holland, 1992.

21 Goal Representations in Imitative Actions

Harold Bekkering and Wolfgang Prinz

21.1 Introduction

Currently, imitation, or performing an act after perceiving it, is in the focus of attention of researchers from many different disciplines. This chapter concentrates on possible cognitive mechanisms that underlie imitation performance in human infants and children. The chapter first introduces some important notions about what imitation actually is and what it is not. Then, some comments about the when, how, and what of imitation are made. Here, "when" refers to the temporal relationship between the perceived event and the imitated movement. The "how" section discusses how imitators can guide their own movements to match the movements they have seen, while the "what" section points out that what is imitated might be the ends rather than the means of an imitative act. Therefore, a new theory of goal-directed imitation is proposed, and some recent evidence in favor of this theory is mentioned. Finally, concluding remarks are made that point out the necessity of a goal-directed concept for understanding the mechanisms involved in imitation.

21.2 Imitation

The notion of "imitation" has probably been under debate for as long as the concept has existed. Thorndike's (1898) pragmatic definition of "learning to do an act from seeing it done" focused on the key role observation plays in imitation without specifying any details about which aspects of the model are imitated or how imitation is achieved by the imitator. Nevertheless, Thorndike already found it necessary to differentiate between imitative acts and pseudo- or semi-imitative ones. Somewhat later, Spence (1937) pointed out that what people typically refer to as imitation might be *stimulus enhancement*. That is, seeing some act done in a particular place, or to some particular object, has the effect of increasing the observer's probability of going to that place or interacting with that object, and many observations that were formerly considered imitation were thereby explained away. The view that stimuli can be seen as a reinforcer for social learning has later been called *observational conditioning* (Mineka et al. 1984). More recently, Tomasello (1990) introduced the concept of *emulation*. Emulation refers to the possibility of learning about the physical situation as an indirect consequence of another's behavior. In other words, many things may be learned from what happens to objects in the environment as a result of individual's actions, quite apart from learning the actions themselves. For instance, strength, brittleness, weight, what an object is made of or contains, and so forth. In emulation, actions of equivalent ultimate effect on the environment are replicated without the particular nuances or techniques of the behavior copied (see also Call and Carpenter, chapter 9 of this book). In summary, several ideas have been formulated that might explain how certain aspects of social learning can occur without the notion of imitation.

Imitation Criteria

A list of criteria has been proposed to classify a certain behavior as an imitative act. For instance, Byrne (in press) argues that only when an act requires:

1. sufficient complexity to trace its origin
2. that the copying depend on observing a model
3. a lack of environmental constraints that could otherwise reinforce or shape the behavior
4. that the behavior is novel to the imitator

can it be said that we have observed imitation instead of a more general type of response facilitation as described above. The criteria seem to be more or less straightforward. Sufficient complexity implies that the imitator needs to produce errors in action reproduction; a criterion that can be easily examined.

An often used experimental technique to discover whether the action performed depends on or copies the action observed is to compare the probability of the occurrence of an observed action in relationship to baseline. Imitation is operationally defined as a significant elevation in the frequency of an observed action over the normal probability of its occurrence (e.g., Byrne and Russon 1998). Important improvements to this basic technique have been developed. In animal research, for instance, two groups of animals are typically used, each seeing the same problem solved by a conspecific (the demonstrator) but in different ways. Importantly, the groups can then be compared to each other in the frequencies of performing each technique. Imitation is then defined as a significant divergence between the groups in frequencies of using the two actions, matching the actions observed (see also Whiten and Ham 1992; Whiten 1998). In developmental psychology, typically one of a set of several different target gestures is repeatedly performed by an adult in front of an infant. Imitation is then defined as the selective increase in the frequency of matching one gesture to baseline performance and not the other gesture. For example, significantly more infant tongue protrusion after observing adult tongue protrusion than after observing adult mouth opening has been reported and vice versa (Meltzoff and Moore 1977, 1983).

The third criterion of environmental constraints might be viewed as a combination of the first two criteria. That is, first of all, (initial) errors should be observed while learning a specific action, and second, a variety of actions should be observed by different species to master the same action goal. In other words, if a fruit can only be eaten after one specific sequence of actions, we will never know whether the members of the population have learned to eat the fruit in this specific way by imitation or by a personal process of trial-and-error learning, inevitably leading to the same, singular solution.

The fourth criterion of novelty seems more cautious and much harder to define. Defining novelty as a necessary condition for imitation would require full access to the behavioral history of the imitator. More important, the concept of novelty ignores the view that most (developmental) psychologists think that new information is constantly being integrated into preexisting programs to enable the animal to become adapted to new circumstances. The new information is not used instead of old information, rather, it is intimately woven into programs by a mutual process of assimilation and accommodation (e.g., Piaget 1952). Assimilation refers to the process of incorporating an internal operative act through which environmental data are acquired. Accommodation is the outwardly directed process of adapting an overall structure to a specific case. In this sense, it always includes an element of novelty, but it is an already present structure that becomes differentiated through observational learning. From this perspective, it is difficult to see how the definition of novelty could be reconciled with such a dynamic and mutual process of learning (see also Huber 1998).

These arguments over the definition of imitation have historically dominated the literature on social learning, thereby obscuring the more interesting questions of when, how, and what imitators imitate from watching a model. In the next sections, we will focus on these three aspects of imitation.

21.3 The When, How, and What of Imitation

The *When* of Imitation

By *when*, we don't mean the age at which actors start to imitate; rather, *when* refers to the temporal relationship between the perceived event and the imitated movement. If one is to contemplate seriously the hypothesis that imitation is not only a certain kind of response facilitation, but instead reflects a behavioral acquisition through observation, it would be useful to show that deferred imitation can span a long delay of at least several hours or even days. This is exactly what Meltzoff and Moore were able to report. First, Meltzoff (1988) investigated imitation performance in 14-month-old children on six actions previously observed after a 1-week delay. One of the six actions was a novel behavior that had a zero probability of occurrence in spontaneous play. In the imitation condition, infants observed the demonstration but were not allowed to touch the objects, to prevent them from any immediate imitation. The results showed that infants in the imitation conditions produced significantly more of the target actions than infants in control groups who were not exposed to the modeling. Interestingly, there was also strong evidence for the imitation of the novel act. In another study, Meltzoff and Moore (1994) tested imitation performance both immediately and after a 24-hour retention interval in 6-week-old infants. First, this study replicated earlier studies by showing that these infants immediately imitated actions like mouth opening, tongue protrusion at midline, and tongue protrusion to the side (however, see, for a critical note on imitation in newborns, Anisfeld 1996). In addition, the study showed that in the memory trials, in which the previous adult model maintained a neutral passive face in all treatment groups, the 6-week-olds showed a significant higher frequency of the adult facial demonstration seen before compared to a baseline frequency of this behavior. Together, these studies were pathbreaking for the notion that young infants are already able to learn and memorize a behavioral acquisition through observation.

The *How* and *What* of Imitation

The how and what of imitation are, of course, fully intertwined. How can we describe how something takes place, without stating what it is? Therefore, it will be impossible truly to disentangle these two aspects of imitative behavior. Nevertheless, we will try to make separate comments on each aspect when possible. The very intriguing, and probably most basic, puzzle of imitation is the question of how can imitators guide their own movements to match the movements they have seen? This issue reflects at least three different aspects: (1) the difficulty of copying an act performed from another's individual perspective, (2) the issue of integration of different modalities, and (3) the difficulty of building complex behaviors from several parts.

The first aspect in itself includes several subaspects. Let us have a look at the example in which a small child attempts to imitate an adult throwing a basketball into the basket. That is, how can a child learn a novel act from an adult model, who already has years of experience in performing this task, while watching him? The child perceives this action from a different perspective, it has to overcome large differences in body size and available motor skills, and so forth.

The second aspect is about how an observer is able to translate the visually gathered information into an action. One possible answer to the translation problem of matching different modalities within different actors has been the notion that observing actions performed by another individual directly activates a matching motor program (e.g., Butterworth 1990; Gray et al. 1991). Infant imitation of diverse facial and manual gestures is taken as evidence that imitative behavior entails a direct matching between the visually perceived input and the motor output. For instance, the active intermodal mapping theory (AIM) of Meltzoff and Moore (1977, 1983, 1997) claims that humans have the inborn ability to actively match visible movements of others with nonvisible but felt movements of one's self. The theory assumes a supramodal representational system in which the information stemming from both the perceptual system and the action system are registered. This supra-modal representational system is supposed to match the perceptual information about the organ relation end-states of the model's act with the configurable relations of the imitator's organs. A matching-to-target process will be activated until the model's act and, for instance, the infant's act, match.

One possible solution to the third aspect—that of building a complex behavior from multiple parts—has recently been offered by Byrne and Russon (1998). They suggest that great ape imitation depends on interpreting observed actions as hierarchical structures. That is, Byrne and Russon propose that the imitation of complex behavior can in principle be a rather mechanical, statistical process. This process of imitation can occur by string parsing (Byrne, in press). Several aspects of string parsing can be separated:

1. Interruptibility. The elements within modules are tightly bound together, as a result of their practiced and frequent co-occurrence.
2. Omission. Unnecessary stages or modules can be omitted.
3. Repetition. Modules, used as subroutines in a hierarchical organization, may be employed iteratively until some criterion is reached.
4. Natural end-points and starts. Planned behavior leads to the achievement of a goal.
5. Invariant elements. The characteristics that always occur must be the necessary ones, other things might vary.
6. Modularity. A subroutine may be used in more than one program, or one program may be used as a subroutine in another.

All the details needed to fabricate an imitative copy of a novel organization of actions can be perceived or recognized without any understanding of the overall purpose of the behavior. Two components are necessary for this hypothetical system to become practical. The first is the segmenting of perceived action into units. These units reflect a vocabulary of primary elements out of which more complex behavior can be built. These units must also already be in the repertoire of the observer to be of any use for imitation. What is needed then is a system for matching gestures in the observer's repertoire with those same actions in the observed behavior of another individual. The other essential component is a string-parsing mechanism capable of extracting the statistical regularities that characterize organized action. This approach brings us to the issue of what is imitated.

Although most views described above contain something of a direct sensorimotor mapping, it has also become clear that this mapping must be rather flexible in order to be successful. Meltzoff and Moore's supramodal representational system is supposed to match the perceptual information about the organ relation end-states of the model's act with the configurable relations of the imitator's organs in order to overcome the *how* issues of different perspectives, and so on. In other words, Meltzoff and Moore, based on their facial experiments with young infants, propose that the organ end-states are the critical elements of what to imitate.

Byrne's string-parsing system is also assumed not to be a slavish duplication of the parsed elements, and he argues that this would seldom be effective in learning an efficient technique. Only the perspective transformation as described above implies that for exact copying of movements this would inevitably be a slow and difficult process. In order for imitation to be successful, Byrne and Russon (1998) suggest that the behavior that is observed is to be understood in the sense of a represented hierarchical organization rather than a linear string of actions. That is what they call "program-level imitation." Unfortunately, although their description of the processes involved in action observation is based on a fine-grained idea of primary elements and statistical string parsing as briefly described above, their notion about the execution of imitative action is restricted to the idea of a system for matching gestures in the observer's repertoire with those same actions in the observed behavior of another individual. The question they leave open is how the resulting hierarchical programs can be translated into matching gestures already available in the observer's repertoire.

21.4 Action Effects

An alternative view about the *what* of imitative actions derives from traditional, general perspectives on action control. As Lotze (1852) has already pointed out, while we as actors know much about what we intend, or are going to do in a particular situation, we do not have the slightest idea about the motor-related mechanisms that underlie the execution of these intended acts. In other words, although we are able to give a number of reasons why we want to undertake an upcoming action, or where our actions are aimed, we are not able to describe consciously how we can realize the action in terms of the muscles we need for it, the forces necessary to initiate the muscles, or the coordination processes between the muscles, and so forth. According to Harleß (1861), the solution to this puzzle has to be found in cognitive representations of action effects, or *Effektbilder* (effect images) as Harleß has called them (see the action concept model of Hommel 1997, 1998 for a recent elaboration of this view). These effect images are assumed to emerge as a result of self-perception of the actions undertaken and their perceived effects on the environment. That is, from birth on, we will experience a tight relation between the actions initiated and the sensory consequences of an action on the environment. A closely related concept to the question of how actions are selected and initiated was offered by James (1890). James postulated the ideomotor principle—that is, the idea that an anticipatory image of feedback from an action participates in the selection and initiation of that action. More recently, the ideomotor principle has received renewed attention. For instance, Greenwald (1970) elaborated the idea of ideomotor control in action by stating that (a) voluntary responses are represented centrally in the form of images of the sensory feedback they produce, and (b) such images play a controlling role in the performance of their corresponding actions. By this, he referred to situations where responses are mapped to stimuli such that the stimuli that trigger them exhibit some resemblance, or feature overlap, with feedback that arises from their required responses (see also, for a more detailed overview, Prinz, 2000).

21.5 Goal-Directed Imitation

With the above in mind, let us now return to the issue of imitation. If cognitive representations of action effects are emerging as a result of perception of the actions undertaken, the reverse might also be true. That is, we might also be able to "recognize" another individual's action by observing the effects on the environment. In other words, it might be that when we observe an action, we do not so much use a kind of string-parsing mechanism to sequence the action elements observed, rather, we might try to extract the perceivable action effects. Further, it might be that perceiving such an action effect automatically activates the motor program most strongly associated with this action effect, thereby ignoring greatly the motor output observed. Evidence in favor of such an action-

Figure 21.1 An illustration of the six hand-to-ear movements as used in experiment 1 of Bekkering et al. (2000).

effect hypothesis in imitation was recently found in some of our studies (Bekkering, Wohlschläger, and Gattis 2000; Gleißner et al. 2000; Wohlschläger et al. submitted; for an overview see Gattis, in press).

In an imitational setting, it was observed that young children always moved to the correct *goal*, such as an object or a particular ear to reach for, but widely ignored the agent (a particular hand to move with), or the movement path (ipsi- or contralateral to the object); see figure 21.1 for the gestures used. This led us to assume that the action-recognition process was strongly affected by the observed action effects. We proposed that imitation entails representing an observed behavior as a set of goals—possible action effects—which subsequently automatically activates the motor program most strongly associated with this action effect (Bekkering, Wohlschläger, and Gattis 2000). Goals may include objects (for instance, a particular ear), agents (a particular hand), a movement path (crossing the body or moving parallel to the body), or salient features (crossing the arms). We also proposed that these goals are represented hierarchically with some goals dominating others. When processing capacity is limited and multiple goals compete for capacity, goals higher in the hierarchy are reproduced at the expense of goals lower in the hierarchy. Our results suggested that objects occupy the top of this hierarchy—children nearly always grasped the correct ear, but in cases of substitution errors used the wrong hand and the wrong movement path. Because young children have difficulty processing multiple elements and relations, their failures to reproduce all the goals of a movement are more noticeable. This proposal predicted that children's imitation errors are malleable, depending on the number of goals identified in the task as a whole. We tested this prediction in several additional experiments. One experiment limited the movements to only one ear, thereby eliminating the necessity for children to specify the goal object. Nine children, with a mean age of 4:4 years, copied the movements of a model who always touched her right ear (randomly with either the left or right hand), or who always touched her left ear (again randomly using left or right hand).

In this circumstance, children made virtually no errors, grasping the ear contralaterally whenever the model did so. Eliminating the necessity of specifying the goal object thus enabled children to reproduce other goals in the imitative act, such as using the correct hand and the correct movement path. A further experiment compared the presence and absence of objects in the action set while keeping the total number of modeled gestures constant. Children (32 children with a mean age of 4:4 years) sat at a desk across from a model who made four unimanual gestures—that is, with a single hand, similar to those described above, but directed at the desk rather than at her ears. Half of the children saw four dots on the table, two in front of the model and two in front of the child. The model touched her dots ipsilaterally and contralaterally, sometimes with her right hand and sometimes with her left hand. Children were encouraged to copy the model, and directed their own actions at two corresponding dots. No dots were placed on the table for the other half of the children, and the model and child instead directed their actions at locations on the table. Children in the dot condition produced the classic error pattern, substituting ipsilateral for contralateral gestures. In contrast, children in the no-dot condition who saw the identical movements directed at

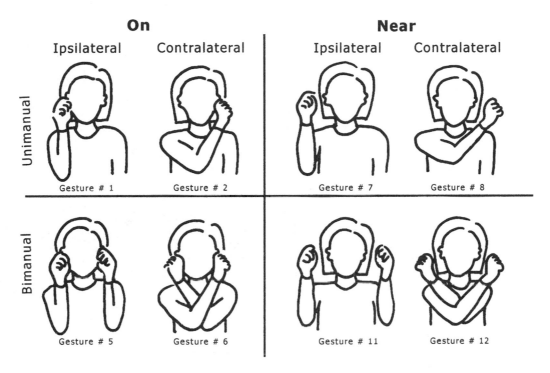

Figure 21.2 An illustration of 8 of the 12 hand-to-ear movements as used in Gleißner et al. (in press). Note that half of the movements end on the ear(s), while the other half of the movements end near to the ear(s). The same 12 movements were also performed on and near the knee(s).

locations in space rather than dots produced significantly fewer contralateral errors. We concluded that manipulating the presence or absence of a physical object had effectively manipulated the necessity of specifying objects as goals. Despite the fact that the movements of both model and child were identical in both conditions, removing the dots from the table eliminated the object goal, and allowed children to reproduce other goals in the imitative act, such as the agent and the movement.

Further research has explored the question of how those goals are specified and organized. Using a similar paradigm to the one described above, Gleißner and colleagues (2000) manipulated whether gestures were directed at locations on the body, or locations near the body; see also figures 21.2 and 21.3. A model performed ipsilateral and contralateral movements with her right or left hand or with both hands. The model either touched a body part (an ear or a knee), or directed her movement at a location in space near the body part. Three-year-olds imitated less accurately

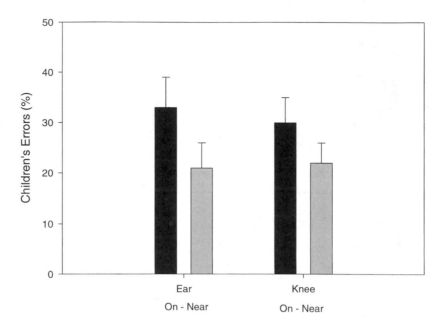

Figure 21.3 The results of the Gleißner et al. experiment (in press). Note that the children make less errors when the movements were directed near the knee or ear(s) than when directed on the knee or ear(s).

when the model's actions were directed at locations on the body than when her actions were directed at locations near the body.

These results confirmed the proposal of Bekkering, Wohl-schläger, and Gattis (2000) that objects (such as an ear or a knee) are high in the goal hierarchy and are able to displace other goals, such as agent and movement. Also, these results provide evidence for the view that perceiving unambiguous action effects automatically activates the motor program that is most strongly associated with this action effect, thereby ignoring greatly the motor output observed. Whether the body part was visible or not (the knee versus the ear) did not significantly influence imitative behavior, suggesting that visual feedback does not play an important role in specifying goals in gestural imitation.

Clearly, the goal-directed view described above deviates from the two alternative theories presented earlier. First, it contrasts with the active intermodal mapping (AIM) theory of Meltzoff and colleagues. We propose that imitation entails representing an observed behavior as a set of goals—possible action effects—but not, necessarily, means. Subsequently, the perceived action effect automatically activates the motor program that is most strongly associated with this action effect. For instance, the fact that the children in our study reached for the correct goal (ear or dot) but sometimes ignored the course of the hand movement suggests that infants may learn how to build the necessary motor structures by an active matching-to-goal process instead of an active matching-to-target perspective as postulated in AIM. Second, the goal-directed view of imitation also clearly deviates from the ideas put forward by Byrne and Russon. They (Byrne and Russon 1998; Byrne, 1999, in press) argue explicitly that string parsing does not depend on comprehension of the intentions of other agents. The goal-directed theory of imitation, on the contrary, argues that the action-recognition process is guided by an interpretation of the motor patterns as a goal-directed behavior, and that these goals, in turn, activate a motor program that will fulfill these goals.

Further Evidence for Goal-Directed Imitation

There are several other studies that provide additional support that goals or action effects are inferred from observing actions. For example, it was found that 16- to 24-month-old children imitated enabling sequences of events more accurately than arbitrary sequences of events (Bauer and Mandler 1989; Bauer and Travis 1993). The novel-arbitrary sequences involved novel actions with simple objects, such as putting a sticker on a chalkboard, leaning the board against an easel, and drawing on the board with chalk. Novel-enabling sequences also involved novel actions with objects, with the difference that actions in the novel-enabling sequence enabled other actions in the sequence, and ultimately led to a salient novel event, such as a toy frog "jumping" into the air. The frog-jump sequence, for example, involved putting a wooden board on a wedge-shaped block to form a lever, placing a toy frog on one end of the board, and hitting the other end of the board, causing the toy frog to appear to jump into the air. Children of all ages performed the modeled actions in the modeled order more frequently for novel-enabling sequences than novel-arbitrary sequences, clearly indicating that the presence of an unambiguous, observable goal leads to more accurate imitative behavior in young children.

Also, Travis (1997) demonstrated that the presence of an end-state goal in a modeled action sequence led to more frequent imitation of those actions compared to action sequences omitting the goal action. Twenty-four-month-old children were shown interleaved pairs of three-step action sequences similar to the novel-enabling sequences described above. They saw either all six actions (three actions for each pair), or only five actions, with the goal action for one sequence omitted. Interestingly, when shown two-goal pairs, children imitated both action sequences equally. In contrast, when shown one-goal pairs, children imitated more actions from the goal-present sequence than from the goal-absent sequence. In addition, children in both conditions performed actions leading to a particular goal as a temporally contiguous sequence—despite the fact that goal-related actions were not temporally contiguous in the modeled sequence, since they were interleaved with actions from another sequence.

Another line of evidence in favor of goal-directed imitation derives from a study by Want and Harris (1998). In their experiment, subjects were shown how to poke an object out of a horizontally mounted transparent tube in which there was a "trap." Only if the poking is done from one end can the object be obtained. Half of the children saw the action performed perfectly, while the other half saw the model put the stick first into the wrong end, then remove it and poke from the other end (the same successful performance as shown to the other group). Interestingly, the children who saw the incorrect sequence did not copy this; however, they did learn significantly more quickly than those who saw only error-free demonstrations.

Thus, a variety of experimental data indicates that observers interpret the actions observed above the level of elementary perceptual-motor maps. For instance, the presence of an end-goal in a sequence of actions increases the likelihood that those actions will be imitated and, presumably, organizes subsequent behavior. It is worth noting that the end-goals used by Bauer, Travis, and colleagues were physical acts involving movement, noise, or both. However, Travis points out that a goal, strictly defined, is "a mental state representing a desired state of affairs in the world" (1997, p. 115), and can therefore only be observed in the outcome of intentional actions. Identifying the goals of an observable action requires an inference beyond any mapping or parsing method as described previously.

Interesting examples, stressing that goals play an important role in imitative behavior, come from developmental psychologists interested in children's understanding of the intentions of others (Carpenter, Akhtar, and Tomasello 1998; Meltzoff 1995). These experiments demonstrate that even very young children are capable of inferring goals from observed actions, and that inferred goals influence imitative behavior. Meltzoff (1995) compared 18-month-old children's reenactments of an attempted-but-failed action, or an attempted-and-achieved action with five unique test objects. For example, an adult experimenter moved a rectangular wooden stick toward a rectangular recessed button on a box, and either inserted the stick in the hole, activating a buzzer, or touched an adjacent area on the box, missing the hole and not activating the buzzer. When given the opportunity to manipulate the objects immediately after the adult's demonstration, children shown an attempted-but-failed act were just as likely to perform the target act (for example, inserting the stick in the hole and activating the buzzer) as children shown an attempted-and-achieved act. This result is especially surprising because children shown a failed attempt never actually saw the target act performed. Children in both groups performed the target act approximately four times as often as did children in control conditions. That 18-month-olds imitated intended acts just as often as achieved acts suggests that even very young children infer the goals of others' behaviors, and imitate those inferred goals.

In a similar paradigm, Carpenter, Akhtar, and Tomasello (1998) compared 14 18-month-old children's reenactments of verbally marked intentional and nonintentional acts. An experimenter performed two unrelated actions on a unique test object—for instance, lifting the top of a bird feeder and pulling a ring on a string attached to the feeder. These actions were accompanied by vocal exclamations marking each action as either an intended act ("There!") or an accidental act ("Whoops!"), with some children seeing first an intentional and then an accidental act, and others seeing the opposite order. After both actions had been performed a salient event occurred (e.g., a party favor attached to the bird feeder moved and made noise). Irrespective of the order of the modeled actions, children reproduced the intentional acts approximately twice as often as nonintentional acts.

Together, these experiments suggest that imitation in children relies on the presence of unambiguous, observable goals and, importantly, also on inferences about the actor's intentions of the observed act. Furthermore, strong support was found for the notion that these (inferences about) goals or intentions influence subsequent imitative behavior.

21.6 Concluding Remarks

1. The present chapter suggests that instead of concentrating on whether or not a specific action can be called imitation, it might be more fruitful to concentrate on the when, how, and what questions in imitation.

2. Studies were reported that indicated even young infants are able to learn and memorize a behavioral acquisition through observation, which reflects the idea that imitation is not only a certain kind of response facilitation.

3. Two functional approaches (AIM and elementary string parsing) have been discussed as providing first examples of possible functional mechanisms underlying the *how* and *what* of imitational behavior. However, it was questioned whether describing the means of imitation would be sufficient to understand imitative behavior adequately.

4. Alternatively, a goal-directed theory of imitation was proposed. It was suggested that imitation in children is mediated by processes that enable the observer to achieve the *goals* or the intentions of the observed actions, but not, necessarily, the means. Imitation of goals clearly involves more than merely perceptual and motor maps. In addition, motivated by traditional views on action control, it was proposed that these goal-directed processes, in turn, activate a motor program to fulfill these goals.

Acknowledgments

We acknowledge the intellectual contributions made by Andreas Wohlschläger and Merideth Gattis in conceptualizing the goal-directed theory of imitation.

References

Anisfeld, M. Only tongue protrusion modeling is matched by neonates. *Developmental Review* 11: 60–97, 1996.

Bauer, P. J., and J. M. Mandler. One thing follows another: Effects of temporal structure on 1- to 2-year-olds' recall of events. *Developmental Psychology* 25: 197–206, 1989.

Bauer, P. J., and L. L. Travis. The fabric of an event: Different sources of temporal invariance differentially affect 24-month-olds' recall. *Cognitive Development* 8: 319–341, 1993.

Bekkering, H., A. Wohlschläger, and M. Gattis. Imitation of gestures in children is goal-directed. *Quarterly Journal of Experimental Psychology. Section A: Human Experimental Psychology* 53A: 153–164, 2000.

Bizzi, E., F. Mussa-Ivaldi, and S. F. Giszter. Computations underlying the execution of movement: A biological perspective, *Science* 253: 287–291, 1991.

Butterworth, G. On reconceptualizing sensori-motor coordination in dynamic system terms. In H. Bloch and B. I. Bertenthal (eds.), *Sensory Motor Organizations and Development in Infancy and Early Childhood*, pp. 57–73. The Netherlands: Kluwer Academic Press, 1990.

Byrne, R. W. Imitation without intentionality. Using string parsing to copy the organization of behavior. *Animal Cognition* 2: 63–72, 1999.

Byrne, R. W. Seeing actions as hierarchically organized structures. Great ape manual skills. In A. Meltzoff and W. Prinz (eds.), *The Imitative Mind: Development, Evolution, and Brain Bases*. Cambridge University Press (in press).

Byrne, R. W., and A. E. Russon. Learning by imitation: A hierarchical approach. *Behavioral and Brain Sciences* 21: 667–684, 1998.

Carpenter, M., N. Akhtar, and M. Tomasello. Fourteen- through 18-month-old infants differentially imitate intentional and accidental actions. *Infant Behavior and Development* 21: 315–330, 1998.

Gattis, M., H. Bekkering, and A. Wohlschläger. Goal-directed imitation. In A. Meltzoff and W. Prinz (eds.), *The Imitative Mind: Development, Evolution, and Brain Bases*. Cambridge University Press (in press).

Gleißner, B., A. N. Meltzoff, and H. Bekkering. Children's coding of human action: Cognitive factors influencing imitation in 3-year-olds. *Developmental Science* 3: 405–414, 2000.

Gray, J. T., U. Neisser, B. A. Shapiro, and S. Kouns. Observational learning of ballet sequences: The role of kinematic information, *Ecological Psychology* 3: 121–134, 1991.

Greenwald, A. G. Sensory feedback mechanisms in performance control: With special reference to the ideo-motor mechanism. *Psychological Review* 77: 73–99, 1970.

Harleß, E. Der Apparat des Willens. *Zeitschrift für Philosophie und Philosophische Kritik* 38: 50–73, 1861.

Hommel, B. Toward an action-concept model of stimulus-response compatibility. In B. Hommel and W. Prinz (eds.), *Theoretical Issues in Stimulus-Response Compatibility*, pp. 281–320. Elsevier Science B. V., 1997.

Hommel, B. Perceiving one's own action—And what it leads to. In J. S. Jordan (ed.), *Systems Theories and A Priori Aspects of Perception*, pp. 143–179. North-Holland, Elsevier Science, 1998.

Huber, L. Movement imitation as faithful copying in the absence of insight. *Behavioral and Brain Sciences* 21: 694, 1998.

James, W. *The Principles of Psychology* (vol. 2). New York: Dover Publications, 1890.

Lotze, R. H. *Medizinische Psychologie*. Leipzig: Weidmann, 1852.

Meltzoff, M. A. Infant imitation after a 1-week delay: Long-term memory for novel acts and multiple stimuli. *Developmental Psychology* 24: 470–476, 1988.

Meltzoff, M. A. The centrality of motor coordination and proprioception in social and cognitive development: From shared actions to shared mind. In G. J. P. Savelsbergh (ed.), *The Development of Coordination in Infancy*, pp. 463–496. Amsterdam: Free University Press, 1993.

Meltzoff, M. A. Understanding the intentions of others: Re-enactment of intended acts by 18-month-old-children. *Developmental Psychology* 31: 838–850, 1995.

Meltzoff, M. A., and M. K. Moore. Imitation of facial and manual gestures by human neonates. *Science* 198: 75–78, 1977.

Meltzoff, M. A., and M. K. Moore. Newborn infants imitate adult facial gestures. *Child Development* 54: 702–709, 1983.

Meltzoff, M. A., and M. K. Moore. Imitation, memory, and the representation of persons. *Infant Behavior and Development* 17: 83–99, 1994.

Meltzoff, M. A., and M. K. Moore. Explaining facial imitation: A theoretical model. *Early Development and Parenting* 6: 179–192, 1997.

Mineka, S., M. Davidson, M. Cook, and R. Keir. Observational conditioning of snake fear in rhesus monkey. *Journal of Abnormal Psychology* 93: 355–372, 1984.

Piaget, J. *The Origin of Intelligence in Children.* New York: International University Press, 1952.

Piaget, J. *Nachahmung, Spiel, und Traum. Die Entwicklung der Symbolfunktion beim Kinde.* Stuttgart: Ernst Klett Verlag, 1975.

Prinz, W. Kognitionspsychologische Handlungsforschung (Research on cognition and action). *Zeitschrift für Psychologie* 208(1–2): 32–54, 2000.

Spence, K. W. Experimental studies of learning and higher mental processes in infrahuman primates. *Psychological Bulletin* 34: 806–850, 1937.

Thorndike, E. L. Animal intelligence: An experimental study of the associative process in animals. *Psychological Review Monograph* 2(8): 551–553, 1898.

Tomasello, M. Cultural transmission in the tool use and communicatory signaling of chimpanzees? In S. Parker and K. Gibson (eds.), *"Language" and Intelligence in Monkeys and Apes: Comparative Developmental Perspectives.* Cambridge, UK: Cambridge University Press, 1990.

Travis, L. L. Goal-based organization of event memory in toddlers. In P. W. van den Broek, P. J. Bauer, and T. Bourg (eds.), *Developmental Spans in Event Comprehension and Representation: Bridging Fictional and Actual Events*, pp. 111–138. Mahwan, NJ: LEA, 1997.

Want, S. C., and Harris, P. L. Indices of program-level comprehension. *Behavioral and Brain Sciences* 21: 706–707, 1998.

Whiten, A. Imitation of the sequential structures of actions by chimpanzees (*Pan troglodytes*). *Journal of Comparative Psychology* 112: 270–281, 1998.

Whiten, A., and R. Ham. On the nature and evolution of imitation in the animal kingdom: Reappraisal of a century of research. In P. J. B. Slater, J. S. Rosenblatt, C. Beer, and M. Milinski (eds.), *Advances in the Study of Behavior*, pp. 239–283. San Diego: Academic Press, 1992.

Wohlschläger, A., M. Gattis, and H. Bekkering. Imitation in young children: Mapping means or mapping ends? Towards a goal-directed theory of imitation (submitted for publication).

22 Information Replication in Culture: Three Modes for the Transmission of Culture Elements through Observed Action

Oliver R. Goodenough

22.1 Introduction

Human imitative processes create the possibility of cultural transmission and underlie an evolutionary theory of culture. A better description of the proximate mechanisms of this transmission will provide a clearer understanding of cultural evolution. This paper argues that cultural transmission occurs through the imitation of actions, rather than of ideas, a process that leads to a significant bottleneck in what can be passed on culturally. These actions can be usefully classified into three modes—nonlinguistic transmission, stories, and formulas. Language plays a critical role in two of these three modes, which can partially overcome some of the limitations inherent in direct copying. Stories and formulas may be transmitted successfully at the level of linguistic action, but may or may not motivate any action based on the behavioral message they purport to contain. Furthermore, the pathways to behavior from formulas may simply be weaker than those translating non-linguistic behavior models into action. Elements from these different modes can be bundled and clustered together. External storage methods such as writing and the recording of sound and video greatly extend the power of each of these modes but do not change the basic mechanisms. The means of replication in each of these modes is an important factor in the differentially successful transmission of culture elements.

22.2 Need for a Better Understanding of Cultural Evolution

It has been widely suggested that culturally transmitted behavioral information exhibits a Darwinian evolutionary dynamic (e.g., Blackmore 1999; Boyd and Richerson 1985; Cavalli-Sforza and Feldman 1981; Dawkins 1976; Dennett 1999; Durham 1990; Flinn 1997; Gabora 1997; Goodenough and Dawkins 1994; O. R. Goodenough 1995; W. H. Goodenough 1999). The argument is straightforward. Darwinian evolution has three basic elements: (1) replicative descent with (2) variation, subject to (3) a form of selection. Bundles of cultural information as diverse as language, religious practices, and how to bake bread pass with imperfect fidelity from generation to generation. Some of the variants created by these imperfections are passed, nonrandomly, to the next generation with greater frequency. Dawkins suggested the term "meme" for such cultural elements (Dawkins 1976), and a subdiscipline applying evolutionary theory to human culture has come into being (generally, Flinn 1997). This approach is sometimes called "memetics" (*Journal of Memetics*; Blackmore 1999).

The study of cultural evolution has been slowed by a tendency to fall back on explicitly biological models of description and analysis. Recent studies (e.g., Blackmore 1999; Gabora 1997) have recognized the need both for a more general approach to evolutionary phenomena, of which cultural and biological processes can be seen as specific cases, and for better, sui generis descriptions of the proximate mechanisms through which cultural elements replicate, vary, and have differential replicative success. This paper suggests a way of looking at a part of these proximate processes—a model for the replication of cultural elements through the imitation by humans of the remembered actions of others. There are two basic ideas in this model: (i) cultural replication involves the observation, storage, and re-creation of contextualized *actions* and (ii) these action-based transmissions can be usefully categorized in three broadly applicable modes: nonlinguistic transmission, stories, and formulas.

22.3 Replication in Culture: Imitation of Action

Cultural replication involves the observation, storage, and re-creation of contextualized *actions*. "Ideas" as such do not replicate —there is no direct brain to brain link that allows the transmission of the internalized information structure. Computers, of course, with the proper interconnection, can transfer data directly to each other. Even my son's relatively simple Game Boy comes with a cable that can connect it directly to others, allowing for a machine-to-machine trade of the more exotic Pokémon characters. Humans have no such intercranial pipe. What we do observe, and can recreate, is *action*. An idea must become an action if it is to spread. Reflecting this necessity, Gatherer (1998) has suggested that the entire "thought contagion" metaphor should be abandoned for cultural evolution.

Of course, storage through mental modeling of the action in the brain of a human is also a critical link in the replicative chain. In this sense, the brain is part of the medium of copying, and this mental modeling, while not the focus of this paper, is an object of lively study in its own right (e.g., Lynch 1998; Richardson 1999). Furthermore, the presence of this modeling in our cognition can both affect our thinking more generally and lead to other actions, actions that can be nonreplicative. Action-to-action imitative replication is not the sole realm of human cognitive functioning, nor is it the sole realm of learning. Nonetheless, cultural replication—the core of the memetic claim—occurs when an action (or in some cases, a result from which the action can be inferred—see Whiten and Ham 1992) is repeated by an observer and observed and repeated by others in their turn. Those aspects of culture that follow an evolutionary dynamic will necessarily reflect this pattern. The importance of action in the transmission of culture has been recognized by writers as diverse in time and subject matter as Jane Ellen Harrison (1903) and Marvin Harris (1998).

Role of Language in Avoiding a Bottleneck

In what looks like an "idea" transfer, actions can be linguistic — that is, the repetition of a word formula. As will be more fully discussed below, these linguistic actions can, as stories or formulas, carry embedded behavioral and cognitive messages piggybacked, as it were, on the linguistic action itself. But while a secondary meaning can be created through language, and modeled in its turn if properly "decompressed" in the observer's mind, the thing replicated from one person to the next is the linguistic action, and not the meaning itself. Indeed, the linguistic action can be learned and relearned by rote, perhaps as a matter of ritual, by a chain of people ignorant of the language in which it is phrased.

As a boy living for a year on a small, traditional island in Micronesia, where most of the residents did not speak any English, I was on the receiving end of just such a chain. Shortly after my arrival, several children approached me and rhythmically chanted "Gary Cooper is an actor." The coded content of this short sentence meant literally nothing to the speakers, but they knew it was English, and they wanted to make me feel welcome.

This action-to-action step in the transmission process creates a very narrow doorway through which human culture must pass, a true bottleneck. This kind of bottleneck has been described in the context of language (e.g., Kirby 1999). It will also constrain other aspects of cultural transmission. In the absence of some way to encode or compress information, what can be passed on culturally will be limited to action/context combinations *actually observed* in a context of direct experience, imposing significant limitations on both the quantity and the type of information that can be passed. Human language, together with two important modes of its use, has provided powerful tools for the coding, compression, and preservation of behavioral information that would be difficult or impossible to transmit by nonlinguistic means.

22.5   Three Modes

Action-based transmission of cultural information between humans can be usefully classified into three general modes: non-linguistic (uncoded), stories (partially coded), and formulas (fully coded) (figure 22.1). Other modes are certainly theoretically possible, and may well exist in practice, but these modes appear widely encompassing for human behavior as it exists. The approach suggested provides explanations for such phenomena as hypocrisy and the separation of law and morals, but it has not yet been tested in a systematic way.

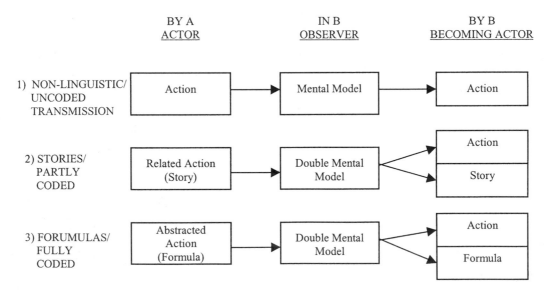

Figure 22.1   Modes of action-based cultural replication.

Nonlinguistic/Uncoded Transmission

Nonlinguistic, uncoded transmission depends upon the direct observation that forms the bottleneck described above. In its simplest form, an action by person A in a particular context is observed by person B. The action and the context for it are stored in the brain of B, waiting for the context to reoccur for B. When this contextual trigger happens, the behavior is reproduced, and, if observed by C, the context and behavior are stored again. While the behavior rests in the brain in a modeled, or symbolized, form, and can be abstracted and generalized by the brain in connection with various thought processes, it is uncoded in the sense that the context/action pattern does not depend on language or some other form of coding to aid in its modeling or transmission. In this, it is somewhat analogous to phenotypic transmission, something observed in traditional biology in RNA replication (Joyce and Orgel 1993).

Language is not used directly in this mode, although it may be used secondarily to initiate a teaching session, to register approval and disapproval, and to help make corrections. Notwithstanding the usefulness of language for facilitation, this mode of transmission exists without it. Indeed, this kind of simple imitative process, which can be assumed to be developmentally "programmed" in humans, could be how language comprehension gets constructed in the developing brain, at least in the early stages.

Stories/Partly Coded Transmission

Once language enters the human repertoire, it can be used to tell a story. Of course, this is only one of the many possible uses of language, but one that can be recruited into the process of cultural transmission. When the linguistic message is understood in the brain, the action/context mix carried by the story is "observed" in a virtual world of the represented experience. From this "observation," a nonlinguistic behavioral model can be created, based on the implicit "moral of the story," and this model can form the basis for an action in its turn. At the same time, a separate memory can be implanted of the story itself—it too becomes an item for replication; its telling is an action for separate imitation. The transmission can become nonlinguistic again, when the action produced by the model derived from the story is observed by people who haven't heard the story. Because the transmission is language based but the behavioral model is not, this can be called partly coded transmission.

The story can be told and retold, and its embedded behavioral message can be passed on across generations, in contexts where the embedded behavior itself is never called upon to occur. Sometimes, the action becomes impossible or obsolete—and yet the story gets attached to a context in which it is retold ritualistically for its own sake. Many children's stories, set in far-off or even mythical contexts, have this characteristic. Nor must the "story" be a coherent narrative. Advertizing jingles can work as partially coded transmissions. The overall point is this: there are often multiple streams of replication through stories—those relating to the actions taught by the story and those relating to the replication of the story itself. Different neural pathways and mechanisms may well be employed in the storage and recreation of the story, on the one hand, and of the behavioral lessons embedded in the story, on the other.

Several benefits accrue from even this level of linguistic transmission. Since it is no longer necessary to be an actual observer of an action/context pairing to learn transmitted behavior, some of the subject matter bottleneck limiting uncoded, nonlinguistic transmission can be avoided. Stories can preserve infrequently needed information, as well as infrequently needed vocabulary. After all, we don't need stories to pass on behavior for frequently experienced contexts. In this light, the somewhat exotic or out-of-date settings of many children's stories can be seen as preserving behavioral information for a "rainy day." There is also a safety factor. Stories about dangerous or unpleasant circumstances can teach survival lessons without the hearer having to witness or experience problematic episodes in person.

The human appetite for stories, and the ability to remember and tell them, suggests that this mechanism, like language itself (Pinker 1994), has had time to root itself in the genetic portion of our human inheritance. For generations, people have paid good money, and lots of it, to consume stories, in contexts from *People Magazine* and the *National Enquirer* to *Pride and Prejudice* and *The Odyssey*. One reason for the prevalent use of stories may be that they require relatively little additional cognitive power once language is in place. The events need to be described, "observed," and modeled, but their underlying behavioral message need not be abstracted in the language system. The decision about action can still be made through the nonlinguistic pathways already established to direct conduct. *Describing* events in words probably has a long history in humans, involving highly developed neural structures. *Generalizing*, abstracting principles, and making decisions about action through the language system, may simply be more demanding and may work through a less fully evolved piece of mental equipment. Drawing on the admittedly subjective observations of a number of years as a graduate law teacher, I suggest that for most of us, stories are interesting and easy; word-based formulas are dull and hard.

Formulas/Fully Coded Transmission

The third mode, "fully coded" transmission through linguistic formulas, uses language to transmit abstracted behavioral information. Here, the replication is of an explicit formula of context and action—a recipe, recommendation, or rule. The authority for these formulas for action can be varied—it might be legal, religious, parental, or simply observational. When it is functioning well, fully coded transmission can greatly increase both the type and the quantity of behavioral information passed through the bottleneck. There are drawbacks, however.

The very creation of such a formula is a task of some mental complexity. Good generalization into language may well require significantly more cognitive innovation than does simple linguistic description. In light of this kind of difficulty, it is no surprise that human word-based analysis is so often flawed. Even trial-and-error correction is at best imperfect. Nor is up-front error the only source of inaccuracy. In such highly coded form, replication must be exact. Memory becomes crucial, particularly in a preliterate society. Stories can often be passed on successfully with some latitude in their need for word-by-word exactness; they are informationally robust. Formulas, however, are more fragile. Their benefit is that they are much more compressed, but with such compression even a relatively small transmission error can turn into a disaster. In a preliterate world, devices such as rhyme, rhythm, melody, and labeling could help to prevent mistakes. Remembering and passing on the ten commandments is helped by the repetition of "thou shalt not" and by the fact that you need to come up with ten of them. "Red right returning," the formula for buoy coloration in ocean navigation, relies on alliteration to defend its accuracy in transmission and recall. The development of writing, of course, greatly strengthened the ability to create and transmit durable recipes and rules of considerable length and complexity. Our formula-challenged brains are still struggling to catch up with this increase in stability.

The process by which a linguistic formula gets translated into its embedded action—requiring both decompression as to its sense and translation into motivation for the embedded action—is also likely to involve complicated and relatively newly evolved neural pathways. There is certainly no guaranty that this translation will occur. One frequently effective step involves rehearsal, where a series of practice re-creations models the formula-inspired action in nonlinguistic, uncoded pathways as well. As with stories, the formula can be transmitted as a linguistic artifact separate from any role it may actually have in determining action on the express "content" of the formula.

Nonreplicating Information, Clusters and Bundles

It is important to recall that many—perhaps even most—linguistic messages are *not* replicating elements of cultural transmission. Among the other things that language does is to help exchange current information on the state of the world: the weather, what's for dinner tonight, where the predators are hiding right now. Only when the message has itself the property of provoking its repetition by an observer, or is linked in a bundle that overall has such a property, will it enter the perpetuating culture stream. At the relatively raw end of this continuum, a "mind virus," like a chain letter, can be as simple as a copying command and some kind of crude threat that creates a compulsion to obey (Goodenough and Dawkins 1994).

The contents of bundles need not be drawn from a single mode. All three modes of replication can mix, cluster, and combine into more-or-less tightly bundled packages of differing elements (Fontana 1998; Gabora 1997). Language itself, at least as learned in childhood by a native speaker, is largely a bundle of uncoded information, which does not use language to form its mental model (O. R. Goodenough 1995, 1997). Some of the other elements in the cultural mix are best viewed as "junk memes" intertwined with more effective elements, unexpressed in action and along for the ride. Some linguistic actions may be excellent at their own replication as formulas or stories, but quite ineffective at producing any behavior other than the copying of the story or formula itself. There are many, many rules, laws, and commandments that are observed "in the breach," rather than "to the letter," and many, many stories that are told but not acted upon. The old adage "do as I say, not as I do" represents a memorable and deeply ironic attempt in the language system to combat this tendency. Hypocrisy may be as much a reflection of the strengths and weaknesses of people's brain architecture as of the strengths and weaknesses of their character.

Indeed, the bundles themselves can carry inconsistent, even conflicting behavioral guides. In genetic replication, it should be remembered, the instructions of the different parts of the genome can be in direct conflict, a phenomenon sometimes linked to parental imprinting of the genes in question (Haig 1993; Haig and Grafen 1991; Mochizuki, Takeda, Iwasa 1996). Source differentiation may also be a factor in the behavioral expression of culturally transmitted information.

The coded formulas on certain subjects—including those rules encoded in the law—may or may not be congruent with the model passed through uncoded transmission for behavior in the same context (O. R. Goodenough 1997). With this potential for discrepancy, it is almost inevitable that in some instances "the law is a ass, a idiot" (Dickens 1837–39). The law is not the only example of cross-modal description. Ethnography in cultural anthropology can be viewed as an attempt to map models from the uncoded or partly coded system of the culture under study into coded rules in the language of the ethnographer (e.g., W. H. Goodenough 1994, 1970).

22.6 External Storage

Each of the modes of cultural replication are strengthened by the development of relatively high-fidelity methods of external storage (figure 22.2). The brain is prone to error as a medium of replication. If the actions can be preserved in decently accurate and durable external storage, the error rate will fall off considerably, and the breadth of preserved experience increased. External storage removes yet another aspect of the bottleneck. Of course, the action of making and accessing the external storage must be passed on at least partly through unstored processes.

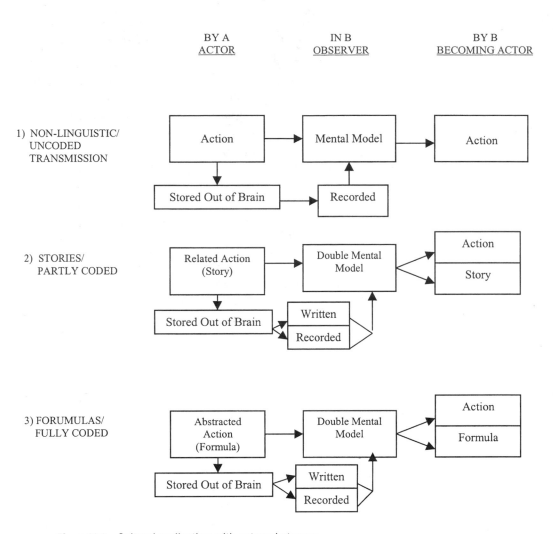

Figure 22.2 Cultural replication with external storage.

Sculpture and pictorial representations, with a history stretching back through stained glass to cave paintings and beyond, provide direct, uncoded messages and can also prompt and reinforce partially and fully coded transmission. Writing, by preserving language, has helped to transmit both stories and formulas. The difficulty of recreating infrequently practiced ritual in a preliterate society acts as a limit on cultural processes (e.g., Williams 1940). Literate cultures faced with a similar problem can invoke the aid of prayer book or other written guide.

The effect of writing—particularly printed writing—on the preservation and transmission of recipes is striking, as anyone who has used a cookbook to make an exotic dish will recognize. The effect of writing on rules is even more dramatic, as anyone who has waded through such laws as the United States Internal Revenue Code can attest. The availability of writing to strengthen the two linguistic modes has only recently been rivaled in the arena of direct transmission by the development of film, television, and other means of audiovisual preservation. The possibilities raised by the external storage and dissemination of non-word-based cultural elements are striking, and are likely to come at some expense to the word-based systems. The possibility of external storage strengthens and complicates the process of cultural replication in all three modes, but it does not change its basic foundation.

22.7 Variation and Selection

The focus of this chapter has been on the proximate mechanisms for replication in human culture. The mechanisms of variation and selection will also repay exploration (e.g., Blackmore 1999; Dennett 1999; Dawkins 1976; Fog 1997; Gabora 1997; O. R. Goodenough 1995). Although an extended treatment of the selection process at work on human cultural elements is beyond the scope of this discussion, the means of replication suggested here may be helpful in such a context. After all, the ultimate selection criteria is a failure to replicate. In the context of this chapter, the key to cultural "survival" is provoking the imitation of action by others. In the same way that sexual selection, so critically tied to reproduction, can embed otherwise nonadaptive traits in genes, so too will psychological selection on the replaying of actions be critical in the passing on of cultural elements. Success at some task, accuracy, truth, and such other seemingly important criteria of selection (e.g., Gabora 1997) can take a back seat to pure action-producing compulsion.

My elder son recently received a computer chain letter whose sole informative content was:

Five people actually got killed by not sending this piece of mail. The creator of this mail has a program that will track down everyone who sent this mail and whoever that didn't send it will DIE DIE DIE DIE DIE DIE DIE DIE DIE DIE because this program can actually track down your address. Send this to 15 people within the next 15 minutes or you will die die die die, what do you have to lose? Your life?

While the proposition is patently ludicrous, its replicative success appears high. A number of long-lived and robust human belief systems with little demonstrable benefit to their adherents are propagated by only slightly more sophisticated psychological goads. The saving grace is that the purported content of these systems is often ignored, while the coded recitation is faithfully handed on.

22.8 Conclusions

Progress in understanding the evolution of culture will depend in large part on the elaboration of increasingly concrete and accurate understandings of the replicative mechanisms that make culture possible. Viewing cultural transmission as the replication of actions, rather than of ideas, focuses us on a key bottleneck. In humans, replicating actions can be broadly categorized into three modes: nonlinguistic transmission, stories, and formulas. Decoupling the transmission of language-based elements from their translation into action can help us to understand such human questions as hypocrisy and failures in the legal system, and suggests a number of projects for further research.

Acknowledgment

The author would like to thank the Gruter Institute for Law and Behavioral Research for its support in this work.

References

Blackmore, S. *The Meme Machine*. Oxford: Oxford University Press, 1999.

Boyd, R., and P. Richerson. *Culture and the Evolutionary Process*. Chicago: University of Chicago Press, 1985.

Cavalli-Sforza, L. L., and M. Feldman. *Cultural Transmission and Evolution: A Quantitative Approach*. Princeton: Princeton University Press, 1981.

Dawkins, R. *The Selfish Gene* (2d ed.). Oxford: Oxford University Press, 1989 [original edition published 1976].

Dennett, D. C. The evolution of culture: The Charles Simonyi lecture, Oxford University, 17 February 1999. Available: ⟨http://www.edge.org/3rd_culture/dennett/dennett_p1. html⟩.

Dickens, C. *Oliver Twist*. Originally published in London in *Bentley's Miscellany*, 1837–1839 (variously reprinted).

Durham, W. H. Advances in evolutionary culture theory. *Annual Review of Anthropology* 19: 197–210, 1990.

Flinn, M. R. Culture and the evolution of social learning. *Evolution and Human Behavior* 18: 23–67, 1997.

Fog, A. Cultural r/k selection. *Journal of Memetics—Evolutionary Models of Information Transmission* 1(1): 1997. Available: ⟨http://www.cpm.mmu.ac.uk/jom-emit/1997/vol1/fog_a.html⟩.

Fontana, W. Personal communication, 1998.

Gabora, L. The origin and evolution of culture and creativity. *Journal of Memetics—Evolutionary Models of Information Transmission* 1(1): 1997. Available: ⟨http://www.cpm.mmu.ac.uk/jom-emit/1997/vol1/gabora_l.html⟩.

Gatherer, D. Why the thought contagion metaphor is retarding the progress of memetics. *Journal of Memetics—Evolutionary Models of Information Transmission* 2(2): 1998. Available: ⟨http://www.cpm.mmu.ac.uk/jom-emit/1998/vol2/gatherer_d.html⟩.

Goodenough, O. R. Mind viruses: Culture, evolution, and the puzzle of altruism. *Social Science Information* 34(2): 287–320, 1995.

Goodenough, O. R. Retheorizing privacy and publicity. *Intellectual Property Quarterly* 1: 37–70, 1997.

Goodenough, O. R., and R. Dawkins. The St. Jude mind virus. *Nature* 371: 23–24, 1994.

Goodenough, W. H. *Description and Comparison in Cultural Anthropology.* Chicago: Aldine, 1970.

Goodenough, W. H. Toward a working theory of culture. In R. Borofsky, ed., *Assessing Cultural Anthropology.* New York: McGraw Hill, 1994.

Goodenough, W. H. Outline of a framework for a theory of cultural evolution. *Cross-Cultural Research* 33(1): 84–107, 1999.

Haig, D. Genetic conflicts in human pregnancy. *Quarterly Review of Biology* 68(4): 495–532, 1993.

Haig, D., and A. Grafen. Genetic scrambling as a defence against meiotic drive. *Journal of Theoretical Biology* 153: 531–558, 1991

Harris, M. *Theories of Culture in Postmodern Times.* Walnut Creek, Calif.: Altamira Press, 1998.

Harrison, J. E. *Prolegomena to the Study of Religion.* Cambridge University Press, Cambridge, UK, 1903 (reprinted, Princeton: Princeton University Press, 1991).

Journal of Memetics—Evolutionary Models of Information Transmission. Available: ⟨www.cpm.mmu.ac.uk/jom-emit/⟩.

Joyce, G. F., and L. E. Orgel. Prospects for understanding the origin of the RNA world. In R. F. Gesteland, and J. F. Atkins, eds., *The RNA World.* Plainview, N.Y.: Cold Spring Harbor Press, 1993.

Kirby, S. Learning, bottlenecks, and infinity: A working model of the evolution of syntactic communication. In K. Dautenhahn and C. L. Nehaniv (eds.), *Proceedings of the AISB '99 Symposium on Imitation in Animals and Artifacts*, pp. 55–63. Brighton, UK: The Society for Artificial Intelligence and Simulation of Behaviour, UK, 1999.

Lynch, A. Units, events, and dynamics in memetic evolution. *Journal of Memetics Evolutionary Models of Information Transmission* 2(2): 1998. Available: ⟨http://www.cpm.mmu.ac.uk/jom-emit/1998/vol2/lynch_a.html⟩.

Mochizuki, A., Y. Takeda, and Y. Iwasa. The evolution of genomic imprinting. *Genetics* 144(3): 1283–1295, 1996.

Pinker, S. *The Language Instinct.* William Morrow, New York, 1994.

Richardson, K. Hyperstructure in Brain and Cognition. *Psycoloquy* 10(31): 1999. Available: ⟨http://www.cogsci.soton.ac.uk/cgi/psyc/newpsy?10.031⟩.

Whiten, A., and R. Ham. On the nature and evolution of imitation in the animal kingdom: A reappraisal of a century of research. In *Advances in the Study of Behavior*, vol. 21, San Diego: Academic Press, 1992.

Williams, F. E. *Drama of Orokolo: The Social and Ceremonial Life of the Elema.* Clarendon Press, Oxford, 1940.

Appendix

As another outgrowth of the Scottish symposium, a special double issue on "Imitation in Natural and Artificial Systems" appears as volume 32, numbers 1–2, 2001, of the international journal *Cybernetics and Systems* published by Taylor and Francis [ISSN print 0196-9722, ISSN on-line 1087-6553]. The reader may wish to access these recent research papers on the topic of imitation. The contents of the special double issue and the page numbers of the articles are listed here:

Contributors

Michael Arbib
Computer Science Department and USC
Brain Project
University of Southern California
Los Angeles, California

Harold Bekkering
University of Groningen
Groningen, The Netherlands

Aude Billard
Computer Science Department
University of Southern California
Los Angeles, California

Cynthia Breazeal
MIT Artificial Intelligence Laboratory
Cambridge, Massachusetts

Josep Call
Max Planck Institute for Evolutionary
Anthropology
Leipzig, Germany

Malinda Carpenter
Max Planck Institute for Evolutionary
Anthropology
Leipzig, Germany

Kerstin Dautenhahn
Adaptive Systems Research Group
Department of Computer Science
University of Hertfordshire
Hatfield, United Kingdom

John Demiris
Institute of Perception, Action, and
Behaviour
Division of Informatics

University of Edinburgh
Edinburgh, United Kingdom

Dorothy M. Fragaszy
Psychology Department
University of Georgia
Athens, Georgia

Johannes Fritz
Konrad-Lorenz Research Station
Grünau, Austria

Oliver R. Goodenough
Vermont Law School
South Royalton, Vermont

Gillian Hayes
Institute of Perception, Action, and
Behaviour
Division of Informatics
University of Edinburgh
Edinburgh, United Kingdom

Louis M. Herman
Kewalo Basin Marine Mammal
Laboratory
University of Hawaii
Honolulu, Hawaii

Cecilia Heyes
Department of Psychology
University College London
London, United Kingdom

Scott Hurst
School of Computer Science and
Engineering
University of New South Wales
Sydney, Australia

Dana Kedzier
School of Computer Science and
Engineering
University of New South Wales
Sydney, Australia

Kurt Kotrschal
Konrad-Lorenz Research Station
Grünau, Austria

Henry Lieberman
Media Laboratory
Massachusetts Institute of Technology
Cambridge, Massachusetts

Maja J. Matarić
Computer Science Department and
Neuroscience Program
University of Southern California
Los Angeles, California

Donald Michie
The Turing Institute
Glasgow, United Kingdom

Robert W. Mitchell
Department of Psychology
Eastern Kentucky University
Richmond, Kentucky

Chrystopher L. Nehaniv
Adaptive Systems Research Group
Faculty of Engineering and Information
Sciences
University of Hertfordshire
Hatfield, United Kingdom

Jason Noble
Center for Adaptive Behavior and
Cognition
Max Planck Institute for Human
Development
Berlin, Germany

Michael Oliphant
Language Evolution and Computation
Research Unit

Department of Linguistics
University of Edinburgh, United
Kingdom

Irene M. Pepperberg
The Media Lab
Massachusetts Institute of Technology
Cambridge, Massachusetts

Wolfgang Prinz
Max Planck Institute for Psychological
Research
Munich, Germany

Claude Sammut
School of Computer Science and
Engineering
University of New South Wales
Sydney, Australia

Brian Scassellati
MIT Artificial Intelligence Laboratory
Cambridge, Massachusetts

Peter M. Todd
Center for Adaptive Behavior and
Cognition
Max Planck Institute for Human
Development
Berlin, Germany

Elisabetta Visalberghi
Institute of Psychology
National Council on Research (CNR)
Rome, Italy

Stefan Vogt
Department of Psychology
Lancaster University
Lancaster, United Kingdom

Andrew Whiten
Scottish Primate Research Group,
School of Psychology
University of St Andrews
Fife, Scotland

Index